The Elementary School Teacher

THE

ELEMENTARY SCHOOL TEACHER

VOLUME IX

SEPTEMBER, 1908—JUNE, 1909

CHICAGO
The University of Chicago Press
1909

Published
September, October, November, December, 1908
January, February, March, April, May, June, 1909

Composed and Printed By
The University of Chicago Press
Chicago, Illinois, U. S. A.

INDEX TO VOLUME IX

INDEX TO ARTICLES

INDEX TO AUTHORS

INDEX TO BOOK REVIEWS

VOLUME IX NUMBER I

THE ELEMENTARY SCHOOL TEACHER

SEPTEMBER, 1908

CONSOLIDATION AND TRANSPORTATION: A RURAL SCHOOL PROBLEM

ALBERT FREDERICK PROBST
School of Education

I. ORIGIN AND EXTENT OF THE CONSOLIDATED SYSTEM

It was Massachusetts that led the way in the development of the district system and to her is also due the credit of pointing out the way for consolidation. As early as 1869 Massachusetts passed a law which provided for the transportation of pupils to and from the public schools at public cost. Probably Quincy was the first town in the state to act under the law of 1869, having closed two schools in 1874 and transported the children to other schools. Consolidation was complete in Montague Township, Massachusetts, as early as 1875, and was begun in Concord in 1879. From this time on, consolidation spread rapidly throughout the state until in 1904–5, her expenditure for transportation alone amounted to $213,221. Other neighboring states have readily adopted the Massachusetts plan until now the movement reaches not only every one of the New England States but extends to the northern, middle, southern, and western states as well, while the question of consolidation is being agitated in every state in the Union. State Superintendent H. A. Ustrud, of South Dakota, reports May 5, 1908, that South Dakota has about fifteen centralized schools. Superintendent Ustrud adds the following: "A number of townships have voted this spring to centralize, so that in a short time we hope to be right along with other states with the plan."

Francis G. Blair, State Superintendent of Public Instruction of Illinois, reports April 22, 1908, that there is but one consolidated school in the state of Illinois that transports the pupils at public expense.[1]

Georgia has consolidation to a greater or less extent in more than sixty counties of the state, while in Iowa, more than one-half of the counties of the state report consolidation in one or more townships of the county.

Maine and Vermont expend about one-thirtieth of their school money for transportation alone, while Massachusetts' expenditure of $213,221 for transportation of pupils is only about 1.18 per cent. of the total expenditure for her public schools.

While consolidation and transportation have made remarkable advancement in many of the eastern states, and particularly in Maine, Vermont, Massachusetts, and Connecticut, perhaps no greater progress or more rapid advancement can be seen anywhere than in Ohio and Indiana.

It was at Kirksville, in Ashtabula County, that the Ohio plan of centralization or consolidation had its origin in 1892. The erection of a new building in one of the districts of Kingsville Township brought up the question whether or no it would be better to abandon the school in that district and take the children to the village school at public expense. In the first case of consolidation in Ohio the schools were centralized at the village school. Finding special legislation necessary in order to consolidate and transport children at public expense, Ohio passed a bill, April 17, 1894, providing for transportation. April 27, 1896, the Ohio legislature passed another bill for the relief of the counties of Stark, Ashtabula, and Portage, and still later a general law was enacted permitting the people of any township at the annual town election to vote "yes" or "no" on the proposition to centralize the schools of that township; i. e., to abandon the small districts and transport the children at public expense to the central school. Under the law of 1904, the board of trustees may abolish all the subdistricts providing conveyance is furnished to one or more central schools for pupils living more than one-half mile from

[1] Due, perhaps, to the large number of township high schools in the state.

the schoolhouse. "Under this section the schools of a township can be centralized without submitting the question to the electors" (State School Commissioner). This law also provides that centralization, once effected, shall not be discontinued within three years, and then only by petition and election. A central graded school must be maintained in centralized townships, and a high-school course of not less than two years is authorized. Transportation must be furnished all pupils living more than three-fourths of a mile from the central building. Such, in brief, is the history of the legislation in Ohio on consolidation of schools and transportation of pupils.

II. CONSOLIDATION AND TRANSPORTATION IN OHIO

Ohio has done much toward solving the rural-school problem. Her rural schools have attracted the attention of many schoolmen of other states and have been made the subject of frequent reports by visitors from all parts of the country. Consolidation has become so widespread in Ohio that at the present time, April, 1908, there are about two hundred townships in which the schools are centralized.

Ohio's first centralized school, the Kingsville school, is a typical example of rural and village consolidation, and perhaps I could do no better than to quote from the *Arena* for July, 1899, concerning the advantages and the satisfaction which it gives to the people of Kingsville Township. This report was made after the school had been in operation eight years and had outgrown the experimental stage, and while this school has made great progress in the nine years since this report was written, yet this same testimony might now be given of many other consolidated schools, not only of Ohio, but of other states both sides of the Mississippi. The quotation is as follows:

> The residents of the subdistricts of Kingsville Township which have adopted this plan would deem it a retrogression to go back to the old subdistrict plan. It has given the school system of Kingsville an individuality which makes it unique and progressive. Pupils from every part of the township enjoy a graded-school education, whether they live in the most remote corner of the township or at the very doors of the central school. The line between the country-bred and the village-bred youth is blotted out.

They study the same books, are competitors for the same honors and engage in the same sports and pastimes. This mingling of the pupils from the subdistricts and the village has had a deepening and broadening influence on the former without any disadvantage to the latter. With the grading of the school and the larger number of pupils have come teachers of a more highly educated class. Higher branches of study are taught; the teachers are more conversant with the needs of their profession; the salaries are higher; the health of the pupils is safeguarded, because they are not compelled to walk to school in slush, snow, and rain, to sit with damp and perhaps wet feet in ill-ventilated buildings. Nor is there any lounging by the wayside. As the use of indecent language is prohibited in the wagons, all opportunities for quarreling or improper conduct on the way to and from the school are removed. The attendance is larger, and in the subdistricts which have taken advantage of the plan it has increased from 50 to 150 per cent. in some cases; truancy is unknown. It has lengthened the school year for a number of the subdistricts; it has increased the demands for farms in those districts which have adopted the plan, and real estate therein is reported more stable. The drivers act as daily mail carriers. All parts of the townships have been brought into closer touch and sympathy. The cost of maintenance is less than that of the schools under the district plan; the township has had no schoolhouses to build; it has paid less for repair and fuel. Since the schools were consolidated the incidental expenses have decreased from $800 to $1,100 per year to from $400 to $600 per year. In the first three years following its adoption Kingsville Township actually saved $1,000.

Green Township presents an example of consolidation distinctly rural. The people of Green Township had watched the school in a neighboring township for two years and had become so thoroughly converted to the new plan that they voted to bond the township for a long term of years to erect a $6,000 modern and up-to-date school building. This building stands in the center of the township eleven miles from one railroad and six miles from another. The building contains six schoolrooms, with two additional rooms, one of which might be used for a library room and the other for a reception room. It is heated by steam and has a basement under the entire building, part of which might be utilized for laboratories, gymnasium, etc. To this building are brought all the children of the entire township. The enrolment the first year was 180, an increase of thirty over the last year in the scattered schools. Eight wagons are employed in transporting the children to the central building. The school grounds comprise about three acres, much of which is now used for gardening and elementary agriculture.

III. CONSOLIDATION AND TRANSPORTATION IN INDIANA

Indiana is fast taking the lead among the states, if she has not already taken it, in the matter of consolidation and transportation. The number of schools abandoned has grown from 679, in 1904, to 1,314 in 1908—449 schools being abandoned from September, 1907, to April, 1908. The number of consolidated schools has increased from 280, in 1904, to 418 in 1908, while the number of children transported has increased from 5,356, in 1904, to 16,034, in 1908. The cost per day at the present time, April, 1908, for transportation of pupils in Indiana is $1,749.24, while the cost per wagon per day is $1.87. Such has been the progress of the consolidated system in Indiana in the last four years and even greater progress will be made in the immediate future owing to the large number of small, one-teacher schools which still exist in the state and the recent enactment of a law by the last legislature which went into effect April 10, 1907. At the present time there are 387 schools in the state with an attendance of fewer than twelve pupils, and 699 schools with an attendance of fewer than fifteen pupils.

The legislature of 1907 enacted a law making compulsory the abandonment of all schools in which the average daily attendance is twelve or fewer, and gives the trustees the authority to abandon all schools where the attendance is fifteen or fewer; provided, the conditions as to roads, streams and bridges permit of such discontinuance. The law provides further that

> it shall be the duty of the township trustee to provide for the education of such pupils as are affected by such or any former discontinuance in other schools, and they shall provide and maintain means of transportation for all such pupils as live at a greater distance than two miles, and for all pupils between the ages of six (6) and twelve (12) that live less than two miles and more than one mile from the schools to which they may be transferred as a result of such discontinuance. Such transportation shall be in comfortable and safe conveyances. The drivers of such conveyances shall furnish the teams therefor and shall use every care for

the safety of the children under their charge, and shall maintain discipline in such conveyances. Restrictions as to the use of public highways shall not apply to such conveyances. The expenses incident to carrying into effect the provisions of this act shall be paid from the public school funds.

E. C. Crider, County Superintendent of Tippecanoe County, submits the following statistical report showing centralization from 1899 to 1906.

Townships	Schools Abandoned	Additional Teachers	Number of Hacks	Number of Pupils Conveyed
Lauramie	10	7	9	197
Randolph	5	4	5	90
Jackson	2	0	1	8
Wayne	3	1	2	44
Union	1	0	0	...
Wea	7	3	6	100
Sheffield	2	1	1	12
Perry	4	3	3	48
Washington	7	2	5	76
Tippecanoe	2	1	1	9
Wabash	3	0	2	26
Shelby	6	2	1	10
Fairfield	2	0	0	...
Total	54	24	36	620

NOTE.—Of the additional teachers two were for rural schools, eight were for high schools, fourteen were needed because of centralization. Length of transportation routes, from 2½ to 7 miles. Cost per day for hacks, from $1.00 to $2.50. Total daily cost of service, $63.75. Number of children per hack, from 8 to 27. Total number of pupils conveyed in the county, 623. All drivers but six provide their own hacks.

Mr. Crider reports that many of the rural schools of Tippecanoe County were so small that they could hardly be designated as schools. Animation and life were lacking. Very often there was but one pupil in a grade, so there were no companionship and competition in the work. The inexperienced teacher was often present. One school had not had an experienced teacher in ten years. Of the 123 rural schools of the county, fifty-four have been abandoned. As a rule, the idea of centralization has generally been well accepted. There are sometimes some objections made to the details in carrying out the plan but the idea has been seldom opposed. The principal complaint concerning transportation is in regard to the hack, the driver, the length of time on the road. A frequent complaint is that children have to start too early.

In contrasting the new plan with the old, and after several years' experience in Tippecanoe County, Mr. Crider says: "The complaints about consolidation, as I see it, are not more numerous nor as serious as the complaints made about poor work and inexperienced teachers under the old plan. The greatest proof that centralization gives general satisfaction is that these fifty-four schools are not missed."

In 1899 there were 164 township teachers in Tippecanoe County. In 1906 there were 133 with nearly one-half the schools of the county abandoned.

In Wea Township six wagons, each heated by a stove and made comfortable, are used to convey the one hundred pupils to a modern, central building heated by a furnace and provided with all the necessary appliances of a well-equipped city school. A well-selected library of nearly one thousand volumes is one of the great advantages of this school. The trustees have built a barn large enough for ten horses and buggies for the high-school pupils who drive. One teacher who can do high-grade music work is employed to give instruction to all the pupils of the school.

Lauramie Township employs nine wagons whose drivers are carefully selected and their routes carefully laid out. One feature of their contract should be generally adopted:—every driver whose route crosses a railroad is required to get out of the hack and lead the team across the track, thus avoiding all chance of being run down by a train.

Shelby Township, after four years of experience with consolidation, makes the following report: (*a*) It has made it possible to increase the length of the term from 6½ months to 7½ months. (*b*) Schools made better. Pupils placed in larger classes, which permitted a fuller discussion of the lesson. It gave them a chance to measure themselves with others. (*c*) Interest raised in the school. Parents quick to realize the advantages and are anxious to keep their children in the high school. (*d*) The building, one of the finest in the county, has a large assembly room for lectures, public meetings, etc. (*e*) High school of four years. Graduates receive credit for work done in the high school in nearly every college and university in the state.

Mr. S. D. Symmes, trustee of Union Township, Montgomery County, says: "The success of the consolidated school is in getting the children to and from school in the most approved way and in the shortest time. Our drivers are men of good reputation and are paid good wages. Each route is run on schedule time, so that the children know to the minute when the wagon

TRANSPORTATION WAGON, DELPHI WAGON WORKS

will arrive, and thus they can be ready to go. Drivers are not expected to wait over two minutes for children to get ready. They carry a book which shows the time they arrive at every home. Routes are from four to six miles in length and can be made in an hour and a half. The wagons are made specially for the conveyance of pupils, having a door and steps at the back, a door on the side for the driver, a window in front, roll side curtains, and are provided with foot warmers, lap robes, etc.

Lima, Lagrange County, a village of about six hundred population, gives the following interesting account of her experience with consolidation: Seventy per cent. of the children are from the country. Town and school centrally located. Length of school term is nine months. There are nine years of grade work and four years in the high school. There are 160 pupils in the grades and 90 in the high school, with a total enumeration of 269. This was the first township high school in the state to be commissioned by the State Board of Education. It is placed on the accredited list of the North Central Association. It employs a special teacher of music and there are two pianos in the high school and an organ in each grade room. The high school maintains choruses and orchestra, and a glee club. There is a school hall with a raised floor and an equipped stage. A $400 lecture course is sustained. The school is provided with a library and reading room with one thousand volumes and a paid librarian; a laboratory well equipped for scientific investigation; a school garden of two hundred plats for the study of agriculture throughout the grades and high school; a free kindergarten and an athletic field; a five-acre playground and a separate building for gymnasium, well equipped.

There are four teachers in the high school—all college graduates, and five professionally trained teachers in the grades. The high-school course of study includes four years each of English, Science, Music, and Latin; three years each in mathematics, history, and German; common branch "review," household science, bookkeeping, public speaking and agriculture.

The following show conditions in the centralized school of Lima township:

Number of days in session	180
Number enrolled in the school	250
Number enrolled in the grades	160
Number enrolled in the high school	90
Average per cent. of attendance	96
Number of teachers	10
Total school enumeration	269
Total number of foreign pupils	40
Total expenditures for school purposes	$7,159.60

One of the most remarkable schools in Indiana is located at Graysville, a small village in Sullivan County. This school is of unusual interest as a rural school from the point of view of the large amount of industrial work which is being done throughout all its departments. Friday afternoon is given up to industrial work in all the departments of the school. The rest that is accomplished in the industrial line is all done outside of school hours—at noons and recesses, after school hours at night and on Saturdays.

Some of the things that are being attempted are sewing and stitching, basket weaving, venetian iron, pounding brass and copper, book-binding, rug-weaving and leather-tooling for the

CONSOLIDATED GRADED SCHOOL BUILDING, UNION TOWNSHIP, JOHNSON COUNTY

girls; cabinet-work, carpenter-work, cement-laying, venetian iron, pounding brass and copper, wood-carving, setting type and printing, leather-tooling and book-binding for the boys. There are tools for doing all this work in the school, some owned by the township, some owned by the principal, and some by the pupils. Immediately adjoining the school-yard is a two-story building which has been fitted up for a workroom for the boys, and here, at noon and recesses, at night and on Saturdays, some twenty boys are busy. Some of this work is done for the township in the way of cement walks around the schoolhouse, building of outhouses, making bookcases, etc. The industrial work is correlated with the textbook work in the various subjects in a way that not only gives a larger and richer meaning to these subjects but also an added value to every production in the shop.

These are some of the advantages which the great state of Indiana, great at least in an educational way, furnishes to more than a quarter of a million country boys and girls.

From the large number of reports from all parts of the country, from state superintendents of public instruction, from county superintendents, from principals of consolidated schools, from the parents and from the children themselves, wherever consolidation has been tried, can be gleaned this common and almost unanimous sentiment which can be summed up under three heads. First, better health, less exposure in going to and returning from school, better heat, better light, better ventilation, and better sanitary conditions. Second, better education: morally, socially, and intellectually. Third, greater economy of money, time, and effort.

Perhaps the best proof of the universal satisfaction with which consolidation meets, is the fact that so few schools ever return to the old plan, no matter how little or how great the cost to make the experiment. From the large number of reports examined, there was found but one school out of the several hundred that have tried the new plan that has gone back to the small, one-teacher school and that was because of an accident in transportation and before the new plan had been given a fair trial.

IV. ADVANTAGES OF CONSOLIDATION

To sum up, then, the many advantages which the system of consolidation and transportation offers:

1. Consolidation provides for better and more modern school buildings: better lighted, better heated, better ventilated, with better sanitary conditions; all of which tend to improve and promote the health interests of the school and of the community.

2. Consolidation is more economical than the many small schools. Under the consolidated system, the cost is less for repairs, fuel, apparatus, etc. Consolidation lessens the expense and equalizes, more nearly, the cost.

3. Consolidation provides for better teachers and, because of

the more favorable social conditions which exist among them, they have greater enthusiasm and interest in their work. Teachers are engaged for a longer term and are paid better salaries, enabling the trustees to secure teachers who have had a normal school, college, or university training. Trained and experienced teachers for special subjects, such as music, drawing, agriculture, nature study, etc., are secured.

4. Closer and better supervision is made possible by consolidation. There are fewer schools for the county superintendent to supervise and much of the time spent in traveling the many miles necessary to reach a hundred or more small schools can be utilized to better advantage. Then, too, wherever the consolidated school has taken the place of a half-dozen or more small schools, there is an added advantage in having a principal at its head, who is competent to manage and supervise the educational and disciplinary affairs of the school.

5. Under consolidation there are fewer and better school officers; there are less politics and less favoritism and, hence, better school conditions.

6. Under consolidation there is a longer term of school than many of the small schools now have, and at less cost.

7. The consolidated system provides for a greater variety of studies, including manual training, domestic science, agriculture, music, gymnastics, etc., hence a greater incentive to boys and girls to continue in school long enough to finish the high-school course.

8. Consolidation engenders that healthy educational spirit which can only come with the association of numbers. It provides for larger classes from which teachers are able to secure the interest and healthy rivalry which does not arise in the small district school. Parents take greater interest in the educational affairs of the community.

9. Consolidation tends toward a more healthy social spirit in the school and in the community; rural and village children mingle together upon a common plain, the one securing much from the other. Parents and teachers become better acquainted with each other through frequent social gatherings at the common

meeting-place—the schoolhouse. Home and school are brought into closer relation to each other.

10. Under consolidation a better system of grading pupils, together with departmental teaching, is made possible. The teacher is no longer required to instruct in all the common branches pupils of all ages, but only in those subjects which she is especially prepared to teach. With better grading the teacher

PREPARING A LESSON IN AGRICULTURE, GRAYSVILLE HIGH SCHOOL

has fewer and longer periods of recitation and is able to give her pupils more individual attention.

11. With consolidation come better roads, giving the farmer the best facilities for transportation and thereby increasing the valuation of the farm.[2]

12. Consolidation has made possible the solution of the problem of agricultural education, and it is the only complete solution that has been offered.

13. Consolidation is the only plan tried or proposed by which

[2] Once when a man wished to sell his farm he advertised, "A school near." Now he advertises, "Children conveyed to good schools." "Good graveled roads all the way to town."

the country child can secure such an education as modern conditions demand, and such as is already afforded the city child.

14. Through consolidation, country boys and girls are furnished a good education from the kindergarten through the high school without disturbing the home either by separation of members of the family or by "moving to town to educate the children."

15. Consolidation provides for a paid janitor, who is able to keep the school building and grounds in a neat, attractive, and sanitary condition.

16. Consolidation also provides for better supervision and better discipline in the building and on the playground at noon and recess.

17. Athletics is one of the factors in the solution of the problem of "how to keep boys in school" and consolidation furnishes even better advantages for athletics than the city school.

18. Consolidation is one of the means of solving the problem of "compulsory education" and under it there is practically no need of a truant officer.

20. Consolidation brightens and broadens country life and rationalizes the movement toward population centers.

V. ADVANTAGES OF TRANSPORTATION

Some of the advantages of transportation of pupils.

1. Under transportation there is far better attendance. No tardiness.

2. Transportation tends to the formation of habits of punctuality not only on the part of the pupils but on the part of the parents in getting their children ready for the hack on time.

3. Through transportation, pupils are provided with warm, comfortable conveyances instead of having to walk through rain, slush, and snow and then sit through the day with wet feet and clothing.

4. In transportation there is no opportunity for loitering by the wayside or fighting on the road to and from school. Vulgar and indecent language, which was frequently used in the presence of the larger girls and the small children when returning from the small school, is now turned to conversation concerning the social

welfare or the work of the school as suggested by the driver or by some of the older pupils.

5. The many trolley lines throughout Ohio and Indiana with half-fare to schools, puts the consolidated school within easy reach of many school children of these states.

VI. SOME OBJECTIONS TO THE CONSOLIDATED SYSTEM

1. Perhaps the chief objection is in the abandonment of the old district school and the erection of a new central building. This objection is anchored partly to tradition, but is more largely a question of expense in the way of increased taxation for a modern school building.

2. Another objection which is frequently raised is that consolidation tends to decrease the value of farm property by abandoning the nearby school. As a matter of fact, reports generally show that by consolidation the value of farms has increased through good roads, better school conditions, and a more united educational and social sentiment throughout the whole community.

3. Some parents object to consolidation on the ground that they are obliged to get their children ready for school much earlier than when they walked to the nearby school, and that they are too long on the road in going to and returning from the central school. While this objection is well grounded, it might be questioned whether even the pupils who live farthest from the central school are on the road longer when conveyed than when they walked from school.

4. Again, parents of young children frequently complain of the little ones being so far from home for so long a time. Every true mother has experienced a feeling of lonesomeness when the little one entered the school, and especially where the school was a small, delapidated country school, and where the teacher had little or no leisure time to give the little folk. But in the modern consolidated school building, with bright, cheerful, well-equipped kindergarten, rest, and playrooms in charge of an experienced and well-trained kindergarten teacher who has learned to take the place of the kindest of mothers, with telephone lines from the

school to every home by which parents can keep in communication with the teacher, mothers have little to fear.

5. Some parents object to having their children eat cold dinners at school on the ground that it is not healthy. This, too, is a valid objection; but why not provide a kitchen and lunch-room in every consolidated building where children can get a warm lunch and have a clean and respectable place to eat it? This is being done in many of the city schools. Why not in the consolidated school, where there is even a better opportunity than in most city schools. Every consolidated school, with four teachers or more, should have a course of training in domestic science, and the well-managed, well-equipped lunch-room will furnish a part of such a course.

6. As the success of consolidation depends largely upon the facility of transportation, it is perfectly evident that not all states and sections of the country present as favorable conditions for the carrying out of the plan as do Ohio and Indiana. The climate and topography of the country, the density of population, the wealth interests of the community—all these are determining factors in the solution of this great problem; yet country people everywhere are at last beginning to see that while they pay more for elementary instruction alone than city schools cost, including the high-school course, their schools are far behind the city schools in instruction, supervision, and in the character of buildings. These people are beginning to realize more keenly than ever before the need of better educational advantages and they are determined to have them through the one solution of the problem—that of consolidation; and when the consolidated school has all the advantages of the city school in addition to those which the country already affords, it will then be the best in the land.

BIBLIOGRAPHY

Report of the Committee of Twelve on Rural Schools.

Advance Sheets on Current Topics. U. S. Bureau of Education.

Ohio School Reports. Indiana School Reports.

Ohio School Laws. Indiana School Laws.

Arena for July, 1899.

Questionnaire Method:

Reports from State and County Superintendents, and Principals of Consolidated Schools.

A NEW DEMAND UPON PROFESSIONAL SCHOOLS FOR TEACHERS

JESSE D. BURKS, PH.D.
Principal, Teachers Training School, Albany, N. Y.

1. It is a common experience for principals and teachers in elementary schools to be called upon by pupils and their parents for advice concerning the prospective careers of pupils. Whether or no a pupil shall continue in school or enter at once upon an apprenticeship in a trade or in a commercial pursuit; whether he shall plan to enter a high school and, if so, in what course; whether it would be advisable for the pupil to prepare for a professional career and, if so, for what profession—these are practical problems such as parents and their children are constantly facing. Recognizing their own inability to work out satisfactory solutions to such problems, many pupils, with or without the knowledge and support of their parents, turn with significant confidence to teacher or principal or superintendent for counsel or guidance.

Though teachers and school officers are not altogether loath to tender their good offices in such cases, it may be seriously doubted whether the advice given often has value other than advice of friendly interest. Excepting the cases where strong native tendencies in children leave little or no doubt as to the vocations for which they are fitted, there is apparently little basis upon which either parents or teachers may make reliable forecasts as to the probable success or failure of a given child in specific vocations. The individuals having native abilities most strongly marked are, of course, least in need of specific guidance in the choice of vocations. It is the great majority without well-defined or clearly recognizable tendencies who must have such guidance if we are to substitute for the present practice of purely fortuitous choice of vocations a more rational practice based upon the adaptation of the individual to his work.

The results of the present random selection of vocations are widespread and evident. Commercial failures, incompetent mechanics, disgruntled professional men, unsympathetic and mechanical teachers, prosaic poets, uninspired preachers, briefless lawyers, honest politicians, and dishonest bank clerks—these and similar evidences point to a deplorable maladjustment.

2. The present organization of elementary education is not designed, even in its later years, to make children aware of their special abilities. The elementary-school course is based upon two radically erroneous assumptions; the first, that the great majority of the pupils in the schools will finish the elementary grades; the second, that the needs of the pupils in the elementary grades are identical as to the so-called "fundamental" education extending through eight years of the school course.

Accurate data as to the dropping out of pupils in the elementary grades are not available, but it is a matter of common knowledge among teachers that pupils drop out with increasing frequency after the fifth school year. This tendency is commonly attributed to economic causes; and without doubt the desire of many parents to have their children begin to earn a livelihood does account for the dropping out of many children. If the facts were known, however, it could probably be shown that economic pressure is not one of the strongest influences in producing this tendency. There is undoubtedly, among parents and pupils, a widespread feeling, not without reasonable basis, that the latter years of the elementary-school course are not highly essential to the welfare of the children and that there is a greater economic advantage in several years of apprenticeship than a like number of years in the upper grades of the elementary schools.

An indication of the truth of this statement may be found in the fact that the organization of technical and commercial courses in high schools commonly has the effect of increasing registration and of raising the percentage of pupils continuing to the end of the outlined course in such schools. The influences that determine the dropping out of pupils in high schools are probably not very different from those operative in elementary schools.

The deliberate choice of a considerable proportion of the

pupils in elementary grades to leave school and enter upon some vocational pursuit, even when economic pressure is not unduly strong and parents advise against the discontinuance of school work, is evidence of a distinct psychological need that arises in the early period of adolescence. The indication is clear that pupils at this stage of their development require greater differentiation and specialization of training than the elementary school is providing. There is actual call for something that leads to a definite outcome in terms of the world's work, especially in terms of that part of it for which the powers and prospects of the individual pupil specially qualify him. There is an impulse, almost an instinct, among many pupils, to try their powers on "real" things; on things that mean much and count much in human affairs.

It is this impulse that gives much of the force possessed by the "manual-training movement." Even the manual training as commonly organized, however, fails to meet adequately the psychological demand for work that bears directly upon the problems of individual and social life. The subject is still too far away from the real social world in which vocations play so commanding a part. Manual training does not "help" in a way sufficiently direct and definite to meet the demands under consideration.

Not only are teachers and administrative officers unable, then, to give pupils trustworthy guidance in the matter of a choice of vocation, but the school is ill adapted, in its last few years, to the peculiar psychological needs of children whose powers are clearly differentiating and whose interests are potentially or actually of a strongly practical nature. There is an obvious call here for the reorganization of the last few years of elementary education in such a way as to provide more effectively for the needs of the various groups of children differing in native capacity, in social and industrial surroundings, in power of self-support, and, consequently, in prospective career.

The familiar objections to early specialization will readily come to mind in this connection. These objections were employed in the long since abandoned fight against the system of election in college courses. They are still retained as stock arguments by the conservatives and reactionists in the field of secondary education. They will no doubt be similarly used by the opponents of optional courses in elementary education. The problem is really identical throughout the whole range of educational organization, and the final solution must inevitably conform to the fundamental facts involved. Briefly stated the question is: how may we provide for the most effective development of the capacities of a group of individuals who differ widely in moral and intellectual inheritance in cultural surroundings, in acquired taste and powers, in economic status, and in prospective career; are the interests of individuals and of society, under these conditions, best subserved by a single, undifferentiated, prescribed programme of studies or by a flexible system of optional courses designed to meet the specific needs of the different classes of individuals in the group?

If a completely social basis for education be accepted, it is difficult to see how this question can be answered other than in one way. The facts of genetic psychology and the facts of normal social life alike demand that adequate provision be made for special training whenever special aptitudes and special tastes come to be strongly enough marked to serve as the basis for separating individuals into distinct groups.

There is a prevailing notion that, in a democracy such as ours, equal educational opportunities must be offered to all children alike. This principle is indeed somewhat generally regarded as a fundamental corollary of democracy itself. When, however, we interpret "equal" educational opportunities to mean the "same" education for all, we are pushing the principle to an unwarrantable extreme. What to one child or group may be an educational opportunity of highest value, to another child or group may be no opportunity at all. It is not what is offered but what can be utilized in the way of education that is to be accounted genuine opportunity. "Completely rounded manhood," "a fundamental common-school education for all children," and similar statements of the aim of elementary education are superficially attractive to an uncritical audience; but they must be relegated to the educational lumber-room along with a good many other worn-out traditions.

Our conventional distinction between elementary and secondary education is, in fact, without completely rational meaning. The practical distinction in organization may easily be explained historically, but it has little if any direct relation to existing social relations. It is difficult to find any tenable reason for an eight-year "elementary" course, planned for all children, to be followed by a four-year "secondary" course planned for all children who survive the so-called elementary course, and designed primarily to meet the requirements for admission to college. A rational distinction between elementary and secondary education would appear to be that secondary courses of instruction should be provided when children reach the secondary stage of development; that is, a stage of fairly distinct differentiation of interests and capacities. The elementary education, from this point of view, should be distinctly fundamental and social in character and should extend through the period when children are relatively unspecialized in their development. The facts previously discussed in this paper indicate that the point of division between elementary and secondary education belongs much earlier in the school course than it is now placed.

3. The mere organization of special courses and special schools designed to meet the specific needs of various groups of children will not, however, be of itself sufficient to assure us of a properly effective and democratic system of education. We must go farther and find a way to bring boys and girls to a definite consciousness of their specific abilities and thus make it possible for them to make rational choice among the courses open to them and, ultimately, of their respective vocations. Merely capricious choice of a course of instruction would certainly be as likely to result disastrously as capricious choice of a vocation. The undesirable results of capricious choice in both directions are to be avoided, if at all, by giving careful consideration to the influence of mental and moral traits upon success in various specific undertakings.

It is by no means certain, to be sure, that all of the persons at present accounted unsuccessful in given vocations could have been assured of success in other vocations by even the most accurate determination in advance of their mental and moral traits. It must be evident, however, that under given environmental conditions these traits are the sole influences in determining success. Conversely, if an individual's mental and moral makeup be known we should be able to forecast his success in a given activity and thus furnish him with reliable guidance, provided we have also sufficient knowledge of the qualities required for success in given directions.

It may be suggested that the elements entering into individual character and the factors determining success in various careers present complications that make it impossible to find reliable solutions for such problems as those under consideration. But while it must be admitted that the difficulties are great, it may be confidently denied that they are insurmountable.

The application of modern statistical method to the measurement of mental traits has already demonstrated the possibility of a knowledge of mental and social life, both of individuals and of groups, far more extensive and thoroughgoing than any yet attained on a large scale. Recent investigations concerning the influence of heredity, notably that of Dr. F. A. Woods, on *Mental and Moral Heredity in Royalty,* have made clear the preponderating influence of inheritance in determining the mental and moral attainments of individuals. The direction for safe advance seems quite clearly marked. What good reason can there be for ignoring the plain facts of biology and of psychology; for assuming that children are really as clay in the potter's hands; and for leaving to chance and the vagaries of unenlightened impulse the important function of selecting, for the mass of our boys and girls, the activity to which each will devote the main part of his life?

4. A reasonable procedure would appear to call for: first, a system of psychological tests calculated to determine the chief mental and moral traits of each pupil; second, precise study of the co-relations between specific traits in individuals and success in typical vocations; third, the accumulation of properly recorded

data which, in subsequent generations, may serve as the basis for determining the probable tendencies due to inheritance.

If such a plan be sound, and if it is to be generally accepted, schools for the professional training of teachers must take an active part in developing its possibilities. Teachers must be equipped to recognize, to search for, and to interpret the evidences of special aptitude in pupils. In order that teachers and school officers may be thus equipped, it is necessary that the influence of heredity upon mental and moral traits be frankly recognized, and that we find a conception of genetic psychology more vital and practical than any yet widely prevalent.

It should hardly be necessary to present arguments in support of this assumption that professional schools should take a leading part in educational research and educational experimentation. It is a curious historical paradox that the study of the educational process, in many the crowning interest of mankind, should so signally have failed to profit by the example furnished in the unparalleled success attained elsewhere by the method of science. If teaching is to be in fact as well as in name a genuine profession, the spirit of investigation, of the pursuit of new truth, should pervade every school for the training of teachers.

Nor should it be necessary to answer the oft-repeated objection that "experimenting with children" is a reprehensible practice, incompatible with the best interests of the children. Every intelligent teacher is an experimenter, in the sense that he is constantly seeking to find better means and better matter to carry out the aims of education. The person trained in the method of scientific research simply has an advantage over a person not so trained, in the directness and facility with which he is able to carry on his experiments. As Professor Dewey has aptly said, "The experimentation is *for* the children, not *with* the children." The perennial freshness of interest, the attitude of inquiry, and the open-mindedness that must inevitably characterize the professional work of a person trained to habits of scientific inquiry, are in themselves a sufficient reason for placing marked emphasis upon methods of research in all institutions for the professional training of teachers. The solution of the main problem proposed in this discussion, therefore, constitutes a new and urgent demand upon schools for the professional training of teachers.

SUMMARY

1. School officers and teachers, though often called upon by parents and pupils for advice concerning the prospective careers of pupils, in general are as helpless as the parents themselves to give advice that may be relied upon.

2. The school as organized is not able to bring boys and girls to definite consciousness of their specific abilities such as might enable them to adjust themselves rationally rather than fortuitously to the requirements of social life. This fact is partly accountable for the relatively unsuccessful careers of the great mass of our population.

3. With proper data concerning the inheritance and the personal development of individual pupils, it would be possible for teachers and school officers to determine, with considerable accuracy, the career for which individuals are best fitted.

4. In order that this result may be attained, professional schools must equip teachers to search for, to recognize, and to interpret the evidences of special aptitude. This will necessitate a clear recognition of the influence of heredity upon mental and moral traits, and a more vital and practical view of genetic psychology than is yet widely prevalent.

THE RELATION BETWEEN THE IDEAL AND THE PRACTICAL IN THE KINDERGARTEN PROGRAMME

LUELLA PALMER
Kindergarten Critic Teacher, Speyer School, New York City

Every individual is living out, each moment, his own view of the relation between the ideal and the practical, between ultimate purpose and immediate necessity. Unrest comes from the constant changing of relationship necessary to growth. A quiescent state in individuals, in groups, in institutions, would show deterioration, for the elevation of the ideal with the consequent adjustment of the practical is the activity which indicates the expanding of life.

The relation between the ideal and the practical in the kindergarten programme is therefore not a static condition; yet if it is a valid relationship, it must be based upon the same principle as that relation in the world at large. In this paper it will be assumed that the relationship is one of unity, not identity, that both are aspects necessary for reality, the ideal being the power, and the practical the means, by which the potential becomes actual.

Every act which rises above the threshold of an impulsive or an instinctive action, is by its very nature ideal-practical. It implies in varying degrees that there is a purpose, that the immediate action is not left on the plane of the present, but is lifted somewhat toward the possibility of the future. Except with the pessimist, it implies the attitude which learns from the past, and which interprets by faith, believing that the future will excel the past by the help of the present.

In attempting to define the position held toward the relationship between the ideal and practical in the kindergarten programme, it will be well to seek in the past for that which will aid in leading toward the goal mapped out by far-sighted interpreters. To Froebel we will turn, as it was not possible to have a kindergarten (to educate consciously a child of five years) until he had brought to consciousness certain educative principles. Froebel is also one of the philosophers who will point out the goal.

Froebel saw all living and consequently all education as a process of interaction. His observations led him to discern that it was carried on from the beginning of the new life to the last days. His educational aim was to bring to consciousness in the individual, the idea that strength of personality was dependent upon the degree to which interaction was carried on. It was for the purpose of encouraging a child to develop this principle in his daily living, and also to see it in perspective as fully as his few years made possible, that the kindergarten was established. This was the step in the revelation of the principle which the five-year-old child was to take.

It was Froebel who saw that interaction occurred in three different directions in the universe: between an individual and (1) a higher level, God; (2) the same level, man, and (3) a lower level, nature. It is the differing attitudes of human beings which make it possible to appreciate these different levels. There are all gradations of attitudes and so there are feelings of many different levels, but these three are different enough in degree to be designated as distinct types. The attitude toward (1) a higher level is that of worship, toward (2) the same, comradeship, toward (3) a lower, control. The first attitude involves a feeling of an ideal to be copied, an end to be attained; the third, a feeling of material to be impressed, a means to be used to gain some end; the second attitude involves a feeling of the possibility of both copying and impressing, of using as means or as end.

The kindergarten, as Froebel suggested it to us, was to show the principle of interaction working in the form in which it was found in the universe, in its three different directions. The teacher was to stand for (1) the higher level; she was to call forth the feelings of love, faith and obedience. The playmates were to stand for (2) the world of humanity, and the spirit of co-operation was to be cultivated; opportunities were to be given for each one to lead and to be led. (3) Materials were to be used for carrying out and enlarging the child's expressions of his purposes, and in order that this functional use might be accomplished in the best way, the possibilities of the materials were to be considered. These are the three factors in the kindergarten programme (teacher, playmates, materials [1]), which are to be so used that a child will be able to comprehend better the working of interaction in his later life.

The kindergartner is the one to whom a child should look for guidance. She is the sympathetic leader who stands to the child, relatively, as the philosophers do to the adult. It is she who will develop his behavior toward a standard; it is she who will give the cue as to his association with other children; and it is she who will suggest his attitude toward materials. It is the kindergartner who determines what a child shall gain from the other factors. She stands to the child as an embodiment of an ideal and also provides means by which he can strive toward it. The most important connecting link then, between the ideal and the practical in the kindergarten programme, is the kindergartner.

The next point is the consideration of the motive which will determine a teacher's influence in the kindergarten. If every individual is living out, each moment, his own view of the relation between the world's purpose and immediate necessity, he will give back to the world what he feels the world has given him, he will give back the meaning which the world has for him. Professor James says, your philosophy "is your individual way of just seeing and feeling the push and pressure of the cosmos." [2] The philosophy of the kindergartner governs the programme. It will indicate the goal toward which to strive and also point out the path by which this can be reached. Let us consider the attitude of the kindergartner toward a few of the philosophical problems which will most strongly affect the programme.

The attitude which the kindergartner will try to create toward herself will depend upon her own feeling toward the spirit in the

[1] The word "materials," as here employed, covers everything that a child uses as a means in gaining control of his experience. Conversation, song, and story are materials for the tongue, rhythm and games for the body, handwork of various kinds for the hand.

[2] William James, *Pragmatism*, p. 4.

universe. She could hold one of three differing views (1) that spirit is transcendent only, (2) that it is immanent only, or (3) that it both enfolds and is in matter. If (1) God is transcendent only, the kindergartner will rule her little world with absolute authority, requiring blind obedience, probably controlling with kindness, but considering no appeal possible. With this attitude there is a tendency to ignore the child's impulses and instincts, using artificial means to make growth. If (2) spirit is immanent solely, there will be no attempt to set a standard. The decision of the children will be as important as that of the teacher. Her idea will be, that a child will force his best growth if allowed to follow his own wish. If (3) the same spirit is in and around all, impulses and instincts will be utilized to make toward the highest ideals known. The children will be helped to work for self-control by exercising their own power of making decisions, but these will be aided by the suggestion and example of the adult. This adult will reserve to herself the final authority, where permanent injury, either physical or moral, might result.

Kindergartners may have differing views concerning the relation of the past to the present. This will affect the development of the social spirit among the children. If (1) the values recognized by the best men of today are the only ones of worth, children must be made to conform to those standards. If (2) the ideals of the past are as important as those of the present, children may be allowed to form their own ideals as a group without advice or aid. But if (3) the values found by the race in its gradual development have had their share in forming the models of the present, which represent the highest aspirations of the race, the kindergartner will recognize the place which childish standards should have in the growth of the group; but by example and suggestion she will seek to elevate the ideal to what more nearly approximates the best of today. There will be the gradual evolution of a society growing in a way similar to man's, founded upon the desire for activity and the gregarious instinct. First, (*a*) the children will all do the same thing at the same time; (*b*) a little later the result of the activity will be put together to form a common product. Then (*c*) will come the choice of a leader with all the children following. Next (*d*) will come the planning of a purpose by contributions from many individuals; this purpose will then be carried out by each child in his own way. Finally (*e*) will come the planning of a common purpose which can be accomplished only by each child perfecting the particular share which falls to his lot. The kindergartner will use these methods with all materials, progressing as far as she can with each as she will realize that between four and six years of age is the period for the most rapid development of social ideals.

The attitude cultivated toward materials will depend largely upon what the kindergartner considers most real in life. (1) The extremists, such as the early Christians, held that reality was spirit only, appearance was to be despised. (2) Others, as the later Greeks, believed that reality was only in what stimulated the senses. (3) Some philosophers of the present maintain that reality is the complete union of the spiritual and the material, the latter being the form in which spirit, in order to exist in this world, must embody itself. If (1) spirit is the solely important, that time is wasted which is spent dealing with the concrete; conversations, stories and songs which treat of virtues and other abstractions will be the only valuable parts of the programme. There will be a constant play of moods, but the essence of each will be lost because not embodied in form. If (2) on the other hand, the material side is solely valuable, materials will be used as ends in themselves; acquisition of facts, perfection of form and ability to practice technique will be the aim. Each thing, even the kindergarten itself as a whole, will be so complete that it will show a finish very pleasing to the adult. If (3) reality is the unity of the spiritual and the material, the kindergartner will lead a child to feel that there should be a guiding thought which seeks expression through all the materials at his command, through conversation, story, song, rhythm, game and handwork. Balance will always be preserved; the creative spirit will be called forth and take form in something adequate to the significance of the moment. A child will gain a feeling of the self as an organic unity; thought and expression in perfect accord will intensify the personality.

The kindergartner's yearly and even daily plans will be influenced by her view concerning the teleology of the universe. She may think that (1) God's design is static and unchangeable, in which case, she can have a fixed programme which will be of use everywhere. She may believe that (2) there is no preconceived plan, that the purpose is gradually evolving as the universe develops, then she will use any momentary suggestion of the children as a basis for work. But if (3) God's purpose is a living, growing one which man is helping to embody, the kindergartner will have a definite plan in mind, but it will be a principle rather than a design, so flexible that it will allow for variations which would be more valuable for the children at the particular time and place than the detail she had prepared.

In the kindergartner's attitude toward good and evil will be found the key to her discipline. If (1) because the body contains a soul, every human being is naturally good, mature ideals will be held up for copy in the belief that this is all that is necessary to bring a child back to rectitude. If, on the other hand, (2) being in a fleshy body means a natural inclination to sin, the evil must be driven out at all costs even by negative, compulsory methods. There may be another view (3) that "goodness" is a relative term, according to the standards of society, which are constantly changing. If evil is untrained impulse, the teacher will generally notice an offending action by suggesting a more virtuous way to free the energy.

Lastly, the view which the kindergartner holds of the nature of unity will be at the basis of her attitude toward the principle of interaction and will determine her choice of topics and method of treatment. If (1) she leans to the ideal side, the adult will give much and the child little. Any subject which the adult feels of value will be presented, trusting that the child will gain something from its consideration. If (2) emphasis is placed on the practical side, the respective shares will be reversed. Whatever interests the child will be taken up in the same way that a child uses it, for its momentary significance only. If (3) unity means the combining of two equal though unlike elements, both adult and child must have equivalent parts in carrying out the principle of interaction. It will fall to the child's lot to select the points of interest for discussion (these for a five-year-old child will be in his immediate surroundings), and to the adult to find wherein they can be stamped with the values which will lead toward the acceptance of race judgments.

In summing up, if it were possible to mention all the methods included under numeral one (1) under each point, they would be seen to carry out a very consistent philosophy. A totally opposing view, and yet consistent in itself, would be found under (2); and the middle view under (3). Very few people are extremists, yet there is a tendency to lean more to one side than the other. Along the middle line lies truth. Emphasis on either the ideal or the practical in the kindergarten programme makes it one-sided. The true relation is the union of the two and the degree to which this relationship is maintained depends upon one factor. That factor is a personality.

The usual programme states the topic chosen, the idea which the children are to gain from its consideration, and also the particular method and purpose of each part of the day. The real programme can never be written, for the personal touch of the kindergartner arouses the controlling ideas, and is the most powerful method.

CONSTRUCTIVE ACTIVITIES AS AN ESSENTIAL AND IMPORTANT FACTOR IN THE ELEMENTARY SCHOOL COURSE

EUPHROSYNE LANGLEY
School of Education, The University of Chicago

"Constructive Activities in the Elementary School"— that is my topic, and any discussion of it must be prophecy rather than history, for as yet the elementary school has had no constructive activities. Ten years ago a wave of criticism to the effect that the schools were impracticable, and could not hold the children, led to a widespread determination to put in manual training. That was to be the specific for the ills diagnosed by the critics, but our specific, it is now said, has failed to work a cure. And why? For the very good reason that though the manual-training prescription was duly written out, the medicine was never actually administered to the patient. I cannot find a school in this country where shop-practice for boys and girls is found throughout the elementary school.

The name manual training appears often in courses of study, but, when analyzed into its actual constituents, it is, outside of shop-work for boys in the seventh and eighth grades, hardly more than a chaotic assemblage of various forms of "busy work," relieved now and then by a bit of knife-work for boys, sewing for girls, or, for the younger children, a dip into the realm of the aesthetic in what Mr. Veblein calls "clay-muddling." Few subjects have been so handicapped as manual training; at the outset there was little in the way of equipment, no kilns, no looms, no benches. There was no time, the subject being superinduced on an already overcrowded curriculum. There was no pedagogical experience. There was no real understanding of the place of handwork in the educational state, and, at the best, manual training has never been more than an unnaturalized foreigner *in* the body politic, not *of* it.

Can handwork be made an effective part of the elementary school? Yes, but there must be a new point of view. We must be ready to put into practice what the best psychological theory has given us. There must be an entire reorganization of subject matter. The handwork must not be a new subject elbowing out space for itself and squeezing up the other subjects. No subject must be allowed to stand isolated. We must break down the pigeon-holes into which kinds of knowledge have been separately bunched. The three R's, though hoary with respectability, are not the pivots on which the educational system turns. No child has an intellectual appreciation of the value of reading, writing, and arithmetic as such. They become of importance to him only when they are the means through which he attains some desired end. Take a child in the first grade. Give him the simplest forms of constructive activity, let him build a playhouse, make jelly or dry apples, dye wool and weave tiny rings. The wooden house, instead of being "so big" by hand is a definite number of inches on the ruler. The materials that enter into the making of jelly are weighed and combined in definite proportion. The weaving of rings demands careful laying out of spaces before the design can be put in. Thus through the actual making of things, number work, in terms of measurements and weights is levied upon each activity. The record of the work in the child's own notebook turns into reading and writing. In a perfectly natural, simple fashion the child reaches out through his social occupations to the more formal studies, which, under such circumstances, cease to be formal or even formidable.

As the "three R's" become the tools which express and reinforce the activities, on the one hand, so, on the other, history, geography, and nature-study, a group in which each is the complement of the others, should form the industrial and social background from which the activities themselves spring. It is illogical and arbitrary to tear apart subjects which rightly belong together in order to build a series of separate coops in which to house a curriculum.

Constructive activities demand a constructive method, and a constructive method insists that the order of introducing handicrafts should be from the kindergarten up, rather than from the eighth grade down. A right constructive method also implies that the handicrafts should not follow along a line of prescribed models arranged from the point of view of the tool and of the adult organizing mind, but should be based absolutely on the subject-matter taught and should be vitally related to each other.

One of the effects of such reorganization is a saving of time. With such fusion of studies as I have briefly indicated, all the formal subjects usually taught in the grade, plus actual shop work in *all* the handicrafts, can be adequately taught without the expenditure of an extra half hour of time. The cost of such reorganization would be chiefly the initial expense in the way of additional space and equipment, and the permanent expense of perhaps two additional teachers in a school of average size. And finally, to make such reorganization effective, there must be mental organization on the part of both grade teacher and special teacher, and the special teacher should add to a broad pedagogical outlook a sound technical training.

What would be the effect of such school work on children? The most startling fact concerning the elementary school is the fact that of those who enter the first grade 80 per cent. do not reach the eighth, an educational leak which, if paralleled in business, would mean bankruptcy. It is my belief that no possible agency could so effectively hold a child in school as a right readjustment of the elementary course on the basis of handicrafts, and I say put the handwork in from the kindergarten up, because the children fall out chiefly in Grades 3, 2, and 4, and in that order. Consider for a moment the agencies which the modern feeling of responsibility for the child brings into co-operative guardianship around the third-grade boy who wishes to play truant. A recent report lists them for us: The truant officer, the factory inspector, the probation officer, the charity worker, the sociologist, the social settlement worker, the woman's club, the teacher, the principal, and the humanitarian—all these to make one boy stay in the third grade. And yet he slips through the meshes of the educational system and escapes to his true school, the street. This small boy has more ingenuity and more energy than the school in its present organization can use, an ingenuity and energy certain to be destructive unless we can make them constructive.

If the money spent, and now necessarily spent, on restraint, constraint, reformation, were turned over into the school funds and expended on prevention, children and communities would be immeasurably the better therefor. That constructive activities would hold the child is clearly apparent from our truant schools, where the most difficult children are so held, and the report of their desirable activities comes with pathetic emphasis to the good little boy who has no such opportunities. We can quite understand the inoffensive little chap who in Chicago was found deliberately throwing stones at windows that he might be sent to Bowmanville (the parental school) "where they make things."

Now if we do succeed in holding the children through the eight grades our educational problem is practically solved. It is because we have not been able to do this that the manufacturers have come forward with their remedy, which is to push the trade ideal down into the grades. Appalled at the lost 80 per cent., at the mass of raw material not converted by the school into marketable stuff, dismayed by their own inability to get skilled workmen, they say, give us the child at the earliest possible moment, at the place where you no longer hold him; let him select a trade, and we will at least make a tolerable artisan of him. There can hardly be a movement more significant and more important than to have the proverbial apathy of communities toward educational questions broken in upon by the alert interest of business men. They are progressive, practical, accustomed to see a weakness and remedy it without any beating around the bush. They command money and influence. What they ordain is almost certain to come to pass. I heartily agree with their plan of establishing trade schools. They are an imperative need. But I am strongly of the opinion that the trade school should not begin its especial work till the close of the elementary school. In other words, I do not believe in the two sorts of elementary school, one bent to fasten on to a trade school, the other bent to fasten on to a "culture" school. Handwork in the elementary school should be the same whether the child is destined for the carpenter's bench, the professor's chair, or any of the vast range of occupations between these. Differentiation can seldom come wisely into play in the elementary school. Vocational selection, if imposed upon the child while still in the grades, is likely to be a disastrous mistake. No teacher, no parent even, holds the divining-rod whereby may be discovered the secret springs of a child's best future activity. Even voluntary early vocational selection is not to be trusted. It is liable to be whimsical, uncertain, determined by temporary influences. If the kind of occupation fervently made by every boy of ten were to reach mature realization, the army and the navy, the police force, the livery business, would be steadily overcrowded. It is hardly reasonable to expect a child of ten or twelve to select out of the great industrial forces of the world that particular line in which his contribution to those forces should run, nor should it be the purpose of the elementary school to urge such selection.

Courses in the elementary school should be planned with the idea of giving to each child the utmost in the way of general development possible to him. It is on this basis alone that constructive activities should be put into the first eight grades. I think of the child as at the hub of a wheel. All his studies and activities are the spokes that connect him with the rim, or the world in general. And he must be led to look along each spoke to each section of the rim. Each handicraft, each subject, should be considered as a means in throwing what Browning calls "films of connection" between the child and his environment. If you set him too early in an appointed groove you unduly narrow his experience. You compel him to look along one spoke to one section of the rim, instead of to all. You strengthen one film of connection at the expense of the others. Every child, whether he is to be later in trade or in scholastic life, has a right to the widest opening out of his personal resources, the most varied activities, the most freely experimental stretching-out of tentacles, that the best-planned, best-equipped elementary school can offer. By all means give every child a chance at a trade, but first give him the opportunity of being a developed individual.

Reorganization such as I believe in, a reorganization called for by two expert opinions, that of the business man and that of the small boy who plays truant at the third grade, would, I am confident, serve even the manufacturer's need better than his own method which, indeed, he does not propose as ideal but as a practical meeting of a present situation. Business statistics are as relentless as those of the schools and show that boys who go directly into some trade at fourteen to sixteen usually come to the limit of their advancement by eighteen, while those who can get more training are the ones who go on to higher positions.

To sum up: I believe in handwork in the elementary school, from the kindergarten up. I believe not in one or two activities, but in all the activities taught in real shops, in a workmanlike manner, from the standpoint of industrial history, to both girls and boys. I believe that the result of such training will be a product of greatly increased value to trade, to the college world, and to life in general, and I believe that this ideal can be widely accomplished only when the business man and the pedagogue make it their common problem.

A MORNING EXERCISE [1]

THIRD GRADE—FRANCIS W. PARKER SCHOOL

PEARL BACKUS CARLEY
Third Grade Teacher

The following reports were given by the children of the third grade at morning exercises. They are the outgrowth of a year's work in the study of the history of Chicago, and illustrate one phase of the development of transportation.

Last year the third grade studied about early Chicago, and the different ways of traveling in the early days. We decided to make a train of cars in the sloyd shop. We chose the cars because they are made just outside of the city, and because Chicago is such a very large railroad center, and because going by train is the most rapid way of traveling.

The reason we did not make a passenger train is because there is so much shipping and commerce going on in the city, and the passenger cars are too hard to make.

We also made plans for the truck, the wheels, and the track. We thought it would be nice to give the cars to the kindergarten children.

JOSEPHINE PALMER

Two people worked on a car. If each child made one car, there would be too many cars, and we would not get them finished. One worked at the sides and floor; the other one made the ends, the top, and the running-board. We put two coats of paint on them. One child put on one coat of paint, and the other put on the last coat. We grooved the sides and ends with a carving tool to make it look like boards running up and down. We used large staple tacks for the steps. We named each car and planned the lettering. We called the cars the "F.W.P. Fast Freight."

MILDRED ZENOS

We did not go to the carshops to measure the cars, as we had all seen freight cars, and we had a good book[2] with pictures and measurements given.

[1] This article is reprinted from the January, 1905, issue of the *Elementary School Teacher*. It furnishes the rounding-out of the series of lessons on the History of Chicago, which have appeared in the issues of this JOURNAL for October and December, 1907.

[2] American Car and Foundry Co.'s publication.

Each child used the book and selected the car he liked the best. I chose the coal car. It was 34 feet long. We decided upon the scale to use in making the cars. We first thought we would make them 1 inch to 1 foot, but 34 inches would make them too long. Then we thought that ½ inch to 1 foot would be better.

This is the plan of my car. HELEN STAUFFER

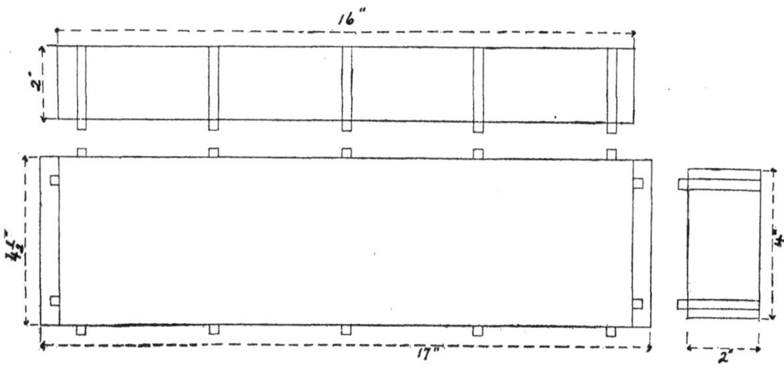

We wanted to know the capacity of our cars. We used inside measurements. The box car is 18½ inches long, 4 inches wide, and 3 inches high. I made a drawing of the floor of the car. We used 1-inch cubes to see how many cubic inches there were in one layer. We found 74 cubic inches. In three layers there were 222 cubic inches.

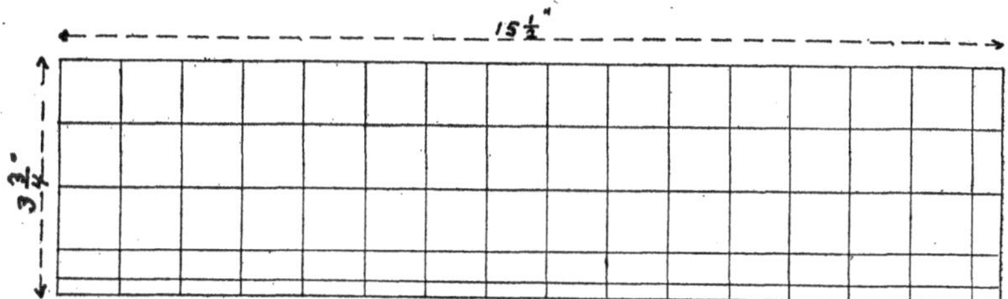

I made a drawing of the floor of the coal car too. In the first layer there were 58⅛ cubic inches. In two layers there were 116¼ cubic inches.

FRIEDA MAYNARD

How we made our wheels: We wanted to have iron wheels for our cars, but we could not make them. We used Frank's wooden model for casting wheels in lead because we wanted to know how they cast large wheels. We took two flasks and pounded molder's sand into one of the flasks, and set the wooden wheels half way in. Then we sprinkled dry sand on so that the molder's sand in the other flask wouldn't stick. Then we put the other flask on it and the pegs held it in place. We then took the two flasks apart and

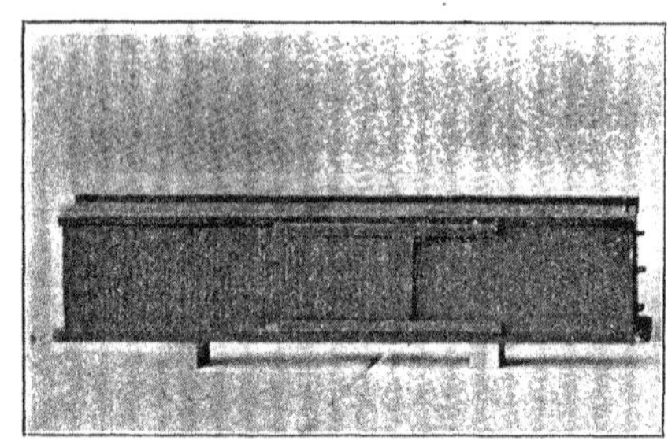

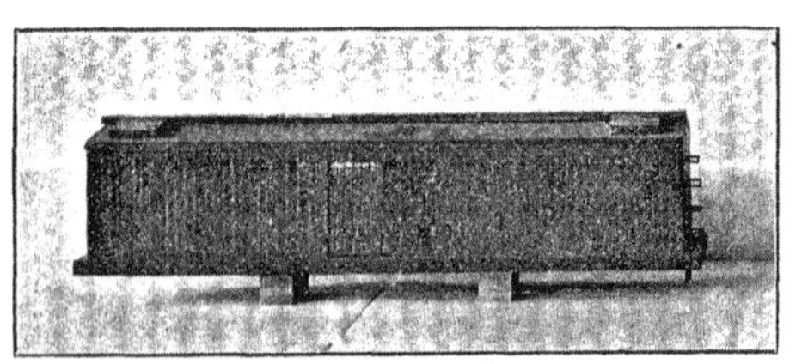

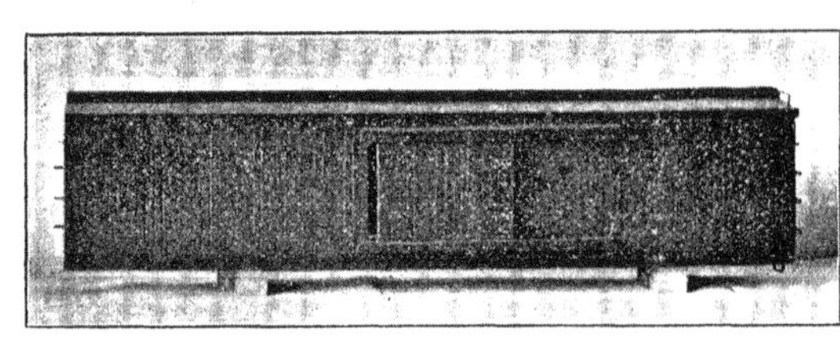

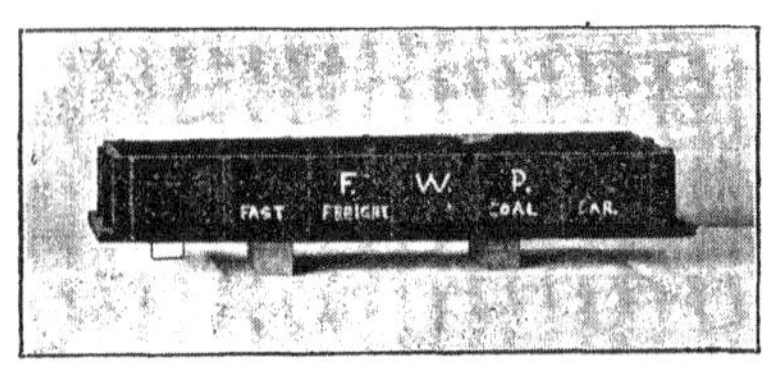
F. W. P.
FAST FREIGHT COAL CAR

took the wooden model out. We made air holes in the flask on top with a hatpin and a larger hole to pour the melted lead in. We put the flasks together again and poured the lead in the hole. When cool we took the flasks apart and this is the way the lead wheels looked. The reason there are these holes in them is because there were not enough air holes in the flasks and the melted lead couldn't push the air out.

DOROTHY WING

When we made the wheels we used the same scale that we did in making the cars, only we made the flange bigger. The reason we did this is because the little cars are not heavy enough to stay on the track.

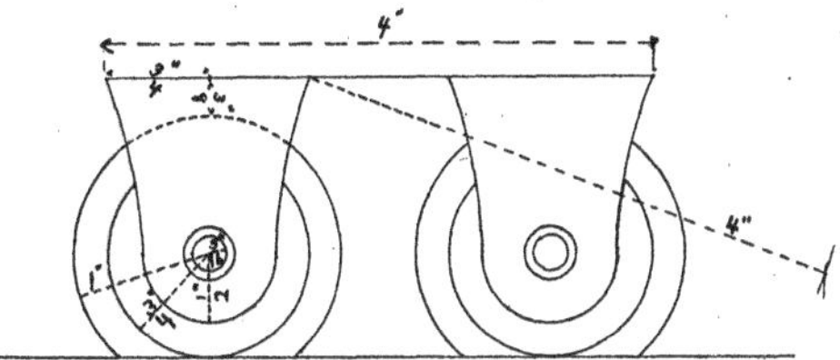

I made a model of the wheels on the lathe. Here is the plan of my wheels.

FRANK PACKARD

Everybody in the third grade last year made a drawing for the truck for our cars, and we at last decided upon this one. The truck is made of some metal. It fits on the bottom of the car and holds the wheels onto the car. We are going to screw our truck to the car so it can turn a little when going around curves. We did not plan to keep the side of the truck from hitting the wheels, and if it did the car could not move very easily, so we think we will put a washer between the truck and the wheels. The wheels are ⅜ inch below

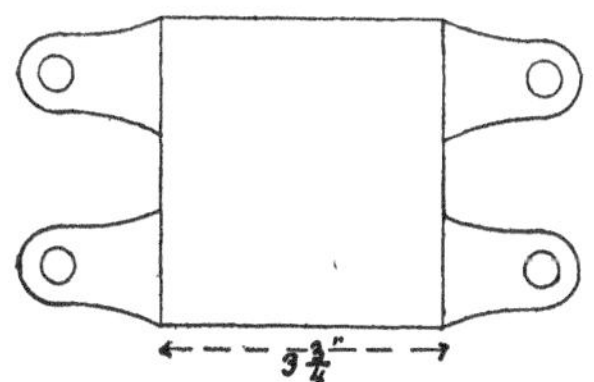

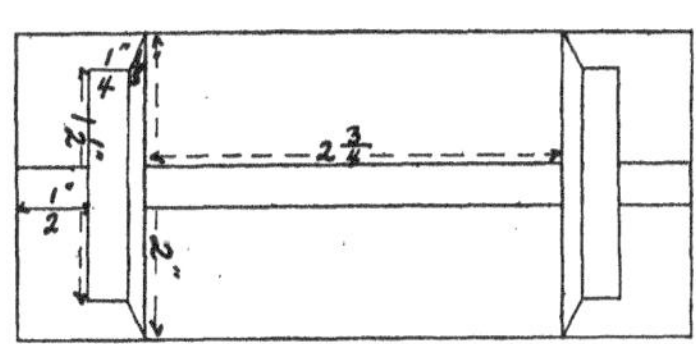

the bottom of the car. We made them that way so the wheels will not hit the bottom of the car. We shall make the hole that we shall put the axle in larger than the axle, so it will have plenty of room to turn around.

LUCY SMITH

If we were to use these cars we would send the stock car west to the cattle ranches to be filled with cattle and bring it back to the Stock Yards to unload. The refrigerator cars we would send to the Stock Yards, fill with fresh meat, and ship to the East where the people need it most. The coal car we could send right down in Illinois and fill with coal to help carry on the great manufacturing in the city. The furniture car we could fill with furniture made here and ship west where the people need it most. The box car we could take to Minnesota to fill with grain, or it might be used for any common freight. The caboos is used for the people who work on the train, and the men who look after the stock.

We went down to measure the kindergarten circle, and found it was 16 inches in diameter. We found there was room just outside of the circle for the track. It is to be made in sections so it can be stored away when not in use.

As we have done all we can on the cars, we have asked the big boys to help finish them, so the kindergarten children can use them very soon.

OWEN WHITE

There were many problems in arithmetic not suggested in the children's reports, such as finding the capacity of real cars, and finding the number of board feet and the cost of the lumber used in making the cars.

READING LEAFLETS, FRANCES PARKER SCHOOL PART I

THE HARVEST

JENNIE HALL

The following reading-lessons were made for a second grade during the process of reaping their harvest of corn from the school garden, of grinding it into corn-meal, and of cooking the meal. The sources of other kinds of flour interested the pupils, and they made the experiment of grinding and sifting rice, barley, wheat, peas, acorns, oat-meal. They also collected and mounted samples of various grains and the foods produced from them. Strange ways of cooking, too, were of interest; the children liked to hear about them and to try them. Among the Keystone Views are many stereoscopic pictures which were of great value in this piece of work.

AN INDIAN CORNFIELD

It was deep in the forest.
Great trees stood around it.
A little brook ran at one side.
Houses made of bark stood near it.
Paths led from the houses into the forest
It was cool and dark in the woods.
But the sun was shining on the cornfield.
Tall dead trees stood among the corn.
Once there had been no cornfield there.
Then the trees grew close together.
Bushes grew under them.
But the Indians needed a cornfield.
They cut down the bushes.

They pulled up the roots.
They cut down the small trees.
But it was hard to cut down the large ones.
"We will let them stand," the Indians said.
But their leaves kept out the sun.
The corn needed sunshine.
So the Indians made a fire at the foot of each tree.
It burned the trunk.
The trees were strong and full of sap.
So they did not burn down.
But they died.
The leaves fell off.
The sun shone down on the corn.
The dead trees spread their bare branches above it.
The corn waved its green leaves below them.

CORN TENTS

It was September.
We children were playing in the cornfield.
Big corn shocks stood about on the field.
Big yellow pumpkins lay here and there.
The ground was black and warm.
The sun was hot.
We sat in the shade of a shock.
"The corn shocks look like Indian tents," said Edith.
Then we all cried,
"Let's play Indian!"
Each child ran to a shock.
He pushed himself into it.

There we sat in the doors of our tents.
We looked out at one another.
But John sat still on the ground.
He was working with his knife and a cornstalk.
"Why don't you come, John?" we called.
"I am a white man making a fiddle," he said.
"I will play it and you Indians may come and dance."

EDITORIAL NOTES

When a movement is passing through an experimental stage, it requires courage and a certain degree of hardihood to respond to the educational public when they request the publication of some statement as to what is being attempted and what accomplished.

Reconstruction of the Kindergarten Movement

During the past decade the kindergarten movement in education has experienced some painful throes in the process of reconstruction. It has, however, stood the test of this crucial transition, thus disappointing the critics who saw in its externals and technique nothing more than a passing educational fad. But it is arising from its own ashes by outgrowing the superficial practice and traditions of its early history, thus fulfilling its promise of a valuable contribution to education. This development was prophesied by students whose faith was unshaken by the early mistakes, because they saw more implied in Froebel's philosophy than shown in his own applications or those which his more recent exponents had realized. In this promising process of reconstruction the effort is being made to build up a practice and application more worthy of Froebellian philosophy and theory.

Froebellian Philosophy and Elementary Education

It is generally conceded by the more thoughtful leaders in modern educational theory that the philosophy of Froebel, while incomplete and unsystematized as a whole, is marvelous in its intuitive insight and worthy of most serious study. Until recently, those men who had given the most scholarly study to the theory of education promulgated by Herbart, were utterly ignorant of the equally valuable contribution made by Froebel. The great Froebel is now coming to his own. Students of elementary education are no longer blinded by the sometimes puerile expression of his deep philosophy of life and education as typified in the kindergarten; they are beginning to see the Froebel who is larger and greater than any of the specific technicalities in which he often most inadequately attempted to realize his own philosophy. One might venture the statement that as the debt of the elementary school to Herbart is universally understood and conceded, and his theory quite thoroughly worked out, many of the masters in our universities are now turning their attention to Froebel, bringing to bear upon his philosophy the scholarly research and analysis bestowed upon Herbart a generation ago.

Thus the Froebel who was in the sole possession of the kindergarten and of a limited number of school men, such as Dr. William T. Harris, Dr. William N. Hailman, and Col. Francis Parker, is now coming into the possession of the elementary school as well. It is not generally appreciated that Froebel had applied his voluntaristic philosophy to the process of education in the elementary school with recognized success before he concentrated his study upon the stage of development for which he planned the activities and instrumentalities of the kindergarten.

It is deeply significant and prophetic of the only true solution of the union between the kindergarten and the elementary school that some of our leading universities are offering courses in the theories of Herbart and Froebel. The masculine gender is generously represented not only in the staff of instructors, but in the enrolment of the classes. Here are to be found men who are preparing for the positions of principal and superintendent of schools and for instructors in our normal schools affiliated with state institutions or universities.

Thus Froebel is no longer in the exclusive possession of the kindergarten and the feminine gender. It behooves the kindergartners of the future to bring to the study of Froebel a scholarly preparation or we will find our birthright taken from us. We will be left with a conception of our own great leader which will be narrow and meager as compared with that of the masculine students of Froebel in these universities.

As was to be expected, this more critical study of Froebel is bringing to light his limitations as well as his genius, his ofttimes faulty applications as well as his great principles. This broader interpretation of Froebellian philosophy and its application to the problems of the elementary school, is not only demanding a reconstruction of the traditional methods of the elementary school, but an equally radical reconstruction of the traditions and practice of the kindergarten. This must be done if the latter is to survive and hold a dignified position in the educational systems of the future.

This need for regeneration within the kindergarten itself, has caused some anxiety among kindergartners. There is a more or less vaguely defined tendency to divide into factions in favor of or opposed to reconstruction. Some feel the urgent necessity for increasingly modifying the practice as laid down by Froebel himself; others are equally certain that such an attempt will be most disastrous to the movement and that the kindergarten must be maintained in its entirety of theory and practice if its true value is to be passed on to future generations. On the whole a fair majority of kindergartners are coming to realize that a respectful, scholarly criticism is not only inevitable but desirable.

Scholarly Criticism of Traditional Method Desirable

Those who believe that the kindergarten must be rescued from its own formalism and traditionalism have faced the serious necessity for experiment and research in attempting to apply Froebel's principles in a more consistent practice. This experimental work has been so absorbing, the attempt to evolve a more worthy practice so demanding, that the participants have had little time to devote to the publication of articles which would explain the work being done in this forward movement in kindergarten circles. In other words the kindergartners actively engaged in the attempt to find worthy substitutes for a sane reconstruction of the traditional procedure, have been too absorbed in the experimental demands to record the results of research, too conscious of the tentative value of the results of experiment to draw conclusions, too eager to move forward toward a more ideal vision to accept as final any results so far attained.

However, as the kindergarten is being incorporated in the public school system, superintendents, principals, and school men generally are urging kindergartners to make known from their point of view its present status and future needs. There is an increasing demand for a fuller understanding of the progress being made by the so-called "new movement" and the time has come when kindergartners must meet this responsibility if superintendents and principals are to participate in and give intelligent supervision to the kindergartens under their charge.

A group of kindergartners who early affiliated with the reconstructive movement in the kindergarten have responded to this call and there will be, through the coming year, one article on the theory and practice of the kindergarten in each number of the *Elementary School Teacher*. The contributors are Mrs. Alice H. Putnam, Froebel Training School, Chicago; Miss Bertha Payne, The University of Chicago; Miss Alice Temple, Mrs. Mary Boomer Page, Chicago Kindergarten Institute; Miss Nina Vandewalker, Milwaukee State Normal School; Dr. Jenny B. Merrill, Supervisor New York Public School Kindergartens; Miss Caroline T. Haven, Ethical Culture School, New York; Miss Patty S. Hill, Columbia University, New York.

Projected Articles on Theory and Practice of Kindergarten

These contributors were selected, not on the basis of intellectual uniformity in either theory or practice, but rather on the basis of a unity of purpose, a purpose which grew out of an earnest desire to see the kindergarten go forward in the realization of its prophetic greatness, even at the cost of death to its dearest traditions; if by dying to the letter of the outer form, the divine spirit of the kindergarten could be born in the light of the new day.

These articles are an effort to state to educators in general, in as simple terminology as possible, what is going on in the kindergarten world, what progress has been made, and what reconstructions found necessary in the light of recent developments in philosophy, psychology, and sociology. The ground is new and the attempts to improve upon the earlier practice will necessarily often be faulty. The interpretations, the inferences and conclusions will quickly be improved upon and possibly superseded, as more scholarly study is brought to bear upon the problems under consideration. This is but the price of progress and the time has now come when attempts which are being made to better our best in the kindergarten should be made known to all educators, including our professional co-workers who hold opposing points of view.

These articles are published with the sincere desire that they may provoke discussion and study, and that through the fire of criticism the gold may be separated from the dross and only the most worthy elements survive. If this great movement is to grow and the kindergarten be liberated from the faulty traditions which are necessarily mixed with its illuminating truths, we who desire to participate and contribute to this reconstruction, even in the humblest way, must not be too fearful of being found in the wrong. As explorers in a new land, too vast for any one person to investigate thoroughly alone, let each return from the search, eager to contribute to the whole the small knowledge gained and in turn to have his personal impressions rectified and illuminated by the contributions of the whole. Such a spirit will in time prove the true value of the principles of the kindergarten to all education and make it possible for both the kindergarten and the elementary school to absorb the eternally true in Froebellian philosophy while eliminating the limitations growing out of his education, training, personality, temperament, and period.

If these articles be found worthy of collecting into a volume for publication at the end of the year for the use of kindergartners, elementary teachers, principals and superintendents, all is well. If the discussion and criticism which they call forth bring the kindergarten to a higher level of attainment, and, having done this, they perish, all is well. If, as a result of the discussion and criticism provoked, the new movement in kindergarten outgrows these articles on the upward way to the realization of higher ideals, the contributors will feel satisfied to see their personal contributions fade in the light of any newer and better thought which they may call forth.

Those who help us to detect our errors will contribute, not only to the kindergarten movement, but will place the contributors themselves under everlasting obligations.

PATTY SMITH HILL

TEACHERS COLLEGE
COLUMBIA UNIVERSITY

NOTES AND NEWS

George B. McClellan, mayor of New York City, is to preside at the second annual congress of the Playground Association of America which meets in that city the second week of September. The congress will endeavor in every possible way to arouse a strong public sentiment in favor of playgrounds. Among the prominent speakers will be Governor Hughes, George E. Johnson, Professor Royal Melendy, Dr. E. E. Arnold, E. B. DeGroot, Professor C. T. Hetherington, Dr. Luther Gulick, and Joseph Lee.

Dr. W. S. Cornell has an article in the *Psychological Clinic* on "Mentally Defective Children in the Public Schools." His work is based upon personal investigations made in pursuit of his official duties as a school medical inspector of Philadelphia. He finds that there are four distinct groups of children: (1) children who are apparently mentally defective, but are really only undeveloped because of poor general health, poor eyesight, or improper home surroundings; (2) dull children; (3) backward children, and (4) feeble-minded children. He compares dull children with bright children with respect to their physical defects, and finds that while 70 to 80 per cent. of the bright children have no defects, only 44 to 60 per cent. of the dull children are without such defects. About 10 per cent. of the bright children have nose and throat defects, and very nearly 30 per cent. of dull children have such defects. He calls attention to the large number of feeble-minded children in the public schools. He estimates that 0.1 per cent. of the children in the public schools are actually feeble-minded, 0.5 to 1 per cent. are truly backward, and about 10 per cent. are dull.

The Children's School Farm movement, which was started by Mrs. Henry Parsons in New York City, some seven years ago on park land, has spread so rapidly throughout the country that there is now a scarcity of efficient teachers to take charge of the various "school farms" in hundreds of different localities. Nature-study teachers are fairly plentiful, but while it was thought sufficient recruits could be gained from their ranks to carry on the school farm movement, it has been found that, without special training, these teachers, in many cases, are as unsuccessful in conducting a children's garden as an ordinary carpenter has often proved to be when tried as a teacher of a large class in manual training in the public schools.

To meet this demand for efficient teachers of children's gardens and elementary agriculture the International Children's School Farm League carried on a special six weeks' course in the practical making and management of children's gardens, at the summer school of New York University this past year. The fine old garden of the Schwab estate was placed at the disposal of the university, as a laboratory and outdoor classroom.

"The ordinary assumption that school gardening is merely the conversion of garden work into a pleasure for children is altogether wrong," says Mr. Parsons, secretary of the League. "Neither is the work taken up merely to show the children how to grow vegetables. The gardens are nature's laboratories, in which her laws take on reality, through the simple garden experiments which illustrate processes of life. Educators now realize that such instruction increases the benefits to be derived from textbooks by fully one hundred per cent."

The American School Hygiene Association is to issue a monthly paper entitled *School Hygiene*. The first number, though small in size, contains thirteen articles and abstracts on such important subjects as eye-strain in school-children, school baths, prevention of tuberculosis, playground legislation, the department of hygiene, and the education of the public in scientific medicine. The journal "stands for an attempt made to call the attention of as many persons as may be reached to the existing school conditions in the country and to methods of improving them." At the same time it aims to foster an increase of knowledge on topics of school hygiene, most of the data concerning which is tied up in reports of scientific societies and in other technical volumes.

One of the most suggestive summer-school experiments we have seen comes from Newton among children of a tenement district, and is reported by the *Springfield Republican*. The school authorities rented a three-room tenement not far away and the class proceeded to make it fit for living purposes, by scrubbing, painting, papering, whitening, repairing, and furnishing. The boys set window-panes, repaired wood-work, made furniture and wove rugs. The girls made draperies and other furnishings. Curtains of unbleached muslin were stenciled by the primary department. With the exception of a range, bed and bureau, which were donated, all of the furniture was made by the class. It included chairs, tables, such conveniences as towel-racks, towels, and wash-cloths, every detail of an adequately furnished tenement. A window-box of geraniums was added for ornament. The total cost, including two months rent at $6 a month, was $25.

BOOK REVIEWS

The Auxiliary Schools of Germany. Six lectures by B. MAENNEL, Rector of the Mittelschule in Halle a. d. Saale. Translated by FLETCHER BASCOM DRESSLAR, Associate Professor of the Science and Art of Teaching in the University of California. Department of the Interior, Bulletin No. 3, 1907. Pp. 137.

This is a timely publication of the history of a movement now some fifty years old in Germany which has for its aim the solution of the problem of the education of backward or defective children. At a time when in the United States the consideration of this problem is being attacked with seriousness, the experience of Germany will be welcomed by all who desire either for scientific or practical reasons to know what have been the results of this half-century of effort.

The lectures of Rector Maennel are replete with information of the sort one requires in order to form an idea of just what the procedure of such schools is. This feature is worthy of special emphasis and renders the publication especially valuable for reference. Following an interesting historical sketch of the movement in Germany and elsewhere throughout Europe and in America, there are chapters on reasons for the establishment of auxiliary schools, admission procedure, the parents and the whole environment of auxiliary school pupils before and during the school period, health conditions of auxiliary school pupils, the pupils of the auxiliary school and their characterization, the building for the auxiliary school, classification of pupils in an auxiliary school and the number in each class, the daily programme, the curriculum, methods of instruction, discipline in the auxiliary school, preparation of auxiliary school pupils for confirmation, the community and the state in their relations to the auxiliary school, the teachers and the principal of the auxiliary school, the pedagogical significance of the auxiliary school. The bureau of education has done the teachers of this country a service by making this material available.

W. B. O.

Linguistic Development and Education. By M. V. O'SHEA. New York: The MacMillan Company, 1907. Pp. 346. $1.25.

The relatively large part assigned to instruction in language, both the vernacular and foreign, in our elementary and secondary schools, seems to warrant the attempt to put that instruction on the best attainable scientific basis. This basis the book under review aims to set forth. As the author states in his preface, the field is a large one and in attempting to cover it one would of necessity be restricted to the exposition of principles, with the use of just enough concrete material to serve as illustration. The author further states that the book owes its origin to his own desire to work out these principles in the course of observing the linguistic development of his own children and of their mates. The author has used the researches of other workers in the field with full bibliographical references, so that the result is a fairly comprehensive survey of the course and scope of investigation up to date.

It is not unfair, perhaps, to say that the chief value of the book lies in the organization of material scattered about in special articles and separate treatises, so as to present a comprehensive view of the whole process of linguistic development, rather than in the new facts reported, or new theories propounded. To have made this body of opinion accessible in the form of an outline of theory is to have performed a worthy service to education.

There are thirteen chapters in the book of 347 pages. There is a general bibliography in addition to the foot-notes and a subject index. In the thirteen chapters two general phases of the subject are treated, non-reflective processes in linguistic development (Part I), and reflective processes in linguistic development (Part II). Under the first heading, there is the discussion of prelinguistic expression; early re-action upon conventional language; parts of speech in linguistic activity; inflection, agreement and word-order; development of meanings. Under the second are treated acquisition of word-ideas in reading, acquisition of graphic word-ideas, development of meaning for word-ideas in reading, development of efficiency in oral expression, processes in graphic expression, development of efficiency in composition, acquisition of a foreign tongue.

W. B. O.

The Welfare of Children: A Reading List on the Care of Dependent Children. By the BROOKLYN, N. Y., PUBLIC LIBRARY. Pamphlet, pp. 44.

The Welfare of Children is a most excellent reading-list which includes both books and magazine articles. It is compiled by Miss Mary F. Lindholm of the Brooklyn Public Library staff, and is published by the Public Library. The annotations are brief and the references are classified under the following headings: I, Bibliographies; II, General Sources of Information; III, Factors Tending to Produce Juvenile Delinquency and Dependence; IV, Methods of Prevention and Reform of Juvenile Delinquents.

IRENE WARREN

SCHOOL OF EDUCATION

The Kindergarten in American Education. By NINA C. VANDEWALKER. New York: Macmillan, 1908. Pp. 274. $1.25.

There is a relation beteen American education and the kindergarten which is very intimate. One may have heard of the lack of interest in Froebel on the part of the Germans, yet he is unprepared to find how thoroughly many German educators still leave him out of account. A prominent schoolman was fairly shocked at the space and prominence given to Froebel by Professor Monroe in his textbook in the *History of Education,* and said to me, "I cannot understand you Americans. With us in Germany Froebel is an old woman." There is another side to this matter but that is found in those who are most alive to the new movements. But in the America of the last fifty years and the kindergarten there are common elements which may well make this period in the development of the institution the most important that may come to it.

This significant relationship has been sketched in part by various writers, but we are fortunate in having the full statement from so well qualified a person as the author. Miss Vandewalker has an acquaintance with the elementary school that few kindergartners possess, and she also combines the training and view-point of the normal school with that of the university. While she is recognized as a representative of the newer movement in the kindergarten, yet she shows evidence of an appreciation and understanding of the valuable elements in the position of those who belong to the older school.

The book is encyclopedic in nature. The student of almost any phase of the subject will find an abundance of material well selected and well organized. The first chapter and the last place the kindergarten with reference to the general educational movement both retrospectively and prospectively, while the ten intervening chapters, taking the Centennial and Columbian Expositions as stations, show the gradual development of the movement in relation to the surprisingly large number of organizations and associations which have contributed to its progress.

There is an appendix which gives references in kindergarten development in the different states. The index is fairly adequate but not complete, as one finds occasional material to which there is no reference. The large amount of detail in some of the chapters leads one to inquire whether, in a later edition, a calendar may not be included which will give in small compass the most important dates to which reference is made. The work is necessarily largely descriptive rather than critical, and one needs to consider some parts of its contents, as for instance certain books referred to from the standpoint of the complex social problems in which kindergartners are involved rather than from that of the most advanced educational standards. When, however, the author does undertake criticism the sifting usually is well done, as in the case of the Herbartian movement, and the tendencies in kindergarten philosophy. One could wish that the child-study movement had been handled more critically.

The material here brought together makes an excellent foundation upon which it is hoped there may be formulated a statement of educational theory and practice with reference to the needs of young children and also a thoroughgoing communication of the philosophy which lies back of the best practice of today. In the future the kindergarten may be less distinct from the rest of the school than it has been, but whatever synthesis the future educational system may reveal, the development of this half-century in the kindergarten will be an important factor.

Frank A. Manny

New York City

BOOKS RECEIVED

HENRY ALTEMUS CO., PHILADELPHIA

Work and Habits. By ALBERT J. BEVERIDGE. Pp. 96. Cloth, $0.50; ooze calf, $1.00.

Good Citizenship. By GROVER CLEVELAND. Pp. 78. Cloth. $0.50.

THE ARCADIA PRESS, NEW YORK

A Little Land and A Living. By BOLTON HALL; with a letter of introduction by WILLIAM BORSODI. Cloth. Pp. 287.

A. S. BARNES & CO., NEW YORK

The Child World Primer. By ALYS E. BENTLEY AND GENEVA R. JOHNSTON. Cloth. Illustrated. Pp. 128.

THE UNIVERSITY OF CHICAGO PRESS

The Seventh Yearbook of the National Society for the Scientific Study of Education: Part II, The Co-ordination of the Kindergarten and the Elementary School. (Supplement to Sixth Yearbook, Part II.) Paper cover. Pp. 66. $0.78 postpaid.

CLARENDON PRESS, OXFORD

Trois semaines en France. A French Reader. By L. CHOUVILLE. Edited by D. J. SAVORY; with questions for conversation and grammatical exercises by FRANCES M. S. BATCHELOR. Cloth. Pp. 127. *2 s.*

THE MACMILLAN CO., NEW YORK

The Last Days of Pompeii. (Macmillan's Pocket Classics.) By SIR EDWARD BULWER LYTTON. Edited, with Introduction and Notes, by J. H. CASTLEMAN. Cloth. Pp. 481. $0.25.

The Wonderful House That Jack Has. A Reader in Practical Physiology and Hygiene. By COLUMBUS B. MILLARD. Cloth. Illustrated. Pp. 359. $1.50.

How We Travel. A Geographical Reader. ("Home and World Series.") By JAMES FRANKLIN CHAMBERLAIN. Cloth. Illustrated. $0.40.

CHARLES E. MERRILL CO., NEW YORK

The Bender Primer. By IDA C. BENDER. Cloth. Illustrated. Pp. 128. $0.30.

VOLUME IX NUMBER 2

THE ELEMENTARY SCHOOL TEACHER

OCTOBER, 1908

FUNDAMENTAL FACTORS IN THE MAKING OF A KINDERGARTEN CURRICULUM

EARL BARNES

In the past, most curricula have been made to fit a theology or a philosophy. Today it is almost universally recognized that a curriculum should be made to fit the children who are to be affected by it. It is the crowning glory of the kindergarten that it has generally started its theories and its practice directly with the child and has studied to understand his nature and to meet his needs. Its successes have been based on the wisdom of its founder and on the splendid devotion of the master's followers; its mistakes have been the errors common to human nature.

During the last twenty years we have had a great deal of really scientific study devoted to little children. On the whole, the results of this study agree with the teachings of Frederick Froebel; they restate the earlier discoveries of great educational leaders, with here and there a modification or an addition. This paper seeks to state the fundamental factors in the making of a kindergarten curriculum from the point of view of modern genetic investigations.

If a scientist were set to study a child under six years old, the first thing to strike his attention would certainly be the marvelous activity of the specimen. He wriggles, squirms, gurgles, laughs, claps, creeps, walks, trots and tumbles about. He talks, cries, shouts, and rubs himself into every object he can reach, so that a student like Professor Dresslar is able to write a long article in merely enumerating the acts of a three-year-old for a half hour.

But the scientist will hunt in vain for any steady axis of organization running through this chaos of doing. This is why all records of infancy, like those of Miss Shinn or of Mrs. Moore, or even the volumes by Preyor, are such uninteresting and almost impossible reading for anyone, except students of childhood. A well-organized mind moves easily along the lines of its normal action; compelled to turn hither and yon in an attempt to follow the accidental movements of a child's mind it is quickly tired out. This is also the reason why any real work with little children is so fatiguing; and it explains the constant struggle between kindergartners and boards of education over the question of double sessions in kindergarten work. It is true that there is little difference between children in the last days of the kindergarten and the first days of the primary grades; but there is a vast difference between kindergarten children and primary children as a whole, and this difference is mainly due to the quality of fragmentariness in the activity and in the attention of the little ones.

The third quality that must strike the scientific observer of little children is their remarkable desire for, and facility in, social intercourse. Even in extreme infancy the baby longs to have someone near him. In his first days, he prefers to lie in a lap rather than in a cushioned crib. Only with protestations and cries will he break his social bonds and voyage off into the lonely land of sleep. In the first year he greets animals and babies as his peers; after the first year any child who seeks solitude is something of a monster. This intelligent interpretation of and response to the social forces about him early marks the child as the master of all living things. He learns quickly whom he can control and how to do it; whom he must obey, and why. At three years old he reads a face as adults read books; and at six he has passed through, and at least partially assimilated, most of the social experiences of life.

This social sensibility makes little children strangely imitative. Whatever any of us thinks that he tends to do; what we think with admiration tends doubly to pass over into action and hence into conduct. We live by our admirations; and that which we love, we become. Later in life, fixed habits and accepted ideas and ideals will inhibit this imitative tendency, but little children are the prey of all the suggestions that play upon them.

And because a little child is weak and unformed, and his ideas run always before his powers, he seeks to realize himself in imitative play. As I write these pages, three children are playing with a cart on the lawn. They have just made a little journey by sea and so the cart is a ship; the child in front is the captain; the one who pushes behind says he is the sailor; the smallest one, who, because he is the smallest, has been crowded into the back of the cart, cries lustily because he wants to be a sailor. "No," explain the others "you are the passenger; here is your ticket." Already, as I write these words, they have deserted the ship and have gone to play in the garden. Here you have an epitome of young childhood with its activity, its fragmentariness, its social demands, its openness to imitation and its attempt to realize life and prepare for it through imaginative play.

This, then, is the material we have to work upon—an undeveloped human being, active, chaotic, social, and hence imitative, ineffective and so driven to imagine, invent, and play at all sorts of actuality. The curriculum must be made to fit this individual and it must also anticipate and lead toward the life that we wish the child to grow into. That life is very different for different groups of children. It depends largely upon the philosophy, theology, and social and political theories of those who are in charge of the children. A kindergarten in a convent must care most to secure success in the life that follows this one; a select kindergarten in an aristocratic neighborhood will care especially to fit the children for the walk of life to which they have been called by their parents' wealth; a slum kindergarten must always be used as an instrument for improving the slums. In this paper, we shall take it for granted that the kindergarten is secular, democratic, and American.

To train a creature with the qualities we have described it is clear we must depend on his activity for our motive power. It is a sad thing when a school for little children neglects to train them; it is a sadder thing when it destroys the driving desire to do things. To maintain the hunger for activity we must have a curriculum providing for pretty constant physical play or work. This can be secured in organized indoor games, in industrial exercises, in gardening, in playground exercises, or in excursions. The children's corners in the recreation centers of Chicago are admirably devised to encourage activity, wide sand piles, ample wading pools, with swings and teeters to provide a succession of activities that can be combined in endless variety.

But this activity is merely opportunity for training. Play will keep activity alert, but work must organize this fragmentary activity into significant sequences. A recreation center may be merely a place for discharging unused energy; but a kindergarten must shape life, if it is to justify its existence. Here we meet the universal paradox of education. We must keep initiative unchecked and activity alert, and still shape desire and direct activity to ends that will be of deepest value in life. It is the old struggle of wind and rudder for the control of the ship; without wind, nothing is done; without rudder, no port is gained.

The directive work in the kindergarten, so far as guiding activity is concerned, must lie mainly in the direction of organizing the tyrannical but necessary reflexes that we call habits. Infant education should be mainly concerned with stocking and directing the subconscious nerve centers. The child should learn to walk well, to carry his head erect and his chest well forward, to step lightly, to run and dance, to shake hands, bow, pass articles or move a chair aside. He should learn to articulate clearly, speaking distinctly and agreeably; the pitch of his voice should be properly regulated, and harshness worked out of his tone; he should learn to sing and recite little poems agreeably. Laughing, grimaces, tricks of mouth and eyes, all these should be constantly shaped toward excellence. Wearing the clothes well, eating and drinking properly, should be reduced to habits, and then forgotten.

Of course, if the teacher is stupid she will make the children into self-conscious prigs, into little automata. That is why the teacher of little children should be wise and carefully trained, well bred and experienced in the usages of good society. The well-to-do have always looked after these matters with great solicitude, and hence they have been able to retain social leadership for themselves and for their children. Some day the children of the people will be trained in this early period, when life-long reflexes are being established, to act like cultivated boys and girls, and the action will strengthen the thoughts and the feelings that make a man truly cultivated. When that time comes, America will have a cultivated and humanized democracy capable of protecting itself against all class aggression and ready to live life with the grace and dignity that human life deserves.

And in the kindergarten all this training of lower nerve centers takes place in a social atmosphere to which the children are fully alive and to which they freely respond. Sympathy, emulation, hope, fear, selfishness, altruism, all the passions that gather round social life and intercourse are available for the teacher who knows how to use them. Hence the work and play must be directed to group activities that will give wide and ordered activity to all the feelings of social life. Just as the child is trained to walk erect, so he must be trained to play the game of life fairly and generously. As he is trained to articulate distinctly, so he must be trained to speak honestly. Most of us are good because we have been trained to be good, and we have the habit.

The teacher, standing as the embodiment of authority, can and should command absolute obedience; in the various combination of the group she will find all the other relations that go to make up our human institutions. The kindergarten is an enlarged and self-conscious home, and a miniature state. So, too, in groups, the industrial games can be carried through all stages of simple production and distribution; while in dramatic combinations, they can figure forth the relations and the crises of life. Probably all sex distinctions had best be, as far as possible, ignored in the kindergarten period. They are far too important in our adult life; they had best wait on older years.

To work out these basal conceptions of industry, society, and life the teacher must depend largely on imitation. All the surroundings of little children's lives should be simple and capable of childish imitation. The teacher should stand and walk well, she should have a cultivated voice and should dress with taste and variety. The kindergarten should look more like a living room than a school; and bad children should be quickly eliminated by making them good. We cannot afford to reform bad children, whether from rich homes or poor, by having them associate with good children four or five years old.

The imagination, as we have said, enables the child to accomplish through play what his powers cannot compass in reality. Hence, industrial games are very effective, but they should always be organized on the basis of some actual observation and experience. That is what imagination can do at this time; it can make observation real, through tactual and muscular experience. Nowhere else does the ordinary kindergarten curriculum lay itself open to graver criticisms than in the imaginative plays. They must be developed directly out of experience, even if they do not recapitulate the experiences of the race.

Dramatic activity, based on imagination, should deal also with the affairs of the home and the neighborhood. And here again they must really appeal to the children as connected with life; otherwise they are not exercises for imagination, but mere mimicry. Instead of gripping the feelings and shaping them, they stultify them. The real life of the homes from which the children come should be represented, but lifted and glorified by the play of imaginative fancy.

On the side of aesthetics we are coming to realize that little children have not the ability to grasp wholes, to feel the charm of proportions and of suggested associations in which all developed art rests. They like brilliant colors and strong sounds and they are especially fond of rhythmic repetition. Dress is the form in which beauty appeals to them most strongly and here it is doubtless blended with egotism, in their own case, or, when others are concerned, with admiration for the wearer. The kindergarten can do little more than give plenty of sense experiences, properly related, out of which the children in later years may build up forms of beauty.

Institutions have all the selfishness of human beings, with few of their generous impulses. They tend to usurp the proper functions of other related institutions and to gather everything into their own hands. The church illustrated this tendency during the Middle Ages. The public school now tends to take over the functions of the home, the neighborhood and the state itself. But the business of the school should be to supplement the home and related institutions. It is true that the teacher should have a complete philosophy of life in mind to guide her in her work, but in the country village the kindergarten curriculum should give much of what the city home naturally furnishes, while in Boston it should bring the child into contact with what the village child sees *daily all* about his home.

There are then these two reasons why we cannot formulate a universal curriculum for kindergartners. In the first place, the kindergarten must take up and use the experience the child has already met; and in the second place, it must supplement the home. It might be possible and desirable to work out type curricula for well-to-do country village homes, for industrial centers like Manchester, for congested slum districts, and for fashionable city homes. Where life is so fluid, however, as it is with little children, it must generally be better for the teacher to be well grounded in fundamental principles and then to work out a daily course of exercises, following the seasons, knitting her work on to daily experience and filling out the acreage of interest and need, not cultivated by the home. To do this, she must be well acquainted with the development of little children, she must have a vivid and complete philosophy of life, and she must be trained to think of her institution as one of several, all working to give the children life more abundantly.

The older school of kindergartners will say that in all this I have touched but the surface of the subject. They will say that this world of ours is knit together in a sane and comprehensible system and that the teacher of little children should always have this final scheme of things in mind and should present in the exercises and games types of universal and eternal excellence. They will tell me that only a great philosopher can see these universals in types and that Frederick Froebel has done this work for us and has given us a permanent frame work of symbolic exercises that we must be content to follow.

To this I can only reply that I doubt the finality of any interpretation of life. The theology of Froebel's day has largely disappeared; as Christian Scientist, as Agnostic, or as a Catholic, I must work over again my conception of the Eternal Cause of all things and of my relation to him. The political absolutism of Froebel's day, surrounded by French Revolution ideas, is giving place to something that looks more and more like cosmopolitan socialism. The formal modes of thought of the earlier nineteenth century have given way to investigation guided by hypothesis; and the next great synthesis may very well care less for form and color and more for spirit and life.

For myself, I am content to study the past in the light of present needs, to live in the present and hope forward. This is a time of transition and I do not dare chain my mind to any dogma. At the same time I realize the danger of going on without a definite sense of where I am going. I may waste my life and the lives of the children intrusted to me in an idle quest, but such is life. I cannot return to fixed dogmas in religion nor in politics—why should I in education?

PRIMITIVE SONGS AND DANCES: A SECOND-GRADE ASSEMBLY

MABEL RAY GOODLANDER
Ethical Culture School, New York City

THE CAVE MEN'S CHANTS

The immediate inspiration for these cave men's chants came from Miss Dopp's story, in *The Early Cave Men,* of the death of the saber-toothed tiger, who was killed by the hero Strong Arm. The people celebrated their deliverance from this terrible animal by a feast, where they rejoiced with chants and dances.

Before making their verses, the children were asked to imagine what the cave men probably said in their chants and decided on a few simple points, such as the following:

1. The cave men were glad Saber-tooth was dead.
2. He was a terrible beast and all the people feared him.
3. Strong Arm was a brave man and a hero.

As many of the children did not know the nature of a chant, this was explained and illustrated for them. In their own productions, however, the chant as differing from the more lyrical form of song was not insisted upon. The work was all oral; in some cases words and music were given together, but most of the children made their lines first and the music afterward.

The words and music are given here in their original form, except two verses, where individuals were helped by other members of the class in correcting the rhythm of their lines. The author of No. 3 borrowed his tune from No. 1, with some very slight changes. Chant No. 7 was composed by several children, each giving a sentence, which was written on the board by the teacher. The music was supplied afterward by one child.

The monotony of the music, with the repetition of phrases, noticeable in these verses, give them a form resembling in character the music of early peoples. Children's original songs often fail to have such a characteristic form because the demands of their subject are not so simple.

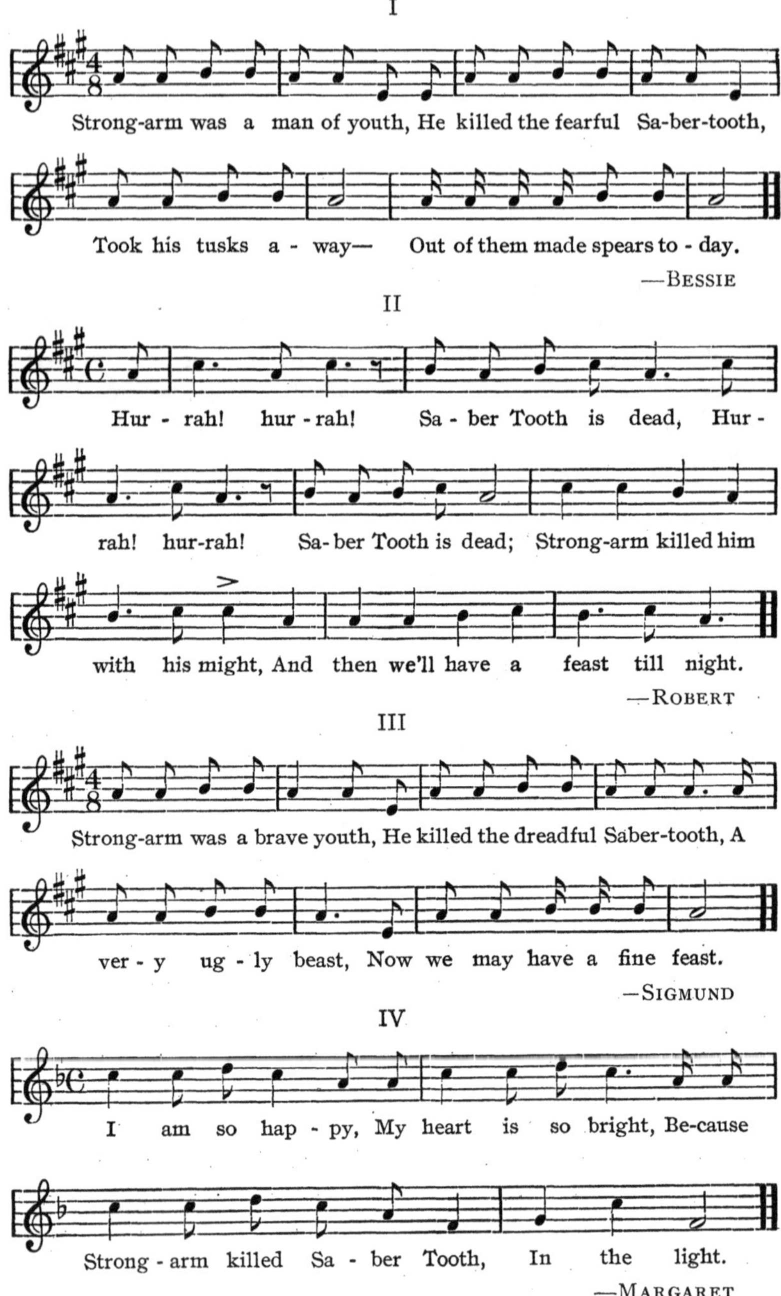
I
Strong-arm was a man of youth, He killed the fearful Sa-ber-tooth,
Took his tusks a - way— Out of them made spears to - day.
—Bessie
II
Hur - rah! hur - rah! Sa - ber Tooth is dead, Hur -
rah! hur-rah! Sa-ber Tooth is dead; Strong-arm killed him
with his might, And then we'll have a feast till night.
—Robert
III
Strong-arm was a brave youth, He killed the dreadful Saber-tooth, A
ver - y ug - ly beast, Now we may have a fine feast.
—Sigmund
IV
I am so hap - py, My heart is so bright, Be-cause
Strong - arm killed Sa - ber Tooth, In the light.
—Margaret

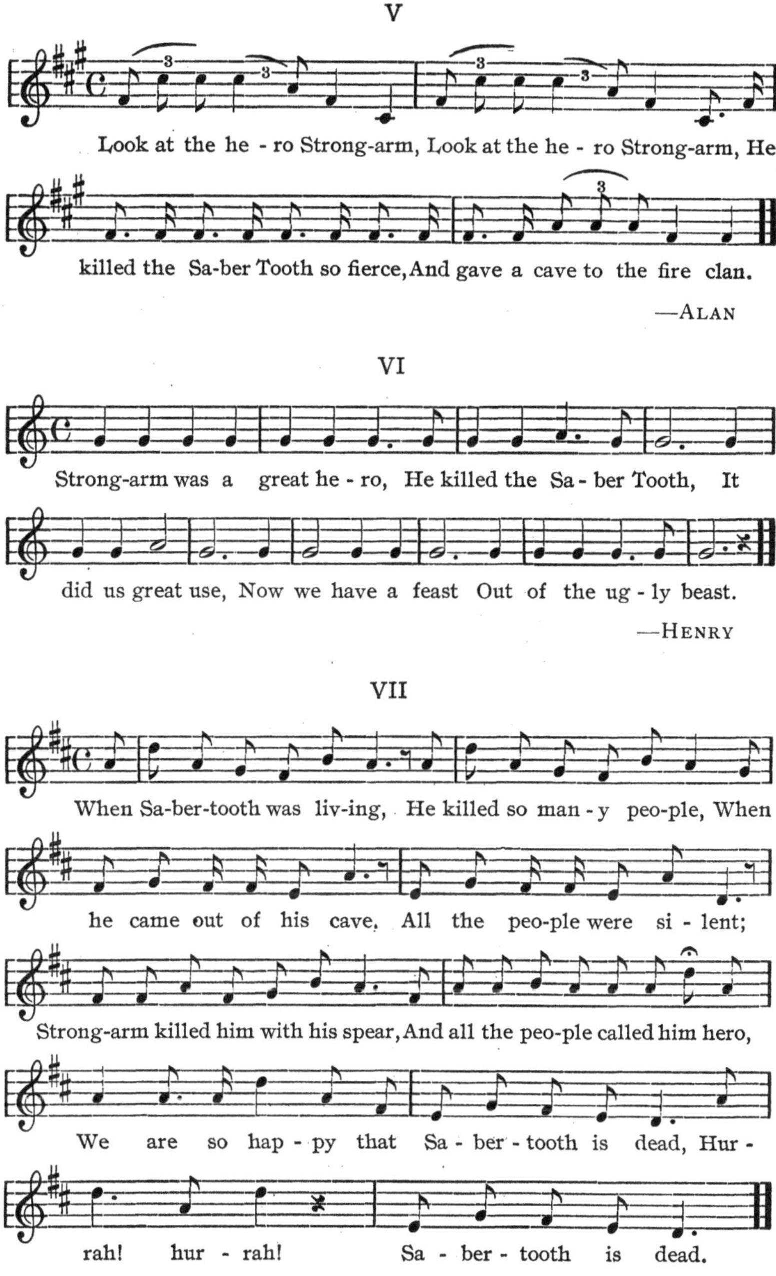
V
Look at the he - ro Strong-arm, Look at the he - ro Strong-arm, He
killed the Sa-ber Tooth so fierce, And gave a cave to the fire clan.
—Alan
VI
Strong-arm was a great he - ro, He killed the Sa - ber Tooth, It
did us great use, Now we have a feast Out of the ug - ly beast.
—Henry
VII
When Sa-ber-tooth was liv-ing, He killed so man - y peo-ple, When
he came out of his cave, All the peo-ple were si - lent;
Strong-arm killed him with his spear, And all the peo-ple called him hero,
We are so hap - py that Sa - ber - tooth is dead, Hur -
rah! hur - rah! Sa - ber - tooth is dead.
—Warren and the Class

VIII

—Marion

IX

Some brave men once lived in a cave,
They were very strong and very brave,
And Strong Arm killed Saber-tooth,
And they called him their brave youth.

—John

X

Strong Arm was so brave and good
He killed the fearful Saber-tooth.
He took his fur and tusks away,
And from his flesh made a feast all day.

—Howard

XI

Strong Arm was a brave old man,
He killed Saber-tooth, the beast of prey.
Let us praise him all we can,
Let us dance and sing today.

—Louise

XII

Strong Arm is a hero,
He killed the Saber-tooth.
Now we have a feast today
Until the neighbors go away.

—Dorothy

XIII

Saber-tooth was fierce and wild,
And he killed all the people.
Strong Arm climbed up in a tree
Where Saber-tooth was sleeping,
Strong Arm threw a spear down
And killed the Saber-tooth.

—Margaret R.

THE CAVE MEN'S DANCE

Miss Dopp's story tells how the cave people beat upon bones for their dancing and the children suggested the use of stones upon logs of wood. They tried both of these instruments, using the simple two-pulse rhythm characteristic of most primitive music. This was produced in primitive fashion, the weak accent being formed by the fall of the hammer after the rebound from the stroke which gives the strong note.

In their efforts to fit suitable steps and movements to the music, some of the children undoubtedly applied knowledge gained from the Indian shows so often seen in New York, and the less ready members of the class imitated the others. The teacher organized their suggestions and drilled them in the rhythm. The dance in its simplest form consisted of two springs upon each foot, bending the knees, but lifting only the heel from the ground. As the dance went on it grew faster, the arms were waved over the head, and the steps were elaborated. This was done by lifting the whole foot from the ground, when springing on the strong accent, and by crossing one foot in front or throwing it out in front or behind, while springing on the other foot. The knees were bent and the body inclined slightly forward throughout the dance.

When the results of the work were presented at an assembly the chants were sung by their authors and the dance followed. Two musicians beat upon bones and logs, a dozen braves danced one after another round the circle, while the chorus of cave people sang over and over in time to the drums:

Strong Arm was a man of youth
He killed the fearful Saber-tooth, etc.

In the development of the chants and dances, several English, music, and game periods were used. The music teacher co-operated with the class teacher in the work.

HISTORY STORIES WRITTEN BY THIRD-GRADE CHILDREN

GUDRUN THORNE-THOMSEN
The University of Chicago Elementary School

The following stories were composed by children of the third grade after a year's study of early trade and transportation. The class was divided into two groups, each consisting of twelve members. In one group the Homeric Greeks, in the other the early Norsemen were selected as types for this study. Each group desired to give the result of their study to the other group, and for this purpose the stories were written. The plot of these stories is entirely original. In planning, the children chose the topics, and points under each topic, which were to be covered: Leave-taking; incidents on the sea: (1) storm, (2) battle, etc. Around these points the plot was woven. Generally speaking, all members of the group contributed, although to a varying extent. It was of great interest to the teacher to note how differently the children responded in this group undertaking. One child, for instance, who in ordinary individual composition expressed herself very meagerly, under the stimulus of the group became one of the best contributors. Another child from her enjoyment of the picturesque language of the Odyssey gave the choicest expressions, and in this way set a standard for the group. Criticisms and suggestions were given, and taken in the kindliest spirit.

THE NORSE TRADER

Harold, king of Norway once decided to take a journey to Spain.

He took four boats, one for provisions, for armor, food, clothes, and trading goods, the other three for his men. When the boats were ready to sail all the women and children were gathered on the shore to say farewell.

Before the sails were furled they offered up prayers and sacrifice to Odin, the all-father, and asked him to give them fair weather, and to Thor, and asked him to give them victory over their foes.

For six days and nights they had pleasant weather; the north wind helped them along toward Spain. But on the seventh day a storm broke out. The sun was hidden behind the clouds, the waves dashed over their boats. King Harold ordered the sails down and the men to the oars. The boats were tossed about and were driven far out of their course.

The men hardly thought anything of this storm. They sang and laughed —it was just fun for them. At noon the next day the clouds passed over and in the faint light there appeared a winged dragon.

"Now, ready for a fight!" cried King Harold. "If I'm not mistaken that's the dragon of King Thorstein."

There was a clashing of swords, spears and arrows flew like the flashes of Thor's hammer. Many a brave warrior on King Thorstein's boat fell dead that day.

King Thorstein begged for mercy and gave rich presents to King Harold, and King Harold let him go.

After fifty days they arrived in Spain. The people came down in crowds to the boats to see who were coming.

King Harold said: "We are Norsemen come to trade."

"We welcome you Norse traders!" said the strangers. "And what have you to trade with us?"

King Harold answered: "We have skins of bears, silver foxes, wolves, ermine, also tin and amber."

The strangers said: "And what do you want of us?"

King Harold answered: "We want gold, silver, silks, and rugs."

Then a trader came forward and invited King Harold into the town to see his goods.

King Harold took his skins, amber, and tin, and loaded them on a cart and took ten men with him and went into the town. There were high walls around the town and it was built on a high hill.

King Harold and the trader went into the trader's shop and King Harold looked at his goods. He saw a beautiful piece of silk which he liked very much, and King Harold asked:

"Where did this piece of beautiful silk come from?"

The trader said: "It came from far off India."

"And how did you get it?" King Harold asked.

The trader said: "I was down in India and saw this piece of silk and liked it very much, so I bought it with a great many other things which I will show you. We were twelve traders with our camels and traveled for thousands of miles through the desert. We brought our goods to Phoenicia where our boats were ready for us. From there we sailed to this country. Here is a lovely vase with drawings on it from Greece; here are spices and perfumes from Arabia. And all this silver is found here in this country of Spain."

"What is this piece of silk worth?" asked King Harold.

"Three weights of amber, or you may give me a man of gold."

King Harold then weighed out the golden amber, and gave it to the trader.

King Harold bought vases and other pottery, perfume, and gold. He paid with silver foxes, tin, and amber. Then he saw the silver and asked how much ten weights of silver were worth.

"Three weights of gold," said the trader.

Then King Harold took off his arm ring, cut off a piece and weighed it. It was three weights of gold, and he gave that to the trader.

King Harold said farewell to the trader and thanked him for his kindness, and started toward his boats. On his way he met a young man from Greece and talked to him and liked him very much. He invited him to his ship where he told him about his life in Norway, about the many battles he had fought and won, and finally asked him to go to Norway with him.

Glaucus, the Greek, thanked King Harold, and said he would like to go very much.

It took two days to get provisions for the home journey, and then they sailed.

After forty nights and days they saw the coast of Norway, and their hearts were glad within them.

Queen Gyda had been watching for many days from the hills for the white sails of King Harold's ships. One morning she came running down the hill. Quite out of breath she told the people: "King Harold and his men are coming home. Hurry to get the feast ready."

At noon a crowd of people were gathered on the shore to welcome King Harold home. When he landed Queen Gyda ran up to him and said:

"Long have I been watching for you to come home. This morning when I saw the wings of your dragon I thanked the gods for bringing you home to me. Come to the feast hall, the tables are set and the mead is ready."

King Harold said: "This is Glaucus, a Greek, whom I met in Spain. Make a place for him at my side."

Then they went forward to the feast hall. The fire blazed and sparkled, and the shields on the wall glittered like the sun. At one end of the table sat King Harold and at the other end sat Queen Gyda. By King Harold's side sat the stranger from Greece. And all around the walls on wooden benches sat King Harold's men.

King Harold told all his adventures and showed the things he had brought from Spain. And Glaucus told about the old Olympic games, and how many victories he had won in similar games. When the mead horns were brought in, King Harold made a vow that he would be foster brother to Glaucus and would help him always. Then he distributed rich gifts to all his friends, and there was much joy and merrymaking.

Then the skald Eivind sang this song:

King Harold went across the sea
To trade for silver and gold.
Four ships to far-off Spain took he
With a hundred men right bold.

One day at sea a storm broke out,
The thunder roared and rang;
Their ships were driven all about,
The men but laughed and sang.

From out the mist a dragon came,
It was a fiery foe;
The swords and spears flashed like a flame
And hundreds went below.
All hail to Harold, glorious king,
And hail to all his men!
Long life and joy to them we sing
And victories again.

THE GREEK TRADER

Once upon a time King Menelaus wanted some beautiful things and he sent for a trader.

Now the trader's name was Aeson. When Aeson reached the palace the king's servant came out to greet him. The servant said, "Welcome, Aeson, come in and rest."

Immediately the king sent a servant with water in a golden pitcher who poured it over Aeson's hands into a silver basin and brought him a chair whereon was a rest for his feet. Another servant brought platters of meat and baskets of bread and Aeson satisfied his hunger.

Then Aeson went and bowed down before the king, and the king said,

"Some beautiful things I need; rugs, ivory, silks, jewels, armor, and purple cloth. How soon can you sail?"

"Oh, brave Menelaus," said the trader, "I can sail in my black-hulled ships on the tenth sun-rise."

On the tenth day Aeson came again to the palace and said to the king,

"Oh brave Menelaus, I am ready to sail. I have five ships with twenty well-armed men aboard each ship. I have abundance of food and water in goat-skin bottles."

"A safe journey to you," said Menelaus.

Before sailing Aeson and his men gathered on the seashore and offered sacrifice to the gods. While the smoke ascended to Zeus, Aeson poured wine into the sea and prayed: "Oh strong and mighty Poseidon, give me smooth seas and gentle winds, that my black-hulled ships may safely reach port."

Then Aeson called his men aboard the ships and bade them loose the cables and take their places on the rowers' benches.

The ships sailed lightly over the sea, skimming the water like sea-gulls on the wing.

One day Aeson and his men spied a ship approaching them. Aeson said, "Be ready for an attack if it proves to be an enemy."

As they drew nearer many arrows came swiftly flying over the water. Aeson's men returned the fire and the battle raged fiercely for three hours. At the end of that time Aeson captured the pirates' ship and took the men prisoners. When Aeson boarded the ship he found gold and silver money and armor.

Two months after leaving Greece Aeson reached the island of Cyprus and got food and water. In another week he entered a Phoenician harbor.

From his ship Aeson saw a walled city on a high hill. He anchored his ships in the harbor and went ashore.

When he entered the city he went at once to the market-place. He met a trader with purple cloth.

"What do you want for this cloth?" said Aeson.

"What have you to trade for it?" said the trader.

"I have wool, vases, and ox-hides."

"I should like to have some wool. How much cloth do you want?"

"About 100 cubits. How much wool do you want for it?"

"Three pounds for each cubit," said the trader.

"All right," said Aeson, and bought the cloth.

The trader then showed him some ivory from Africa, some of it carved and some uncarved.

"How much is it worth?" said Aeson.

"Fifty talents for the uncarved and seventy-five talents for the carved," said the trader.

Aeson thought this was too much and offered the trader forty-five talents for one and seventy talents for the other and they finally agreed on this price.

Next Aeson bought bronze armor from the armor-maker for fifty pieces of gold for each suit of armor.

Another trader said, "Here are some beautiful silks and precious stones from India. It was very hard work to bring these things to Phoenicia. It was dusty and hot crossing the desert with the caravan. We suffered for water. One day we saw palm trees in the distance and hastened to get the water we knew was there. As we drew near the trees disappeared. It was only a mirage. Later we did find some water which we made haste to get. We filled our goat-skin bottles and went farther toward Phoenicia. By and by our bottles were empty and we again suffered from thirst. For three days we saw no water and then found a very small quantity.

Another day a great sand storm came up and we had to lie down and cover our heads until it passed. Two of our men were smothered. At last we reached home after our struggle and thirst."

When Aeson had bought all the things he needed he loaded them on his ships and sailed for Greece. He had a pleasant voyage with only one day of storm.

He went immediately to the palace, his men following with the goods. The palace shone brilliantly with gold and silver and gleaming bronze.

Helen came in with her ladies in waiting. Menelaus waited impatiently on his throne. All the servants and soldiers crowded in to see the things Aeson had brought.

The king said, "You must have had a good voyage to get back so soon."

As Aeson unpacked the things everybody became very much excited and crowded closer to see them. When he held up the silks and purple cloth Helen and her ladies said, "Oh, how beautiful." When the armor was brought out the men began to put it on.

"Part of this armor I got for nothing," said Aeson. We met some pirates and in the course of a three-hours' fight I captured the ship."

"It makes me think of the scenes of Troy," said the men.

Then Aeson brought out the ivory and the glistening jewels. He gave to Helen a beautiful amber necklace.

"How beautiful it is!" said Helen. "What is it made of?"

"It is amber—found in the cold seas of the far north."

Then Aeson said, "Oh brave and mighty Menelaus, I have found out how to make the gleaming bronze. Here is copper from the mountains of Cyprus and tin from far-away England."

Instantly the whole palace was in an uproar and King Menelaus said, "Aeson, I shall reward thee greatly for this."

Then the king ordered the servants to prepare a great feast for Aeson and his men.

A PLAY FESTIVAL BY THE SEVENTH GRADE

MICHALENA CARROLL
New Paltz, N. Y.

The following paper is a report of a play festival held by the seventh grade of the New Paltz Training School in June, 1907. The subject is treated from its original beginnings, and embraces the following points of view: (1) The historical basis and the scheme pursued in imparting the instruction; (2) The manner in which the play was organized; (3) The general scheme in the preparation for the play; (4) The explanation of the play's phases: (*a*) the tableaux; (*b*) the crusade in the streets.

> .... The true old times
> When every morning brought a noble chance
> And every chance brought out a noble knight.

Before a man can derive the full benefit from his own period and thereby contribute worthily to the future, he must realize by what struggles his predecessors purchased the privileges which he now enjoys. This retrospect should be taken early in life when the imagination is keen. The child should live through the trials and triumphs of his race. He should unconsciously measure himself with his hero brothers of the past. Thus a closer relation will be established between him and his fellow-men.

In accordance with the above ideas, the seventh grade of the New Paltz State Normal School studied the history of the Crusades. To give the children an idea of the magnitude of the Crusaders' inconvenience and perseverance, a few lessons were given on the geography, physiography, and history of Palestine. The children reviewed their Bible history from the time of Abraham, through the life of the Israelites in Egypt, up to the time of the Crusades.

Throughout the work the children were encouraged to make their own inferences, and to discover an effect from a cause. The following reason for the establishment of government among the

Israelites, given by a child of twelve, is a good example. He said that when the Israelites were shepherds, in order to obtain good grazing land, they were obliged to travel from place to place, and therefore the people became scattered. When they undertook agriculture, they became localized where they tilled their soil, and formed groups, and later as the groups felt the need of a leader and laws, they originated a simple form of government. In every case the teacher was especially careful to make each child feel that his influence was valuable. A series of lessons on the life of Mohammed was presented, and, so far as explanation was legitimate, the Mohammedan religion was explained.

In dealing with the Saracen apart from his religion, emphasis was laid upon his customs, occupations, inventions, conquests, his contributions to the world, and his character. The spirit of adverse criticism was avoided as much as possible. The children were led to realize their indebtedness to all peoples of the past, thus reducing their deficiencies to minor importance.

During the study of the Saracens' conquests and life in Morocco and Spain, an opportunity was afforded to give the children a glance at the Alhambra, its use, its architecture, its ruin, and its importance today. At this point the Mohammedans were left for a time and attention was given to pilgrims and pilgrimages, beginning with the origin of pilgrimages, and continuing through the various phases of the subject up to the pilgrim's burial.

To establish an appreciation for the significance of events which prefaced the Crusades, it was necessary to give a few lessons on the conditions in various countries and on the relation of countries to one another. In this connection, the Greek Empire was studied as to its power as a nation, its ruler, its capital, and the importance of the location of the latter to Europe. From the last point, the children were able to infer the result to Europe of the possible fall of Constantinople into the hands of the Saracens, and likewise to understand why the Saracens were eager to seize the city.

The latter point introduced the subject of the Crusades. Three Crusades were studied in detail and one in general.

In studying a Crusade, the specific causes were discovered first which included the study of councils held by the pope and by monks. Then followed the social and military nature and incidents of the army, including the battles fought (with their causes, events, and results) which battles were turning-points, classification of the Crusade as successful or unsuccessful and why, and the results of the Crusade to Europe, to the world then, and to the world today. In following the different leaders through a Crusade, an excellent opportunity to compare courage with cowardice and wisdom with ignorance was afforded, but comparisons were made by the children almost unconsciously.

The last step in the sequence of work was the summing-up of the results of the particular Crusade in order to find out the general results to the world. The general results were classified as (1) agricultural; (2) social; (3) military; (4) commercial; (5) intellectual; (6) political.

As exercises the children wrote essays, made outlines of work, and made maps, marking the routes followed by the various crusading expeditions.

THE PLAY FESTIVAL

At the end of the year, the children were eager to give an exhibit of their work. They decided upon a series of tableaux which should represent the sequence of their work by depicting the decisive events in the history of the Crusades. The tableaux were to be preceded by a street pageant. The selection and assignment of the characters that should appear were made by the class. This phase of the work was very interesting because of the manner in which the children ignored the personal element.

The character of the festival necessitated considerable handwork, which called upon the children's knowledge of manual training, sewing, and art, as well as history.

After the tableaux and pageant had been arranged, the problem of costuming was considered. It was thought best to keep the attire very simple and merely suggestive of mediaeval costumes. The children made and helped make their paraphernalia. During one period, two boys came into the assembly where the teacher was arranging material, and, securing a needle and thread, they sewed yards of cheesecloth together, on which their scenery was to be painted. The armor was made of gray cambric painted to represent link armor.

Before making their shields, the children studied the history of the cross and various styles of shields, drawing the different forms. From their drawings they selected the shield and cross which they preferred. Having arranged the cross in an appropriate design on the shield, they worked out the color scheme, adhering to the idea of complementary pairs, which was one phase of the color theory studied in the grade. With their small shields as models, they made their large ones of pasteboard in the Manual-Training Department. These were brought to the art class and decorated according to the small patterns.

Pennants were next worked out very much as were the shields, except that they were made entirely in the art and history periods. The sail for the boat which should appear in the parade was constructed in the Manual-Training Department under the direction of the History Department. The boat was a real rowboat placed on a wagon, and draped with orange and green cheesecloth to match the sail.

The horse trappings were very simple. They consisted of a blanket and a sash tied with long ends in front, all of which corresponded in color with the cross on the rider's breast.

Each participant, except the monks and pilgrims, carried a spear or a pennant and a shield.

All the costuming and dramatization were done in one week. Only two of the rehearsals were in costume. At the first rehearsal, conditions seemed to point to failure. The next rehearsal looked more promising, and by the third, the children had lost all self-consciousness and entered fully into the spirit of the work. Each child had his individual opinion regarding the attitude he should assume. Some would kneel and lean forward as though eager to listen to Peter and Urban; some looked down in sorrow; some assumed an expression of joy. They all entered into the spirit of the time. Of course some required more time than others to forget themselves, but all seemed eager to make the affair a success.

THE MARCH

The pageant was called "An Original Crusade," because not only one Crusade was depicted; but it showed a typical crusading army on its way to the Holy Land, the stations in life from which Crusaders and pilgrims came, their method of travel, the leaders of various expeditions, the nations which contributed most toward the movement, the instigators of the wars, and the Christians' opponent, the Saracen.

The underlying spirit of the Crusade is perhaps best expressed in the motto, "Live pure lives, think pure thoughts, right wrongs." In order to emphasize the Crusade idea, the characters were arranged so as to form a cross (see illustration). Here the sequence of work was still maintained. The Saracen, or the one who made war necessary, was the foremost figure; a typical French and a typical German Crusader (the Saracens' two greatest opponents) followed, carrying a white banner bearing the motto, *Deus vult! Deus vult!* Peter the Hermit and St. Bernard, being the two who did most to arouse the people's enthusiasm, followed, the latter on horseback; the four leaders of the first Crusade were on horseback and spaced so as to form the horizontal limb of the cross; in their rear were Conrad III and Louis VII, the leaders of the second Crusade; next came a typical pilgrim and Frederick Barbarossa of the third Crusade; Richard I and Philip II followed on horseback, and last came the boat in which were Crusaders and pilgrims on their way to the Holy Land.

At an appointed hour, the children assembled at the Town Hall and put on their costumes; then they organized their line of march and paraded the streets of the village, returning to the hall. As soon as the children had rested, they formed in single file, and, led by Pope Urban, entered the auditorium, singing the Crusaders' hymn, in which the rest of the school joined. Thus the procession slowly marched to the stage at the opposite side of the auditorium, where the players took their places behind the curtain at the rear of the stage, ready to present the tableaux which followed.

"An Original Crusade"

THE TABLEAUX

1. Saracen conducting a merchant's quarter or bazaar.
2. Peter the Hermit addressing his wayside audience.
3. Urban conducting the Council of Clermont.
4. The four leaders of the first Crusade.
5. Saint Bernard and followers at Vezelay.
6. Philip II, Richard I, and Frederick Barbarossa with followers.
7. All Crusaders singing the "Pilgrims' Chorus."

In order that the tableaux should be better understood by the audience, the children advised having some explanation of each scene. Therefore pupils were selected to introduce and explain each tableaux.

Inasmuch as the Saracen through his threatening attitude toward Constantinople was really the one who caused the first Crusade to be organized, he was given the first place. In order that he might be shown in a purely Saracenic environment, he was represented as the keeper of a bazaar, sitting huddled up among his wares counting his coins. Back of him and back of all the succeeding scenes, was a large screen, painted by the teacher, which showed the towers of Jerusalem just above a hill, surrounded by trees. This was done in order to emphasize the fact that through all the struggle, the recovery of the Holy City was uppermost in the Crusaders' hearts. The thought of Jerusalem was back of all they did or anticipated doing.

Scene 2 showed the first man who made an attempt to arouse the world to the true state of affairs in the East. Just before the curtain was dropped, Peter raised his hand and repeated the passage from Eph. 6:10–17.

Scene 3 enabled the class to show the great sympathy shown by Pope Urban, and the means by which he transmitted his wonderful enthusiasm to his hearers in the Council of Clermont. Suddenly, some knelt and the others stood upright and exclaimed, *Deus vult! Deus vult!* Thus was shown the transition from the pilgrim spirit to that of the Crusader. Then Urban raised his arms and said, "This day has been fulfilled in your midst, the saying of our Lord, 'Where two or three are gathered together in thy name, there am I in the midst of them.'"

Scene 4 was purely a tableau; the four leaders stood in front with their followers grouped back of them. This scene showed that the pope's efforts had been of some avail.

Scene 5 showed the great preacher of the second Crusade at his famous Council of Vezelay, with the two rulers who were influenced by him to enter upon the Crusade.

Scene 6 represented the three leaders of the third Crusade with their followers.

The exhibit would not fulfil its purpose if closed by the last tableau, therefore three children were chosen to state the results of the Crusade to the world at large, thus making the audience realize the meaning of the study.

After results had been given, all the characters appeared and sang the "Pilgrim's Chorus," in which intermediate pupils and normal students joined.

HELEN KELLER AND THE LANGUAGE-TEACHING PROBLEM

JEAN SHERWOOD RANKIN
Minneapolis, Minn.

If the Society for the Scientific Study of Education—formerly known as the Herbart Society—would but consent to look into the methods whereby Helen Keller acquired her remarkable command of English, the results might, in the course of a few eons, come to have some perceptible effect upon the absurd performances now going on all over America in the name of "language work." Probably the most interesting character of the present century from an educational standpoint is this blind and deaf girl whose name is a synonym for marvelous achievement in the face of stupendous obstacles. But what she has accomplished is of less importance to the school world than the manner in which she was enabled to accomplish. It would be well for the rising generation if every grade teacher could be persuaded to read with care Helen Keller's *Story of My Life* (Doubleday, Page & Co.), and then to study also the "Supplementary Account of Helen Keller's Education," to be found in the same volume, written by John Albert Macy, now editor of *The Youth's Companion.*

Miss Annie Sullivan, teacher of Helen Keller, had herself been blind for many years, although she later regained her sight. During the six years which she spent at the Perkins Institution for the Blind, in Boston, she had been in the same house with that other famous blind-deaf-mute, Laura Bridgeman. She had thus become especially fitted by previous experience for the unusual work to which she was called. That she was, moreover, by nature a great teacher, whose name will be honored side by side with those of the world's most famous educators, is conceded by all who know how great is the work she has done.

With the kind permission of Mr. Macy I give here a number

of short extracts from his valuable account of Miss Sullivan's work, in the hope that many teachers of more favored children may thus be led to a thorough study of the original account, as well as to a practical application in their own work of the methods used by Miss Sullivan in the training of Helen Keller.

Helen Keller was born June 27, 1880; Miss Sullivan came to her March 3, 1887. Thus the little pupil was less than seven years old. It was however full time that she have a teacher, for, having no means for the communication of her desires, she was becoming less and less manageable. She was to all intents a savage little animal, without affection or understanding. Often kicking, screaming, and striking became her sole means for asking for what she wished; but with the gift of language, gentleness displaced violence.

The story throughout is intensely interesting. The gains were at first obtained solely through imitation, Miss Sullivan spelling the words *doll* and *cake* into Helen's hand and trying to get her to associate the spelling with these objects. Helen imitated the letters very well, but did not for some time acquire the associations. I quote from Miss Sullivan's letters:

March 11, 1887. Helen knows several words now, but has no idea how to use them or that everything has a name.

March 13, 1887. She has learned three new words, and when I give her the objects, the names of which she has learned, she spells them unhesitatingly; but she seems glad when the lesson is over.

March 20, 1887. Helen has learned several nouns this week. "M-u-g" and "m-i-l-k" have given her more trouble than other words. When she spells "milk," she points to the mug, and when she spells "mug," she makes the sign for pouring or drinking, which shows that she has confused the words. She has no idea yet that everything has a name.

March 28, 1887. She knows twelve words now.

April 3, 1887. The hour from twelve to one is devoted to the learning of new words. *But you mustn't think this is the only time I spell to Helen; for I spell in her hand everything we do all day long, although she has no idea as yet what the spelling means.* . . . . On March 31 I found that Helen knew eighteen nouns and three verbs. Here is a list of the words. Those with a cross after them are words she asked for herself: *Doll, mug, pin, key, dog, hat, cup, box, water, milk, candy, eye* (x), *finger* (x), *toe* (x), *head* (x), *cake, baby, mother, sit, stand, walk.* On April 1 she learned the nouns *knife, fork, spoon, saucer, tea, papa, bed,* and the verb *run.*

April 5, 1887. Helen has taken the second great step in her education. *She has learned that everything has a name, and that the manual alphabet is the key to everything she wants to know. . . .* This morning, while she was washing, she wanted to know the name for "water." When she wants to know the name of anything, she points to it and pats my hand. I spelled "w-a-t-e-r" and thought no more about it until after breakfast. Then it occurred to me that with the help of this new word I might succeed in straightening out the "mug-milk" difficulty. We went out to the pump-house, and I made Helen hold her mug under the spout while I pumped. As the cold water gushed forth, filling the mug, I spelled "w-a-t-e-r" in Helen's free hand. The word coming so close upon the sensation of cold water rushing over her hand seemed to startle her. She dropped the mug and stood as one transfixed. A new light came into her face. She spelled "water" several times. Then she dropped on the ground and asked for its name and pointed to the pump and the trellis, and suddenly turning round she asked for my name. I spelled "T-e-a-c-h-e-r." Just then the nurse brought Helen's little sister into the pump-house, and Helen spelled "b-a-b-y" and pointed to the nurse. All the way back to the house she was highly excited, and learned the name of every object she touched, so that *in a few hours she had added thirty new words* to her vocabulary. Here are some of them: *Door, open, shut, give, go, come,* and a great many more.

P. S. I didn't finish my letter in time to get it posted last night; so I shall add a line. Helen got up this morning like a radiant fairy. She has flitted from object to object, asking the name of everything.

April 10, 1887. I have decided not to try to have regular lessons for the present. I am going to treat Helen exactly like a two-year-old child. It occurred to me the other day that it is absurd to require a child to come to a certain place at a certain time and recite certain lessons, when he has not yet acquired a working vocabulary. I sent Helen away and sat down to think. I asked myself, *"How does a normal child learn language?"* The answer was simple: *"By imitation." . . . But long before he utters his first word, he understands what is said to him. . . . I shall talk into her hand as we talk into the baby's ears. . . . I shall use complete sentences in talking to her,* and fill out the meaning with gestures and her descriptive signs when necessity requires it; but I shall not try to keep her mind fixed on any one thing. I shall do all I can to interest and stimulate it, and wait for results.

April 24, 1887. The new scheme works splendidly. Helen knows the meaning of more than a hundred words now, and learns new ones daily. . . . If I say, "Get your hat and we will go to walk," she obeys instantly. The two words, "hat" and "walk" would have the same effect; *but the whole sentence, repeated many times during the day, must in time impress itself upon the brain, and by and by she will use it herself.*

May 8, 1887. I am beginning to suspect all elaborate and special systems of education. They seem to me to be built up on the supposition that every child is a kind of idiot who must be taught to think; whereas, if the child is left to himself, he will think more and better, if less showily. Let him go and come freely, let him touch real things and combine his impressions for himself, instead of sitting indoors at a little round table, while a sweet-voiced teacher suggests that he build a stone wall with his wooden blocks, or make a rainbow out of strips of colored paper, or plant straw trees in bead flower-pots. Such teaching fills the mind with artificial associations that must be got rid of before the child can develop independent ideas out of actual experiences.

Helen had signs for *small* and *large* long before I came to her. . . . . The other day I substituted the words *small* and *large* for these signs, and she at once adopted the words and discarded the signs. I can now tell her to bring me a large book or a small plate, to go upstairs slowly, to run fast, and to walk quickly. This morning she used the conjunction *and* for the first time. I told her to shut the door, and she added, "and lock."

Since I have abandoned the idea of regular lessons, I find that Helen learns much faster. *I am convinced that the time spent by the teacher in digging out of the child what she has put into him, for the sake of satisfying herself that it has taken root, is so much time thrown away* [italics mine]. *It's much better, I think, to assume that the child is doing his part, and that the seed you have sown will bear fruit in due time.*

May 16, 1887. It is wonderful how words generate ideas. Every new word Helen learns seems to carry with it the necessity for many more. . . . . Helen is eager to tell her mother everything she has seen. *This desire to repeat what has been told her shows a marked advance in the development of her intellect, and is an invaluable stimulus to the acquisition of language. I ask all her friends to encourage her to tell them of her doings, and to manifest as much curiosity and pleasure in her little adventures as they possibly can.* This gratifies the child's love of approbation and keeps up her interest in things. . . . . Thus her vocabulary grows apace, and the new words germinate and bring forth new ideas; and these are the stuff out of which heaven and earth are made.

May 22, 1887. Helen is a wonderful child, so spontaneous and eager to learn. She knows about three hundred words now *and a great many common idioms,* and it is not three months yet since she learned her first word.

We have reading-lessons every day. Usually we take one of the little *Readers* up in a big tree near the house and spend an hour or two finding the words Helen already knows. *We make a sort of game of it* and try to see who can find the words most quickly, Helen with her fingers, or I with my eyes, and she learns as many new words as I can explain with the help of those she knows. When her fingers light upon words she knows, she fairly screams with pleasure and hugs and kisses me for joy, especially if she thinks she has me beaten. It would astonish you to see how many words she learns in an hour in this pleasant manner.

June 2, 1887. Helen begins to spell the minute she wakes up in the morning, and continues all day long. If I refuse to talk to her, she spells into her own hand, and apparently carries on the liveliest conversation with herself.

I gave her my braille slate to play with, thinking that the mechanical pricking of holes in the paper would amuse her and rest her mind. But what was my astonishment when I found that the little witch was writing letters! . . . . One day she brought me a sheet that she had punched full of holes, and wanted to put it in an envelope and take it to the post-office. I asked her what she had written to Frank. She replied, "Much words. Puppy mother-dog—five. Baby—cry. Hot. Helen walk—no.—Sunfire—bad. Frank —come. Helen—kiss Frank. Strawberries—very good. . . . ."

Helen is almost as eager to read as she is to talk. I find she grasps the import of whole sentences, catching from the context the meaning of words she doesn't know.

She has a perfect mania for counting. She has counted everything in the house, and is now busy counting the words in her primer.

June 19, 1887. Helen will be seven years old the twenty-seventh of this month. . . . . *She knows four hundred words besides numerous proper nouns.*

[Mark this, Oh Famous Educators, who are wont to talk publicly, but foolishly, about the size of the vocabulary of the average citizen! And these four hundred words were learned *by spelling each one,* and wholly without the aid of eye and ear associations!]

In one lesson I taught her these words: *bedstead, mattress, sheet, blanket, comforter, spread, pillow.* The next day I found that she remembered all but *spread.* The same day she had learned, at different times, the words: *house, weed, dust, swing, molasses, fast, slow, maple sugar,* and *counter,* and she has not forgotten one of these last. . . . . She can count to thirty very quickly, and can write seven of the square-head letters and the words which can be made with them. . . . . She discovered a hole in her boot the other morning, and, after breakfast, she went to her father and spelled, "Helen new boot Simpson (her brother) buggy store man." One can easily see her meaning.

July 31, 1887. Helen's pencil-writing is excellent. I am teaching her the braille alphabet, and she is delighted to be able to make words herself that she can feel.

She has now reached the question stage of her development. It is "What?" "Why?" "When?" especially "Why?" all day long. . . . . I know now that these questions indicate the child's growing interest in the causes of things. The "Why" is the door through which he enters the world of reason and reflection. On the whole, her questions are analogous to those that a bright three-year-old child asks.

August 21, 1887. She remembers all that I told her about it [a drive], and in telling her mother *repeated the very words and phrases I had used in* describing it to her.

August 28, 1887. . . . . The readiness with which she comprehended the great facts of physical life confirmed me in the opinion that the child has dormant within him, when he comes into the world, all the experiences of the race. These experiences are like photographic negatives, until language develops them and brings out the memory images.

September 18, 1887. I kept a record of everything she said last week and I found that she knows [that is, used; she would not use all her words in any one week!] six hundred words. This does not mean, however, that she always uses them correctly. Sometimes her sentences are like Chinese puzzles; but they are the kind of puzzles children make when they try to express their half-formed ideas by means of arbitrary language. She has the true language impulse, and shows great fertility of resource in making the words at her command convey her meaning.

October 25, 1887. She has begun to use the pronouns of her own accord. This morning I happened to say, "Helen will go upstairs." She laughed and said, "Teacher is wrong. You will go upstairs." This is another great forward step.

FROM MISS SULLIVAN'S PUBLISHED LETTER IN THE PERKIN'S INSTITUTION REPORT

October, 1887. Only those who are with her daily can realize the rapid advancement which she is making in the acquisition of langugage. . . . . Neither the length of the word nor the combination of letters seems to make any difference to the child. Indeed, she remembers *heliotrope* and *chrysanthemum* more readily than she does shorter names. At the end of August she knew 625 words.

I now thought it time to teach her to read printed words. [This refers to a previous date.] I took an alphabet sheet (with raised letters) and put her finger on the letter "A," at the same time making "A" with my fingers. She moved her finger from one printed character to another as I formed each letter on my fingers. She learned all the letters, both capital and small, in one day. Next I turned to the first page of the primer and made her touch the word *cat,* spelling it on my fingers at the same time. Instantly she caught the idea, and asked me to find dog and many other words. Indeed, she was much displeased because I could not find her name in the book.

December 12, 1887. Helen is as eager to have stories told her as any hearing child I ever knew. She has made me repeat the story of Little Red Riding-Hood so often that I believe I could say it backward. She likes stories that make her cry—I think we all do; it's so nice to feel sad when you've nothing particular to be sad about. I am teaching her little rhymes and verses, too. They fix beautiful thoughts in her memory. I think, too, that they quicken all the child's faculties, because they stimulate the imagination. Of course, I don't try to explain everything. If I did there would be no opportunity for the play of fancy. *Too much explanation directs the child's attention to words and sentences, so that he fails to get the thought as a whole.* I do not think anyone can read, or talk for that matter, until he forgets words and sentences in the technical sense.

January 1, 1888. The Christmas season has furnished many lessons, and has added scores of new words to Helen's vocabulary.

For weeks we did nothing but talk and read and tell each other stories about Christmas. Of course I do not try to explain all the new words, nor does Helen fully understand the little stories I tell her; but constant repetition fixes the words and phrases in the mind, and little by little the meaning will come to her. I see no sense in "faking" conversation for the sake of teaching language. It's stupid and deadening to pupil and teacher. Talk should be natural and have for its object an exchange of ideas. If there is nothing in the child's mind to communicate, it hardly seems worth while to require him to write on the blackboard, or spell on his fingers, cut-and-dried sentences about "the cat," "the bird," "a dog." I have tried from the beginning to talk naturally to Helen and to teach her to tell me only things that interest her and to ask questions only for the sake of finding out what she wants to know. When I see that she is eager to tell me something, but is hampered because she does not know the words, I supply them and the necessary idioms, and we get along finely. . . . . What would happen, do you think, if someone should try to measure our intelligence by our ability to define the commonest words we use? I fear me, if I were put to such a test, I should be consigned to the primary class in a school for the feebleminded.

March 5, 1888. Miss E. came up to help me make a list of words Helen has learned. We have got as far as P, and there are 900 words to her credit. [The letter does not state what the total list numbered; but when we recall that Miss Sullivan spelled into Helen's hand all day often, we may be sure that the computed list is much less in number than the words actually known by the child.] I had Helen begin a journal March 1. I don't know how long she will keep it up. . . . . Just now she finds it great fun. She seems to like to tell all she knows. This is what Helen wrote Sunday:

"I got up, washed my face and hands, combed my hair, picked three dew violets for Teacher and ate my breakfast. After breakfast I played with dolls short. Nancy [a doll] was cross. Cross is cry and kick. I read in my book about large, fierce animals. Fierce is much cross and strong and very hungry. I do not love fierce animals. I wrote letter to Uncle James. He lives in Hotsprings. He is doctor. Doctor makes sick girl well. I do not like sick. Then I ate my dinner. I like much ice cream very much. After dinner father went to Birmingham on train far away. I had letter from Robert. He loves me. He said, Dear Helen, Robert was glad to get a letter from dear, sweet little Helen. I will come to see you when the sun shines. Mrs. Newsum is Robert's wife. Robert is her husband. Robert and I will run and jump and hop and dance and swing and talk about birds and flowers and trees and grass and Jumbo and Pearl will go with us. Teacher will say we are silly. She is funny. Funny makes us laugh. Natalie is a good girl and does not cry. Mildred does cry. She will be a nice girl in many days and run and play with me. Mrs. Graves is making short dresses for Natalie. Mr. Mayo went to Duckhill and brought home many sweet flowers. Mr. Mayo and Mr. Farris and Mr. Graves love me and Teacher. I am going to Memphis to see them soon, and they will hug and kiss me. Thornton goes to school and gets his face dirty. Boy must be very careful. After supper I played romp with Teacher in bed. She buried me under the pillows and then I grew very slow like tree out of ground. Now I will go to bed.— HELEN KELLER."

This from a child not yet eight years old, who just one year before knew not one word of verbal speech! Few normal children of eight years can equal this composition, and the schools may well take heed of Miss Sullivan's just criticisms upon their wooden methods.

May 15, 1888. It is as easy to teach the name of an idea, if it is clearly formulated in the child's mind, as to teach the name of an object. It would indeed be a herculean task to teach the words if the ideas did not already exist in the child's mind. If his experiences and observations hadn't led him to the concepts, *small, large, good, bad, sweet, sour,* he would have nothing to attach the word tags to. . . . . The child learns from many experiences to differentiate his feelings, and we name them for him—*good, bad, gentle, rough, happy, sad.* It is not the word, but the capacity to experience the sensation that counts in his education.

We visited a little school for the deaf. . . . In every classroom I saw sentences on the blackboard, which evidently had been written to illustrate some grammatical rule, or for the purpose of using words that had previously been taught in the same, or in some other, connection. This sort of thing may be a necessity in some stages of education; but it isn't the way to acquire language. Nothing, I think, crushes the child's impulse to talk naturally more effectual than these blackboard exercises. The schoolroom is not the place to teach any young child language, least of all the deaf child. He must be kept as unconscious as the hearing child of the fact that he is learning words, and he should be allowed to prattle on his fingers, or with his pencil, in monosyllables if he chooses, until such time as his growing intelligence demands the sentence. Language should not be associated in his mind with endless hours in school, with puzzling questions in grammar, or with anything that is an enemy to joy.

October 1, 1888. When traveling, she [Helen] drinks in thought and language. Sitting beside her in the car, I describe what I see from the window. . . . . In this way she learns countless new expressions without any apparent effort.

From the day when Helen first grasped the idea that all objects have names, and that these can be communicated by certain movements of the fingers I have talked to her exactly as I should have done had she been able to hear, with only this exception, that I have addressed the words to her fingers instead of to her ears. . . . . While not confining myself to any special system of instruction, I have tried to add to her general information and intelligence, to enlarge her acquaintance with things around her, and to bring her into easy and natural relations with people. *I have encouraged her to keep a diary.* [An extract from this has been already given.]

FROM MISS SULLIVAN'S REPORT READ AT CHAUTAUQUA

July, 1894. During the first two years of her intellectual life I required Helen to write very little. In order to write one must have something to write about, and having something to write about requires some mental preparation. . . . . Too often, I think, children are required to write before they have anything to say. Teach them to think and read and talk without self-repression, and they will write because they cannot help it.

Helen acquired language by practice and habit rather than by study of rules and definitions. Grammar with its puzzling array of classifications, nomenclatures, and paradigms, was wholly discarded in her education. She learned language by being brought in contact with the living language itself; she was made to deal with it in everyday conversation, and in her books, and to turn it over in a variety of ways until she was able to use it correctly. . . . . I think much of the fluency with which Helen uses language is due to the fact that nearly every impression which she receives comes through the medium of language. . . . . The constant companionship of good books has been of supreme importance in her education. . . . . It is not necessary that a child should understand every word in a book before she can read with pleasure and profit. . . . . I am convinced that original composition without the preparation of much reading is an impossibility. Helen has had the best and purest models in language constantly presented to her, and her conversation and her writing are unconscious reproductions of what she has read. Reading, I think, should be kept independent of the regular school exercises. Children should be encouraged to read for the pure delight of it. The attitude of the child toward his books should be that of unconscious receptivity.

The following extracts are from Mr Macy's own notes upon Miss Sullivan's methods:

Helen Keller is supposed to have a special aptitude for languages. It is true rather that she has a special aptitude for thinking. . . . .

When at the age of fourteen she had had but a few lessons in German, she read over the words of "Wilhelm Tell" and managed to get the story. *Of grammar she knew nothing and she cared nothing for it. She got the language from the language itself, and this is, next to hearing the language spoken, the way for anyone to get a foreign tongue, more vital and, in the end, easier than our schoolroom method of beginning with the grammar.* . . . .

She was taught by a method of teaching language to the deaf, the essential principles of which are clearly expressed in Miss Sullivan's letters. . . . . And it can be applied by any teacher to any healthy deaf child, and *in the broadest interpretation of the principles, can be applied to the teaching of language of all kinds to all children.* [These italics are mine.]

The style of every writer and, indeed, of every human being, illiterate or cultivated, is a composite reminiscence of all that he has read and heard. Of the sources of his vocabulary he is, for the most part, as unaware as he is of the moment when he ate the food which makes a bit of his thumbnail. . . . . The child mind gathers into itself words it has heard, and they lurk there ready to come out when the key that releases the spring is touched. . . . .

All use of language is imitative, and one's style is made up of all other styles that one has met.

The way to write good English is to read it and hear it. Thus it is that any child may be taught to use correct English by not being allowed to read or hear any other kind. In a child, the selection of the better from the worse is not conscious; he is the servant of his word experience.

Whoever makes a sentence of words utters not his wisdom, but the wisdom of the race whose life is in the words, though they have never been so grouped before. . . . .

The educated man is the man whose expression is educated. The substance of thought is language, and language is the one thing to teach the deaf child and every other child. Let him get language and he gets the very stuff that language is made of, the thought and the experience of his race.

No better subject-matter for close study and discussion by teachers' reading-circles could be found than this "Supplementary Account of Helen Keller's Education," which is a most important contribution to the problem of teaching the mastery of the mother-tongue to all children. Just as soon as the truths here formulated shall have come to be generally recognized, there will be a linguistic renaissance throughout the school world.

DECORATIVE DESIGNING AS A STUDY FOR CHILDREN

RUTH RAYMOND
The School of Education

This paper begins like a creed: "I believe." I believe that everyone can design. A little patience, a little coaching in the means of expression, and every person who reads these words could make a pattern. I believe it, but you do not. If you were given pencil and paper and told to make the simplest kind of a scheme—an arrangement of embroidered dots and scallops for a centerpiece, a braiding pattern for a gown, a design in cross-stitch for collar and cuffs—a good many of you would look aghast and say, "I can't do it." If I tell a child that he can make a design he believes me and forthwith, he makes one. Why is it? Perhaps there are several reasons for this. First, the child does not suffer from that curse of our oversensitized generation, self-distrust. Decorative designing is only one means of self-expression. The child does not share our morbid fear that there is nothing within worth expressing. With a self-confidence that has not yet been ofttimes shaken he believes in himself and in his own ability, and dares to try.

The child believes in his *message*. A design is only one way of telling a story and the child is an enthusiastic story-teller. How many times have you had him run to you breathless, eyes big with the wonder and the thrill of the encounter which he has just witnessed between a dog and a squirrel. His nature is stirred to its depths over the dramatic side of what would have seemed to you a trivial incident. For it is one of the penalties of becoming an Olympian that we lose the Arcadian scent for the dramatic, the significant, in the little happenings of every day. He tells the story as would the practical raconteur, not slurring over any of its details, not fumbling blindly for a place to stop lest you are already bored, and, unless you are one of those hopelessly "grown-up" people, you are interested with him in his tale. He believes in his story and in his material.

The power to *create* is part of our divinity, and the child, still "trailing" his "clouds of glory," has not yet bartered that power. The desire to create appears in all the child's activities. His imagination gives the spark of life to inanimate objects. He breathes upon them the breath of his own superabundant life, and they become instinct with life to him. As he is untrammeled by many precedents, and has no preconceived ideas of the world's standards, his Galatea always seems to him beautiful, and he takes in her the joy which is the necessary accompaniment of art. That painful ecstasy we find in the bodying forth of a bit of our own life and thought Oliver Wendell Holmes describes in telling of the poet's sensations at the birth of a poem. He says:

> A lyric conception hits me like a bullet in the forehead. I have often had the blood drop from my cheeks when it struck, and felt that I turned white as death. Then comes a creeping of centipedes running down the spine, then a gasp and a great jump of the heart, then a sudden flush and a beating in the vessels of the head, then a long sigh, and the poem is written . . . . not copied, but written. . . . . It is enough to stun and scare anybody to have a hot thought come crashing into his brain and plowing up those parallel ruts where the wagon trains of common ideas were jogging along in their regular sequences of association.

Have you felt it? To the child oft comes this joy in the things which he creates, and with the creator's joy he sees that "it is good," and "behold, it *is* very good." It is good because it is frank, sincere, a true expression of the child's thought. It is good in the way the Aztec pottery, the Indian rugs and baskets are good. And if we can foster in the child, not crush these primitive instincts, we can lead him by the path mankind has followed, from the first rude imitations of the patterns his handcraft has suggested toward such an expression of beauty as Milan Cathedral or the Parthenon.

But what is *beauty* and how are we to know that the standards of beauty which we set up are not false standards? In an interesting series of articles in the *Craftsman,* Ernest Batchelder says:

The beautiful thing is invariably sane and orderly in arrangement, clear and coherent in expression, frank and straightforward in its acceptance of all the conditions imposed by questions of use, environment, tools, materials, and processes.

Surely this is a safe standard; but do we accept it? Think of the various decoratively designed objects in our own homes: walls, curtains, floor coverings, table linen, dishes, silver, picture frames, toilet articles, books, costumes, jewels,—the list might be prolonged indefinitely. Do they exemplify the beauty that is sane and orderly in arrangement, clear and coherent in expression, and frank and straightforward in accepting the conditions imposed by questions of use, environment, tools, materials, and processes? Or do they show, rather, our blind acceptance of any design the manufacturer chooses to foist upon us, even when that design is only a servile copy of forms which, to quote,

were once fresh, real and significant because they embodied in their expression something of the thoughts and feelings of the times in which they were used, but which now appear as misapplied finery.

Granted, then, that we are in sad need of real *designers,* and granted that every child is a designer in embryo, how shall we cultivate his instinct for self-expression, how foster his childlike faith in his message and in his power to create, how help him to develop that creative power, not binding him by the work of the past, as a convention, but helping him to profit by the mistakes and successes of others, through the ages, in their efforts to express what appeared to them as true and beautiful? We must use care in presenting to the child the treasures of the past. Imitation is perhaps as strong an instinct with him as creation, and unless he is guided in his choice of material, he will unite Egyptian scarabs, the Roman sacrificial ox, the salamander of Francis I, and Edward Penfield's hounds in one "happy family"!

Many writers adopt the theory that the *racial development in design* begins with the geometric forms undoubtedly suggested by the weaving, plaiting, tying, of the primitive industries; that side by side with this grows the desire to imitate graphically the human form and features and the various objects of nature that surround the embryonic artist. This, then, seems the logical order to adopt in teaching the child to design. He must treat Nature and the art of the past as a storehouse from which to draw the materials he needs to express his own thoughts.

We find him quick to see analogies and to grasp the principles that apply equally to all forms of artistic expression, whether graphic, musical, or literary. He sees easily that the story of the little boy who hated to bathe in the sea, and therefore spent his days dipping up water in his little tin pail—dipping up water and pouring it away, dipping up water and pouring it away, dipping up water and pouring it away—may be very efficacious in putting a baby to sleep, but is somewhat lacking in dramatic interest. He realizes that one note drummed over and over on the piano does not make music, and that a sheet of clean white paper neatly ruled with even lines does not make a design—and he begins to understand the first great principle of designing—that of *variety*. He is willing to excuse us, perhaps with a little reminiscent twinge of conscience, for the times he has needed excuse, when we rap upon the table to show him that a monotonous, cadenceless rapping is as annoying as the dripping of water and is lacking in the element of interest, but that the instant we introduce a rhythm, he is on the alert to see whether we will repeat it—the element of *interest* has been introduced.

He will make a design for a striped gingham, using only the material which we despised in the case of the ruled sheet of tablet paper—straight lines all running in the same direction, by merely varying these intervals. He will see that he can whistle his design, making a bird call out of its meter. He will see that widths of mouldings, arrangements of braid and tucking on garments, and all the various stripes and plaids in fabrics are but the illustration of this one simple principle.

In a similar manner he gains knowledge of the principle of *unity*. He sees that, as the wind blows sticks and dead leaves and swirls of dust about, or the current of the swift-flowing stream influences the flotsam and jetsam on its surface, compelling them into the semblance of a pattern, so his will and the underlying current of his thought can lead all sorts of unrelated forms into harmony and make of them a unit, an entity. He learns that a form, without which his design is complete, is an intruder and must be shut out; that a form, no matter how pleasing in itself, which does not help the harmony of the whole, is a disrupting member and, unless it can be influenced by the prevailing spirit of the whole, must be dispensed with. He learns to be a peacemaker between warring elements, modifying them in unessential characteristics that they may uphold and strengthen their neighbors and establish harmony in the group.

He comes to understand *symmetry* in its simple form where the two halves of his pattern are identical and also the subtler form of symmetry where the balance is maintained by carefully calculated opposing masses differing in color and value. He learns the part color plays in a scheme of design and discovers how to oppose and blend hues to obtain the wonderful effects he admires in nature.

It is but a step from the division of a space into interestingly related masses arranged in stripes to the breaking up of a square panel into dominant and subordinate masses, working always from the big to the smaller, not filling up a space with small detail.

From the problem of the square we proceed to the circle, the oblong, the border, the all-over pattern, and each problem is developed into an object for which the child can see definite purpose (for example, the square is stenciled in a sofa pillow, the triangle in leather or metal becomes a blotter corner, etc.), thus helping the child by the works of his own hands to fit into the great world of adult life in which he is so often only the eagerly curious looker-on.

I might tell you how we bring to the child's attention the ideas of proportion, balance, of rhythm and movement in design, and how quickly he applies the ideas to his everyday problems, but I am anxious to suggest one other phase of the subject for your consideration. I am convinced that the study of design has a distinct ethical bearing; that, rightly taught, it should aid in character building as well as in the acquirement of mental and manual dexterity in combining lines and forms. Surely the frail germ of beauty in the child's soul, brooded over in the effort to give it adequate expression, grows and develops, and only spreads its wings to leave room for another beautiful thought.

The study of design strengthens the child intellectually; he must learn to give a reason for his intuitive choice of one form instead of another. His study of proportion, of emphasis, and of the gradual unfolding of a design teaches him lessons which philosophy only states in another language. In his strivings for rhythm he is brought into accord with—to quote Hamilton Mabie —"the flow of rivers, the procession of stars, the antiphony of day and night, the silent but inviolate order of the seasons." He begins to realize the melodic tendency in all kinds of action, "as if nature drew into the vast flow of things all lesser works or sounds," and that "to move with it is to be part of the fathomless movement of life which the universe reveals and illustrates." When the child has proved this in his own experience, he feels that he has allied himself with all the constructive forces that are moving in an orderly and stately way toward the upbuilding of the true and beautiful in this world.

A "NEW SCHOOL" IN AMERICA

MARION FOSTER WASHBURN
Elgin, Ill.

Prospectuses littered my library table, and John and I, looking them over, were hopelessly bewildered by the multitude of good things which they offered—none of them, however, the kind of good things for which we were looking. John is my thirteen-year-old son. Owing to a severe illness in his childhood he has been unable to endure the eye-strain and the close confinement of the usual public school. So now we were trying to find a boarding-school for him where he might have an active out-door life, as few hours of book-work a day as possible, and yet that social discipline which no child can get at home. He needed contact with many other boys to socialize him, and make him a useful member of society.

But these prospectuses before us offered nothing of the kind. There were pictures of beautiful buildings, there were descriptions of military drills and uniforms, and promises in regard to college preparation. We read a good deal about athletics, but a glance at the programme and a rapid computation of the hours that must be devoted to study made it quite plain that few boys would be able at once to attain excellence in mental work, and get in any kind of out-door living.

While we were yet facing our discouragement there came the postman's ring, together with the prospectus of the Interlaken School, at La Porte, Indiana. At once, as I read the description of the German Rural Educational Homes, upon which this school is based, I remembered a talk which Colonel Parker once gave to his faculty on Dr. Lietz's schools in Germany. He told us how the boys there rose early in the morning, took a cold shower, and an out-door run, ate a simple but abundant breakfast, and were ready for school work at half-past seven, with eyes and brains fresh from the night's rest. He told us how full of vigor the boys were, how robust their health, and how clear their minds. Here in this prospectus I read that the founder of Interlaken, Dr. Edward Rumely, had taught in Dr. Lietz's school for some time before returning to his home in America, and that Interlaken was indeed another school of the same sort, transplanted to American soil.

Later I found that the first school of the group now known as "The New Schools" was founded by Dr. Cecil Reddie, at Abbotsholme, England. Dr. Reddie's recent visit here as a member of the Mosely Commission, sent by the English Parliament to investigate our educational system, has made him known probably to many readers of this article.

Dr. Lietz was one of the first to work with Dr. Reddie at Abbotsholme, and he wrote a very Germanic, idealistic, but most valuable and suggestive, book about it, called *Emlohstobba*—which name, you perceive, is just Abbotsholme spelled backward. Dr. Lietz now has three schools, one at Elsenburg in the Hartz Mountains, one in Thuringia, and one near Frankfort. There is another school of the same sort on the shores of Lake Constance, and still others are located in Sweden, Poland, and France. The boys who attend these schools for the most part wear red caps, and as part of their course includes a *Wanderjahr,* during which they travel over Europe on foot and on bicycle, they have come to be widely known as the Red Cap Boys. It is well to add, perhaps, that they are favorably known; for when a group of them stop over night at the farm of a peasant they don't make him suffer for their visit, but, on the contrary, give him a good lift with his morning's work before they depart.

Well, John and I, and John's father, were so well pleased with the prospectus that we all started at once to visit La Porte. We found the school located in a substantial, old-fashioned, roomy mansion, set well back from the road, and surrounded by seventeen acres of varied land, including an orchard, a large garden, fields, woods, and the shores of an inland lake. Here, surely, was opportunity for that varied country life which we had been led to expect. The boys could fish, row, or swim in warm weather, while in the winter the ice would give them a field for skating, tobogganing, and ice-boating. In the house were laboratories, and a large manual-training workshop, besides classrooms, and a library with an open fire where the boys gathered at the end of the day for what the directors called a "family evening." This was in agreeable contrast to those evening study hours which had dismayed me as part of the routine of other boys' schools.

Without describing further my own personal experience—for that would stretch the description beyond the limits of this article—I will say briefly that John entered the school, and that when he came home for the Christmas holidays, looking as hearty as possible, he said that he liked the school just as well for school as he did home for home. So at the end of the vacation he went back again, quite happy and contented. Is not that exactly the way a boy ought to feel about his school?

In the diminutive community of a school located, like this, on a farm, many of those processes which have disappeared altogether from city life are still in daily use, and the pupils learn of them by seeing them performed, as well as by actual participation in the work. Here are Dr. Dewey's and Colonel Parker's ideas practically carried out.

The boys make frequent excursions on foot or by wheel to neighboring factories and mills. Near La Porte there are various industries operating with wood, metal, and fibers as raw materials. The visits of the boys are encouraged by the factory owners. In fact, many business men and manufacturers are taking a deep interest in the school, and have told the directors of their willingness to co-operate in every way and to receive the pupils in their plants. The boys study at first hand noteworthy industrial feats like the damming of a river, the sinking of deep tubular wells, or the building of a city like Gary.

As may well be imagined, a visit to a foundry to see all the stages of the smelting process greatly rouses their interest. The lining of the ladles with clay, the charging of the cupola with iron and coke, the opening of the blast, the making of molds and cores, the pouring of the molten fluid, the dumping of rattling finished castings—how intently the boys observe these things! The experiences of such excursions are employed as illustrative material in classes of physics, chemistry, history, and geography. This discussion of the underlying laws knits the fragmentary information together into an organic whole in the mind of the pupil.

OUT-DOOR WORK IN MANUAL TRAINING, INTERLAKEN SCHOOL

In the field and garden the school repeats wherever practicable the experiments reported in the publications of the United States Department of Agriculture. In this work the school attempts to rouse the boy's interest early in the coming age, greater perhaps in importance than that of steel and steam, in which man shall mold like wax the plant forms to suit his needs.

In conclusion let me quote directly from the prospectus:

> The basis of the educational home is healthy environment that surrounds, like the walls of a house with large windows, the space in which youthful freedom can move and develop. The boy should feel that he is free and unhampered, that the spirit of the house concedes to him the right of self-government, that it can and does have confidence in him. With a limited number such education can be carried on successfully, while with a larger number freedom must make way to rules and prohibitions, and spontaneous buoyancy must yield before overemphasized discipline.
>
> Religion and morals are, of course, inseparable, whether we are in a chapel offering prayers and thanksgiving; or in class; or in the fields studying the marvelous works of God; in history or natural science; or wandering by the river, in the wood or on the hill; or are standing under the starry heavens and gazing into the dark abyss—always and in all places we are offering up divine service. Religion is too sacred and too subtle a matter, too much an affair of the feelings and affections, of the inward life and will, to be adequately handled in class or taught like an ordinary subject, say mathematics.
>
> We do not try to lecture on religion to our pupils, but live religion before them and with them. Our pupils must never see or hear us scoff about sacred things, nor find us indifferent or indulgent about what is wrong. They must observe in us reverence for what is holy, indignation at wrong doing, pitying gentleness for weakness, and boundless readiness at all times to help every one. They ought to see their teachers attempting to do that which the Great Master did to His disciples and to all men—forgiving, helping, reproving, healing, consoling, encouraging; in a word—loving.

With the limited number of pupils—the school admits only fifty boys at a time—it is entirely possible for the directors to carry out their promise of sharing very fully the daily life of the pupils. They lead them on the morning run, eat at the same tables, help and direct them as older friends in the classroom, dig with them in the garden, and take part in their manual work. They swim or row with them in the afternoon, accompany them on excursions, and read or listen with them at the evening family gathering.

In spite of all this varied activity and its comparatively light insistence upon book-work—or rather, perhaps, exactly because of this state of affairs, a state which keeps the boys' minds fresh and responsive, and their bodies full of vigor—the school prepares its pupils for entrance to any college. But it does not make this the end and aim of its being. On the contrary, the boy who has five years at Interlaken is already pretty well prepared for life.

The school has a branch in the Black Forest, at which the plan contemplates a stay during the last year of the course. I say a stay, but the school is scarcely more than headquarters for the boys, who spend most of that year traveling about Europe in charge of their tutors. These travels are very simply pursued on foot or on bicycle, the trains being only occasionally brought into requisition over particularly difficult bits of country. The boys camp out by the roadsides, or put up at country inns, or with the peasantry. The cost of the trips averages only $1.50 a day.

At Interlaken the boys learn to speak German and French, and in some cases Spanish. These languages are perfected, of course, during the stay in Europe; and in the meantime, the fact that they are going to be actually in use within a short time makes the boys eager for their acquisition. Nor is this by any means the only advantage of the year of foreign travel. The knowledge acquired at Interlaken is from the beginning linked with actual observations of its living forms, and the European travel knits together those loose ends of the study of history, or the languages, and sciences, of which the living forms are in other countries. In short, to quote Dr. Lietz:

> The boy who at eighteen has tasted some of the best thoughts of Hebrew, Hellenic, and Christian antiquity, and has drunk of the choicest vintage of Italian, French, and Spanish, Norse, and Anglo-Saxon literature; who beside telescope and microscope, can use pencil and violin; who is at home not only in library, museum, or laboratory, but also in workshop or garden, farmyard or forest; the boy who can run and jump, dance and sing; who is at ease in river or boat; who can cast a line and bring down a bird on the wing; the boy to whom geography and history and the institutions of his fatherland are not unexplored continents; the boy who knows how to live healthily, and how to defy, not only wind and weather, but the demoralizing influences of modern life—this boy does not belong in the least to the regions of fable; he is the realizable ideal of our school.

READING LEAFLETS, FRANCIS PARKER SCHOOL
PART I

THE HARVEST—*continued*

JENNIE HALL

MY MOTHER'S STORIES

I. CORN HUSKING

When I was a little girl I lived on a farm.
I liked corn husking.
The corn was ripe in August.
My father and brothers cut it with long knives.
They tied it into bundles.
They set the bundles together in large shocks.
These shocks stood in the field waiting for husking time.
But there was no hurry about that.
There was much other work for the men to do.
Sometimes the shocks stood until snow came.
At last, one morning, my father said:
"Well, boys, the plowing is done. We will husk corn today."
Each man got his husking-pin.
It was a little, sharp, wooden peg.
He strapped it to his middle finger.
Then they all went to the cornfield.
Each man went to a corn shock.
He cut the cord that tied it together.
He pushed it over and pulled it apart.

He sat down on a pile of the stalks.
He pulled others into his lap.
The ears hid among the leaves.
He pulled them out.
He ripped the husk with his wooden pin.
The dry leaves made a great noise.
The man broke the stem with a snap.
Out flashed the yellow corn.
He threw it to the ground.
Then he husked other ears.
Soon he had a big yellow pile.
So the men went from shock to shock.
At last all was done.
Then a wagon came.
The men picked up the corn and threw it into the wagon.
The driver took it to the corn crib.
Then he came back with a hay-rack on the wagon.
The men piled the stalks upon it.
They drove to the cow-yard.
They threw the stalks into it for the cows to eat.

EDITORIAL NOTES

The National Education Association at its Cleveland meeting recognized the importance of industrial education by giving this subject first place in the declaration of principles and aims adopted. But the way in which the "plank" was framed seems to us most unfortunate, although we have no doubt that the specific emphasis and still more, the omissions, were unintentional. The declaration reads as follows:

Industrial Education in the Cleveland Platform

Fully realizing that trained and skilled labor is a primary essential to the industrial and commercial welfare of the country, we cordially indorse the establishment by municipal boards of education of trade schools, industrial schools, and evening continuation schools; and further recommend that the instruction in these schools be practical and efficient and have the advice and the approval of the trade interested, to the end that graduates of these schools may at once become advanced apprentices or journeymen.

The Four Interests Concerned

Four interests, at least, claim consideration in this new movement for industrial education: (1) the employers; (2) the workmen in the various trades; (3) the boys and girls who are to follow the courses; (4) the general public, in so far as it is not identified with any or all of the three preceding groups. Further, both the children and the general public are interested, not only from a financial standpoint but from that of human welfare in its broadest sense.

We can imagine conventions of employers of labor, of trades-unionists, of parents, and of those interested broadly in public welfare considering the several phases of industrial education which appeal to them. The first would naturally emphasize the need of skilled labor. The second would demand a sufficiently high standard to prevent an influx of ill-prepared workmen and a consequent lowering of the wage scale. The third would feel the need of preparing children for other occupations than clerkships or the learned professions, and, if the parents were broad-minded, of preparing children to be men as well as laborers. The fourth would no doubt consider the industrial and commercial prosperity of the country as one element of public welfare, but would not fail to bring forward other things as worthy of mention in planning a school system.

Which Does the Teacher Represent?

Which of these four interests does the teacher represent? Certainly, like the supposed convention of parents, the teacher should represent the children. No less certainly he should speak for the welfare of society conceived in its broadest aspects. He is doubtless glad to have the employer find competent skilled workmen. He will also sympathize with the labor union which does not wish to see wages depressed. But these interests will not be primary. Society expects the representatives of these interests to express their needs. It looks to the teachers for something else. But in the Cleveland declaration the only reason urged for industrial education is that "trained and skilled labor is a primary essential to the industrial and commercial welfare of the country." We do not believe that the committee which drew this statement, or the body of active members which adopted it, would on reflection wish to place themselves in the position of considering only the importance of "trained and skilled labor" when planning a course of study. This might be appropriate for a manufacturers' association; it does not represent the larger function of an educational gathering.

What Difference Does it Make?

But it may be asked, What difference does it make? If we get the public to adopt the system, why quibble over the motives? It may make a great difference. There is little doubt that some form of industrial education is to be organized in the near future. But the lines along which this is to proceed are still to be worked out. If courses are organized solely or chiefly to "supply labor" they will be planned in one way; if they are organized with the motive of making intelligent and cultured workmen as well, they will be planned in another. In one case attention is likely to be centered on the narrowly technical aspects of the trade; in the other its historical development, its aesthetic values, its relation to the whole industrial process will not be overlooked. This in our view is of fundamental and far-reaching importance.

The movement for industrial education has thus far been not altogether fortunate in its management. It is to be hoped that the teachers of the country will stand for the broader significance of the movement. If they do not, who will? The unfortunate emphasis in the declaration at Cleveland should stimulate teachers and educators generally to make sure that their influence is on the right side in future plans for industrial education.

J. H. T.

NOTES AND NEWS

"The early withdrawal of pupils from school is a fact universally recognized," says the United States Commissioner of Education in his report for 1908, "but up to this time there have been few investigations of the extent and the causes of the evil." The United States Department of Education in 1900 reported that over 50 per cent. of all public-school pupils were in the first and second grades and were less than nine years of age; 87.5 per cent. were in the first five grades and were under twelve years. All investigations on this point in particular cities, however widely they may differ, agree in indicating "a marked decline in attendance between the fourth and fifth grades, and continued decrease thereafter."

Religious education having failed to find for itself a method acceptable to more than one country at a time, an International Congress on Moral Education is now being held in London (September 23–26). Papers in three languages are on the programme, discussing everything from discipline to juvenile literature, and the ethical penetration of the whole curriculum. Unwillingness to relegate moral instruction to an hour by itself, and a desire to introduce its application in "history, geography, literature, languages, composition, mathematics, natural history and other subjects," is a strong note of this congress. The problem of moral education, in so far as it is distinguishable from religious education, is practically virgin soil. The papers of the congress will be issued in a book as a sort of encyclopedia on the subject.

Four at least of the articles in *Child Labor and Social Process*, a publication containing the proceedings of the fourth annual meeting of the National Child Labor Committee, deal with the bearing of education on child-labor. This is another sign of the growing recognition of the relation between education and the wider problems of society. Lewis Parker contends that laws of compulsory education are a much more direct solution of the problem than laws for the repression of child labor. The former legislation would include the latter, and would prove, in many parts of the country, a much more popular measure. Especially in the south, where legislation against child-labor seems immediately to take the form of a class attack on the owners of cotton-mills, a compulsory education law would be much less objectionable. In fact the Cotton Manufacturers' Association of South Carolina has itself made a written plea for a law compelling school attendance for children between eight and twelve, though this same association quite naturally refuses to support "measures heretofore introduced intended to require school attendance on the part of cotton-mill operatives only." Registration of births is also requested by the association, in order to insure the possibility of obedience to the other laws mentioned.

BOOKS RECEIVED

AMERICAN BOOK COMPANY, NEW YORK

Chinese Fables and Folk Stories. By MARY HAYES DAVIS AND CHOW-LEUNG. Cloth. Illustrated. Pp. 214. $0.40.

Japanese Folk Stories and Fairy Tales. By MARY F. NIXON-ROULET. Cloth. Illustrated. Pp. 191. $0.40.

Swift's Gulliver's Travels for Children. By JAMES BALDWIN. Cloth. Illustrated. Pp. 172. $0.35.

Goethe's Hermann und Dorothea. Edited, with notes and vocabulary, by WATERMAN THOMAS HEWETT. Cloth. Pp. 325. $0.60.

A Spanish Reader for Beginners in High Schools and Colleges. By CHARLES ALFRED TURRELL. Cloth. Pp. 256. $0.80.

Avellanda's Baltasar. Edited, with introduction and notes, by CARLOS BRANSBY. Cloth. Pp. 224. $0.65.

Latin Prose Composition Based on Caesar. By HENRY CARR PEARSON. Cloth. Pp. 195. $0.50.

Maury-Simonds Physical Geography. By M. F. MAURY; revised and largely rewritten by F. W. SIMONDS. Half leather. Pp. 347. $1.20.

HENRY ALTEMUS COMPANY, PHILADELPHIA

How to Dress a Doll. By MARY H. MORGAN. Illuminated boards. Illustrated. Pp. 95. $0.50.

MACMILLAN, NEW YORK

Emerson's Earlier Poems. (Pocket Series.) Edited, with introduction and notes, by OSCAR CHARLES GALLAGHER. Pp. 161. $0.25.

Hawthorne's Mosses from an Old Manse. (Pocket Series.) Edited, with introduction and notes, by CHARLES ELROY BURBANK. Cloth. Pp. 286. $0.25.

Whittier's Snow-Bound and Other Early Poems. (Pocket Series.) Edited, with introduction and notes, by A. L. BOUTON. Cloth. Pp. 288. $0.25.

Shakespeare's A Midsummer Night's Dream. (Pocket Series.) Edited, with introduction and notes, by ERNEST CLAPP NOYES. Cloth. Pp. 147. $0.25.

Lesson Stories for the Kindergarten Grades of the Bible School. By LOIS SEDGWICK PALMER AND GEORGE WILLIAM PEASE. Cloth. Pp. 127. $0.75.

THE HALTING OF A CARAVAN BESIDE THE NILE

Third-Grade Work. (See "Social Life in Geography")

VOLUME IX NUMBER 3

THE ELEMENTARY SCHOOL TEACHER

NOVEMBER, 1908

SOCIAL LIFE IN GEOGRAPHY

LUNA E. BIGELOW
State Normal School, New Paltz, N. Y.

The aim of education as stated by the greatest educators of our day is that of social efficiency. The educational method employed is that of more social life in the schoolroom. This social life as an educational means is begun in the kindergarten. It should be continued throughout the grades.

How does geography further this living of a real life in the schoolroom? This question leads us to ask several others. First, What is geography? Second, What are the aim and purposes of teaching geography? And third, What is the importance of geography in the curriculum if the aim of education is social efficiency?

Geography is defined as the relationship of things organic and inorganic. It involves some knowledge of geology, physics, zoölogy, botany, astronomy, and history, but it is only with relationships that the geography has to deal.

The aims and purposes of geography should be, first to show these relationships and man's control of his environment. Second, to broaden the child's horizon and develop the powers of perspective study. Third, to develop the power of scientific reasoning and observation. And fourth, to have the child able to question intelligently and weigh the evidences of newspaper and magazine articles as well as that of the text in geographical subjects. He should know his own environment and should have some knowledge of the world as a whole and its relation to the people who inhabit it.

The importance of geography in the curriculum is manifold. I will mention only four reasons: First, the dependence of other subjects upon geography; second, the interdependence of man on man; third, the moral and social forces of the world as controlled by geographic conditions, and fourth, by far one of the most important, the broadening of the child's sympathies through a knowledge of the controls of social life widely different from his own.

In the grades of the elementary school man is the central feature of the geography work. With the children of the lower grades the curriculum leads from man in his social environment to the control of that environment. With the children of the upper grades it leads from the physiographic conditions to man's utilization and control. It is with the former that this paper will deal, and the emphasis will be placed on interrelationships.

When the child enters first grade from the kindergarten he has a rather clear idea of home life. He has studied the home of the smaller animals, of birds, as well as the home of the human family, at different seasons of the year. He has done this by observation, construction, excursion, and dramatization. He is now ready to understand and to enjoy the homes of children whose environment is far different from his own.

What boy of from six to ten does not enjoy playing Indian or being a Filipino? How he works to build a snow house in which he lives and labors in his childish efforts to be an Eskimo! This very playing at being a child of another land can be turned to excellent use in the schoolroom. By careful suggestion and direction from the teacher the children can be lead to dramatize the phases of Indian life which show their geographic controls. They can build the tepees, make and decorate their suits, their bows and arrows, their quivers, their clay pottery, and their basketry. They can have the bear hunt, and deer hunt, and the fishing scenes. Even the feast can be held at the return of the huntsmen. The agricultural methods of the Indians can be carried out in the school garden and contrasted with our own agricultural methods.

The Eskimo home can be built in the school yard during the winter season. The children dressed in their warmest furs can live in this house for a few minutes, and, by so living, can more fully realize the necessity for the fur clothing of the little Eskimo baby. The children can make the few crude household utensils which these people have. They can make the harness for the dogs. If some child has a pet dog which can be harnessed to the ice sled, a ride around a snow hut will make Eskimo life more of a reality to him. Having led the children through these activities to understand some of the difficulties and hardships in the life of their little Eskimo brothers and sisters, they can now be lead to appreciate the effort of these people of the snow. They should learn how to get their food and what is to be obtained. They should also learn the necessity for eating the animal food, and the relationship of that necessity to the food supply of that cold climate. The children should feel the great advantage of their life and opportunity rather than to consider themselves a superior race.

As the hot months of summer come on a primitive village of Central Africa can be built in the place of the Eskimo village of the winter. This is easily done as the house needs only the four posts, covered with straw, and the sides and floor made of branches of leaves. Mats of braided leaves will serve as beds, and only some crude clay pottery is needed for household utensils. Although the children can only imitate the dress of the African native they will enjoy decorating themselves with shells and bright stones, and tying on the girdle. They will go to the make-believe forests to gather rubber. They will tramp round and round the school yard to carry this rubber to the place of shipment, and receive their reward for gathering their assigned quantity. While these are gathering rubber another squad of boys will return from the elephant hunt laden with ivory and other trophies. They, too, will give up their treasures to be sent to the civilized world. All this can be dramatized and much more. Then let the children follow by pictures and discussions the rubber as it leaves the hands of the African until it is on their own feet. By this means they will see the relationship of the savage life to ours and our obligation to them.

In many schools this outdoor work is not feasible; but in many far more can be accomplished than has even been suggested. When no open-air work is possible much can be done in the schoolroom. A corner of the schoolroom can be transformed into another country and the geography lessons each day lived instead of recited. The children will be able to bring many articles brought from foreign lands to equip this miniature country. Many children will construct wondrous things, and frequently the mothers will co-operate in this work.

The sand board should be used. I know, from practical experience, that we have not as yet begun to realize the value of the sand table in the schoolroom. When the country studied is less primitive, or the environment more complicated, the children should construct on the sand board the life of the country studied. They should dress the dolls, make the homes, contribute the animals from among their toys, gather the foliage, and obtain the covering for the board. They can make rivers and lakes, build mountains and even have a glacier or a smoking volcano whenever anyone of these are needed to emphasize the life of the people.

Last year, a fourth-grade class studied the life of Mexican children, illustrating each main feature on the sand board: the palm trees and cacti; the packed burros and the Mexican steer harnessed to the wide wooden-wheeled carts; the adobe houses with the public water fountains and the hacienda with its bells. The study of the palm leaf fiber and the hemp brought the children in touch with the industrial life of Mexico; and a knowledge of the great cathedral made them appreciate the religious life of our neighbors (see illustration on opposite page).

In one schoolroom, the children have constructed the rural life of Italy—its home life, its people, its vineyards, its irrigation ditches and the distant Mt. Vesuvius sending forth its puffs of smoke. This vineyard had row after row of vines, from which the pickers were gathering and carrying grapes to the preservers

MEXICO

and wine makers. Some of the boys had written letters to importers and had received samples of the products of the vineyards, accompanied by a pamphlet describing the process of curing and methods of importing.

At their homes several children have made themselves aprons, shawls, and kerchiefs, which they wore as they told the rest of the school how the Italian children worked in the vineyards. Another group of children showed me pictures they had found of these people in books of travel. Another group dramatized some of the quaint manners and customs of these children. One child told of their religious life. All were able to show on both globe and map the route which they would take from their own city, not only to Italy but to the vineyard country near Naples. Some of the boys could name railroads and steamship lines and state the price of tickets. This school had a large collection of Italian home-manufactured articles which the children had brought. They knew what Italy imported and exported; and discussed intelligently the interrelationships and interdependence of one country upon another.

As this phase of geography teaching draws to a close in the fourth or fifth grades, an excellent review is obtained by holding a conference of nations. The children should choose their own parts, and work them out. Each child should give from the globe or map of the world his journey, carefully planned as to route, expense, and time. Then they should dramatize the manners and customs, should set forth the needs and the advantages of their chosen country, its contributions to the world and to particular peoples, and the help or benefits it receives from these peoples. In fact, here again interrelationships should be emphasized. One of the best conferences of this sort I ever saw closed by the Japanese and Chinese serving tea in true oriental style. The children sat on bright crape paper rugs and drank their tea off tables made of cardboard covered with dark glazed paper to imitate the lacquered tables of the Orient. This method of review is vital and alive with social interest. It is not difficult to carry out such a programme.

Assign to each country a portion of the schoolroom wall, and leave the decorations to the children. They will find pictures, dress dolls, collect all sorts of specimens. Let them study pictures and arrange their own costumes. It might be well to tell them how much can be done with crape and tissue paper, and to limit expense if some children of well-to-do parents are apt to "show of." The construction work and costumes will be crude and unfinished. They are made quickly for effects and not for the purpose of manual training.

This work should be the spontaneous, initiative effort of the children, and not a play dramatized for spectators. I doubt if it is advisable to invite visitors at all. The presence of adults, unless they take an active part in the exercise, often creates in some child a strained consciousness of effort which thwarts the purpose of the lesson.

In carrying out any or all of this work the children should have access to a large number of children's books, to books of travel and to magazines. The older of these children should keep in touch with the daily papers and the progress made by all people. Their assignments should be individual or in small groups, and the subject-matter should appeal to the individual tastes of the children. Except for the geographical locations, main exports and imports and principal cities, etc., each child should be left free to absorb and assimilate that phase of life in any country which suits his temperament and purposes. These assignments may often be an excursion to some other part of the town to visit our immigrants and see how they live and to be able to compare what they see with the meager descriptions in the textbooks; or to some factory to see our process of manufacturing some article which in a foreign land is made by hand; or to see one of our bridges and its approach and compare with noted ones in Europe. All should gradually learn to see the physiographic controls.

Some pupils may write for railroad and steamship schedules and advertising matter; others may write to our large manufacturing establishments and corporations requesting educational series of their goods; and still others can open correspondence with schools and institutions in foreign countries. Thus they will feel the real necessity of studying geography.

These are only a few of the ways by means of which more social life can be lived in the schoolroom. But these will develop in the child those habits of study and thought for which we aim. He will see and live relationships, his judgments will be based upon well-weighed evidences and his sympathies will embrace all people.

THE CONSERVATION OF CHILDHOOD

FRITZ KOCH
Lake Geneva New School
Chataigneraie sur Coppet (Vaud), Switzerland

Henry Ward Beecher has said that no man is a man unless he has some of the boy left in him. Fortunate is the man of that type and fortunate too the woman that has some of the girl left in her, for the boy and the girl and the child element in the adult adds greatly to the realization of the universal happiness we are all striving for.

This paper is, however, not so much concerned about youthful adults as about the conservation of that original naïve, playful mental attitude which we find in typical children.

The list of things that man considers as absolute necessities is steadily growing and consequently an unnatural stress is forced on the ability to earn money. This not only prevents adults from living a full, well-balanced life but it reaches clear down into childhood. The relentless money hustler arrives finally at that state of narrow-mindedness where he can no longer appreciate the reasonable right of a child to live the full life of a child with all its fanciful dreams and delightful make-believe.

We, wise adults with our great mass of accumulated knowledge, have found certain ways, which, if strictly followed, may lead one rapidly to much desired results. Our faith is very great in this course, because this or that man "got there" by doing so and so. One sometimes gets the impression that the text is "Seek ye all the other things and the Kingdom of Heaven will be added as you hustle along." The rapidly growing craze of today to make the utmost show of actual or borrowed wealth has created in the brain of some shrewd fanatic the brilliant notion that a training in trades and commerce and make-money-quickly processes should commence even as the child emerges from the cradle. Every minute in life being represented by a coin it is highly essential that children become grown-ups as rapidly as possible. The sooner the young infant learns to grasp and reproduce the methods and manners of adults, the greater is the applause, for the adult ways and manners are the only ones that bring "tangible" results.

Now wouldn't it be strange if we should wake up some day and discover that an overfed, swell-housed, swell-automobiled nation is after all not such a desirable achievement as we imagine it to be—at least not worth the sacrifice it costs. Perhaps those who have enjoyed a glorious childhood will discover some day that their children, not having had the same advantages, have grown up pitiable specimens of humanity, utterly unable to enjoy either the wealth they accumulated or any of the worthier pleasures that money cannot buy.

If an education given to a child shall enable him to live a full life later on as well as during this school period his education must be such that when he finally enters upon his vocational career he will be deeply interested not only in his vocation but also in many other things including at least one hobby of some kind distinctly different from his chosen vocation.

Whereas it may be an excellent idea to have pupils, from their thirteenth year on, gradually, tend to a specialization along vocational lines, we must not lose sight of the fact that adults work eight hours a day and that most of the worst mischief in the world is done by those who do not know what to do with themselves in the hours when they are free from work.

When twelve years of reading fails to interest children in good literature and in the secrets of nature to which books furnish a key, something is wrong somewhere. When twelve years of practice in writing does not enable one to express in legible characters an account of some common event that flows glibly from the end of the tongue, something is wrong somewhere. A lack of interest for the things written and read about are to my mind one of the reasons for such unsatisfactory results. Who knows but that, notwithstanding the heroic efforts of reformers, the subject-matter still lacks genuine adaptability to a childish nature and that the methods are *still too much akin* to those by which venerable adults enlarge their store of abstract knowledge. It seems to me that because the more mature and cultured mind keenly enjoys the highest in art, literature, and music, one is often inclined to demand an appreciation on the part of the child which is forced and unnatural. The process of urging children to form and express personal opinions about the most sublime achievements of great men is wrong because children have neither a natural desire nor any business to do so. The method, too, of early forcing a crystallization of opinion by having children read a great deal *about* the highest literature and art is most disastrous to the development of a strong personality because a child has not lived long enough to corroborate or supplement the book-material by results from personal experience. Such opinions are consequently without backbone and we have, as a result, on the one hand those who are puffed up and conceited and on the other hand those who, a few years later, have forgotten both the subject and their opinion. An opinion that is formulated unverified by personal experience, is only borrowed property and very frequently proves to be valueless.

As to hearing and seeing music, literature, and art much of the very best acts beneficially and successfully upon the child even in cases where it is not altogether adapted to his interest and emotional nature. The mistake is made when we *expect reactions* from these influences in forms of expression identical to our *adult* view of looking at things.

But not only through adult school-subjects is the child spirit in the child suppressed when it has scarcely commenced to blossom. There are other agencies that encroach with equally harmful results. Children to thrive best, should be much with children. The child that is always with adults assumes adult ways and cuts out of his career experiences that leave him mentally crippled when he has reached maturity. He can never be a full man. Children that frequent theaters, balls, etc., are forcibly influenced by the conversation and ideals of adult performers and try to be grown-ups in their thought and expression. There is a vast difference between the serious (sometimes unconscious) attempt of the precocious child to be an adult and the playful make-believe of natural children when for the mere novelty of it they dress up in big people's clothes.

Not least among the detriments to a natural development of children is fashion, a forced culture of vanity and extravagance. Not only do the parents but also the teachers set the example. To follow slavishly all the extravagance of fashion appears to be a far stronger tendency than the desire to be refined and simple. It is so utterly common to be fashionable, nowadays, that I should think teachers, at least, would refuse to imitate the great mass of humanity, unless the fashion happens to be adaptable to the particular personality of the wearer. For the benefit of the children I would recommend that all "self-crippled" exponents of vanity be banished from the schoolroom.

Dressing fashionably, dressing elaborately is often so strongly impressed even upon the youngest children that it prevents them from concerning themselves about things of much greater value to them. This is particularly noticeable not only among the wealthy but among children of the great middle class and among those who believe it necessary to live up to the very limit of their income.

Cleanliness is a virtue not demanded from the factory hand while at work, but children, while at play, are constantly reprimanded because of their dirty hands, spots on their clothes, etc. So frequently are they called away from their real life because of this, and so dressed up are many of them (because the father can afford it and the mother likes it) that natural, intense, wild play is gradually replaced by occupations of lesser value, or by systematic games, like tennis, basket-ball, and baseball. As, however, the systematic games are indulged in by only a small section of the children generally, owing to an insufficient number of places, this does not affect the great majority; and, excellent as they are, *systematic games* should not be the only ones played by children. The free plays of their own making, and such simple games as hide and seek, or hare and hounds give more scope to the exercise of the imagination because they are bounded by very few rules.

Spontaneous action and natural growth take place when

children are least encumbered by critical adult supervision during their free play hours. They are naturally diggers in the dirt, waddlers in puddles, climbers of trees and fences and balustrades. Real boys and girls are rovers in fields and forests, in alleys and dangerous places. They play hide and seek until it is pitch dark and come home all perspiration and mud and radiant happiness. They are awfully hungry and yet a genuine sleepiness overtakes them even while they eat their bread and milk.

Real boys and girls are fascinated by the most gruesome ghost-stories and they listen to the most impossible fairy tales with breathless attention. They keenly enjoy the inner battle between fear and courage. The child that never knew fear has never intensely felt the glory of a victory when courage wins out. The child that has never tried to down hatred, jealousy, or revenge is probably the child that never played intensely to the very limit of his strength. When children play intensely there is noise and lots of it—and that is right. It should be so. Children who play noiselessly never test their capacities to the uttermost and fail to expand as they should. Growth of mind, body, and character takes place not nearly so thoroughly and successfully in the peaceful kindergarten or the well-ordered classroom as in the clash-bang hour of genuine, exhaustive play.

But how are boys and girls going to play like this when they are constantly dressed-up in Sunday clothes? And how is it possible so long as parents have a thousand foolish fears and when they feel terribly disgraced upon beholding their children all mussed up?

Children up to fourteen should wear play-clothes designed on the simplest lines and made of tent canvas if needs be. Children should wear stockings and sandals only when the weather gets to be too cold, but run barefooted otherwise. Rubbers are inventions to please the housewife. To the children they are the cause of more sickness than their not wearing them would bring. Why not let them exchange their sandals for slippers as they enter the house. Talks about rubbers and leggings and this wrap and that and all kinds of temperature have created a greater wave of fear and sickness and worry than all the written and unwritten ghost-stories put together, and furthermore such over-anxious adjustments to weather conditions have prevented the child from freely exercising his real inner forces. I have seen small children on a bright winter day so encumbered by great quantities of beautiful clothes that they could not possibly spoil them for they could scarcely waddle around in them. Of course, real play was out of the question. The natural child that has not already been spoiled by elementary lessons in vanity cares very little for costly clothes. It is the vain parent that early inoculates these tendencies, irrespective of the child's more normal demand for clothes that are first of all practical. Such clothes can be quite artistic. In fact, much more so than the questionable finery that ignorant parents often select as the best.

We are living in an age when the well-patched garment is no longer a sign of thrift and economy but rather a sign of poverty. The man is considered a pauper who does not keep his children constantly dressed in new and fashionable clothes. But I question the wisdom of this attitude, as it is not only the cause of much unhappiness among those who cannot keep pace with the more "fortunate"(?), but a constant supply of new garments creates either a vain passion for clothes or it becomes such a common event that children grow indifferent. They fail to enjoy the keener pleasure that comes to the child who on rare occasions is surprised by the gift of a new suit, which for a long time is childishly treasured and worn at first only on holidays.

City life is, of course, very detrimental to the natural growth of children, but even those families who decide that it is wisest to live in a flat, can do several things by way of solving the playground problem for children. Wherever back yards are to be found there perhaps, by an agreement between all the neighbors, a common playground can be established by putting doors in the dividing fences. Such a larger playground, with its many nooks and corners, is very essential to *intense, free play*. Children should be provided with plenty of old dry-goods boxes, odd board, and bits of worn-out rugs, etc. The fantastic houses made of this material stir up the imagination and furnish manual work most closely related to their ideals. The crude model of a ship whittled and rigged in the most primitive manner has an educational value which we frequently underestimate. We criticize a child's work because we fail to find in it those elements that happen to constitute our *preconceived* notion of what the thing ought to be, and we are blind to any of the originality expressed because it is foreign to us and obliges the lazy mind to adjust itself to new conditions.

I once saw a class of 32 slum children produce 22 different inventions for strengthening four legs attached to a table-top. The vital imagination in these children had not been prematurely adjusted to our notions of what is right and proper. Without having had some opportunity to experiment children do not fully appreciate the achievements of the race. A most refreshing diversity and many suggestive improvements characterized the whole work of this class, but, above all, these children lived intensely *the life of people eleven years old.* They were not forcibly drawn into work-ideals of people twenty years their senior. The delusive fact that children can early be trained to act very much like adults, and skilfully to accomplish tasks equal in workmanship (if not excelling) those of adults, is not at all a sign that children should be made to do these things. Such evidence is rather significant of the fact that adults are not nearly such wonderful creatures as they imagine themselves to be. Adults are often occupied in their regular business with things that children can learn to do in a few years of apprenticeship under the right kind of a leader. It is commonly known that the art productions of children ten years old are usually in every way superior to the artistic attempts of inexperienced adults.

One of the greatest mistakes we make is to consider children inferior beings. It is just as bad as the habit of making unnatural sacrifices for them. When a family in Germany goes out to a picnic, the men carry canes, the women carry the babies, and the children drag along the heavy lunch-basket. But also in America are children often made to feel that they are "only" children. I take exception to the word "only." Those who look upon children in that light are unreasonable, unjust, and ignorant of a true attitude toward life. Such people possess a remarkable lack of humility and get a good share of my profoundest sympathy whenever, and as soon as, I am able to down my grudge against them.

Let us recognize children as children, neither granting them all the privileges of adults nor depriving them of their particular rights as *junior members* of our race. Picture to them with fervor all the fun and glorious opportunities that their special plays and occupations bring, and children will enthusiastically live their happy life and ardently love it until they have outgrown it or even beyond that time which, by the way, is no serious fault.

THE VALUE AND LIMITATIONS OF FROEBEL'S GIFTS AS EDUCATIVE MATERIALS
PARTS I, II

PATTY SMITH HILL
Teachers College, Columbia University

This article will attempt to treat Froebel's gifts from the following points of view:

PART I. Froebel's gifts as one phase of the modern tendency to introduce activities and materials into education.

PART II. The fundamental aims which Froebel had in mind when planning the activities and materials of the kindergarten.

PART III. The degree of success attained by Froebel in attempting to apply his educational principles to the use of materials in the kindergarten.

PART IV. Some present-day conceptions of the aim of materials in the kindergarten.

PART V. Some present-day conceptions of the application of Froebelian principles to the use of materials in the kindergarten.

PART I

FROEBEL'S GIFTS AS ONE PHASE OF THE MODERN TENDENCY TO INTRODUCE ACTIVITIES AND MATERIALS INTO EDUCATION

A broad, philosophical interpretation of the term material would have to include all the varied agencies of the modern curriculum; but this article will limit the term to the more ordinary, external conception of materials; for example, the interpretation of the term as "supplies" for such modes of expression as art, construction, etc.

Froebel's philosophy of life and education demanded materials as a fundamental element in his scheme.

He had been preceded by Comenius, Pestalozzi, and others in the use of activities and materials as educational agencies;

but no predecessor had placed these in the philosophical setting, seeing them in their organic, basic relationship to the other phases of the curriculum.

In other words, the activities and materials of the kindergarten are the result of Froebel's most serious attempt to apply his voluntaristic philosophy to the smallest detail of child-life; and while the vastness of the attempt often betrayed him into puerile applications, his very errors should provoke a certain respect, for they are evidences of his unwillingness to voice a philosophy which was not firmly rooted in life and which, in turn, would illuminate the smallest detail of life and educational practice.

Unfortunately, the terminology in which Froebel voiced his educational theories and christened the technique of the kindergarten is not always intelligible to educators in general, and has been one of many other causes for the separation which often exists between the kindergarten and the elementary school. Now that the kindergarten has become a part of the public-school system, its peculiar terminology is growing more familiar, and "gifts" and "occupations," Froebel's technical terms for the kindergarten materials, are more generally understood.

It is taken for granted that readers of this article know what the Froebelian materials are, and therefore no description will be given.

The proper perspective for a valuation of Froebel's gifts and occupations is secured when viewing them—(1) In their relation to the other instrumentalities of the kindergarten or as only a small part of the whole; (2) As one phase of the modern tendency to introduce activities and materials into education.

This latter tendency is evident all through education—from the plays and games, the gifts and occupations of the kindergarten, the art, manual training, domestic science, and laboratory method through the elementary and secondary schools, to the departments of technology in higher education.

How far this change of ideal from the passive to the self-active conception of education is directly or indirectly due to the educational philosophy of Froebel cannot be discussed here; but the statement that all education is growing more active, more closely related to life, with a tendency to lay more emphasis upon development than abstract instruction, needs no argument.

We are inclined to call his the "new education," and while it must be acknowledged that it is a present-day reaction from the formal, abstract method of instruction of an earlier day, in reality it is an attempt to reinstate that early racial method of education *in* life, used unconsciously in primitive society, but now consciously illuminated by the richness of the knowledge and highest spiritual ideals of civilization.

An exhaustive study of the significance of materials in an ideal of education based upon self-activity and development would presuppose a knowledge of philosophy, psychology, sociology, science, art, and industry far beyond the attempt of this article. To be adequately understood materials would have to be studied from at least three typical view-points: (1) philosophical, which would involve the consideration of some of the oldest and most fruitful problems of philosophy—i. e., the relation of matter to the development of mind, of the objective to the subjective life, of body to spirit, of nature to man, of the not-self to the self; (2) psychological, which would require a study of the relation of sensation and motion, and of stimuli and response to the life of feeling and thought; (3) sociological, which would demand a knowledge of the part activities and materials have played in deepening the sense of social consciousness through the medium of social co-operation.

While such a study of materials would illuminate the problem of activities and materials in the kindergarten and subdue the tendency of kindergartners to make an educational fetish of the gifts and occupations, the limitations of this article require concentration upon the discussion of Froebelian materials in general and the so-called gifts in particular.

PART II

THE FUNDAMENTAL AIMS WHICH FROEBEL HAD IN MIND WHEN PLANNING THE ACTIVITIES AND MATERIALS OF THE KINDERGARTEN

It requires the most patient, sympathetic study of Froebel to select what must have been the most fundamental aims which he had in mind when he planned the technique and instrumentalities of the kindergarten.

Two principles must be mentioned which seemed to be the "seed thoughts" out of which all the lesser aims grow: (1) Froebel's conception of (*a*) mind as activity, (*b*) of the child as a self-active, creative being, (c) and education as a process of development by which man comes into harmonious development with nature, man, and God.

These convictions are voiced on every page of his writings and are the burden of his thought in a somewhat unsuccessful struggle to systematize his philosophy and express it in terms which could be understood.

With his deeply religious nature he bases the necessity for manual training, not primarily upon the necessity of earning a livelihood, but upon the creative principle inherent in man as a child of God. The line of argument is as follows:

a) "God creates and works productively. . . . . Each thought of God is a work, a deed, a product. . . . . The spirit of God hovered over chaos and moved it; and stones and plants, beasts and man took form and separate being and life."[1]

b) "God created man in his own image;

c) "Therefore man should create and bring forth as God. His spirit, the spirit of man, should hover over the shapeless and move it that it may take shape and form and a distinct being and life of its own.

d) "We become truly Godlike in diligence and industry, in working and doing which are accompanied by the clear perception or even by the vaguest feeling that thereby we represent the inner in the outer; that we give body to spirit; form to thought."

(2) Froebel's conception of mind as activity would seem to demand as its counterpart an acceptance of the reality of the world of nature as the condition of human activity, offering limitations which furnish the necessity for effort in a process of self-realization. The ideal of the child as a self-active, creative being, requires that education should offer materials which are in a sense complementary to mind, yet offering through their

[1] *Education of Man*, pp. 30, 31.

apparent oppositions and limitations the conditions for activity, effort, and development.

While it is claimed that Froebel did not entirely escape the dualistic conception of nature and humanity, he feels deeply the oneness of all life in spirit and essence, apparently without denying the reality of nature. Dr. Cole thus states a general misconception of Froebel's attitude toward reality:

> Contrary to a prevalent impression Froebel is distinctly for reality in education. Realizing to a greater extent than Fichte, or than Herbart, that nature is real, and to a degree objective, Froebel took his educational materials from the near at hand, developed occupations from contact with visible and tangible objects and studied nature for what it is, as well as for what it may symbolize.[2]

With the emphasis laid upon the child as primarily a doer, the possibilities of any material in the educative process will depend upon—(*a*) The possibilities of this material considered in itself, i. e., what can be done with it; (*b*) The degree to which this same material responds to the activities, capacities, and powers of the doer.

Froebel thus describes what, from the child's point of view, is required of materials:

> Therefore the child likes best that plaything, whatever its outward appearance may be, by which and with which he can form and accomplish most.[3]

That Froebel felt that materials should be carefully selected in the light of finding those which are a true counterpart to the self-activity of the child, and those which are a means of nourishment to mind is quite evident. He writes,

> An object must therefore be given to the child, not merely for his outward bodily activity, but rather for his inward activity, the activity of his soul and for the development and cultivation of this activity. It is by no means unimportant, it is, on the contrary a thing of the highest importance, what kind of an object is here provided for the child as a true *counterpart* of himself. . . . . It is to be an object like the child, but at the same time his pure opposite.[4]

Or again,

> As a being complete in himself, bearing life in himself, developing and appropriating life to himself . . . . the child seeks also a counterpart to him-

[2] Percival Cole, *Herbart and Froebel*, p. 14.

[3] *Education by Development*, p. 200.

[4] *Op. cit.*, pp. 180, 181.

self an object which is opposite to, yet like himself. It must therefore, firstly, as a similar object, be such a one as will enable the child, for the free unfolding of his self-determined nature, to make from it everything which he wishes.

Thus out of many minor aims growing out of these major ones, the following might be selected as giving the *raison d'être* for his educative materials.

a) *Self-realization and self-knowledge.*—The conviction that self knows self—that thought comes to consciousness through its objectivation in outward form, as a mirror to mind is marked in Froebelian literature.

As the child comes to know its own face through its mirrored reflection, so man has come to self-knowledge through his effort to stamp his own image on nature and society. Thus, thought comes to itself, through externalization, what Froebel describes as "making the inner, outer," "the internal, external," "giving body to spirit," and "form to thought." Froebel thus describes the necessity for the ceaseless activity of childhood:

> The child's activity . . . . has its foundations in the effort, first of all, to make known his inner life in and by means of outward phenomena, as soon as it comes to his perception—to place this life objectively before himself and externally to himself; and next to appropriate the inner life of things around him, and indeed to come to a knowledge of it by this reproduction.[5]

b) *Control* (1) *over material,* (2) *over social experience.*—Froebel is deeply imbued with the value of limitations and oppositions in calling forth effort. The theory of effort as conditioned in the necessity for overcoming the difficulties which interpose or obstruct the self in the process of realization is evident. Dr. MacVannel says regarding Froebel's theory of opposites and their reconciliation:

> When with Fichte he emphasizes opposites, antagonisms, or a system of limits as the condition of activity, effort, work and self-development, Froebel is surely on the right track.[6]

The value of outward form, in calling forth the effort of the ego when mastering the difficulties which arise in trying to body

[5] *Op. cit.*, p. 64.

[6] John Angus MacVannel, *The Educational Theories of Herbart and Froebel,* p. 90.

forth thought is emphasized. As one child in the manual-training class expressed it, "Teacher, I tell you there is a big difference between looking at a chair and making one."

The spiritual unhealthiness of the child whose early life has been sacrificed to the dangers of the "boundless" and "formless" by lack of materials and opportunities for externalizing thought and feeling is thus described by Froebel:

> If this requirement of the human being in general is not fulfilled for the child by suitable objects coming to him from without, he seeks to satisfy this requirement of his nature by means of his power of imagination (fancy). But the images of fancy lead the human being, and even the child, very easily into the boundless and formless, as they at the same time more weaken than strengthen the human being and this even in his early development.[7]

He values work, play ("self-employment") with materials for these reasons:

> They free man from the life of empty, formless, vacant, as well as measureless imagination and fancy, which is inwardly full of disturbance and outwardly demoralizing and annihilating.[8]

Not only control, but continuous progress in control must be provided. This need Froebel endeavored to meet by a sequence of geometrically related materials progressing from the simple to the complex in the analysis and synthesis of form. The inability of the child to control materials in good form was to Froebel the indication of his need for materials which provide gradually increasing difficulties, which would guarantee steady progress in power and ability to organize and control experience:

> Therefore (as every one who has watched the impulse of healthy children will have been convinced) the as yet slight power of the child is not in a condition to obstruct his impulse to creative activity, but, on the contrary, he seeks to strengthen and elevate this impulse by increasing demands on the efficiency of his power.[9]

c) *Social co-operation.* When viewed from the social point of view activities and materials are rich in values for deepening a sense of social consciousness.

In race development materials have brought social dependence to consciousness in the need of social co-operation in realizing

[7] *Op. cit.*, pp. 179, 180. [8] *Op. cit.*, p. 201. [9] *Op. cit.*, p. 65.

social ends, industrial, aesthetic, and religious. The social contributions of many were necessary to meet the individual and social needs. There was the constant interchange of ideas necessary for the reconstruction of experience among the mature members of society; and the transmission of experience from the mature to the inexperienced apprentice in that progressive control necessary to the skilled artisan.

Even the competition of festivals where rival social groups vied with each other for supremacy was rich with the social suggestions necessary to progress in the reconstruction of experience within the group.

"If," according to Dr. John Dewey, "society is a number of people held together because they are working along common lines, in a common spirit, with reference to common aims"[10] we can readily appreciate that "common needs and aims demand a growing interchange of thought and a growing unity of sympathetic feeling."

d) *To promote a sane balance and proportion between the intellectual and emotional life on one hand and the practical and executive on the other in a life of social service.*—To Froebel this is a principle of individual and social hygiene necessary to maintain health of mind and body in the individual and the relation of privileges and obligation in the social organization. In the following quotation it is to be remembered that religion must be interpreted in its broadest sense as a consciousness of relationship to God and man.

> As for religion, so too for industry, early cultivation is highly important. Early work guided in accordance with its inner meaning confirms and elevates religion. Religion without industry, without work, is liable to be lost in empty dreams, worthless visions, idle fancies. Similarly work or industry without religion degrades man into a beast of burden, a machine.[11]

e) *The interpretation of life through the reproduction of ideal modes of human experience in the educative process.*—Froebel endeavored to use the activities of play and work as a means of clarifying, expanding, and deepening the child's social experience and vision of the significance and meaning of social

[10] *The School and Society*, p. 23.

[11] *Education of Man*, p. 35.

life. Dr. John MacVannel defines Froebel's conception of the kindergarten as,

a society of children engaged in play and its various forms of self-expression, through which the child comes to learn something of the values and methods of social life, without as yet being burdened with too much of intellectual technique.[12]

Froebel expresses the interpretative value of play as one of his fundamental aims:

to develop man's inner as well as his outer eye from an early age, for the near and distant relations of life, for perceiving them rightly and for seeing through their inner coherence, is one of the ultimate and highest aims of these plays for the welfare and blessing, for the joy and peace, for the individual human being as well as of humanity.[13]

f) To bring to the child's consciousness, intellectually, the objects and qualities of objects in space.—It must be acknowledged that this was one of the aims of Froebel most painfully prominent when one turns from his inspiring theory to his more imperfect practice. This aim and application of Froebel often betray him into an apparent abandonment of his theory of development and into a reversion to the method of abstract instruction far afield from the nature, the needs, and the experiences of the child. His division of forms of expression with the gifts into (1) forms of life; (2) forms of beauty; (3) forms of knowledge, while a sincere attempt to provide a broad culture in utility, art, and knowledge is at present under the fire of pedagogical and aesthetic criticism which will require an educational adjustment in the kindergarten.

[12] MacVannel, *op. cit.*, p. 100.

[13] *Pedagogics of the Kindergarten*, p. 131.

[*To be continued*]

MICHIGAN'S PREPARATION OF TEACHERS FOR RURAL SCHOOLS

ERNEST BURNHAM
Western State Normal School, Kalamazoo Mich.

"I shall teach a country school if I can get one," said a young girl who had barely reached the minimum age requirement of eighteen years. "The best teachers I have had in my home district were beginners. I believe they are the best teachers unless you can get a real old one, who has made teaching a life work." The exuberant life speaking in every word and glance and bodily gesture of this young girl made it possible to believe her estimate of the beginner. Youth has been the chief asset of Michigan rural teachers. And this is not forgetting the small number who, keeping the enthusiasm of youth, have added with maturity the strength of knowledge. In the way of offering to the young teachers opportunity and provocation to grow, the rural schools of Michigan have been normal schools in a true sense. The irony of the fate of the rural school is that in so far as it has been a training school for teachers this work has been done for the urban schools to which a very large proportion of notably successful rural teachers have gone. It is true that the urban high schools are paying annual instalments on this debt by sending out their graduates to teach in the country districts. These high schools have been the best source of supply for the rural teaching force. The normal school graduates, worth having, have until very recent years practically all gone to the urban schools. As late as 1900 less than 2 per cent. of the rural teachers in Michigan had any normal-school training, while, according to the statement of the Department of Public Instruction, 75 per cent. of urban teachers had some normal-school instruction.

The miscellaneous agencies for the improvement of teachers such as state and county association meetings and institutes, reading circles, and private study have rendered service to rural teachers. The state association has had at almost every annual session some topic directly or indirectly relating to rural schools. In the programme for the annual session of 1904 the most advantageous of the general sessions was given to a direct study of rural schools. In 1907 the executive committee of the state association, at the request of the county normal training class teachers, organized a section for rural teachers. To this action the rural teachers responded enthusiastically, making their section the most largely attended one of the association. In this section for the first time work was *with* rather than *for* country teachers. County teachers' associations have communicated progressive ideas and these ideas have been made vital by the social and spiritual novelty of the occasion. The longer county teachers' institutes have been directed specifically to the aiding of rural teachers, and the shorter or inspiration institutes have been of value according as they have had speakers who could perform the soul-feeding function. Approximately one third of the rural teachers of the state take advantage of the state reading-circle course. This involves the study of three books annually. One of these books is pedagogical, another bears directly on some one of the common-school subjects, and the third is a general culture book. This is the best of the miscellaneous agencies for teacher improvement. Circumstances of previous preparation and present convenience make the number of rural teachers who do private study very small.

In 1903 the state legislature authorized the establishment of county normal training classes for the preparation of rural teachers. These classes are established in connection with a high school centrally located in the county. Instruction is by two teachers; one, specially in charge of the class, who teaches reviews of the various common-school subjects, with some reference to their pedagogical aspect, and directs the observation and practice work of the members of the class. Practice is had in the various grades of the town and observation to a limited extent is in rural schools. The second teacher is composite, usually including the superintendent who teaches psychology and management, with the special town teachers of music, drawing, and manual training.

Candidates for admission to these classes must have schooling equivalent to ten grades of public-school work. All who are successful in the year's work outlined receive legal qualifications to teach in the rural schools of their county for three years with a possible extension to six years if they succeed. In the five years of their service these classes have added 1522 teachers to the state's corps of rural teachers. The indications are that approximately one half of these teachers will renew their certificates at the expiration of three years of service. Suggestion has been made that the admission requirement for these classes be advanced to an extent to put their graduates on the same footing scholastically as the graduates of the best high schools. This now seems to be the most likely line of progress for the county normal training classes, since it points directly at their greatest weakness —abbreviation.

A state law passed in 1897 established reciprocity and uniformity in the courses of study of the state normal schools and specified the courses of study and the certificates to be granted. This law made mention of special courses for rural teachers. An act passed by the state legislature in 1903, authorized the State Board of Education to prescribe the courses of study and issue certificates. Under this act the State Board of Education passed resolutions continuing the uniformity and reciprocity features and providing for three distinct courses of study leading to three distinctly different certificates. A life certificate given to high-school graduates upon the completion of a course of two years of normal-school work; a three-year certificate given to high-school graduates upon the completion of one year and one summer term of normal-school work; and a certificate restricted to use in one- and two-room rural schools, this certificate to be given to graduates of common schools on the completion of two years and one term of normal work. The rural-school course which was put in operation deliberately fixed a very low standard for admission and graduation on the theory that in view of the existing absence of trained teachers from the rural schools it would be better to add a considerable number having very limited training than to add a smaller number having better training.

In 1908 the State Board of Education authorized a more advanced course of study for rural-school teachers. This is a two-year course open to graduates of ten grades of public-school work and its completion is intended to be fully equivalent to the completion of the work of the best twelve-grade high school. This advanced course gives a rural-school certificate good for five years.

The foregoing paragraphs indicate, in brief, the differentiation which has thus far taken place in Michigan in the training of teachers for ungraded rural schools and graded urban schools. That differentiation is necessary was clearly pointed out by Dr. W. T. Harris, some years since, when he said that a distinct difference should be made between training teachers for a school having a few large classes all within one or two grades and a school having many small classes scattered through six or eight grades. That Dr. Henry Barnard also appreciated this condition appears from his statement made in 1892 that the raising-up of teachers for country service was an unsolved problem. The industrial and social revitalization of country life in this generation is concentrating public attention upon this unsolved problem. Solution is being attempted chiefly along three lines: First, the reorganization of the rural-school system with a view to grading and the utilization of the present graded-school methods and teachers; secondly, the institution of local training classes; thirdly, the introduction of specially adapted courses in the state normal schools. The consolidation or centralization solution has been acclaimed by the most active and influential educators of the state for many years, the best arguments advanced being the probability of better trained teachers, and the certainty of securing free secondary instruction for country children by this method. Occasionally a community will centralize several schools and where this is done the better trained teachers and the free secondary instruction will be secured. Then, too, conditions of taxation and population in some localities will enforce the consolidation of two and sometimes three districts to form a one-room school of sufficient financial resource and large enough enrolment to make possible a first-class rural school, including a trained teacher.

The problem of the provision of efficient teachers for country children cannot await solution by this method alone, for it seems certain that the vast majority of country children will be sent in Michigan for many years to come to one-room rural schools for their elementary training. The second attempted solution of this problem of providing trained teachers for rural schools—the county normal training class—has already been discussed. This solution has really made a large contribution in a short time, but it has the fatal weakness of perpetuating by its brevity the belief that little preparation is needed for teaching rural schools. It is this belief that must be destroyed before a just solution of the problem can properly proceed. In spite of the brief course it is possible for the county training classes through the attitude of their teachers really to create a demand for more extended training for rural teachers. In so far as a real love of teaching is inculcated it will of itself breed ambition for more training and appreciation of the great need of trained service in the rural schools will induce some to return to these schools after being prepared by further training to better meet the need. Its brevity will not at present depreciate the value of training in the minds of the public, if the quality of service is good within its limitations. Brevity is not significant when compared with nothing.

The state normal schools are mature, well-organized, and expensive public agencies which were purposely instituted to solve the problem of providing trained teachers for the public schools. The adequate preparation of teachers fitted to teach rural schools must be secured through the state normal schools, else these schools admit failure in a conspicuous proportion of the only task they have been given and that they are being paid to do. The Michigan normal schools have begun the development of courses for rural teachers as herein stated. All of the four state normals have the same course, the only difference between the normal schools in this respect being in the administering of the course. In the western normal at Kalamazoo, at the inception of the school in 1904, a rural school department directed by a man ranking officially with other heads of departments was instituted. This was a new departure in normal-school administration in America, and to trace the development of this idea in practice is one purpose of this article. This plan concentrates the administration and promotion of rural-school interests in the normal. The very elementary course authorized by the State Board of Education, in 1903, was the only course used for training rural teachers in the first four years of the school. The enrolment in the rural-school department in the regular year has been one-fifth to one-fourth of the total enrolment, and in the much more largely attended summer sessions the enrolment of rural teachers has been more than one-half of the total. Adverse criticism has been directed at the content of the course and at the meager requirement for graduation. There has been a continued effort to amplify the course and this effort has resulted in the present year in the authorization of a new course making an advance of two years in the entrance and graduation requirements.

Instruction along pedagogical lines is of necessity very meager because of the immaturity of the students. Almost without exception the students in this department have been country bred and they are consequently responsive when the peculiar characteristics of country children are pointed out. Ungraded school conditions are continually kept in mind in discussing methods of classification and instruction. The attempt is made through nature-study and agriculture to empower prospective teachers to more richly interpret the natural and industrial environments of the rural school. Common-school subjects of study are closely reviewed and the secondary subjects taught are presented with conscious intention of creating a vigorous desire for further academic instruction. The right attitude toward education and a conception of the rural school, which makes it a vital factor in national progress and in the characters of a multitude of individuals, are consistently sought. Special agencies have been invoked to convince the young people going out to teach in the rural schools of the absolute necessity of greater daily happiness in country life, and their attention has been systematically called to the social as well as the industrial sources of contentment and joy.

In the first year of the school the students of the rural-school department organized a seminar for the study of rural social conditions. The organization has grown in interest and service. Monthly meetings are held and research reports and debates dealing with historical and current rural progress topics have made up the programmes. This somewhat miscellaneous work has been systematized and supplemented in the last term of the course by a brief formal study of rural sociology. This study attempts to fix the present rural social status and to discover and become familiar with the present agencies making for rural betterment. In 1907 a series of annual rural progress lectures was begun under the management of the rural-school department. The series was initiated by President Kenyon L. Butterfield of the Massachusetts Agricultural College with a lecture on "The Social Factors in Rural Progress." The second lecture was given in 1908 by Dean L. H. Bailey of the New York State College of Agriculture. His subject was, "The Outlook for Rural Progress." In connection with these lectures the rural students, assisted by the faculty, receive their parents and friends from home, and the students in other courses, making the lecturer the guest of honor. Public appreciation of the rural progress study undertaken in the school has been proven by the presence at these lectures of representatives of the State Board of Agriculture, the Agricultural College, the State Association of Farmers' Clubs, the State Grange, and the State Superintendent of Farmers' Institutes.

The immediate frontier in the better adaptation of the rural teachers' course to its purpose is in the discovery of the necessary differentiation in the observation and practice work of the students from that required of students preparing for graded-school teaching. It is probably true that teachers will be less inclined to teach in ungraded schools after practice in a highly organized graded training school and it is possibly true that such practice would render them less likely to succeed in an ungraded school. Directed observation in both graded and ungraded schools has been required. The rural schools observed have presented various degrees of efficiency, and no doubt helpful suggestions have been secured. Observation made in the graded training school has been carefully discussed and many valuable ideas capable of application in ungraded schools have been gained. In the present year a conveniently located rural school is affiliated with and controlled by the normal. It is proposed to make this rural school a laboratory for the observation and development of expert rural teaching. The instituting of this rural observation school; the development of the industrial and social possibilities of the course of study; the promotion in the state, through various means, of a better appreciation of rural-school teaching; and the amplification by two years' work of the state normal course for rural-school teachers are steps marking the progress made. These are initial steps in the inevitable progress in the preparation of teachers for rural elementary schools dictated by the spirit of the times.

THE HARVEST—*continued*

JENNIE HALL

MY MOTHER'S STORIES

II. A HUSKING BEE

Sometimes the plowing and other work lasted long.
The corn-husking had to wait.
At last it was too cold for husking out-of-doors.
Then the men hauled the bundles of corn to the barn.
They threw them upon the floor.
One of the boys rode to the neighbors' houses.
"Come over to our house tomorrow night," he said, "we are going to have a husking-bee."
At each house he borrowed a lantern.
The next evening we lighted all the lanterns.
We hung them in the big barn.
The floor was covered with cornstalks.
Soon the neighbors began to come.
We took them to the barn.
We all sat down on the corn.
Then we all began to husk.
It was great fun.
We told jokes.
We laughed and sang songs.

The corn leaves rustled.
The corn ears went thump on the floor.
Soon all the corn was husked.
Then we pushed the stalks into a corner.
We swept the floor.
Mother and the boys went to the house.
Soon they came back.
They carried big pans of doughnuts and pots of hot coffee and pitchers of cider.
We all sat down on the floor and ate and drank and talked and laughed.
At last a fiddle squeaked.
We all shouted and jumped up.
The music began.
We danced and danced.
That was a husking-bee.

THE BARLEY MOWERS' SONG

Barley Mowers, here we stand
One, two, three, a steady band;
True of heart and strong of limb,
Ready in our harvest trim:
All a-row with spirits blithe;
Now we whet the bended scythe;
Rink-a-tink, rink-a-tink, rink-a-tink-a-tink.

Side by side, now bending low,
Down the swaths of barley go,
Stroke by stroke, as true as chime

Of the bells, we keep in time;
Then we whet the ringing scythe,
Standing 'mid the barley lithe.
Rink-a-tink, rink-a-tink, rink-a-tink-a-tink.

MARY HOWITT

INDIAN RICE HARVEST

Rice grows wild in many places.
It must have much water.
It grows in swamps and in the edges of little lakes.
Sometimes it grows in the edges of slow rivers.
The tall stalks stand up out of the water.
They are green.
The tops are feathery.
Here grow the seeds.
They are heavy and they make the heads bend down.
When the rice is ripe the stalks and leaves turn yellow.
Then the Indian women gather it.
They lay mats in the bottom of their canoes.
Upon them they set large baskets.
They push the canoes into the water.
They paddle to the rice patches.
They push their canoes among the rice patches
They bend the stalks over their canoes.
They hit the heads with sticks.
The ripe rice falls out into the canoes.
Soon the mats on the bottom of the canoes are covered with rice.

The women pour it into their baskets.
Then they gather more.
Long ago wild rice grew in the edges of the Chicago River.
Indians lived here then.
Indian women gathered the rice.

IN THE MOONLIGHT

The farmer's family were eating supper.
"There is a good moon tonight," the farmer said,
"Shall we shock the wheat?"
"Yes," said the boys.
So after supper they went to the field.
The stubble cracked under their feet.
The moon made black shadows.
The bundles of wheat lay on the ground.
"Joe, you go down the north side," the farmer said,
"George, you go down the south side.
I will take the middle."
Then the work began.
Each man bent down, picked up a bundle, set it up on end, bent down for another.
His shadow bent with him.
Field mice ran from the bundles.
The stubble cracked.
One shock was done, another, another.
Soon there were three long lines of shocks.
A shadow lay behind every shock.
A little breeze blew.
"It is cool working at night," said Joe.

THRESHING IN ITALY

The threshing-floor is out of doors.
It is a flat place paved with stones.
The floor is covered with yellow corn.
The men are going to shell it today.
Four of them come with their flails.
The flail is made of two sticks of wood.
They are tied loosely together at one end.
Two men stand on each side of the threshing-floor.
They swing their flails over their shoulders.
Down they come on the corn—first this two and then that two.
Whack! Whack! sound the flails.
The yellow corn flies.
The white cobs peep out.
After a long time the men stop.
They take wooden forks.
They lift the corn and cobs.
The corn falls through the forks.
The cobs stay on.
The men throw them away into a pile.
But some cobs still have corn on them.
The men take up their flails again.
So they work until all the corn is off.
It lies in a clean, yellow pile.
On another day the men thresh wheat in the same way.

THRESHING IN GREECE

It looks like a circus.
There are two or three threshing floors in a field.

One is covered with bundles of wheat.
A man is driving four horses around over the field.
The horses are dragging a little board.
The man stands on this board.
He cracks his whip.
The horses run around and around over the wheat.
The straw cracks under their feet.
The wheat falls out of the heads.
At another floor the threshing is done.
The horses have been driven off.
The straw is all broken up.
The wheat is beaten out of the heads.
It lies on the floor under the straw.
Men are winnowing it now.
They stand so that the wind blows from behind them.
They take wooden forks.
They toss the straw and wheat into the air.
The wheat falls again.
But the wind blows the chaff and straw away.
The men keep tossing it for a long time, until the wheat is clean.
At the other threshing-floor women are at work.
The clean wheat is raked into a pile.
The women lay blankets on the floor.
They spread wheat on the blankets.
They look it over and pick out the sticks or straws or stones.
Then they put it into bags and tie it up.

The bags are striped brown and white or red and black or yellow and brown.

So at the three floors many things are going on at once.

Here men are driving their horses around and around.

There men are tossing the wheat and the chaff is blowing away.

Here women are filling gay bags.

DR. MEYER ON THE DANGERS OF KNOWING THINGS WITHOUT DOING THINGS

JAMES H. TUFTS
Department of Philosophy, The University of Chicago

An extremely valuable article by Dr. Adolph Meyer in the *Psychological Clinic* has a much broader significance for teachers and superintendents than is at first evident from its title: "What Do Histories of Cases of Insanity Teach Us Concerning Preventive Mental Hygiene During the Years of School Life?" Although prompted by a study of cases of insanity the conclusions reached have a direct and vital significance for our whole educational programme. For they bear not only on the treatment of the children who fall by the way, but as well on the treatment of the very large number who fail to make the fullest success of life. They touch also the core of one type of moral failures.

Dr. Meyer first points out that the seclusive, dreamy children, characterized at times by depth of thought, are peculiarly liable to develop that type of insanity known as *dementia praecox*, a precocious or early dementia in contradiction to the dementia of senility.

The early history of persons admitted to the insane hospitals shows that as a rule they were peculiar, rather than defective, and that they were characterized rather by *repression* than by aggressive mischief. They "are the very ones whom a former generation might have looked upon as model children." Dr. Meyer does not think most of these cases due to such organic causes as to make them in any sense hopeless, if proper educational methods are used. The trouble is due to a "perfectly natural, though perhaps unusually persistent development of tendencies difficult to balance." "Tendencies of day-dreaming, a reading craze, or sexual imagination, the meeting of failure by dreaming or by dodging consequences, if not corrected by actions, may develop an ever-widening cleavage between mere thought-life and the life of actual application, such as would bring with it the corrections found in concrete experience." Then under some strain which a normal person would be prepared for, a sufficiently weakened and sensitive individual will give way. Moreover many who do not break down completely have their lives partly spoiled or their success seriously interfered with. "Most failures are persons who withdraw from straightforward and wholesome activity into seclusion, into flights of imagination, or so-called "deep thought," all of which tends to make ordinary concrete activity appear as shabby and inferior." Dementia is chiefly a deterioration of instincts of action.

What can be done for such children? The remedy is obvious. "If opportunities for doing and accomplishing simple and enjoyable things could be furnished mere *dreams* of doing and accomplishing would be less tempting." We must find the proper level and avoid for the time at least the strain of disappointment or of unhappy comparison. Dr. Meyer sums up in these two paragraphs which deserve the most serious consideration:

"To sum up, I should urge that we spread among teachers and pupils a realization of the fact that knowledge must be a knowledge of doing things, and next a knowledge *ready for doing* things. Even in cultivating the instincts of play and pleasure we must aim to make as attractive as possible those games and diversions which require decision and action, and carry with them a prompt demand for correction of mistakes and reward for achievement: actual play with others and for others, and not the play of mere rumination. We further must aim to find levels of activity with moderate demands and well within the limitation of even the less brilliant or less vigorous children and yet giving full enough satisfaction to remain attractive and truly stimulating.

"It is lamentable to hear youngsters, encouraged by their elders, refuse to do certain things because they already know how to do them. When doing things becomes less attractive than knowing things, an avenue for disappointment if not for failure has been opened before the pupil. It is evidently the plain duty of those who have to map out curricula and those who have to advise as to the life of children who are in danger, to see that the doing of things is made infinitely more attractive than is usually the case. I do not see why the success of efforts directed toward this object should not appear more glorious than, or at least as glorious as, the devising of some new plan of cramming the pupil with the subjects of a conventional curriculum. Thus it is that through training in wholesome action as well as in physical culture a real hygiene is making its way into the schools."

EDITORIAL NOTES

The N. E. A. Resolution on Industrial Education

In the last number of this journal editorial comment was made upon the resolution of the National Education Association with reference to industrial training. The failure of this great body of teachers to emphasize the higher intellectual and educational interests for which they stand called not only for comment but criticism.

European Continuation Schools

It may, however, be said in defense of this resolution that its recommendations correspond closely with the achievement of such schools elsewhere. The continuation schools in Germany, France, and England in which the larger part of their industrial education is given, have curricula which answer simply to the immediate demands of the trade for which the laborer is trained. There is, to be sure, some attention given to the vernacular, but this with strict reference to its uses by the laborer in his later occupations. This European schooling is built upon the old apprenticeship system. It aims to do what, relatively to the former situation, the training of the apprentice accomplished.

American and European Educational Situations Compared

We have in America, in the first place, hardly the remainder of an apprenticeship system, and in the second place, nowhere should the advantages which America possesses in her democracy show themselves so definitely as in the education of her workmen. The limitations of European industrial schooling are quite comparable to those of the European common schools, which are distinctly schools of a lower social class. Neither the task of enriching the common-school education by the interests of the trade, nor that of interpreting the trade activities through instruction in the schoolroom is seriously undertaken by these continuation schools. These tasks are appropriate, and indeed imperative, in America.

The absence of social classes has constituted the profoundest difference between America and Europe. Industrial training in this country should aim to give to the laborer not only professional efficiency but the meaning of his vocation, its historical import, and some comprehension of his position in the democratic society into which the artisan enters.

It will be a distinct acknowledgment of failure of American common schools if they undertake industrial training without recognition of broader intellectual and spiritual interests. These have been constantly present in the common schools, both in the grades and the high schools, often surcharging the curricula and inadequately taught. But these so-called culture studies have stood for the demand that the meaning of life in our community belonged to every citizen and should not be reserved for an upper social class, with especial educational privileges.

Technical Skill as the Sole Aim a Confession of Failure of the American Common School

It is perhaps the most serious evil which has come in the wake of European immigration that public opinion has insensibly set up a different and lower standard of life and training for the factory and unskilled laborer. We are encouraging a class distinction which must be destructive of American democracy if it persists, and at no point can it be either rendered more permanent or be more successfully fought than in the industrial training of those who are to labor with their hands. American industrial training must be a liberal education.

Illiberal Industrial Education an Acceptance of Class Distinction

G. H. M.

NOTES AND NEWS

Professor Charles H. Judd, of Yale University, has accepted a call to the Deanship of the School of Education and Headship of the Department of Education in the University of Chicago, and will enter upon the duties of the position next June.

The Northern Illinois Teachers' Association, at its meeting in Joliet, November 6 and 7, centers attention upon the topic of "Moral and Religious Education in the Public Schools." Professors Coe of Northwestern, Starbuck of Iowa, Cook of DeKalb, and Soares of Chicago, speak at the general session Friday afternoon; President Judson of Chicago and State Superintendent Blair, Friday evening; Professors Bagley of Illinois and Votaw of Chicago, Saturday morning. Besides this central topic the following resolution will be discussed Saturday morning:

Resolved, That the minimum annual wages of all qualified teachers in the public schools of Illinois should, in no event, nor under any circumstances, be less than $365.00, and that whenever a school district by taxing itself to the limit authorized by law is unable to pay this amount, the deficit should be supplied by the state or the school district annexed to another district in which the payment of a minimum wage as large as the one specified in this resolution can be paid.

At the section meetings Friday afternoon the "Function and Autonomy of the High School with Relation to the Elementary School and to the College," will be considered by Superintendent Bryan of St. Louis, Professors McMurry and Libby of DeKalb and Northwestern, Principals Smith and Loomis of Harvey and Chicago, and President Lord of Charleston.

The annual meeting of the National Society for the promotion of Industrial Education will be held in Atlanta, Ga., November 19, 20, and 21.

It is significant of the growing importance of the playground movement that so eminent a worker in the educational field as Dr. Luther H. Gulick should resign his position as director of physical training in the schools of Greater New York to devote himself to playground work. The moral value of this movement is only beginning to be appreciated. Communities that try it under proper management soon discover that it is as necessary in its place as the school. The report of Henry S. Curtis, secretary of the Playground Association of America shows that the sixty-six cities maintaining playgrounds a year ago have been increased to one hundred eighty-five, of which one hundred and sixteen are supported publicly.

Charities and the Commons for October 3 has an extended account of the second play congress held in New York for five days beginning September 8. Governor Hughes urged the value of play in developing honor. "There is no better way to teach a boy to be honorable and straight than to give him the opportunity to play normally with his fellows. He acquires it without the sense of rebellion he sometimes feels in obeying precept. The natural outcome is the establishment of fair play. He develops the spirit of give and take, of generosity in defeat, and of lack of assertiveness in victory."

"Can the Child Survive Civilization?" was Dr. Woods Hutchison's thought-provoking subject. "The boasted organization of our civilization is an organization for grown-ups and has left the child out of its calculations." The city child has scarcely breathing room and no play room. He has lost his most precious birthright—the backyard. The streets have become impossible as places for play. "We have not improved matters much by substituting the school because the child is deprived of the proper opportunity to develop his body. We build beautiful palaces for his incarceration during the hours of daylight so that we may overdevelop his brain. The schoolroom must relinquish at least half its claims upon the time and strength of our children. The playground should be organized as a vital and co-ordinate branch of our system of education."

A recent report made to the Chicago Board of Education indicates an alarming number of underfed children. Forty nurses have been engaged to investigate the individual cases to determine how far the condition of the children is due to poverty and how far to ignorance on the part of the mothers.

The National Society for the Promotion of Industrial Education has issued *Bulletin No. 6*, which may be obtained from the headquarters of the society, 546 Fifth Avenue, New York. This contains addresses made at the annual meeting in New York. Dr. Graham Taylor in his address said:

> The interest of the whole people, however, would have to be safeguarded from the abuse of an unlimited apprenticeship by the monopoly of natural resources and by the limitation of the opportunities for skilled labor. For the wages and standard of living, even in skilled trades, would be at the mercy of monopolists whenever or wherever they could control the access to natural resources and the tools of machine production, and at the same time command an unlimited supply of skilled labor. If exploitation be barred by just legal safeguard and by the organized self-protection of the group or class most in danger of being exploited, the wealth-producing capacity of our whole people will undoubtedly be promoted by trade schools placed within the reach of all.

At the same meeting Luke Grant, the labor editor of the Chicago *Record-Herald*, made an address wherein he said:

> The attitude of the wage earner toward industrial education at the present time is not clearly defined. Suspicion and distrust does not represent the real attitude toward industrial education or even toward trade schools. There

are good and bad trade schools and I believe that the wage earner appreciates this as truly as the employer. But there is another phase of this question which concerns the intelligent wage earner even more than questions of productivity. He sees, I think, more clearly than the employer, the human side of this problem. I believe this is the most important phase of the entire problem and that the wage earner is justified in placing it above every other consideration. The production of men and women is more important than the production of manufactured material.

At the suggestion of the New York City Board of Education's Committee on Trade Schools, of which Mr. Frederic R. Coudert is chairman, the board has determined to establish two vocational schools. Said Dr. Haney in a report prepared for Mr. Coudert's committee:

This preparatory vocational work, it is entirely possible to organize in the seventh and eighth years of the elementary schools and in the two years immediately succeeding, i. e., from the twelfth to the fifteenth year inclusive. One plan would be to set aside certain of the elementary schools throughout the city as centers in which this teaching might be given in the seventh and eighth years. This would obviate the temptation for the boy to leave the elementary vocational school when the compulsory school-age limit is reached by bringing him to an early recognition of the advantage which the completed course offered, and subjecting him to the influence of teachers who might restrain him from a hasty determination to go to work with his preparation only half completed.

City Superintendent Maxwell has also called attention to the possibility of offering this kind of training to the so-called "over-age pupils," who are found in considerable numbers in the lower grades of the grammar schools. These boys are mentally slower than their mates and are at the present time left to work their way as best they may through the grades, or are segregated in special classes and coached in number and language work. For these pupils vocational work of the kind suggested for the elementary school would offer manifest advantages.

In Portland, Oregon, the Board of Education announces that at the beginning of the school year in September there will be established, under the direction of the board, the Portland School of Trades. The object of this school will be to furnish instruction to the boys of Portland in some trade that they may be better fitted for their life-work. Opportunity will be given for instruction in the following trades: carpentry, cabinet making, pattern making, molding, electrical construction, machine-shop practice, mechanical and architectural drafting, and plumbing. Such academic branches as English, mathematics, applied physics and electricity, and industrial chemistry will be included in the course. Special attention will be given to these subjects as they relate to or have bearing on the trade work. The course will be three years. The equipment will cost nearly $20,000.

The management of the Alaska-Yukon-Pacific Exposition, which will be held at Seattle, opening June 1 and closing October 15, 1909, is planning for an interesting educational exhibit. A large portion of one of the largest exhibit buildings on the grounds, the Manufactures, Liberal Arts, and Education Building, will be devoted to the housing of the displays pertaining to education. This structure is now well under way and will be completed in the near future.

It is the intention to erect two up-to-date school buildings, one a model of a city school and the other a model of a country school building. These buildings will contain all of the modern equipment used in furnishing schools, and classes will be in session at different times during the day. Illustrated lectures by prominent speakers on public schools and their value to society will be a feature of the exhibit. One of the features of the educational exhibit will be the display of the progress made in the development of the school system of Alaska and the results of the work accomplished by the pupils of the North.

Professor Manny, Kalamazoo Normal School, sends us the following:

The new report of the Decatur (Ill.) schools is noteworthy in that it is the first issued under a new administration following Mr. Gastman's forty-five years of continuous service. Apart from this, however, the section on meetings is important. We find "professional meeting," planned "to facilitate the basic adjustment to each other of the teaching corps and superintendent and to further the immediate study and the probable tentative solution of the problems confronting us." The general subject "Education in a Democracy" is worked out in a way that shows definite consciousness of the problems of originality and independence and of the distinctive features of democratic education. These meetings were for the cabinet, but other teachers were free to attend, thus taking them out of the duty class and making them opportunities with the result of large voluntary attendance.

The "general meetings" brought in speakers from neighboring colleges and normal schools and from Boston, New York, and elsewhere. "Principals' meetings" "building meetings" and "grade meetings" dealt with more specialized topics—the high-school section worked on the special function of the secondary school and the agencies it employs. A good subject none too often taken by itself is "The Physical School Plant." In the grade meetings evidently live work was done on "motivizing" and dramatization.

Most significant of all were two janitors' meetings held in August and November. The subjects were "The Relation of the Condition of the School Plant to the School's Efficiency" and "Factors Detracting from the Best Results in Our Work." It is only a question of time when we shall require experts as janitors—men thoroughly trained in schools for this work. What institution will lead in this educational development? Meanwhile Superintendent Wilson is making progress of which account needs to be taken.

BOOK REVIEWS

Mind in the Making. A Study in Mental Development. By EDGAR JAMES SWIFT. New York: Scribners'. Pp. ix+329. $1.50.

Although consisting of ten essays bearing titles which imply a variety of themes, a single purpose is everywhere evident in this strong and highly suggestive book. It is, in the author's words, "a plea for the personal element in education, and for the extension of the experimental method." Professor Swift believes that "the most significant tendency in educational literature today is the substitution of the individual for the course of study as the basis of constructive pedagogy." This book is likely to prove one of the most influential in this direction, for although many of its chapters are based on careful study of some single phase of the problem there is nowhere any tendency to conceal the results from the general reader by means of technical terminology. We can scarcely conceive that any teacher or thoughtful parent would not be interested in nearly all the essays, and no one engaged in educational or social improvement can rise from its reading without both stimulation and encouragement—stimulation, because it points out so many things that ought to be changed, encouragement, because it shows the value of experiment, and the possibility of correcting the evils.

The first, third, and ninth chapters enforce a somewhat similar thesis under different aspects. The first, "Standards of Human Power," shows from a great number of cases how futile our school standards often are for the measurement of ability. A large number, certainly, of the geniuses of modern times have been very unsuccessful in their school studies. This of course by no means proves that every boy who is stupid in school is to be a genius in later life—unless we keep him so long in our grind that he finally becomes tamed to it, and spoiled for anything original—but it does show that no teacher or parent has any right to treat a child as hopeless or as below par, merely because he cannot do mathematics or learn foreign languages, or because his mind has too much latent logic to yield admission to English spelling. Failure in school studies may be due to lack of ability, but it may occur because the supposedly negligent, indolent and dull are like the cases studied, "too forceful natures to be satisfied with a narrow range." School studies "require a certain specialized ability, just as puzzles do, but it does not follow that those who cannot do them successfully are dull." "What then," the bewildered teacher and parent may cry: "Are we to abandon all our scheme of studies, the fruit of all our science and culture?" Doubtless not this, but we ought at least, instead of looking on our curriculum as sacred and jamming our children into it, to look at the child on the one hand and the studies on the other as somewhat evenly balanced in value. Then if the child does not fit into the curriculum, we shall consider it as possibly the fault of the curriculum, rather than of the child. Chap. iii on "The School and the Individual" is a plea for a study of individual children on the part of the teacher. "The dominant sin of the schoolmaster is the attempt to make children homogeneous." Chap. ix, "School-Mastering Education," challenges many of the present "idols," and demands greater freedom for the individual teacher as well as a greater flexibility in all lines of instruction.

Chap. ii, "Criminal Tendencies of Boys," is based on a *questionnaire* sent to teachers and others who presumably are not living a violent or desperate life. Professor Swift finds their boyhood ideas and performances not very different from the histories of boys in the Wisconsin Reform School. Most men with red blood in their bodies know these facts, but it is impressive to have them brought together. It is a defect in the chapter that the author draws mainly on Letourneau for his pictures of primitive morality. To one who has pondered the careful studies of Spencer and Gillen, such a sentence as that quoted on p. 57, "The Australian language has no words for justice, error, or crime" is too much like arguing that there are no gentlemen in Germany and no homes in France because there is no precise equivalent in German and French for, "gentleman" and "home." This, however, is merely incidental. The main thesis of the chapter is not affected: "It is doubtful whether in three-fourths of the cases criminal tendencies are anything more than a convenient name with which to cover our social sins and failure in education."

Chaps. iv and v deal with the influence of physical conditions upon the mental life. Chapter vi, on "The Psychology of Learning," gives the results of experiments in learning both manual dexterity, in ball-tossing and typewriting, and vocabulary in a new language. The whole study is highly instructive for the teacher in his everyday work. It shows that progress must not be expected to be uniform, that there must be "plateaus" when there is seemingly no progress, and many "off-days" when there is seeming retrogression. The teacher who has read this chapter need not be discouraged by such periods, and will have more sympathy for the learners as he appreciates that "equal amounts of work do not produce equivalent results" at different times. "Overstrain and hurry tend to mental confusion, rather than clarification."

The final chapter, "Reconstruction of Nature" (and the concluding pages of the preceding chapter) is an impressive demand for a larger conception of education than that of merely adapting the child to the existing civilization. "The animal method of education is for static life—stability; with man it must be for dynamic life—change, improvement." Social progress is at present impeded, friction is produced by any attempt at reform, largely because "education has been engrossed in the comparatively petty rôle of teaching lessons." The current method is to impede social transitions; the intelligent course is to facilitate them." When educators rise above mere scholmastering, social deadlocks and cataclysms will be of the past," and in urging that the teacher must know society if he is to fit for membership in it, he strikes a note like that which Chancellor sounds so forcibly. We shall see increasingly that education if it is to do its own work cannot take orders passively from other interests. If the economic order or political institutions interfere with education, self-respect and duty command a larger outlook and a greater independence for the educator's work. The society of tomorrow for which the educator works has its claims as well as the order of today.

J. H. T.

School Reports and School Efficiency. By DAVID S. SNEDDEN AND WILLIAM H. ALLEN. New York: Macmillan, 1908. Pp. 183. Price $1.50.

"The origin of this study of school reports dates back to 1904," we are told in the Introduction, and is to be found in a discussion which arose in a meeting in New York City, in the course of which someone asked a simple question about the schools, which no one could answer. In the agitation which began at that time, it was made plain that there were no records of many things about schools and pupils which intelligent people might and should wish to know. In May, 1906, the Committee on Physical Welfare of School Children was organized. One definite purpose of this committee was the "effort to secure establishment of such a system of school records and reports as will disclose automatically significant school facts—e.g., regarding backward pupils, truancy, regularity of attendance, registered children not attending, sickness, physical defects, etc."

Three papers by this committee were ready in 1907 for publication, one on home conditions, one on school buildings in their relation to physical defects, and the one here presented, on school reports. The book is, therefore, a report of the New York Committee on Physical Welfare of School Children, of which Dr. Snedden and Dr. Allen are members.

After the Introduction there are seven chapters, of which the first is on "The Purposes of Educational Statistics," the second on "The Beginnings of School Reports in American Cities," and the third on "Efforts of the N. E. A. to Improve School Reports and to Secure Uniformity." The next three chapters contain examples and discussions of statistical tables which have been published, with their merits and faults, and suggestions for improvement. The book closes with a "Practical Study of One School Report" from New York City. A good index adds to the usefulness of the report.

One great purpose of good school reports, according to Professor Snedden, is to make it possible for "the layman of average intelligence, but of more than average interest," to acquire "the information he seeks." It is plain then, that, though this report of the committee is of special value to superintendents and administrative officers, it will also be suggestive to anyone who is interested in the schools and their improvement. It is true, as the report in one instance points out, that figures may deceive; but it is made obvious that there is a great deficiency in the matter of reports, and great consequent difficulty in getting information. This book should do much to improve the conditions.

J. M. C.

Studies and Observations in the Schoolroom. By HENRY ELTON KRATZ. Boston: Educational Publishing Co., 1907. Pp. 220. Price $0.80.

There is of course no question that in order to perfect the science of education we must fix our attention on the child, and improve our knowledge of him indefinitely. It is of course true that the teacher has a rare opportunity, if he have sufficient intelligence and interest, to record and report the facts of childhood and youth, and so furnish priceless material for the scientist and philosopher. Every teacher who is making such observations and reports, and every book which publishes them, does valuable service. It is unfortunately equally true, however, that the putting of questions to children, especially about themselves, may be carried too far; that it is easy to ask profitless questions; that persons who set great store by *questionnaires* often exaggerate the weight of evidence afforded by pupils' answers; and that in presenting the records of such investigations there seems a strong tendency toward the picturesque and amusing.

In this volume there are seventeen chapters, besides a brief introduction by E. A. Kirkpatrick. In general, the subjects are treated by quotation from pupils in different schools. Some titles are particularly interesting, e. g., "Children's Knowledge when Entering School," "Children's Reading," "How May Fatigue in the Schoolroom Be Reduced to the Minimum?" One chapter giving an "Outline of a Manual-Training Course," while it has admirable definiteness, is quite different in subject and treatment from the rest of the books. It is not adverse criticism to say that another, on "The Building of Character," suggests, like thousands of other dissertations, our need of a deeper and more scientific conception of the subject, with a careful definition of terms. Perhaps the most valuable chapter for its suggestion is entitled "A Study in Study," and deals with the most fundamental failure in our education.

It would not be difficult to point out certain illustrations in the book of the dangers which beset child-study by the child-answer method. But the long service of Superintendent Kratz in this field and his interest in the subject must attract attention to the volume and give it value. Altogether, it is very readable —often entertaining; it touches important, practical questions; and it gives helpful hints and suggestions.

J. M. C.

BOOKS RECEIVED

AMERICAN BOOK COMPANY, NEW YORK

Teaching a District School. A book for young teachers. By John Wirt Dinsmore. Cloth. Pp. 246. $1.00.

Latin Prose Composition Based on Cicero. By Henry Carr Pearson. Cloth. Pp. 171. $0.50.

Algebra for Secondary Schools. By E. R. Hedrick. Half leather. Pp. 431. $1.00.

Heyse's "Er Soll Dein Herr Sein." Edited by Martin H. Haertel. Cloth. Pp. 106. $0.30.

Hyde's Primer. By Amelia Hyde. Cloth. Illustrated. Pp. 112. $0.25.

HENRY ALTEMUS COMPANY, PHILADELPHIA

Americans of Today and Tomorrow. By Albert J. Beveridge. Cloth. Pp. 133. $0.50.

ATKINSON, MENTZER & GROVER, CHICAGO

Applied Arts Drawing Books. Grades 3, 4, 5, 6, 7, and 8. Edited by Wilhelmina Seegmiller. $0.15 each.

A. S. BARNES & CO., NEW YORK

Folk Dances and Games. Edited by CAROLINE CRAWFORD. Cloth. Pp. 82. $1.50.

GINN & CO., BOSTON

Fairy Tales, Vol. II (The Open Road Library). Edited by MARION FLORENCE LANSING. Cloth. Illustrated. Pp. 180. $0.40.

D. C. HEATH & CO., BOSTON

Rhyme and Story Primer. By HELEN A., MARIE M., AND ANNA M. MCMAHON. Cloth. Illustrated. Pp. 126. $0.30.

HINDS, NOBLE & ELDREDGE, NEW YORK

First Year in United States History, Books I and II (2 vols.). By MELVIN HIX. Cloth. With maps and illustrations. Pp. 172, Pt. I; pp. 201, Pt. II. $0.40 each.

MACMILLAN & CO., NEW YORK

The Administration of Public Education in the United States. By SAMUEL TRAIN DUTTON AND DAVID SNEDDEN; with Introduction by NICHOLAS MURRAY BUTLER. Cloth. Pp. 601. $1.75.

Shakespeare's "King Richard II." Edited by JAMES HUGH MOFFATT. Cloth. Pp. 280. $0.25.

First Course in Biology. (Part I, Plant; II, Animal; III, Human.) By L. H. BAILEY AND W. M. COLEMAN. Cloth. Illustrated. Pp. 204+224+164. $1.25.

The Tortoise and the Geese, and Other Fables of Bidpai. Retold by MAUDE BARROWS DUTTON, and illustrated by E. BOYD SMITH. Cloth. Pp. 125. $1.00.

LITTLE, BROWN & CO., BOSTON

The Wide Awake Third Reader. By CLARA MURRAY. Cloth. Illustrated. Pp. 224. $0.40.

The Pig Brother, and Other Fables and Stories. A supplementary reader for the fourth year. Edited by LAURA E. RICHARDS. Cloth. Illustrated. Pp. 142.

OXFORD UNIVERSITY PRESS, NEW YORK

A Book of Verse for Boys and Girls. Parts I, II, and III. Compiled by J. C. SMITH. Part I, 60 pp., 3*d*; Part II, 160 pp., 6*d*; Part III, 288 pp., 1*s*.

SILVER, BURDETT & CO., NEW YORK

The Little Helper, Book Two. A supplementary primer to accompany the rational method in reading. By MILLICENT BAUM. Pp. 128. $0.28.

VOLUME IX NUMBER 4

THE ELEMENTARY SCHOOL TEACHER

DECEMBER, 1908

PREPARATION IN THE ELEMENTARY SCHOOL FOR INDUSTRIAL AND DOMESTIC LIFE

A. WATSON BAIN
Teachers College, Columbia University

The aim of public-school education today, whatever it may have been in the past, is not to drive knowledge into the pupils nor even to draw it out. It is a much broader and higher one, viz., individual and national efficiency. This general aim involves at least four special aims in the case of each individual pupil—bodily well-being, vocational ability, a modicum of culture, social service. These, unfortunately, while their importance is admitted by most educators, do not all receive a fair share of attention in the elementary school. Some attention is usually paid to the first and, in the best schools, a little to the last; but by far the most time is devoted to means leading toward the third (culture), while the second item in the analysis (vocational ability) is almost wholly neglected. The schools thus prepare directly for commercial and professional life, in which the three R's are the primary tools; but hardly at all for the various walks of industrial and domestic life, in which other tools are needed. This is doubtless due to the fact that our grammar schools, as their name indicates, are lineal descendants of the schools attached in mediaeval times to churches and monasteries, whose function was to teach boys to read and copy classical manuscripts and to prepare for the priesthood. The great majority of boys, who were destined for agricultural and industrial life, got their training on farms or as apprentices to members of trade-guilds; while girls, naturally, got their training for domestic life in the home. All this has been changed within the past century by the rise of the factory system, the consequent growth of cities and inrush to them from the country, the decay of the system of apprenticeship, the disappearance of domestic arts and activities, and the establishment of free public schools. These last, while they have rendered incalculable service to the nation, have none the less tended to create and perpetuate an academic prejudice against manual work; and it is only in recent years that educators have been learning to realize the dignity of labor.

It is generally admitted that the public schools do not prepare their pupils for industrial and domestic life; and it seems reasonable to attribute to this defect the lack of interest in school work, on the part of many boys and girls, and their rapid dropping out of school from the age of twelve and upward. This tendency is shown clearly and graphically in Professor Thorndike's recently published study entitled *The Elimination of Pupils from School,* issued as a bulletin of the Bureau of Education, Washington. Professor Thorndike, dealing first with elimination by grades, estimates "that the general tendency of American cities of 25,000 and over is, or was at about 1900, to keep in school out of 100 entering pupils 90 till Grade IV, 81 till Grade V, 68 till Grade VI, 54 till Grade VII, 40 till Grade VIII, and 27 till the first year of high school." Putting the matter in another way, Professor Thorndike estimates the dropping out from Grade IV to Grade V as 9 per cent. of those entering school, from Grade V to VI as 13 per cent., from Grade VI to VII as 14 per cent., from Grade VII to the last grammar grade (usually VIII, but sometimes IX) as 14 per cent., and from the grammar school to the high school as 13 per cent. Dealing with elimination by age for a group of 25 cities in different parts of the country, he tells us that, of 100 pupils in school at eight, practically none drop out before twelve, while 9 leave when twelve years old, 18 at thirteen, 23 at fourteen, 17 at fifteen, 13 or 14 at sixteen, and 8 at seventeen.

Of the large number of boys and girls who thus leave school as soon as possible, between the ages of thirteen and fifteen, a considerable proportion, as trades are not open to them, drift into unskilled or low-grade work. This is brought out clearly in the *Report of the Massachusetts Commission on Industrial and Technical Education* (April, 1906), which states that "33 per cent. of the children of this state who begin work between fourteen and sixteen are employed in unskilled industries, and 65 per cent. in low-grade industries; thus a little less than 2 per cent. are in high-grade industries." The following is the first of the general conclusions arrived at by the commission as a result of its investigation:

> For the great majority of children who leave school to enter employments at the age of fourteen or fifteen, the first three or four years are practically waste years so far as the actual productive value of the child is concerned, and so far as increasing his industrial or productive efficiency. The employments upon which they enter demand so little intelligence and so little manual skill that they are not educative in any sense. For these children, many of whom now leave school from their own choice at the completion of the seventh grade, further school training of a practical character would be attractive and would be a possibility if it prepared for the industries. Hence any scheme of education which is to increase the child's productive efficiency must consider the child of fourteen.

As a result of special inquiries at the leading textile centers of the state, the Massachusetts report goes on to say "that neither power nor advantage is gained by entering the industry at an early age; that the child who does enter closes behind him the door to progress to a fair living wage; that that child associates himself with our most undesirable population; that the work performed by the children is passing gradually to poorer and poorer classes of foreigners; that industrial education or education of any kind will mean that the children will not enter the industry." Those who at present do so depend, as a rule, on casual employment, become in many cases idle and discontented, are always on the verge of poverty, and are centers and causes of much social unrest.

It is thought by many people that the educational preparation in question is supplied by the manual-training high schools. This is not so: the manual-training high school does little more than the elementary school to prepare for industrial and domestic life.

It does not profess or aim to do so. Like other high schools, it undertakes to prepare for college—hence its course is predominantly academic, rather than practical; and as a consequence it attracts few pupils who mean to become ordinary workmen and workwomen. Moreover, it teaches its graduates to look beyond the workshop—to go to technical schools or colleges, to aim at industrial leadership, not to remain in the rank and file. Finally, it holds its pupils even less well than the ordinary high school. This is brought out by the following figures, the first set, taken from Professor Thorndike's study above referred to, showing the elimination from 49 high schools in different cities in terms of the median ratios of the number of pupils in the second, third, and fourth years respectively to the number in the first year; and the second set, prepared by Mr. Selvidge, a graduate student at Teachers College, doing the same for 16 manual-training and technical high schools.

TABLE I: 49 HIGH SCHOOLS

Boys—	$\frac{n_2}{n_1}=0.66$	$\frac{n_3}{n_1}=0.39$	$\frac{n_4}{n_1}=0.25$
Girls—	$\frac{n_2}{n_1}=0.70$	$\frac{n_3}{n_1}=0.45$	$\frac{n_4}{n_1}=0.31$

TABLE II: 16 MANUAL-TRAINING HIGH SCHOOLS

Boys and Girls—	$\frac{n_2}{n_1}=0.65$	$\frac{n_3}{n_1}=0.35$	$\frac{n_4}{n_1}=0.22$

These tables—where n_1 stands for the number of pupils in the first year, n_2 for the number in the second, and so on—show clearly that the retention of pupils by the ordinary high school, expressed in each succeeding year as a percentage of the number in the first year, is greater than that by the manual-training high school.

Nor does the ordinary trade school answer the purpose of holding pupils between the ages of twelve and fifteen. For these schools—which are practically all outside the public-school system—do not, as a rule, admit pupils under sixteen years of age, and in any case few boys or girls are ready to learn a special trade before fourteen or fifteen at the earliest. It is clear, therefore, that work is needed of such a nature as will appeal to the vital interests of boys and girls from twelve to fourteen, who leave school in such large numbers from Grade VI upward, and who cannot enter a skilled trade before sixteen. Accordingly this work must be given in Grades VII and VIII, though it might well continue for a year longer, when special trade-work might begin. Public opinion is, apparently, not yet prepared for the establishment of a system of vocational training for trade, though we have already public education for commerce, law, medicine, engineering, and the teaching profession. The Massachusetts report, previously quoted, groups the callings for which children and youth need special preparation into four classes—professional, commercial, productive, and domestic—and shows that, while the first and second classes are sufficiently provided for, the other two (apart from a few scattered agricultural schools) are almost wholly neglected. The scheme about to be submitted is an attempt to fill at least the bottom of this gap in our educational system, a gap that appears in the upper grades of the elementary school. The training which should there be given should not, in the opinion of the writer, be a preparation for any particular trade, but should be directed to the cultivation of the motor powers, of habits of steady work, adaptability, and resourcefulness, and to the study of industrial processes in history and in modern life. In short, the objects aimed at should be intelligence, manual skill, and the appreciation of good workmanship.

It has been said that modern industry is machine industry, that the machine is the prime element in industrial life and must therefore form the center of any scheme of industrial education. As my scheme of work is not based on this principle, it may be well, before submitting it, to state my grounds for dissent. These are as follows: (*a*) The factory system, in its most familiar form, is not universal and not necessarily permanent, and educators must "look before and after." (*b*) There is still room for craftsmen, if they have sufficient originality and skill. (*c*) The "handy man" is not only very useful in ordinary domestic city life, but is invaluable in the country and especially as a pioneer in new lands. [The objects aimed at can be obtained through work with hand tools.] (*d*) A proper machine equipment would involve considerable expense, which few schools could afford to bear. (*e*) Boys of thirteen and fourteen are too young to work much with machines. (*f*) They can obtain sufficient elementary knowledge of machines by demonstrations on a few working models and by occasional visits to workshops and factories. (*g*) It is difficult to make a study of machines sufficiently representative and at the same time enable the pupils to acquire adequate mechanical knowledge and skill. (*h*) There is a strong tendency to approach machines from the technical side, by analyzing their mechanical elements and classifying them from the standpoint of the engineer, and thus making the study formal and (probably) uninviting to young boys, who are interested in products rather than in means and processes of production, which, as a rule, arouse only a temporary curiosity.

Having thus cleared the way, I shall proceed to set forth the curriculum I have in view, which may be entitled "An alternative course of study in Grades VII and VIII for boys of motor type who intend to follow a trade and for girls who wish to prepare for domestic and industrial life." In other words, the course is meant to be parallel with the ordinary academic course and to be open only to pupils who have passed through Grade VI. These might not be more than twelve years old, but doubtless the majority would be thirteen at least. The guiding principles of the proposed course may here be stated. They are these:

1. The course is quite unfettered by ordinary school traditions.

2. Manual work is the core of the course and receives rather more time than the academic work.

3. Shopwork for boys—in wood, metal, and (possibly) leather—is broad and varied, thus appealing to their diverse motor interests.

4. Manual work for girls includes (*a*) housewifery—cooking, sewing, dressmaking, millinery, laundry; and (*b*) domestic science and art.

5. The work is correlated as far as possible, but not slavishly so. (As Professor Dewey says, the best correlation is in the mind of the pupil.)

6. There is provision for physical training for both sexes.

7. The English read in class should be distinctly literary, and should be studied for appreciation, not for dissection. All formal work should be done in connection with composition.

SUGGESTED COURSE

GRADE VII

Boys	Periods per Week	Minutes	Girls	Periods per Week	Hours
Shopwork (wood)— Individual work......10; Group work.......... 5	15	675	Sewing, knitting, darning (⅔ yr.); Machine sewing (⅓ yr.)........	5	3¾
Drawing (freehand and mechanical)...............	5	225	Cooking (plain)..............	5	3¾
Practical mathematics.......	5	225	Freehand drawing, brushwork, design..................	6	4½
English....................	4	180	Practical mathematics........	5	3¾
Industrial geography and history..................	3	135	English.....................	6	4½
Singing....................	1	45	Industrial geography and history.....................	3	2¼
Physical exercise..........	2	90	Singing.....................	2	1½
			Physical exercise.............	3	2¼
Total...............	35	1,575	Total..................	35	26¼

GRADE VIII

Boys	Periods per Week	Hours	Girls	Periods	Minutes
Shopwork— in metal (⅓ yr.); in metal or leather (⅓ yr.); in wood (⅓ yr.)	15	11¼	Cooking (plain, fancy, invalid).................	5	225
Mechanical drawing..........	6	4½	Dressmaking and embroidery (⅔ yr.); Machine sewing (⅓ yr.)......	5	225
Applied science..............	4	3	Millinery (⅔ yr.), laundry (⅓ yr.)..................	5	225
English.....................	4	3	Domestic art...............	6	270
Civics......................	1	¾	Domestic science............	4	180
Economic and business methods................	3	2¼	English.....................	4	180
Physical exercise.............	2	1½	Civics......................	1	45
			Business conditions and methods...............	2	90
			Physical exercise............	3	135
Total................	35	26¼	Total................	35	1,575

8. Pupils should be encouraged to read books at home and report on them in school, especially biographies, histories, and books of travel.

9. The aim should be to prepare boys and girls to become industrious, skillful, and resourceful workers—not mere tenders of machines—and also honest, intelligent, and public-spirited citizens.

10. The school day consists of seven 45-minute periods, and there should be a minimum of home-work.

Some details may be added as to the work that should be attempted under some of the various heads.

SHOPWORK

In wood.—Trays, bookshelves, hat-racks, plate-racks, towel-racks, foot-stools, picture-frames, handkerchief-, tie-, and collar-boxes, chairs, tables, book-cases, desks, cabinets, etc., including articles for school-room use and decoration.

In metal.—Trays, bowls, vases, candlesticks, lamp-shades, picture-frames, etc.

Study of materials and tools. Original design should be encouraged.

PRACTICAL MATHEMATICS

Fundamental processes, with whole numbers, common and decimal fractions; approximations; methods of checking.

Weights and measures, including the metric system.

Practical applications, including the following: (*a*) Accounts—personal, household, business, bank; (*b*) Buying and selling—commercial discount, gain and loss, etc.; (*c*) Borrowing, lending, and investing money—notes, simple interest, bank discount; savings banks, stocks and bonds, life and property insurance; building and loan associations; (*d*) Canceling indebtedness—checks, drafts, postal money orders, express money orders.

Easy practical geometry and mensuration.

Graphical methods.

Use of simple algebraic methods, when feasible.

Note.—All the above could not be done in one year in the time allotted. The mathematical classes in any case would probably need to be taught in two sections, the lower section covering the more elementary part of the work, the upper the more advanced.

ENGLISH

Reading of good literature in prose and poetry; adequate practice in composition, especially friendly and business letters, replies to advertisements, and discussion of magazine articles and current events; occasional debates.

INDUSTRIAL GEOGRAPHY AND HISTORY

Sources of supply of raw materials—wood of different kinds; coal, iron, steel, copper; leather; wool, cotton, flax.

Location, origin, and growth of the leading industries.
Transportation by land and water—historical development.

BUSINESS CONDITIONS AND METHODS

Trade conditions; relations of employer and employed; division of labor; supply and demand; wages; healthy and unhealthy occupations; companies, unions, strikes, etc.; laws affecting labor; bookkeeping and office methods.

APPLIED SCIENCE

Personal, household, and municipal hygiene—lighting, heating, ventilation, drainage; simple mechanical and electrical applications; bacteria and infectious diseases; accidents and first aid; tobacco, alcohol, and narcotics.

DOMESTIC SCIENCE

Personal and household hygiene; waste products; baths and ventilation; clothing materials; dietetics, including milk and water supply; infectious diseases and their treatment; accidents and first aid; sick-nursing and rearing of children.

DOMESTIC ART

Model-, plant-, and figure-drawing; lettering and illuminating; pottery and leather-work; study of pictures, rugs, and drapery; house-furnishing and decoration.

A suitable time-table for the suggested course of work would be a school day of seven periods, beginning at 9 A. M. and ending at 4 P. M., with assembly from 9 to 9:15 A. M., recesses from 10:45 to 11 A. M., and 3 to 3:15 P. M., and a dinner interval from 12:30 to 1:30 P. M. It would not be advisable, at least in the first instance, to have work lasting longer than the usual school hours. If the course could be extended to three years, the academic work in the third year should be of a nature similar to that above outlined, while the manual work should be specialized and elective, becoming direct preparation for a particular trade.

It may be interesting, for purposes of comparison, to give the time-schedules of two English schools with much the same aim. First, that of the Borough Technical Institute Day School, London, with a three-year course for boys only; second, that of the Holbeck Preparatory Trade School, Leeds (boys). Here the second-year course is on lines similar to the first-year, but the more advanced and best pupils are encouraged to specialize. There is also specialization for a particular trade or group of trades in the third year of the London Borough Technical Institute School.

There has been much recent discussion as to whether schools

BOROUGH TECHNICAL INSTITUTE (LONDON) TIME-SCHEDULE

HOURS PER WEEK

	First Year	Second Year	Third Year
Mathematics	5	4	4½
English subjects	6	3	3
Science	4	4½	6
Mechanical drawing	4	5	5
Art	2	1½	..
French	..	3	3
Workshop	5	5	7½
Physical exercise	1½	1½	1
Total	27½	27½	30

HOLBECK PREPARATORY TRADE SCHOOL (LEEDS) TIME-SCHEDULE

HOURS PER WEEK

	First Year
Practical mathematics	5
Mechanics	3
Technical drawing	4½
Metal work	6
Woodwork	2
English	6
Drill	1
Total	27½

should prepare for vocation or avocation. The course of study suggested is frankly and primarily planned as a training for vocation; but it would be a preparation for avocation as well, culture and the proper use and enjoyment of leisure being directly aimed at in the work in English—designed to encourage reading and the love of good literature—and also in the work in art. I believe that such a course would attract and hold many boys and girls to whom the ordinary school curriculum makes little or no appeal and who at present leave school at the earliest opportunity. They would thus be greatly aided to become, not only more efficient bread-winners and home-makers, but also happier men and women and better citizens.

BRIEF BIBLIOGRAPHY OF RECENT BOOKS AND ARTICLES

The Elimination of Pupils from School. By E. L. THORNDIKE. Bureau of Education, Washington, 1908.

Report of Massachusetts Commission on Industrial and Technical Education, April, 1906. Teachers College Reprint.

Continuation Schools in England and Elsewhere. By M. E. SADLER. [Esp. chaps. xiii and xiv.] Manchester, 1907.

Beginnings in Industrial Education. By P. H. HANUS. Boston, 1908.

Our Children, Our Schools, and Our Industries. By A. S. DRAPER. *New York State Commissioner's Report,* 1908. Albany, N. Y.

Report of Committee on Education, Syracuse Chamber of Commerce, January, 1908. Syracuse, N. Y.

Charities and the Commons, October, 1907; ten articles on industrial education.

School Review, May, 1907: three articles on the basis of an efficient education, and three articles on industrial education

"The Technical High School of Cleveland," *School Review,* June, 1908.

"Vocational Work for the Elementary School." By J. P. HANEY. *Educational Review,* November, 1907.

Educational Review, February, April, and May, 1908: articles on various aspects of industrial education.

Social Education Quarterly, June, 1907: seven articles on industrial education.

"Industrial Education." By P. H. HANUS. *Atlantic Monthly,* January, 1908.

"Manual-Training in Public Schools." By E. R. SNYDER. *California Education,* September, 1906.

"Vocational Training and Industrial Education." By H. C. MORRISON. *Educational Review,* October, 1908.

"The Relation of Manual Training to Industrial Education." By C. R. RICHARDS. *Manual Training Magazine,* October, 1907.

"Manual Training at Hampton Institute and Its Relation to the Trades." By J. H. JINKS. *Manual Training Magazine,* February, 1908.

"The Effect of Trade Schools on the Social Interests of the People." By GRAHAM TAYLOR. *Manual Training Magazine,* April, 1908.

"Industrial Education in the Elementary Schools." By F. M. LEAVITT. *Manual Training Magazine,* June, 1908.

"Differences Among Varying Groups of Pupils Should Be Recognized." By DAVID S. SNEDDEN. *Manual Training Magazine,* October, 1908.

THE ELEMENTARY SCHOOL AND INDUSTRIAL OCCUPATIONS

ERNEST B. KENT
Director of Manual and Industrial Training, Jersey City, N. J.

In view of the fact that 90 per cent. of the population begin to earn a living at the age of fourteen, the demand seems reasonable that the manual-training course in our elementary school concern itself first of all with preparation for more intelligent choice of vocation; aiming both to discover mechanical tastes and aptitudes, and to impart knowledge regarding the relative advantages of different industries. It is true that when a boy reaches the right shop he will surpass in a few weeks the skill which he has acquired at school, but the important and the difficult thing is to have him reach the right shop. That the conventional course accomplishes this in certain cases is of course a matter for congratulation, but the question is whether it is accomplishing one-fifth or one-tenth of what it might.

The question arises at once as to the value of interests and abilities which may be discovered before the fourteenth year in determining vocation. No one denies that in many individual cases these early tendencies have proved to be totally misleading, but some types of aptitude, like that for music, make themselves known in early childhood, and there is much to indicate that mechanical talents and interests appear early, if at all. In a study made by the writer, of the boyhood of a large number of leading engineers, it was found that the great majority of them were absorbed almost from infancy in mechanical interest of one sort or another and have displayed remarkable ability in mechanical work—coupled in many cases with noticeable lack of either interest or ability in such foreign subjects as history and literature. And further, these early interests often showed very close relation to the special line of success in later life. Many of the mechanical engineers had built working steam-engines in boyhood, while the play of great electricians had been with telegraph relays, dynamos, and telephones.[1]

Every teacher of manual training knows boys from ten years of age upward who had been failures in school and enigmas at home, but, on entering the shop emerged into a new life, and worked there with a persistence and interest amazing to parent and principal. One such may develop an initiative which suggests a future engineer, while another is so dependent on oversight as to promise no more than the journeyman grade of ability, but the suggestion gained regarding vocation is equally valuable to both pupils, and the school is rendering a most important service in developing such interest in the industrial life.

Industry, however, is not one but many. It demands from its workers a great variety of talents, mental and motor. Psychology and experience unite in assuring us there is really no such thing as "mechanical ability," but rather a multitude of mechanical abilities, and these scattered in a most promiscuous way. Frequently, of course, one person proves to be endowed with a group of them but it is always dangerous to prophesy which ones will appear together. They may appear singly or in almost grotesque combinations. That a boy, therefore, lacks enthusiasm for bench work in wood, even when supplemented perhaps by work in decorating leather and in hammering copper, by no means stamps him as one of the non-mechanically minded. He may easily prove a first-class plumber, electrician, or even machinist, not to mention a host of other specialized trades.[2] Consequently the school should make persistent efforts to open up these other industries to its pupils, if only in a crude way, and in spite of obvious lack of equipment and of classroom time.

[1] *The Constructive Interests of Children*, pp. 58–65.

[2] The writer's experience in an evening trade school has furnished frequent illustration of this. Boys were constantly applying to "learn a trade" with not the slightest notion of trade-preference (there was no manual training whatever in their schools) and again with a purely a-priori bias for electricity. These were encouraged to experiment upon themselves in one course after another, and some who had been the despair of the instructor in pattern-making appeared later as the shining lights in electrical construction. Others who had been completely bewildered by the electrical work found themselves thoroughly at home in the foundry room.

No selection of industries for such study can have general application since attention should of course be focused upon the important local industries. The proper group for Pittsburg would be wholly out of place in Grand Rapids. The following list, however, contains the topics which in the writer's opinion would be most frequently appropriate:[3]

Machinery: Its operation, adjustment and repair.

Metal-working: The foundry and machine shop.

Woodworkirg: The requirements of carpentry, cabinet making, pattern making, and the planing-mill.

Electricity: Bells and simple circuits, telegraph, structure of motor.

Building trades: Carpentry, masonry, plumbing, structural iron work, reinforced concrete construction.

As to time-allowance and mode of treatment, the writer's thesis is that anything at all will be better than nothing at all. At least there may be a brief discussion of such occupations with explanation of the general conditions of work in each, i. e., their desirability in regard to wages, hours, and seasonal fluctuation, —ways of learning the trade, the time required, opportunities for later advancement, etc. The processes of the industry may be illustrated with photographs, magazine illustrations, and trade catalogues. Frequently, however, the teacher will take his class to visit the industry itself. Such visits should involve an actual study of the industry, including discussions beforehand of the things to be noted and explanations afterward of the things seen and of their interrelations.[4] Still further, some of these indus-

[3] Agriculture should appear in this list, of course, but for the fact that the school is accustomed to dealing with it as nature-study rather than as manual training.

[4] The value of such work is supported in an interesting way by the testimony of a number of eminent engineers in the study mentioned above. To quote from four of them:

1. "My actual work was undoubtedly an incentive to apply my decided taste for mechanical work later, but it was rather watching mechanics at their work that led me on. I spent my boyhood time in such ways constantly—whole days in engine rooms of mills, etc.—but I actually made and finished few things of importance, if any."

2. "In my own case I feel that my constant love for seeing machinery at work, and learning by questioning and observation the what and why of things, had most to do with my taking up engineering."

tries may be effectively reproduced in miniature by the pupils within the school shop. This is the ideal conclusion for such a study, giving to the pupils an actual feeling of the materials and actual experience in solving some of the problems involved and of discovering and overcoming one obstacle after another which had escaped their notice when they were simply looking on at the work of others. Such reproduction, by boys of twelve and fourteen years, crowded into the compass of a few lessons, will necessarily be a greatly simplified affair, and the results will be exceedingly crude, but this is not a serious objection, provided that some elementary problems of the trade or industry in question are faced and solved in a fairly typical way, not in a merely imitative fashion. To illustrate: the study of carpentry through making cardboard houses would be purely imitative while the building of a properly braced house frame out of laths would be more nearly typical.[5]

Machine-sense, under modern conditions, seems a fundamental industrial asset. Ability to understand, operate, adjust or repair machinery is doubtless a determining element in the success of the great majority of workers who rise above the level of unskilled labor, and as all machines have so much in common, the study of machinery probably comes the nearest to being a "general mechanical training." In visits to factories the various devices for the transmission of power and motion should receive attention as well as the successive transformations of the product. Then, in the manual-training room, a more intensive study of mechanisms is entirely practicable. The lock on the door, for instance, is always at hand for dissection before the class, and

3. "I was fond of watching the machinists in the factory and spent as much time there as I was allowed, with the result of quickening my power of observation until I had the faculty of carrying in my mind complex mechanisms."

4. "What I consider of eminent importance for the future engineer would be much observation especially if it can be done under a competent teacher. With a bright student this develops into a comprehensiveness that can never be overvalued." Pp. 71–3.

[5] For detailed accounts of such industrial studies see Richards, "The Thought Side of Manual Training," *Manual Training Magazine*, December, 1902; McNary, "A Study of Transportation," *Teachers' College Record*, VIII, 57–66; Wahlstrom, "Industries in the School," *Proceedings E. M. T. A.*, 1906, pp. 89–105.

many other examples, such as toy steam engines, old clocks, sewing-machines and bicycles,[6] may be analysed in the same fashion. The making by the pupils of mechanical projects like waterwheels, windmills, and various moving toys is also of course a most desirable phase of such a study.

Foundry work, electrical construction and plumbing should each have some attention, not only because of the large number employed in these lines but because they make use of such radically different kinds of ability, both mental and manual. Plumbers earn excellent wages, but they seldom surprise with the fine quality of their woodwork, and probably many of them could never be taught to do good woodwork. The molder requires delicacy of touch, while the electrician's main need is not manual dexterity but is a mind that can pick its way rapidly through tortuous circuits and connections. A great variety of electrical tinkering may be done in the shop at small expense, and small wooden molding-flasks made in the shop may be used extensively even at home in the making of castings from lead. In all of the more concrete and experimental studies it should be borne in mind that it is the whole industry which is being studied, and care should be exercised in keeping prominent the relationship between an entire industry and the part which has been selected for reproduction.

The suggestions thus far offered concerning subject-matter have assumed both the conventional time-allowance of one lesson per week, and the conventional organization which treats all elementary pupils exactly alike. That much can be accomplished under these conditions has been proved by a number of schools. The question must arise however whether a course that is not excessive for the less mechanical pupils can be at all adequate for the more mechanical. As Professor Kennelly has shown,[7] almost any course of study may be either vocational or cultural,

[6] The bicycle seems a peculiarly fortunate combination of mechanical-movements, adjustments and resistances to strain. It would be interesting to know how many machinists were first faced toward their careers by the experiences which it furnished them in boyhood.

[7] "The Basis of an Effective Education," *School Review*, May, 1907.

according to the vocational purpose and interest of the pupil. The work outlined above will have a certain vocational value for the mechanically minded pupils while for the others its value will be cultural. But the boy who is destined for industry needs a larger time-allowance, so that while getting the general view of the industries he may also have contact, as adequate as his age will permit, with the different types of work. He needs the actual experimenting with tools and materials,—which should rather be called experimenting with himself and his own abilities.

The idea of an elective course of any sort in the public schools is certain to be unpopular, and it is true that the programme of the regular teacher might be complicated by its introduction. Still it seems to the writer that the situation is one which must be met sooner or later by the formation of special classes. The possibility of holding such special classes outside of regular school hours at once suggests itself. There are obvious objections to such a plan, but the writer has seen it carried out quite effectively. The classes, which met twice a week in the late afternoon, were open to the sixth and seventh grades of one public school. They were taught by the same teacher who had the manual work of these entire grades within school hours, and were attended by 30 per cent. of the boys belonging to these school grades, with a rate of absence very low for any type of voluntary course—3 to 10 per cent.

This experiment under typical public school conditions indicates that such work is a strongly preferred form of play for the more mechanical third or fourth of the school population, and suggests opportunities of which the school should not be slow to take advantage.

Thus far we have been considering the boy under fourteen years of age—the boy under legal obligation to attend school. In turning now to the case of the boy who has passed fourteen, a glance is necessary at further conditions which govern his entrance into gainful occupation. The investigation of the Massachusetts commission furnishes our best data.

The commission concluded that the average boy leaves school at fourteen, not so much from economic necessity as from lack of interest in the course of study now offered to him; that this feeling is due sometimes to mere impatience of books and craving for a more active life, sometimes to the inability to see how the work of a year or so more in school would be of any real value to him, either personal or vocational; that while in many cases the parents require or demand the boy's wages after fourteen years, more often his going to work is against the protest of parents who would prefer to have him remain there longer.

While the school does make a real effort by moral suasion to retain its pupils, it is possible that comparatively small changes in curriculum and course of study might be far more effective. We are justified in believing that more emphasis upon manual and industrial training would be the most effective single means toward a lengthening of the school life.

It seems to the writer that special courses may be offered by the elementary school for the benefit of this pupil without requiring any serious readjustment of school programme or of the work offered to other pupils. Such a special class could occupy two or more of the afternoon school sessions per week. Its enrollment should probably be limited to boys who have passed fourteen years of age—boys upon whom the school has no further legal hold. It should presumably be placed before the pupil as an inadequate substitute for a secondary course, and none need be admitted except upon evidence of inability to afford or to profit by the conventional high-school course, and upon written permission from parents.

The work in this course might relate to a number of industries or it might be confined to one, according to local conditions. In either case it could of course be much more thorough, systematic and technical than the work given previously and should therefore make a much clearer contribution to industrial intelligence and efficiency. Pupils taking this course would continue for the remainder of the time in the regular school classes, the programme being so arranged that they would drop the whole of certain subjects rather than parts of different subjects. The more important subjects would naturally be confined to the forenoon, and in these no distinction would be made between special and regular pupils. The dropping of certain subjects would of course mean giving up the high school, but the provisions already suggested would prevent entrance to the special course except by those just on the verge of leaving the school; and for these both the industrial training and the additional drill during the forenoon upon the fundamentals would be just so much clear gain.

In conclusion it may be well to make more explicit the thought that the suggestions which have been set forth do not contemplate new schools nor even new shops. All the plans proposed seem to the writer to belong naturally within the curriculum of the elementary school and to interfere in no way with its present organization. All the work proposed seems to him practicable within the elementary manual-training equipment—somewhat supplemented. Three steps have been suggested to increase the contribution of manual training to industrial efficiency: that the present work should aim primarily at developing intelligence in vocational choice; that special classes should be provided outside of school hours for the specially apt pupils under fourteen years of age; that special introductory trade classes within school hours should be provided for those between fourteen and sixteen who cannot look forward to secondary training. All such opportunities, it may be added, seem especially necessary in our present situation, but there is every reason to believe that they would continue to be of great value even after this country has acquired an adequate system of industrial-continuation schools.

AGRICULTURE IN THE PUBLIC SCHOOLS

WALTER H. FRENCH
Michigan Agricultural College

Agriculture is a broad and complex subject. It is both a science and an art. As a science it is a study of the soil, its composition, fertility, care, and uses; the vegetation growing therefrom and the animals subsisting thereon. As an art it is the application of scientific principles and knowledge in actual production from the soil, through the culture and development of vegetable and animal life. In general, then, agriculture may be defined as the theory and practice of producing and utilizing plants and animals useful to man, the soil and its management being the basis of the work.

It is not necessary in this place to deal with the history of the subject or the steps by which it has come to be recognized as one of the most important fields of knowledge. Agriculture, like medicine and the law, is a science; and like them, having a sound foundation, it is being developed rapidly along lines which will make it most useful to mankind.

There may be those who think it not practicable to teach agriculture in the public schools because of its range and complexity. We would call the attention of such to the fact that mathematics also is a broad subject and no one claims that all mathematics should be taught in the public schools; but the subject in its simpler phases is nevertheless a proper one to be presented in these schools. In the same way it is not possible to teach all the science or the art of agriculture in the public schools, but since it touches life in a way even more important than mathematics does, it becomes a proper subject for the public-school curriculum.

From the science of psychology we learn that the mental faculties of an individual are active at all stages of his life, but that certain mental faculties are more active at certain periods than at others. We may make three general divisions of these periods of activity. The presentative or the perceptive faculties are most active in childhood, the representative faculties most active in youth, and the reasoning power reaches its highest activity during the maturer years.

A course of study in any subject should be so arranged as to harmonize with the natural activity of the mind at different stages; that is to say, the order of the phases presented must be so arranged as to exercise the presentative, the representative, and the reasoning faculties at the proper time and to the proper degree.

In accordance with this principle, the subject of agriculture may be separated into three divisions, which we may term the elementary, the secondary, and the college courses, corresponding almost exactly to the periods of mental activity named above.

ELEMENTARY COURSE

This course covers the period below high school and is concerned almost entirely with the actual doing of things. The subjects to be presented in this course may include a study of the germination of seeds, the selection and care of seed, the actual planting and producing of flowers and vegetables; also, the observation of soils. The child may be led to know the different kinds of soils, and the effects of cultivation, moisture, and air upon the soil. In addition to this, the care and use of tools needed will be a proper subject of study. The observation of birds, insects, animals, and especially the raising of poultry may also properly be included in this elementary course. The foregoing work will constitute an introduction to the study of crops in general, horticulture, and animal industry; and while the work will consist chiefly in having the child actually do these things, work will consist chiefly in having actually do these things, every step taken must rest upon a scientific basis. In all this work the perceptive faculties will be used most.

SECONDARY OR HIGH-SCHOOL COURSE

This course will mainly treat of agriculture as an art, but of necessity will include certain sections of scientific work. High-school students pursue the subjects of physics, botany, zoölogy, and chemistry, sciences which are all related directly to agri- include laboratory studies and experiments in the fundamental operations of the farm, including work belonging to the subjects of horticulture, botany, soils, crops, and animals. The subjects culture, and in the presentation of each of them, this relation should be made clear. The high-school course may properly of entomology and ornithology as a part of zoölogy closely touch agricultural operations, and these subjects, therefore, may be given some special attention in the high school.

The thought and reasoning powers are more developed in this period, and the high-school course may include a study of the feeding, care, and breeding of animals. The elements of economics as presented in commercial geography, describing the packing, transportation, and marketing of farm products, will lead the high-school student further into the real atmosphere of practical thought and reason.

If we consider the subjects taught in the high school purely from the educational standpoint, supposing that the sole purpose is to train the intellectual faculties and furnish general culture, no one subject is better adapted to this purpose than the subject of agriculture; and we may safely say that any subject which deals with the problems of real human life and at the same time produces acuteness of perception, clearness of memory, and soundness of reason is unquestionably a proper one to be included in the high-school course.

Elementary Agriculture

The following outline of work is specified for the advanced grades, that is, from the fifth to the ninth. No attempt has been made to divide this work according to terms or grades, but a natural order of presentation is given. Graduates from county normal training schools, and others who have had some instruction in agriculture willl be competent to arrange the lessons and present them in an interesting and attractive way. The study of seeds and the manner of planting them can be illustrated in the schoolroom. The various kinds of soil to be found in the neighborhood may be collected and stored in boxes for examination. Small boxes or pails may be used for the planting work in horiculture and wherever possible it is advisable to have a small garden wherein the common vegetables may be planted in the spring. In the fall a flower garden may be prepared and bulbs secured and planted for flowering in the spring.

Through the lessons in the schoolroom the children may be taught to give special attention to their home garden, to flowers, to the care and uses of animals, and may practice also learning the various trees and shrubs on the way to school. A recitation period of one hour per week may be set apart for this work in agriculture; say the last hour on Friday afternoon or the first hour in the morning of some other day. This time will give sufficient opportunity during the school year for the presentation of all the subjects indicated in the outline.

It is to be understood here, as well as in the course in nature-study, that many valuable lessons may be presented and taught outside of school hours.

The chief purpose of this work is not mere instruction. Agriculture is the art of producing from the soil, and in all elementary work we must appeal principally to the motor activity of the child. The child will here learn to do by doing, and he will also learn to love and respect the subject of agriculture as one of the great vocations of mankind.

In working out this outline the teacher may use any of the textbooks now available on the subject of elementary agriculture. The teacher, not the student, should have these books.

OUTLINE

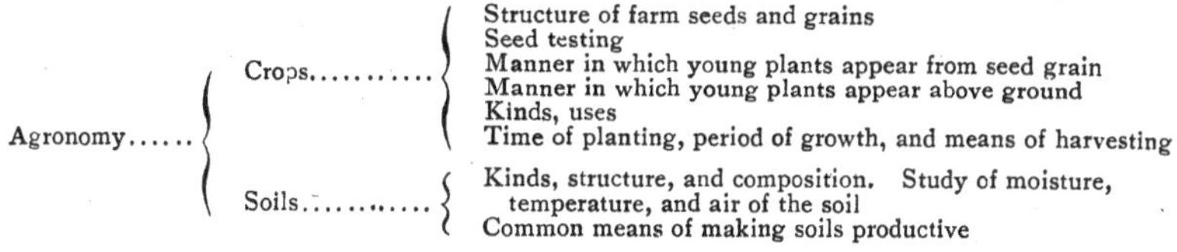

Agronomy......	Crops...........	Structure of farm seeds and grains Seed testing Manner in which young plants appear from seed grain Manner in which young plants appear above ground Kinds, uses Time of planting, period of growth, and means of harvesting
	Soils...........	Kinds, structure, and composition. Study of moisture, temperature, and air of the soil Common means of making soils productive

- Horticulture
  - Germination of seeds
  - Propagation of plants
    - Seeds
    - Layers
    - Runners
    - Budding
    - Grafting
  - Garden vegetables and plants
    - Planting
    - Culture
    - Harvesting
    - Uses
  - Laboratory methods and work
  - Materials needed
    - sharp knives
    - boxes of earth
    - raffia
    - wax
  - Common sprays for fruit trees and plants
  - Flowers
    - Seeds
    - Bulbs
    - Slips or cuttings
      - Manner and form of planting
      - Proper effects
      - Window gardens
- Forestry — Common trees and shrubs of the locality
- Botany
  - Common weeds—a few from the locality
  - Structure, flowers, seeds, distribution, destruction
- Entomology—a few insects
  - Recognition
  - Harm done
  - Means of destruction
- Ornithology—birds
  - Recognition
  - Song
  - Habits
  - Nests
  - Usefulness
- Animal husbandry — Animals, kinds, uses, care
- Mechanics — Tools, care and use

HIGH-SCHOOL COURSE IN AGRICULTURE

9th Grade	10th Grade	11th Grade	12th Grade
Botany ½ year Agricultural botany ½ year	Horticulture ½ year Crops ½ year	Livestock and poultry ½ year Dairying and farm mechanics ½ year	Soils ½ year Farm management ½ year

OUTLINE OF HIGH-SCHOOL COURSE

- Sciences related to agriculture
  - Physics
  - Chemistry
  - Botany
  - Zoölogy
    - Entomology
    - Ornithology
    - Physiology
- Botany
  - General plant-study
    - Composition
    - Structure
    - Physiology
  - Agricultural plants
- Horticulture, laboratory practice, and field
  - Culture and breeding
  - Vegetable gardening
  - Flower gardening
  - Orchard
  - Protection, spraying, etc.
  - Marketing
  - Landscape
    - Drawings
    - Sketches
- Agronomy
  - Soils
    - Elements
    - Kinds
    - Fertility
    - Management
    - Ventilation
    - Moisture
    - Temperature
  - Crops
    - Seeds
      - Selection
      - Care, treating for diseases
      - Testing
    - Planting
    - Culture
      - Soil needs
      - Climatic needs
      - Improvement
    - Rotation
    - Adaptation
    - Marketing

- Animal husbandry or live stock
  - Breeds
    - Cattle
    - Horses
    - Sheep
    - Swine
  - Uses
  - Care
  - Feeding
  - Judging
  - Marketing
- Poultry
  - Breeds and breeding
  - Incubators
  - Care and feed
  - Marketing
- Dairying
  - Care of milk
  - Tests, Babcock, etc.
  - Testing individual cows
  - Separators
  - Butter making
  - Cheese
- Farm mechanics
  - Tools
    - Kind
    - Care
    - Purchase
  - Repairs
    - Tools
    - Harness
    - Fences
    - Buildings
  - Architecture
    - House
    - Barns
    - Out-buildings and silos
  - Study and comparison of team draft, use of dynamometer
- Farm management
  - Arrangement of field, pastures, rotation
  - Cost of crop production
  - Most profitab e crops
  - Most profitable stock
  - Housing of machinery
  - Study of farm buildings in vicinity
  - Drainage, tile, ditches, etc.
  - Sanitation
  - Accounts
  - Crop values, by current prices
  - Average yields in this state compared with the best known
  - Uses of soil

THE VALUE AND LIMITATIONS OF FROEBEL'S GIFTS AS EDUCATIVE MATERIALS PARTS III, IV, V

PATTY SMITH HILL
Teachers College, Columbia University

PART III

THE DEGREE OF SUCCESS ATTAINED BY FROEBEL IN ATTEMPTING TO APPLY HIS EDUCATIONAL PRINCIPLES TO THE USE OF MATERIALS IN THE KINDERGARTEN

Froebel's attempt to apply his philosophy gives evidence of both his greatness and his limitations, his strength and weakness as an educator.

In common with all great inventors, his applications often violate his principles. His greatness lies in his effort to put all his theories and application to the severest test.

He not only tested them himself in work and play with children, but urged his co-workers to bring him the criticism resulting from experience in using them.

In spite of this earnest attempt to test the value of his theories in experience, disappointment awaits any student who imagines that even a genius can entirely reconstruct earlier habits of educational practice by the leavening influence of the most regenerating and revolutionary theory. Froebel's embodiments of his philosophical theories as a guide for the practical procedure of the home and the kindergarten are to be found mainly in three volumes: *The Mother-Play, The Pedagogics of the Kindergarten,* and *Education by Development.*

The *Mother-Play* is a practical exposition of Froebel's theory of the educative process as one of interaction or interplay between the insight, wisdom, and experience of the mother and the native instincts, the blind impulses, and the inexperience of the child, which, through the medium of plays and games, are to be illuminated with the significance and meaning of social life.

A study of these three volumes would seem to indicate that Froebel had more successfully applied this theory of interaction in his plays and games than in his methods for the use of the gifts and occupations in the other two volumes. The following criticisms of the practical procedure of the kindergarten as laid down in *The Pedagogics of the Kindergarten* and *Education by Development* might be offered.

a) Though the Froebelian theory of knowledge was that it should grow out of the needs of the child's life, and come to consciousness through the child's own activities, in these volumes we find him frequently falling back into the practice of giving instruction and information unrelated to the needs of child life and in no way leading to an increasing appreciation or control of the child's own experience. "Knowledge," he says, "is for the purpose of use in life," and yet he plans plays with his gifts in which geometric knowledge and philosophical abstractions were sung to the child through an educative process in which the self-activity of the mother or teacher, much more than that of the child, is developed. Being deeply interested in the philosophic and geometric problems of space, we find such extraneous information as the following imposed upon the child:

> The sphere takes up the space you see,
> So where it is the cube cannot be.[14]

Again in a play with the cube:

> Though one side was all you saw,
> Yet my hand shut up five more.[15]

Or as in another play

> I twist and turn, go high and low,
> Three sides at once is all I show.

Here we have quite the method of "object-teaching," a method Froebel was earnestly attempting to supersede with activity as a substitute for sense impression.

b) Froebel's intuitive insight into the educational value of the symbol inspired an enthusiasm which frequently led him to

[14] *Pedagogics of the Kindergarten*, p. 79.

[15] *Ibid.*, p. 84.

read artificial symbolic meanings into simple natural facts; and betrayed him into puerile applications of an inspiring, but ill-understood educational value.

c) Froebel's attempt to relate and unify all the experiences of the child lead to his idea of unified playthings— the gifts. It was believed that the external unity embodied in the gifts, based upon geometric evolution, would lead to inner unity, especially if these unified materials were used in a related method ("sequence plays"). Some of the methods suggested by Froebel would seem to be based upon the desire to bring to the child's consciousness the geometric unity embodied in the gifts. Thus the geometric analysis of the material leads not only into intricate and complex divisions, but to play materials so small and limiting as to call forth the criticism of the psychologist and the hygienist.

The criticism has been made that the gifts are more logical than psychological—the unity being embodied in the materials, rather than in furnishing that more living unity—the unity between the impulses of the child and complementary materials. Thus the method of using these materials has often degenerated into artificial and unnatural methods of dictating to the child certain definite ways of handling and using them which would lead to the consciousness of the geometric relations and unity of which they are an embodiment. In other words instead of these materials being used as a means of organizing the child's present experiences, illuminating them so as to bring to the child's consciousness the unity of life, they were used to increase his consciousness of the unity in the material.

With all the fair criticisms that may be passed upon the gifts, the attempt to select materials in the light of a high standard of merit was most unique and worthy, and, after all, is still the most notable effort in this line.

Some of the gifts are much more successful than others, and, provided they may be used on the basis of selection and elimination, rather than as a related whole whose value is lost if the "charmed circle" of unity be broken, they are and ever will be materials of great worth in the education of the little child.

PART IV

SOME PRESENT-DAY CONCEPTIONS OF THE AIM OF MATERIALS IN THE KINDERGARTEN

It is interesting to compare the conception of some of the contemporary leaders of education with the Froebelian ideal of the educative process as the reciprocal relation, the "give-and-take" between the maturity of the teacher and the immaturity of the child. The constitutive elements in this interchange were (1) the impulse, the activity, the need manifested by the child; and (2) the standard, the interpretation, the insight contributed by the teacher, the adult, in the modification and reconstruction of the child's experience.

The Baroness von Bülow gives the spirit of this in her *Reminiscences of Froebel:*

> Therefore it is of the greatest importance that the understanding of the grown-up should come to the help of the dark striving of the young child, in order to point out to the blind impulses that are endeavoring to express themselves the right way of reaching their aim.[17]

Dr. John Dewey gives as his conception of the educative process,

> The fundamental factors in the educative process are an immature, undeveloped being; and certain social aims and meanings incarnate in the matured experience of the adult. The educative process is the due interaction of these forces. Such a conception of each in relation to the other as facilitates completest and freest interaction is the essence of educational theory.[18]

The early manifestations of self-activity are in the form of native instincts and impulses. To the child these are mere tendencies and impulses to act with no future beyond their own pleasurable results; to the teacher they are indications of awakening powers and interests which with a guidance in accord with their significance and possibilities may lead to all the values in the accepted curriculum and the standards of worth in an intelligent society and civilization.

While the impulses of the child are the only points of de-

[17] P. 105.

[18] *The Child and the Curriculum,* pp. 7, 8.

parture in a self-active process of education, they must be accepted only upon a basis of selection and elimination in the light of the judgment passed upon them in the experience of an enlightened civilization. When isolated from the part their higher development has played in the creation and preservation of the signal achievements of civilization, impulses stand on a level of merit with no principle of selection; but when they are tested in the accomplishment of the elevation or degradation of society, education is in a position to elect only those which are worthy of a position of dignity in the activities of the school.

Dr. Cole thus expresses the relation of impulses and instincts to the curriculum:

> Freedom in education seems to be that instincts and impulses are to be utilized, not eliminated. For these are the obvious contributions of the self to the educative process. If they be not respected, or in some way maintained, it is difficult to see how there should be talk of freedom. Yet it is one thing to respect instincts and impulses, and another to admire them as they blindly perform an unassisted work. . . . . Then instincts and impulses may be thought of, not as the opposites to ends, ideals, or values so much as the possibilities and cravings for these very realizations and satisfactions. The educational situation ought then to be, not impulses versus the curriculum, but impulses for it.[19]

Miss Blow states the Froebelian conception of the relation of the impulsive manifestations of the child in play to the achievements of civilization:

> Through his study of the different forms of childish play Froebel became aware of the fact that some of them point toward the practical arts, some toward the fine arts, some toward science and literature and some toward the ethical life of man as incarnated in social institutions. In these creations of the human spirit Froebel found his standards of value. In different native forms of play he recognized the germinal tendencies of which these values are the higher expression.[20]

In the light of this discussion of the relation of impulses to their mature forms of expression, one might submit the following line of thought:

a) The most far-reaching instincts, those with the most varied implications in their later emergence in the curriculum

[19] Percival Cole, *Froebel and Herbart*, p. 33.

[20] *Educational Issues in the Kindergarten*, p. 143.

and in social life, seem to be: (1) The impulse to communicate—conversation;[21] (2) The impulse to find out—inquiry; (3) The impulse to make—construction; (4) The impulse to artistic expression—arts.

b) The two essential points to be emphasized here are: First, impulses are self-contributions to the educative process, and should culminate in the spiritual investments of civilization—art, science, industry, institutions, and religion; second, as preserved by civilization these achievements represent the same impulses that are germinal in the child, emerging on higher planes of creativity sifted of the trivial and the transient, and thus representing the eternal values of human progress on its highest level.

c) While these achievements are the educational inheritance of the child, civilization's bequest of its noblest and best, they can be appropriated by him only through a self-active process of reproduction, through the creative development of the same germinal powers, emerging on higher levels in the curriculum and social progress. In other words, the child must re-create before he can appreciate, must reinvent before he can appropriate and win his inheritance through his own self-active powers.

d) To reachieve, to re-create and reinvent on the lower levels of development demands material as a stimulus and necessary condition to this creative process.

e) The differentiations of the creative impulse as manifested in art, science, industry, etc., together with the different phases of this impulse from which they spring, require as their counterpart a differentiation of materials for two reasons: (1) the ends to be attained—art, science, industry, etc., require for their realization certain specific materials so that each may find its own legitimate medium of expression. (2) The early manifestations of these impulses which culminate in the varied arts and industries require differentiation of materials as nourishment and as the condition of their activity.

f) This differentiation of materials, to meet the requirements of the ends to be attained and to supply the nourishment and

[21] Dewey, *School and Society*, p. 57.

activity of the germinating impulses, would result in a unified but not closely organized system of selected materials. Here the unity would be, not only a unity in and among the organized materials (in that no one could supply the need for the other), but would meet the psychological requirement of unity between the impulses of the child and materials.

In an all-round education all these worthy instincts are to be fed and started on the upward way to their goal. If any one is omitted or unduly sacrificed to another we rob (1) the child of its individual development and inheritance; (2) society of its right to receive from its members the contributions necessary to its fullest maintenance.

PART V

SOME PRESENT-DAY CONCEPTIONS OF THE APPLICATION OF FROEBELIAN PRINCIPLES TO THE USE OF MATERIALS IN THE KINDERGARTEN

If the Froebelian conception of the educative process as one of developing interaction between the child and the teacher in a social environment be accepted, this demands four essential factors: (1) the self-active child; (2) child society; (3) the enlightened and sympathetic guide or teacher; (4) educative materials as selected stimuli to the interaction process between child, children and teacher.

That we may realize the organic unity in which these elements cohere, let us imagine certain abnormal conditions where some are withheld. First, imagine a normal, self-active child without suitable materials as an outlet for his creative impulse; second, add to this situation the educative materials without child-society or mature guidance; third, imagine the self-active child provided with educative materials, under mature guidance and withhold child-society—the ideal social situation in which all of these function; fourth, and finally, place the self-active child in child-society where selected educative materials are provided as stimuli to social interaction under the guidance of an enlightened, sympathetic, mature guide, and you have Froebel's ideal process of education.

With these factors in an organically related whole let us consider the function of each to the other and the whole—especially the relation of children to child, and of teacher to children and child. What does the presence of social equals, with like impulses, powers, privileges and rights imply to the child? What is the function of the teacher in adjusting these to each other in the educational situation?

These might be answered by asking a counter question—What are the different ways in which society demands social co-operation in preserving the rights of all its members to lead and to follow, to be led and to be followed? Society would seem to demand social co-operation in these four typical ways: (1) ability to co-operate with one's equals in working out purposes suggested, offered or planned by a superior; (2) Ability to secure the co-operation of others in working out one's own purposes; (3) Ability to co-operate with others in working out a purpose suggested by one's equals; (4) Ability to co-operate with others in working out a plan made up of purposes suggested by the different members of the social group, with or without the guidance of a superior.

There is much discussion in education at present as to the possibility of maintaining individual freedom and development under conditions where the ego is working out purposes which are not self-originated. This would be more easily answered if man were not social as well as individual in his nature, and if man did not often realize self through adopted purposes in social co-operation. Also the significance of suggestion and imitation in the development of individuality would have to be reckoned with.

The origin and development of purpose in child-life, and its relations to social suggestion, social co-operation and the demands of democratic society are too subtle and too vast to attempt to discuss. However one might venture to state that in child-life purpose gradually emerges out of: (*a*) originally aimless activity, (*b*) accidental activities, representations and arrangements, (*c*) imitation and suggestion from (1) equals and (2) superiors.

In the light of the problems of democracy the following practical methods might be submitted as an economic means of preserving for each individual in child-society the right to lead, to follow and to co-operate with one's equals under the guidance of a superior.

1. Each child may be provided with materials for experimentation with no purpose suggested by the teacher or the other children. Here each child works as an individual with no direct attempt to develop the sense of group.

2. The teacher looks over what each child has done to grasp the first opportunity to suggest purpose, or possibilities of purpose in some accidental representation, arrangement, or activity which has been stumbled upon by the child.

3. The teacher suggests a purposeful repetition of an activity originally aimless.

4. Teacher suggests that the children each should look at the other's representations or arrangements to discover possible purpose each in the other's work.

5. The teacher suggests a standard of "better" and "best" and with that in mind has the children select which of the varied contributions is the best to adopt as a social purpose for the whole.

6. The teacher suggests a child-like purpose to the whole group—(*a*) All making the same representation in the same form; or, (*b*) All making the same representation in a variety of forms; or, (*c*) All making different things to contribute to a common end or plan demanding individuality and social co-operation through a variety of social contributions.

These are purely suggestive and are only a few of many means the thoughtful teacher might use in her effort to develop individual initiative, self-determination, and leadership while seeking to increase and deepen the child's sense of kind, group, consciousness, and co-operation on a gradually ascending scale.

Democratic society demands this sane balance between the right of the individual and the social good, under the conditions of freedom and development. Here we have interaction between the individual and society as the social situation and requirement.

Hence with this goal in mind the school should gradually develop the little individualistic ego, with latent social tendencies into its social privilege of working *under, over,* or *with* its equals under conditions of freedom and development.

Mazzini tells us that "democracy is the progress of all, through all, under the leadership of the best and wisest."

READING LEAFLETS, FRANCIS PARKER SCHOOL
PART II

MAKING FLOUR

JENNIE HALL

MY MOTHER'S STORIES

MILLS

Our flour is made in big mills.
Steam turns all the wheels.
Our grandfathers had water-mills.
Water made their wheels turn.
Some people have windmills to grind flour.
In Greece windmills have white sails.
They look like ships on land.
Long ago people made horses turn their mills.
Some people have little handmills.
They turn them with their hands.
Some people use mortars.
They make their own mortars.
They get a big stone.
They make a hole in it with a stone ax.
It is hard work.
At last the hole is big enough.
But it is not smooth.
The people make it smooth by rubbing it with another stone.
It takes many weeks to make a stone mortar.
Many people make mortars of wood.

That is not such slow work.
My grandfather told me how to make one.
He made one for skinning hominy.

THE MILL WHEEL

It is pleasant to go to the old mill race.
I sit on the green bank.
The water rushes past me.
It drops upon a mossy old wheel.
Slowly the big wheel turns.
It drips with water.
Below the water runs out.
I look down there.
It splashes and whirls and foams.
At the side of the wheel stands the mill.
It is made of brown logs.
Around the windows the logs are white with flour.
The miller looks out of the window and smiles at me.

AN OLD FLOUR MILL

I like an old flour mill.
I like to look through the window at the water wheel.
It turns slowly all the time.
The water falls over it.
It splashes, splashes!
Inside the mill everything is white with flour.
The floor is white, the walls are white.
The miller's hair is white.

So are his clothes.
The big millstones rumble.
There is a long chute above the millstones.
The miller opens a little door in this chute.
I see the wheat falling upon the millstones.
There is a big box around the millstones.
The miller opens a little door in this box.
I see the white flour falling from the millstones.
I hear a man call, "Miller!"
The miller goes to the door of the mill.
There is a man with bags of wheat in a wagon.
"I have a grist to grind," he says.
"Put it into the corner," the miller says.
"I am busy to-day."
"How many bags?"
"Ten," the man says.
"I get two for toll," says the miller.
"Put mine into the bin."

PLAYING MILLER

I saw some children playing miller.
They had a coffee mill and a wire sieve and some dishes and some ears of corn.
Helen shelled the corn.
Then Ruth put it into the coffee-mill and ground it.
"I am the steam engine that turns the mill," she said.
At last she had ground all the corn.
She opened the drawer.
It was full of yellow meal.

"But some of it is too coarse," said Helen.
She put it into the sieve and sifted it.
Fine yellow meal fell into the dish.
This milling was fine.
The children worked at it for three or four days.
Then they had six quarts of good cornmeal.
"Let's have a bon-fire," somebody said.
"And we will cook like Indians," another one said.

HOW TO MAKE HOMINY

We put some water into a dish.
We put some lye into the water.
We weighed a cup of corn.
It weighed 8½ ounces.
We put the corn into the lye water.
We let it stand for two nights and two days.
Then we skinned the corn by rubbing it with our hands.
We washed it many times in clear water.
Then we cooked it in a double boiler.
Some children had three cups of hominy.
It weighed 19 ounces.
But each child used only one cup of corn.
That cup of corn weighed 8½ ounces.
How could it make so much hominy?

HOMINY

My grandmother used to make hominy.
A big iron kettle was always on the stove.
It was full of hominy.

My grandmother made her own lye for the hominy.
She burned wood in her stove.
She took out the ashes.
In the yard was an ash hopper.
An ash hopper is a big box with a hole in the bottom.
My grandmother put the ashes into this hopper.
Then she put water into it.
The water slowly went through the ashes.
It dropped out at the bottom into a pan.
When it dropped out it was lye.
My grandmother used this lye to make hominy.

HOW WE MADE A MORTAR

We took a big piece of wood.
It was two feet long and one foot wide, and eight inches thick.
We took some hot coals from the furnace.
We put them on the wood where we wanted the hole.
We left them for an hour.
Then we took them off.
They had burned the wood under them.
It was black and soft.
We cut it out with chisels.
We had a little hole.
Then we put more coals into the hole.
We left them for an hour.
Then we took them off and cut out the burned wood.

So we did many times.
At last the hole was big enough.
But it was black and was not smooth.
We sandpapered it.
We used our mortar for skinning hominy.

FLOUR

There are many kinds of flour.
Germans like rye flour.
The Japanese taught us to make rice flour.
We make flour from buckwheat.
The Indians taught us to make cornmeal.
They grind it in stone mortars.
Indians make flour from acorns.
They dry the acorns.
Then they grind them in stone mortars.
Scotch people grind oats into oatmeal.
Then they make gruel with the oatmeal.
They also make oat-cakes.
They put them upon a piece of iron.
They put the iron before the fireplace.
The cakes bake there.
Scotch people also make flour from barley.
They make barley cakes as they do oat-cakes.
They also make flour from peas.
But most flour is made from wheat.

ACORN FLOUR

The Indians dry acorns.
They take off the shells.

They pound the acorns in a stone mortar.
That makes acorn flour.
But the flour is bitter.
The Indians must get that bitter taste out.
They get some clean sand.
They pile it up on the ground.
They make a hole in the top of the sand.
They put fir leaves into the hole.
They put the flour into a basket.
They put warm water with it.
They stir it.
It is thin dough.
They put the dough into the hole.
The fir leaves keep it from the sand.
The water runs out of the dough.
The bitter taste goes with it.
The Indians put more hot water on the dough.
They do that until the bitter taste is all gone.
The flour is done.

HOW THE INDIANS COOK ACORN FLOUR

One Way

They put warm water with the flour.
They make it into a thin dough.
They put it into a basket.
They heat small stones in the fire.
They put the hot stones into the dough.
The hot stones cook it.
It is acorn mush.

Another Way

They heat a big flat stone.
They pour the thin dough upon this hot stone.
The hot stone cooks it.
It is a thin acorn cake.

HOW THE INDIANS HEAT WATER

They have no iron pots.
They have only baskets.
They cannot hang baskets over the fire.
The baskets would burn.
They put the water into a basket.
They heat small stones in the fire.
They put the hot stones into the water.
The stones make the water hot.

AN OUT-DOOR OVEN

It was built against the end of the house.
It was a little shed built of stone.
On one side was a little round door.
The woman was ready to bake.
She filled the oven with sticks and set them on fire.
The fire leaped up in the oven.
The smoke came out at the door.
The stones grew hot.
When they were very hot, the woman raked out the fire and ashes.
She cleaned the oven floor with a cloth.
She brought her bread out from the house.

There were many loaves in a long wooden box.
She took a wooden spade with a long handle.
She put a loaf on the spade.
She put the spade into the oven and pushed the loaf off upon the floor.
So she put in all her loaves.
They lay close together on the hot floor.
The woman put a piece of iron over the door.
She piled hot ashes before it.
The hot stones of the oven cooked her bread.
In almost an hour her bread was done.
It had a nice brown crust all over it.
Sometimes every house has an oven.
But sometimes a whole village has only one oven.
Then it is very large.
Many women bake bread in it at one time.

"ALICE'S SUPPER"

Far down in the valley the wheat grows deep,
And the reapers are making the cradles sweep:
And this is the song that I hear them sing,
While cheery and loud their voices ring,
"'Tis the finest wheat that ever did grow,
And it is for Alice's supper; ho! ho!"

Far down on the river the old mill stands,
And the miller is rubbing his dusty hands;
And these are the words of the miller's lay,
As he watches the millstones grinding away,
"'Tis the finest flour that money can buy,
And it is for Alice's supper; hi! hi!"

Down stairs in the kitchen the fire doth glow,
And cook is kneading the soft white dough.
And this is the song she is singing today,
As merry and busy she's working away;
"'Tis the whitest dough whether near or far,
And it is for Alice's supper; ha! ha!"

To the nursery now comes mother at last,
And what in her hand is she bringing so fast?
'Tis a plateful of something, all yellow and white,
And she sings as she comes, with her smile so
    bright;
"'Tis the best bread and butter I ever did see,
And it is for Alice's supper; he! he!"

EDITORIAL NOTES

Two articles in this number of the *Elementary School Teacher* discuss the orientation of the Elementary School, with reference to industrial training. Mr. Kent attacks the problem in its simplest form and suggests practical changes and additions which would involve hardly any increase in school expenses. What he presents is a change in point of view in giving the manual-training course in the elementary school, its extension by classes out of school hours with voluntary attendance, and a special course for boys a year or two after the elementary-school period. Mr. Kent lays especial stress upon the possibility of using this work to discover and emphasize different forms of "mechanical abilities," which should be the basis of trade choice. Mr. Bain attacks the problem with a view to an alternative curriculum for the two last years in the elementary school following in the steps of the English elementary technical schools; that should prepare the child, boy or girl, to approach industrial occupations after having gained a general grounding in their common methods and the opportunity for more intelligent vocational choice.

The Articles of Mr. Bain and Mr. Kent on Industrial Training

Both writers recognize that work at this period cannot be specialized trade-school work. Both appreciate that this type of training must react back into the elementary-school curriculum, that this foundation for industrial training has its cultural value as well as its specialized industrial import. Thus the problem of industrial training in our elementary schools appears definitely in these articles. It must be general, selective, and in the best sense instructive. It should gather about the motor processes, but the work suggested is as really educational as any that the elementary school offers.

The Problem of Industrial Training in the Elementary School Presented

General consent among educators and employers of skilled

labor, and skilled workmen, calls for an unspecialized industrial training up to the fifteenth or sixteenth year. If this position is frankly accepted, many who have feared the trade school will be relieved. At least in the elementary school, the training will remain educative in an unspecialized sense. Here the interpretation through the history and literature of mechanical activities will remain. The undeveloped character of the child saves him from too early specialization. Another count is added to the advantages Professor Fisk has detailed of a prolonged period of infancy.

The Child in the Elementary School Protected from Specialization

This type of education can and should be distinctly liberal in its character. On the one side its history and geography and on the other its presentation of civic and industrial conditions relate the trade occupations both to their social origins and their immediate social conditions. The economic conditions, so far as children of that age comprehend these, can be touched upon in connection with the raw materials and the market. Out of this will arise an interest in the whole product which may lay the foundation for that intelligence which can in some measure resist the narrowing influence of the specialized labor in the factory.

The Character of Such an Industrial Course in the Elementary School

There are, to be sure, those who see little if any purpose in such attempts at increasing the general occupational intelligence of the factory laborer. Except for the opportunities which will develop the unusual boy who is to be the high-grade mechanic or foreman, the only ideal they will recognize is that of speed in operating the individual machine with the necessary bondage of the factory worker to the machine itself. Beyond the reply that the right to think and to comprehend can never be deliberately denied to anyone by our community, there is a very pertinent consideration which needs emphasis—that our tools (and these include our machines of the most complicated sort) are invented and constructed as much with reference to those who are to use them as to the product which they are to turn out. The increased intelligence of the workmen is as sure to affect the type of machine as is the demand for specific goods. The mod-

The Legitimacy of Increasing the Intelligence of the Factory Laborer

ern factory looks as definitely toward the immense supply of cheap, unintelligent labor, as it does toward the vast market for inexpensive articles which our methods of transportation make possible. Many a recent labor-saving device has arisen in answer to so temporary a labor condition as a strike; and whole factories have been built and equipped to make use of the cheaper labor of women and children. If the history of invention in industry proves anything it is that increased intelligence in the laborer will inevitably reflect itself in the form and function of the tool he uses.

NOTES AND NEWS

Dr. James P. Haney, director of art and manual training in the public schools of New York, with Professor Arthur W. Dow, represented the United States on the programme of the Third International Congress for the Development of Art, in London last summer. Dr. Haney, who is secretary of the National Society for the Promotion of Industrial Education, made a plea for the broader use of drawing in education and urged its immediate relation to many school subjects and its great importance in all phases of training for a vocational life.

The older teaching emphasized the technical side, and spent much time in copy-work. The subject was made dry, formal and imitative. Later teaching in America has seen much more free and creative work. The drawing is not now taught as a mere end in itself, quite apart from other school subjects, but has been made a means to many ends and has been successfully introduced from the kindergarten to the high school. Our present teaching sees drawing made of use in all forms of constructive work. The boy in school now learns the use of plans, and how to make and read them. This knowledge is an invaluable asset to one who later enters the vocational field, as so many boys must. Many hundreds of pupils are yearly taught in our elementary schools how to make, directly from the model, a working-sketch properly lettered and dimensioned. Thus the work has been taken out of the formal and theoretical field and made immediately practical.

Beside this both our boys and girls are constantly called upon to use drawing in connection with their work in design. The latter subject not only gives excellent training in taste, but is daily becoming of more importance in our industries. We have learned that good form and pattern must appear in all our manufactured products which are to compete with the well-designed goods made in foreign markets. Teaching of design in the public schools not only educates prospective workmen and designers, but also is fast developing an appreciative public which understands the practical side of art and each year demands higher standards in all forms of dress and furniture.

One of the most important problems for educational theory and practice is that of the "spread of training," or "transfer of training." Does training in one subject or process help in another? The most recent contribution to this subject which has come to our notice is by Dr. G. C. Fracker, of the University of Iowa, "Studies in Psychology—No. V," issued as a monograph supplement of the *Psychological Review*. Dr. Fracker made experiments to determine whether memory for various tests, e. g., poetry, order of nine grays, order of tones, order of nine numbers, etc., could be improved by training. In the case of some, e. g., the order of tones, the training was very similar to the test; in others it was dissimilar.

The results of the experiments tend to show an improvement where the training was closely similar to the tests, but not much, if any, in cases where it was not similar. Training in remembering the order of tones and colors did not apparently prove of any value in the ability to remember poetry.

The most novel and suggestive result was the importance of "imagery." Improvement seems to depend upon the consistent use of some form of imagery. "Improvement depends also upon the fitness or adequacy of the imagery to do the thing for which it was adopted." Perhaps this opens up a great field for the teacher of the multiplication table, and other of the similar tasks: to find imagery that shall help the children. But who can devise any imagery that shall be adequate for English spelling?

The state of Washington reports will show an expenditure of $51.32 a pupil, the highest, it is expected, of all the states in the Union. Spokane is also proud that the last government report showed it as first in its investment per capita in school buildings and grounds, and second only to Pueblo in the per capita cost of maintaining schools. Newton, Mass., is third in this latter regard.

The interest excited by the exhibition of representative industrial educational institutions of the United States, under the direction of Charles H. Morse, at the Chicago meeting of the National Society for the Promotion of Industrial Education is further accentuated by the second annual report of the Massachusetts Commission on Industrial Education, recently published. Mr. Morse, as secretary of the commission, states that the narrative and illustrative material collected for use in connection with this exhibition is of such value that it will be published as a bulletin of the commission.

Evening schools for industrial workers have been established by the commission at Cambridge, Beverley, New Bedford, Waltham, and Taunton. Upward of a thousand children, young men, and young women in the state of Massachusetts are now attending industrial schools which are under the direction of the commission.

Professor H. Heath Bawden is about to publish a volume entitled: *The Principles of Education.* This book is the result of the author's study and teaching of Professor Dewey's educational philosophy for the past eight years. Part I treats of the "Problem of Education." Part II treats of the "Subject-Matter of Education" on the psychological basis of child-development. This part of the volume contains a statement of those important psychological and sociological grounds for a radical reconstruction of the elementary curriculum for which Professor Dewey's educational philosophy stands. Part III discusses the "Method of Education" on the logical basis of adult experience. The various phases of "special method" are treated as corollaries of the great fundamental social and psychical laws recently brought to light in biology and psychology.

B. F. Scales has a plea in the *New England Journal of Education* for "out-of-school" musical organizations for school children, under the direction of qualified instructors. He feels that it removes the strain of the regular routine, while giving aesthetic training. In the William Penn Charter school, the number of applicants for such clubs has tripled in eight years, and visiting artists have noticed a decided increase in the appreciation of good music.

Boston is to spend $58,000 during the next twelve months in improving and increasing its playgrounds. Athletic fields for the high schools, and instructors for those fields are included in the appropriation. The rest of the money will go for improving school playgrounds, and providing local playgrounds for the older grades. Military drill in the high schools will be continued as at present.

Neurasthenia is the most common disease given by New York teachers to the board of retirement as the cause of their withdrawal from active service. In the three years since this board was organized 351 have applied for pensions on the plea of length of service; 124 gave neurasthenia as the reason for no longer continuing at work; 31, the next largest number, gave heart-disease. Nearly all of the applicants had been in service over thirty years.

Postal cards as a means of education is the latest fad, fresh from Germany. The school museum at Breslau has undertaken to make a collection of all postal cards which might be useful in imparting knowledge. Manufacturers are asked to forward samples. Many cards have already been printed in Germany which illustrated natural and political history, and some which aim to give instruction in the German language.

"Compulsory education laws have not yet been adopted in any of the southern states, except Kentucky and Missouri," says G. F. Milton in *Child Labor and Social Progress.* Great progress has been made in education during the past twenty years, yet in 1900 27.9 per cent. of all the illiterate white voters of the Union were found in southern states containing only 14.9 per cent. of all the white voters. The South is the only section of the United States in which attendance on public schools between the ages of six and fourteen is not compulsory. Many of the much-criticized cotton-mills supplement the public-school deficiencies by running schools of their own in connection with other kinds of "welfare-work." "But in nearly every 'mill-school,' says Alfred Seddon, writing in the same publication, "the teachers speak most discouragingly of their work. The children attend until there is a demand for mill-labor; then they leave. Out of 110 on the roll, only 34 may be present at classes. Mill schools can never be a substitute for compulsory education by the state."

BOOK REVIEWS

The Condition and Tendencies of Technical Education in Germany. By ARTHUR HENRY CHAMBERLAIN. Syracuse, N. Y.: C. W. Bardeen, 1908. Pp. 108.

Technical Education is a brief but very complete classification and account of the industrial and technical continuation schools of Germany.

The chief function of the schools is viewed as vocational training. The commercial demand for such training is naïvely accepted as the sufficient reason for their being and the psychology of manual work in the schools is not considered.

While we may not agree with Mr. Chamberlain in the very few deductions which he makes, and though the book is very poorly printed, it is an exceedingly valuable report of existing conditions in the home of vocational schools.

WM. C. PAYNE

HARRISON PRACTICE SCHOOL
CHICAGO, ILL.

Father and Baby Plays. By MILLIE POULSSON. Illustrations by FLORENCE STORER. Music by THERESA GARRISON AND CHARLES COMICH. New York: Century Co., 1907.

The modern awakening of parenthood and the strong interest in the child-study movement has been steadily gaining ground under the influence of the mothers' congress, the parents' and mothers' clubs of schools and the general trend of modern pedagogical literature. No one has done more to further this, in a simple, sympathetic way, than Miss Millie Poulsson with her insight into the child's needs and her power of putting these so that the "grown-up" must feel their importance.

In this book of *Father and Baby Plays* Miss Poulsson has given us a charming collection of verses and games which would tempt any father to stray into the world of baby play. They are so natural that they are almost a spontaneous expression of the things that the right kind of father would do without teaching —but being arranged in an interesting and related order, they suggest a purpose and meaning that would not be seen otherwise. The music is simple and attractive, and not the least interesting parts of the book are the well-chosen selections and suggestions which precede each group of plays. Among the best of these little songs are, "Funny Fishes," "Chasing Speck-o' Dirt," "Two White Ducks," "The Rabbit," "The Squirrel," "The Trotting Plays" and "The Shadow Plays," while of the lullabys "Gapo," "Nid, Nod," and "Slumberee" are such as all mothers will want to use.

It is true that the relation between the Father and the Baby might easily be less beautiful if it became self-conscious, no matter how thoughtful or educational it was. As Professor Royce says there are limitations to the too thoughtful attitude of mind. Only the most highly developed intelligence will carry us as freely as wholesome instinct. But used as suggestively as Miss Poulsson has intended, this book will prove to be a delightful inspiration to many fathers, will educate many others in ways that they would be chary of entering on undirected, and will give many little children happy hours of fun and frolic.

Merry Animal Tales. By MADGE BIGHAM. Boston: Little, Brown & Co., 1908.

Stories to Tell to Children. By SARA CONE BRYANT. New York: Houghton, Mifflin & Co., 1908.

These are two books of stories for children, collected and edited by Miss Bigham and Miss Bryant; and both the compilers have included advice and suggestions for the teacher, though in Miss Bigham's book it consists only of a few pages of explanatory notes.

The *Merry Animal Tales* have a good deal of spontaneity and the action and interest do not drag, but there is a doubtful wisdom in taking away an old friend's individuality of appearance, however attractive the new dress may be, and these tales are our old friends, the well-worn fables—thirty-seven of them, adapted from La Fontaine and put into prose in the form of a series of stories in which continuity is preserved by introducing the several incidents into the lives of a family of rats.

The fables are enlarged, the terse, pithy sentences which find their way into the memory become long conversations, and the whole has a somewhat artificial setting. The teacher is advised to use seat work of a rather mechanical kind to illustrate these stories in a way in which their value as literature would be still more lost. It is true that these suggestions might give a new impulse to the teacher in the rural districts that are mentioned, but possibly this impulse might be aroused in a more valuable way.

The stories to tell to children collected by Miss Bryant will be found useful by many teachers and her suggestions about telling stories are even better than the stories themselves. Miss Bryant's point of view is very sound and her criticisms are direct and helpful. The stories are collected from many sources and are often new and interesting The story of Epaminondas has already become popular, and several of the others bid fair to follow suit. The serious criticism to be passed on both these books is that the style is not finished and the construction is often weak. The English in many instances is crude and unsatisfactory, "I guess," "Hurry up," "Right here," and so forth, being common expressions, and there is a certain affectation of the child's talk in one or two of Miss Bryant's which endangers their sincerity. The books of stories for children are improving each year. But it is earnestly to be hoped that our clever collectors and editors, of whom there are so many now-a-days, will in time study English composition and literature more thoroughly and develop that fine taste which alone can give us the best editions of books for children.

ALICE O'GRADY

CHICAGO NORMAL SCHOOL

The First Book, Song and Story for Little Children. Edited by E. E. SPEIGHT, B.A., AND CLARA L. THOMSON. The Norland Press. Shaldon, South Devon, England. Pp. 223.

At last we have found "something new under the sun"—a first reader which begins with something worth reading and maintains that standard throughout the book. There is not one page of mere device for teaching words, regardless of content.

The First Book, edited by E. E. Speight and Clara L. Thomson, is an English publication of the Norland Press. "It is," as the preface states, "the outcome of an idea which is in the air—the idea that the endless scroll of beautiful and wonderful stories which research in folklore is steadily unfolding is not only a matter of interest to students of psychology and anthropology, but one of great moment in the education of little children. Ardent collectors in all parts of the world are providing a rich heritage for the children of today and tomorrow, to take the place of the old-fashioned reading-books with their undesirable subject-matter and impossible manner of writing."

All of us who have plowed through the drift of primers and first readers which have threatened to bury the best educational ideals of what children's reading should be, look upon this new attempt with delight. Those of us who have had our hopes of rich material raised high by the attractive binding, beautiful printing, enchanting pictures, only to be dashed to earth by the inane content, and who have felt that this sugar-coated mockery was not only an indignity to rational children but a serious pedagogic evil, welcome with heartfelt gratitude this honest attempt to make a book for very little children which should be rich in the best literary material.

Here we have the good printing, beautiful pictures, plus real content. The plan of the book, too, shows that technical difficulties have been considered, and children's ability has been measured so that we find much repetition of words and phrases and an orderly gradation in the difficulties of reading. That this arrangement is not entirely for the sake of learning words adds to its interest. The editors say, "The stress is laid on the idea of order, for from the simplest rhymes, such as 'Graufa Grig' or 'Doodle, doodle, doo,' to elaborate stories like 'Cinderella' or 'Hine Moa,' there is for each variant only one proper sequence of events and one right choice of words and phrases, which must be strictly observed, and insistence upon this observance is good training for little minds."

Part II is unique in its attempt to "re-introduce the singing of folksongs into our homes." We hope it may give children a basis of merry melody which will direct their taste into such lines that afterward they may be able to distinguish between real song and the rubbish which so often passes for music in this country.

When the World Was Young. By ELIZABETH V. BROWN, Supervisor of Primary Schools, Washington, D. C. New York and Chicago: Globe School Book Publishing Co. Pp. 160.

When the World Was Young is another sign that times are changing and that content is beginning to be considered in the making of a reader.

The general idea of this reader may be gotten from some selections from the

Table of Contents as follows: "The Story of the Food Quest," "Homes of Many Lands," "Queer Clothes for Queer Weavers," "The Story of Transportation," "Killing of Time," "Music of Many Centuries." The preface states that, "Playing Indian is perhaps the modern child's closest contact with primitive life. The warpath, the hunt, the chase, revive the aboriginal instincts; but the patient steps by which men have climbed from savagery to civilization, through the exercise of invention and industry, are often overlooked. It is the aim of these stories to stimulate an interest in culture history and from a knowledge of past conditions to build up an idea of the meaning of the arts of life in our own time."

To the teacher who is using this industrial history the book is suggestive. The material is carefully selected and the trend of the work evident. One wishes that each topic had been more dramatically and more fully developed and that something more of grace and literary quality had gone into the telling. Nevertheless let us be thankful for these signs of a better day when we shall have material so rich that it will be worth while for a child to make the necessary effort to read.

E. A. W.

Rhymes and Stories and Fairy Tales. Compiled and edited by MARY FLORENCE LANSING. The Open Road Library. Boston and New York: Ginn & Co., 1907. Pp. 182 and 179.

The first of these little books represents the effort to furnish reading-matter for little children which will contain the essentials of interest and of good form, and at the same time secure such repetition of words and phrases as will carry the beginners on to a control of the ideas expressed with the least possible obstruction. The rhymes from Mother Goose and other sources which fill the first part of the book are well selected for this purpose. The stories which follow are drawn from nursery classics and are very simply told—perhaps too simply to be artistic in form. However, the simplicity makes them readable by children and they are superior in childish charm to much of the pointless matter that fills too many beginners' readers.

Fairy Tales is a first volume of a series. It contains some of the old fairy tales with which every child should be familiar. The compiler has left the popular modern versions with their often fanciful and irrelevant additions and has gone to the best sources among the earlier compilers. In the list of writers whose forms she has preferred stand the names of Dasent, Grimm, Perrault, and Madame D'Aulnay. These names should insure a certain measure of literary merit, and prefer a claim to attention. Whether for supplementary reading at school or for home browsing the book should be appropriate for children who are still in the fairy-tale phase of interest in stories.

Gulliver's Travels for Children. By JAMES BALDWIN. New York: American Book Co., 1908. Pp. 172. $0.35.

Gulliver's Travels for Children is a successful attempt to abridge and paraphrase that classic in something of Swift's own simple, unadorned style, omitting the coarseness, bitterness, and tediousness, while preserving the humor which will always endear these adventures to the young reader.

JESSIE ELIZABETH BLACK

BOOKS RECEIVED

AMERICAN BOOK COMPANY, NEW YORK

How the World Is Clothed. A Geographical Reader. By FRANK GEORGE CARPENTER. Cloth. Pp. 340. Illustrated. $0.60.

A Punctuation Primer. By FRANCES M. PERRY. Cloth. Pp. 103. $0.30.

Arnold's Fritz auf Ferien. Edited by MAY THOMAS. Cloth. Pp. 112. $0.30.

Practical Elementary Algebra. By JOSEPH V. COLLINS. Cloth. Pp. 240. $1.00.

Physics for Secondary Schools. By CHARLES F. ADAMS. Cloth. Illustrated. Pp. 490. $1.20.

Elements of Physics. By GEORGE A. HOADLEY. Cloth. Illustrated. Pp. 464. $1.20.

A. S. BARNES & CO., NEW YORK

Some Living Things. Primary Lessons in Physiology. By ELLA B. HALLOCK; edited by C. B. GILBERT. Cloth. Illustrated. Pp. 214. $0.36.

Graded Games and Rhythmic Exercises. By MARION BROMLEY NEWTON; edited by ADA VAN STONE HARRIS. Cloth. Illustrated. Pp. 110. $1.00.

THE CENTURY CO., NEW YORK

The American College: A Criticism. By ABRAHAM FLEXNER. Cloth. Pp. 200. $1.00.

HOUGHTON, MIFFLIN & CO., BOSTON

The Story of the Greek People. By EVA MARCH TAPPAN. Cloth. Illustrated. Pp. 257. $0.65.

Children's Classics in Dramatic Form. (A reader for the fourth grade.) By AUGUSTA STEVENSON. Cloth. Illustrated. Pp. 181. $0.40.

King Arthur Stories from Malory. By LILLIAN O. STEVENS AND EDWARD F. ALLEN. Cloth. Illustrated. Pp. 188. $0.40.

Selections from the Works of John Ruskin. Edited by CHAUNCY B. TINKER. Cloth. Pp. 328. $0.50 .

MACMILLAN & CO., NEW YORK

Austen's Pride and Prejudice. (Pocket Edition.) Edited by JOSEPHINE WOODBURY HEERMANS. Cloth. Pp. 338. $0.25.

Hughes' Tom Brown's School Days. (Pocket Edition.) Edited by CHARLES SWAIN THOMAS. Cloth. Pp. 296. $0.25.

MUSEE PROVINCIAL CHARLEROI, FRANCE

Méthodes Américaines d'éducation générale et technique. Par OMER BUYSE. Paper cover. Illustrated. Pp. 744.

VOLUME IX NUMBER 5

THE ELEMENTARY SCHOOL TEACHER

JANUARY, 1909

RELIGION IN THE PUBLIC SCHOOLS

HARRY PRATT JUDSON
President of The University of Chicago

In discussing the possibility of teaching religious truths in the public schools, the first thought which will occur to anyone is the great number of forms which religious organization and expression have taken in our country. There have been times in the history of mankind when the people of a given nation were connected with but one church. That time has long since passed. Especially in our own country is it true that no form of religious activity can command anything like a majority of the people. In other words, any one church is in a minority, and the main question of difference numerically between churches is merely how small this minority may be.

Remembering also that the public schools belong to all the people, and not to any one portion of them, it at once becomes imperative that we should consider whether it is possible to isolate out from the phenomena of religious thought, as expressed in its manifold forms, those which are common to all, which, in short, belong to religion in itself, and not only to any of its particular modes of expression. If that should prove possible, it would at once become practicable to embody such common truths in the teaching of the public schools, as belonging to all, and not to a few. Such truths would almost fall under the ancient category, "Quod ubique; quod semper; quod ab omnibus."

Attempts have been made thus to isolate common religious doctrine. One such attempt may be cited as an example. Professor Votaw of The University of Chicago, in a paper presented at the meeting of the Religious Education Association, in 1908, expressed his view in the following words:

What do we mean by religion? Is religion to be identified with ecclesiastical organization, creed, ritual, and emotionalism, so that when those are dismissed nothing remains? In most of the discussions over the Bible and religion in the public schools, this seems to be the point of view. The partisan advocates of particular sects, the zealous guardians of religious liberty, and the vigorous opponents of everything called religious, all join hands to keep the Bible and religion out of the public schools.

But this conception of religion so generally held by Christians differs from that held by Jesus, whom we Christians profess to follow. He did not make religion to consist in ecclesiasticism, or in doctrinal belief, or in ritualism, or in emotionalism. He gave to his followers no ecclesiastical organization, no theological creed, no ritual or ceremonial system, no standard type of emotional experience. To him religion was an ideal of life. Religion meant righteousness, the doing of God's will, the possession of the qualities of character described in the Beatitudes, the doing of the good and helpful deeds described in the Sermon on the Mount and the parables, the love to God and love to men in which the law and the prophets were summarized, the practice of justice, mercy, and faith, the weightier matters of human obligation which men were leaving undone. This was what religion meant to him, and this is what religion should mean for us.

Religion, therefore, as interpreted by Jesus, and by all Christianity that has been faithful to his teaching, and by the Hebrew prophets upon whose foundation he built, means reverence, trust, obedience, faithfulness, industry, sincerity, honesty, truthfulness, righteousness, justice, purity, honor, kindness, sympathy, helpfulness, health, and happiness. Religion is an ideal of life. For all these qualities and acts the actual teaching of Jesus can be cited, and his own example shown. These qualities and acts therefore set forth the ideal of life which religion at its best proposes.

This list of the essential religious ideas is extremely interesting. It seems to me, however, that it is fatally defective. It comprises a code of conduct—a code perhaps complete, and certainly very comprehensive and important. Such a code of conduct in its essentials, it is true, is found in every form of religion. It is found also in every formulation of ethics. It seems to me, however, that the code in question is not itself either a system of ethics or a system of religion. Ethics, as I take it, comprises two essentials: the first being a code of conduct; the second being the motives for action under this code.

It is not enough to present to anyone a mere list of desirable moral actions. Least of all is that possible with one who is young. He may be told never so often that he should not lie or steal, but always the question occurs, Why? The natural instinct is to do that which seems to give an immediate advantage; falsehood and theft are obvious means to such ends. Queen Elizabeth, we remember, is said to have defined a lie as a convenient means of meeting a difficulty. That which so commended itself to the great queen it will readily be seen commends itself even more pressingly to young and untrained minds. How, then, shall one be taught that this immediate advantage, if gained at all, is at the sacrifice of a far greater advantage, and one which can plainly be shown to be pressing and important? In other words, the motive for each form of moral regulation must be present, must be clear, must be pressing in its nature, or the regulation in question becomes a mere abstract dictum with no practical bearing on life.

Passing a step farther, it may readily be admitted that ethics, in other words a system of conduct and a system of motives for such conduct, is an essential part of every form of religion. But it is also equally plain that religion means more even than this. No system can be considered a religion unless it embodies certain ideas with regard, for instance, to God, to the human soul, to the relation of the human soul to the Divine, the future life, and the relation of conduct in this life to the life hereafter. It will at once be seen that in these ideas we find the motives for ethical conduct which transform ethics into religious ethics, and which supply the powerful springs of action in daily life. Strip away the ideals relating to the Divine Being, or to the future life, or to both, and we have left a system of ethics for which some other motive must be supplied than the religious. Other forms of motive may be supplied, but in this case we have secular ethics and not religious ethics.

Such secular ethics may plainly be shown to exist. There are other motives for right conduct than the religious motive. The motive of desire to attune one's own soul to what is believed to be the Divine purpose, on the one hand; or the motive either of hope or fear regarding the future life, on the other, may be regarded as obvious forms of religious motive. On the other hand, the desire on the whole to do that which accords with the general social welfare, either now or in the far future, is a purely secular motive, and yet one conceivable as operating powerfully to influence conduct. Again, it may fairly be claimed that a large proportion of right conduct in society, as we understand it, results from one or two other motives: either a sense of self-respect leading one to avoid actions which he regards as beneath him, on the one hand; or a desire to confirm the respect of one's associates, on the other hand. All these together are secular and non-religious motives.

Turning now to religion in this sense, it is plainly apparent that theology, if we may use that term as applied to the body of doctrine which seems to be associated with every form of religion, can by no means be dissociated from sectarianism. Of course I use the term "sectarianism" in no derogatory sense, and merely for the lack of a better and more colorless word to express the idea. It is impossible to formulate any body of doctrine with regard to God or the relation of the human soul to the Divine, or to the future life, without embodying some particular form of theology, which will be in accord with the views of a certain class of people, from which other classes will strongly dissent—and this is sectarianism. From this fact it at once appears that religion, or even religious ethics, cannot be taught in the schools without teaching some form of sectarian religion. Practically, this is even more obviously the case, because such teaching must from the nature of things be in the hands of one who is actuated by the ideas of some form of sectarian religion, or possibly by one who is antagonistic to any or to all forms of religion. It is extremely difficult for anyone to teach either the history or the philosophy of a form of religion which meets his own approval without being more or less unconsciously biased against those which do not meet his approval. Such teaching, it needs no argument to show, would be out of place in the public schools which belong to all the people of all classes.

Again, even if it were desirable to teach religious truths of this character in the schools, it is extremely unlikely that they could be taught to advantage by the ordinary secular teacher. These teachers are trained to educate in certain lines of life. They have, in general, a more or less definite idea as to their own form of religious doctrine and practice. They have not, however, been trained in the really difficult science of theology, and much less trained to educate in such science.

It follows, therefore, that if such instruction should be given it could hardly be done adequately excepting by the clergy, and this at once, if the instruction were given in the public schools as now organized, would import into those schools the clergy of every form of religious thought in the country. It needs only to state this supposition to show at once its impossibility. One need not dwell on the very obvious results in the way of contention and infelicity which would be found in every school of this kind. It has sometimes been suggested that such teaching might well take place in the school building after school hours, children attending only such lessons as might be given by the pastor approved by their respective parents. It is difficult to see how the situation would be affected by having the instruction given after four o'clock rather than before four o'clock, for instance. Surely there is nothing sacred in a particular hour of the day. The conditions would be essentially the same, whatever the hour, and the results would invariably follow.

There remains, of course, another hypothesis. Religious schools, that is, schools under religious control, might be organized by any denomination, and taxes for school purposes assigned them proportionately. This would make it possible to support at the public cost schools like the present public schools in which no religious instruction is given at all, and at the same time schools in which instruction is given by Catholics, by Methodists, by Presbyterians, or any other religious body, as the case might be. It may be said that not a few in our community urge this as being just. Their ground is that they regard no teaching as adequate unless religious teaching is made a part of it; that one fundamental principle of education from their point of view is the religious atmosphere in the school; and that if the present system is maintained they are compelled from a sense of duty to establish and maintain schools at their own cost to carry out these ideas. Inasmuch as they at the same time must pay taxes to support the schools in which religion is not taught, it is very obvious that they must pay doubly toward education. This they regard as unjust.

If we consider this suggestion we are at once confronted with the fact that there is hardly any political doctrine which our experience has more firmly embedded in the national consciousness than that of the separation of church and state. This is not merely a vague political theory, either; it is a conclusion reached by our people as the result, in the first place, of a long experience of the union of church and state in Europe, and what we believe to be the extremely unfortunate consequences in leading to repression of free thought, and to dissension of the bitterest description. In the next place, it is based on experience in this country. The Virginia Statute of Religious Liberty of 1776 was brought about because the people of that state became convinced that there was no safety for democratic institutions if the state supported any one form of religion. Again, in Connecticut, one church was supported by taxes until 1817, when the constitution was changed to put that state also on the general basis of separating political and religious activities. It is true that the Constitution of the United States puts no inhibition on the states in this respect, and that therefore any state may, if it sees fit, provide for supporting either the public worship or the education of any particular church or of all churches, at its will. At the same time, in the constitution of every state will be found a distinct prohibition on the state government toward using the public funds for any such purpose; and this is the expression, as I have said, of a public conviction almost universal and deeply rooted. Whatever benefits might be conceived to follow from the plan contemplated I greatly fear would be far more than counterbalanced by the innumerable and complicated evils of a partnership between the state and the churches, or any of them. The possibilities of dissension, especially of contention over the proper distribution of the public funds, are interminable.

Another grave result would follow. Many of us believe, and believe strongly, that whatever benefits may be conceived to flow from the atmosphere of religious life in which those of the same faith live and work together, and teach and are taught apart from others, are far less than the incalculable benefit to the national life derived from the union in the same school of those of all political parties, of all religious views, of all races. It is the fusion of these which forms a republic such as ours, which makes it possible for people of conflicting races and creeds to live together in peace, in mutual respect, working out the common interest of the Republic, without confusion, without dissension. This would be lost if we should isolate those of each faith in its own separate church schools, and the loss would be enormous. Moreover, as a part of this loss would be, I greatly fear, that mutual respect which those of different views learn for one another when they live and work together. Isolation almost invariably means a lack of common understanding, and that means prejudice, and prejudice means hostility. In the interest, then, of the welfare of the Republic, based on union of thought and action, our common schools, as they are, seem to many of us as yet the last word of social science in the direction of an enduring republic.

There remains the important question as to whether ethics, secular in character, can be taught in the public schools; and, further, as to how it should be handled. This question is a vital one in our public life. I am convinced that those who insist that character is the first consideration in our early education are right, and that the state cannot afford by its education to bring up a set of young people who are intelligent and intellectually acute, but conscienceless. The proper training of character, therefore, in the public schools should be, undoubtedly, a matter of the most earnest attention. We should cease merely talking about it and it should be carried into practice in every schoolroom in the land. It should be made a part of the training of every professional teacher, and should be foremost in the thoughts of all to whom are intrusted the destinies of our young. It is obvious that ethics of this character involves, as has been pointed out, a code of conduct, and at the same time an adequate presentation of the motives of action which lie back of the code. It is not enough to have a formal teaching of these principles, although that in its place is valuable, but the teaching should permeate the entire school life; should be made a part of the instruction in every school subject; should be present in the life of the school in its every day and every hour of work; should be the primary thought in the mind of all the teachers all the time. This is entirely possible, and if handled in that way there can be created in every school not merely a definite body of knowledge to be imparted, but what our friends of the religious schools call an atmosphere of the utmost inspiration. In the organization of this work I repeat that among others it seems to me that the most important and the most easily presented motives are the two of self-respect and the respect of one's associates. Few things are more powerful in determining one's conduct than the opinion of his fellows, and the teacher should endeavor in every way to build up in the school a body of opinion with regard to certain specific lines of conduct which will powerfully reinforce what may come from his lips. Other motives are so remote that they become very shadowy. It is true that to some extent children can be taught the duty of certain lines of conduct as, on the whole, improving the society in which they live. It is not impossible to make this a motive, but with the many it will be so far removed as to have little force; and so far as benefit to remote posterity is concerned, one is tempted to remember what Sir Boyle Roach said, "Why should I benefit posterity? What has posterity ever done for me?" On the other hand, I am inclined to believe that a vast number of very upright persons are affected slightly or not at all by the religious motive of conduct, and that their correct conduct comes primarily from one of the two motives to which I have referred. A sense of personal dignity and self-respect it seems to me should be the first; and many a man refrains from falsehood or dishonesty not because he fears the Divine displeasure, not because, on the other hand, he fears the penalty of courts of law, but because he respects himself so much that he scorns what he regards as an unworthy action. This is a worthy motive, and entirely capable of translating into constant action, even with the very young.

Of course it may be added that such treatment of ethical questions by no means displaces a further treatment which superadds to the secular motive—which in fact all should have—the possible religious motive, but leaves that to be added in the home and in the church, by parents and by the clergy. It is true that in many cases parents are not keenly responsive to these questions. It is true, also, that in many cases children outside of the schoolroom are not subject to church control, and that the Sunday school has a far smaller part in their lives, if it has any part at all, than have the daily hours in the schoolroom. All that that means, however, is that the church needs—and by the church I mean every form of religious activity—the church needs to devise new and more efficient ways of influencing the public life. We are acting on old lines devised and carried on in centuries past; we need new lines of activity to be devised as applied to the conditions in the twentieth century. This is the problem of the church today, and if it is losing its hold on the public mind it is not, I believe, because it is not put in control of the schools, but because it has not learned as yet what the twentieth century means. When the church has learned that it will resume its former position of powerful influence on the entire community.

One thing more should be said. There is one matter with regard to religion in the public schools which the church may legitimately claim, and that is negatively, if you please, this: that the school should not teach directly or by indirection anti-religious doctrines. It is no more the right of the public school to teach atheism than it is to teach any form of religion. Moreover, in this same connection, the public schools should teach a respect for every form of religious organization, and the utmost fairness and justice in dealing with them. It is impossible to discuss history without crossing the lines of religious controversy. It is impossible to teach many forms of social thought without coming in contact with the diversities of religious doctrine and action, as found in daily life.

We should discuss this question without bitterness. It is not wise, on the one hand, for those who disapprove the present system to stigmatize our public institutions as Godless schools; it is not wise, on the other hand, for those who believe in the advisability of maintaining this secular character of public education to assail others as bigoted religionists. There can be no doubt that each side embraces people of the utmost integrity of thought and of earnest moral purpose. The question should be discussed solely on its merits, and we should try to reach conclusions as a body of American citizens, respecting one another, recognizing the weight of opposing convictions, and seeking only the highest good of the young intrusted to our charge. In the words of our great President, in short, we should act "with malice toward none; with charity for all."

A REPORT OF THE SECOND ANNUAL MEETING OF THE NATIONAL SOCIETY FOR THE PROMOTION OF INDUSTRIAL EDUCATION

LILLIAN S. CUSHMAN
The School of Education, The University of Chicago

THE AIMS OF THE SOCIETY

To those who are not familiar with the initial efforts and aims of this association a word of explanation may be of interest. The society states that it has resulted from the conviction "that we are no longer fitting our youth for their opportunities in the way in which they must be fitted."

With a plea for greater social efficiency they present their purposes: First, "To bring to the attention of our national life, of our people, this realization of our shortcomings;" second, "To bring together the people most directly interested in this problem: first, those who have to do directly with industrial callings; next, the great manufacturers who depend on skill in these trades, and the schoolmasters who are to train the boys and girls; and, lastly, the great American public itself, which, after all, in all such questions is as directly concerned as any other party, but which is the one the most often left unconsulted." The society further emphasizes the belief that this problem is to be worked out "in a spirit of industrial peace, not in a spirit of industrial war," "because it is equally to the interest of the workingman, of the manufacturer, of the teacher, of the citizen, that the boys and girls may find an open door to opportunity by which they may fit themselves to be effective men and women in the industrial life of our nation."

THE WORK OF THE SOCIETY

During the past year the society has been actively engaged in the circulation of propaganda. Last spring a committee of ten was organized. The personnel of this committee is sufficiently representative and distinguished to insure a careful hearing for its first report which is as follows:

REPORT OF THE COMMITTEE OF TEN

The committee appointed to consider the relation of industrial education to the general system of education of the country is composed of members living in widely separated parts of the country. Since the appointment of the committee in the spring of 1908 it has been found practically impossible to prepare a final report. The following is therefore offered as a preliminary statement with regard to this matter.

The need for industrial training and the facts concerning our own lack of it have been so often repeated that they may be accepted. All who are acquainted with education in European nations know that in the matter of industrial education we are far behind such countries as Germany, that our apprenticeship system, even if materially extended, can offer industrial education to only a few; that there are practically no facilities for the training of the youth between the ages of 14 and 18 for industrial pursuits, and the opportunities for those who are in the trades to improve their skill by theoretical training is confined to isolated and occasional schools. It is also perfectly clear that this is an industrial age and that the education which is to serve for a whole people must take account of vocational training.

TWO GROUPS CONSIDERED

Assuming these facts as clearly demonstrated, it is evident that two distinct groups of our population are to be considered: (1) boys and girls between the ages of fourteen and eighteen who leave the grammar school and at present have no systematic opportunity for training in the industries; (2) the men and women now in the industries who desire to increase their skill and efficiency by further study. The problem of industrial training seems, therefore, so far as the schools are concerned, to be divided into practically two parts, according as it applies to one or the other of these groups.

THE INDUSTRIAL TRAINING OF YOUTHS

The vast majority of children leave school at the end of the grammar-school period, a number in fact leaving the school before that time. Any vocational school which has to serve this great group of citizens must evidently fulfill the following conditions:

(*a*) Such school must articulate at some point with the public-school system of the country, preferably with the grammar school. In other words, the grammar school must at some point in its course lead a boy or girl naturally into some vocational school, if such schools are to be fruitful to the great mass of youth.

b) If the grammar schools are to make this connection with the vocational schools, it is clear that the grammar schools should at some part of their course do their part in developing the vocational purposes of the pupils on the basis of enlightenment concerning the advantages of skilled vocations, including the trades. It is clear, also, that every study should be so taught as to bring out its application to life, particularly to the skilled vocations, although these studies should not be so taught in the grammar school as to provide preparation for any particular trade. It is clear, too, that the grammar school should introduce elementary industrial training in some form, either in the form of manual training at the bench or at the forge or in household pursuits wherever the training could be effectively given. Such an introduction of subjects for industrial training must come through the substitution of these subjects for something in the curriculum. The way of industrial education lies not in a more complex curriculum in existing schools, but in a larger variety of schools, each with a simpler programme and each seeking to do well the work it sets out to do.

c) Such schools as may articulate with the grammar school for the training of youths will therefore most likely assume the form of training schools for particular industries. They will be local in their character and will seek to serve the needs of the local industry. The boy or girl trained in them will not be a skilled journeyman in any trade, but will have received a fundamental training in those things which will make him a skilled journeyman in a short time and will at the same time prompt him to a higher form of vocational efficiency than he is likely to have had otherwise. In this respect the industrial training school for youth is likely to have much the same relation to the preparation of a skilled journeyman as the high-grade engineering school has to the preparation of a practical engineer.

SCHOOLS FOR THOSE ALREADY IN THE INDUSTRIES

Experience would seem to indicate that the schools which seek to serve those already in the industries will assume one of two forms:

a) Industrial-improvement schools.

b) Trade schools.

The industrial-improvement school has so far, as it is likely to do in the future, assumed the form of an evening school in which are taught the fundamental sciences upon which a trade rests, together with such technical information as can be given in a physical, chemical, or mechanical laboratory. For example, those who are engaged in the power station of an electric railroad, as motormen, as electricians, or as linemen, may in such a school learn the fundamental theory of electricity, the method of insulation, of electrical measurement, and of the transformation of energy, All of these principles may be illustrated before their eyes in the electrical laboratory, and they may thus acquire a foundation of knowledge which will enable them to become in time foremen, managers, or perhaps inventors. Such a school appeals only to the men of more than usual ambition and energy.

The pure trade school, on the other hand, undertakes to teach not alone the fundamental processes of a trade, but its technique. It therefore lays chief emphasis upon giving to its students such continuous practice as may bring them up to the point of expertness. It seeks to reproduce as nearly as possible the conditions of actual practice.

GENERAL CONCLUSIONS

It seems clear to your committee that schools of all the types which have been mentioned here, both for the youths and for the adults, are likely to be attempted, and in fact are being attempted in the various parts of the United States. The committee believes that all these types of schools are to be welcomed as experiments in the general problem which we are trying to solve. Success in industrial training does not depend upon the adoption of one type of school. A measure of success is likely to be achieved by all of these efforts, and in the judgment of your committee it is wise for those who have to do with industrial education to welcome during the next decade of experimentation all these forms of industrial education, whether they be in the form of a trade school for boys, an industrial improvement school for boys and adults, or a trade school for the workers of a trade. Ultimately, all these efforts will, by the force of educational gravitation, relate themselves to the public-school system of the country, partly by the adaptation of the public-school system itself, partly by the adaptation of these industrial schools. No series of schools can finally survive which does not so relate itself to the public-school education, since the source from which pupils are to be drawn must in the long run be the public schools. The committee, therefore, feels that any of these efforts undertaken in an intelligent, sympathetic, and proper spirit, is to be welcomed as a new contribution to the general problem of industrial education in the United States.

THE COMMITTEE OF TEN

Following is the membership of the committee:

Henry S. Pritchett, president Carnegie Foundation for the Advancement of Teaching, *chairman.*

Paul Hanus, Harvard University.

M. W. Alexander, General Electric Co., West Lynn, Mass.

Thomas M. Balliet, dean School of Pedagogy, New York University.

Elmer E. Brown, U. S. commissioner of education, Washington, D. C.

William Maxwell, superintendent of public schools, New York City.

President E. J. James, University of Illinois.

L. D. Harvey, superintendent of schools, Menomonie, Wis., and president National Educational Association.

THE BUSINESS MEETING

Certain legislation enacted at the business meeting defines the intention of the association concerning its campaign of the immediate future. An officer was authorized who will represent the society personally everywhere in the country as its officially delegated commissioner. This action was the result of the recommendation of the president, Carroll D. Wright. In his opening address he urged the importance of such an official, claiming that he should be a high-priced man, one of broad culture and experience, who could meet equally well the representative of the government, of educational, or industrial interests. The national congress was memorialized in recommendation that the Bureau of Education, now a branch of the Department of the Interior, be created a department. This recommendation carried the important corollary that a new cabinet officer be established, whose duty will be to conserve the educational interests of the country.

THE PROGRAMME

The text of the meetings was contained in the statement of Gov. Hoke Smith when he said that our government supplied a liberal education for the few and nothing for the 75 per cent. engaged in manual labor. Enlarging upon the natural resources of the country he emphasized the fact that development of the individual could obtain only when there was fair support for the family. He dwelt upon the need of statistics and information and expressed the belief that the national government should contribute directly to the solution of educational problems and distribute information to all parts of the country.

The national government was represented by Dr. Elmer Ellsworth Brown, United States Commissioner of Education. Dr. Brown spoke on "The Unifying Influence of Industrial Art." He dwelt on the fact that trade schools or technical schools of any kind should be intimately connected with the general movement of public education. He said in part:

We shall get a much better system of industrial education in this country if the new movement can be kept in close alliance with our great systems of public schools as already established, than if we undertake to set up an entirely new system that has no part nor lot in the general education movement of our time. The special phase of this subject of which I wish to speak is the unifying influence which is to be exerted within the next few years by industrial art and by the spirit of art as it is to be found in our general education and also in our industrial education.

It is difficult even at this day to speak of art before an American audience without seeming to belittle the subject under discussion. We have not yet got beyond the idea that art is something very like millinery. When I speak of the tendency of our time to emphasize the art side of education, what I have in mind is something much more serious and substantial. Art is that part of education which lays emphasis, first, on the excellence of the work done, apart from any extraneous consideration; and, secondly, lays emphasis on good taste in the product of the work. Our modern education has allied itself with modern science. That alliance is to be maintained and extended. But it has begun to ally itself also with modern art, and that alliance is to be one of the most important in the education of the future. It is already so well begun that we may count on it with confidence in the immediate future.

I am not forgetting that the topic of the evening has to do with industrial education as related to national prosperity, but let it not be forgotten either that the markets of the world are profoundly influenced already by the spread of popular education, and will be more widely influenced by popular education in the course of the twentieth century.

It was not until the nineteenth century that a majority of the population of the civilized world was able to read and write and had come under the influence of organized schools. In the course of the nineteenth century a large proportion, certainly more than three-quarters of the population of Western Europe and America, became a literate population—a people who had tasted the learning of the schools. Now that proportion will be still further increased in civilized communities within the twentieth century. Not only science but art is to be in the schools. The markets of the world must respond not only to a growing demand for modern appliances of comfort and convenience but also to a growing demand for excellence of finish and design.

For forty years or more this demand for fineness and beauty in manufactured products has been steadily gaining ground. Its influence has been clearly manifest in the great world-expositions. It has become a well-recognized element in international competition. But who can tell what momentum this demand will acquire when popular education shall become ten times as great a power in the world as it is today and when the schools shall become, to an incalculable degree, more alive to artistic ideals than they are today! The commercial advantage in that near future will rest with the nation that can make the finest combination of science and art, the finest combination of inventive skill with beauty of design and workmanship.

SCIENCE AND ART TO WORK TOGETHER

Science and art will have to work together to this end. Inventive skill and the ideals of genuine art do indeed work over into each other and each reinforces the other in the finer manufactures, where the higher grades of intelligence are already in demand. But the disciplines which go to make an educated man, all of them work together in the making of a high-grade artisan. Except for an occasional freak or a still more occasional genius, our main reliance for artistic performance must be a class of workers and designers who have ideas focused by training and training backed up by ideas. Industrial training alone, and particularly industrial training under teachers who themselves have been narrowly trained and never educated, will utterly fail to give us that great army of producers in the field of the finer manufactures which will be needed to supply demands that have already begun to appear. Our industrial education must be carried forward in the full sweep of our great systems of schooling for intelligence, schooling for character, schooling for citizenship, if they would keep from falling into a petty, mechanical, unproductive routine.

SPECIAL SCHOOLS MUST BE CONNECTED WITH PUBLIC EDUCATION

This does not mean that there should be no distinctive trade schools, or agricultural schools, or technical schools of any kind. Such schools, indeed, we must have. The need for them is imperative. But these special and technical schools must be brought into some intimate connection with the general movement of public education or they will fail. I am confident that they will not fail in the end. But they will win their success by bringing over into their new and difficult work of special training a full measure of that general intelligence and insight and strength of ideals which has made the public schools and the public-school teachers of our land so true a source of national pride and power.

The programme was centered upon three phases of industrial training, viz., the apprenticeship system, trade schools, and industrial education in the public schools.

The apprenticeship system of a new type, and adequate to the needs of modern industry, was ably presented by Mr. E. P.

Bullard, Jr., president E. P. Bullard Machine Tool Co., and by the vice-president of the society, Mr. Magnus W. Alexander; of the General Electric Co., Lynn, Mass. Mr. Bullard urged that manufacturers give more attention to training their own apprentices. He said in part:

It is admitted by all that we need more skilled men and that some means must be devised for developing the inefficient and unskilled so that they may be valuable to themselves, their employers and to the community in which they live.

Where can these men be found? The supply is inadequate to the demand. Our public schools do not educate for any particular trade, our colleges do so broadly, but not specifically, our technical schools lay the foundation of engineering professions but relatively few have an opportunity to avail themselves of the courses offered. According to a writer in a recent periodical, which I beg leave to quote:

"Less than 5 per cent. of all the millions of school children in the United States ever reach the secondary school and it is safe to say that not more than 25 per cent. of the whole number ever go above the fifth grade; that is to say—of approximately 24,000,000 children enrolled in 1907 at least 18,000,000 will leave school between the fifth and sixth grades."

Think what this means industrially; it means that every year millions of American boys and girls—for all grow up to be Americans no matter where they were born—are sent out wherever workers are needed; to factories, to trades, to commerce, to all industries. They are turned out into a world of fierce competition utterly unfit to compete, into a world of splendid opportunities without the training of intellectual power to enable them to take advantage of these opportunities. Is it strange that skilled workmen are so few, or that the unskilled, low-wage occupations are so overcrowded, or that our armies of unemployed are larger every time depression brings them into notice?

Carefully devised apprenticeship systems successfully operated in the majority of our factories would do much to augment the existing supply of skilled and efficient workmen. They would insure workmen being educated along definite lines, thereby meeting the demand for competent leaders and executives. They would offer to young men of limited means, who would otherwise be forced into that large and growing class of unskilled labor, an opportunity to learn a trade. They would increase the efficiency of a plant, an industry, a people.

APPRENTICES PAY FOR THEMSELVES

Many large and successful concerns who have had apprenticeship systems in operation for a period of years, are unanimous in their statements that apprentices do pay. If properly instructed and intelligently directed, their employment is more profitable than the employment of the so-called skilled workman who has been available in the past. Apprentices pay as producers during their term of service; as competent skilled journeymen when they have completed their course; and as industrially intelligent foremen and executives later on. These boys who leave at the termination of their apprenticeship course become staunch supporters of the mother shop, always ready to say a good word for it, as loyal as college graduates to their Alma Mater, an unequaled advertising medium.

Does it pay the employee to serve an apprenticeship? I firmly believe it does. He is raised from the ranks of unskilled labor and given an earning power which he could not otherwise command. He is taught to work intelligently and to apply his mind to his work, thus increasing his opportunities for further development and advancement.

An apprenticeship should make the following provisions for the employee: A proper term of service to insure ample time for thorough instruction; sufficient remuneration to support the apprentice during his term of service; instruction in the technique of the trade and allied studies; instruction in the manipulation and care of the appliances of the trade; the fostering of a spirit of ambition and a desire for increased knowledge; and full recognition, upon the completion of the course, of what has been accomplished, by a diploma such as has been adopted by the National Machine Tool Builders' Association.

Magnus M. Alexander, of the General Electric Works at West Lynn, Mass., spoke on "An Effective Apprenticeship Programme." He offered suggestions drawn from the big apprenticeship school established by the General Electric Works, saying in part:

MANUFACTURERS SHOULD HAVE SCHOOLROOMS IN THEIR FACTORIES

A rational apprenticeship system in its final analysis is, after all, a trade school conducted in a factory. This at once implies that provision should be made whereby the apprentices are taught skill and at the same time receive a training of the mind. Any effective system of industrial education, whether promoted through apprenticeship in the factory, private trade schools, or the public-school system, must be based on the broad principle of correlated instruction in the trade itself and the related sciences, and an adequate amount of general culture.

Large manufacturers can take care of both sides of the apprenticeship question by initiating the boys into the trade and also giving them such classroom instruction as will enable them to carry out their work intelligently. Smaller employers can achieve the same general result by calling upon the public schools or existing private educational agencies, for the educational development of the boys, while they themselves teach the trade in their shops where, after all, the trade can best be taught. Manufacturers of a community may also combine by establishing joint schoolrooms for their apprentices. In any case, there should be close relation between theory and practice; the theory should be taught in as practical a way as possible and the practical work developed along educational lines.

COMMERCIAL WORK ADVOCATED

Inasmuch as apprentices are trained for industrial life, they should, as far as possible, be trained in industrial life, or in other words, should work from the beginning under conditions that approximate those under which they will later on earn their living as industrial workers. Accordingly the apprentice should start on commercial work, for this shows him his position as an economic unit in the factory organization and thereby clinches his interest. He sees that the product of his work is to be a part of some useful machine rather than a plaything or an object of exhibition in some show-case and therefore learns to appreciate the value of time and money.

For this commercial work, apprentices should of course be paid. While the amount of wage will depend to a large degree on local conditions and the prevailing compensation for labor, experience has shown that a liberal treatment of the apprentice-wage question will prove beneficial in the long run; it will enable the employer to select a high grade of apprentices and will allow the boys coming from poor homes and distant places to take advantage of this opportunity of trade training. Classroom instruction should be carried on during the working period for one or two hours every day and apprentices should be paid the same wages as when working at the bench or machine. It is a mistake to expect boys to come to school in the evening physically buoyant and mentally alert after a long day's work; they are then not in condition to reap the greatest benefit from the instruction.

Employers have so far refrained from taking boys under sixteen years of age, believing that they are neither physically nor mentally able to serve an apprenticeship at an earlier age. My experience has proved, however, that excellent material can be found among healthy boys from fourteen to fifteen years of age.

TRADE SCHOOLS

The subject of trade schools was discussed by Mr. George M. Carman, of Lewis Institute, Chicago, John H. Shrigley, president of Williamson Free School of Trades, and Florence M. Marshall, director Boston Trade School for Girls. Mr. Carman distinguished sharply between technical training and trade training. He said:

Much of the special or technical instruction that is needed today can be obtained after leaving school better than in school, if the school had furnished that broad and generous foundation which the education of after-life cannot supply. Too much technical training cannot be given, but it can come too soon and at too great a cost if it crowds out other instruction which cannot be had except in school.

We must distinguish between technical instruction and the trade school. Technical instruction may be given throughout the entire school period. There is a place for it in the education of the child in the elementary school and of the youth and adult in the secondary school, the college, and the university. Technical instruction may be preliminary to the actual work of a trade or supplementary to it. The trade school is a secondary school that fits its students for a trade just as other secondary schools may fit their students for colleges.

MAKE ELEMENTARY EDUCATION MORE INDUSTRIAL

Elementary education should be much more industrial than at present. Technical instruction has a place in the elementary school. It should be adapted to the needs of all children regardless of differences in sex, aims, and future occupations. I agree with Professor Dewey that the child in the elementary school should be led to consider and to get some practical hold of the activities that center in the family—the house and its structure; clothing and its construction; food and its preparation; that the only adequate basis for that unity and correlation of studies that gives interest to the work of the elementary school and makes it effective, is the child's own activities of primary expression—his constructive powers.

Mr. Shrigley, of the Williamson Free School of Trades urged a school of practice making nothing for sale. He said in part:

SCHOOLS CAN TURN OUT JOURNEYMEN

I recommend that the trade-school day be made eight hours long on five days of the week and about three hours on Saturday; that the trades taught be governed to some extent by the school's environment; and that the shops be well equipped with tools and appliances embodying the types of those the pupils must handle after graduation. The teachers should be masters of their respective trades; they must have had good general educational advantages, be well versed in mechanical drawing and mathematics and capable of readily imparting their skill and knowledge to the pupils. It will not answer to have schoolmen with a limited practical knowledge of trades as mechanical teachers.

It is advisable to have representatives of mechanical avocations on the Boards of trade schools. All trade work should be instructional and nothing should be made for sale. To manufacture for the market would not be scholastic, neither should schools be run as competitors of legitimate business enterprises or paid labor. Manufacturers should be fair in their treatment of school graduates. It is entirely practicable to have the trade-school course so thorough in practice as well as in theory, that the graduates will be at once qualified to work as journeymen.

Miss Florence M. Marshall, director of the Boston Trade School for Girls, spoke on behalf of women in industry:

TEACH TRADES TO GIRLS

All history proves that women have a right to industry. Moreover, many lines of industry are dependent on woman's skill, such as industries dealing with clothing and household products, and woman herself is dependent on the opportunity to participate in constructive industry in order to reach her highest development. The fact that a number of industries are able to use women's labor in the unskilled processes, and that the present organization of industry prevents their becoming skilled workers without training, necessitates provision for trade education.

Assuming that a study of the locality has revealed that three-fourths of the girls enter industries with a grammar-school training or less; that there is no opportunity for them to enter skilled industries because of lack of training, even though the industries are in need of skilled workers; and that the kind of work girls are doing is detrimental physically and morally, is lowering to their standard of living and hence having a bad effect on our future homes, the following scheme for a school is mapped out.

NO TRADE TEACHING BEFORE END OF COMPULSORY SCHOOL AGE

The requirements for admission should be at the limit of the compulsory school age. The course of study should combine a school and a workshop, the type of workshop to be determined by the skilled industry of the locality. The academic work should be definitely applied to the trades being taught. The technical work should be organized so that each year should fit for some definite step in the trade, so that the girl who could spend but one year could at least gain entrance to a skilled industry, even though her work be of the simplest character. The academic teacher should have the power to adapt the work to the demands of the trades, giving practical problems aimed at practical results. The managers of the workshops should be trade workers with teaching power, but the shops should be conducted according to the principles of the trade.

Such a plan presents many difficulties. None are insurmountable. The disposition of the product of such workshops, even in large cities, could never mean serious competition if the main aim is to produce workers, and the product is used as a means to that end. The individual character of instruction, necessitating small classes, might seem to present a serious difficulty in per capita cost, but the experience of the two schools conducted on the workshop plan shows that the per capita rate can be reduced to a figure less than that of the manual-training high schools. The necessity of conducting such a school during working hours rather than school hours has presented no difficulties in the places where it has been tried.

In a debate on the round table on evening-school work, Louis Rouillion, director of the educational work of the Mechanics' Institute of New York, stated that training at night schools was the most practical form of trade teaching. He said in part:

EVENING SCHOOLS BEST FOR REAL VOCATIONAL WORK

In great Britain the evening vocational schools are wielding so large an influence that all attempts at day training are almost eclipsed. In this country by far the larger amount of real vocational training that is definite and effective, is being done in the evening schools. The reason is not far to seek.

The evening school does not interfere with the pupil's present earning capacity, nor with his hours of labor. It only asks for some of the time that would otherwise be lost in idleness or in the pursuit of amusement. In vocational training the evening school has a decided advantage in that it does not have to force or urge a boy to select this or that trade, but finds him already employed as a plumber, a mason, or a carpenter, with his ambition aroused to excel in his trade. The mere fact that a lad elects to attend an evening school puts him in the select class of the actively ambitious. This is one reason why the tone of the evening trade schools and mechanics' institutes is pitched to a higher and truer key than obtains in similar day-school work. The earnestness and intensity of purpose of these students is a well attested fact.

There is heard much talk about the self-sacrifice and hardships in a boy attending evening school after eight hours labor at his trade. Any one who has had to do with evening-school work knows how misplaced is such sympathy. The school work is seldom a burden to the student, in most cases it is a real pleasure, as attest the faces of these students at their school work. This actual joy in their work is frequently reflected in the attitude and feelings of the teacher. The reaction upon him is not one of exhausting his nervous vitality, but quite the contrary.

EVENING SCHOOLS TO SOLVE THE PROBLEMS

Evening schools will, undoubtedly, be the solution of our problem that will be the most generally accepted in the immediate future and it is along these lines that we may look for the major part of all real vocational training.

There are two somewhat clearly defined types of evening technical schools along which lines the immediate development of vocational training will probably occur. One type is the trade school pure and simple where instruction is confined to the technique of the trade. The other type gives instruction only in such school subjects as will add to the efficiency of the boy as a mechanic. A school may advantageously combine these two types. If a carpenter attends a school of the former type he constantly has his hammer and saw in hand and is confronted with the intricacies of stair building or house framing. If he attends a school of the second type he is taught to make and read architectural drawings, to estimate on a job, to cypher, and is, perhaps, taught something of the properties of the materials with which his trade brings him in contact.

Schools of these two types may run into highly specialized forms and contribute largely and effectively toward increased industrial efficiency.

Mr. L. D. Harvey, Superintendent of Schools, Menomonie, Wis., and president of the National Educational Association, and Thomas M. Balliet, dean of School of Pedagogy, New York University, presented the claims of the public schools to an adequate system of industrial education. The *Atlanta Journal* reports Mr. Harvey as follows:

"I am glad to see that Georgia has established the type of school that has heretofore been lacking in our country, the secondary schools, the district agricultural schools, for the country boys and the country girls, to teach them how to intelligently and efficiently live their lives in the country."

This tribute to Georgia's pioneer work in secondary education that reaches the farm was enthusiastically applauded. Mr. Harvey said that until recently a tremendous majority of country children over city pupils has gone almost without recognition.

Mr. Harvey told of industrial training in the schools of his own town. The boy pupils, he said, especially are realizing the attractive inducements offered them by the training in the way of increased learning capacity. They are each year continuing in greater numbers their grammar-school work to the high-school grades. Only two pupils dropped out from the promoted eighth-grade classes this last term, he said, and the year before every scholar moved up to the high school.

When a boy can step from the second grade of the high school with two years of manual training into certain lines of work and earn from $2.50 to $3 a day, more than his father is making after forty years of work, as he can in Menomonie, said Mr. Harvey, his parents and the boy himself all say there is something to the new training, and generally the boys want to continue through the other two years of the course, in the belief that even greater advantages will accrue to them.

WHAT IS NEEDED

"I want to see some system that will hold our boys and girls in the public schools as long as possible. I don't want to see any system that will put a premium upon early withdrawal from school."

Mr. Balliet said in part:

MAKE MANUAL TRAINING PRACTICAL

So far as the elementary schools (apart from special vocational schools) are concerned, the following forms of vocational and industrial training are possible: cooking and sewing; manual training for all through the entire course; drawing, color work, design and the elements of industrial art for all. The closest possible co-ordination between the drawing and manual training should be made.

In manual training mere exercises should be eliminated and "projects," which appeal to the interest of children, made. The teacher may be interested in the exercises involved in the "projects," the pupil is interested solely in the thing made. When children make things which they are not even willing to sell, then manual training for them is industrial education. The product has high value for them, although it may have no market value.

Manual training of this kind appeals most strongly to children's interest, forms a natural transition to strictly vocational industrial training, and forms the broader training on which specialization in vocational training should be based. It bears the same relation to the latter as a liberal education does to professional training in the higher institutions of learning.

SHOULD ESTABLISH ELEMENTARY VOCATIONAL SCHOOLS

Special vocational schools should also be provided which would take the pupils at the age of twelve, regardless of the grade to which they belong in school, and give them a four years' course fitting them for some trade or vocation. Most communities will not be ready for several years or more to undertake the establishment of this type of schools although several cities have already done so.

In this type of trade school it will be difficult to hold boys until they complete the course. There is therefore danger of "flooding" the market with half trained boys to which just objections can be made by labor unions. Labor unions themselves can do much to prevent this by refusing to admit to membership boys who have not completed their course in school or as apprentices. Labor unions must ultimately have a voice in the management of trade schools as they now have in Germany.

We must establish evening trade schools in the shops of manual-training high schools. This has been done in a certain number of cities where there is such a day high school, and as this is the easiest sort of trade school—and the least expensive—to establish, it should be, under such circumstances, the first one to be undertaken.

OVERHAUL EVENING-SCHOOL SYSTEM

Our whole evening-school system needs overhauling. Our evening schools ought to provide for instruction in English and give the elements of the elementary school studies to foreigners. This is a problem which no other nation has to solve on so large a scale. They should provide facilities for pursuing the studies of the day elementary schools and high schools, to pupils who are forced to leave these schools. They ought to develop a large variety of vocational schools, the number and kind to be determined by the industrial and commercial conditions of the community. Extensive provision should be made in our evening schools for a high grade of instruction in industrial art and for this the instruction in drawing and design in the elementary schools should serve as a good preparation.

We should open trade schools in the shops of technical high schools where such exist. This would involve only very moderate expense. The preference should be given to men who are already at work either as apprentices or as journeymen. There are enough of such to fill this type of schools. This policy can, to some extent, also be followed in other evening trade schools. It will win the support, or at least disarm the criticism, of labor unions.

It is interesting to note the attitude of organized labor as expressed by its representative at this meeting.

Leon C. Sutton, editor of the *Labor World* of New York and New Jersey, spoke on "The Wage Earners' Benefit from an Effective System of Industrial Education." He urged the point of view of the wage earner, saying:

ORGANIZED LABOR MUST BE RECOGNIZED

To some few manufacturers in the United States who want to have educated, at public expense, young men and young women, who, upon their graduation from an industrial school, can be used as a club to lessen the rate of wages or can be used as strike breakers, an effective system of industrial education means one thing. To the wage earner, on the other hand, who wants to have his children taught better than he was taught, it means something far different. He has a different standard. He wants the children taught not merely dexterity of hand but he wants them taught in addition to the theory of mechanics, the reading of blue prints and the use of tools, also the history of commerce, the ancient guilds, the origin and growth of trades unionism, the story of the struggles through which it has gone, something of what real, true unionism means in the betterment of the men and women of our country today, so that after their years of study in the industrial school they do not come forth with their diploma to eat up their fellow human beings by inferior work at lesser wage during longer hours, and thus be an aid in undoing just what trades unionism has struggled so long and earnestly to win. They must start on their career at the foot of the ladder, well-drilled, of course, with a loyalty to their trade and a pride in their craftmanship and yet a feeling that they have much to learn by practical experience.

ORGANIZED LABOR MUST AID

We believe that in any effective system of industrial education from which the wage earner is to derive a benefit, organized labor must have a part. The young men and the young women educated in the various handicrafts which they have chosen in the trade schools, will be either the friends or the enemies of organized labor.

It is not necessary that the pupils should be taught to be rabid unionists or to be strike breakers, but they should have their consciences awakened and they should learn what trades unionism means, what it has accomplished, and what it hopes to attain. When once they have been taught to think we will risk the rest and an effective system of industrial education can confer no greater benefit upon the future workingmen and workingwomen than to teach them to think, in addition to using their hands.

We have said that an effective system of industrial education must include the co-operation of the trades unionist. The pedagogue sees in theory the value of such a training, the manufacturer sees the value of its productiveness, the trades unionist sees its human side and these young men and young women are to be his successors. He remembers his trials and his sacrifices and he goes with natural caution, but admit him to his proper place among the boards of control and among the practical instructors, give due weight to his advice, and then his attitude of suspicion will be turned to one of cordial co-operation.

INDIVIDUAL ASSIGNMENTS IN GEOGRAPHY

LUNA E. BIGELOW
State Normal School, New Paltz, N. Y.

In a previous article,[1] mention was made of individual or group assignments. These individual assignments in the classes of the elementary school, especially of the fifth, sixth, seventh, and eighth grades, can be made a potent factor for strong work.

The social instinct of the child rebels against repeating recitations made by other members of the class. But he eagerly adds to those recitations, or offers to search for further information, whenever the opportunity offers. This very eagerness on the part of the child to contribute something of vital interest to the class is the foundation for this individual work. With this impetus the child will work diligently and long that he may entertain well, as he takes great pride in making his contribution worth while.

Although this method can be carried out in all subjects of the elementary school curriculum, geography and history are most easily adapted to it. There is, of course, a certain body of facts that every child must know. But beside all this there is a wide range of geographical knowledge from which the child may select to suit his own taste. Here the teacher should guide the child to cultivate what is best suited to his temperament, and teach him to enjoy much that he had ignored. To guide the child thus, means strenuous effort on the part of the teacher; but such effort pays.

Much work can be saved if a card catalogue containing a list of countries to be studied is kept, as in selecting assignments for one country those for others will be noted.

The material for this work is found in magazines, books of travel, works on art and architecture, series of geographical

[1] November number, p. 113.

stories, some of the classics, and in many United States government publications. With a public library to use the teacher will find little difficulty in making a beginning.

Little can be said as to selection and elimination of material, as each teacher must adapt the subject-matter to her class. After a teacher has selected and organized her material, she must then consider her class and give each pupil an article suited to his particular temperament and so of real interest to him. The child should then study his article and report on it the following day. This report should take the form of a short lecture. The little lecturer should stand before his audience and talk to them, showing any illustrations he may have to emphasize his talk, or dramatizing any of the manners he may choose to.

It is well to have several children give reports from varied sources on a large topic. Then they will be able to organize the reports and work out for themselves that body of facts which must be known.

This method of study will train them to compare and question intelligently the textbooks, and to weigh the evidences of books, magazines, and newspapers. It will teach them where and how to look for information on any given subject. It will also be one aid toward forming good habits in reading for later life.

Its influence on oral language is powerful. In one seventh grade class which I took, not a single child would give a recitation of more than one short choppy sentence. I immediately began individual assignments in the geography and in one month every child could talk for at least five minutes in reporting an article or chapter of a book. At first the vocabulary was meager. pronunciation incorrect, and grammatical construction atrocious. Nevertheless, no child was corrected while talking before the class; but gradually by private discussions the children freed themselves of all this and were able to talk fluently.

Occasionally, written reports are advisable, as a result of the children's own search. The written papers of a meager two or three lines of errors at the beginning of the month changed to one or two pages of fairly well written subject-matter at the end. This shows that when the children have definite and interesting knowledge on a subject they are able to put it into written expression.

The general results of work of this kind are far-reaching. It oftentimes awakens an interest in the home of the child and shows the parents their opportunities. It broadens the child's horizon so that he appreciates other conditions than his own. It puts a vital life and enthusiasm into the schoolroom that has not existed there before. It makes for general culture not only for the pupil but for the teacher as well.

The illustrations given below are ones which have been used in the seventh grade here within a year. Those of the industries are being worked out as this goes to print. No geographical series nor government publications are on these lists, although they were used and furnish excellent material.

INDUSTRIES

"Our Mines and Quarries," *The National Geographical Magazine,* July, 1905, p. 234.

I. SILVER

"Cobalt, a City of Silver," *Harper's Weekly,* April 11, 1908, p. 18.
"The Alamos District of Mexico," *Harper's Weekly,* April 11, 1908, p. 21.
"Bullfrog and Its Suburbs," *Harper's Weekly,* April 11, 1908, p. 20.

II. GOLD

"Gold and Silver Production of the United States," *Scientific American Supplement,* March 20, 1907, p. 26119.

III. COAL

"How Long Will Our Coal Supply Last?" *Review of Reviews,* September, 1907, p. 335.
"Will Our Coal Reserves Last?" *Review of Reviews,* April, 1907, p. 479.
"Our Great Grandfathers' Coal," *Harper's Weekly,* April 25, 1908, p. 29.
"Coal Reserves of the United States," *Scientific American Supplement,* February 1, 1908, p. 77.
"Advantages of Being a Coal Miner," *Harper's Weekly,* May 16, 1908, p. 31.

IV. PETROLEUM

"A Great American Industry," *Independent,* March 5, 1908, p. 511.
"Petroleum and Its Refinement," *Scientific American Supplement,* May 4, 1907, p. 26195.
"Oil Transportation Industry," *Review of Reviews,* December, 1907, p. 738.

"Standard Oil on Its Industrial Side," *Review of Reviews,* November, 1907, p. 610.

"The Large Corporation," *World's Work,* August, 1908, p. 10571.

"Production of Oil," *Outlook,* September 28, 1907.

V. IRON

"Iron Ore Reserves," *Scientific American Supplement,* March 14, 1908.

"Position Occupied by the United States in the World's Products," *Scientific American,* January 19, 1907, p. 71.

Rocheleau, *Geography of Commerce and Industry,* p. 118.

VI. COPPER

Rocheleau, *Geography of Commerce and Industry,* p. 115.

INDIA

I. LIFE, SOCIAL

William E. Curtis, *Modern India,* chap. xx, "Famines and Their Antidotes;" chap. xxiv, "Caste and the Women of India."

"Children of the World," *National Geographical Magazine,* February, 1908.

John Finnemore, *Peeps at Many Lands—India,* chap. xiv, "At the Court of a Native Prince;" chaps. xvii, xviii, "In the Jungle;" chaps. xix, xx, "In an Indian Village."

Herbert Compton, *Indian Life in Town and Country,* chap. iii, "Manners and Customs;" chap. ix, "The Indian at Home."

"Caste, the Curse of India," *Cosmopolitan Magazine,* December, 1906.

"Letters from an Indian Bungalow," *Outlook,* September 5 to October 3, 1908.

Stoddard's *Lectures,* Vol. IV.

II. CITIES

William E. Curtis, *Modern India,* chap. ii, "The City of Bombay;" chap. xvi, "The Quaint Old City of Delhi; chap. xxvii, "Benares the Sacred City;" chap. xxx, "Calcutta the Capital."

"The Buried City of Ceylon," *National Geographical Magazine,* November, 1906.

John Finnemore, *Peeps at Many Lands,* chap. i, "The Gateway of India;" chap. xi, "The Sacred City of the Hindoos;" chap. xii, "The Capital of India."

Stoddard's *Lectures,* Vol. IV.

III. ARCHITECTURE AND ART

"Discoveries of Grandhara Art in British India," *Scientific American,* October 3, 1908.

William E. Curtis, *Modern India,* chap. xiv, "The Architecture of the Moguls;" chap. xv, "The Most Beautiful of Buildings—Taj Majah."

IV. COMMERCE

"Canals and Railways," *Scientific American,* April 21, 1906.

William E. Curtis, *Modern India,* chap. viii, "The Railways of India."

"A Nation in the Making," *Review of Reviews,* October, 1907.

"Commerce of India," *World To-Day,* November, 1907.

William E. Curtis, *Modern India,* chap. xxix, "Cotton, Tea, Opium."

"Post-Office of India," *Blackwell's Magazine,* December, 1907.

V. RELIGION

"Christianity in India," *Contemporary,* May, 1908.

Stoddard's *Lectures,* Vol. IV.

John Finnemore, *Peeps at Many Lands,* chap. xv, "The Religious Mendicants."

"The Parsees and the Towers of Silence at Bombay, India," *National Geographical Magazine,* December, 1905.

SPAIN

I. LIFE IN SPAIN

The World and Its People—Modern Europe, Vol. V, chap. xvi, "In Sunny Spain and Portugal."

The World's Famous Places and People, Vols. I, II, "Spain."

Stanford's Compendium of Geography, Vol. I, chap. x, "The Kingdom of Spain."

"Spanish Impressions," *Scribners,* October, 1907.

"Home of Holy Grail," *Harper's Magazine,* April, 1907.

"Nineteenth-Century Spain," *Quarterly Review,* January, 1908.

II. ARCHITECTURE

Washington Irving, *The Alhambra,* "The Journey;" "The Palace;" "The Mysterious Chambers;" "The Court of Lions."

"Southern Spain," Burton Holmes' *Lectures,* Vol. IV.

III. PEOPLE

Our Little Spanish Cousins, chap. ii, "School Days;" chap. iii, "Visit to Hacienda;" chap. vi, "The Holidays;" chap. vii, "Easter in Seville;" chap. x, "Games and Sports."

RUSSIA

I. ST. PETERSBURG

M. H. Wade, *Our Little Russian Cousins,* pp. 10–12, "Origin of St. Petersburg."

E. R. Shaw, *Big People and Little People of Other Lands,* pp. 73, 74, "The Ice Palace."

Taylor, *Northern Travel in Greece and Russia,* chap. xxx, "The Kremlin;" chap. xxxiv, "The Palaces of St. Petersburg."

Stoddard's *Lectures,* Vol. VI, pp. 246–57.

"The Hermitage Museum of St. Petersburg," Burton Holmes' *Lectures,* Vol. VIII, pp. 33–39.

II. GOVERNMENT

Palmer, *Russian Life in Town and Country,* chap. ix, "Rural Self-Government."

Sanford, Compendium of Geographical Europe, pp. 666–68, "Government of Russia."

I. Hapgood, *Russian Rambles,* pp. 228–30.

"The Russian Duma," *Independent,* July 9, 1908, p. 66.

"The Duma Holding Its Own," *Review of Reviews,* September, 1908, p. 280.

"The Power behind the Czar," *Independent,* March 19, 1908, pp. 610–20 (long).

"Punishments; The Russian Torture Chamber," *Outlook,* September 5, 1908, p. 7.

"Happenings in the Russian Empire," *Review of Reviews,* September, 1908, p. 280.

Shaw, *Big People and Little People of Other Lands,* pp. 50–55, "The Crowning of the Czar."

I. Hapgood, *Russian Rambles,* chap. i, "Passports, Police, and Post-Offices in Russia."

III. RELIGION

Sanford, *Compendium of Geographical Europe,* Vol. I, pp. 677–79.

Burton Holmes' *Lectures,* pp. 144–57.

"Church Festivals."

I. Hapgood, *Russian Rambles,* pp. 115–20.

I. Hapgood, *Russian Rambles,* pp. 220–28, "Catacombs in Cathedral of the Assumption."

Taylor, *Northern Travels in Greece and Russia,* pp. 296, 297.

Shaw, *Big People and Little People of Other Lands,* pp. 28–35, "Cathedrals of Russia."

I. Hapgood, *Russian Rambles,* pp. 228–30.

Stoddard's *Lectures,* Vol. VI, pp. 237–42.

Taylor, *Northern Travels in Greece and Russia,* chap. xxxiii, p. 371.

"Christmas in Russia and Her Provinces," *Travel Magazine,* December, 1907.

IV. COMMERCE

Rocheleau, *Geography of Commerce and Industry,* chap xii, p. 362, "Russian Commerce."

Shaw, *Big People and Little People of Other Lands,* pp. 73–79, "The Great Fair of Nizni-Novgorod."

I. Hapgood, *Russian Rambles,* chap. xii, p. 348.

M. C. Smith, *Life in Asia,* pp. 241–46, "The Country through Which the Great Siberian Railway Passes;" pp. 246–48, "The Great Siberian Railway;" pp. 249–51, "Travel before the Great Siberian Railway."

I. Hapgood, *Russian Rambles,* pp. 111–15, "The Russian Market."

Shaw, *Big People and Little People of Other Lands,* pp. 36, 37.

"Russia's Caviar Export," *Harper's Weekly,* September 19, 1908, p. 31.

V. SOCIAL LIFE

Morfill, *Russia,* chap. xiii to p. 344, "Social Life before Peter the Great;" pp. 352–57, "Manners and Customs."

Palmer, *Russian Life in Town and Country,* chap. iii, "Country Life in Summer;" chap. xvii, "Country Life in Winter;" chap. xi, "Jewish Town Life."

Shaw, *Big People and Little People of Other Lands,* pp. 42–48, "A Peasant Village."

Burton Holmes' *Lectures,* pp. 130–35, "Theaters of Moscow."

"Tolstoy's Birthday," *Outlook,* April 25, 1908, p. 904; *Harper's Weekly,* September 16, 1908, p. 16.

Stoddard's *Lectures,* Vol. VI, pp. 312–16, "The Foundling Hospital;" Vol. VI, pp. 244–46, "The Alexander Column."

VI. LITERATURE

Morfill, *Russia,* pp. 317–21, "Early Literature;" pp. 335, 336, "Change in Literature."

VII. OCCUPATIONS

Sanford, *Compendium of Geographical Europe,* pp. 679–85, "Agriculture and Manufactures."

VIII. THE EUROPEANIZATION OF RUSSIA

Review of Reviews, July, 1908, p. 107.

IX. PASSING UPON RUSSIAN FINANCES

Review of Reviews, July, 1908, p. 28.

THE KINDERGARTEN PROGRAMME

BERTHA PAYNE
The School of Education

The kindergarten programme is to the kindergarten what the course of study is to the school. Usage has established the word programme, in this particular sense, until it is now so firmly fixed that the difficulty of dislodging it, to secure more uniform terminology, would probably cost more effort than it would be worth. Moreover, "course of study" has a connotation of definite conscious purpose on the part of the pupil, which scarcely describes the very playful and indirect modes of learning in the kindergarten. Suffice it to say then, that by programme we mean such organization of children's interests and activities as may fitly be made for children of from four to six years of age. The experiences chosen for them, the materials used, the playthemes and their treatment all represent a selection of what seems to offer the best conditions for growth.

This paper is a discussion of the governing principles of selection, those that we find in Froebel's theories and those that have been reinforced or modified by modern thought, with some illustrations of typical differences in method and aim engendered by different emphasis of principles.

I. FROEBELIAN PRINCIPLES

Froebel left no kindergarten programme as a distinct model to be followed, or as a type illustrative of his ideas of organization. Apparently he had the simplest possible form of organization of their total activity from day to day and from week to week. It is certain that his children took walks, worked in the garden, played games out of doors and in, looked at pictures, listened to stories, sang songs, and played at making and building. Through it all there is no indication of a typical treatment of subjects, no hint of a logical development of "subject." Whether one searches the *Mother Play Book,* the *Pedagogics of the Kindergarten,* or the *Education of Man,* the result is the same. We find continuity in short sequences, short steps in organized play, but not long series of related incidents, "worked out" in handwork, songs, games, and stories.

This simplicity is found in the imitative plays and tiny dramas of the *Mother Play Book.* These plays have been taken by many American kindergartners as a long sequential basis for a year's work on which the activities of the kindergarten are founded. That Froebel intended this kind of use is not only problematic but impossible. They are types of experience which a child has and directions to the mother of the way in which to treat these experiences to make them fruitful through play, in which the mirror is held up to the world about of animal life and to the activities of people in the home, in industrial occupations and in festivals.

The same simplicity is to be seen in most German kindergartens today, but too often without the spontaneity and naïveté of the Froebel whose call from table-work to games, was, "Komm' Kinder, lass' uns singen and springen."

It is easily seen that while Froebel was the apostle of continuity in education and while he found it both in "short steps" and in the "long run," the programme as a highly organized continuous course of topics and developing method is a post-Froebelian achievement. The kindergartner has been forced to organize on the basis of the gift sequence in forms of life, beauty, and knowledge, modeled on those suggested by Froebel, on the typical plays of the *Mother Play,* if she be orthodox, or upon some scheme of her own devising. The programmes that are printed in the magazines, that are seen in operation in the kindergartens, show the individual bias and temperament of the kindergartner, her training, and, in general, her philosophy of life. The evolution has been away from the primitive spontaneity of Froebel and often toward over-intellectualization and formalization.

There is great diversity in the modern programme, so great

that it is difficult for the layman to determine what the kindergarten actually stands for. This diversity arises not only from natural causes, but from the varying stress that is laid upon one aspect or another of Froebel's many-sided theories. The person who believes, by temperament and training, most in his gospel of freedom and individual development, lays stress on creativeness and initiative. She who believes most strenuously in the doctrine of order and sees the gifts and the exercises with them as a demonstration of orderly process, leans toward the method of direction. The one who is imbued with belief in symbolism will choose her exercises to embody and convey to the little souls the ultimate truth of which the gift forms or the plays are outward signs, that the child's mind may, by "a series of effluxes," "impose its native forms upon the objective data of experience."

The remarkable contribution of Miss Susan Blow [1] to this subject comes at a most opportune time, and by its vigorous expositions and clear-cut definitions will be of great value in focusing attention on attempts that have recently been made to shape the current of children's ideas and habits under the guidance of definite principles. We shall not all agree with Miss Blow's classification, and many of us will not admit that her characterizations are typical of the largest and most sane existing movements in each type programme. But that is a matter of course and does not impair the value of the book to the thoughtful reader.

Truly, as Miss Blow shows us, influences have drifted in upon the kindergarten from the world of social and educational theory and have left their characteristic mark upon the molding of the kindergarten plan. Each breeze has brought influences for both good and evil, without doubt, but the general effect will be wholesome in the final summing up. It is a merciful fact in the make-up of the human mind that it cannot keep its psychology, its social theory, and its daily living in water-tight compartments and keep on moving. The children are not wholly suffer-

[1] Susan E. Blow, *Educational Issues in the Kindergarten*, Appleton & Co., 1908.

ers from this law of our consciousness. Having lived through the many phases through which the kindergarten has passed it is my belief that these phases are not the microbe diseases of its infancy, but stages in its evolution in which it has fed upon the thought found in its habitat and that it has absorbed nutriment, cast off, appropriated, assimilated, and is, by these acts of assimilative energy growing into a larger stature and finding by this means a more discriminating focus for its activities. The kindergarten has not been deformed by its stretching and groping after a clearer light, nor is it necessary to put it into a straight-jacket to bring it back to the exact form and measure of Hegelian mold out of which it sprang and from which it has begun to evolve.

It seems a most necessary thing at this juncture of kindergarten affairs to restate some of the familiar Frobelian principles of education, to reinterpret in part, and to indicate the emphasis, the reinforcement, or the departures that the general trend of modern psychology and evolutionary theory demand.

Froebel's doctrines and his life-work have a significance, even to those who are not directly interested in forwarding the kindergarten as a step in education; they have a place in the history of modern thought. Belonging as he does to the group in which we may put Goethe, Schiller, Lessing, Coleridge, and Wordsworth, he forms with them a kind of link between the German idealistic school of philosophy and modern thought. These men, the poets, the dramatists, the novelist, and the educational reformer, brought what were to them root principles from the regions of pure thought and realized them in the world of people and social forces through the medium of their art. In them the germinal principles of Hegelian thought become vital and dramatic, and through art they were made the possession of the world. Through them this idealistic philosophy created a hospitable atmosphere for the doctrine of evolution that followed, and which has remade our physical, our social, and our mental sciences.

The concepts of unity, the unity of man and nature, the process of growth as development, the indwelling of energy which is one energy in all creation and the meaning of creative acts as self-revelations, the finding of truth in the symbol, all these are the basic principles, which are as warp to the art of their weaving. Goethe says:

Wouldst thou truly study nature?
Seek the whole in every feature
Whole at each point, at each point canst thou learn all;
Only examine thine own heart,
Whether thou shell or kernel art.

Tennyson, reflecting this viewpoint writes his lines:

Flower in the crannied wall,
I pluck you out of your crannies,
Hold you here, root and all, in my hand.
Little flower, could I but understand
What you are, root and all, and all in all
I would know what God and man is.

Schiller in his poem of the "Artist" says:

The truth that had for centuries to wait;
The truth that reason had grown old to find
Lay in the symbol of the fair and great,
Felt from the first by every child-like mind.

And as a final whip to the flagging creative energies of the doubting human Goethe says:

Produce, produce, produce! Though it be the smallest infinitesimal fraction of a worldkin, yet—produce!

Wordsworth writes of the significance of nature:

Wisdom and Spirit of the Universe!
Thou soul that art the eternity of thought
. . . .
not in vain
By day and starlight thus from my first down
Of childhood didst thou intertwine for me
The passions that build up one human soul;
Not with the near and vulgar works of man,
But with high objects, with enduring things
With life and nature.

Not only does Froebel's theory bear this quality of binding the old to the new but in himself, in his own life, he combined the attributes of philosopher and observer. While his method of procedure was distinctly governed by a priori premises he nevertheless went to children with a most open feeling for the worth of their expressions as giving cheer to their processes of growth. This feeling of respect for the meaning of childrens' acts, this respect for their impulsive tendencies, for their primitive desires at once places Frobel in touch with modern thought despite his a priori philosophy.

While Froebel left no "ear's outline" he did make provision for continuity. He planned for plays that would progressively utilize his powers of discovery, invention, and control in the adaptation of the play materials.

The previous papers [2] in this series have dealt with the gifts, that important set of Froebelian materials, a succeeding paper will deal with the scarcely less important kindergarten occupations. But as we cannot deal with the organization of activities in the kindergarten programme without touching these topics it is necessary at least to review the principles embodied in them by Froebel, in order to be clear on points of criticism or emphasis. On this ground the indulgence of the reader is begged, if there is in this paper something of repetition.

In these gifts and occupations themselves, in the descriptions to be found of the gifts in Froebel's Pedagogics, in the *Mother Play Book* and the *Education of Man,* we find asserted and reasserted definitely and comprehensively the basic principles on which any course of study or programme for kindergarten or school must rest. These principles may be classified by the student of Froebel into psychologic, social, and religio-philosophic principles according as they are directed toward the development of mind in the individual, in the working out of social relationships or in securing an interpretation of the plan of the universe.

Psychological

1. The child is a self-active being whose impulses lead to all-sided growth.
2. The mind is a unit.

[2] Patty Smith Hill, "Value and Limitation of Froebel's Gifts," *Elementary School Teacher,* November and December, 1908.

3. Growth is continuous.

4. Being continuous, growth proceeds by stages, each stage growing out of the preceding, conditioned by it, and showing special powers and characteristics.

5. Infancy is the stage in which the child is gaining control over his own movements, through sensori-motor adjustments, and gaining through them an apprehension of meanings bound up in the objective world.

6. In early childhood the rise of speech, locomotion, and imitative play brings him into possession of a wider range of bodily control, more definite imagery, and a larger consciousness of related meanings.

7. Truth is felt by the child before it is clearly perceived. Play nourishes the "feeling" for the true and implicit in play creations.

8. As boyhood follows childhood, play merges into work, play ends are replaced by ends which the boy recognizes as on a plane more nearly approaching those of adults. Persistence and self-criticism are the powers which enter into productive work.

9. During boyhood the individual becomes capable of reflection, of discovering principles of connection, and of holding them clearly in consciousness.

One contribution of Froebel's psychology is his stress upon the *act* as the point of departure in the knowing process. The increment of impulsive act is knowledge and the renewal of the impulse. In this he anticipates the emphasis of modern educational psychology.

> You will foster his impulsive movements, exercise his strength, prepare him through doing, for seeing through the exertion of his power for its comprehension. In a word you will seek through self-activity to lead him to self-knowledge.[3]

Another citation from the *Commentaries* has a most modern ring:

> How different are the motor activities from the activities of sense, and yet how each reacts upon the other. Each one of our little plays has shown the recoil of movement upon sensation, or of sensation upon movement![4]

[3] *Mottoes and Commentaries of Froebel's Mother Play,* p. 74.

[4] *Op. cit.,* p. 185.

In the following quotation we find a clear statement of the sequence of mental development on the side of knowledge:

> In your education of your child, therefore, let your point of departure be an effort to strengthen and develop his body, his limbs, and his senses. From the development of body, limbs, and sense, rise to their use. Move from impressions to perceptions, from perceptions to attentive observation and contemplation, from the recognitions of particular objects to their relations and dependencies, from the healthy life of the body to the healthy life of the spirit, from thought immanent in experience to pure thinking. Ascend thus from sensation to thought, from external observation to internal apprehension, from physical combination to spiritual synthesis, from a formal to a vital intellectual grasp, and so to the culture of the understanding, from the observation of phenomena and their relation to the recognition of their final cause and hence to the development and culture of life-grasping reason.[5]

Social

1. The child is a being actuated by impulses that relate him to others from the dawn of intelligence.

2. Recognition is mutely sought before speech begins; sympathy is sought in the child's pleasures, griefs, knowledge, and discoveries.

3. Speech and imitation become the great means of communication and social learning. By means of imitation the child wrests the meaning from the acts of others, while by speech he enters into conceptual systems, his own and others. Speech becomes a useful instrument for the satisfaction of desires, whether material or intellectual.

The emphasis laid by Froebel upon the community of playing and working individuals as an indispensable condition for securing education, even the education of a little child, constitutes another contribution to education.

Philosophical

1. Unity embraces all things.

2. The divine essence pervades all things.

3. All things are creations of the divine.

4. That which God creates partakes of his nature, and is in turn essentially creative.

[5] *Op. cit.*, p. 59.

5. The human being is the highest earthly expression of this creative energy, must be developed through creative activity.

6. The end and aim of all things is to develop and so reveal this divine essence.

7. The last stage of this self-revelation is in the recognition of his destiny, his oneness with the source of all things.

Educational Propositions

1. Education can but remove obstacles to self-revelation, and assist its course. Education should therefore be following, not prescriptive. Freedom is the condition essential to development.

2. Since all things have proceeded from the divine unity, the child can find himself mirrored in the lesser things of nature, in the forms and laws, structures and functions of plant, and animal. Therefore a study of nature is one great means of approaching clear consciousness of divine unity. To the little child this comes in the form of impersonations and play.

3. The family is the type of social organization. A co-operative community is the requisite environment for the growing child, into which he enters by play and by actual participation in its industries and festivals.

4. Intellectual analysis, synthesis, and reflective thought belong to the stage of the boyhood and youth, rising through education nearer to the goal, which is clearness toward his relations to the trinity—nature, man, God.

What is the basis afforded by the theory of evolution? How does it differ from Froebel's thought? What effects has its adoption on kindergarten procedure, and especially upon the programme? These are some of the questions that naturally arise.

II. MODIFICATIONS SUGGESTED BY THE EVOLUTIONARY POINT OF VIEW

The theory of evolution makes the child one with all nature in these essential points:

1. He is a growing and changing organism.

2. Growth goes on by means of his own efforts to adjust himself to his environing world.

3. His equipment for this adjustment is his stock of reflexes, instincts, and impulses to act which throw him into contact with the objective world.

4. Out of these contacts come stimuli which are registered, held to, or avoided, and which furnish him through his reactions upon them with sensations, perceptions, and images which he can manipulate as memory or imagination and from which he derives his concepts and conceptual world. His reactions to stimuli either grow into larger, more efficient ways of dealing with this world of things and forces, or harden into fixed habits.

Educational Propositions

1. The clue to education consists in controlling the stimuli so that the responses which the child makes will be the most fruitful for him in terms of imagery, concept, and control.

2. As the individual shapes his growth by reactions upon stimuli, so society has shaped itself. The school is one instrument of society for perpetuating its ideals and habits, or for enlarging and purifying them according as it selects school conditions.

Psychological Modifications

What have we in this evolutionary theory not already given us in the psychologic insights and philosophic outlook of Froebel? An examination of the two plans readily yields a parallel. It shows almost every important generalization that Froebel made on the process of mental growth with this most weighty addition: *We now know not merely that such and such is the order of growth, but we know with some definiteness how such and such processes affect later processes. In other words, we know more about the causal links in the series.*

We know, for example, both in brain terms and in mind terms more of the interrelation of sense and motor processes. We know also that certain brain conditions parallel mental states. We know something of the physiological accompaniments of emotional states and their consequent reaction on body conditions, as well as the converse. We know more intimately the instinctive side of life. We have at our command a remarkable study of the mode in which imitation provides for the intellectual control demanded in invention. The unitary nature of consciousness is affirmed by Froebel; and since his time this conception has replaced the old faculty psychology. The motor nature of consciousness which Froebel assumed is verified. But when we come to the subject of the growth of concepts we do not find the same confirmation for Froebel's belief in the inner norms or germs of thought which project themselves, so to speak, upon the objective world and in this world find their correspondences. This belief of Froebel's gave rise to his symbol, the awakener of the inner germ which rises thereby into a general idea or feeling of truth.

Modern psychology shows that the concept gradually emerges as the running together of like elements met over and over again in varying complexes, until they become in themselves *one,* an experience, a thought, which is the result of a long process, from dimness to clearness. The view of symbolism, then, which holds, for example, that the reason why a babe is charmed with a clock is because of his presentiment of the meaning and value of time is not supported by modern psychology. Nor is the belief that as an infant gazes at a ball it has a dim presentiment of the great truths of which it is a symbol. The view that makes many, countless, typical experiences yield their gradually rising increment of thought, until it climbs above the threshold into clearness is justified.

It follows therefore—and this is a main line of cleavage—that whatever in individual kindergarten exercise or programme seems to force the earlier point of view, regardless of children's own interest or continuity, is questioned.

To sum up, this difference is also one of emphasis. Froebel and many of his followers emphasized the *innate mocrocosmic germ,* while evolutionary thought emphasizes the effort of the mind-body-organism to adjust itself to the stress and strain, the push and pull of the outer world. The stress of modern thought falls upon the value of the inner impulse to act, rather than the inner germinal idea, not upon the innate prescience of meaning in the symbol, but upon the *act which converts the symbol into meaning.*

Social Affirmations

What does modern evolutionary theory contribute to Froebel's views on social education? It gives most absolute affirmation of their validity. It is scarcely necessary to review the modern grounds of justification, they are so familiar to all. The biological significance of play is undoubted. The relation of instinctive modes of play to racial activities is a hypothesis that adds weight to Froebel's view of racial stages and their reflection in child life.[6]

The creative character of play is recognized. The need of direction and partial control of play-activities is insisted upon for educational ends. No class of educators looks upon the Santa Barbara experiment in the "free-play-programme" as final in this regard. Belief in play has resulted in a great national organization for its promotion through the establishment and maintenance of playgrounds and play festivals. It has spread upward through the social settlement to play and art for young people of all ages.

The game is a recognized social instrument to entrain to group action, leadership, and self-subordination. The social imitation play is recognized as an adjustment by the child to the social aspects of his environment, yielding social comprehension. Similarly constructive plays add to this increment that of intellectual control of materials and forces.

The school is recognized as ideally a community, not an aggregation—a working and playing group of children, taking upon themselves social initiation. A comparison of Froebel's ideal school sketched in the chapters on the "Boyhood of Man" and "Man as a Scholar and Pupil" [7] with the school of Dr. Dewey's "School and Society" shows how prophetic was Froebel's social insight.

[The conclusion of this article which will appear in the February number will be upon "The Present Situation."—Ed.]

[6] Froebel, *The Education of Man*, pp. 40, 41.

[7] *Op. cit.*

EDITORIAL NOTES

One of the features of the recent meetings was a tendency to enrich and liberalize the content of technical training of all kinds.

A Broader Interpretation of Technical Training

"Teach our children to think, and we will risk the rest" summarizes the attitude of organized labor. How far this attitude has exerted a chastening and restraining influence upon the association an outsider could not judge. It was noticeable that the men chosen to represent the manufacturers were those who were able to approach the subject in the scientific attitude of the trained student. It must have been reassuring to the labor representative as well as to the educator to hear Mr. Alexander say, "Industrial education must prepare for both work and recreation" and also that "a rational apprentice system is nothing but a trade school," that, "skill,. mental training, and character must result from this training," that "nothing but this is worthy the name under modern industrialism," and "skill must be accompanied by intelligence which animates all work and tells the why."

Certainly if the apprentice system or the trade school attains this result it will have succeeded where the public-school system has too often failed. There was unanimity as regards the proposition that the student should be made an independent thinker with the power not only to fit into conditions but also to *create* the conditions.

Discussion naturally developed variance of opinion concerning the most effective machinery for bringing about this result. There was encouraging recognition of the fact that the best kind of a school for one community was not necessarily the best kind for another, and an undercurrent of suggestions that the government should aid in experiments leading to the solution of the problem. In fact the speakers at this last meeting approached the question of industrial education as students who realized the weightiness of the problem and were willing to devote to it, time, money, and their best intellectual efforts.

To those of us who look upon the world through the windows of the schoolroom, the needs which have aroused this effort may not seem imminent. Our rank and file in school are kept busy on the task of caring for the 25 per cent. who do not drop out between the fifth and sixth grades, and we have enough to occupy our minds in providing in the best way for the 5 per cent. who remain through the high-school course. It is well, therefore, to see the situation through the eyes of those on the outside. To them it it a question of the most important of all assets—the intelligent workman. The Massachusetts report has been conspicuous in every discussion. The 18,000,000 children who in 1907 left the public schools between the fifth and sixth grades constitute a waste-product which for economic reasons alone must be redeemed.

The Point of View of the Man Outside of the School

The discussion so far seems to point to the conclusion that eventually technical schools must be articulated with the public-school system. The organization of the elementary curriculum along the lines of general industrial training would seem to be the logical beginning for such an organic system. With certain fundamental industrial experiences as a working capital, the trade school would have time to do its own work effectively without imposing the much-dreaded vocational idea upon the lower grades. If the school people realized the strategic importance of this they would hasten the reorganization of the curriculum. It is not possible, however, that a system which already has its traditions can effect changes rapidly enough to control the situation. Probably other states will rapidly follow New York in offering material encouragement to the trade schools. At the start they will be somewhat isolated, and it will take the double time of readjustment on both sides to bring them into effective harmony.

The Relation of the Technical School to the Present System

During the past year the society has more clearly defined its function. The first report of its Committee of Ten and the authorization of a special officer in the field indicate an active proselyting campaign. It is to be hoped that it will stimulate an equally careful consideration of the subject on the part of every teacher in the country. L. S. C.

NOTES AND NEWS

The Post Express (Rochester, N. Y.) for Saturday, November 14, contains a full page of school problem material which is of considerable importance. It will be recalled that eight years ago a new board came into office and undertook in a vigorous but not revolutionary manner to reorganize the city schools which were in a somewhat backward condition. Three weeks ago a citizens' committee began work as a result of a general meeting held in September. This committee has now formulated twenty requests which it has discussed with the board of education. The remarkably sane and courteous spirit of the latter body has averted any danger of serious trouble and has taken much of the wind out of the committee's sails.

The situation remains, however, somewhat precarious and the effect of what has been done in Rochester upon other cities in which the issues first stated in Aristophanes' *Clouds* are ready to come up at any moment cannot well be predicted. A summary of the requests is as follows: "that dramatization and the three group system be made entirely optional with the grade teacher; that moral discipline be strengthened; that exhibition be stopped; that the making of books be cut down; that school supplies be furnished to the children and that free textbooks be favorably considered; that pencils be substituted for ink in rough work; that the time for formal drill in spelling be increased and the question of more formal drill in grammar be investigated; that a better textbook in arithmetic be introduced; that the the formal drill in geography be increased; that the fundamental take precedence of the 'expression work;' that some kinds of expression work be dropped from the curriculum; that the waste of time before festivals be checked; that the strain of the artistic studies be relieved by the employment of special teachers or the interchange of work between teachers; that the proportion of men be increased; that some home work be required of the grammar grades; that a formal and uniform test be applied in the grammar grades; that the salaries of the teachers be increased; that the established practice regarding tenure of office be made plain, and that such causes of irritation as may exist in the teaching force may speedily be allayed."

The board meets these recommendations by showing that some of the grievances are not well founded, others have been and are being carefully considered in comparison with the work of other leading cities; still others, as the overstress on celebrations of festivals, are an inheritance which has been steadily reduced; the need of men teachers cannot be filled by wishing and the larger salaries depend upon taxation and not the school board.

The most interesting consideration appears in the failure to place the matter upon a basis of expert judgment. Pastors, college and theological seminary professors are not necessarily experts on elementary education. The suspicion that the persons concerned may not be expert is not reduced when one meets the recommendation concerning arithmetic "to introduce a textbook which will be more in line with the good old Robinson." Again the committee finds that mothers are disturbed because children daub their clothes with ink, therefore "we recommend that the children be permitted to do all rough work with lead pencils." There is no home work in the elementary school and it is asked that it be put in. Quite apart from the individual's views on pencils and home work the danger of settling these by popular sentiment is evident. I recall the withdrawal from one high-school room the same day of two girls—one because the room was overventilated, the other because the air was too close.

The expert problem comes out again in the recommendation that a committee be appointed "to advise with the board in the preparation of tests" in the grammar schools. This committee is to consist of two members of the university faculty, two from each of the high-school faculties, and three from the citizens generally. Does it not occur to the reformers that there may be grammar-school people whose services would be of value in testing grammar schools? If there are none the reforms had better begin in finding some who can help.

One inference from some of the items is that teachers have been complaining about requirements which they misunderstood. So often school troubles would be straightened out if there were franker relations between the various members of the force. If teachers would take their grievances direct to supervisors both would learn much that they need.

The reaction in this instance is on a higher plane than has usually been the case. The partisans of "fundamentals" recognize the unfortunately named "expression work" as a factor and instead of calling for its removal only demand that it be put in its properly "subordinate" place.

The names of the superintendent and assistant superintendent do not appear but it is evident that both of them are in mind. How largely the former's opposition to Regents' Examinations plays a part cannot be readily seen. Mr. Carroll and Miss Harris have placed us all in their debt for suggestions and experiments and we hope that the board may combine its present graciousness with equally necessary firmness on central necessities so that the work begun may go on, reconstructed perhaps by a larger view of community needs but not put upon a lower plane by non-expert limitations.

The reports of W. L. Bodine, superintendent of compulsory education, and of D. P. Macmillan, director of the Department of Child-Study and Pedagogic Investigation, upon the conditions in Chicago schools, have called out wide notice so far as the general conclusions are concerned. Five thousand children habitually hungry and ten thousand more who do not have sufficient nourishing food, as estimated by Superintendent Bodine, is certainly distressing enough to compel attention. Dr. Macmillan's report brings out the close connection of malnutrition with retardation. Of 10,090 children observed in 12 schools, 1,178 were rated as "necessitous." The distribution of these by grades is significant! Among children of kindergarten age the percentage of underfed is 15.9, and for grades one, two, three, four, five, and above, the percentages respectively are 13.8, 11.2, 9.6, 9.0, and 5.9. The inference that the larger number of ill-nourished children in the lower grades is due in part at least to retardation is confirmed by Dr. Macmillan's data concerning subnormal children. Of some 2,100 subnormal children examined in the past three years it was found "that in the case of approximately 55 per cent. the subnormality, in part, at least, was attributable to malnutrition and insufficient food."

The Probation and Juvenile Court movement in Italy is reported in *Charities and the Commons* by Miss Lucy Bartlett. Beginning with a band of volunteer workers who undertook to supervise boys "conditionally condemned," the society in Rome now numbers three hundred subscribers and forty one active workers, and similar societies have been formed in Milan, Turin, and Florence. In May of 1908 a ministerial circular provided for the establishment of special courts, analogous to juvenile courts in this country, in which the judge "shall endeavor to treat juvenile cases in a psychological rather than a punitive spirit."

School gardens were found highly suitable work for defective children in the Cleveland schools the past year.

Wherever the statistics of over-age children in the public schools have been collected and studied, the school authorities and the community have been shocked to discover the large number of children who are retarded in their progress through the schools, and are over age for the grades in which they happen to be. Dr. Roland P. Falkner, commissioner of education for Porto Rico, has made a study of retardation in school work in *The Psychological Clinic* for May.

The five cities studied are New York, Boston, Philadelphia, Kansas City (Mo.), and Camden (N. J.), the only cities from which statistics can be obtained for the purpose of a comparative study. The theoretic age limit for the first-grade child is seven years. All children over seven years in the first grade may therefore be regarded as beyond the age limit of that grade; similarly, all children over eight years in the second grade, nine in the third grade, and so on throughout the eight grades in the school system. In the February number of *The Psychological Clinic* Dr. Cornman, district superintendent of Philadelphia, had shown that in Boston 21.6 per cent. of the school population are one year or more behind the proper grade for their age, in New York 30 per cent., in Philadelphia 37.1 per cent., in Camden 47.5 per cent., and in Kansas City 49.6 per cent.

Dr. Falkner subjects Dr. Cornman's figures to a searching analysis, and finds that the statistics used by Cornman are not directly comparable, because they are computed by a different method in each of the five cities. After eliminating the discrepancies due to differences of method, and basing the figures upon the total enrolment, which was the method originally used in Camden and Kansas City, Dr. Falkner finds the results to be even more striking than those reached by Dr. Cornman. The percentages of retardation for Camden (47.5 per cent.) and for Kansas City (49.6 per cent.) remain unchanged, of course. For Boston the showing is much better, being only 12.5 per cent. instead of 21.6 per cent. For Philadelphia and New York, however, it is somewhat worse, being 42.5 per cent. instead of 37.1 per cent. for Philadelphia, and 35.0 per cent. instead of 30.0 per cent. for New York.

These figures have an important bearing on the question of the causes of retardation. Why should Boston have only 12.5 per cent. of children behind a satisfactory age limit, and Philadelphia and New York have respectively 42.5 per cent. and 35 per cent.? The populations of these cities are not sufficiently diverse to account for this marked difference to the advantage of Boston. Dr. Falkner points out that it may be partly due to the fact that in Boston the children appear to enter the school system at a much earlier age than they do in the other cities. But both Dr. Cornman and Dr. Falkner believe that the methods by which the city of Boston succeeds in getting the children up through the grades are well worthy of study by the rest of the country.

Comparisons of American with British education have often been made to the disadvantage of the former on the score of efficiency. What efficiency means is interpreted differently, of course; certainly, no one would long be able to maintain that inability to pass the college-entrance examinations should be the final proof of inefficiency. But that charge was made, practically, in the September *North American Review* by Lieutenant Larned, of the West Point Academy. Over against the rather doubtful statistics there given, we may set some reports of the results of entrance examinations at the universities of Glasgow and Edinburgh, held last September. At Glasgow, out of 250 candidates who took the entrance examination in English, 26 passed, i. e., 87 per cent. failed. At Edinburgh, 83 passed and 89 failed in English, while in French, 44 passed and 82 failed.

A good many signs point to the rise of what may specifically be called an "international consciousness of the problem of education." The sense of the failure of educational practice along specific lines as indicated in these various statistics, has its darker aspects relieved by the positive work of the First International Moral Congress which met at the University of London in September. More than a thousand educational leaders from all parts of the world were present. Aside from the discussions of specific phases of the general problem of moral education, in which nothing new of importance was suggested, the positive gain that will come from reflection upon the congress as an accomplished fact, with the correlated meanings of the fact, will be very great. Beyond any mere discussions of moral training rises the fact that moral education is seen to be a real function of our world-life, international in its bearings, and no longer merely an individual or even a national issue. With it is wrapped up the whole question of national ideals and sincerity in international relationships. Japan, Germany, Russia, and England, not to mention other countries, met to discuss "moral education." If that fact is anything more than a polite international sham, it must certainly come to have some bearing on the relationships between England and Germany, Russia and Japan.

A new departure has recently been made in the school system of New York State. A special Department of Trades Schools has been organized under the Education Department of the state. After certain set requirements as to qualifications of teachers and equipment of buildings have been fulfilled, the state will allot to schools whose boards will agree to maintain a session of not less than forty weeks, with not fewer than twenty-five pupils, the sum of $500, with additional allotments for each additional teacher required. The aim as set forth by the department is the development of craftmanship. But it is difficult to see how the regulations as to the schools are in all points consistent with this aim. There will be two classes of the schools: (1) factory schools, training for work in factories where machinery predominates; (2) trades schools, training for the constructive trades, along the lines of individual interest and ability without regard to the demands of machinery-work. This latter provision seems excellent. Full information as to the exact trend of the former is not at hand, but it hardly seems to be in line with the best developments in industrial education.

The postmaster-general has asked for the co-operation of all schools in the instruction of children in the organization of the Post-Office Department and in the operation of the postal service. Special materials for use in such instruction is being forwarded by the department to all local post-offices. The reason for this effort is found in the fact that the dead-letter office receives about 40,000 pieces of mail daily.

Kindergartners are rejoicing over the prospect of an early death of the Sunday comic supplement. The *Boston Herald* has already discontinued its publication, and it is thought that other leading papers will follow the lead of Boston. Kindergartners have always maintained that the normal child has no real interest in this particular form of "children's literature."

The demand for a more thoroughgoing application of science to the ordering of the household underlies one phase of modern industrial education, and furnishes one of the liveliest of topics of contemporary discussion. Superintendent Van Sickle, of Baltimore, has recently been saying that our schools have not made as adequate provision for girls as for boys. The boy is prepared, as schools go, for a great many lines of work after school. But the girl is prepared for very little, nothing beyond bookkeeping and stenography. He suggests that the girls should have the benefit of a polytechnic training fitted to their future needs, and as comprehensive in its way as is the work for boys. The work of such a school should center about household economics in the larger sense, i. e., the application of scientific principles to the whole course of daily life.

The next convention of the American Physical Education Association will be held in Philadelphia in April. Among the topics announced for discussion we note: "The Place of Physical Education in the Public-School Curriculum;" "The Playground as an Educational Force;" "Physical Education for Girls in the Public High School;" "Administrative Problems Connected with Physical Education in the Public Schools." Attention to this phase of education is being enforced both in this country and in Europe by journals and associations, and by the work of leading educators.

Dr. Witmer, of the University of Pennsylvania, discusses a topic correlative with this in the November number of the *Psychological Clinic.* He deals with the problem of feeble-mindedness, and its relation to bodily conditions and brain states. He contends that the right kind of medical and educational work given by a man who understands the situation and given at the right time may mean all the difference between imbecility or marked subnormal efficiency and some relatively high degree of efficiency. An "Orthogenic School" has been organized in connection with his work for the purpose, as the name indicates, of cultivating a "right or normal development" in children for whom there is, in his opinion, a fighting chance of restoration to normal life.

In the same journal, Dr. Felix Arnold discusses the classification and education of afflicted children in the public schools. He points out the necessity of establishing classes in which will be treated separately (1) backward children, (2) crippled children, (3) deaf and dumb children, (4) blind children, (5) feeble-minded children, (6) delinquent children, (7) morally defectives. He outlines the educational treatment which should be applied in the public schools to each of these classes. He insists that as long as the public allows afflicted children to be born into the world, and to live, the only logical thing is to educate them on a par with other children.

It may not be amiss, in this connection to call attention to the suggestive description in the *Outlook,* for December 5, of the Forest School of Charlottenburg in Germany where about two hundred and fifty children from the town, who are suffering from various defects, are educated at public expense in a school in the forest, under simple conditions. The annual expense of the school is above $12,000, most of which is paid out of the general taxes of the community. But after four years of testing the merits of the case, it is generally felt that the money is well invested, for it means the producing of two hundred and fifty self-supporting individuals. During the past year the school was copied at Dresden, at Elberfeldt, and at Borstal Woods, near London. And a school organized along similar lines has more recently been opened for the children of well-to-do parents on the eastern side of Berlin.

Current Events gives the following account of an interesting experiment. For some years a Sicilian named Antonio Parisi has been giving historical "puppet-shows" in the Sicilian quarter of New York City. His plays deal chiefly with events in the life and times of Charlemagne. The Drama Committee of the People's Institute has now taken notice of Signor Parisi and is to test the puppet-show as an aid to education in history. The show, moved to a retreat near Washington Square, is to be accessible to 600,000 school children and their teachers. The school authorities of the city are said to be very much interested in the experiment. The Sicilian children, according to enthusiastic advocates of the plan, know the history of Charlemagne "like a book," wholly through these shows.

A recent number of the *Blätter für die Fortbildung des Lehrers und der Lehrerin,* published at Berlin, has the following items relating to women in German schools:

The lack of men teachers in Gotha is so great that the wife of a schoolmaster was obliged to step in at Sundhausen, as no master was to be had.

The Catholic women teachers' union in Bavaria has petitioned for authority to permit unmarried women teachers to assume the title "Frau" in place of the "less worthy title" "Fräulein"—this to apply both to speech and to official communications in accord with historical authorities. According to which "the unmarried also have a right to the title."

BOOK REVIEWS

Chinese Fables and Folk Stories. By MARY HAYES DAVIS AND CHOW LEUNG. With an Introduction by YIN-CHAN WANG TSEN-JAN. New York: American Book Co. $0.40.

This is a recent addition to the series of Eclectic Readings. It lays claim to being "the first book of Chinese stories ever printed in English that will bring the western people to the knowledge of our fables which have never been heretofore known to the world." The general belief of the occidentals has been that the Chinese had no fables, but the research of the translator and compiler of this little volume has brought to English-reading children a varied collection. They are, according to the testimony of the writer of the introduction, fair examples of the folklore of this ancient people. The book is intended to give "not . . . . a full idea of Chinese literature, but it shows the thinking reader a bird's-eye view of the Chinese thought in this form of literature."

To one who is not a student of oriental thought the book gives glimpses of a different life, a conception of the ideas of life and a mode of embodying these ideals in forms so alien to our own and yet in ways so human that it carries with this sense of difference the indescribable feeling of charm. While affording a series of pictures of manners, customs, and ideas not our own, it still draws a remote people nearer to the one who enters into these sympathetic human records. For this reason the book seems worth while as reading-matter for children of the later years of the elementary school. The fables have been taken, not only from the common stock of the story-teller, but are found recorded here and there in advanced literature and historical books. For this reason they have been most difficult of access to the foreign student of Chinese writings because they have been lost to all who had not a perfect control of that all-but-impossible written language. Much credit is therefore due the compilers.

Japanese Folk Stories and Fairy Tales. By MARY F. NIXON-ROULET. New York: American Book Co. Pp. 191. 40 cents.

This is a later book in the same series as the *Chinese Fables.* It is a collection of popular stories from Japanese mythology and folklore. Like the other collection they are especially suited to the interests of the older children not to say adults, for they require a certain maturity of mind and experience to appreciate the subtlety of meaning in many and the poetic significance and grace of diction. As a means of giving a reflection of their habit of thought, their attitude toward people and events, their feeling for nature, and their religious sentiment, these stories must be unrivaled and should occupy some place in relation to the study of peoples which is now an illuminating phase of the study of geography.

The Louisa Alcott Reader. A Supplementary Reader for the Fourth Year of School. By LOUISA M. ALCOTT. Boston: Little, Brown & Co. Pp. 222, illustrated.

Just why this book should be designed for fourth-year and not for third- or fifth-year pupils is not quite clear. Of course Miss Alcott is a prime favorite with girls, but most girls can be trusted to read her books if they are in any degree accessible at home. An old-fashioned idea of school may be dominating the commentator who feels that something more significant as literature on the one hand, or really valuable related information on the other, such as may reinforce his study, should form the bulk of a child's school reading. The charm of Miss Alcott's books is undeniable. They furnish the sweet meat and sugar plum of children's reading at a certain period.

B. P.

A Little Land and a Living. By BOLTON HALL. New York: Arcadia Press, 1908. Pp. 287. $1.

Two years ago there appeared a book of striking title—*Three Acres and Liberty*—but a book of equally striking content. It was designed to make clear to overcrowded, underfed, and more or less uncomfortable city people that the small farm can be made to make a good living for a family, and that the amount of energy expended by a worker in the shop will give larger returns upon the small farm. We now have from the same author a second book, *A Little Land and a Living,* this being a sequel to the first and having been designed to help solve the problems of who shall go to the farms, how shall they be got to go, to what kind of farms should they go, and what should they try to grow upon the farms.

Mr. Hall asserts that "there is more money to be made out of the soil, if you go at it intelligently, than there is in any endeavor that is open to every one." It is urged that if those who are living in conditions that render adequate food and good hygienic conditions impossible, were to secure a small piece of ground, an acre or less, usually they would find that this small piece of ground would make possible plenty of food, good air and the feeling of independence that comes with doing something that is worth while. Often these people should secure this land sufficiently near the city to make possible a daily trip to city work when such may be had. Abandoned farm lands may be had for small sums, and under the free guidance of the United States Department of Agriculture, they may soon be made productive. The availability of the market must always be kept in mind. Vacant lot gardening has never been fully developed, and offers very great opportunities. All well-organized plans for utilization of vacant lots have given valuable money returns, but have done a much greater service in giving new purpose and opening new opportunities to fully or well-nigh discouraged people. Intensive farming makes possible much valuable farming within most city limits, and a very large amount of it quite near all cities. Meantime the general health, attractiveness, and land values are enhanced. "One-sixth of an acre planted in radishes and lettuce, followed by egg-plant and cauliflower, and the next year to radishes alone followed by egg-plant, yielded at the rate of over $1,200 an acre per year."

Record yields of various crops are given and certainly look tempting to anyone who loves country life. The large number of crops that may be grown profitably will surprise many readers who thought they already knew about the possibilities. "Animals for Profit" includes a discussion of a snail park, frogs, turtles, bass, pheasants, dogs, cats, silver foxes, and bees. The résumé of the enormous advances in agricultural practice within the past ten years, opening of new agricultural territory by dry-land farming, irrigation, and by reclaiming of swamp areas, treatment of soils to retain or bring back or develop a high degree of fertility, can have no other result than to stimulate the general interest in farm life, and in this a great service has been done.

It must be said that there is no adequate solution of the great problem of who is to leave the city for the farm, and just how land is to be secured from them. There are many people who gladly would accept the tender of a good farm, but such a ready settlement of the difficulties does not seem immediately forthcoming.

Methods in Teaching. By ROSA V. WINTERBURN. New York: The Macmillan Co., 1907. Pp. 355. $1.25.

During the World's Exposition held at St. Louis, many teachers were attracted to the exhibit of the schools of Stockton, California. The interest in this exhibit stimulated the preparation of a book upon *Methods in Teaching,* intended to present the Stockton methods, rather than a solution of general educational problems. The first seven chapters of the book are given to literature, language, and word study, two chapters are given to arithmetic and one each to plant study, animal study, non-living things, geography, history in the primary grades, civics, and a closing chapter upon drawing, music, physical culture, and sewing.

Obviously the author believes either that literature, language, and word study should occupy most of the attention of the grades, or that more emphasis is needed to get a proper amount of work well done. The suggestions for work in these subjects are quite detailed, and more than one-third of the entire plan is given to this aspect of the work. In justification of this large emphasis the author says, "He who knows how to read, and who desires to read valuable and instructive books has gained a great part of his education." With this sentiment many school people would agree, but it would not follow that so large a proportion of the time should be given directly to the language work. As evidenced in the above quotation the value of reading depends quite largely upon the selection of reading about things that are worth while. It is important that people give more time to thinking about interesting and valuable material than that they should give so much of their time to consideration of forms of expression. I do not mean to minimize the importance of the latter, but to call attention to the fact that if more time were given to definite, clear, trustworthy thinking in arithmetic, history, etc., such would give the real basis for development of good forms of expression. It is difficult to secure good expression unless good impression precedes it.

The chapter on "Plant Study" was prepared by Mr. Edward Hughes, supervisor of nature-study in the Stockton schools, and it and the succeeding chapters upon natural history subjects will prove most helpful to many teachers. We cannot agree with the author when he says "nature-study is a common-sense subject and does not require special preparation of the teacher." If it is not "a common-sense subject" it has no place in the schools—indeed it and all other worthy subjects are common-sense subjects. The claim that it demands "no special preparation of the teacher," is just the thing that has so often brought nature-study into disrepute. In order to make nature-study fully justifiable in the schools the teachers need some familiarity with nature materials—some knowledge of nature. The proper point of view is also necessary, just as in a study of history or mathematics, but we should scarcely argue that point of view is all that is needed in any of these things.

The material included in the chapters that deal with nature subjects is all good and teachers will find most helpful suggestions as to methods of organizing these materials. The whole book should be studied by teachers who are looking for the best in education.

The Boy Geologist. By EDWIN J. HOUSTON, PH.D., with illustrations by HERBERT PULLINGER. Philadelphia: Henry Altemus Company, 1907. Pp. 320. 4 illus. $1.

The Boy Geologist is an attempt at combination of story and presentation of a few ideas upon elementary science—mainly geology—and upon the methods of teaching elementary science. The first and second chapters, in addition to introducing the author's characters, are used in comparing the book-memorizing method of study, and a method of interpreting the real meaning of the text. It would have been more in keeping with the modern notions of science teaching had the author presented some kind of an argument for an interpretation of book discussions as based upon a previous or accompanying study of nature materials. It seems strange nowadays to have presented an argument against verbatum memorizing of books. Does anyone practice such a method?

Beside a discussion of the above point, the character representing the teacher is made to discuss with his boys a few minerals and the leading types of volcanoes. The latter discussion is interesting, but interwoven with it, and composing the rest of the book is a frivolous discussion of a more or less make-believe life of school boys, all of which greatly obscures the small amount of real merit the book possesses.

O. W. CALDWELL

Trois Semaines en France. A Reader. By L. CHOUVILLE AND D. L. SAVORY. Clarendon Press, 1908. Pp. 127.

The subject of this little book is a trip that three young men take through some of the most interesting parts of Brittany and Normandy. It forms a continuous narrative in which are introduced conversations on diverse subjects, pictures of French life, and historical anecdotes of the two provinces. It is very attractively illustrated with twelve views of different places visited by the travelers. The book is not intended for beginners. It is planned for students of high-school age, who have had two or three years of French. After each chapter (and the chapters are short) there is an exhaustive questionnaire on the text, followed by four or five articles of grammar exercises based on the material just studied. It is a well-planned and interesting little reader.

Simplicité. A Reader of French Pronunciation. By JULIUS TUCKERMAN. New York: American Book Co., 1908. Pp. 128. $0.50.

The aim of this book is to teach French pronunciation in as brief a time as possible. Each lesson takes up two or more new sounds which are explained by the vowel sounds in English words. Following this explanation is an exercise of a few lines, made up of sentences whose only *raison d'être* is that the words contain the sounds presented in the lesson above. The result is sentences of this type: "It snowed all the week. Paris is situated on the Seine. The sick man broke a vein. The queen was pained at the death of her sister. Have you seen the whale?" etc. It may be a simple way to teach pronunciation, but it is simplicity bought at the expense of interest and enthusiasm. How a student can gain any *Sprachgefühl* from such a method is difficult to understand. At the end of the book there is some general reading matter, which, the author says, "'combines the useful and the good'—a notable departure from the usual fairy tales." The first part of this section deals with the human body—head, eyes, mouth, trunk, arms, and legs. This is followed by the story of a loaf of bread, from the breaking of the earth, and the sowing of the seed, to the baked loaf as it comes from the oven. And finally there are a couple of pages on the animal, vegetable, and mineral kingdoms. The book is not in harmony with the present movement in modern language teaching.

JOSETTE E. SPINK

SCHOOL OF EDUCATION
THE UNIVERSITY OF CHICAGO

A Baker's Dozen for City Children. Music by ISABEL VALENTINE; words by LILEON CLAXTON. New York: The Kindergarten Magazine Co., 1907. Pp. 16. $0.50.

The subjects embodied in these thirteen songs for kindergarten children are well chosen, but the songs themselves are below the average. The texts lack charm and the melodies are commonplace. The small people to whom they are offered will sing them for the sake of the ideas expressed but will gain nothing from them of aesthetic value. Poor art for little children is especially to be deplored.

M. R. KERN

SCHOOL OF EDUCATION
THE UNIVERSITY OF CHICAGO

BOOKS RECEIVED

THE CENTURY COMPANY, NEW YORK

The American Executive and Executive Methods. (The American State Series.) By JOHN H. FINLEY AND JOHN F. SANDERSON. Cloth. Pp. 352. $1.25.

GINN & CO., BOSTON

Book of Alphabets. For use in schools. By H. W. SHAYLOR. Pp. 24. $0.10.

LONGMANS, GREEN & CO., NEW YORK

Moral Instruction and Training in Schools. A report of an international inquiry. Edited by M. E. SADLER. Cloth. Vol. I, pp. 538; Vol. II, pp. 378.

THE MACMILLAN CO., NEW YORK

The American as He Is. By NICHOLAS MURRAY BUTLER. Cloth. Pp. 104. $1.00.

Textbook of School and Class Management: Theory and Practice. By FELIX ARNOLD. Cloth. Pp. 409. $1.25.

Special Method in Reading in the Grades. By CHARLES A. MCMURRY. Cloth. Pp. 351. $1.25.

CHARLES E. MERRILL CO., NEW YORK

The Vision of Sir Launfal and Other Poems. By JAMES RUSSELL LOWELL. Edited with Introduction and Notes, by JULIAN W. ABERNETHY. Cloth. Pp. 172. $0.25.

NEW YORK CHARITIES PUBLICATION COMMITTEE

Medical Inspection of Schools. By LUTHER HALSEY GULICK AND LEONARD P. AYRES. Cloth. Pp. 276. $1.00.

CURRENT EDUCATIONAL LITERATURE IN THE PERIODICALS[1]

IRENE WARREN
Librarian, School of Education, The University of Chicago

Adams, Victoria A. Delphi and the teacher of history. Educa. Bi-mo. 3:135. (D. '08.)

Adamson, John William. Some impressions of the international moral congress. School World. 10:412–14. (N. '08.)

Arnold, Felix. Classification and education of afflicted children. Psycholog. Clin. 2:180–91. (N. '08.)

Bain, A. Watson. Preparation in the elementary school for industrial and domestic life. El. School T. 9:167–77. (D. '08.)

Bascomb, John. Co-education. Educa. R. 36:442–51. (D. '08.)

Bedinger, George Rust. Japanese college students. Out. 90:626–28. (N. '08.)

(The) Berea college case. Out. 90:757–58. (D. '08.)

Boone, Cheshire L. A course of study in manual training. Man. Train. Mag. 10:123–33. (D. '08.)

Bush-Brown, Henry K. Work, study, and play for every child: a system of education that would make for better mental, moral, and physical development. Craftsman. 15:330–37. (N. '08.)

Butler, Nicholas Murray. Training for vocation and for avocation. Educa. R. 36:471–74. (D. 08.)

Daly, W. E. The education of a marine engineer. Cassier. 35:73–78. (N. '08.)

DeGroot, E. B. Recent playground development in Chicago. Amer. Phys. Educa. R. 13:462–67. (N. '08.)

De La Paz, Fabian A. Education in the Philippines. Educa. 29:239–47. (D. '08.)

Dorey, Milnor. Should secondary schools teach the Bible? School R. 16:680–82. (D. '08.)

French, Charles W. Social education. Educa. Bi-mo. 3:136–47. (D. '08.)

[1] *Abbreviations.*—Amer. Phys. Educa. R., American Physical Education Review; Atlan., Atlantic Monthly; Chaut., Chautauquan; Educa., Education; Educa. Bi-mo., Educational Bi-monthly; Educa. R., Educational Review; El. School T., Elementary School Teacher; Harp. W., Harpers' Weekly; Journ. of Educa. (Bost.), Journal of Education (Boston); Lib. Journ., Library Journal; Man. Train. Mag., Manual Training Magazine; Out., Outlook; Pop. Sci. Mo., Popular Science Monthly; Psycholog. Clin., Psychological Clinic; Pub. Lib., Public Libraries; School R., School Review; South. Educa. R., Southern Educational Review; Teach. Coll. Rec., Teachers College Record.

FRENCH, WALTER H. Agriculture in the public school. El. School T. 9:186-91. (D. '08.)

GOWDY, JEAN L. The educational value of the essentially motor activities. Man. Train. Mag. 10:97-103. (D. '08.)

GRIFFITH, IRA S. Methods and arrangement of subject-matter in grammar-school woodworking. Man. Train. Mag. 10:148-60. (D. '08.)

GUTHRIE, MARY G. Some principles of history teaching. Educa. Bi-mo. 3:110. (D. '08.)

HAMANN, ALBERT. The higher education of women in Prussia. Educa. R. 36:433-41. (D. '08.)

HANEY, JAMES P. The London art congress. Man. Train. Mag. 10:110-22.

HARPER, PAUL VINCENT. Student life in Bonn: the impressions of an American student. Chaut. 52:427-33. (N. '08.)

HETHERINGTON, CLARK W. Report of committee on a normal course in play. Amer. Phys. Educa. R. 13:472-74. (N. '08.)

HIBBARD, GEORGE. The playground from the standpoint of the executive officer of the city. Amer. Phys. Educa. R. 13:455-61. (N. '08.)

HILL, EDWARD E. The value of the study of society in elementary and secondary schools. Educa. Bi-mo. 3:129-34. (D. '08.)

HILL, PATTY SMITH. The value and limitations of Froebel's gifts as educative materials. Pts. 3, 4, 5. El. School T. 9:192-201. (D. '08.)

HOSIC, JAMES FLEMING. The elementary course in English. Pt. 2. Educa. Bi-mo. 3:159-89. (D. '08.)

HULL, M. W. The value of time and material. Man. Train. Mag. 10:161-63. (D. '08.)

JERNEGAN, MARCUS WILSON. An unsolved problem in secondary education. Educa. Bi-mo. 3:111-22. (D. '08.)

JOHNSTON, W. DAWSON. The library of the bureau of education. Educa. R. 36:452-57. (D. '08.)

KAUFFMAN, EUNICE HUGHES. A school in the forest. Out. 90:793-95. (D. '08.)

KAVANA, ROSE M. Concerning method in history. Educa. Bi-mo. 3:128. (D. '08.)

KENT, ERNEST B. The elementary school and industrial occupations. El. School T. 9:178-85. (D. '08.)

LANE, WILLIAM COOLIDGE. A central bureau of information and loan collection for college libraries. Lib. Journ. 33:429-33. (N. '08.)

LARSSON, GUSTOF. Otto Solomon. Man. Train. Mag. 10:104-9. (D. '08.)

LUCK, F. C. Ethics of education. Educa. 29:201-12. (D. '08.)

MARK, E. H. Compulsory school attendance. South. Educa. R. 5:119-30. (N. '08.)

MARTIN, EDWARD S. President Eliot—a great man. Harp. W. 52:7. (N. '08.)

MARVIN, GEORGE. The American spirit in Chinese education. Out. 90:667-72. (N. '08.)

MILLER, KELLY. Forty years of negro education. Educa. R. 36:484-98. (D. '08.)

NELSON, J. RALEIGH. A revival of the Megalensian games. School R. 16:660-63. (D. '08.)

NOYES, WILLIAM. Function of constructive activities in education. Pt. 1. Journ. of Educa. (Bost.) 68:589-91. (D. '08.)

PAYNE, WM. C. The trend of the elementary school. Educa. Bi-mo. 3:148-57. (D. '08.)

PEARSON, H. G., BENNETT, MARTHA T., AND WARD, ANDREW H. New England Association of Teachers of English: report of the standing committee on entrance requirements. School R. 16:646-59. (D. '08.)

PRICHETT, HENRY S. The organization of higher education. Atlan. 102:783-88. (D. '08.)

(The) problem of adapting history to children in the elementary school. Teach. Coll. Rec. 16:1-348. (D. '08.)

RIIS, JACOB. Riis on play and playgrounds. Journ. of Education. (Bost.) 68:591-92. (D. '08.)

SCHWARZ, HERMANN. The study of experimental pedagogy in Germany. School R. 16:633-45. (D. '08.)

SHEARIN, HUBERT C. Trend of education in the South. South. Educa. R. 5:131-34. (N. '08.)

SIES, RAYMOND W. The study of education in the high school. School R. 16:670-79. (D. '08.)

SISSON, EDWARD O. Reading versus translating. Pt. 2, methods. School R. 16:664-69. (D. '08.)

(The) springs of Australian character. Educa. R. 36:475-83. (D. '08.)

STECHER, WILLIAM A. The playgrounds under the Philadelphia board of public education. Amer. Phys. Educa. R. 13:468-71. (N. '08.)

STEVENS, W. LECONTE. College standardization. Pop. Sci. Mo. 73:528-39. (D. '08.)

THILLY, FRANK. Paulson on modern education. Educa. R. 36:458-70. (D '08.)

VINCENT, GEORGE E. The individualizing duty of the library. Pub. Lib. 13:391-97. (D. '08.)

WAHLSTROM, LEONARD W. A school print shop. Man. Train. Mag. 10:134-47. (D. '08.)

WITMER, LIGHTNER. The treatment and cure of a case of mental and moral deficiency. Psycholog. Clin. 2:153-79. (N. '08.)

VOLUME IX NUMBER 6

THE ELEMENTARY SCHOOL TEACHER

FEBRUARY, 1909

THE PHYSICAL NEEDS OF THE GRAMMAR SCHOOL GIRL

NELLIE COMINS WHITAKER
Salem, Mass.

The motion of a heavenly body, say the astronomers, is the resultant of all the forces acting upon it. It may not be in the direction of any one of them. In a somewhat similar way the course that a teacher follows is the resultant of many forces; the direction in which she would travel is only one element in the way which she takes. More and more the grammar-school teacher is finding that the pressure, even from a point as far advanced as college, is transmitted beyond the high school and is making itself felt farther back in the grades. Every year more things must be done during the thirteen years—or twelve years of public school. Manifestly not all the additional work can be done in the last four grades.

The grammar-school teacher is influenced by what she learns of the situation of her pupils in their homes and in their community. It becomes evident that for a large number of these children there is now no schooling after the grammar grades. Whatever learning the greater part of these young people are to have the grammar school must give them. And this applies not to book-learning alone but also to instruction in cooking and sewing and similar subjects which children are apparently no longer taught at home.

It lies with especial weight upon a teacher's mind that the pupils before her are potently related to the state, and that one of her first duties is to give them some instruction that shall furnish a basis of intelligence for the coming generation of common people with whom our political destiny must rest. Her standing with her superintendent may be largely influenced by the way in which she responds to some particular hobby of his; her general professional reputation depends to a great degree, she knows, upon the percentage with which her pupils pass their high-school examinations. With all these forces acting upon a teacher, what wonder that she sometimes finds she is moving in an orbit surprising even to herself? The importance of the physical preservation and upbuilding of her pupils is seldom indicated in the course of work laid out for a teacher, yet physical development is the most important element in the life of a child between the ages of eight and fourteen. Is not this what we should wish considered first in the case of our own children? Students of education and of health are saying now with impressive emphasis that the years between ten and fourteen are the critical period of a girl's whole life for the establishment of her physical well-being. Unquestionably this care of the health should be provided in the girl's own home, but it is evident that in the majority of instances the demand is not adequately met there. In such cases the girl's only hope for guidance is in her teacher. To meet this demand, however, a teacher needs to know just the existing conditions. Often this knowledge has been offered her neither in normal school nor in supplementary instruction at teachers' institutes nor by supervisors. She sees evidences of nervous strain in her girls and understands in a general way what it indicates. For definite information it is worth her while to read Professor John Tyler's *Growth and Education.* Here, in the chapter on the "Grammar School," she will learn that while the death rate is low at this time, morbidity is rising to its first maximum at about the age of thirteen. This is not a period when sickness and death are to be feared; it is rather a time of foundations, foundations either for health or for weakness:

At this critical period of puberty every organ in the body is more or less modified. A girl's future happiness, if not her life itself, depends upon the successful accomplishment of this metamorphosis. She is making her final preparation for Nature's second and most searching examination. Almost anything except readiness for this test can be postponed or even neglected without irremediable loss. But failure to meet Nature's requirements here means ruin, and a low mark means lifelong disabilities, if not weariness and pain. The test will soon be applied once for all and must be final. There is no appeal from the verdict and no forgiveness for those who even ignorantly have sinned against Nature's laws.

In the same chapter Professor Tyler tells us that the years before ten furnish opportunity to store up vitality against the lean years of puberty. The increased morbidity of girls later is attributed to poverty of blood, due to accumulation of waste material, or deterioration through loss of appetite or decrease of assimilative and digestive powers. Now may be the time when fatal diseases gain entrance into the system. In the upper classes in England, as a case in point, the death rate from consumption in girls between fifteen and twenty is three times that of boys. But the seeds of inability to resist disease are sown in earlier years:

The time to begin to take precautions is at seven or eight. Few seem to think that the health of the girls in the grammar grades needs any care or attention. There could hardly be a worse or more dangerous mistake.

We gain from Professor Tyler a conviction that there is upon some one a great responsibility for these girls—a responsibility that they are in no way qualified to take upon themselves. And when a teacher realizes that for the girls in her room, their future health and so their ability to become successful students or wage earners or housewives may be determined in these months, we may be sure that she will inquire what she can do about it. And what *can* she do?

In the first place she must carefully consider existing conditions for each girl—her physical condition, the conditions surrounding her in her home, the effect of school and its demands upon her.

The chapter on "Periodicity" in President Hall's *Adolescence,* or the little volume, *Sex in Education,* by Doctor Clarke, which aroused so much discussion a score of years ago, explain fully the demands which nature is making for each girl at her time of puberty. At this period she is developing an extremely important element of her being, in the eyes of nature her most important system, one to which all other systems should give way. To this development a girl's nourishment and blood and vitality should be directed for many months. If the nurture that belongs to these organs is diverted from them they are stunted permanently and the result is irregularity of function, life-long suffering, a woman "not very strong," and incapable of meeting the demands which life has a right to make of her. And her fate is often settled while she is in the grammar school —you have the word of educator and biologist and physician for it. No less an authority than Dr. Engelmann maintained that the appalling burden of ill health upon American women could be greatly lessened by preventive measures at the time of puberty.

This is the physical condition, the anatomical condition, we might almost say, of the school girl at the time of puberty. What are the conditions surrounding her in her home? She requires generous nourishment now and it is especially important that waste matter should be completely eliminated from both her digestive and her respiratory systems, that her blood may be kept clean. Proper exercise and unlimited fresh air are literally vital. Suitable clothing also is especially important, such clothing as does not impede growth and movement, and properly protects the body from cold. It is an important question whether her home is looking out for these things, and also keeping her from unsuitable and exhausting amusements.

School conditions for pupils are, we expect, under the control of the teachers—or the superintendent—and ought to be made as favorable as possible for the adolescent girl. But we hear of pupils hardly in their teens who cannot sleep for fear of pending examinations, who have somehow become morbidly nervous in relation to their school and its requirements. They are almost hysterical if there is danger of a mark for tardiness or absence, or a paper that is a day late. A great many teachers sacrifice their pupils and work much evil at this time through their desire to report a high percentage of attendance. It is very important that a girl should be interested and prompt, but these are not the most important matters just now.

If the conditions for the adolescent girl are as critical as we have tried to show, again we must ask, what can the teacher do about it? As soon as she has determined what is to be done she will naturally inquire what she can get the mother to do. The acquaintance between mothers and teachers varies much in different places, depending chiefly upon the individual teacher and upon the superintendent. In relation to the maturing girl there is the greatest need for confidence between the mother and the teacher. The mother should be shown what needs to be done and the tremendous importance of her doing it.

The very least that the mother can grant is an expression of her willingness that the teacher attempt to give the girl the direction that she ought to receive at home. I believe that the average mother would be glad to have these matters put rightly before her daughter; often a mother says, "I know I ought to tell my daughter about these things, but I keep putting it off because I do not know just what to say."

It will be the teacher's business, a somewhat difficult business, perhaps, to know what to say. Probably before the end of her grammar-school years the young woman has come under the periodic law, and periodic rest is requisite to her development. This means no less than that just as soon as a girl is governed by a wave of increasing and diminishing vitality, as she is for more than thirty years of her life, this rhythm must be respected. For at least two years she must give up two days in every month to complete rest, mental and physical. She ought to stay out of school for those two days, though sometimes a girl very strong in body and nerves goes with no immediate signs of harm. But she must be kept free from any exertion that will divert nutrition from developing organs. Staying out of school of course causes some interruption to her work, but her teacher knows that she can keep her standing nevertheless if she tries. Many a high-school girl is obliged to be absent two days every month during the latter part of her college preparation or, at least, is unable to do any effective work because of pain, and yet keeps front rank in her class. Even if her absences did affect the standing of the grammar-school girl they would be worth while because they are necessary to the establishment for her of a vigor which many American women have missed. We all know women who are invalids because, their physicians tell them, they "are no more developed than are twelve-year old girls."

In many cases a girl would be better off if she could be taken from school entirely and given a year for physical development under right conditions. Frequently, however, it is quite as well for her to be in the regularity of school life under a judicious and watchful teacher because the care at home is not judicious.

The home conditions of a girl's life at this time it seems almost impossible for a teacher to affect, yet she can do much toward bringing the girl herself to know what is good for her in food and clothing and amusements. Physiology is one of the subjects that has been forced back from the high school to the grammar grades; and a teacher who has definitely in mind what her girls ought to know will find in her textbook many texts for teaching the facts of hygiene vital now when "every organ of the body is affected by the change." In mixed schools one lesson for the girls alone, easily arranged while the boys are occupied at an athletic meeting, for example, can give emphasis to the other instruction; in the case of the older girls they can be given an idea, so far as girls of that age can comprehend it, of the importance of the physical change that has come to them.

In relation to school work the teacher must consider in general what seems proved, that nervous and mental exertion at this time robs the developing organs of the blood and vitality needed for their perfecting even more than would great physical demands upon the undeveloped limbs of the child and for exactly the same reason.

> We need [says Professor Tyler] teachers with clear and watchful eyes who can lighten worry, fret, and weariness, and can see when leniency is needed and when firmness is kindness, who know when not to notice a bad error or recitation or even a day's work; who can pass over or advise a day's absence from school now and then.

Though there are so many demands upon the mind and the minutes of every teacher, yet we have faith in her and reason for the faith that she will find time and strength to do at any rate the duty that is most worth while.

AN OUTLINE FOR THE PRESENTATION OF A COUNTRY—AFRICA

ROBERT M. BROWN
State Normal School, Worcester, Mass.

In the teaching of any grand division, it is essential that the physiographic factors be clearly outlined and, then, that the responses which organic functions make to these be understood. The responses to a certain sum of physical surroundings are constant; and, as between two situations, a variation of one or more terms of the sum must account for the differences in the life elements. An analysis of the physiographic features and their resultant effects upon life can be made an aim in geography work. The fulfilment of such an objective would free many courses of study from excessive repetition, would give a unity to the geography work, would make the work of the various grades more progressive, and would furnish a logical basis for the study of the grand divisions so that they may be approached not as unknown subjects but as continuations of a former study under new combinations of controls. I am not offering a panacea for all ills, but the results of a large number of trials make me assert with considerable confidence that the idea herein presented, if undertaken, of course, in good faith, will be helpful to the teacher, and much more will be contributive to interest and knowledge and mental exercise in the pupils. The tenacity with which the terms "torrid" and "hot belt" are applied to all areas lying between the two tropics is an indication of an ignorance of the other controls of climate. It is natural to begin with sun insolation as the first factor in climatic condition, but never to grow away from the elemental notion is deplorable. By easy stages, topography, migration of wind belts, wind direction, etc., are to be added, and a comprehensive view of the variations of the climates, even in the equatorial regions, is to be obtained. The system presented in this paper is directed to the analysis of the physiographic factors and the responses resulting therefrom, then to the synthesis of these same factors, with their more complicated resultants. For this a series of eleven maps is used, as follows:

I. Map showing the outline with parallels and meridians. Shape and position are the subjects of discussion.
II. Map of topography.
III. Map of winds for January.
IV. Map of winds for June. Maps III and IV show the limits of migration of the wind belts of the world.
V. Map of rainfall.
VI. Map of soils.

This ends the presentation of the physiographic factors of Africa. Up to this time the discussion of the vegetation, the animals, and especially mankind, has been mainly inference, based upon our knowledge of certain combinations of physiographic factors and their accompanying responses. Our inferences are verified or not in the maps which follow:

VII. Map of vegetation.
VIII A and B. Maps of vegetable products.
IX. Map of animals.
X. Map of commerce.
XI. Map of population.

If the deductions are verified, as they should be in the majority of cases, there will be gained a working knowledge of the factors of geographic science, and a background for all subsequent study. On the other hand, when deductions do not accord with fact, there is afforded a chance to investigate the discrepancy, a form of exercise that is of value. The double process of deduction, and later the presentation of the facts, serve as checks on the work. The source of the variance may be an error in fact or may be accounted for by fashion or by custom. Under any circumstances, the system does not allow one to go very far afield from the truth, although generalization must play a large part at this stage. A few years ago I presented[1] this scheme, using South America as an example. The present paper enlarges upon the former, fills in certain vacancies of treatment and supplements the outline by applying the principles to Africa.

MAP I—OUTLINE, WITH PARALLELS AND MERIDIANS. Upon

[1] *Journal of Geography,* IV, 273 (1905).

any wall map the outline is sufficiently clear to read, but few wall maps give any prominence to the parallels and meridians. The subordination of the lines of latitude and longitude is a necessity if clearness of outline or detail is desired. The wall map must be adapted to many uses, but it generally brings into prominence the physical or political subdivisions of a country; and those maps are the most successfully used which emphasize an essential feature to the neglect of others. However, latitude and longitude are elements in geography, and special emphasis must be made in order to direct the pupil's attention to them. In Map I a study of the outline and position of Africa is made and only outline and position is presented. The stages of the presentation follow:

The facts of this map are (1) regular outline with no large estuary, (2) an extent in latitude corresponding with that from Raleigh, North Carolina, to Buenos Aires, (3) an extent in longitude such that five time meridians, 15 degrees west to 45 degrees east, cut the country. The time meridian of London passes through the western bulge and the time meridian of Vienna along the Nile to the extreme south. Longitude is used merely for position. The inferences are these:

A. *Climate.*—Map I furnishes us with two climatic controls, latitude and distance from the sea. The deduction, based on latitude and the inclination of the sun's rays, would be that the climate is for the most part warm. This inference, if latitude alone is the determining cause of climatic states, should be correct. The introduction of the other controls of climate shown on later maps indicates that latitudinal lines are not boundaries of climatic zones. A second statement would be that there is a great deal of rain, and this we base on the capacity of warm air for moisture and a recognition of the influences of the planetary wind circulation in equatorial regions.

B. *Soil.*—No evident relationship. However, frequently a fiord coast is an indication of glaciation and therefore glacial soils.

C. *Vegetation.*—Basing our statement on the knowledge of the vegetation of the home country or the vegetation zones as there shown, we may expect a luxuriant growth. This approaches a climatic control more nearly than a position control, but it is not easy to keep the two apart.

D. *Animals.*—No positive law of distribution dependent upon outline is known. However, latitude may be a barrier to migration and this again approaches closely to the climatic control.

E. *Population.*—The outline shows no indentations which are apt to be centers of population, and if this feature was the only control, the population would be sparse. As interiors of continents are secondary to coast centers and are generally subsequent in development, our conclusion may be made for the whole of Africa. In regard to the character of the people, if civilization in its varying degrees has been spoken of in terms of latitude, a statement to the effect that the people are not very far along in civilized customs is admissible.

F. *Commerce.*—Commerce and population are to a large degree complementary. Commerce is developed by harbors, and if it depended upon re-entrants alone our conclusion in regard to the commercial status of a country should be at once definite and accurate. The commerce of Africa, so far as this factor is concerned, is a negligible quantity. It may be found later that some ports and cities are developed on a regular coast line, as, for example, Iquique, Chile. The reason for this situation, which would appear in the course of the development, emphasizes the leading factor of the city's growth.

MAP II.—TOPOGRAPHY. Now are added the facts of relief. The fourfold division, which may be designated mountains, highlands, uplands, and lowlands, as shown on the map, is a convenient one to use as one or more of the forms is within the experience of pupils and they are sufficiently general in character to embrace all sorts of variations, yet specific enough to be differentiated. The inferences made during the study of Map I are to be modified if need be by the facts of this map and new inferences made from the additional data.

A. *Climate.*—Two more controls of climate, altitude and slope exposure, are added by this map. The general statement of an extensive warm area in Africa, based on position, has to be changed to meet this new control. Furthermore, mountains are

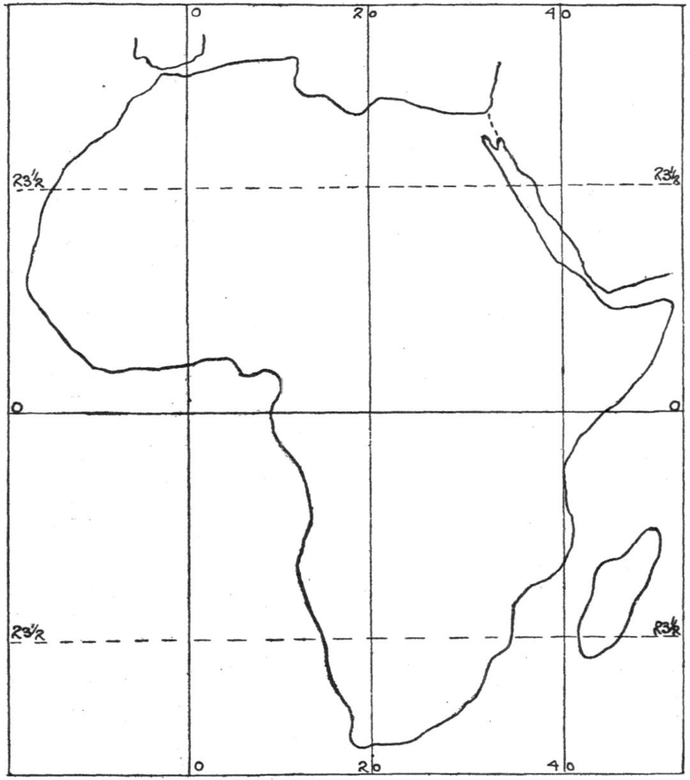

Map I.—Outline Map, Showing Farallels and Meridians

Map II.—Topographic Map

Above 6,500 feet
From 1,650 to 6,500
From 650 to 1,650
From 0 to 650

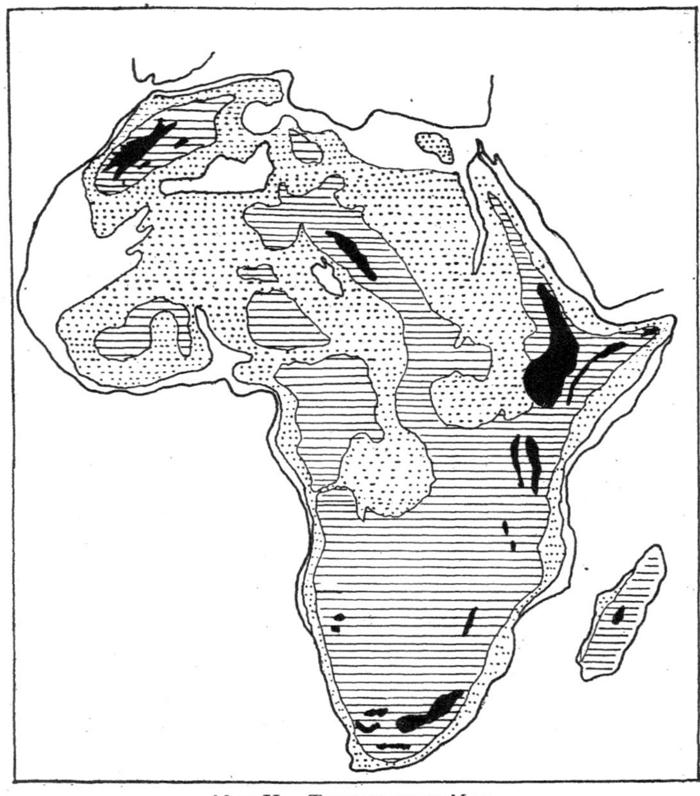

regions of heavy rainfall; they act as deflectors of wind, so that on one side of the mountain there may be moist regions and on the other arid regions. To determine this accurately, wind direction must be known.

B. *Soil.*—Mountains are in the process of denudation, consequently they contain but little soil. Most commonly, metals and minerals are exposed in these regions; this is, in part, the resultant of the erosive processes which shapes the peak or chain. Lowlands are generally being aggraded, from their position, and the rocks are being buried with fertile soils. Mining is not possible to any large degree except where rivers, in the natural process of erosion, deposit in their beds precious minerals, as gold and diamonds. Between these two extremes of topography, the uplands and highlands may be expected to have coatings of soil, the amount varying roughly in inverse proportion to the height.

C. *Vegetation.*—In all localities, Alpine conditions may be experienced by the ascent of some lofty mountain. In equatorial Africa, a height of 15,000 feet would be equivalent to a latitude of 60 degrees. There is, however, this advantageous feature of high latitudes over high altitudes, namely, a longer duration of sunlight during the growing season. Vegetation would be more luxuriant in lowlands than in highlands. Here again there is demanded a restatement of the deductions made under Map I so as to accord with the topographic factor.

D. *Animals.*—Mountain sides offer in many instances good pasturage. The open country is essential to some animals as the antelope, zebra, etc., and high mountains are inhabited by species of goat and ibexes. Again, the mountain chain is apt to be a barrier to types, so that the fauna on opposite sides may be different.

E. *Population.*—Mountain chains may separate peoples by acting as barriers, may form political boundaries, and may promote social unity and independence through protection (Abyssinia). On the other hand the low countries must contain the trade centers and be the more densely populated.

F. *Commerce.*—All forms of earth surface promote or hinder trade: the mountain in proportion to its inaccessibility restrains

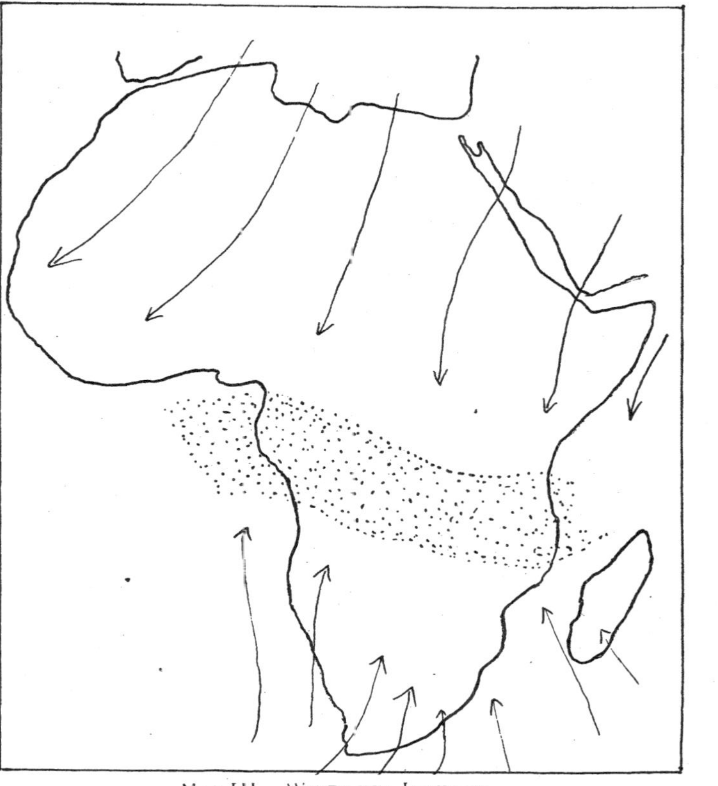

Map III.—Winds for January
Dotted areas show ascending currents. Arrows fly with the wind

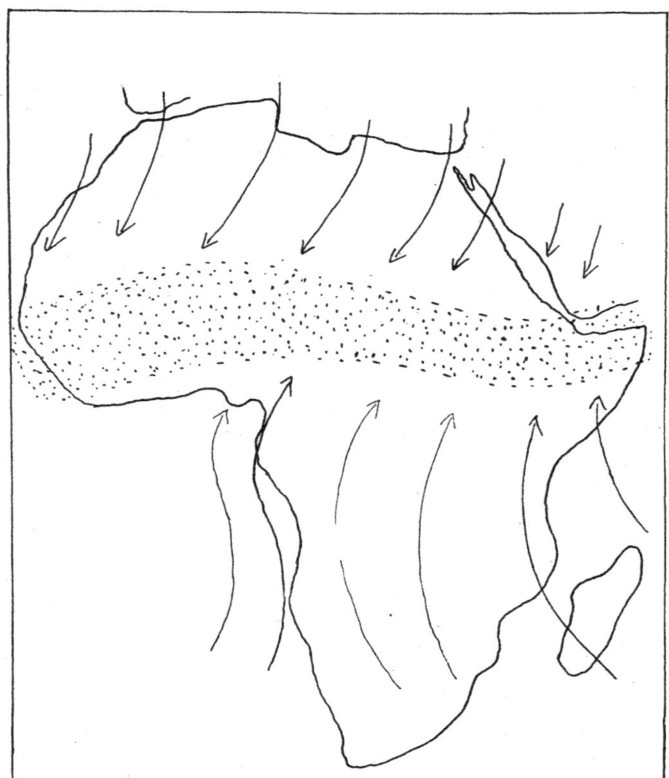

Map IV.—Winds for July
Dotted areas show ascending currents. Arrows fly with the wind

it; plains and valleys facilitate transportation and thereby stimulate industry and manufacturing.

MAPS III AND IV.—THE WIND MAPS FOR JANUARY AND JULY. On these maps are shown the wind system of Africa and the limits of the migration of the wind belts.

A. *Climate.*—Winds are transporters of climates. Winds which blow from the water to the land bring to it a marine climate and moisture; winds blowing over the land are drying winds and if they blow from the interior they bear the extremes of the continental type of climate. In regions of ascending currents, warmth and moisture result; in regions of descending currents, we find cooling temperatures and prevailing clear weather. The combination now of the effects of outline, topography, and winds gives a clue to the climate of the various parts of Africa.

B. *Soil.*—Where winds absorb moisture, sand and salt may be expected. Sand will be found also on the leeward sides of mountains. On the windward sides of the mountains, especially at their bases, there will be much fertile soil. Sand will travel in the direction of the prevailing winds.

C. *Vegetation.*—The winds affect vegetation especially by the dispersal of seeds and, in individual cases, by shifting the centers of gravity to leeward. In regions of ascending currents the vegetation is luxuriant; in regions of parching winds, sparse; in regions of moist winds, moderate. These latter effects may be considered as resulting from rainfall, but the wind movement largely controls the precipitation.

D. *Animals.*—No noteworthy effects.

E. *Population.*—No noteworthy effects apart from such as are instanced under commerce.

F. *Commerce.*—Winds affect commerce by determining sailing routes. This cannot be said to have a large valuation today in the time of steamships. The direction of the prevailing wind in any locality determines in some measure the harbor privilege. A wind blowing toward the land and into an estuary may make an otherwise good harbor undesirable as a place of safety. This difficulty is overcome to a large degree by breakwaters, as at Algiers.

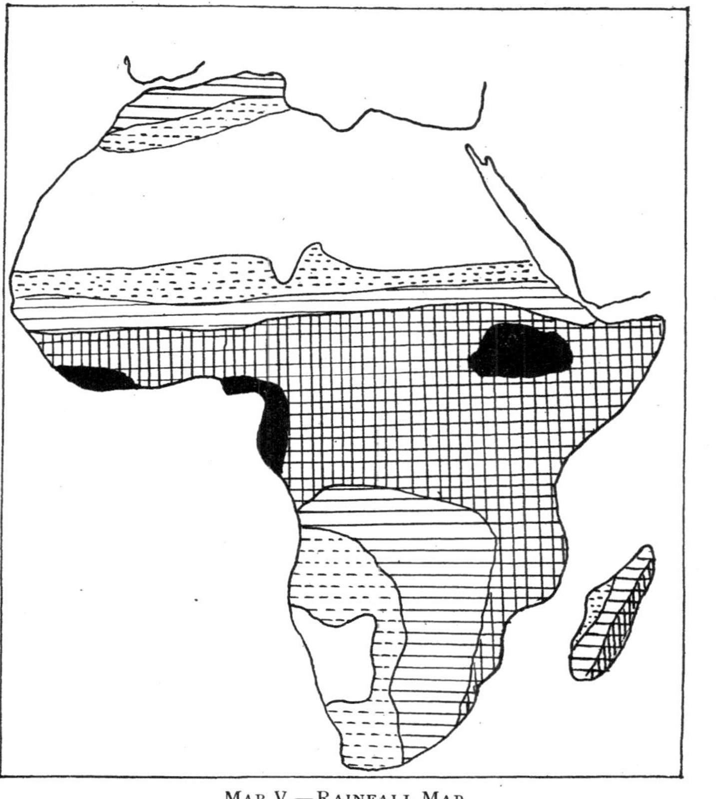

Map V.—Rainfall Map

Under 10 inches annually
10 to 20 inches
20 to 40 inches
40 to 80 inches
Over 80 inches

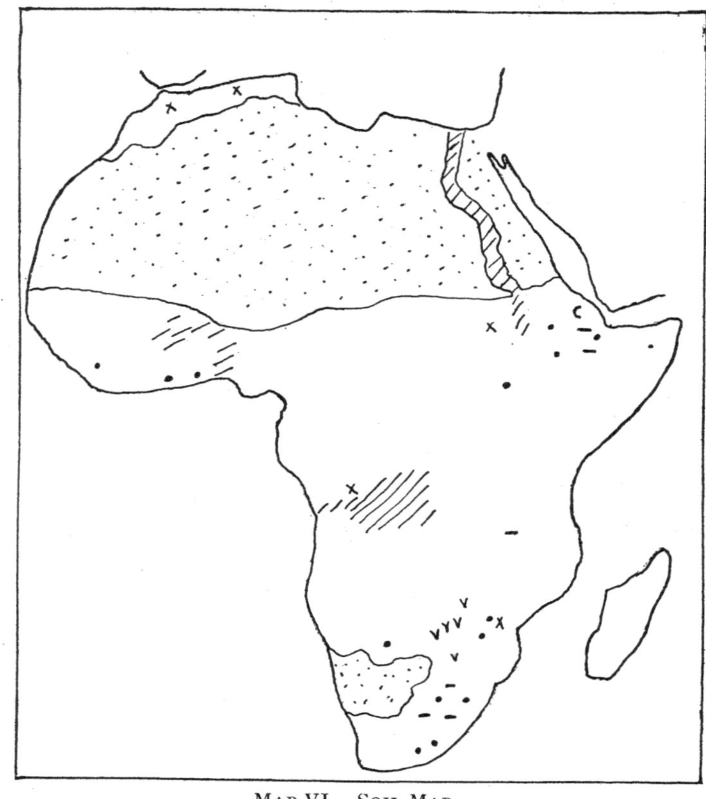

Map VI.—Soil Map

Sand. Alluvium. • Gold. — Coal. x Copper. c Silver.
v Diamonds

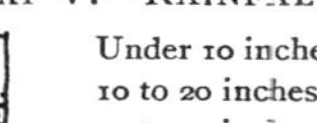
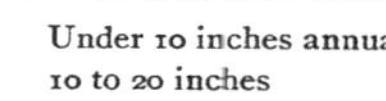
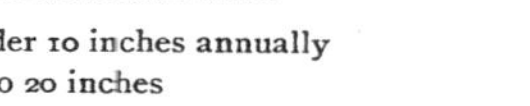

EXERCISE

The rainfall controls have been considered. A summary of these may be introduced at this time, and, if they are correctly interpreted, a rainfall map may be made by the pupils which should approach closely to the one to be presented later. On an outline map of Africa, plot the rainfall, using a fourfold classification; the regions of heavy rainfall (over 80 inches annually), the regions of moderate rainfall (20 to 80 inches), the regions of sparse rainfall (10 to 20 inches), and the regions of little or no rainfall (less than 10 inches). When this is done the rainfall map may be presented for comparison.

MAP V.—RAINFALL. This is the last of the climatic elements to be presented and the climatic condition of Africa in general terms ought to be known. It is possible to introduce the rivers of Africa at this point to good advantage. The sources of the rivers are in the mountains as the mountains are the regions of rainfall. The size of rivers depends on the amount of rainfall. The floods of rivers result from the seasonal migration of the rainfall belts as in the case of the Nile. When highlands approach near the coast, as in the case of most of Africa, falls are apt to block the river for sailing craft.

A. *Soil.*—Soil is transported by rivers and forms floodplains and deltas. The regions of interior drainage are salt, as Tchad. Mountains are in their early stages devoid of soil cover. The wearing down of the mountains is a natural mining process and yields gold and diamonds in river deposits.

B. *Vegetation.*—Climate probably influences vegetation more than any other factor. The high temperatures and heavy rains produce such luxuriant growths that clearing for agriculture is not profitable. Under more temperate conditions staple foods may be cultivated. Less than ten inches of rain annually makes vegetation a negligible quantity; when the rainfall is between ten and twenty inches, the vegetation is sparse; more than twenty inches and less than eighty gives the best conditions for cultivation of crops. Within the limits of the rainfall suitable for agriculture, an increase of rainfall is conducive to a larger yield per acre. Kinds of plants may, in the rough, be determined by

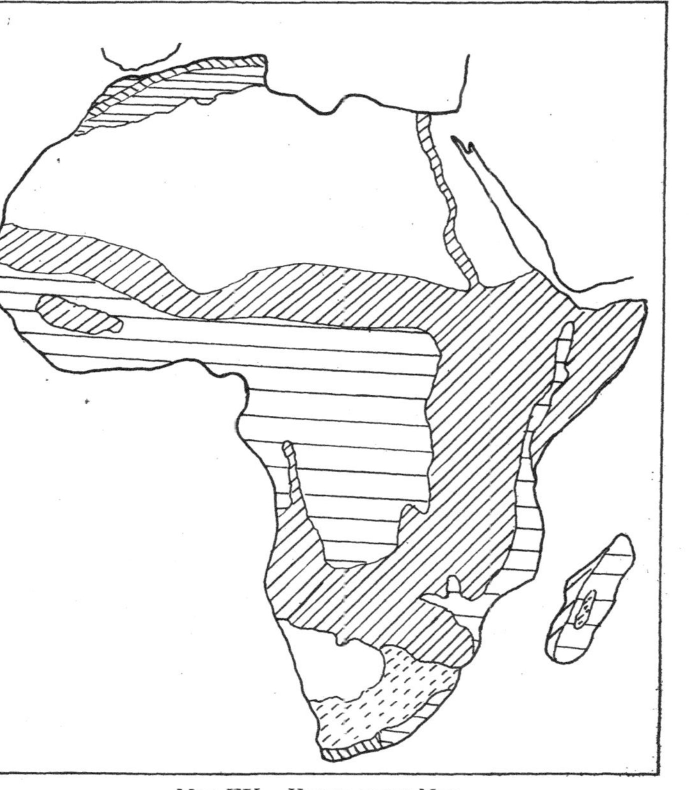

Map VII.—Vegetation Map

- Tropical Forests and Cultivable Lands
- Sub-tropical; Grass Plains
- Temperate; Firs and Pines prevailing
- Temperate; Grass Lands, part needing irrigation
- Desert

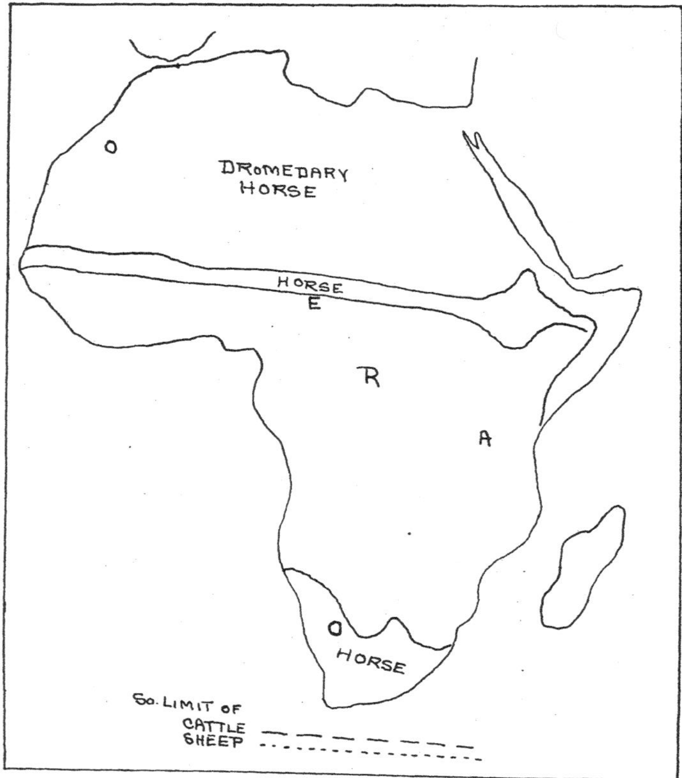

Map IX.—Animal Map

O. Ostrich. A. Antelope. R. Rhinoceros. E. Elephant

the amount of water; there are the drouth plants, as the cactus; water plants, as the flags, lillies, and willows; and intermediate conditions of plant growths, ranging from Alpine carpets, prairies, deciduous forests to broad-leafed evergreens.

C. *Animals.*—Climate cannot be said to be the direct determining cause of the distribution of animals, although there are animals which must fall under such a factor of distribution, and isothermal lines are barriers to migration. Animal increase is limited by the food supply and animal migration is also so limited. Vegetation is the important function in the consideration of most animals.

D. *Population and commerce.*—Responses are many but not important enough to find a place here.

MAP VI.—SOIL. A soil map may show the larger tracts of alluvial soil as flood plains and deltas, sandy areas and the location of the mineral products.

A. *Vegetation.*—Sandy soils do not retain moisture and are therefore not adapted to much plant growths. Alluvial plains are fertile. On leeward sides of sandy areas vegetation may be destroyed by drifting sand.

B. *Population and commerce.*—Minerals attract people to almost uninhabitable mountains. Certain minerals in the process of mountain destruction are borne by rivers and deposited in river gravels and loams, as gold and diamonds, and these influence the distribution of population and are of commercial value. Around coal outcrops population gathers. The sandy wastes are devoid of a settled population except here and there where water issues from the earth. In lesser ways soil and rocks affect people by furnishing or limiting building material.

All the physiographic factors have now been presented. The remaining maps show the responses to these and the lessons from this time on are in the main a verification or a correction of the inferences made. Before the next map is presented, it is possible to introduce an exercise which may also serve as a review. From the factors already discussed which influence vegetation, construct a vegetation map. This map will of necessity show quantity, not kinds.

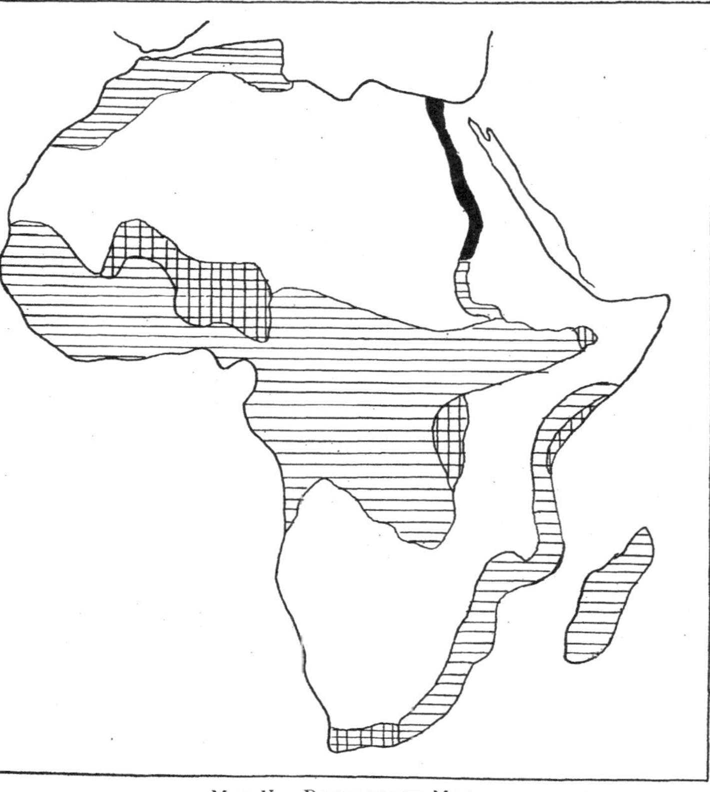

MAP X.—POPULATION MAP

Over 500 to a square mile
50 to 100
10 to 50
Less than 10

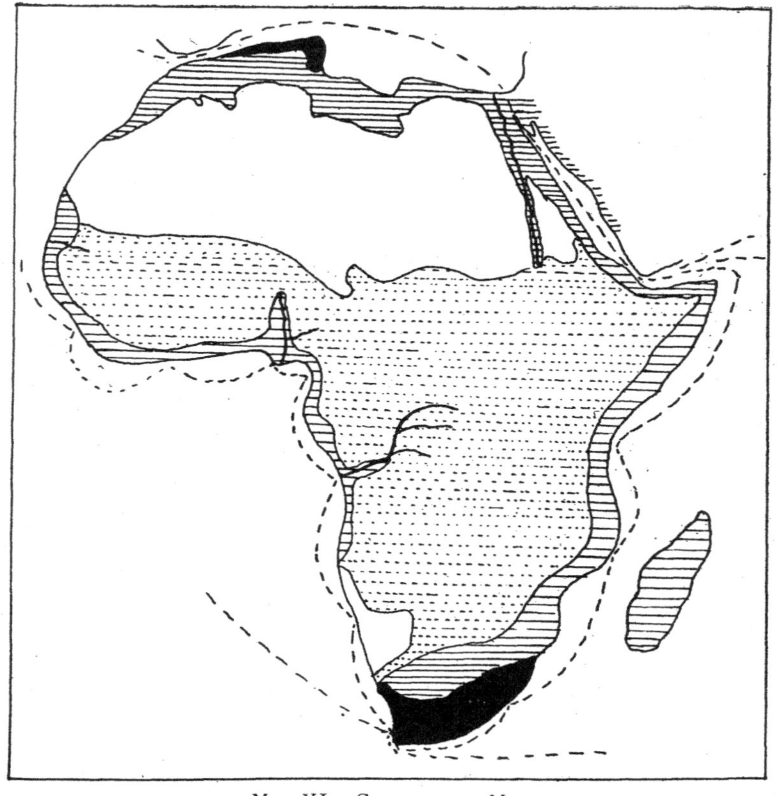

MAP XI.—COMMERCIAL MAP

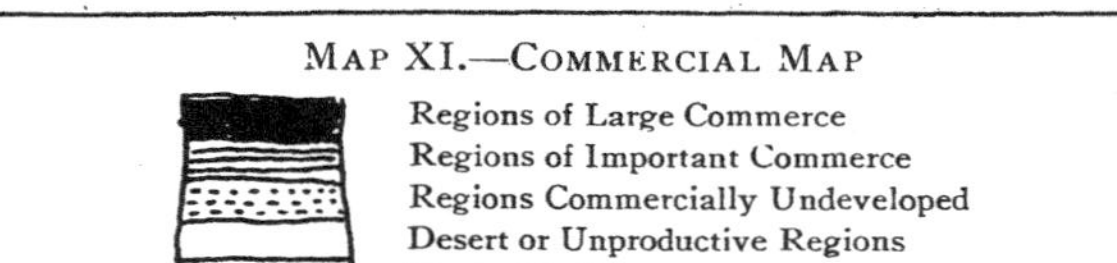

Regions of Large Commerce
Regions of Important Commerce
Regions Commercially Undeveloped
Desert or Unproductive Regions
Navigable Rivers
Steamer Lines

MAP VII.—VEGETATION. Introduced for verification of statements deduced from the conditions.

MAP VIIIA AND VIIIB. These maps may show the areas where wheat and rice are raised. Two forms of exercise may be used in this connection. From similarity of conditions of growth, kinds may be located, and from location of kinds, the condition of the climate may be inferred. For example: Rice requires 60 to 80 degrees for ripening, an abundance of moisture and the nourishment of low alluvial lands within the tropics. This is the condition of growth. From what has been found out concerning the climate of Africa, locate where rice may grow. Compare with Map VIIIB. Again, given Map VIIIB, infer the conditions of the climate and soil in those regions of rice-culture shown and note how the inferences agree with the conclusions already reached. The same sort of exercise may be carried out for sugar cane, cotton, coffee, wheat, and dates.

MAP IX.—ANIMALS. This map shows but a limited number of features, namely, the ranges of cattle and beasts of burden and the locations of a few typical native animals. In this portion of the subject it is well to omit much generally included under this heading. Large grazing areas and the distribution of wild animals which yield a product of commercial value are legitimate topics. In order to avoid confusion, but two or three of the wild animals should be mentioned. The items that determine the distribution and the increase of animal life have been considered under previous maps; there remains now the restatement in terms of the facts presented. Mountain ranges, rivers and arms of the sea, isothermal lines, deserts and forests act as barriers limiting the range of animals.

MAP X.—POPULATION. Before this map is presented, the construction of a population map may be tried by the pupils after a review of the factors determining the distribution. The facts are obtained for comparison afterwards from Map X. A study of the native population, the true negroes of Central Africa, and the related types, as the Negroids and the Bushmen, as well as the Arab invaders, may be introduced here if desired.

MAP XI.—COMMERCE. As before, a commercial map may be

constructed by the pupils in anticipation of the facts. The effects of elevation upon industry and commerce may be seen in the plateau region of Africa; of lack of rainfall in the Kalahari Desert and the Sahara; of alluvial plains in the Nile Valley; of

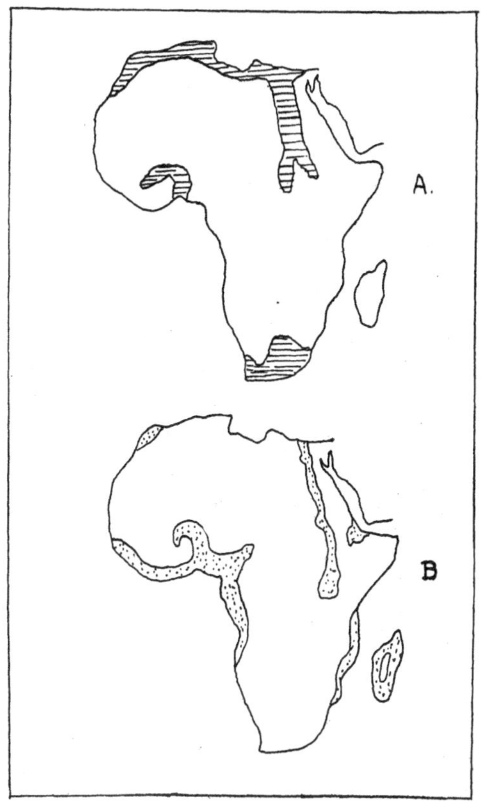

MAP VIII A.—DISTRIBUTION OF WHEAT
MAP VIII B.—DISTRIBUTION OF RICE

underground waters in parts of the Sahara; of minerals in the gold and diamonds of South Africa; of animals in the grazing and ostrich culture of South Africa; and of location in Tripoli's caravan trade. In further explanation of certain conditions, it should be added that a bad government is detrimental to commerce as is illustrated by the case of Morocco.

The presentation of the political divisions follows naturally the study of the larger view. It is generally the custom to take up in some detail and order each country of a continent. In the presentation by means of the maps nearly every feature of value in the study of any one of the subdivisions may be presented, consequently there remains nothing new but to give a name to certain sections of the continent and to explain one or two social, political, or historical phases which have been instrumental in the development. Thus, the study of the individual countries, as Egypt, South Africa, Abyssinia, and so on, may be now used as a review or an exercise.

Some avoidance of names of cities, rivers, etc., has been exercised in this paper. This was intentional in order to satisfy a double demand. In the first place, in the great uncertainty concerning what names ought to be taught and what names ought to be omitted, I did not desire to dictate; again, inasmuch as the plan herein presented is applicable to other grand divisions and as well to limited portions of them, I wished to furnish an outline as free from specific references to Africa as possible. The teacher knows to a great degree what names she is expected to use and these are easily fitted into the study at the proper time.

THE KINDERGARTEN PROGRAMME. II

BERTHA PAYNE
The School of Education

THE PRESENT SITUATION

The emphasis which Froebel placed upon unfoldment caused him to invent the geometric series of the gifts with their logically unfolding use. In these sequences the "forms of knowledge," "forms of beauty," and "forms of life" following the canon of unfoldment are to reveal to the child such principles as "inner and outer," "part and whole," "unity and diversity." The plays and games are chosen to reveal similar truths.

The kindergartner who places her emphasis on adjustment as Nature's method of enabling the young human being to find himself and his powers by his reactions on the objective world asks whether he has a use and need for these geometric forms in carrying out play purposes of his own. She questions the beauty form sequence and tries to make it the outcome of the child's appreciation and feeling rather than something imposed by herself without his inner concurrence. She wants it to be the outcome of his volition and not the result of a mechanical obedience to dictation. This type of kindergartner in choosing representative plays asks herself not only, "What truth does this symbolize?" but, "Does it fall in line with the child's interests; and does it come close to him through his experience?"

The application of the principles of adjustment causes us to look on knowledge, such knowledge as that of the interrelation of geometric planes or solids, as first, an increment of efforts to adjust, and second, as a tool for new adjustment. For example, a child first discovers a law of balance in mere piling of blocks; this new knowledge becomes now his tool in the execution of further purposes.

A study of children's activities shows that adult sequences of thought are not always logic to a child's mind. To be true he must proceed on premises of his own—premises of his own discovering—not on those we force upon him. Through the sequences that he himself has responded to actively, or evolved for himself, he proceeds to sequential thinking. His realities, his truths must be won for himself by his own efforts to adjust; we can help him to short cuts, by helping him to the right premises, and we can help him to the right premises only by controlling the presentations, or stimuli from which he derives them through his own self-activity. We herein affirm and reaffirm the validity, nay more, as most central and essential this principle of Froebel's psychology—*self-activity* which becomes *creative activity.*

The first order of childish invention lies in the free making of the "copies" of things with which the child is familiar and which have meaning for him. Through these play-creations children discover principles of construction and strengthen form and number concepts, before they are ready for gift or occupation exercises which deal with the *systematization* of form and number concepts; such systematizations or classifications as are found in conventional geometric sequences in block building, tablet, stick and ring laying, sewing, and folding.

Children are impelled by the force of their growing ideas to strive for wholeness. This Froebel fully recognized as a "striving for unity," but his way of reaching that wholeness was sometimes in accord with a child's natural process, and sometimes quite an unchildlike course of thinking. Experiences of our earlier years of kindergarten teaching showed a line of cleavage, sharp and distinct, between the ready response to suggestions or directions that meet a natural impulse, and that mechanical and listless following of orders to do that which was not suited to the child's concepts or interests. Dr. Dewey points out the necessity of recognizing in the child's intellectual progress the same conditions that hold true for an adult. The child's particular ends, problems, points of departure, and interests the adult has probably passed by, but both child and grown person achieve by the same type of mental action.

No one seriously questions that, with an adult, power and control are obtained through the realization of personal ends and problems through personal selection of means and materials which are relevant, and through personal adaptation and application of what is thus selected, together with whatever of experimentation and of testing is involved in the effort. Practically every one of these conditions of increase of power for the adult are denied for the child. For him problems and aims are determined by another mind. For him material that is relevant and irrelevant is selected in advance by another mind, and, upon the whole, there is such an attempt made to teach him a ready-made method for applying his material to the solution of his problems, or the reaching of his ends, that the factor of experimentation is at the minimum. With the adult we unquestioningly assume that an attitude of personal inquiry, based on the possession of a problem which interests and absorbs, is a necessary precondition of mental growth. With the child we assume that the precondition is rather the willing condition to submit to any problem and material presented from without. *Alertness* is our ideal in one case; *docility* in the other.[1]

There is a widely accepted type of programme which is stamped with this attempt to select ends, problems, and methods to such a degree that the values of experimentation and discovery are depreciated. The plan of work for one week which is given below may serve to give point to this contention.

GENERAL TOPIC: COMING AND GOING, WITH SPECIAL EMPHASIS PLACED ON THE RETURN

The child's own coming and going is to be more definitely brought before him. Talks will be given on the coming and going of mother and father; also talks on the coming and going of the seasons, the flowers, birds, etc. Among all of the childrens' experiences thus far the most significant has been that of estrangement and return.

STORY: THE THREE BEARS

Bring out the following points: the home of the bears and the home of the child, the straying from home and returning to home. The child leaves home and comes back, the bears leave home and come back. The little girl wanted to go home; she finds her mother. Bring out also the difference in the size of the bears; objects in their house, etc.

TALKS

I. Use natural objects within reach. Flowers; notice color and formations of golden rod, color and dark center of "Black-eyed Susan," color and structure of "butter and eggs," star shape of aster.

II. Develop "A Little Boy's Walk"[2] as preliminary to the "Pigeon

[1] John Dewey, *Psychology and Social Practice,* pp. 13, 14, The University of Chicago Press.

[2] Emilie Paulsson, *Finger Plays.*

House." Tell poem as a story. Draw picture on board. Put emphasis on "telling mother." Encourage children to share their experiences. Develop tendency to communicate experiences.

III. Give period to learning words and music. Suggest games that bear upon the idea of estrangement and return, but do not make idea conscious to the child.

Games: Visiting, wandering, hiding, ball games, travelers, lads and lassies, sunbeams, steam train.

MONDAY

Gift exercise.—First Gift: Review movements; round and round, forward and back, right and left. Develop movement up and down in a rhythmic manner. Give children a chance to use strings of things they have brought in up and down exercises. Children asked to tell the names of all things that *go* up and down, that *are* up and down. Develop attention. Test children's attention to what you say by such games as "Simon says thumbs up."

Develop new color. Count balls of different colors. Find out how many children can really count. Play hiding ball in connection with color exercises.

Occupation.—Clay modeling. Make balls and flatten them out. Cut edges with a cake-cutter. Make indented line near edge around each clay circle. Children model two balls of equal size and place on this plaque. Make a good-sized oblong plaque. Divide into five equal parts, by means of lines made with the finger. Make balls, two at a time, and place on the divisions of the oblong in the same manner as on the circular one. Let the child count the balls and spaces.

TUESDAY

Gift exercise.—Third Gift: Cut cube into two parts, then put together again. Repeat. Refer to house made for Thumbling, and play cube is house. Furnish bedroom. This room chosen as being perhaps the most familiar room to child. Make a bed, return to cube. Make a chair, return to cube. Make table, sofa, washstand, wardrobe, etc., returning to cube after each form. Let children make anything else we have in the house.

End lesson by going over all the forms given in the series of bedroom furniture, without, however, going back to the cube after each form.

End with cube *illustrating the principle of estrangement and return.*

Occupation.—Sewing. Use card having three concentric circles, or card having three circles in a row, differing in size. Use one color or three. Emphasis placed on difference in size. Refer to big and little objects in this connection. Sand may be used for house in this period if preferred.

WEDNESDAY

Second Gift.—Have large gift in sight. Give each child box containing either spheres, cubes, or cylinders differing in size, using three sizes. As teacher calls for different forms have children hold them up. Have children bring forms to teacher and place them in three rows upon the floor: a row of spheres of different sizes, a row of cylinders of different sizes, and a row of cubes of different sizes. These forms may also be seen in rows of three, a sphere, a cube, and a cylinder in each row. Redistribute the forms and let each child arrange independently, according to size.

Play matching game, with the following words:

Use your eyes, use your eyes,
Look carefully now and see,
And if your ball is the size of mine
Roll it across to me.

Use nests of boxes, tin cans, spools of different sizes for this work. Main point to be brought out is that of difference in size.

Occupation.—Pasting. Paste a row of circles on an oblong piece of paper. Count circles. Tell what other things have the same color. Take completed work home as a bookmark for mother.

THURSDAY

Gift exercise.—Third Gift. Use fifth-gift boxes, second-gift cubes, and ordinary third gifts. Divide according to child's suggestion. Make the same furniture built on Tuesday, using three sizes of blocks. Contrast in size is the point to be brought out. Re-tell story of "Three Bears" in this connection.

Occupation.—Sewing, or milk weed exercise. If sewing, finish card. Milk weed exercise: Use pod for little boat. Have children make mast and sail of stick and paper, and sail pod on dish of water. In this connection recall traveling experiences.

Observe resemblances of seeds to fish. Give each child a seed and let him watch its expansion in the sunlight. Let the children blow seeds from the window. Tell the children how the wind carries the seeds.

FRIDAY

Gift exercise.—Rings. Contrast in size is the point to be brought out. Give three rings of different sizes. Let child arrange as he chooses. Dictate form of concentric rings. Have fingers *jump* into large, small, and middle-sized rings. Have children tell where rings are, making a complete statement each time for the sake of developing language. Have small and middle-sized rings placed outside of large rings.

Arrange in vertical row, in horizontal row. Replace in form of concentric rings.

Give three more of each size and repeat figure, forming straight row of concentric rings. Give exercises on "in and out." Alternate front and back placing.

Occupation.—Stringing. Use a variety of natural objects, or, represent with natural objects some previous arrangement of rings or circles. Show connection between natural objects and conventional types.

Our criticism upon this programme is that it shows tendencies that are opposed to a child's process of growth.

1. The topic for the week is based upon a principle (estrangement and return) which, while perfectly true and absolutely fundamental, is one that needs no week of special application. It is as wide as life. Its meaning is sure to come to us and the children *in the day's work,* without resorting at a given week to special impressions in the shape of talks, stories, songs, games, and gifts and occupations.

2. A too obvious knowledge standard. Connections are sought by means of similarity in number, form, size, and color rather than by related meanings, such meanings as a child can appreciate while he explores the significant and relevant aspects of things in such plays as that described by Baldwin[3] in which the older child plays mother to the younger who impersonates the baby.

An objection to this method is that five-year-old children have outgrown the stage when mere quality or appearance, apart from function, has any charm. Similarities and contrasts of these qualities *per se* will not hold attention but when used as signs of function as clues to meanings, as pegs to hang their ideas on they are distinctly necessary and fill their higher place in the educative process.

In trying to teach large and small, red and blue, etc., we are underestimating a child's power. He is ready to use these qualities in play arrangements and representations drawn from life and with reference to life.

3. Play is at a minimum. Spontaneity is at a minimum.

4. There is too much talking about the plays as a means of focusing attention on the play, or of giving knowledge. If the

[3] J. Mark Baldwin, *Social and Ethical Interpretations.*

play is well chosen it brings its own response. Otherwise it is not a play, "The image constrains the child to play."

5. Adventitious exercises are indulged in to give focus to attention on details of form or number that have apparently no inherent interest, such as, "Have the fingers jump into the large rings, the small, the middle sized." This is a most pernicious teaching vice.

6. Artificial and meaningless connections are emphasized, such as the three different sizes in rings, balls, cubes, spheres, and sewed circles with the three bears of the story.

7. A forced return to the fundamental form of the cube after each piece of furniture is built quite opposed to the natural movement of the child's mind is insisted upon for the sake of impressing the fundamental unity of all structural forms, as well as the principle of "estrangement and return."

To sum up the contentions on which we make the above strenuous objections let us see the power which a four-and-a-half-year-old brings to the kindergarten with him. He has explored the world of form and size, texture, density, and weight by shaking, throwing, biting, and pounding everything within reach. He has set up objects and knocked them down, pulled things apart and put them together, piled them in heaps, and distributed them. He has felt all roundabout the furniture, doorways, stairways, windows, and implements in his own home until he has some apprehension of the long and short, round and flat, rectangular and curved, rough and smooth, high and low, in terms of his own muscular movement as well as by his eyes.

He has played with boxes, blocks, spools, balls, apples, sticks, books, sand, and earth. He has therefore much acquaintance with the qualities of things and has a basis for selection in his new life of representative play. He comes into the kindergarten in the full tide of his energy. His dominating impulse is the desire to make a record of his transforming power, on the thing with which he is surrounded. This he does through imitation and play with the motor force of ideas and images to shape the form with a personal stamp. We believe the above programme is in general thwarting, underestimating, and artificial, aiming to teach what is already known, drawing far-fetched principles out of bare concrete forms and contrast, and in part reversing the normal mental movement.

We see children in the play period of growth continually taking bits of their experience, and piecing them together, living them over, informing them with imagination. By this means they get the meaning of that which is fragmentary, and create fuller wholes.

Children exploit and explore environment in their adjustments in the shape of question, experiment, imitation, and invention. Immediate experience is the field of their operations. People and their doings furnish stimuli of prime interest. These social play adjustments are not only of prime interest to them but of prime value. It is life that children want, and that abundantly.

Dr. Dewey points out that the statement so frequently made that education means "drawing out" does not sufficiently recognize that children from four to eight years of age need no drawing out, being already "spilling over with activities of all kinds," and that we are neither to repress nor humor these crude impulsive activities, expressive of correspondingly crude ideas and interests, but are to organize and direct them. This is an excellent statement with which to combat a notion prevalent among the more orthodox that the modern view of instinct and of impulsive activity in general is that it is to have its fling regardless of consequences. A more scientific attitude toward the place of instinct in the upward movement of the little human individual is that it gives a powerful push in certain directions, such as imitation and the tendency to imitate some things, rather than other things, and that the intelligence of the child supplements and controls the original primitive instinct. The business of the kindergartner or teacher is to see that the motor force of the impulse is not lost, nor the act hardened into habit in its crude state, but that the child's intelligence shall supersede and control.

Miss Blow[4] points out another type of programme which she calls the industrial. The type programme which she quotes is an

[4] Susan Blow, *Educational Issues in the Kindergarten,* pp. 238–80.

extreme one on the industrial side and not typical of the largest and most elastic of its kind. The significant things in the programme are a social ideal, and a psychological principle. The social ideal is that of the interdependence of people, in work, in service, or in festival. It is grounded in the principles which shape community life. It seeks to take the situation in which a child finds himself at home, on the street, in the playground, the garden, the shop, the fields, and by reviewing some of these experiences in play to enter as far as a little child can enter into their meaning. The psychological principle is that of the use of immediate experience through imitation and play, through participation, and through the observation which these forms of activity entail. The aim of this plan is not to induce prematurely the attitude of work, but to let the play cluster about the social activities as the child's play does normally and naturally. This principle can be elucidated further as a recognition of the fact that children seize upon activities of others as giving "copy" that is worth while. They engage in them instinctively and are equally interested in a circus the rush of the fire engine, store keeping, the building of a shelter, or a funeral. The effort is made by the kindergartner to select those themes that are freighted with individual and social meaning, from forms of work to festival celebrations. It is believed that a better quality of attention is secured, a more vital living interest, by following this plan. Nor is the child's representation all work by any means. It is a just criticism upon this programme if the making of real tools, utensils, or other articles becomes forced, if the real work engaged in takes precedence of play or if the make-believe loses its quality of choice and selection. If the aesthetic element is crowded out, then surely the values have lost balance. But this is not true of the best type of programme formed largely on social activities, and which I refuse to call an industrial programme. In these play themes dramatization takes first rank as a mode of entering into such situations as going to a fire, playing store, or any social function, such as making visits, or going to church. Next come play makings with kindergarten gifts, or with paper, clay, sand, or paint. If the making a toy thing, such as a little broom, a store window, a fireman's cap, will enhance the meaning of the play, and if it can come within the scope of a child's constructive imagination, with no more of dictation, and no more highly organized material than he would get in the kindergarten folding paper or sewing card, then by all means let the article be made. It becomes the most potent kind of symbol of the real activity out of which it has grown and of which it is a part.

Nor do some household occupations fail of a happy use here and there. What more natural than that these five-year-old children should undertake some activities ordinarily classed as "work" and which grow out of their life together. They delight in brushing up the crumbs, the paper scraps, dusting the piano, washing the milk cups, and scrubbing the tables, provided these occupations are alternated so that each may take his turn at each kind of work. It is not work so much at first as it is play, but in either case it is not at all forced or un-childlike. Through the dusting and wiping he becomes acquainted with properties of sponge, cotton cloth, woolen, he loves to splash in the water and to manipulate the soap and the brush. The meaning of household work becomes his own in an intimate way beside which the consciousness of it brought home solely by such a story as "Charlotte and the Ten Dwarfs" becomes a pale and meager thing. If the story be *added* to this participation, it meets and adds charm to a genuine appreciation.

The alternation from actual participation to play representations of work contains no contradiction. The impulses to both are in a child's heart. He can go with the greatest satisfaction from helping to prepare something for luncheon to the play building of store or table with the greatest naturalness, and out of each kind of experience he gets a different and vital reaction. As an illustration of this simple play process, note the description that Froebel gives in his *Pedagogics of the Kindergarten* [5] of the way in which the mother plays with her child using the building blocks to follow out a little play of making the stove on which the soup is being prepared for the father's dinner, the table around which all are soon to sit, or again, the garden benches, and the

[5] Froebel, *Pedagogics of the Kindergarten,* pp. 178, 179.

summer house into which they must run to escape an impending rain storm. Here are sequences of meaning as well as form, natural, familiar, and vital, into which the children enter with ready response. Froebel recognized the joy which children take in the sharing the work of older people, and gives a strong emphasis to the learning process that goes on in such participation:

My neighbor's son, scarcely three years old, tends his mother's goslings near my garden hedge. The space to which he is to confine the lively little creatures in their search for food is small. They escape from the little swain, who may have been busy in other ways, seeking food for his mind. The goslings get into the road, where they are exposed to injury. The mother sees this and calls out to the child to be careful. The little boy who, by the ever-renewed efforts of the goslings for freedom, probably had often been disturbed in his own pursuits, retorts, "Mother, you seem to think it not hard to tend goslings."

Who can indicate the present and future developments which the child reaps from this part of the parent's work and which he might reap more abundantly if parents and attendants heeded the mother and made use of it later on in the instruction and training of their children?

Behold here the little child of the gardener. He is weeding; the child wishes to help, and he teaches the little fellow to distinguish hemlock from parsley, to observe the differences in odor and brillancy of the leaves.

There the forester's son accompanies his father to the clearing that at some previous time they together had sown. Everything looks green. The child sees only young pine plants; but the father teaches him to recognize cypress-spunge and to distinguish it from the pine plant by its different properties.

. . . .

In another place the child sees his father striking the hot iron, and is taught by the father that the heat makes the iron softer, and again as the father tries to push the heated rod through an opening through which before it passed easily that heat expands the iron.[6]

This kind of learning through sharing occupations cannot go on in our highly organized households as it did in the simple village life of rural Germany of Froebel's day. It is therefore the more necessary to provide occasions in kindergarten and school for the interest that it stimulates and the control it involves. Here children can take part in simple occupations which can

[6] Froebel, *Education of Man* (Appleton), pp. 84–86.

either be initiated by them or observed, shared, and continued by them.

In this scheme the child is the center, his budding interests are followed and the most fruitful selected for culture. As he lives a life with many points of contact so the kindergarten plan must include many phases of interest. The child's interest is fragmentary and his thinking is fragmentary, and yet he is seeking for wholeness, he is trying to fill in his *schema,* to dig out its essential meaning, and any plan which we pursue must follow his own method of pursuing this completeness. If all our hand occupations are merely disjointed exercises, having no relation to a purpose which, however fleeting and small, is *his* purpose, they have not achieved what he can really achieve for himself, namely, an explanation, implicit in his acts perhaps, but still an explanation of various phases of the moving world about him.

Nature has its place. In the garden we find a typical opportunity for gaining a set of related meanings in which children can play and yet really plant and tend. The insects that are on their plants, the earth worms in the soil of their plot claim unusual attention. The worms feed upon their cabbages, the aphis on their rose leaves, the bees suck honey from their flowers. The attempt to make the garden grow may not be a very successful one from the standpoint of results. No very reliable habits of work may be formed, and yet it is a play with point, it goes on from day to day with increasing interest, and the small by-products as are indicated above are the invaluable accompaniments that lend wholeness to the picture which he is gaining from day to day. Another typical theme in this kind of programme is found in the preparation for a festival such as Thanksgiving or Christmas.

Now, if this be open to the objection that it is developing a succession of topics, separate centers, as it were, I would answer, so does apperception proceed. A little child is non-resistant, open to all stimuli. Those attended to and acted upon become organizing centers for later experiences to tie to. He may have a dozen or five hundred "apperception centers." This is not mental disintegration but the progress toward integration. As his experience widens and his attention grows in span these centers get into relation as inevitably as the raindrop-circles on the surface of the lake coalesce; nothing remains unrelated.

The *child* is the center. His organizing activity makes him not the passive, receptive vehicle into which experiences pour, sorting themselves out into different knowledge groups, but the creative as well as the assimulative individual. It is this creative principle which makes the "apperception centers," referred to above, vastly differ in meaning from the Herbartian signification.

Nor is this or any programme suited to the play period of growth unless it is elastic, giving room for experimental learning, which, it must be remembered, is learning through trial and error, failure and success.

When it is proposed to cause a programme, prepared by one person or set of people, to be adopted by others, we would say, "To what end?" and ask in the words of Dr. Dewey whether "any teacher can receive from another a statement of the methods by which his ends may be reached and not become hopelessly servile in his attitude."[7]

This paper has, by reason of its necessarily general nature, given no typical programme of the order which the fundamental principles to which we hold would demand. If space permits some illustrations may be given in succeeding numbers of the application of these principles in daily work for a given period.

[7] John Dewey, *Psychology and Social Practice,* The University of Chicago Press.

AMERICAN SCHOOLS AS SEEN BY A BELGIAN EDUCATOR[1]

FRANK A. MANNY
Western State Normal School, Kalamazoo, Mich.

"Real life enters into the American school by doors and windows." This expresses the impression our schools make upon many foreigners. M. Buyse, who has charge of the industrial museum and school at Charleroi, province of Hainaut, Belgium, is a most appreciative student of what we are doing. He is so much delighted with what he finds here that in the course of seven hundred and fifty pages he raises scarcely a question and seems to consider practically all of our difficulties overcome. In a letter apart from the book he expresses the hope that we should "continue in the same progressive way and avoid, as much as possible, European influence which would disturb the admirable concordance between your systems and your national spirit."

One wishes that there was evidence of more discrimination in the work. There is not the evaluation of what we are doing that is found in Dr. Kuyper's *Volksschule und Lehrerbildung in den Vereinigten Staaten,* neither is there as clear a line between the theoretical discussions and the description of what is done. This does not mean that the report is not in many respects well made. There is a remarkable absence of misstatement and one can gain a better detailed view of some of our interests than is available in our own language. As much praise as is here given is especially valued coming from a leader in industrial education in Belgium. One of our best informed students of this important field, Professor Mary Schench Woolman, considers the work in Belgium most instructive for Americans to visit. It takes considerable experience in progressive education to enable a man to find in our schools all that M. Buyse finds there.

The seven divisions treat of: (1) elementary education;

[1] Omer Buyse, *Méthodes américaines d'education générale et technique.* Paris, M. Dunod & E. Pinat.

(2) secondary technical education; (3) industrial education; (4) trade schools; (5) education of backward races; (6) commercial education; (7) higher technical schools. There are seven hundred and ten illustrations from a wide range of subjects.

The recent reports of the National Society for Industrial Education will prove a boon to the industrious European student of American schools. He has availed himself usually of the monographs prepared for the Paris Exposition, but beyond that his task of gathering together what he needs from the mass of papers, reports, and pictures represents a great amount of labor. Our government reports have not been of the value in this respect that they should be. The new administration offers more hope in this direction.

In order to appreciate the significance of the material the reporter selects for presentation it is well to bear in mind the condition of affairs in the country from which he writes. We have few careful, connected accounts of the schools of the smaller countries of Europe. In Belgium I was impressed by an emphasis upon individual liberty which at first seemed promising. A prominent education official told me "We would not dare, in Belgium, to propose either compulsory education or compulsory military service." I learned, however, that the latter is non-compulsory only in the sense that when a man draws a lot calling for service he is excused if he can hire a substitute! The other non-compulsion is somewhat more genuine and its evidences are apparent. But this is true of France also. The latest report of our commissioner of education states that school attendance is one of the most serious questions in French primary schools. It will be found that in many other respects the schools of the two countries have much in common. M. Ribot in the noted report of the commission of 1898 says:

The crisis is not then limited to our own country. But it is complicated in France with the ever-present contest between public and private instruction. This contest shows here a character seen nowhere else save in Belgium. Liberty of teaching has ended in France with a monopoly divided between the State and the Catholic church. Individual initiative is crushed. We do not have all the benefits of liberty, but we do have all the inconveniences, not to say perils, of liberty.

While these statements had reference to secondary education the problem of the relation of secondary and primary education is one even though one finds its unity in France often to consist of mutual hatred and distrust. Nowhere have I found more contempt by teachers of secondary schools for those trained for the (to them) purely utilitarian work of the lower schools than in France, and in that anomalous institution, the middle school, where teachers of the two trainings meet, the situation is often tragic. I never felt so near to the French Revolution as during an hour spent in a class in which boys were almost in revolt against a teacher of morals who had come up from the lower school. I understood the attitude of the boys better when I had talked more with teachers in the same school, trained from the standpoint of the privileged class. We are fortunate in having at last an adequate work on the French field by Professor Farrington, *The Public Primary-School System of France.* We need one which will state more adequately than has yet been done the larger problem.

In French writers on education there is a striking unanimity in condemning the lack of opportunity for initiative on the part of young people. In one of the French weeklies there are frequent extracts from the autobiographies of modern Frenchmen. Among these the same note is constantly struck. There is a recognition that what is wanted in life is not attainable without initiative and greater participation in processes than is now permitted. The difficulty, it seems to me, lies in the unwillingness of these men to pay for what they want. Processes like physical labor are to them necessary evils valuable only for what they make possible. This in itself is true in a sense, but there is a marked failure to recognize that flower and fruit and seed are no more ends in themselves than are root, stem, and leaf. Products cannot be isolated, even in appreciation, without a stoppage of circulation. One is reminded of Matthew Arnold's inclusion of the results of processes in the curriculum while he excludes the processes themselves. The direction of processes belongs to the higher class, but the performance of them is menial. A French teacher, who had been an engineer, said to me in reference to the teaching of chemistry: "No, the students do not perform the experiment—a drawing serves just as well. Any servant can be trained to perform experiments—you might as well expect to educate a boy by teaching him to make a fire in a stove as to put iron in a test tube." I have even found it carried so far that boys in classes corresponding to our seventh grade, were taught merely to indicate mathematical operations and only carry them out when that labor was unavoidable. What Professor Palmer calls "the glory of the incomplete" is even less recognized in Europe than in America.

This is not the place to discuss the material in the last six divisions of M. Buyse's book. One needs to go through a work of this kind to see the larger social relations of the American school. It is only in this way that we see how wide a field our responsibilities are coming to include—as, for instance, the significance of the correspondence schools, the present status of the schooling of barbers in America, etc.

But the first section dealing with elementary education may be taken as representative of the whole. There is the usual expression of American faith in education; surprise at the extent of the reading habit, children's libraries, mother's congresses, parents' associations, the variety of programmes, general appreciation of initiative, etc. The European observer sees the constructive activities as the center of our elementary school life. Here however, as is too often the case, these are seen in the manual-training work to the neglect of other phases. One hundred and thirty pages are given to elucidating the four systems found among us. These are: (1) the Froebelian, leading into sloyd; (2) the technical, of Russian origin; (3) the social, as worked out under the influence of Professor Dewey, and (4) the artistic, as directed by Liberty Tadd of Philadelphia. The American art teacher is unprepared for the great vogue of the latter school in Europe. I found more direct evidence of the use of Mr. Tadd's work in a number of the countries on the Continent than of any other American. The only well-equipped room, as to blackboards, that I saw in the visiting of hundreds of schools was one fitted up to carry out the Tadd method. M. Buyse fails to see how much more integrally related are Dr. Dewey's work and that of Froebel than are the latter and sloyd.

While the three chief cities studied are Boston, New York, and Chicago, it is evident that the writer received his focusing impressions in Boston and that he sees much of the whole field in the light of the impression given him that "the Athens of the United States" is "the laboratory in which European ideas upon education are received and passed through the crucible of American thought in order to adapt themselves to the life of the New World." If he had there come into relation with the work of Dr. Scott at the normal, as well as that of Mr. Larson at the sloyd school, he would have had a more adequate standard for organizing his material. However one may regard them, the recent criticisms of Dr. Dewey's work by Dr. Scott in *Social Education* and by Miss Blow in *Educational Issues of the Kindergarten* will, no doubt, aid foreign visitors to undertake a more definite evaluation of what has probably been the most important educational experiment in America. Most of these writers, like Mr. Math of Manchester University, have dealt with this material in a largely descriptive manner.

As has been stated before, it is from the standpoint of description that the present work under discussion is most valuable. The foreign reader will be able to use what is given as suggestion for his own work. It is intended evidently to serve this purpose. Even the illustrations show this, as in the case of modeling, where the exact position of the hands is pictured. But the meaning of the movements studied is by no means so evident. One is reminded by what is seen of the notebooks of city teachers, who frequent the exhibits of other schools, that the motives and movements are lost in materials and methods. The bibliographies given by M. Buyse are fairly well selected. It is unfortunate here, as elsewhere, that such a report, and especially the bibliographies, are not edited or at least proofread by an American, in order that proper names, titles, etc., which vary from French forms might be stated more intelligibly. The titles are representative although here, too, the method side is overemphasized, and some less significant works are consequently cited.

EDITORIAL NOTES

The general interest in moral training in the schools is widening and deepening. The very important volumes on *Moral Instruction and Training in the Schools,* which are reviewed in the present number, reflect this interest most intelligently, in an international inquiry. There are other indications of this interest which are more striking if less enlightening. We refer to the systems of moral instruction which pass under the names of the "Fairchild and Brownlee Systems." These undertake to seize real moral situations in the experience of children, and by striking comment to educate the moral judgment. In the system which is identified with the name of Mr. Milton Fairchild, these situations are found to a large extent in sport or in the child's ambitions for success in later life. Photographs catch and vividly reproduce these crucial situations, and the comment of the lecturer aims to identify these highly exciting and absorbing situations with equally vivid moral judgments. The method has received wide approval and the host of names that cover the circulars imply that in the judgment of many of our clearest minded educators and thinkers a solution had been found for this problem of moral education in what have been termed these "moral nickel theaters." There can be no desire on the part of anyone to discourage an effort which certainly has abandoned the mere moral maxim, and attempts to make use of the child's own experience, to help him to form his own judgment, instead of trying to din the results of adult experience into the boy's mind in the form of ready-made judgments.

Moral Training in the Schools

Novel Systems of Moral Instruction

Approval of the Fairchild System and its Aim

There is, however, an inadequacy in the presentation, which should be emphasized in the interest of the very purpose which has called out these schemes. This inadequacy lies in the fragmentary character of the situations which are seized by the lecturer and his camera. A situation in a baseball game must call out a whole social organization

The Inadequacy of the System

if it is to have the moral value desired. Why is it that American sport to so large an extent, even in our colleges, has led to lowering of morals instead of leading to a higher ethical level? In the English public schools and universities it is fair to claim a morally elevating influence for sport. In America this has not been the case. We have not succeeded and probably never will succeed in organizing the whole social life of the school on the basis of sport as is the case in England. When this is done the judgment of the school and its history and ambitions appear in the conduct of the boy.

Athletic Situations as Moral Situations in England and America

No really moral consciousness will be aroused until the school and its ideals speak in the conduct of the boy on the athletic field. In America the school and its ideals call for success, and it is questionable whether we can ever succeed in identifying the school tradition with the ethics of sport. Our school instructors who must remain the principal personages in the school community are not part of the school games. The presence and character of athletic coaches are sufficient evidence that the ideals of Rugby and Harrow cannot be reproduced in the American school.

But eminent English educational opinion deplores the lack of civic consciousness in the intellectual and moral atmosphere of the English school, and here it is possible to obtain an organized school consciousness which shall be moral and moralizing. In approaching this problem it is of the first importance to recognize that it is only as the school becomes organized as a social whole, and as the child recognizes his conduct as a reflection or formulation of that society, will it be possible to have any moral training in our schools.

Another Phase of Moral Consciousness, and the Condition of Moral Consciousness in the School

G. H. M.

NOTES AND NEWS

The problem of school attendance is one of the fundamental problems of our educational situation. Superintendent D. C. Gile, of Marshfield, Wis., offers some interesting data in connection with the problem. The following tables were prepared in the Marshfield schools:

TABLE I

AVERAGE ATTENDANCE BY GRADES

	GRADE												
	Kg	1	2	3	4	5	6	7	8	9	10	11	12
Boys	37	65	61	42	42	29	36	17	26	26	21	8	11
Girls	29	59	40	33	35	37	25	27	35	32	26	19	13
Total	66	124	101	75	77	66	61	44	61	58	47	27	24

In general the number of boys above Grade 6 is much less than it is below that grade. The boys outnumber the girls as far as Grade 6 but the girls outnumber the boys in grades beyond the sixth. The following table will show the relative numbers of boys and girls in school, by ages:

TABLE II

	AGES																
	Below 5	5	6	7	8	9	10	11	12	13	14	15	16	17	18	19	20
Boys	12	27	37	53	36	32	23	32	26	36	34	38	18	13	2	0	0
Girls	9	24	36	30	31	30	28	32	29	39	40	24	20	18	7	4	1
Total	21	51	73	83	67	62	51	64	55	75	74	62	38	31	9	4	1

This table shows that the boys outnumber the girls up to nine years of age and that beyond this age the girls outnumber the boys except at age 15. Table 1 shows that in grades above the seventh a decided increase in numbers of both sexes is noticeable. This is due to the fact that parochial and rural schools send many of their pupils to the public schools after the eighth grade. Aside from this influx from parochial and rural schools, there is a decided falling off in the numbers of both sexes above the fifth grade, but the decrease is more marked among the l
girls.

ılling off to be attributed to the demanc
h upport of the family? Marshfield is not,

an industrial center. Hence, this reason does not satisfy. We may find some help by comparing averages of boys and girls by grades:

TABLE III

	Grade												
	Kg	1	2	3	4	5	6	7	8	9	10	11	12
Boys	4.8	6.3	7.9	9.1	10.8	11.9	12.6	13.2	14.1	14.8	15.3	15.8	16.9
Girls	4.8	6.2	7.4	9.	10.3	11.5	11.9	13.2	13.7	14.8	15.6	16.5	17.9

It will be noted from this table that in the grades below the high school the average age of the boys is greater than that of the girls. This fact is reversed in the high school. In the grades it means that though the boys are possibly as able, yet they do not progress as rapidly as the girls. In the high school, the boys who have kept up with their grade remain to the end or nearly so; while the girls who have fallen behind their grade do not find it as profitable to go to work as to remain at school.

All this seems to indicate that the work of the grades is more attractive to, or more in accord with the needs of, the girl than the boy. The lagging, backward, quitting boy needs attention. He drops out of school after the sixth grade and becomes a floater. This is, of course, not merely a school question, but a general social problem, in which the parents should have a share.

The parents' side of this question is a rather uncertain field. There is a large amount of doubt, in its way quite natural, mixed with our current feelings toward popular education and the public school. An English school journal reports a mother who took her little boy away from the day school to which he had been sent, because he liked his lessons, and cried if he was kept at home. The mother said that "there must be something wrong" with such a topsy-turvy state of affairs. But, an American daily paper said recently, rather cynically, that "The boy who cries to go to school needs investigating." And, in the same general vein, a writer in a recent number of the *Boston Herald* in refuting some remarks made by that paper on the subject of truancy, said: "With the system now in operation in this city, with the help of twenty-three able and faithful truant officers, the teachers, and the police force of the city, nearly every child of school age is connected with some school and registered there. . . . . There are school districts where a real truant is as rare as a white blackbird."

In the Jefferson City (Mo.) schools the following directions are given to the teachers to be used in studying the health conditions of the individual children in the schools.

Facts to be ascertained:

1. Does the pupil habitually suffer from inflamed lids or eyes?

2. Does the pupil fail to read the majority of the letters in the XX line of the Snelling's Test Types with either eye?

3. Do the eyes and head habitually grow weary and painful after study?

4. Does the pupil appear to be cross-eyed?

5. Does the pupil complain of earache in either ear?

6. Does matter (pus) or foul odor proceed from either ear?

7. Does the pupil fail to hear an ordinary voice at 20 feet in a quiet room? Each ear should be tested by having the pupil hold his hand over first one ear and then the other. The pupil should close his eyes during the test.

8. Is the pupil frequently subject to "colds in the head"? Discharges from the nose and throat?

9. Is the pupil an habitual "mouth-breather"?

If an affirmative answer is returned to any of these questions the pupil is given a printed card of warning to be taken to the parents or guardians. A complete record of the whole transaction is kept.

Professor M. E. Sadler has recently been pressing a rather comprehensive programme upon the consideration of the English school world. It is worthy the attention of American educators, as well. He proposes: (1) to reduce the size of classes in all elementary schools; (2) to institute a competent system of medical inspection and care of children; (3) to provide more and better playground space in connection with the schools; (4) to raise the age limit for compulsory attendance; (5) to make provision for all the children, so that none need be put on half-time; (6) to attempt to provide special, adequate social care for all children through the critical period of adolescence; (7) and he is particularly interested in making thoughtful care for the quality of the coming generation a matter of social provision, by laying a statutory obligation upon all employers of the young, to allow all children to attend classes of some sort up to the age of seventeen. This last consideration lies close to the heart of his demands for a more comprehensive system of continuation schools, which shall be seriously accepted by the public, and for which all employers of boys and girls shall make allowance in their working schedules.

The State Educational Association of Pennsylvania is engaged in making a canvass of the teachers of the state for a larger membership. This association has been in existence for more than fifty years, yet, the president states, most of the teachers of the state seem to hold aloof and are unwilling to lend their influence to the organization. In an appeal to the teachers of the state some rather interesting data are given. For instance, it is reported that Connecticut enrols 90 per cent. of its teachers in the state association; Rhode Island, 88 per cent.; New Jersey, 65 per cent.; New Mexico, 50 per cent.; California, 27 per cent.; Idaho, 25 per cent.; Alabama, 18 per cent. Pennsylvania falls below these figures. Seeking for information from other states, Alabama reports its state association "is decidedly the leading force in educational advancement;" California, that "its voice is very potent in legislation;" Florida, that "the school interests of the state cannot afford to be without such an association;" Kentucky, that "it is the greatest force in the state;" and so on.

It may not be out of place, in this connection, to ask whether Pennsylvania is not suffering from a serious weakening of the democratic ideal, in education, as in a great many other lines. There is, certainly, some connection between the apathy of the teaching forces of the state and that apathy in politics which has become the shame of the state. But, of course, Pennsylvania does not stand alone in these respects.

Syracuse (N. Y.) reports a very interesting effort along the line of industrial training. The Artisan School has been established by the manufacturers of Syracuse to furnish a place where boys can learn certain trades. The boys work seven and one-half hours a day at 8 cents an hour. They have, beside this, an hour of drawing, talks, shop mathematics, etc., and they are required to keep up notebooks covering all their work. The course covers fifteen months, and leads to a good degree of efficiency in the particular trades. It remains to be seen whether, on the one hand, the school will be able to succeed financially, and, on the other, whether such training will really meet the full demands of a democratic citizenship.

Special attention should be called to the meeting of the Department of Superintendence of the N. E. A., which will be held in Chicago, February 23, 24, and 25. Beside the Department of Superintendence, the National Society for the Scientific Study of Education, the Society of College Teachers of Education, the National Committee on Agricultural Education, and the Conference of State Superintendents of Education, as well as the Educational Press Association, will meet at the same time and under the same general auspices as that of the Department of Superintendence. The preliminary programme promises meetings of unusual interest. The question of waste in school work, the problem of the delinquent pupil, industrial education, school hygiene, are among the questions to be discussed in the Department of Superintendence. There will be also the usual round-table discussions which are frequently of so much more importance than the papers presented in the programme. The Society of College Teachers of Education will discuss observation and practice work in university departments of education. The question is one that is peculiarly interesting to superintendents and teachers of elementary schools. Application to Mr. Irwin Shepard, Secretary of the N. E. A., Winona, Minn., will bring information regarding railroad rates, ticket conditions, and other detail.

BOOK REVIEWS

Moral Instruction and Training in the Schools. The Report of an International Inquiry. Edited by M. E. SADLER. London: Longmans, Green & Co., 1908. In two volumes. Vol. I, The United Kingdom, pp. 596; Vol. II, Foreign and Colonial, pp. 396. With Index.

The influence of education upon conduct and character is the subject discussed in this book. Its chapters are the outcome of an inquiry undertaken with the purpose of gathering information as to the methods of moral instruction and training now in use in schools in different countries. They record the judgment of experienced teachers and others as to the efficacy of the various means by which schools may bear part in the task of quickening and defining moral ideals, and of strengthening their influence upon individual conduct and upon national life.

The materials here presented are, of course, very variable as to value. The points of view represent all stages, from that of the most progressive scientific students of education like Prof. Sadler, himself, and Prof. J. J. Findlay, with whose work we have become familiar through their contributions to American school journals, down to the most dogmatic and traditional representative of scholastic education which is still very much alive in certain parts of the world. But there is enough of value in the contributions that do have scientific interest to make the work, as a whole, a very valuable contribution to that larger consciousness of the essentially world-wide character of the problem of moral education.

In the first volume, dealing with the schools of The United Kingdom, attention may be called to the following discussions; Professor Rudolf Eucken discusses, illuminatingly, the "Problem of Moral Instruction;" Professor J. J. Findlay treats of "The Growth of Moral Ideas in Children," and Professor William James, President Hall, and M. Alfred Fouillee, the Bishop of Birmingham, Dr. Bernard Bosanquet, and Dr. Felix Adler contribute to a symposium on the question, "How can the Ethical Efficiency of Education be increased?" Professor James is the only one who really touches the question, and his contribution is short: "I should increase enormously the amount of manual or 'motor' training relatively to the book-work, and not let the latter predominate till the age of fifteen or sixteen."

There is one discussion in this volume which has a considerable value from the standpoint of the organization of the school. Mr. H. Bompas Smith, headmaster of King Edward VII's School, Lytham, contributes a long account of the corporate life of the English public school, which is interesting from the standpoint of the development of the class-morality, upon which English society rests. It is interesting to note, here, however, that some of the leaders of education in England are trying to find a way out of the group or class morality which their schools tend to foster; but most of them seem to have developed no means beyond the method of the Herbartian pedagogy, and that does not seem to solve the problem.

Volume II deals with Colonial and Foreign materials. The French system of non-religious moral instruction is treated in several papers, and other countries receive lesser mention. Mr. Gustav Spiller, General Secretary of the International Union of Ethical Societies, contributes a study of moral training and instruction in the schools of Switzerland, under the title, "An Educational Democracy," in which he uses this sentence, which we in America, with our penchant for "democracy" may well ponder: "It has been assumed without reflection, that no one need be especially prepared for influencing the children morally, though scarcely any part of education requires so much conscious preparation."

The work of American schools is treated from the standpoint of the Ethical Culture School, by Mr. Chubb; the State Normal School, by Principal Baldwin, of the Hyannis Normal School; and from the standpoint of the American school child, by Principal Burke, of the Teachers' Training School, at Albany. Mr. Burke describes the type of the "George Junior Republic," that general retreat for all who would make our American school life "democratic." All in all, the American materials in the book are not very satisfactory.

Finally, we may call attention to a fact that will strike many as peculiar. The western world has been regarding the Japanese as a people who have taken over our western material equipment without caring for our western ideals of culture. Of course, we had our eyes opened somewhat by the medical and surgical work in the Japanese armies during the Russian war. But we shall soon be called upon to wonder still more; for Japan is rapidly taking the lead among nations devoted to education, and to moral education. The Imperial Rescript on Education, of 1890, is the foundation of all Japanese education. Baron Kikuchi gives a very readable account of the spirit of that rescript and the education that has grown up about it. It would be worth the while of anyone interested in education, and in the larger problems of social and international relationships, to read this account and come to an appreciation of the way in which Japan has seriously attacked the larger problems of moral advance.

This book will shortly be supplemented by the reports of the International Moral Congress: the whole gives us a larger comprehension of the real problem of moral education: it is not a problem of individual conduct, in the narrower sense; it is a problem of the realization and acceptance of social relationships, and these social relationships are now seen to be world-wide. From this point of view this collection of materials stands alone today.

J. K. Hart

History in the Elementary School. By Henry Johnson, professor of History, Teachers College, Columbia University. New York: *Teachers College Record,* Novemer, 1908. Pp. 60.

Professor Henry Johnson has given us a work of much more than ordinary importance in his recently published study on *History in the Elementary School.* The need of a good discussion of this subject has long been felt and teachers in general will be delighted. It is one of a series of articles by the heads of departments in Teachers College who are actively in charge of the work done in the practice school, the Horace Mann schools. Professor Johnson is wonderfully well equipped to write such a study. He was an unusually enthusiastic and successful teacher of history in the high school, as the writer well remembers from the happy days spent in his classes, and has had exceptional opportunities for studying the problem later, as superintendent of schools, normal-school instructor, and, at the present time, in the well-equipped Teachers College institution.

The publication of such articles is in itself an encouraging sign of progress in educational work today. All realize the need of having more such centers as the one established at Columbia, among the universities, to provide a large number of opportunities for carrying on such work. We may safely say that the need of trained experts in education has never been felt as at present. We are in a period of transition educationally with many new things pressing for attention. It is imperatively necessary to decide as to their values wisely after subjecting each conception to the most discriminating criticism.

It is evident that Professor Johnson has studied the problem of history work in the elementary school. He makes clear at the very outset that he believes history deserves the place it now occupies, but he as quickly distinguishes between that which is, and that which should be. His ideal of the history for the elementary school is the history as conceived by the historians and not the history of made-over histories, nor the masquerading of myths, romances, and the like, as history. He opposes the idea advocated by the Chicago teacher that, "an ideal history for children would be history written by a child." He opposes also as unnecessary bringing history "down to the child's effortless understanding."

He confesses that at present even historians differ as to the content of elementary school history. In view of this fact it is not to be thought strange that superintendents and others responsible for courses of study in history do wander and lose themselves among a maze of paths, for we all know that in the great majority of cases they are not trained in historical work and should not presume to speak authoritatively about the matter. When he urges that they shall spend less time in portraying the difficulties involved in adapting serious history to the comprehension of the children of the elementary school, and more time in studying the field and arranging rational courses and methods of instruction that will lead the child to get something true and definite, he is altogether to be commended.

Perhaps the most direct profit that comes to one who reads this admirable article lies in his statement of the problem involved in history teaching: Does serious history, the history of trained historians, furnish material for history in the elementary schools? He does not in the least minimize the difficulties involved and which all of us agree do exist. There are adults who try to understand serious history, and who cannot, due to a lack of the development of historical-mindedness. He goes beyond, simply enumerating the difficulties by applying the knowledge of these difficulties in determining what aspects of the past can best be presented to and understood by the child. In this he gives the best and most illuminating treatment of the subject that has recently appeared. The principles he lays down are refreshingly unlike those in so many of the present-day pedagogical studies, in that they smack of actual test and practice.

In general he would aim for concreteness and vividness in the portrayal of the material background of the past; cleave to the characteristic and not the sensational of the past; utilize local history as far as possible; make full use of objective aids; and allow only historians of known authority to supply the summaries that will be necessary from time to time.

These principles he fully elaborates. To emphasize concreteness in treatment he uses two illustrations very effectively: the cotton industry in the South before the Civil War, and the slave power. The study also contains an account of the Puritans in America. These three illustrations offer extremely valuable material to any teacher. They show that history can be made a thinking exercise as well as merely a learning exercise. That it is not done now, and that much of the work is indefinite he shows aptly in citing the following incident: A little girl was once asked if she could tell what sort of a looking man Alexander the Great was. "Why, no," said she, "I thought he was just one of those historical characters." There would be fewer of such historical characters, we believe, if Professor Johnson's admirable study were pondered by the teachers generally.

Other chapters deal with: "History as Determined by Textbooks for the Upper Grades," "Relation of Elementary History to the Question of How Historical Facts Are Established," "Use of Histories," "Problem of Finding What Is Significant in History," and "The Question of Educational Aims and Values." There is also a short list of books suited to the needs of teachers and pupils.

The severe indictment against the majority of the present-day textbooks in history is that they are general, vague, and empty. He urges that the textbook for the average elementary school should be a repository of concrete examples.

The advantages of using source material in the elementary school are presented strongly by Professor Johnson. He urges that the pupils earn the facts of history instead of merely learning them; that this will result in making deeper impressions than merely reading answers; in remembering important facts longer and more definitely; and, when managed by a skilful teacher, in greater accuracy. The cry against this form of history work in occasional exercises will subside when they are used as he suggests.

Questions as to the availability of using some of the histories mentioned by Professor Johnson in the grades that he suggests will come to the minds of many teachers who lack neither "conviction" nor "scholarship." Can Parkman's works be intelligently and understandingly read by a sixth grade? Will Bradford's *Plymouth Plantation* drive other accounts from the field in the seventh? We should have more extensive data on this matter from the average schools.

The study is brought to a close with a brief discussion of the educational aims and values in history for the elementary school. Professor Johnson maintains the attitude shown in the entire discussion of refusing to enter a controversy where at the present time mere opinions held sway and where there is no absolute data to discuss. There must be further study and investigation on this point. It is not altogether unwise, however, to follow his idea, which is to expose the children to serious history and to note the results.

No one can read this scholarly discussion without being abundantly rewarded. Its thoughtfulness invites you to think; its originality is refreshing; its concreteness is helpful. There is in every paragraph the directing power of a man earnest to obtain results that measure up to the importance of the subject, and we may not say that he has not, at least in part, succeeded.

CONRAD G. SELVIG

STEVENS SEMINARY
GLENCOE, MINN.

The Pig Brother and Other Fables and Stories. By LAURA E. RICHARDS. Little, Brown & Co., 1908. Pp. 142.

This book is sent out as supplementary reading for the fourth school year. There are one or two charming poems in this collection, but the book is really a book of modern and original fables. The morals are not attached at the close of each fable as in the ancient models, but they are quite as evident as they would be if so analyzed out of the text. The story element in them is sufficient to hold interest, but it is open to question whether the moral is not so obvious as to be somewhat irritating to the average ten-year-old child. The style is good; the subtle points and turns of thought appeal to the adult much as do the social hits that his knowing countrymen find in the fairy tales of Hans Christian Andersen.

BERTHA PAYNE

BOOKS RECEIVED

AMERICAN BOOK COMPANY, NEW YORK

The Eleanor Smith Music Course (4 vols.). By ELEANOR SMITH. Cloth. Book I, 112 pp., 25 cents; Book II, 145 pp., 30 cents; Book III, 192 pp., 40 cents; Book IV, 255 pp., 50 cents.

Plane and Solid Geometry. By ELMER A. LYMAN. Half leather. Pp. 340. $1.25.

SILVER, BURDETT & CO., NEW YORK

State Control of Courses of Study. By FRED J. BROWNSCOMBE. Cloth. Pp. 125. $1.00.

CURRENT EDUCATIONAL LITERATURE IN THE PERIODICALS[1]

IRENE WARREN
Librarian, School of Education, The University of Chicago

BROENE, J. Nietzsche's educational ideas and ideals. Educa. R. 37:55–70. (Ja. '09.)

BROWN, ELMER ELLSWORTH. Unifying influence of industrial art. Journ. of Educa. 68:703–5. (Ja. '09.)

BURR, WILLIAM H. The study of engineering. Col. Univ. Q. 9:42–49. (D. '08.)

BURRUSS, J. A. Industrial factor in public education in the south. South. Educa. R. 5:163–75. (O.—N. '08.)

BUTLER, NICHOLAS MURRAY. Physics teaching in secondary schools. Educa. R. 37:86–8. (Ja. '09.)

CATTELL, J. MCKEEN. The school and family. Pop. Sci. Mo. 74:84–95. (D. '08.)

CLARK, JOHN BATES. Education and the socialistic movement. Col. Univ. Q. 9:28–41. (D. '08.)

COE, GEORGE ALBERT. Moral and religious education from the psychological point of view. Relig. Educa. 3:165–79. (D. '08.)

COHEN, LEON M. SOLIS. Library work in the Brooklyn ghetto. Lib. Journ. 33:483–84. (D. '08.)

CUSHMAN, LILLIAN S. A report of the second annual meeting of the National Society for the Promotion of Industrial Education. El. School T. 9:250–56. (Ja. '09.)

FREEMAN, MARILLA WAITE. The relation of the library to the outside world. Lib. Journ. 33:488–92. (D. '08.)

FURST, CLYDE. The financial status of the professor. Col. Univ. Q. 9:50–54. (D. '08.)

GARD, WILLIS L. Some neurological and psychological aspects. Pedagog. Sem. 15:439–73. (Ja. '09.)

[1] *Abbreviations.*—Col. Univ. Q., Columbia University Quarterly; Educa. R., Educational Review; El. School T., Elementary School Teacher; Harp. W., Harper's Weekly; Journ. of Educa., Journal of Education; Lib. Journ., Library Journal; Out., Outlook; Pedagog. Sem., Pedagogical Seminary; Pop. Sci. Mo., Popular Science Monthly; Psycholog. Clinic, Psychological Clinic; Relig. Educa., Religious Education; South. Educa. R., Southern Educational Review.

HALL, G. STANLEY. Elements of strength and weakness in physical education as taught in colleges. Mind and Body. 15:326–30. (Ja. '09.)

HERTS, ALICE MINNIE. Dramatic instinct—its use and misuse. Pedagog. Sem. 15:550–62. (Ja. '09.)

JONES, ELMER E. A concrete example of the value of individual teaching. Psycholog. Clinic. 2:195–203. (D. '08.)

JUDSON, HARRY PRATT. Religion in the schools. El. School T. 9:223–32. (Ja. '09.)

K., F. P. The Columbia university summer session. Col. Univ. Q. 9:19–27. (D. '08.)

LELAND, CLAUDE G. The world's largest circulating library. Harp. W. 52: 12–13. (26 D. '08.)

MAGRUDER, W. T. The cosmopolitan high-school curricula. South. Educa. R. 5:195–96. (O.–N. '08.)

MARTIN, GEORGE H. Industrial education and the public schools. Journ. of Educa. 68:675–76. (D. '08.)

MCNARY, SARAH J. The preparation of a class for a lesson in literature. Pedagog. Sem. 15:484–91. (Ja. '09.)

MILLER, DICKINSON S. Mr. Roosevelt's opportunity as president of a university. Pop. Sci. Mo. 74:62–69. (D. '08.)

MORRISON, G. B. The high-school situation. South. Educa. R. 5:187–94. (O.–N. '08.)

ORDAHL, GEORGE. Rivalry; its genetic development and pedagogy. Pedagog. Sem. 15:492–549. (Ja. '09.)

PRICHETT, HENRY S. Professional education. Out. 90:870–73. (19 D. '08.)

PUTNAM, HELEN C. Biological knowledge and morality. Relig. Educa. 3:180–86. (D. '08.)

ROARK, R. N. Modern tendencies in education. South Educa. R. 5:149–57. (O.–N. '08.)

Report of the librarian of the Bureau of Education. Lib. Journ. 33:503– (D. '08.)

RUEDIGER, WILLIAM C. The field of education. Pedagog. Sem. 15:474–83. (Ja. '09.)

RUSSELL, JAMES EARL. The call to professional service. Col. Univ. Q. 9:1–9. (D. '08.)

SEERLEY, H. H. Industrial arts in normal schools. South. Educa. R. 5:158–62. (O.–N. '08.)

SHAW, CHARLES FRANKLIN. The educational principles involved in the religious training of young people. Relig. Educa. 3:182–86. (D. '08.)

SHOWERMAN, GRANT. A co-educational meditation. Educa. R. 37:44–54. (Ja. '09.)

SISSON, EDWARD O. The genius of the American high school. Educa. R. 37:29–43. (Ja. '09.)

SOULE, A. M. Work of the agricultural school in the scheme of state education. South. Educa. R. 5:176-86. (O.-N. '08.)

STARR, M. ALLEN. The duties of the medical profession to the public. Col. Univ. Q. 9:10-18. (D. '08.)

STERLING, E. BLANCHE. Gymnastics as a factor in the treatment of mental retardation. Psycholog. Clinic. 2:204-11. (D. '08.)

STOWE, LYMAN BEECHER. School republics. Out. 90:939-48. (26 D. '08.)
Tenth anniversary of the hall club. October 23, 1898. Pedagog Sem. 15:563-79.

TERRY, H. L. The new movement in physics teaching. Educa. R. 37:12-18. (Ja. '09.)

THORNDIKE, EDWARD L. The influence of the number of men teachers upon the enrollment of boys in public high schools. Educa. R. 37:71-85. (Ja. '09.)

THWING, CHARLES F. The answer of the far east to some American college questions. Educa. R. 37:19-28. (Ja. '09.)

WITTICH, GEORGE. Folk-dances as physical training for the young in America. Mind and Body. 15:321-25. (Ja. '09.)

VOLUME IX NUMBER 7

THE ELEMENTARY SCHOOL TEACHER

MARCH, 1909

THE PRESENT POINT OF VIEW OF THE PLAYS AND GAMES OF THE KINDERGARTEN

MARY BOOMER PAGE
Chicago Kindergarten Institute

The educational value and significance of play in modern life needs no justification—"The more play, the more man." Experts from every profession contribute facts proving the need of free, spontaneous play-life in childhood. The growth of the physical body demands it; the growing powers of the mind depend upon it; the social and moral welfare results from it.[1]

While philosophers, statesmen, religionists, and educators from the classic days of Greece to the end of the eighteenth century had recognized the worth of play in childhood to a certain extent, to Friedrich Froebel is due the honor and credit of utilizing and organizing the play-life of children as the basis and corner-stone of a system of education. In the words of Dr. W. T. Harris: " . . . . these (Froebel's plays and games) are thoroughly humane in their nature and they offer to the child in a symbolic form the treasures of experience of the race, in solving the problems of life. They make children wise without the conceit of wisdom."[2] Jean Paul Richter in his *Levana* has well said, "Play is the first poetry of the human being," and, as

[[1] The bibliography relating to plays and games is so extensive it would be beyond the limits of this article to refer to any but those bearing most directly upon the following outline.]

[2] Introduction to *Mottoes and Commentaries to Froebel's Mother Play*, pp. xiii–xv.

Ruskin says, "all true work is praise, all true play is love and prayer."[3]

A threefold attempt is made in this article: First, to outline briefly the philosophical and psychological implications found in Froebel's writings concerning plays and games; second, to suggest the most important modern points of view; third, to suggest periods and kinds of plays and games for children of kindergarten age.

I

First, Froebel's ideas of education are the result of the philosophical thought and atmosphere of his age. The law of unity, which is basic in every phase of his educational procedure, is, for him, the universal law of all development. It governs the unfolding of natural objects, as well as the mind. "This all-controlling law is necessarily based on an all-prevading, energetic, living, self-conscious, and, hence, eternal unity." "Education consists in leading man, as a thinking, intelligent being, growing into self-consciousness, to a pure, and unsullied, conscious and free representation of the inner law of Divine Unity, and in teaching him ways and means thereto."[4]

Froebel divides education into three periods: 1, earliest childhood; 2, boyhood; 3, manhood. The human being is always to be considered in relation to God, to nature, and to humanity.

> It cannot be doubted that Froebel for the most part kept clearly in mind throughout his work this idea of the educational process as a process of interaction, a process by which the spiritual experience, the *ideal* values of human life, are mediated or communicated to the individual.[5]

To Froebel it was possible to know life only through social relations, for only in response to the demands made upon him by the human family, by nature, and by God, could he come to consciousness of self and the oneness of all things.

"For Froebel, as for Fichte, freedom depends on activity and reflection, and for both the ethical law is, each particular action

[3] *Adolescence,* Vol. I, p. 235.

[4] Froebel, *Education of Man,* pp. 1, 2.

[5] J. A. MacVannal, *Educational Theories of Herbart and Froebel,* p. 87.

forms part of a series, which leads the individual to spiritual freedom."[6]

Play is the highest phase of child-development . . . . for it is a self-active representation of the inner—representation of the inner from inner necessity and impulse. Play is the purest activity of this age . . . . and typical of human life as a whole. It gives joy, freedom, inner and outer rest. It holds the source of all that is good. A child that plays thoroughly, until physical fatigue forbids, will surely be a thorough, determined man, capable of self-sacrifice. Play is not trivial, it is highly serious, and of deep significance.

The plays of childhood are germinal leaves of later life, for the whole man is shown in these tendencies. If the child is injured, if the germinal leaves of the future tree of life are marred, he will only with the greatest difficulty escape the stunting effect of the injury it entails.[7]

In the

period of childhood the aim of play consisted simply in activity as such—in boyhood the aim lies in a definite conscious purpose; it seeks representation as such, or the thing to be represented in the activity.[8]

The nature of play should be the development of the physical nature, but, to Froebel, the physical activity is but an "inner craving," "and has its grounds in his inmost life."[9]

The activity of the senses and limbs of the infant is the first germ, ... the first formative impulse.[10]

With the advancing development of the senses there is development in the child simultaneously and symmetrically, the use of the body, of the limbs; and this, too, in a *succession* determined by *their* nature, and the properties of corporeal objects.[11]

The type of play-activity treated in Froebel's *Pedagogics*, while dealing largely with "means of fostering employment" or, with educative play materials, again and again enunciates very clearly both his philosophical basis and the psychological method for the types of play selected by him.[12]

We have repeatedly said, and everyone can observe, that the child is to *feel and experience,* to *act and represent,* to *think and to recognize,* and

[6] J. A. MacVannal, *Educational Theories of Herbart and Froebel,* p. 89.

[7] *Education of Man,* pp. 54, 55. [8] *Ibid.,* pp. 112, 113.

[9] *Pedagogics of the Kindergarten,* pp. 238, 260, 261.

[10] *Education of Man,* p. 34. [11] *Ibid.,* p. 47.

[12] *Pedagogics of the Kindergarten,* pp. 28, 67, 237, 145, 122, 206.

that in this *threefold yet single* nature are included the totality of his expression of his life and of his activities.[13]

The *Mother-Play Book* contains the type of play most advocated by Froebel and used by the majority of his followers. It gives the key to his philosophy of life, and forms the basis of the so-called "subject-matter" and of the games of the kindergarten used by all who follow the historic method. Froebel's conception of play is relational. The function of the mother or teacher is to present ideals of life in play form; in order that the child himself may have "fore-shadowings" or "premonitions" of his later adult life. Froebel unquestionably recognized that instinctive life of the child in certain aspects, for he frequently refers to activity itself as instinctive. He values both the imitative and social aspects of play, but his treatment of the instinctive life of the child is not unitary, but isolated. The whole emphasis is upon the symbolic nature of play, for the major portion of his writings shows forth his methods by analogues.

Froebel's method of realizing his philosophical ideals was deductive.[14] While we are enjoined not to be "mandatory," or "prescriptive"[15] and are urged to be "following"[16] in our guidance, yet the tendencies indicate that by presenting only such ideals as are true to *all* life, can we truly educate the child. Occasional divergence is permitted,[17] but other than this is unworthy of the nature of man. From the practical point of view Froebel inaugurated the inductive method in his work, and his efforts in the organization of his ideals into a new form of practice was experimental, but as has already been indicated, the trend of his writings evidences the attempt to make the practical working-out of his theory conform to the postulates of his philosophy.

[13] *Op. cit.*, p. 122.

[14] See *Pedagogics of the Kindergarten*, p. 237.

[15] *Education of Man*, pp. 10–14.

[16] *Pedagogics of the Kindergarten*, p. 79.

[17] *Ibid.*, p. 239.

Froebel's general position is that spiritual monism which conceives material and mental evolution as continuous phases of one spiritual movement.[18]

In the *Mother-Play Book* are presented typical experiences of life which the historic kindergarten utilizes today in the same form as when first written, and as Miss Blow says,

By playing all the ideals which interpret nature and human life, the kindergarten flings the rainbow bridge between the heart of childhood and the vision of manhood, and through the allurement of the beautiful impels intellect to wrestle for truth, and persuades will to a prevailing struggle for goodness.[19]

Again,

The merit of the kindergarten games will be more closely discerned if we pause to define accurately the meaning of typical characters. A typical character is the concrete embodiment of some generic or creative aspect of human nature, or of some native passion which collides with generic selfhood.

The characters represented in kindergarten games must have three marks. They must be typical, elementary, and ideal. Children should not waste time dramatizing the merely capricious. They should not represent elementary types of evil. They should not represent complex types of either good or evil.

The question arises, then, do children of kindergarten age respond most vitally, or embody most truly, this class of plays selected by adults? I think not. Would not the best evidence or test of their value be to discover what games or plays are most commonly chosen by children when undirected by adults? "It is this freedom of choice and action at this early age which must inevitably be the criterion of judgment of kindergarten games." To summarize this statement: We present the point of view of the advantage to kindergarten education of philosophic adult ideals, versus the child's own ideals.

II

A. If it is true, as we believe, that freedom of choice and action are fundamental to the pedagogy of the kindergarten,

[18] J. A. MacVannal, *Educational Theories of Herbart and Froebel,* pp. 97–116. See also S. E. Blow, *Educational Issues of the Kindergarten,* p. 271.

[19] *Ibid.,* pp. 66, 74, 140, 143.

then the relation of the children to environment and heredity must be carefully considered. We do not believe that "nature and heredity" are radically false, but that the children can be trusted to select much that will be nutritive physically, mentally, and morally. The young child is non-moral, and only gradually can he grow into a consciousness of moral values, through concrete need in his *own* daily life, and "only by *experience* will he learn the meaning of truth and the value in accomplishing his ends." Often what is true for him is not our view of truth, but is his vividness of imagery, his ideal, and he has not learned, as yet, to distinguish between it and the real world. His consciousness of moral worths is somewhat comparable to his own stages of growth; 1, impulsive; 2, tending toward co-operation; 3, social regard and greater reliability, etc. The child needs, therefore, a social environment that presents a variety of experiences, both from the point of view of the objective world and the possibilities of subjective reactions. This will offer large scope for those instinctive activities that are so essential to all his later life, for out of them, or upon them, it is made.

> They are all impulses, congenital, blind at first, and productive of motor reactions of a rigorously determinate sort. Each one of them, then, is an instinct, as instincts are commonly defined. But they contradict each other —"experience" in each particular opportunity of application usually deciding the issue.[20]
>
> Man has a far greater variety of impulses than any lower animal . . . . Owing to man's memory, power of reflection, and power of inference, they come each one to be felt by him, after he has once yielded to them and experienced their results, in connection with a foresight of those results.[21]

The relation of these instinctive acts to the emotional life of the child is fundamental, but general,[22] and while slight,[23] is significant. While the play-life of the child is undoubtedly instinctive, play is a general term descriptive of many aspects of activity,[24] or is "simply a way of looking at things."[25] In the

[20] James, *Psychology,* Vol. II, p. 293.
[21] *Ibid.,* p. 390.
[22] Angell, *Psychology,* pp. 313, 325.
[23] James, Vol. II, p. 450.
[24] Kirkpatrick, *Fundamentals of Child Study,* p. 50.
[25] Angell, *Psychology,* pp. 106–8.

words of Mr. James, life is all play and fairy-tale and learning the external properties of things.[26] Happily the fairy-tales form a most important part of his life, for they incite to activity of the best order.

The directive work in the kindergarten, so far as guiding activity is concerned, must lie mainly in the direction of organizing the tyrannical but necessary reflexes that we call habits. Infant education should be mainly concerned with stocking and directing the subconscious nerve centers.

And in the kindergarten all this training of the lower nerve centers takes place in a social atmosphere to which the children are fully alive and to which they freely respond. Sympathy, emulation, hope, fear, selfishness, altruism, all the passions that gather round social life and intercourse are available for the teacher who knows how to use them. Hence the work and play must be directed to group activities that will give wide and ordered activity to all the feelings of social life.[27]

In Section I we noted that Froebel's effort was to bring the child to an apprehension of adult truth by analogy. According to the modern point of view

there is a tacit assumption that it is a good indication of future mental ability for the child's expressions and attitudes to show early a similarity to adult types. To emphasize these analogues to adult life is to lay stress on the least important aspects of child-life. The daily spontaneous outgo of energy in play, imagery, and work is of far more importance as an indication of the future than are the clever doings which are often mere imitations—not the sparklings of intelligence that they seem to be to the adult, but simply efforts, along with many others, that the child puts forth to express himself.[28]

This view of the developing life of the child is most clearly and satisfactorily stated by Mr. King in the following words:

The functional point of view emphasizes, first of all, the intimate interrelation of all forms of mental activity, and the impossibility of describing any one aspect of consciousness except with reference to the organization of consciousness as a whole.

It (the conscious state) is no longer regarded as an *imperfect* manifestation of that which it is hoped may mean something in a later stage

[26] James, pp. 401, 427.

[27] Earl Barnes, *Elementary School Teacher,* October, 1908, pp. 60, 61; cf. Irving King, *Psychology of Child Development,* Introduction by John Dewey, p. xviii.

[28] *Ibid.,* p. 4. Note also p. 10.

of life. The conscious state exists here and now, and it must be interpreted entirely with reference to its origin and meaning in the here and now.[29]

The life of the child is to be considered from this unitary point of view, in his developing of consciousness.

Nothing can be more uncertain than to judge of consciousness by its so-called expressions. The conclusions must rest on the assumption that certain activities are necessarily connected with certain conscious states—an assumption that for any particular case must be more or less hypothetical. In others words, we must depend on the mere assumption that such and such an act expresses such and such a conscious state.

The situation is, however, quite different if we know what is the functional relation of consciousness to activity. We know, on the one hand, that the consciousness of the child changes with its growth, from a relatively vague to a highly specialized form. We know also that its activities, its possibilities of movement, change enormously with maturing years.

Consciousness is related, not to activity, but to the growth of activity.

The point to be emphasized is that there must be a unified consciousness from the very first, even though it be a vague one. . . . . Emotion is no more capable of being defined *in* and of itself than is any other mental attitude. . . . . Just as a co-ordinated movement of any kind must occur with reference to some end that is to be accompilshed, so with the emotion that arises within such co-ordination.[30]

In other words, there is no such thing as emotion in general; it is always directed toward something.[31]

Emotional attitudes are as much differentiated products as any other mental function, and it is impossible to postulate their presence before there have been built up consciously co-ordinated sets of activity with reference to definite things and persons. We do not attempt to find the first appearance of emotion. The really important question is to discover the kind of a process or situation that tends to call for the division of labor that the emotional attitude represents. . . . . The true method is to take the experience and note what sort of activity it stands for, how it differentiates and grows in complexity as the demands made upon it increase. . . . . We are not concerned with finding in the child analogues of adult events, but in defining "conditions" in terms of their meaning and significance in the *experience* in which they occur."

[29] *Ibid.*, pp. 5, 6 (italics mine).

[30] *Psychology of Child Development*, pp. 30, 32, 35 (italics mine).

[31] *Ibid.*, p. 43.

[32] *Ibid.*, p. 70.

Imitation in the play-life of the child must be considered from the same functional point of view to derive its full worth.[33] This gives added weight and value to those simple, repetitional forms of play that so often are disregarded by the young kindergartner as too trivial to claim her attention, viz.; arm and leg movements, clapping, etc., play with sand, playthings, etc., repetitional acts.

Sufficient inductive study has been made by many able and sympathetic child students with thousands of children, to make very clear certain tendencies in the plays and games of undirected or self-directed children.[34] But, perhaps, of even greater importance from the point of view of development, are the results of investigation concerning nascent stages.[35] For the period of childhood the two fundamental requirements are that (1) suggestion should play an important rôle, and (2) the spontaneity of the child should have *full* freedom. These needs are fully outlined, and every teacher of young children would do well to take them to heart.

The testimony of all the observers of children in self-directed play is the close relation it bears to the environmental conditions, growth, pleasure and greater power in movement, understanding and initiative result. Whitman adds his tribute:

There was a child went forth every day, and the first object he looked upon he became,
And that object became a part of him, for the day or a certain part of the day,
Or for many years or stretching cycles of years.

A great many of the tendencies to action that we shall have to consider are usually accounted for in a vague and useless fashion by being described as recapitulation from early race history. We shall attempt to state them in terms connected with the immediate life-processes of the child itself. If such a statement is possible, it will certainly be more illuminating than one in which the emphasis is largely on the past.[36]

[33] *Ibid.*, pp. 119, 122, 123, 127, 128.

[34] Dr. Gulick, *Ped. Sem.*, Vol. VI, No. 2; Mr. Cooswell, *ibid.*, p. 315; Dr. McGhee, *ibid.*, Vol. VII, p. 459; E. Barnes, *Studies in Education*, Vol. I, No. 6.

[35] E. B. Bryan, *Ped. Sem.*, Vol. VII, p. 357.

[36] King, *op. cit.*, pp. 154, 156, 157.

The really illuminating category, then, under which to describe the child's activities, and one which includes them all on an equal basis, is that of present function. Their backward reference to the life of a remote ancestry is of far less moment to the educator than the fact that they are essentially the manifestation of a developing psycho-physical organism, and that in some way they make possible the activities of later stages and in the end condition the adequate performance of the functions of maturity. From this standpoint it becomes of even greater importance than before to know accurately from a study of children themselves just what we can call functions and activities of an immature mind. We do not mean to say that the study of the backward reference in the child's life is not necessary, but that the value of such a study for the teacher consists solely in applying it to the elucidation of its significance in the child's present experience. The question then is: What are the activities that characterize an undeveloped or immature mind and body, and in what way do they condition later and more adequate reactions?[37]

In this relation we note the similarity to Froebel's classification of the play-activities of early childhood, but with much clearer statement as to its meaning and value. (Note p. 175 for a fuller statement.) Here (1) we find further corroborative testimony as to the kind of games naturally shown by the children themselves; the succeeding stages of interest center [38] about (2) objects, toys, real things, and (3) the legal period, as described by Dr. Gulick, (ages 7–12). It concerns social co-operation to a higher degree. The interests center about ideas; the requirements of games are more exact. (Note also Miss Sisson's experience.[39]) A comparison with Froebel's *stages* of play is suggestive.[40]

The criterion of value for the future is necessarily one for the observer, one to be applied only after the evolution has been completed, and when we can look back and interpret the incomplete in terms of the complete. It may be perfectly legitimate in philosophy to use such a standpoint, but for psychology the criterion must be in terms of present function. From this point of view we have outlined the unfolding of the child's interests and disposition to certain sorts of action.[41]

[37] *Op. cit.*, pp. 160, 161. Note also pp. 164–166, 180, 181, 187, 188.

[38] A. Tanner, *The Child*, chap. xix.

[39] *Studies in Education*, No. 5.

[40] *Education of Man*, pp. 267, 271, 303.

[41] King, *op. cit.*, p. 40.

The earlier interests of man are not the mystic foreshadowings of what is to come, but the stuff that goes on differentiating until it reaches a degree of co-ordination and specialization that by common consent we call mature. There is no reason intrinsic in any activity at any time that labels it as more or less perfect, or as higher or lower in the scale of development. The boy does not form various clubs and societies with his playmates so that he may be a better member of society, but he does become an efficient and useful member of society because of these youthful co-operations. This is in substance all we can mean by the "development of interests." [42]

B. A few statements as to the nature or theory of play are needful to give meaning to the other sections of this paper. The simplest form of statement,[43] explanatory of the nature of play, is that "playful acts are always performed for their own sake, usually prepare for future usefulness, and are the outcome of inner tendencies of development resulting from past experiences of the race."[44] Or, stated differently, the four theories most suggestive and quite reconcilable are the Schiller-Spencer theory, that of surplus energy; that stated by Gross as the preparatory theory;[45] that by Hall[46] as the motor-habits and spirit of the past persisting in the present, and that "it is an expression of psychic life and reacts on it."[47]

I would not claim too much, but I cannot believe there can be any education in the true sense of the word that does not deeply involve the *emotions* and the *will*, and that does not take root in the inheritances that have come down from the motor-habits of the race; and as these motor-habits, endeavoring to persist in the present, are involved in play, we find there the surest and nearest approach to a true education of the child.[48]

The reader who may chance to be unfamiliar with Groos's book, *The Play of Man*, is urged to read the third section of the

[42] *Ibid.*, p. 216.

[43] Kirkpatrick, *Fundamentals of Child Study*, p. 58.

[44] *Ibid.*, chap. ix, p. 147.

[45] G. E. Johnson, *Education by Plays and Games*, p. 38.

[46] G. S. Hall, *Adolescence*, Vol. I, p. 202.

[47] T. R. Croswell, *Ped. Sem.*, Vol. VI, No. 3, p. 323.

[48] G. S. Hall, *Adolescence*, Vol. I, pp. 183, 204, 235; also Barnes, *Studies in Education*, Vol. I, No. 9, p. 359.

work, and note especially the last three chapters in it; also the second chapter in A. F. Chamberlain's valuable work, *The Child —A Study in the Evolution of Man.* Groos states that biology proves to us that the child does not play because he is young, *but,* he is young because he must play!

Play in childhood is concerned with everything; emotions, acts, thoughts, imaginings, speech, all begin their career under its subtle influence; language, poetry, art, science, all begin in child-play; the seekers after knowledge "play" as surely and as naïvely as the child.

III

In our effort to improve the plays and games of children under the age of seven, or, with more direct reference to their social grouping, in the kindergarten, we need to take closely to heart and mind the criticisms brought upon the kindergarten by scientists, artists, educators, physicians, or the "public." While their criticisms often show a lack of insight or appreciation for what has been contributed to education at large by the kindergarten principle and method, the marvelous change of mental attitude it has produced in many groups and communities of people; while, also, the cause of childhood from *every* point of view has been greatly advanced; yet, it still is true that the cherished ideals of its founder have been far from realized, and the hopes and efforts of child students the world over have not yet borne the fruit so much coveted.

We fully recognize that as a social organism it is impossible to attribute the causes of these unfulfilled hopes and ideals to the one phase of educational life, the kindergarten, but we do need to be self-examining in order that we may be more accountable for our heritage and our stewardship. 1. In the light of unquestionable facts[49] have we met the physical needs of children as fully as we might? 2. Have we so environed them that they have been stimulated, or had occasion to react from objective or subjective stimulus *freely* and *creatively?* 3. What occasions, "according to the nature of the child," have we offered for

[49] A. F. Chamberlain, *The Child,* pp. 13, 18; also *Ped. Sem.,* June, 1908, p. 271.

growth in moral action and ideas? These are the questions, or such as these, that we need to face. We believe that the plays and games of the kindergarten offer a better opportunity than any other one medium for development in these directions. We fear we have not honored, as we should, the fact that the child not only *delights,* but *needs* to realize his own possibilities in the "joy of being a cause," or his powers in experimentation.[50] We have oft-times presented plays and games more suitable for illustrative material for subject-matter, etc. We are beginning in different centers to plan for time when there shall be *no* plan. In other words, free-play has an honored place and time in the newer phases of kindergarten life. Many simple toys, pictures, books, sand-piles, as well as sand-tables, gardens, and play-places, are to be found in our most advanced kindergartens. The latter means of play were considered by Froebel himself the *indispensable* requirements for the children. Unquestionably Froebel was in the most natural play-relation to the children of his kindergartens, but in his effort to fully work out his theories in practice, the preponderant appeal in his own thought was the satisfying of the intellectual needs, and it dominated the form of his writings which have been the main source of training for kindergartners the world over, coupled with the more or less adequate interpretation of his followers.

While Froebel's aim in the plays and games was to develop creative self-expression, the games that are cited in the chapters on Movement Plays,[51] as well as those in the *Mother-Play Book,* are largely of a formal and symbolic nature and the chance for *free* self-expression is greatly limited.

In general, the play-life of a child expresses itself during four periods of life: (*a*) babyhood (1 to 2½); (*b*) early childhood (2½ to 6); (*c*) childhood merging into girlhood and boyhood (6 to 12); (*d*) boyhood and girlhood merging into the adolescent period (12 to 20).

a) The first period is characterized by simple movements for their own sake and the beginnings of instinctive activity.

[50] A. F. Chamberlain, *The Child,* p. 16.

[51] Froebel, *Pedagogics.*

b) The second is a continuation of the first, with new instinctive tendencies manifest, and the plays and self-made games centering more strongly about objects—realities. This is more noticeable till about 5½ years of age. It is the individualistic period. The imagination becomes more active with a growing knowledge of things and vague ideas of the relation of means and ends. "Primarily the imagination is a power of realization, not of fanciful playing with unreals."[52]

c) The third period begins to evidence spontaneous co-operation in social groups and the interests center about social relations. It is the time of competitive instincts and a desire for skill. The relation of means to ends is evident, rather than in immediate realities.

a) Babyhood. The form of play at this first period is largely motor, somewhat rhythmic. Froebel utilizes it largely by use of balls, and through songs. We can add to these opportunity for repetitional play, as previously mentioned.

b) Kindergarten age. During this period the form of play is largely rhythmic (simple individual dance movements, etc.) and imitative. In the latter class almost endless opportunities present themselves. Their chief characteristics will be determined by environmental influence, for they belong largely to the representative group. The beginnings of creative arrangement appear.

c) and *d*) Boyhood and girlhood. These ages witness great changes, for experience has registered much that is new, and so enriched the child, that memory plays an active part. The imagination is therefore more highly developed. Constructive and dramatic plays predominate, and originality is greatly enhanced.

In many kindergartens undoubtedly the swing of the pendulum has gone to an opposite extreme in the use of rhythmic activity, or, the plays and games have been for the "subject's" sake rather than the child's sake. If we bear in mind that the

[52] John Dewey, *Mental Development*, pp. 6, 9, 11; note also Angell, *Psychology*, pp. 170–80.

nature of the child and the nature of play should and do coincide, it will economize effort and make for freedom.

"At the beginning there was rhythm."[53]

In the dark background of history there is now much evidence that at some point play, art, and work were not divorced. They all may have sprung from rhythmic movement which is so deep-seated in biology because it secures most joy of life with least expense.[54]

Rhythmic movement is the inevitable expression of certain moods. By watching for the play of these moods, either (1) in activity itself, or (2) centered about playthings, or (3) centered about ideas or social groups, we can naturally lead the children to create their own play-forms. These may be in simple dances or games.

The main point is, that we shall meet the child upon his own plane of development, note his states of activity, emotion, or idea, and help him to originate of his own initiative his form of expression. We remember from our former statement that only as these activities and interests are considered from a functional point of view, in the "here and now," with reference to "how and why" they came to be, can we adequately help little children to *make ideal* that which already allures them on and out into a fuller, more perfect expression or being.

"Unless we condemn the experience, we cannot condemn any of the activities that have called it into being." This type of activity is a unity in itself, and is adequate to the plane upon which the child lives, moves, and dwells.

If the plays and games of the kindergarten are not developing (*a*) motor-power, (*b*) initiative, (*c*) individual and some degree of social control, is the kindergarten doing what is quite within its own realm?[55] We believe that the kindergarten has not done all that it could along these lines. Sporadic efforts have been evident, but the time is now ripe, with the increasing clearness of view concerning the social function of education, to

[53] G. S. Hall, *Adolescence,* Vol. I, p. 211.

[54] Gross, Vol. II, pp. 383, 392, 394.

[55] Colin Scott, *Social Education,* pp. 33, 34.

further these efforts and we believe the courage born of experience will give conviction of insight and principle.

On the one hand we believe the unchanging influence of undue organization of plays and games will be done away with, and on the other the seemingly aimless, confused, spontaneous activities of the children will, through the guidance of the feeling, seeing, and knowing teacher, be related unconsciously to the social group of which they form a part. In this connection a word as to the function of the teacher will not be amiss. She should not be the leader, but the "occasioner" only, who from the standpoint of larger experience can help the children upon their own path of discovery. Her personality will be the moving power.

The music in relation to the plays and games should be of the sort that integrates with the growth of the child and is a natural counterpart of the acts, feelings, and ideas which are being expressed in play form, and in the main should be quite simple.

In other words, we heartily recommend to every kindergartner who believes that the foregoing statements are worthy of consideration, that she endeavor to follow the requirements for children of kindergarten age (outlined by Mr. Bryan); that her methods be largely those of suggestion and imitation, and that she give children full scope for free, spontaneous play.

When she possesses experience based on such conditions she will realize that her highest obligation will be to enable each little child to live out his own life as fully as possible, according to the ideals of his own stages of growth, not hers. Then she will make occasion for him (1) in his baby days, to reveal in playful, free sense-activity, for the joy of being alive; and again, (2) during his kindergarten days, to imitate and make rhythmic experiences that are worthy, to his heart's content, and while she will endeavor to bring him into contact with nature in every way, yet in his own environment no matter how undesirable, can be found much that is worthy of representation in play, and if life abounds, he can idealize the real that *he* knows, enters into, and possesses, through his *own* creative dramatizations. Then, as he grows into a period (3) when he requires more complex conditions for constructiveness, or larger group games, etc., he passes into the life of the school, he will be better prepared to function adequately there because he has lived out his own life as fully as possible in each previous period.[56]

In conclusion let me recall the main points we have tried to elucidate:

I. That Froebel's plays and games were based on the postulate of idealistic philosophy; that they were to bring *to* the child ideals common to the adult world.

II. That the modern point of view is that ideals possessed by the child himself and the whole group with whom he plays will be utilized as means of gaining higher ones; that only as he functions in relation to those from whom he has come and with whom he associates, can he rise to higher levels later on.

III. That the plays and games of the kindergarten will be expressive of the "life that is in and around all;" that they are *conditioned* by local factors, differing in each center (nationality, numbers, environment, etc.); that "stages of growth" must be the fundamental consideration, or point of departure.

If reality is in the unity of the spiritual and material, the kindergartner will lead a child to feel that there should be a guiding thought which seeks expression through all the materials at his command, through conversation, story, song, rhythm, game, and handwork. Balance will always be preserved, the creative spirit will be called forth and take form in something adequate to the significance of the moment. A child will gain a feeling of the self as an organic unity; thought and expression in perfect accord will intensify the personality.[57]

[56] Teachers of little children of all grades will find suggestions of special value concerning games as typical of the best work along these lines, in Mr. G. E. Johnson's book, *Education by Plays and Games,* published by Ginn & Co. Note especially pages 65–94 for children of kindergarten age. The studious and inventive teacher will be able to help her group of children to utilize their own resources and develop games most suited to their conditions. With such suggestions, as in this and other books arranged to meet the growing, changing child-life, the games will be more in accord with his health and happiness than any other type.

For folk dances see Miss Caroline Crawford's book, published by A. S. Barnes, and *Suggestions for Graded Games and Rythmic Exercises,* a book by Marion B. Newton, published also by A. S. Barnes.

[57] Miss Luella Palmer, *Elementary School Teacher,* September, 1908.

The attitude which the kindergartner will try to create will depend upon her own attitude toward the universe. The spirit of this article on plays and games and the point of view of the writer are in hearty accord with the quotation and article referred to, particularly the third principle which it states:

She (the kindergartner) could hold one of three differing views: (1) that spirit is transcendent only, (2) that it is immanent only, or (3) that it both enfolds and is in matter. . . . . If God's purpose is a living, growing one which man is helping to embody, the kindergartner will have a definite plan in mind, but it will be a principle rather than a design, so flexible that it will allow for variation which would be more valuable for the children at the particular time and place than the detail she had prepared.

In China society succeeds and civilization stands still. With our larger freedom the child throws off some part of the useless burden, expresses anew the ideals of life, and even reacts upon the adult so as to retard his hastening decadence, and civilization advances steadily onward. With increasing freedom in the study of realities and in *living* schools, our children will bring us still larger life with the birth of each new generaton.[58]

May the wondrous confidence of the little child be furthered, may his wonder-world be enriched, and the unfolding of his spirit, in gladsome, free, mirthful, and yet strengthening activity, be made more possible by our fellowship in play!

[58] Earl Barnes, *Studies in Education,* No. 9, p. 360 (italics mine).

POULTRY-RAISING AS A SCHOOL OCCUPATION

W. A. BALDWIN
Principal State Normal School, Hyannis, Mass.

Ever since Comenius said "Things before words" there has been a growing demand for some kind of physical activity upon which to base the so-called "regular work" of the schools. At first one form seemed as desirable as another. Even so wise a man as Dr. E. A. Sheldon, principal of the Oswego Normal School, used to say that it mattered little about the kind of work so long as it was objective. We have been gradually coming to see that it does matter very much and that the right kind of work must possess the following among other characteristics, viz:

1. It must fit into the needs of the community of which the school is a part so that children and parents may see that it is of practical value.

2. It must give opportunities for the child to participate in the work and in the rewards of his work.

3. It must furnish opportunities for typical, basal experiences and so build up important apperceiving concept groups.

4. Things must be seen by the children in their natural relations, and ministering to the life of man.

5. It must furnish a basis for natural correlation with the regular subjects.

In a section like Cape Cod, already known in Boston and New York markets for its fine Cape Cod eggs, and in a school like our Training School, nearly every child of which may have a few hens at home, this poultry industry seems to meet all of the foregoing requirements. I have felt for some time that poultry-raising, properly conducted, might furnish a school activity equal in value to the school garden. We have, therefore, started the experiment to see how much of this work may be safely recommended to the regular public school.

We have a small plant fairly well established and incidentally have done a little educational work of the right sort. Thus far this has been done almost entirely in connection with the Normal School. We hope gradually to find points of connection with the Training School.

In the winter of 1907 a Cyphers Incubator was purchased and I began to experiment with it. The incubator was placed in my library with an experimental batch of eggs. My two little boys, aged respectively 9 and 10 years, watched and assisted in the turning of the eggs and in the care of the incubator. They heard the first faint peeps from the imprisoned chicks and watched with the greatest enthusiasm to see the little fellows struggle out of their enclosing shells. After all were hatched these chicks were transferred to a Cyphers Brooder which was placed on our lawn. The children considered it a great honor to be allowed to help care for them.

The incubator was now transferred to a small house which had been used for the school garden tools and a part of which had been partitioned off by one of our students to serve as an incubator house. This house was built into a sandy hillside and so it was possible to have an incubator room in which an even temperature could be preserved.

The business of incubation was now turned over to an energetic, faithful teacher and the incubator was kept going at its full capacity for two successive periods. It was found convenient to utilize some of these eggs at different stages of their development to illustrate Normal School work in biology. When the chicks began to hatch out the students were taken in groups to watch the process and they showed almost as much enthusiasm as my boys had shown.

After being transferred to the brooders the chicks continued to be centers of interest not only for the whole school but for visitors to the school. The question now arose as to what should be done with these chicks after they should outgrow the brooders. Here was a new problem. We must have a hen-house and we had no money for that purpose. We visited local poultrymen and obtained printed suggestions from the Cyphers Incubator Company, from the Agricultural Department at Washington, and from Orono, Maine.

We decided to make this our manual-training work for a while and to build a poultry-house after plans similar to those described in "Poultry Investigations at the Maine Agricultural Experiment Station, 1906." The School had recently constructed a coal-pocket out of reinforced concrete and had saved the lumber and some stones from the same. We dug into the south side of a very sandy hill and erected a strong retaining wall six feet in height, facing it with concrete. We erected walls of concrete two feet high on the other three sides and made a slightly sloping floor of concrete. We next erected our frame, covered it with the boards, and these with shingles. The concrete work was done in the spring principally by the men who care for the school grounds under the direction of a first-class mason. The framing of the building was done during the summer mostly by instructors and members of the manual-training class of the summer school. The shingling and a part of the interior construction was done during the autumn by the instructor and the Normal School students. As winter was fast approaching it was found necessary to have a carpenter finish up the work.

This chicken-house had thus furnished an excellent kind of manual training for the men of the school. I do not believe that it was an *excellent* kind for the young women, but it was much better for them than is the ordinary wood-working course. In fact, many advantages might be urged for it, not the least being that here was an urgent need for which they might help to provide.

As soon as the house was ready, the fowls were installed in their new and comfortable quarters. I was absent in Europe during the winter and so can only write what has been reported regarding the results. The fowls were put into the keeping of successive Normal School students, each anxious to help earn his way and willing to get some experience in poultry-raising. The instructor who was in general charge found a great difference in the quality of the work done by different students. Certain very important characteristics which were not suspected from the regular school work were clearly manifest in the poultry-house. In fact, enough has already come to me along this line to prove that here is a new and reliable means of applying practical tests and of helping students to see and correct inherent weaknesses, which might never appear in the course of regular school work.

In connection with the incubation such points as the following impressed themselves upon the students: Very much depends upon the ancestors. Eggs should be obtained from a reliable dealer who has standard fowls of a high grade. The general health of such ancestors must be good. Both the cock and the hens must be in a vigorous condition at the time of the egg-production. Even after exercising the utmost care in these matters, some eggs are not fertile and others cease to develop at various stages of the incubation period. Some chicks break through the shells but have not sufficient vitality to free themselves from them. Others are so weak after struggling forth from their shells that they are trampled upon by their more vigorous fellows. The greatest care must be exercised during the period of incubation to keep an even temperature and to prevent any jarring of the eggs. The young chicks must be fed enough but not too much, and must be given some hard food to provide work for their digestive organs. They must be given plenty of fresh air and exercise, not too much heat, and opportunity to gradually accustom themselves to the cold air and other conditions outside of their brooder.

All of these ideas and many more furnish to the Normal School students very forceful lessons which have direct application on the hygienic side of their own everyday lives.

Although not much connection has as yet been made with the children of the Training School I have myself gained some ideas of possibilities along those lines by the experiences of my own children. I have already related some of these.

After seeing their father experiment with the incubator, my boys were anxious to try raising some chicks. We discussed matters at some length and finally it was decided that the older boy might try running a small incubator which I had purchased and that the younger should set a hen. Each was interested in the experiences of the other and so both became well acquainted with the different stages of both methods of chicken-hatching.

When the young chicks were transferred from the school incubator to the brooders a few were thought not able to fight their way with the others. My boys asked for several of these unfortunates. They fed and watered them; put them out into the sunshine in the morning and behind the stove at night. They tried to straighten crooked feet and expended a vast amount of sympathy upon them. Some died and were buried with tears; others grew to be valuable members of the hen colony.

As a result of these chicken experiences and of various garden experiences they are glad to try for this winter (1908–9) the following plan. Each boy has charge of a flock of hens and a cock, one flock consisting of Rhode Island Reds and the other of Barred Plymouth Rocks. The hens are furnished; the boys do all of the work, pay for the food and sell the eggs. Each boy will have half of the profits from his flock. The lessons which they are learning could not be so well learned in any other way, and they are lessons which are becoming a valuable part of their equipment for life.

It is true, as some one objects, that such training cannot well be given to every child at school. But the school can do much. It can help to cultivate the right attitude toward this kind of work, and nearly every family in our villages and even in our small cities would find it profitable, pleasurable, and educational to teach the children how to care for a few hens.

"They knew, as God knew, that command of nature comes by obedience to nature; that reward comes by faithful service. . . . . There was no secret of labor which they disdain."—Emerson.

THE SCHOOL CLUB: ITS RELATION TO SEVERAL EDUCATIONAL IDEALS

A. MONROE STOWE, A.M., PH.D
State Normal School, Hyannis, Mass.

In endeavoring to realize one of the chief ideals of the public elementary schools, the development of intelligent, efficient, and upright citizens, teachers have had to depend upon the curriculum for material from which to develop a knowledge and appreciation of the rights and duties of citizens in a democracy and upon the classroom discipline for opportunities to make vital this knowledge through expression. While such studies as history, literature, geography, and civil government contain a wealth of material from which to develop such knowledge, the teacher is handicapped by the fact that as the government of the schoolroom must necessarily be of a more or less paternalistic character, the opportunities for the application or expression of this knowledge are very limited. Limitation in this case is unfortunate, since the realization of the ideal requires not only a knowledge and appreciation of the rights and duties of citizens in a democracy, but also a habitual proper reaction to those rights and duties. In other words, the intelligent, efficient, and upright citizen not only knows what he ought to do in a given civic situation, but he always actually does what he ought to do. Hence in this training *for* citizenship there should be training *in* citizenship, there should be opportunities to act and form habits of reacting as well as instruction in theory and principles. If, therefore, the schools are to be more successful in their endeavors to realize the ideal they have accepted, they must utilize every agency which makes possible growth in civic efficiency as well as improvement in civic knowledge.

Recognizing the fact that in this training *for* citizenship in a democracy there must be training *in* citizenship in a like democracy, not a few of thoughtful men welcomed the "school state," the "school city," and the "school village" as agencies which might make possible this necessary growth in civic efficiency. This movement, however, met with severe criticism. It was said that the movement created within the school an organization entirely too complex and artificial. Teachers and principals who were working for simplicity in school administration did not favor a scheme involving the complexity of the government of the modern state, city, or town. Why impose upon the school forms of government which are proving themselves cumbersome and unsatisfactory in real life? Such forms could never express the real vital life of the school which must be regarded, not as a civic community, but as a large family in which the teacher stands *in loco parentis*.

Granted that the school is like a large family the artificiality of the "school city" is very apparent. The "school city" is not a real city, nor are the pupils real citizens. While sometimes it may seem almost real, there must always be the realization that after all it is merely a game. The police are not real police. The police court is not a real police court; nor is the criminal (let us be thankful) the real criminal. It is all a play, sometimes a drama, sometimes perhaps a farce, in which the actors are little men and women. Is not this attempt to reproduce the state, city, or town in miniature, with little men and women as its citizens, a retrogression to the seventeenth-century conception of children? Must another Rousseau arise to awaken us again to the fact that children are children, not little men and women?

To reject the "school city," however, does not necessarily mean that we must henceforth depend upon the curriculum and school discipline alone for our material and practice in the development of our ideal. Training *for* citizenship still implies training *in* citizenship, but we must remember that the citizenship of the child is somewhat different from the citizenship of the adult. If our schools are to be made more real to the child, we must find some agency which will express a part of his life as well as make possible growth in civic efficiency through activity. Such an agency can be found only in a careful study of the natural development of the life of the child.

A careful study of the natural development of the child will reveal a period in his life when ceasing to live so completely for himself alone, he begins to reach out in an effort to join his life with the lives of others through some forms of co-operative activity. While at first this reaching out may be unconscious and instinctive and may express itself in gang life as well as friendships, it also becomes conscious, expressing itself in the club or society organized for the accomplishment of definite aims and purposes. At the threshold of this stage of their development the pupils of the last two years of the upper elementary schools stand, anxious to do things, and perceiving that some things can be accomplished only by working together in some form of club, they are eager to organize and enjoy the pleasure of achieving results through co-operation. Club life is to them, therefore, very real and vital. Not only is this true, but, as in the club they learn their first lessons in living and working together in a democratic organization, respecting the rights of others, while maintaining their own and performing their own duties while insisting that others shall not be negligent of theirs, we may almost say that the club is the youths' own state in which they learn the fundamental lessons of citizenship. Shall these lessons be learned only by the wasteful hit-and-miss method of experience or shall the pupils have the helpful guidance of the wise teacher? As the presentation of the proper motive by the teacher will set the pupils eagerly at work on the organization of a school club, it is within the power of the teacher, as advisor to such a club, to exercise this much needed guidance. Indeed, since the school club, when organized and conducted by the pupils, not only meets the need so long felt by the teacher in his endeavors to develop intelligent, efficient, and upright citizens, but also helps make school life more real and vital to the child, is it not the duty of the school to utilize this agency which expresses the civic life of the pupil as well as makes possible a natural and progressive growth in civic efficiency?

While from the point of view of the ideal of the school the function of the school club is to furnish opportunities for making vital through expression the knowledge of the rights and duties of citizens in a democracy acquired through their study of the subjects of the curriculum, from the standpoint of the individual pupil one of the most important functions of the school club is to train its members in the knowledge and practice of parliamentary rules of order. How widespread ignorance concerning parliamentary procedure is among members of organizations of teachers and university post-graduate students, as well as of churches and women's clubs, is well known to those who are acquainted with the way in which the business of these organizations is often conducted or rather misconducted by the members, many of whom feel very deeply their inability not only to conduct meetings as they should be conducted but also to make or put even the most simple motions. Since this knowledge and power will be needed by the great majority of the graduates of our elementary schools, and since in these schools we are endeavoring to develop all of the powers of the individual, do we not owe it to the individual to develop his power and ability to co-operate with others in the conduct of meetings and in the transaction of business in the best ways, or according to recognized rules of order? Is it not the duty of the school to meet this real and vital need by developing in its pupils a working knowledge of these rules of procedure?

Granted that it is the duty of the schools to develop in its pupils a working knowledge of the standard rules of order, how shall the schools develop such knowledge? From the nature of the subject it is evident that formal instruction in it will be insufficient, since to make this knowledge vital requires opportunity to put into practice the knowledge thus acquired. From the nature of the child, furthermore, it is evident that this instruction and practice must not be artificial, since the result desired can be achieved only if the instruction be given in response to a need felt by the child and the practice be found in putting this knowledge to some practical use. As in the ordinary school there is no agency which either calls into being a need for this instruction or presents opportunities for the practical use of this knowledge, if the school is to be successful in giving this training, must it not make use of the school club, organized and conducted by the pupils for the purpose of achieving ends accepted by the child as worthy of his efforts and attainable only through co-operation?

Thus the school club both makes possible a natural and progressive growth in civic efficiency and furnishes opportunities for a vital development of a practical knowledge of the rules of order in such a way as to assist the school in its endeavors to make the school life an expression of the child's life as well as a better preparation for intelligent, efficient, and upright participation in the privileges and duties of American citizenship.

INDUSTRIAL EDUCATION, THE WORKING-MAN, AND THE SCHOOL

GEORGE H. MEAD
University of Chicago

The education of a workman has always been very close to his trade. The dependence of his training upon his trade is expressed in the word apprenticeship. The apprentice has been trained by helping under the direction of a master in the trade. If we go back far enough we find apprenticeship as a necessary introduction to every trade, and indeed the only introduction. The elementary school appeared in the first place to train the clerk and accountant. It was part of the apprenticeship of the commercial trades. In the seventeenth and eighteenth centuries the artisans and laborers were not taught to read, write, and figure. The extensive commercial activity, the constantly increasing use of money, and the growing importance of reading for political and social life, gradually carried the demand for control over the three R's throughout the whole laboring class; though it remained for America in the early decades of our republic to inaugurate the common school with universal education. Under these conditions, the master artisan was expected to allow his apprentices to attend the common schools, but there was little or no connection between the schooling and training in the trade.

The school taught the use of language and number. Apprenticeship taught the vocation. It was true that the exercise of the trade demanded reading, writing, and figuring, but the apprenticeship system simply left training in these to the school. The two vehicles of education remained separate and influenced each other either indirectly or not at all.

This was partly due to the function of the common school in America. It opened the door to all avenues. Our democracy elected men to office who had no more than a common school education. It is not very long ago that boys left the common school to read law and medicine. In a country in which everything was open to everyone and the common school was the door to all opportunities, the relation of schooling to the work of the apprentice was lost in its relation to more ambitious callings. The common school has retained its stamp of the first step toward the learned professions and political preferment.

Thus the education of the workman has been and has remained divided into two parts, the formal training in the three R's and the apprenticeship to a trade. These two parts have not been parts of a whole. The schooling has remained formal, bookish, and literary in its interest. The apprenticeship has suffered severely in the change of modern industry, but even in its better days it did not awaken any interest in its own history, nor in its social conditions, nor in the technique of better methods. The schooling taken by itself was narrow and unpractical, the apprenticeship had no outlook and wakened no interest outside itself. The two did not reinforce and interpret each other. In a certain sense they ought to have been in the relation of theory and practice. The apprenticeship should have presented the problems which the school solved, and the interest in the solution of these problems should have made the work of school vivid and educative. But while it is easy to pick flaws in this training, its results were admirable especially in comparison with the training which children of today get who work with their hands.

Apprenticeship remains in many trades, especially in those under the control of organized labor. The interest of organized labor has been, however, very largely that of keeping down the number of skilled artisans to that which the trade can profitably absorb. Organized labor has not accepted the control over apprenticeship to make out of it a better education. Nor is there uniformity in the trades. In many the apprenticeship system has quite gone by the boards, in others it is not at all adequate. As a system of training skilled laborers the old system of apprenticeship has disappeared and no consistent new system has arisen to take its place. The cause of the changes is evident enough. It is the machine that has taken possession of the trades, has displaced the artisan, and has substituted for the artisan, who makes an entire article, a group of laborers who tend the machines.

The effect of this upon the training of the laborer has been most deplorable. The more the machine accomplishes the less the workman is called upon to use his brain, the less skill he is called upon to acquire. The economics of the factory, therefore, calls for a continual search for cheaper and therefore less skilled labor. The success of the modern type of wholesale manufacture of inexpensive goods has depended upon the vast numbers of unskilled laborers. Women and children have been swept into the factories to displace the more expensive labor of men. We are accustomed to recognize that the sudden use of this type of factory production was made economically possible by the huge markets which steam transportation brought to the doors of the factory. The other determining factor, the surplus of unskilled labor that could be absorbed by the factory and the mine, we are not so conscious of. We are also very well aware of the nicety with which the inventor can adjust the machine to a product which the market demands. We are not so aware of the equal nicety with which the inventor adjusts his machine to the cheapness of labor.

The most serious handicap under which labor suffered with the opening of the modern period of factory industry was the lack of any connection between the training of its apprentices and the technique of the machine. The intelligence of the artisan who made the whole article made of him an admirable citizen of the older community. It was this intelligence very largely which made the success of our early democratic institutions. The apprenticeship system made practical, intelligent, self-reliant men, as well as good workmen who did not have to blush for the work of their hands. The training was not, however, adaptable. The very skill of the artisan stood in the way of his adapting himself to the new régime. The skilled artisan was no more but rather less valuable than the untrained man. And machines invented to exploit unskilled and unintelligent labor in so far fixed the condition of the workman that were thereafter to tend these machines.

It is perhaps idle to speculate as to what the form of the machine, and the method of industry would have been if the laborer had had the training, the science, and the sort of skill which enabled the merchant, the manufacturer, and the engineer to make use of the advent of steam in manufacture and transportation; but we can recognize that invention has shown a suppleness in adapting itself to any kind of product or market, in using every sort of science and technique, and that there is every reason to believe that adaptable intelligence, skill that could be generalized and applied in various ways, if found at that period in the artisans, would have been a more profitable field for invention than the lack of intelligence and adaptability which our present machines are built to use and exploit.

A skill that can be adapted must be based upon some theory. The shop must be reinforced by the school. Such skill can turn from one form of manufacture to another, as the manufacturer himself can turn from sewing machines or steam locomotives to automobiles. Such dependence of the shop upon the school, of practice upon theory, we find in our most up-to-date apprenticeship schools. In those of the General Electric Company, of the New York Central Company, of the Houston, Stamwood, & Gamble Company at Cincinnati, the schooling represents by and large a half of the preparation. The apprentice must understand the technique that he acquires so that he can apply it with intelligence, and this means power to do many things, not one thing alone. It means the creation of intelligence rather than speed in the apprentice. These apprenticeship schools will not allow the foreman to hold the apprentice to a machine because he operates it with greater speed, i. e.: these schools recognize that the man must not be subordinated to the machine if he is to acquire the sort of skill they wish in these upper class workmen. The school and the shop must go hand in hand in modern artisanship. Their lack of connection in the old system spells the disappearance of the old-time system as the old-time artisan has disappeared. There can be no question that the modern artisan demands schooling if he is not to be a mere creature of the machine. He needs the mathematics and drawing out of which the machine has arisen. He must know the formulas which are expressed in the tools that they may be his tools and adapt them to his uses. He must be able to read the blue prints that are the language into which the engineer translates the formula to carry it over into bodily form. This sort of training is the only kind that will free the artisan. It is not until he can comprehend the machine as a tool that he will not be a part of it. Not that the employer desires in his high laborers ignorance. He is building up expensive schools because skill here is money in his pocket. The history of the technical schools at Fall River, Massachusetts, demonstrates that the employee, the employer, and the community all recognized the need of this training in the artisans who were to employ the high-grade machines.

It is in the economic struggle that organized labor fears the apprenticeship school. It has fought to keep down the number of apprentices in order that their wages might be kept up, and their working hours more occupied. Industry being organized on the basis of surplus labor supply, it is natural that labor should suspect the employer of aiming to bring about a surplus of skilled labor not only to make sudden increase in production possible, but to enable the employer to fight the labor union. That many employers have this in view is of course true.

However, as long as advance in wages means skill there will be an inevitable demand among laborers for industrial training. Correspondence schools are profiting by this demand at present, at the expense of the laborer. In the end it would be hopeless for labor to maintain its economic position by entrenching itself behind lack of skill. If the apprenticeship school is the best method of learning the trade it will be adopted. The restriction of the number of apprentices must arise in some other fashion, for with these schools, whether in the hands of employers or in our public-school systems the numbers cannot be fixed by the labor unions, and skilled labor outside the union will be more dangerous than inside the organization. Inevitably the manner in which the commodity of skilled labor is to be controlled will be changed. It will be controlled because it is an economic waste to the country to have a surplus of labor. Our present industries adapt themselves to this surplus and of course exploit it, but this does not in any sense justify it nor make it permanent. Industry has adjusted itself to and exploited child labor. The remedy for this exploitation is not to be found in reducing the birth rate, and thus the number of children. The community itself, becoming intelligent, refuses to permit such economic and human waste as that involved in child labor. It must reject as decisively a system by which industry drops its adult labor into misery when for the time being it is not needed, to pick it up again at a reduced rate when there is a demand for increased production. The social control we demand will come through increase in intelligence, and the laboring class is the last class that can afford to restrict its own intelligence. In our present industrial evolution the race is to the technically equipped or to those who can command such equipment, and in a competitive society those who lack such equipment must be subject to exploitation.

The tremendous revolution brought about by the factory system, the machine, has found every group in society equipped with sufficient free intelligence to enable them to adapt themselves to the changes incident to the revolution. The investor, the producer, the middle man, the technical expert, the engineer, the banker, fitted in with no friction with the new order and have profited financially. The capital of the artisan alone has been lost. His capital is his acquired skill. If this is simply in the form of a fixed group of habits every change in the method of manufacturing will consign workmen to the human scrapheap.

The financial disability of the laborer is that which is generally contrasted with the greater freedom of the capitalist or those who can accumulate a financial reserve. A revolution in industrial methods may annihilate the investment of the capitalist and even wipe out of existence the occupations of officers and employees. Still those whose incomes have permitted the accumulation of a reserve have an indefinitely better chance of getting upon their feet again, than have those whose incomes admit of no accumulation. There is room for them in which to move. They can seek opportunity at a distance. They can wait for it. They can prepare themselves for new and unaccustomed occupations, while the laborer whose income is swallowed up day by day in the necessary outgoes for his and his family's daily bread, must do anything or nothing as it presents itself, at the moment, at his own door. There is no reason to depreciate this disability of the day laborer. It only emphasizes the other disability which has been above presented; the disability of skill without adaptive intelligence. The man who knows why he does what he does, is better able to do something else. Intelligence, the ability to see the relation of means and end in conduct, is the fundamental form of freedom—"and the truth shall make you free." A laborer with acquired skill for which he has no theory, approaches the condition of the purely instinctive animal. He becomes helpless the moment he is out of the environment to which his habits are adapted.

To these general propositions, which may be summed up in the old adage that knowledge is power, a reply comes from our technical schools and our universities. It is said that only a select few can afford to know; that our life has become so complicated that it must be governed by the highly trained expert; that it is the age of the expert who dominates our industry as really as he does our medical practice. And there are social philosophers willing to accept this judgment and build their conceptions of the future of society upon it. We are, according to them, to pass from the control of the political and financial aristocracy to that of the technical expert. Only they will be able really to understand why anything is done in the growing complexities of our society, and they will rule. And the answer to this philosophy is that the expert does not and in human history has not ruled. He has served. His greatest effectiveness is found among those who are intelligent. The expert even in industry demands not blind obedience but intelligent co-operation, and the more intelligent the co-operation can be, the higher the efficiency of the expert. What is wanted in an ideal machine shop, where the tools are made to do certain work, is that the man who uses the tools should be able to criticize the tools. He should be able to go to the man who planned and made them and tell him how they work and where the test of use shows that they fail and need to be improved. If human intelligence consisted in the knowledge of fixed laws and methods the man who knew them would be king. It consists in the constant interaction of theory and practice. Theory is called in to tell us how to act, and what we do shows us where the theory was defective. As long as we have got to check up and reconstruct our theories, our plans, our models by their working, there is going to be as great need of intelligence in those who use the tools, who install the machinery and fit the pipes, as in those who think them out and make the blue prints. No one can estimate the loss which our industry suffers from the lack of trained intelligence among the workmen. The loss arising not simply from injuries and wear and tear due to ignorance, but from the suggestions of inventions that have not been made, from the opportunities for saving and for increased efficiency of equipment that have not been used can never be estimated. The exploitation of ignorance and misery which is involved in machines tended by the unintelligent, the children, the physically and mentally unfit represents losses none the less real because they are not recognized. Any process that adjusts itself to the lack of intelligence is in just so far wasteful—if it might be served by intelligence. If human invention has been able to make use of the ignorant and stupid, it certainly could have adjusted itself the more to those who were informed and skilful.

There is nothing more democratic than intelligence, because the higher the intelligence the more it demands of others for its own best exercise. It is true that intelligence may be used to manipulate brute matter, and brutalized men, and it may so adjust itself to this task that it conceives its function is to use the unintelligent. Those who possess it may conceive themselves an aristocratic class apart, but this only indicates their false and inadequate conceptions. When intelligence goes into action of any sort it demands all the intelligence it can find. It seeks comprehension in its agents; because it never can keep tab upon itself; it can never adjust itself and its constructions to their purposes without working with people who are in so far on a par with itself that they can judge the workings of the machinery and the execution of its plans.

This needs to be emphasized not only to make evident the importance to society of the widest possible spread of intelligence and the fact that industry can afford to pay for it, but especially to indicate the nature of the intelligence and the manner in which it should be acquired. It is the sort of intelligence that is close to its application. Its results are the criticism of methods and means as well as their use, and the suggestions of improvements and economies. This calls for an interest in theory just as far as that is involved in understanding what is being done. Many of our best mechanics get it without going to technological schools. They find out what they need to know and get the textbooks, the formulas, the tables that are necessary for this purpose. It is a result to which many a more ambitious education reduces itself in practice.

It is just the type of education which higher apprentice schools in this country and in Europe give to those whom they expect to be the élite of their workmen. It involves a knowledge of a whole process, if one is to comprehend any part of it. Thus in the approved apprentice school a boy may not be held to a single machine to merely gain speed. He must be familiar with all the machines. Mathematics and drawings are necessary for such a training, at least as far as the control over them helps on with his task. A large part of mathematics is a language in which one can best state his problem. If his work brings problems with it the workman must have the appropriate language in which to state them. It is also a language in which the results of the work of others can be conveyed in the form in which they will help toward the solution of the problems. The same thing can be said of the blue print. The competent workman must be able to read his tables, his formulas, his blue prints. It is fair to assume that any workman who has had the right training can reach this goal. It is important to notice that so much theory as this does more than make an expert workman in a definite calling. It also gives the skill he possesses adaptability and pliability. When he has met problems and has solved them in his own occupation he gains a confidence in his ability to solve the problem brought by a change of occupation. Theory after all is nothing but the consciousness of the way in which one adjusts his habits of working to meet new situations. The man who has never made such readjustments is discouraged at the mere presence of the new situation. The man who has done it, who has some acquaintance with the processes and technical expressions by which it is accomplished has his interest aroused by the new situation. The acquaintance with, and use of, so much of the theory of an occupation as the exercise of the man's own function in it calls for, means that his habits are not fixed, that the man has an adjustable nature. His chances of fitting into a new economic situation are a hundred times better than those of the man who has simply the facility of a single process. In the exigencies of the shop such a man can pass from one machine to another. His speed is not at first what it will be when his reactions become almost automatic, but the knowledge which he has of the whole process and the ability he has of stating the new and the old jobs in the same terms render him a vastly more valuable man than the workman who is nothing but a part of a single machine. The amount of training which an operative, a workman, in any trade should have is that which will acquaint him with all the processes of his trade, and so much theory of his trade which will enable him to understand the tools he uses and the manner in which they operate, that he may both use the tool to the best advantage and be able to check up its efficiency and suggest the sort of changes and improvement that should in his judgment be made.

So much training a mechanic, a farmer, a mill operative, a plumber, every artisan should have. In the bill of rights which a modern man may draw up and present to the society which has produced and controls him, should appear the right to work both with intelligent comprehension of what he does, and with interest. For the latter one must see his product as a whole, he must know something of the relation of the different parts to the whole, and he must know enough of the language in which the problems of his trade are stated and solved to be able himself to criticize his own work and his own tools. This indicates also the manner in which this training should be acquired. The apprenticeship school in which school work and shop work balance each other, in which the school provides the method of stating and meeting the problems which arise in the shop, has become the modern system of apprenticeship. As we have seen, it is distinguished from the older apprenticeship system by its school, and from the later system by the organic relation between the school and the shop. The school work commands attention because shop problems appear there. And the shop becomes educative because its processes are comprehended and thought out. This educational method is ideal from the psychological point of view, for the acquirements of the school are demanded by the practical activities of the boy. This result has never been attained in other public or private schools. The training in these schools has been planned largely with reference to occupations which are not to be undertaken until the pupil has left school. Hence language and number have been dry formal studies meaning little or nothing to the child.

Some schools have attempted to meet this difficulty by introducing what have been called constructive activities in the school, so that the problems of the children might be real problems. The measurements of the boxes they were making should give them their arithmetical problems. In solving the problem they would also be learning what amount of lumber they would need and what lengths they would have to cut off, etc.

With this in view, very varied activities have been introduced in certain private schools. The results have not fully met the anticipations. The children's work has not felt the compulsion which apprenticeship offers. The actual products of the factory set not only problems but they carry with them a discipline that the apprentice accepts. They set the standard which becomes the boy's standard because he wishes to succeed in his calling. No task which the child sets to himself, and no task which the school sets as a school, has this meaning to the child. His own task makes no demand upon him that is bigger than himself and sets no standard that comes upon him with compelling power from the great world of which he wishes to be a part. No tasks of a school can be made to take hold upon the child as the training does which is to admit him to the rank of men. Even in college the students will not work as they will in the law and medical schools where they get their professional training.

In an industrial democracy the citizen must sufficiently understand the tools and the processes to comprehend and criticize the tool and its use. This is not only necessary for the technical efficiency of the industry. It is equally essential for the social control of the conditions of labor. At present the workmen undertake this by controlling labor as a commodity in the market. The artisan has lost the vantage-point of the mediaeval guild. Their control was over the product and the process. It is neither possible nor desirable to reproduce the mediaeval guild. It *is* possible and logical to make the workman's skill the basis of his social position and financial competence. Where labor appears only as a commodity, the unit being any man, the group of laborers can protect their wage only by protecting the weakest man. His wage must be theirs and it follows that their individual outputs must be his. On the other hand, the more highly skilled workmen tend to get out of the unions because on the one hand they do not need its protection and on the other their own earning power is restricted. Or the unions of the more highly skilled trades are able to pursue so different a policy in protecting their wage and hours of labor, that they lose touch with the unions of less skilled labor. This break emphasizes the attitude of the unions of the relatively unskilled trades. It is of the first importance that the working-men recognize that skill—developed intelligence—brings an entirely different factor into the economic situation, from that of the so-called supply and demand of a commodity. That other factor is described somewhat vaguely as the standard of life. It is recognized in the higher salaries of skilled employees—of professional men. When you demand skill you must make possible the conditions under which that skill can be obtained and exercised. Those conditions involve not simply technical training. Intelligence depends upon conditions of physical and social well-being. Every new demand for skill will inevitably carry with it the conditions under which that skill can be obtained. The manner in which a community responds to this obligation will be varied, and will appeal to many motives beside the economic interests.

There is no community in which a more conscious demand is being made for larger skill on the part of its workmen than Germany. There is no community in which society has faced more definitely the necessity of raising the standard of life of its working classes. State insurance seeks to meet the unavoidable accidents and disabilities. Supervision of hygienic conditions undertakes to eliminate the evils to which economic inferiority exposes great masses of men. Universities and schools of every character aim to put the intelligence of the laborer upon the higher level demanded by the self-conscious industry of Germany. And Germany has but begun to recognize the consequences which will follow with unavoidable logic upon her demand that her laborers be adequately instructed. Society cannot demand intelligent workmen without accepting the policy of rendering the acquirement of such intelligence socially possible. What the laboring classes have to fear, at least for the immediate future, is that the demand for skill will be too restricted; that our community will conceive that it can fulfil its industrial functions with an élite of trained workmen and a proletariat of the ignorant and unskilled. If organized labor can raise its eyes for the moment beyond its immediate quarrels with its employers, it will recognize that its most strenuous efforts must be directed toward the widest possible industrial education, and that this demand must be made on behalf of all labor.

There remains the school itself. The apprenticeship system, as it has been worked out by the General Electric Company, is pedagogically and technically admirable. It is possible and probable that such schools will be multiplied among large concerns throughout the country. But even with such extension of the system the demand for this apprenticeship will not and cannot be met. Every laborer who is going into mechanical industry or into allied trades should have this training. It will be a training, if we may judge from the experience already gathered, which will accomplish its task of instruction as the public schools have never been able to fulfil theirs, for it will, under proper conditions, draw upon the interest of all professional training, and it will always have the discipline which contact with the actual process and product brings with it.

Such training cannot be confined to those whom our great industrial companies educate for their shops and designing rooms. It must be the demand of labor that this system of apprenticeship training be taken into the public schools. Manual-training high schools should become apprentice schools. But in this case the curriculum should be one so far liberalized that the history and geography of the trades connect the apprentice's skill with the social and physical conditions out of which it has sprung, and in which it at present exists. The curriculum should also contain the study of the social community into which the graduated apprentice will go. He should comprehend the central and state government not only, but the legal and administrative features of the city within which he is to labor. He should understand the laws that protect him as well as those which threaten him with pains and penalties. He must know to what officials he can appeal and he should have some comprehension of operation of the courts and the city council. He should know something of the conditions which control wages and their relation to the calling he expects to exercise. If his years and interests admit, such a course should be one in elementary sociology, such as are already to be found in French industrial secondary schools, in which the ideas of social obligations, the meaning of social standards, and the relations of man to the community can be discussed. What the child expects to do and what he expects to be provides adequate motive power for study and application. They provide also the natural center from which his relation to the past, in history, and to the present, in the study of society, can be brought within his field of interest and comprehension and through which he can form those fundamental conceptions of social rights and obligations which constitute our morality.

There remains, however, the still more difficult question of the elementary schools, where at the present time the vast majority of Americans get all their formal education. As has been indicated earlier the rest of the community have suffered because the curriculum of the elementary schools has been fashioned to meet the demands of a commercial class, and for those who expect to pursue literary and professional studies. The arithmetics do not present the type of problem that the average child meets when he leaves school. The histories instead of bearing on the occupation and phenomena with which the child is familiar, and toward which he is attracted, are hopelessly political. One would assume, from the study of our school histories, that politics is the only phase of human society that has a history. Geography is abstracted from the actual relations of industry and commerce which would give it meaning to the child living in a world that is given over to the production of wealth.

How the elementary schools will finally adjust themselves to an education that faces toward the occupations which its pupils will enter, remains to be seen. It is, however, beyond question that the training on the farm and in the shop, even of the child who is not yet old enough to enter upon definite apprenticeship, indicates the direction toward which educational theory and practice must turn.

Two great facts stand out. One is that we are forced to reconstruct our whole apprenticeship training, and that when this is satisfactorily accomplished it will carry with it not only satisfactory technical training but a much broader and more liberal education than our schools at present can give to those who enter industrial occupations. The other is that apprenticeship provides an adequate and indeed almost the only adequate method of instructing children. When we recognize that this instruction need not be narrow nor unenlightened the objection to the application of the principle in our public schools finally disappears.

EDITORIAL NOTES

INDUSTRIAL NATURE-STUDY

The Waste in American Forests, Farms, and Mills

The amount of timber taken from the forests of the United States is so great that if piled solidly in a mass one mile wide and one mile high, it would produce a pile more than 852 miles in length. Such a stack of wood would extend almost from Chicago to New York, or from Chicago to New Orleans. We take from our forests 260 cubic feet for each inhabitant of the United States, while the per capita consumption of timber in Germany is 37 cubic feet and in France is 25 cubic feet. Though this annual cutting exceeds by 3½ times the annual growth of new timber, and though some improvement has been made in our forestry methods, still one-fourth of the standing timber is lost in logging processes, and in milling from one-third to two-thirds of the amount delivered at the mill. For forty years forest fires have destroyed an annual average of fifty lives and $50,000,000 worth of timber.

The United States produces "one-fifth of the world's wheat crop, three-fifths of its cotton crop, and four-fifths of its corn crop." But our wheat fields of 50,000,000 acres yield an average of only 14 bushels per acre, while the wheat fields of Germany and England yield respectively 28 and 32 bushels. Our 100,000,000 acres of corn fields yield an average of 25 bushels per acre, although our best agricultural colleges and progressive farmers have demonstrated that 100 bushels and more per acre may be produced on good soil by proper tillage. Our farm crops annually lose through injurious insects an amount estimated at $659,000,000, and farmers and horticulturalists lose through plant diseases additional hundreds of millions of dollars annually. Preventable diseases are largely unprevented, and securable benefits from more intelligent application of knowledge of industrial science are largely unsecured.

The other side of this wastage of natural resources is the interest growing almost month by month in correcting our national besetting sin. And the increase in our national income arising from industrial methods improved by science and practical intelligence arouses not only the absorbing interest of technical and business men. It offers material of equal interest and import for education.

Educational Value of the Efforts to Correct Waste

The motto of efficiency in education can be read from this point of view—education in efficiency. The effect on children of studying the increase of the return from industrial processes through the scientific intelligence is distinctly moral.

The point of view has equal value in organizing the work in nature-study. It gathers the study about specific industries and specific localities. It relates the plant and animal life to each other and the human interests that must after all be the center of all children's interest. Nor need we fear the narrowing effect of the objectionable type of industrial training. The application of science to agriculture, to lumbering, and the manufacture of their products does not mean drill in formulae, but the study of plant and animal life, in its relation to the occupation and locality; the study of savings in human life and well-being. It approaches the study at the point at which system and a better order are being introduced in the industry, and this means an order in the relation of the things studied as well. It means interest in these callings, and their methods. It carries with it the appreciation of their function and value in the community. Nature-study can most profitably be organized and developed from the standpoint of industrial agriculture and forestry. It has already proved its pedagogical value in both elementary and secondary schools.

The Organizing Value of the Standpoint for Nature-Study

O. W. C.

NOTES AND NEWS

Many American teachers will recall the enthusiastic study made of American schools a few years ago by Mr. J. C. Hudson, who, with the assistance of his wife, is now conducting the Home School for Boys and Girls at Inglehome, Highgate N., London. The private school which has grown out of his home work, and this visit deserves more than passing notice. Perhaps nowhere is the immediate influence of Professor Dewey's work more evident today than in this and in one or two other schools in England. A visit to the school during its first year showed a remarkable appreciation of those elements in American education which have bearing upon English conditions. Mrs. Hudson and the other teachers associated in this undertaking are people of unusual ability and the advisory committee includes Professor and Mrs. Patrick Geddes, Alfred C. Haddon and others eminent in British education, and Professors John Dewey and Earl Barnes of America. Mr. Joseph Fels, with characteristic generosity, has furnished a scholarship fund of £100.

The illustrations and subject-matter of the new announcement are suggestive of a well-organized school life leading into all the more important interests.

The English schools make much more of inspection by outsiders who judge a school in operation without reference to its relations to college entrance or other single considerations. A report in this case is made by Professor Geddes which answers many of the questions a parent or a student of education would naturally ask. Even more suggestive are the reports of the medical officers. These are made at the end of each term and so show the effect of previous examinations and of efforts made at progress.

The *School* (England) for January, 1909, reports that in Japan, in 1904, "Discipline in the schools was not well maintained. Strikes were prevalent. One of the paradoxes of the country is said to be that 'whilst elsewhere it is the master who expels a boy, here it is the boys who expel the master.' The usual practice is for the pupils to write and recommend an offending teacher to resign; if he decline they request the director to dismiss him; and failing that, go on strike. Deference to the sentiment of subordinates is a characteristic of Japanese life—a fact upon which Mr. Hearn commented, and it partly explains the apparent weakness of the teacher."

W. H. Winch in the same journal, in connection with the Chicago plan for the promotion of teachers, states: "It hardly seems to me that the scheme carries out the object which the superintendent has in mind. . . . .

Are we quite sure that this never-ending examination of the teacher is just the way to secure it? Is it not of vastly more importance to find out what habits of thought and work he has instilled into his class? What has he done to inspire his boys to thought and action?"

The December number of *School Hygiene* contains some very valuable materials for the guidance of teachers in the observation of their pupils. The time has practically come when, to allow curable defects in school children to remain, is inexcusable. The Massachusetts Board of Education has issued a pamphlet entitled *Suggestions to Teachers Regarding Tuberculosis and its Prevention.* The legislature had passed an act providing that tuberculosis and its prevention should be taught in all grades of the public schools of the state in which instruction is given in physiology and hygiene. This pamphlet gives suggestions to teachers for the observation of children for the purpose of early detection of any symptoms of this disease. It teaches the simple gospel "of fresh air, day and night, sunlight, cleanliness, bathing, plenty of plain, nourishing food, and care of the teeth and bowels. If school children can be taught this hygiene, so simple, yet apparently so little appreciated, a great advance in social progress will be evident." Teachers are very diffident about making suggestions that may reflect upon the intelligence of the home; but movements that have the initiative of the State Board of Education back of them can, certainly, be made educative in a social way without making the teacher obnoxious to the community

There are two very common causes of ill-health in children which the average teacher pays little or no attention to, and which seriously affect the child's power to do work. These are adenoids and decayed teeth. Prof. William H. Burnham discussed the former in an article in the *Pedagogical Seminary* for June, 1908. His list of special symptoms to be observed should prove valuable to all teachers who are interested in the health and work of the children they are teaching. These are:

1. Disturbances of breathing. Breathing through the nose is difficult, so the mouth is kept open.

2. Disturbances of speech. The voice has a nasal sound, since the stopping of the nose hinders clear speech.

3. Disturbances of hearing on account of the swelling of the Eustachian tubes. In this way buzzing in the ears, deafness etc., may occur.

4. Disturbances in the functions of the brain resulting in inattention, so-called *aprosexia nasalis,* and the like.

Investigation shows that from 5 to 6 per cent. of the children in the Boston schools suffer from this disorder, and that in the German schools about 10 per cent. are afflicted. In Leipzig the percentage has run as high as 23.2 per cent. Surely this is not a subject to be treated lightly, since it has been developed that there is a close relationship between mental weakness and the nasal disorders which interfere with good breathing.

The subject of dental decay is treated by *School Hygiene* in a special article. "The medical inspection of school children has demonstrated the fact that one-third to one-half of them stand in need of dental attention." Here is a typical report:

New York Children. (Report of Dr. Haven Emerson on physical condition of poor children admitted to the summer sanitarium at Sea Breeze, Long Island.) An examination of 1,478 poor children, 1 to 15 years of age, showed 278 (18.8 per cent.) with no apparent dental decay, and 1,200 (81.2 per cent.) with dental decay existing.

These revelations point most clearly to the necessity of instruction of both school children and teachers in the care of the teeth, and in the evil effects of decay. A monthly inspection of the children's teeth by the teacher, and an annual inspection by the school medical inspector, are the measures required to bring home to each child and parent a realization of the importance of the subject, ... Not less important is the education of all parents to the relation between sound teeth and good health.

In August, 1907, the San Francisco Board of Education adopted a plan for instruction in Civics in the Eighth Grade which should attempt to make a direct connection of the Individual with the social institutions of which he is an implicit member. The study is based directly upon the actual life and conditions of the city. The following outline will show the general plan pursued, and may serve to stimulate other work, elsewhere, along the same line. The text book used in this connection is Dunn's *The Community and the Citizen.* The outline follows: For the first half-year: The beginnings of a community. What is a community. The site of the community. What the people in a community are seeking. The family. Some services rendered to the community by the family. The making of Americans. How the relations between the people and the land are made permanent and definite. How the community aids the citizen to satisfy his desire for health. How the community aids the citizen to protect his life and property.

The outline takes up in the second part of the year the larger problems of the community life and its relationships to the larger community life of the state and nation. Problems of business, government regulation and control, waste and saving in production and consumption, community life and transportation, educational satisfactions in the community life, provisions for beauty and recreation, community provision for the religious life and interests, community care for the defective and dependent members, provision for the control of those who cannot control themselves, defects in self-government of cities, and the outlying problems of rural, state, and national government, with some consideration of the question of taxes. The effort is made

to stimulate the children to take a deep interest in community life. Have them investigate various topics by observation, inquiry, and reading. Then let their reports be a basis for fair and free class discussion. Try to make the children conscious of what the community has done and is doing for them, and try to make them sensitive to their obligations. Stimulate the spirit of inquiry and analysis from the facts, and encourage the forming of intelligent personal opinions. Work for a proper attitude of mind rather than mere command of facts.

Such work as this is surely more fundamental than the dry abstractions commonly taught under the name of civics.

We are hearing a great deal today about the necessity of individual teaching. Very little definite information is at hand, however, to show the greater value of individual teaching over class instruction. The article by Dr. Elmer E. Jones, professor of education at the Indiana University, published in the current number of *The Psychological Clinic,* is therefore timely.

Professor Jones picked out a first-grade class, and studied their progress in learning words during a period of sixteen weeks. During this time the average child in the class learned 150 words and over. Each week that the test was applied by Professor Jones, a few more words had been added to the child's vocabulary. But there was one boy in the class who at no time during the sixteen weeks had learned more than twelve words, and on the last day of the test, at the end of the sixteenth week, he knew only two words of the total number that had been taught the class. The boy was then given individual teaching. At the end of the second week the test showed that he knew eighteen words, and every week he added a few words to his vocabulary, until at the end of fourteen weeks of individual teaching he knew 130 words, doing just about as well as an average child under class instruction. Professor Jones's results are a strong argument in favor of the establishment of special classes for children who are supposed to be mentally defective, as this boy was supposed to be, but are merely unable to progress because the methods of the classroom do not reach them individually.

The report of educational work in Alaska is very interesting.

In the years 1907 and 1908 the Alaska division has erected twenty-three new school buildings for natives in Alaska; has strengthened the provision for the industrial training of the natives, including the provision for the teaching of agriculture and other industries in the southern districts and the establishment of nine new centers for the reindeer industry and the distribution of reindeer to natives in the more northern region; and has instituted a campaign for sanitary education and the improvement of sanitary conditions with particular reference to combating tuberculosis.

The Legislature of Indiana is considering a very comprehensive bill embodying an "act to protect and conserve the health and lives of school children by providing for their medical inspection, by providing healthful schoolhouses, and by requiring the teaching of hygiene." Little by little we move forward.

BOOK REVIEWS

Special Method in Reading in the Grades. Including the Oral Treatment of Stories and the Reading of Classics. By CHARLES A. MCMURRAY. New York: Macmillan. Pp. 351. $1.25.

This book is a combination of two earlier volumes both of which deal with special method in reading. These earlier volumes—*The Special Method in Primary Reading and Oral Work with Stories* and *The Special Method in the Reading of English Classics*—appear in this new form with but few changes.

In the present form the book will be found to contain in the main three lines of treatment of the subject. In the first place, it is a plea for the teaching of reading in all grades for the sake of its content. Secondly, several chapters are devoted to a consideration of the technique of teaching reading to beginners; and thirdly, the book contains a course of study in reading for each of the grades together with illustrative lessons.

The earlier part of the book lays great stress on the importance of oral work as a preparation for learning to read, and as supplementary to the regular work in reading, especially in the earlier years. Such a method of procedure is based upon the view that it is much more important for a child to acquire a taste for good books than to meet the purely formal requirements of learning to read. Furthermore, even apart from his inability to read, the appeal to the young child through language appears to be stronger when by the medium of the sense of hearing than sight. A number of useful hints to teachers for the acquisition of skill in the oral presentation of stories are given.

The sentence, word, and phonic methods in alternation are recommended for teaching reading to beginners. Some details are given by the author as to how these methods may suitably be applied at different times, but the main point insisted on here is that the reading material should be interesting in content. To this end it should preferably be connected with stories already made familiar to the children in oral form.

One can object to this great emphasis on the importance of content which is the keynote of the book, only when it leads to a corresponding neglect of drill and analysis. The apparently growing number of children in the schools who read incorrectly because the words are apprehended by a process little better than guess work, shows that there is a tendency to go to extremes in this respect.

The bibliographical material of the book is extensive and valuable. A number of illustrative lessons are given and suggestions for the treatment of certain typical stories and phases of literature suitable for the various grades.

Book of Alphabets. For Use in Schools. By H. W. SHAYLOR. Boston: Ginn & Co. Pp. 24. $0.10.

This book is essentially a copy-book designed for practice in lettering. A variety of standard alphabets are presented—Roman forms, French script, Gothic, outline, italic, Lombardic, simple, plain, and skeleton letters, etc. These are so arranged that the letters to be made come directly below the copy. In addition to the alphabets there are a number of illustrations showing the various letters in title-pages, headings, and illuminated texts, and also a page of monograms and ornamented initials.

E. H. CAMERON

YALE UNIVERSITY

Joseph, A Three-Scene Play for Children. By F. H. SWIFT. New York: William Beverley Harison. Pp. 31. 25 cents.

To those seeking to make the incomparable stories of the Bible live again in the experience of the children of today, and to those who in searching for really valuable material have read through innumerable books, painfully compiled but thoroughly worthless, Mr. Swift's dramatization of the story of Joseph comes as truly refreshing.

No really alive educator doubts the value of using the imaginative and dramatic instinct in every child to make him understand different phases of life and to develop that rare trait of putting himself in someone else's place, but few teachers in the actual routine of the daily accomplishment of things necessary, have either time or energy to arrange a story in dramatic form. Here is a play ready to hand, the most dramatic of stories, as truly human today as when told to breathless audiences thousands of years ago. It has world-wide passions, great contrasts of situation, and the great moral principle of forgiveness of wrong.

Mr. Swift has simplified the intricate biblical account, has cut out unnecessary material and has retained the beautiful English of the Bible to a very large extent. He has given the whole unity and good dramatic structure. The book is printed in inexpensive form and only on one side of the page, so that the leaves may be torn out and used by more than one child.

For three years this little play has been used in the Charlton School, New York City. It has served as the climax to the study of the pastoral stories of the Old Testament, which the third grade of this school uses as a part of its literature. In the history period the manners, customs, tent life and nomadic habits of a pastoral people are studied, aided by pictures, sand table work and Bird's story of *Joseph the Dreamer.* The story is read by the children in biblical language. With this as a foundation transition to dramatization is simple and natural.

The conditions in a private school give unusual advantages, for daily the children come laden with photographs of deserts and Egyptian temples and rare trophies collected by fathers and mothers who have traveled through the Orient. With the Metropolitan Museum within a few blocks the glory of Egypt and the greatness of Pharaoh become realities. Yet this very wealth of material has been recognized as a danger, and care has been taken to the end that, after the pictures of ancient Egypt and of the simple nomadic life on the beautiful Judean hills had been built up in the children's imaginations, they then should not be spoiled by any cheap scenic effect. "We had only black cloth over a screen for a tent, and one palm," says a small girl in her composition, "because we like to use our imaginations." The throne room of the monarch of Egypt consisted of the same screen draped with some rarely beautiful curtains loaned by an interested mother. The chair in front of it was covered with the same material. The children grouped in front of these, with their bright oriental costumes falling in soft folds because made of canton flannel and cheese cloth, made pictures long to be remembered.

The simplicity of the scenery and the costumes threw the emphasis on the children and their interpretation of the story. From the first they felt that this was no ordinary play but one to be approached with reverence and lived, because they already loved it. They were quite unconscious of themselves but were too young to fully enter into the passions of hatred, power, or supreme forgiveness. Still the essentially great is always worthy of reflection, even in imperfect mirrors, and the effect on the audience, which perhaps is the best test, was a great surprise even to those who had lived with the children and felt the power of the story.

The value of such work is very well worth while.

ANNA MANSFIELD CLARK

NEW YORK CITY

The Summers Readers, Primer, First Reader, and *Teachers' Manual.* By MAUD SUMMERS. Illustrated by LUCY FITCH PERKINS AND MARION L. MAHONY. New York: Frank D. Beattys & Co.

This series is one of the best that has been produced of late for beginning work in reading. It is far better in our estimation than an earlier work of the same author, *The Thought Reader,* being richer in content and more psychological in treatment. The *Primer* contains short sentences built on familiar experiences and on children's rhymes and also simple commands for movements to be carried out by the children. The *First Reader* contains familiar fairy-tales, rhymes, poems, descriptions of such activities as maple-sugar making, and carpentering, with some "observation lessons" from nature. These are all well chosen and well told and form a valuable addition to our list of First Readers, in which there are too few that are as full of interest and still simple enough for the beginners.

In her *Manual* Miss Summers sets forth most clearly her idea of the process involved in learning to read, and her mode of simplifying and strengthening the elements in the process. She takes up the subject under three headings: Thought, Symbol, and Phonics, treating each element fully with ample illustrations, and without wearisome detail. She places thought first as the all important goal in the teaching of reading and demands that the association of symbol and thought, or symbol and image, be made while idea is vividly present in the child's mind. To this end she recommends the use of script reading from the blackboard from the beginning, with a transition to the printed page, to be made whenever the children show a measurable degree of readiness in reading the script. Her treatment of phonics is full of good suggestions and free of the burdens of technicalities. She deplores the early use of diacritical marks as a useless cumbering of the image. The author emphasizes the prime interest which action has for the little child and develops the first reading lessons through an appeal to his love of performing even the simplest movements at command. To the mind of the reviewer this is a useful device among other devices, but is in danger of being over-worked, or magnified out of its real importance. The earlier pages of the *Primer,* also, do not quite bear out the author's own theory of the value of *thinking.* Some of the lessons seem too trivial. But they are interspersed with so much that is excellently presented that it seems hardly fair to be too critical on these points. The *Primer* is good, beyond the average, and the *First Reader* merits a place in every school. The *Manual* should certainly be of great assistance to the young teacher.

The Wide Awake Third Reader. By CLARA MURRAY. Boston: Little, Brown & Co. Pp. 224. $0.40.

This is not a story-book, but consists in part of sketches of foreign peoples and their customs as seen through the daily doings of foreign children. These include children of Holland, Armenia, Greenland, Japan, Switzerland, and Brazil. This work is excellently done, and the book would be a valuable adjunct to the supplementary reading stock of every school for this alone. Its merits do not end here, however, for there are some delightful animal, bird, and plant studies, some good poems, and the charming "Christmas Monks" of Mary E. Wilkins. Altogether it presents varied and interesting matter for children of about the third or fourth school year.

Fairy Tales, Vol. II. Compiled and Edited by MARION FLORENCE LANSING, M.A. Illustrated by CHARLES COPELAND. Ginn & Co. Pp. 180. $0.40.

This is the second volume in a series of which two other volumes were reviewed in the December number of the *Elementary School Teacher.* The compiler states that the division of the tales into two volumes does not indicate that they are intended for children of different ages. The stories are taken about equally from Perrault, Andersen, and Grimm. She also calls attention to the discrimination of fairy tales from stories of heroic deeds which are supposed to have been carried down from some actual events in time and place. Tales of the latter class are to appear in a succeeding volume under the name, *Tales of Old England.* Like its predecessors this second volume of Fairy Tales is a convenient little book of well-chosen and well-told tales and is eminently suitable for school reading.

The Tortoise and the Geese and Other Fables of Bidpai. Retold by MAUDE BARROWS DUTTON. Boston: Houghton, Mifflin & Co. Pp. 125. $1.00.

These fables are handed down to the modern world from the obscurest of origins, from the early literature of the Orient. Tradition ascribes their authorship to one Bidpai, of India, who wrote them at the command of the king, and delivered them as a treasure into the keeping of his ruler. La Fontaine incorporated some of them into his fables. To represent the aim of this collection we quote from the compiler: "In this selection from the fables of Bidpai only a scant portion of his wisdom and his humor is offered, but it is sincerely hoped that herein lies sufficient to awaken in our children a love for this Indian sage that shall increase with the years until the name of Bidpai be ranked in their affections with Æsop."

Wherever the fable is wanted as reading material in the school, this collection will be a desirable one.

BERTHA PAYNE

Laboratory Lessons in Physical Geography. By L. L. EVERLY, R. E. BLOUNT, AND C. L. WALTON. New York: American Book Co., 1908. Pp. 246. $0.56.

The manual is intended to furnish sufficient exercises for a full year's work but is so written "that some may be omitted by classes that have not time enough for all, without detriment to those remaining." The authors have sought "to arrange some exercises that shall suggest better methods to many teachers, and save time for those who are too busy to work out the details of plans they may have had in mind." The reviewer believes that they have been very successful. The manual contains eight exercises on "Mathematical Geography," nine on "Materials of the Earth's Crust," thirty-one on "Drainage and Land Forms," thirty-two on "The Atmosphere," and ten on "The Ocean." It seems that many more type forms could profitably be added to the map exercises on land forms, while some of the exercises on materials of the earth's crust and the atmosphere might just as profitably be done by the teacher. If the exercises that the instructor selects from the manual are well done they should aid greatly in giving the student a clear concept of the subject. The manual should be adapted and not adopted. It seems to have been prepared with this in view.

GEO. J. MILLER

THE UNIVERSITY HIGH SCHOOL

First Year in United States History. Books I and II. By MELVIN HIX. New York: Hinds, Noble & Eldredge, 1908. $0.40 each.

These little books are admirably adapted to the pupils for whom they are written—"the American school children who leave school by or before the end of the sixth year of school." To awaken and sustain a love for history in early adolescence, the author has avoided the "epitome" pitfall and has treated a few topics fully, securing vigor and vitality through a choice of incidents with action, anecdotes, and interesting details. His treatment is biographical when possible; his style is clear and simple, yet vigorous.

Although the occasional page of important events, with their dates, may be made to serve some purpose, it is doubtful whether the completing of each period by faithful inserting of the less important facts of history (as, for instance, the settlement of New Jersey) is really necessary for immature readers. The books, however, answer a demand created by our modern courses of study.

JESSIE E. BLACK

BOOKS RECEIVED

AMERICAN BOOK CO., NEW YORK

The Human Body and Health. An Elementary Textbook of Essential Anatomy, Applied Physiology, and Practical Hygiene for Schools. By ALVIN DAVISON. Cloth. Illustrated. Pp. 320. $0.80.

Standard Algebra. By WILLIAM J. MILNE. Half leather. Pp. 464. $1.00.

Songs Every One Should Know. Two Hundred Favorite Songs for School and Home. Edited by CLIFTON JOHNSON. Cloth. $0.50.

Choruses and Part Songs for High Schools. By EDWARD BAILEY BIRGE. Cloth. Pp. 184. $0.65.

D. APPLETON & CO., NEW YORK

The Appleton Arithmetic, Primary Book. By J. W. A. YOUNG AND LAMBERT L. JACKSON. Cloth. Pp. 264.

GINN & CO., BOSTON

Control of Body and Mind. (Book Five, "Gulick Hygiene Series.") Cloth. Illustrated. Pp. 267. $0.60.

Merrie England. Travels, Descriptions, Tales, and Historical Sketches. By GRACE GREENWOOD. Cloth. Illustrated. Pp. 200.

Tales of Old England in Prose and Verse. Compiled and edited by MARION FLORENCE LANSING. Cloth. Illustrated. Pp. 180. $0.35.

CURRENT EDUCATIONAL LITERATURE IN THE PERIODICALS[1]

IRENE WARREN

Librarian, School of Education, The University of Chicago

B., G. H. The financial status of the university professor. Liv. Age. 42:375–9. (F. '09.)

BAUGHMANN, JEANETTE G. Informal exercises in the primary grades. Educa. Bi-mo. 3:211. (F. '09.)

BOONE, CHESHIRE LOWTON. A course of study in manual training—6. Man. Train. Mag. 10:235–41. (F. '09.)

CAMERON, J. Y. The fourth modern Olympiad, London England, 1908. Amer. Phys. Educa. R. 14:40–5. (Ja. '09.)

[1] Abbreviations: Amer. Phys. Educa. R., American Physical Education Review; Educa., Education; Educa. Bi-mo., Educational Bi-monthly; Harp. W., Harper's Weekly; Liv. Age, Living Age; Man. Train. Mag., Manual Training Magazine; Psycholog. Clinic; Psychological Clinic; Pub. Lib., Public Library; R. of R., Review of Reviews; Sci. Amer. Sup., Scientific American Supplement.

DEWING, ARTHUR S. Some reasons for decrease of interest in nature study. Educa. 29:291–3. (Ja. '09.)

FAULKNER, ROLAND P. Some uses of statistics in the supervision of schools. Psycholog. Clinic. 2:227–33. (Ja. '09.)

GILBERT, M. B. Dancing: its applications and its advantages. Educa. Bi-mo. 3:212–15. (F. '09.)

GREENWOOD, J. M. Progress of pupils through elementary and high schools. Educa. 29:267–75. (Ja. '09.)

GRISWOLD, SARAH E. The importance of gymnastics in the first grade. Educa. Bi-mo. 3:209–10. (F. '09.)

HORWILL, HERBERT W. Democracy in American education. Liv. Age. 42:231–5. (23 Ja. '09.)

KINDERVATER, A. E. The international gymnastic and athletic competition at Frankfurt, Germany, and Olympic games at London, England. Amer. Phys. Educa. R. 14:27–39. (Ja. '09.)

LARNED, CHARLES W. Athletics from a historical and educational standpoint. Amer. Phys. Educa. R. 14:1–9. (Ja. '09.)

MCMANIS, JOHN T. Reciprocal relation between physical and mental education. Educa. Bi-mo. 3:226–33. (F. '09)

MULLINER, MARY R. Posture as related to efficiency of body and mind. Educa. Bi-mo. 3:201–4. (F. '09.)

OGG, FREDERIC AUSTIN. Harvard's new president. R. of R. 39:196–9. (Ja. '09.)

SCHRADER, CARL LUDWIG. Why physical education in the grammar school? Educa. Bi-mo. 3:205–8. (F. '09.)

SNEED, C. M., AND WHIPPLE, GUY MONTROSE. An examination of the eyes. ears, and throats of children in the public schools of Jefferson City, Mo. Psycholog. Clinic. 2:234–8. (Ja. '09.)

WELLMAN, JAMES. Harvard's new president. Harp. W. 53:27–. (23 Ja. '09.)

VOLUME IX NUMBER 8

THE ELEMENTARY SCHOOL TEACHER

APRIL, 1909

THE OCCUPATIONS OF THE KINDERGARTEN

ALICE TEMPLE

The occupations may be said to bear the same relation to the kindergarten programme that the industrial and art activities bear to the elementary-school curriculum. This paper will discuss the kindergarten occupations as one of its several instrumentalities, attempting to indicate certain points where the traditional occupations fail to meet the needs of child-development, and to state some of the changes and modifications which the modern kindergarten has made in both materials and methods, in the effort to meet such needs.

To the kindergartner of twenty years ago, the term occupation stood for a certain fixed set of prepared materials and a very definitely prescribed series of exercises to be carried out with each kind of material. It seems to mean much the same to the orthodox kindergartner today. To an increasingly large number of radical kindergartners, however, the term occupation has come to mean any sort of industrial or art work with plastic materials which develops the fundamental impulses of the child of kindergarten age, and which is suited in material and process to his mental and motor capacity. In order to illustrate what one school of kindergartners claims to be the "true Froebelian use" of gifts and occupations, I quote below one week's exercises taken from their programme for the year:

MONDAY

Gift.—Fourth.

Notice square faces cut into two oblongs, four oblongs, many oblongs. Find corners; associate with activity; do not make them symbolic; corners on top and below.

Sequence of simple life-forms by imitation, as house, chest of drawers, bureau with glass, washstand, table and chair, bed, crib for baby. If time, children invent.

Occupation.—Sewing.

Horizontal lines, long and short.

TUESDAY

Gift.—Tablets.

Forms of beauty; change (spread and contrast) "giving out and coming back."

Occupation.—Sand.

Impressions of tin cubes; forms of beauty.

WEDNESDAY

Gift.—Sticks.

Squares of different sizes—inventions. Life-forms if the children make them of their own accord. Notice corners.

Occupation.—Folding.

Book. Recall derivation of square from cube of folding paper, crackers, etc. In folding, children crease with closed fist. Book, shed, screen, trough.

THURSDAY

Gift.—Fourth.

Review corners, top and below. Into how many oblongs is front face divided? Emphasize broad and narrow. Make broad gate and path. Make narrow gate and path. Bring cloth, ribbon, paper; broad and narrow, long and short.

Occupation.—Peas and sticks.

Make squares. How many sticks needed? All same length? Give two long and two short for oblongs. Make life-forms from squares and oblongs. Draw things made.

FRIDAY

Gift.—Lentils.

Develop square. Give stick with which to measure distance apart. Give smaller and larger sticks.

Occupation.—Painting.

Long strokes with brush or pasting. Fold square and cut into oblongs, then paste. Combine into border.

A thoughtful reading of this outline suggests among other things the following questions for discussion:

I. What should be the relation between the subject-matter of the programme and the use of materials?

II. Should materials be used for the purpose of making the child conscious of form, size, and number as such, or of the logical derivation of one geometric form from another?

III. Are the opportunities and incentives offered the children for originality and invention well selected?

IV. Is there psychological justification for the division of forms of expression into forms of life, forms of knowledge, and forms of beauty?

I

What should be the relation between the subject-matter of the programme and the use of materials?

The entire programme of which the matter quoted is a part is based upon (*a*) the *Mother-Plays* of Froebel, and (*b*) the gift and occupation exercises suggested by Froebel in the *Education of Man* and the *Pedagogics of the Kindergarten*. There is no relation, apparently, between the subject-matter (*a*) and the use of materials (*b*) with one or two striking exceptions. During the weeks preceding Christmas, for example, the occupation periods are devoted to the making of Christmas gifts. Again, during the week of February 22, all the exercises of the kindergarten, including of course the occupations, center about the general subject or thought for that week—*patriotism*. While one would not select the last subject as a particularly valuable or suitable one to bring to children under six years of age, yet there is a playfulness in the exercises of this week which is sadly lacking in most of the others.

Now if the child as an active, social being is to be the center of correlation (and this was Froebel's ideal) the subject-matter of the programme must be selected with reference to the child's fundamental interests and activities and the instrumentalities of the kindergarten used as various avenues for the expression of his interest in different aspects of such subject-matter. In this way the child is helped to organize his experience in a far more natural and effective way than when unity is sought in the materials themselves on the one hand, and in the philosophical truths underlying the *Mother-Plays* on the other. Either of these methods presupposes an intellectual grasp quite beyond the power of the little child.

In suggesting the home life and occupation as suitable subject-matter for the kindergarten programme, Dr. Dewey says:

> From the child's standpoint unity lies in the subject-matter, in the present case, in the fact that he is always dealing with one thing: home life. . . . . The child is working all the time *"within a unity,"* giving different phases of its clearness and definiteness and bringing them into coherent connection with one another. When there is great diversity of subject-matter, continuity is apt to be sought simply on the formal side; that is, in schemes of sequence, "schools of work," a rigid programme of development followed with every topic, a "thought for the day" from which the work is not supposed to stray. As a rule such sequence is purely intellectual, hence is grasped only by the teacher, quite passing over the head of the child.[1]

Quite in sympathy with this line of thought we find the following expression from Professor Earl Barnes:

> Dramatic activity based on imagination, should deal also with the affairs of the home and the neighborhood. And here again they must really appeal to the child as connected with life; otherwise they are not exercises for imagination, but mere mimicry. Instead of gripping the feelings and shaping them, they stultify them. The real life of the homes from which the children come should be represented, but lifted and glorified by the play of imaginative fancy.[2]

It is quite possible, of course, to make the programme based upon the child's experiences in his immediate social environment as rigid, as formal, as the one criticized, and thus to sacrifice the child's spontaneity and freedom in the effort to secure unity and continuity. It is equally possible to keep it simple, elastic, close to the child's interests, and yet sufficiently unified on the concrete, dramatic basis which the little child can understand.

[1] "Froebel's Educational Principles," *Elementary School Record,* Vol. I, No. 5.

[2] "Fundamental Factors in the Making of a Kindergarten Curriculum," *Elementary School Teacher,* October, 1908.

II

Should materials be used for the purpose of making the child conscious of form, size, and number as such, or of the logical derivation of one form from another?

In many of the exercises given above there is every evidence that the aim is to teach the child the abstract qualities of objects as such. He makes *squares* and *oblongs* with sticks; sews *vertical* and *horizontal* lines; derives the *square* from the *cube;* develops the *square* from lines; brings cloth, ribbon, paper, which is *broad* and *narrow, long* and *short,* etc., and all this in a formal, mechanical, unrelated way. We have an excellent illustration here of emphasis upon technique apart from content or meaning. The little lesson comes first, a lesson in form, size, number, or what not; the making of life-forms follows; there is no real relation between the two. But modern thought emphasizes the fact that knowledge arises normally out of action, out of the individual's effort to realize his ends and purposes. A separation such as we have here is therefore unpsychological.

And, further, the many studies of children's interests go to show that they have no interest in the form of objects except as a means to an end. They are interested primarily in the use of objects, what they are for, what can be done with them.

> Children at first pay little heed to the aesthetic aspect of the things they use or make; the service of objects in ministering to vital needs is mainly considered and crudity will serve as well as refinement in attaining this end.[3]

> Dealing with common objects, the young children attend almost exclusively to their uses; gradually they become interested in classifying them into larger groups and in noticing their qualities.[4]

In the effort to satisfy this interest of the child in use, to help him construct objects of worth from *his* standpoint, the kindergartner of today has found that a greater variety of materials is needed as well as new ways of using them. The processes of sewing, weaving, folding, and cutting are all retained. but the materials have been enlarged in some cases and more

[3] O'Shea, *Dynamic Factors in Education,* p. 72.

[4] Barnes, *Studies in Education,* December, 1896.

durable ones substituted in others. It is the sewing and weaving materials particularly which have been enlarged because they call for a premature co-ordination of the small muscles.

In the matter of motor development, it is clear that the eye muscles and body muscles, as well as the nerve cells of a child of four or five years of age have not attained the degree of maturity essential to perform with safety the ordinary kindergarten exercises of weaving and plaiting and threading. The effort to accomplish these tasks leads inevitably to strain and exhaustion.[5]

Human sympathy founded in a desire for a healthful, robust, physical machine, would naturally help us to avoid such forms as would tend to the use of small muscles or the development of ideas not directly serviceable in the life of children.[6]

Miss Blow[7] in criticizing this general tendency to enlarge the kindergarten materials, quotes Dr. Judd as her authority. Dr. Judd does say that "the finer muscles are in full operation very early in life," that "they are the muscles which in diffuse movements are most apt to be called into action," and that "development means the selection of the right movements out of the total mass of diffuse movements." But following immediately the words quoted last we read,

Only one limitation appears in all this provision of many movements. This is the limitation we have noted. No mechanism could be devised which would not, in the general stimulation of the muscles, affect the small muscles more than the large ones. This limitation in nature's provision for free movement is the first point at which the teacher's rational mode of developing the child must come in to supplement nature's provision. The teacher should see to it that if diffusion tends to emphasize the small muscles, teaching should emphasize in due measure the large muscles.[8]

This seems to the writer to be but another argument in favor of the wisdom of enlarging many of the kindergarten materials.

Much of the modified kindergarten occupation goes by the name of constructive work, corresponding as it does to the constructive work of the elementary school. It is the making of

[5] O'Shea, *op. cit.*, p. 156.

[6] Hatch, "Technique in Elementary Manual Training," *Elementary School Teacher*, November, 1904.

[7] *Educational Issues in the Kindergarten*, pp. 170–72.

[8] *Genetic Psychology for Teachers*, pp. 222–25.

little objects, mainly toys, of any plaster materials which are easily handled by the children and which lend themselves well to the expression of children's purposes. They may involve such processes as folding, weaving, sewing, cutting, and pasting, but the products make stronger appeal to the childish heart than those resulting from the older uses of these processes. They are objects which the child feels the need of in his play life, and the free play with the object made completes the activity and adds greatly to its value. A kindergartner who has been introducing these occupations with children brought up in the traditional handwork, tells me that these children no longer ask for their sewing-cards or weaving-mats, but beg to "make something," often suggesting what they would like to make.

One special value of such handwork has been clearly stated by Miss Hill:

> The steps or processes in the constructive occupations are so self-evident as organic means to an end, that the child can either imitate or originate them more intelligently than in the earlier flat occupations. In many of these flat occupations, the how, or processes of making are so hidden, so disguised, as organic steps leading toward a certain end, that kindergartners have had to fall back on the method of dictation, which the child often blindly follows, and when the unforeseen result is accomplished, the child is allowed to name it according to some resemblance he discovers.[9]

The objections made to constructive work by the conservative kindergartner are that (*a*) it represents the substitution of work for play; (*b*) it makes an appeal to understanding rather than an appeal to imagination; (*c*) it is a substituting of constructive activities for free self-expression.

a) In consideration of the first criticism the question at once presents itself: Is not work of this kind, in which the end to be achieved is a very immediate one and one of great interest to the child, the first and most natural form of work, and does it not belong in the kindergarten period? Interest in the product, great as it is, is not "substituted for delight in the process" but rather *added to it.* When one remembers that there is no real falling apart of means and end, but that both process and product

[9] Patty S. Hill, "The Relation of the Kindergarten and the Elementary School," *Proceedings of National Educational Association,* 1904.

are in one sense means to a further end, viz., free play with the objects made, the whole seems to be one big play-activity including within it attitudes of both play and work. And, further, it must be remembered that the constructive occupation is only one of many instrumentalities of the kindergarten, about the purely play character of which there is no question.

b) As to the second objection, that in constructive work there is appeal to understanding rather than imagination, it may be said that there is a more legitimate appeal to both than is made by the traditional occupations. The model of the object which the child makes may be supplied by the teacher or another child, or he may make his own plan. If in the process he works by imitation, at least it is conscious, intelligent imitation of steps recognized by the child as necessary ones in reaching his end. If he works out each step himself, he is getting the best kind of training in simple, logical thinking which calls for full use of the constructive imagination. Is it not in this sort of work that the child is "beginning to live in little arcs of thought, instead of mere detached points of thought" far more truly than in those sequences when he develops one form from another at the teacher's dictation? If again the child plans and executes all for himself, as he may well do when supplied with a variety of materials, there is incentive and opportunity for the maximum use of creative imagination both in the process and in the play with the product. I think anyone who had seen children as I did the other day, playing with some little cardboard street-cars which they had just completed, would have been satisfied on this latter score. They asked for blocks, built a street of houses, cut paper-dolls, and then played. The dolls came out of the houses, hailed the passing cars, went downtown to shop and returned in time for dinner. The play was a self-organized group play suggested by the little cars which the children had constructed. It is the common experience in kindergartens where toys of this kind are sometimes made, that the free play with them is often self-organized group play. Compare such an occupation and play with the folding exercise given in the Wednesday programme quoted. The children for whom this was planned are supposed to have been in the kindergarten at least four months. They begin with recalling a previous exercise in which the square was derived from a cube of folding papers or of crackers. Then they make *one* fold in the paper according to direction and name the resulting form—book, shed, screen, or trough, as it suggests one or another of these objects. Surely there can be no question as to which makes the more legitimate appeal to understanding and imagination.

c) The third criticism, that constructive work is a substitute for free self-expression, is based upon the assumption that in this sort of occupation there is no opportunity for free self-expression. What the critics mean by free self-expression, Miss Blow illustrates thus:

> In weaving, for example, the child begins with simple combinations of number; discovers patterns as the result of this combination and thereafter through the reciprocal influence of pattern and numerical arrangement *creates interesting and beautiful designs.* In folding the beginning is made by creasing and bending paper in different ways; these creases and bends suggest simple objects and finally the child folds *with intention* to make objects.[10]

In both these illustrations the child is first shown how to manipulate the material; this suggests to him the relation between certain processes and certain results or products; he then creates designs or makes objects with intent, with purpose. The creation, the free "self-expression" seems to come with the purposeful activity. Now in constructive occupation this is exactly what happens except that in the first imitation of process the child knows what result he is going to achieve. After he has learned something of the possibilities of material through imitation, there is the same opportunity to create that is offered in the weaving or folding, with the added advantage that the possible products of his activity are far more attractive and desirable because he can carry on a play-activity with them, giving a still further opportunity for self-expression.

It must be remembered also that the believer in constructive occupation by no means uses it exclusively. Drawing, painting,

[10] *Educational Issues in the Kindergarten,* p. 265 [italics mine].

paper-cutting, clay-modeling, and design[11] have a *large* place in her programme. There is full opportunity given for free expression in all these occupations in which the child is less dependent upon guidance in the beginning.

III

Are the opportunities and incentives offered the children for invention well selected?

In the outline quoted there is some opportunity for invention. After the children have made squares of different sizes with the sticks they are allowed to make life-forms (inventions). Again, after a sequence of forms by imitation with the fourth gift, they invent "if there is time." The question at once arises as to whether this is the best method of developing the child's inventive powers. It seems to make invention as such an end in itself rather than an unconscious means to an end. There is no doubt that in his free play with material the child often hits upon a result that strikes him as valuable. He may then consciously repeat the act in order to get the product, and this may stimulate him to work for other ends. But it is this second act, the effort to realize a desired end that is the really educative one, and the one which gives his inventive powers fullest opportunity. Baldwin, in his treatment of invention, points out that the valuable thought-combinations, the inventions, arise in active mental life in the conscious direction of thought to certain useful ends.

> The whole process is a circular one. . . . . Thoughts issue in movements adapted to these thoughts. Variations in these movements react to produce variations in the thoughts. Some of these thought variations are selected. These are the inventions.[12]

When a child sets out to realize some end of his own, even though model for imitation and materials be supplied him, there is opportunity for originality in the adaptation of means to end. If he selects the material and creates the form there is still larger exercise of his inventive powers. But he is not inventing for

[11] These occupations will have fuller treatment in a later paper of this series.

[12] *Social and Ethical Interpretations*, p. 96.

the sake of inventing. Invention is the unconscious result of his successful effort to accomplish his purpose. While child purposes often originate in aimless activity, the thing which is educationally valuable is the following-up of such accidentally suggested purpose with really purposeful activity, demanding effort and originality. This is the teacher's opportunity. She too often fails to seize it.

IV

Is there psychological justification for the division of forms of expression into forms of life, forms of knowledge, and forms of beauty?

This is a division which Froebel makes in exercises with materials of whatever kind, but it is certainly one which modern thought does not indorse. The little child naturally makes no such artificial distinction between the products of his activity. As has been pointed out in this and other articles of this series, "forms of knowledge," as such, have no meaning or existence for him. The same may be said with almost equal truth of "forms of beauty." He will sometimes like a certain arrangement of units "because it is pretty" but it is practically never his only motive in the things he makes.

After making a study of children's drawings, Elmer E. Brown concludes that the development of symmetric forms merely for the sake of beauty is a late occurrence and due to the influence of older people. Burk finds that "the child has practically no interest in conventional designs nor in abstract geometrical forms."[13] Allison expresses his agreement with this general point of view in these words:

> Neither the conscious production in the interests wholly of aesthetic values, nor production of objects independent of utility, is characteristic of art in its earlier phases nor for children in the elementary schools.[14]

The art-impulse seems to be closely associated with and to grow out of the child's other instincts—the constructive and

[13] "The Genetic *versus* the Logical in Drawing," *Pedagogical Seminary;* Vol. IX, p. 296.

[14] "A Study in Theories of Art," *Elementary School Teacher,* March, 1905.

social instincts especially, according to Dr. Dewey.[15] Use and beauty are as yet undifferentiated by him. It would seem to be a serious mistake then to attempt to develop the aesthetic sense through the production of series of borders or symmetrical forms unrelated to any of the child's play-activities. In her use of design, therefore, the new school kindergartner gives the child opportunity to decorate the objects that he makes—if they lend themselves to decoration—or to decorate the room perhaps. She lets him select his own motive or unit for design in most cases. It is needless to say that this is rarely if ever a square, circle, or oblong. It is rather a pet animal, a flower, a snow man, Santa Claus driving his reindeer, or some other object dear to the childish heart and which it therefore gives him joy to repeat. Earl Barnes finds in his study of what children seven and eight years old think pretty, that their feeling of beauty gathers mainly around flowers, animals, dolls. A similar study of kindergarten children might give many suggestions as to what units for design we should offer them. There is a marked tendency at present to overemphasize this form of art-work.

In conclusion and by way of summary it may be said that the traditional materials and methods of using them are subject to the following criticisms:

1. The unity sought is a formal one, one existing in the materials themselves.

2. Exercises are planned for the purpose of giving the child knowledge of form, size, number, etc., apart from any felt need for such knowledge on the child's part.

3. Some of the processes with the small material demand a premature co-ordination of the fine muscles. A greater variety of substantial materials is needed.

4. There is too little recognition of the child's constructive and play instincts.

5. There is not sufficient opportunity or incentive of the right sort offered for originality and invention.

[15] *School and Society,* p. 56.

6. The threefold division of forms of expression into life, beauty, and knowledge forms is arbitrary and unnatural.

In recognition of the force of these criticisms certain changes in method and material have been made by the new school kindergartner.

1. The materials are used as a means by which the child may express the images, ideas, and play-purposes growing out of his social life. Through such expression he gradually defines and organizes his varied experiences bringing them into some sort of concrete connection with one another.

2. When materials are thus used, ideas of form, size, number, etc., follow as a necessary consequence. Exercises for the special purpose of teaching these things are discarded therefore as out of place at this stage of the child's development.

3. Many of the materials have been enlarged and some substantial ones added which lend themselves to the making of objects which the child feels the need of in his play.

4. To satisfy more fully the constructive and play instincts, the so-called constructive occupations have been introduced.

5. These constructive occupations, when rightly used, furnish both opportunity and incentive for originality and invention as means of securing desired ends.

6. Since all forms of expression are "life-forms" to the child in the sense that they have meaning and functional value to him, there is no division of his products into forms of life, beauty, and knowledge. He uses what knowledge he has in all his creative efforts, getting more as he needs it from his own experiments or the suggestions of his companions or teacher. Doubtless all of his achievements have some elements of beauty to him, although certain of them develop the aesthetic sense more than others.

THE SENTENCE AND THE VERB

JEAN SHERWOOD RANKIN
Supervisor of English, University Elementary School, Minneapolis

Far too many of the modern grammar-texts are at fault in their definitions of the sentence and of the verb. I quote almost at random from a few of the recent publications:

> A complete thought expressed in words is a sentence;
> A group of words expressing a complete thought is a sentence;
> A sentence is the expression of a complete thought in words.

But grammar takes no heed as to whether the *thought* expressed in any sentence be complete or not. Grammar merely demands that the *expression* of the thought be complete, if the result shall be called a sentence. That is to say, every sentence must be a grammatical whole, having at least one subject with its predicate verb.

These definitions of the sentence hark back to the logical definition of a thought as synonymous with a *judgment.* Now the judgment, or logical proposition, is not necessarily the same thing as the sentence, and it is unfortunate for our school children that this fact has not yet been discovered by sundry book-makers. Observe, in its bearing upon this statement, the following definitions, taken from one of the most pretentious of the recent texts:

> The subject of the sentence is the word or group of words which expresses the thought-subject.
>
> The predicate is the word or group of words which expresses the thought-predicate.
>
> The copula is the word or group of words which expresses the thought-relation.
>
> *Why Every Sentence in the English Language Must Have These Three Parts:*
>
> *They beg* is equal to *They are beggars* or *They are begging.*
> *They may write* is equal to *They may be writing.*
> *He must go* is equal to *He must be going.*
> *She does study* is equal to *She does be studying.*

We do insist is equal to *We do be insisting.*
The boy had gone is equal to *The boy had been going.*
They have studied is equal to *They have been studying.*
His brother will have departed is equal to *His brother will have been departing.*

Every sentence in the English language not only may have three parts, but every sentence must have, either actually in it or implied in it, these three parts: subject, predicate, and copula. . . . . No matter how many or how few words a sentence may contain, it is always made up of three parts: *subject, predicate,* and *copula.*

Teaching of this kind is an attempt to fit into the English sentence the laws underlying logical propositions. The result is something that is not good logic nor good grammar nor good English. It is absolutely false that every sentence is made up of three parts; and one proof of this statement is the fact that scores of grammars of German, French, Latin, and other languages, all agree in teaching that two words properly related, namely, the subject and its predicate verb, make a sentence.

Now the term *predicate* as used in logic and the term *predicate* as used in grammar are two wholly different things. In the proposition, "Grass is green," logic calls *green* the predicate; not so grammar. And although it is true that a grammatical predicate always implies a logical copula and a logical predicate, why attempt to teach baby-logic under the name of grammar? Certainly, if this is good teaching for English, it must be also good teaching for all other modern languages; but how absurd it would be for all the Harknesses and the Ollendorfs and the Whitneys, and the rest, to set at reconstructing the texts which have taught common-sense facts about verbs for many generations!

The rather obvious fact that every grammatical sentence must imply a corresponding logical proposition was clearly pointed out in the early grammar of Professor William Fowler, of Amherst College, published over half a century ago. Four chapters of Professor Fowler's voluminous text were given to "Logical Forms." In fact, the comprehensive work was undertaken chiefly for the instruction of college students in elementary logic. But Professor Fowler knew the difference between grammar and logic, and he did not get his subjects nor himself mixed. He expressly stated: "The structure of propositions in language does not always coincide with the structure of propositions in logic." And again: "Propositions which do not contain the copula may be easily resolved into those which do. Thus, 'Gold surpasses all other metals in brilliancy' may be stated, 'Gold is superior to all other metals in brilliancy.' "

Observe that Professor Fowler did not perpetrate the absurdity, "Gold *is surpassing* all other metals in brilliancy"! And is it not evident at a glance that in the pairs of sentences quoted above and declared to be equivalent, there is no real equivalence either logical or grammatical? Even if we could pardon the intolerable English of "She does be studying" and of "We do be insisting," we cannot pardon the untruthfulness of the statement that the first sentence in each pair "is equal to" the second. But is it not marvelous that the simple and obvious facts of English grammar should thus elude the grasp of numerous psychologic and pedagogic educators who feel called to make grammar-books for the mystification of the young? If it were true, as several authors state, that verbs are *necessarily* resolved into the form of predication needful to the logical statement of a judgment, it would at once be necessary to rewrite all the grammars of the modern languages used in our schools. Luckily, the microbe of a misconceived logic has not yet affected the scholarly makers of the French and German language-texts, and these still teach the sound and unassailable doctrine that a verb is a word which makes an assertion. May the infection not spread!

When the fetich of the recent grammar-book makers is not logic, it is usually psychology; and the attempted admixture of this science with grammar is worse, if possible, than in the case of logical theory. The psychological mixture results in the abandonment of words altogether, and the child is asked to wrestle with "ideas." He is told: "The *copula-idea* is that which asserts that an *attribute-idea* belongs to an *object-idea.*" He is taught: "The mind is furnished (!) with five kinds of *ideas:*" and, "Interjections are the signs of *feelings,* but not of *ideas.*" And finally he is told by one normal-school professor, in a recent pretentious text: *"The verb is a word which expresses a thought-relation."* This definition forces its author to classify the verb and the preposition together as "words of relation," which he calmly proceeds to do. But will the educational public receive without protest such distortion of grammatical truth?

It is important that every teacher of grammar in America recognize the fallacy in this position, for almost surely a dozen new texts will hasten to repeat the error within a twelve-month. Is it not obvious that *every possible grammatical construction shows thought-relation of some sort?* And is not the subject of syntax an attempt to reduce to a system thought-relations as shown by words? Predication is no more an expression of "thought-relation" than is apposition or any other construction. The moment two words are used in juxtaposition they express some thought-relation in the mind of the speaker. Whether we say to the baby, "Sugar—sweet," in the natural mother-way of the untutored savage, or, "The sugar is sweet," in the artistic mode of grammatical art, the "thought-relation" is identical in the two expressions.

The preposition is a relation-word not because it expresses thought-relations more absolutely than do other parts of speech, but because it expresses actual relations of every sort which exist in fact, as of place, position, source, direction, and the like. No other part of speech except the preposition expresses relations thus, although subordinate conjunctions shade into prepositions. It is immaterial whether we say, *The dress was blue,* or *It was a blue dress,* or *It was a dress of blue.* The *thought-relation* in these three expressions is identical, whether it is implied by the adjective, or expressed by the preposition, or asserted by the verb.

It is peculiarly unfortunate that this last glaring misconception of the function of the verb should be added to the long list of previous errors befogging the minds of teachers and of pupils. Once again, be it said with all possible emphasis, *every syntactical relation is a thought-relation.*

The failure to see that there is a marked difference between the proposition of logic and the sentence of grammar is usually accompanied by another failure—that of not comprehending the real nature of the verb. Not a text yet published, so far as I am able to determine, recognizes that free and varied communication of thought may occur without the use of verbs. Apparently it has been wholly forgotten that the verb was the last part of speech to be differentiated, and that there are still uncivilized tribes which have not yet developed the verb. It would be absurd to claim that these tribes neither think nor communicate thought. They do communicate thought easily enough, although they have not as yet developed that particular art-form which we call the sentence.

Originally all words were names. In order to show thought-relation of various sorts the simple method of *apposition,* or of placing words side by side, was first invented. Gradually, the adjective and then the other parts of speech were differentiated, and last of all the verb. This fact seems not to have come to the knowledge of many writers who state that "Young children use many verbs among their first words." The reverse is true: very young children use almost no verbs at all. What is mistaken for verbs are the numerous "action words," or verbal nouns, which are as truly nouns to the child and to the grammarian as are any other names of sense-objects. But how long shall this truth be ignored?

The time is almost here when the truth that the modern sentence is an *art-product* must be recognized. The sentence is the norm of cultivated expression, although it is not essential to the communication of thought. Whether or not we think in sentences can be determined in any individual case only by learning the habit of that individual. But that one's thinking depends upon the number and clearness of his ideas, and that these in turn depend upon the vocabulary which has been mastered, is the really vital truth which language-teaching is bound to recognize if it is ever to get upon a sound basis. Luckily for our graded schools, college presidents are at last beginning to take an interest in elementary principles, and one college president, Mr. Edwin W. Doran, of Mississippi, has published rather startling figures as the result of ten years' work in investigating vocabularies of elementary pupils.[1]

Professor Brander Matthews, of Columbia University, very justly said that the modern grammar-texts of America are usually "grotesque in their ignorance." But the most grotesque of them all—those which try to marry logic and grammar, or psychology and grammar—had not been written when Professor Matthews made his famous criticism. Bad as many of the earlier texts were, at least they had not forgotten that grammar deals with *words* rather than with *ideas,* and that a verb is a word which makes an assertion.

It is high time that a reaction should set in against the false grammatical theory now exploited in many recent texts. What the schools need in this line is an elementary course in old-fashioned grammar, unadulterated with logic or psychology. And, incidentally, in steering clear of Scylla, let us not sail into the jaws of Charybdis by trying to unite literature and grammar. Any eighth-grade class which has been well trained in English can easily master elementary grammar in a year, if the grammar is really grammar. But when misunderstood logic is added to equally misunderstood psychology and a heavy dose of literature is spread over all, there is little hope for the floundering child. Then speed the day when every school shall offer a short, intensive, but comprehensive course in grammar pure and simple, divested of every scrap of logic, of literature, or of psychology!

[1] *Pedagogical Seminary,* December, 1908.

THE SCHOOL CLUB, THE SCHOOL GARDEN, AND CORRELATED SCHOOL ACTIVITIES

A. MONROE STOWE
State Normal School, Hyannis, Mass.

While at first thought there may seem to be little possible relation between the school club and the school garden, the former organized and conducted by the pupils of the upper elementary school to accomplish certain results which appeal to them as worthy of their efforts and which can be achieved only through co-operation, and the latter fast becoming a part of the curriculum, still the school club may be utilized by the school not only to make the work in gardening more interesting to the pupils, but also to assist in correlating with that work social and civic activities as well as school studies. It is the object of the present paper to indicate very briefly some of the ways in which the school club may be thus utilized.

The school club has just been defined as a club organized and conducted by the pupils of the upper elementary school to accomplish certain results which appeal to them as worthy of their efforts and which can be achieved only through co-operation. While this implies that the aims of the club must be very definite, yet if the club is to be an efficient agency for assisting the school in its endeavors to realize its educational ideals such as, for example, the vitalization of the curriculum, there must be tucked away somewhere in the constitution of the club an "elastic clause" which will permit it to undertake almost any form of work which may at any time interest the majority of its members. If there is such an "elastic clause" in the constitution of the school club, it should not be difficult to interest the members in the subject of gardening, since in most schools the pupils look forward with pleasure to their work in the garden. Indeed, in the majority of cases this interest will have to be molded rather than created, it will have to be socialized by developing it into a club or community interest. This club interest may be awakened by proposing that the money made from a vegetable garden go into the club treasury to be expended by the club for some specified purpose, e. g., the purchase of books for the school- or village-library. While to some this proposition may appear to savor of the "commercial," the "utilitarian," yet if accepted and worked out, it will offer many opportunities to introduce naturally and to present through vital experiences many school subjects as well as to teach many valuable lessons in the appreciation of the value of money.

If then our school club has become so interested in the subject of gardening that it has decided to organize all or a part of its members—the number depending upon the number who are to take the work—into a Committee on Gardening, entire charge of the garden may be given to this committee who should be impressed with their responsibility to make it as successful as possible from the financial point of view as well as from the standpoint of a model garden. While formerly there may have been little co-operation in the garden work due to the lack of a community feeling, there will now be more and more efficient co-operation as the community interests become stronger and stronger through their development in the organization and work of the Committee on Gardening.

As there is much important work to be done before work is begun in the garden, the organization of the Committee on Gardening ought not be delayed too long. Before proceeding with the election of the chairman and the secretary-treasurer, who is to keep the minutes of the committee and make regular reports to the club concerning what is being done, the committee should take time to discuss what qualifications make for a good officer, especially one to hold the office which it is about to fill. The result of such discussion will generally be the election of a pupil well qualified for the office. If this preliminary discussion takes place before all school-club elections, there will gradually be developed a habit of taking elections seriously, of weighing carefully the qualifications of the candidates, and of casting one's vote for the candidate considered best qualified, a habit which, if once formed and made permanent, will do much to reform political conditions in the near future. Thus even the work preliminary to gardening may be made to contribute toward the training of our pupils in and for citizenship.

After it has organized itself the Committee on Gardening may proceed to a discussion of what should be done before seed-planting time, the chair being occupied by the chairman and the teacher as adviser simply guiding the discussion. Much of this preliminary work, however, can be best taken up in class, leaving some of the following concrete, practical problems for discussion in committee:

1. From what vegetables shall we derive the most profit?

2. What method of caring for the garden shall we adopt? Shall we plant our vegetables in beds, each member having a plot, or shall we plant them in rows, each pupil being responsible for certain rows?

3. Which of these methods is favored by the kinds of vegetables we desire to raise? By the space we have at our disposal?

4. Which vegetables will grow best in this climate and in the soil of our garden?

After the Committee on Gardening has discussed the above problems, a special committee including the teacher might be chosen to draw up a plan for the garden, a task which will enable the pupils to utilize their knowledge of ratio and proportion in drawing the plan to a scale. When the report of the special committee has been approved, the Committee on Gardening with the help of seed catalogs obtained from seed firms will be able to figure upon the kind, amount, and cost of the seeds needed. While this committee is now ready to purchase its seed, it finds itself in the position of a man who desires to begin business but cannot do so until he obtains the necessary capital. What an excellent opportunity for introducing in a perfectly natural way the subject of borrowing money, promissory notes, interest, and even bank discount! How these subjects lose their abstract character when the committee is allowed by the teacher to borrow from some person connected with the school what money it needs for seeds and incidentals, giving a note signed by the secretary-treasurer for the committee and indorsed by the teacher as adviser! What a natural introduction to the subject of banks of deposit is offered when the secretary-treasurer deposits with the treasurer of the club the money borrowed and receives an account book and check book similar to those issued by banks of deposit except that "Treasury of School Club" is substituted for the name of a bank. If possible the other members of the Committee on Gardening should be furnished with duplicate books in order that they may keep duplicate records. There will be considerable practice in keeping accounts on the stubs as well as making out, indorsing, and presenting checks for payment, when checks are made out for money to be remitted with the various orders for seeds. In order to present through vital experience another phase of the subject the teacher may instruct the treasurer of the club how to keep the accounts of the Committee on Gardening and how to make monthly reports so that at the beginning of the following month the treasurer may give to the secretary-treasurer the canceled checks together with a statement similar to those rendered at the beginning of the month by banks of deposit.

The orders to which reference has just been made may be written by all of the pupils, the best copies being chosen to be sent to the seed firms and the secretary-treasurer being instructed to make checks payable to the pupils whose orders are to be sent. The necessity of sending remittances with these orders is a natural reason for introducing the subject of ways of making remittances through the mail, a subject which may be made more concrete to the pupils by allowing each to fill out properly an application for post-office money order in favor of one of the seed firms. When the proper applications have been filled out, a committee of three may be chosen to purchase the money orders and to report what takes place at the post-office. Following upon this report may come an account of what becomes of the duplicate orders as well as how the original orders are cashed, while the study of bills may be looked upon as following naturally upon the receipt of receipted bills for the seeds ordered.

While actual work in the garden, for which the pupils are now prepared, may go on much as in former years, the observant teacher will notice less of purely selfish individual effort and more of healthy and friendly co-operation, for the members of the Committee on Gardening are working out a plan to which all have given their approval and for the success of which all are earnestly striving moved by many motives, not the least important of which is the desire to have a model garden and to make their first financial undertaking a success. Thus by transforming individual effort into social co-operation as well as by offering wonderful opportunities for introducing naturally and presenting through vital experiences a number of important school studies, the school club through its Committee on Gardening may be of great assistance to the school in its endeavors to realize not only its purely educational ideal, the vitalization of its curriculum, but also its social ideal, the development of men and women trained to co-operate for the common good and welfare of their communities.

THE FUNCTION OF THE FARM SCHOOL

Quite a story lies behind the letter printed below. In the spring of 1908 the principal of one of the public schools of Dubuque, Mr. B. J. Horchem, purchased a small farm beyond the outskirts of the city. It was very much run down, as the illustration shows. A tenant was put in possession and by the time the schools closed in June, repairs on the house were well on the way. The new owner did not invest in the farm either for personal profit or for the luxury of a summer residence, but because he wanted to try an experiment. He felt that the city boys, such as those in his school, needed something other than two months of idleness and mere play, and something other than the work in the shops, which in any event but few were old enough to undertake. Having been brought up on a farm himself, it seemed to him that farm life offered a solution of the problem presented.

An invitation having been given to some of the leaders among the boys to "come out and help," nearly twenty responded and came with more or less regularity throughout the two months. The result as far as the boys were concerned, were so satisfactory that Mr. Horchem is anxious to continue and expand his experiment into a permanent summer school. He has two plans in view, one of which might be called the immediate and the transitory, and the other a more thoroughgoing scheme, involving the entire reorganization of the school-system.

In the first place he wants the boys of a manufacturing city to know something of what the farm offers, before the pressure of circumstances forces them into shop or office work or into unskilled labor.

He believes that even one summer can serve to implant the germs of an ideal of the opportunity and rewards of farm life. He said that he would willingly take an entirely new set of boys to his farm next year, in order that others might see for themselves what otherwise they might never appreciate—that there is a world of work outside the factory and that there are other fields of employment to choose from. Nearly one hundred boys are making plans for this farm for the coming summer.

Some of the educational views of the author of this experiment follow the letter.—EDITOR.

PARK HILL FARM SCHOOL

President—ROBERT E. YOUNG
Manager—AMOS F. PALEY
Secretary—ADALBERT T. WALLER
Treasurer—J. RUSSELL JOHNSTON

DUBUQUE, IA.
November 17, 1908

Mr. John Morrison, Dubuque, Iowa:

DEAR MR. MORRISON: Inclosed please find some of the pictures which were taken of some of us boys while at work on the farm during the summer.

No. 1 shows where some of us thought that it would be fine exercise to fix up the roadway.

No. 2 will give you an idea of how the approach looked after it had been finished.

No. 3 will give you an idea of how we used to go and come from work occasionally.

No. 4 shows you how we enjoyed playing or working around the barley stack.

No. 5—We were preparing a park around the tent you so kindly loaned us.

No. 6—We are planning on civic improvement around the tent.

No. 7—How we petted the cows when we had nothing else to do.

We regret that you did not find it convenient to visit us during the summer. As a whole we had a pleasant and profitable vacation. Professor Horchem suggests that we give you a short account of our efforts. In regard to the work we did, we must say that some of us did report to our parents when we came home and did not explain anything in particular. When they would say that they doubted if we did anything, we would reply that we did so many things that we could not remember anything in particular.

We did many different things. We learned much. We hoed vegetables, cultivated, fertilized, picked peas, also other vegetables, husked corn, went to market, and had other experiences in farming.

Our first taste of farm life was hoeing. We hoed the cabbages. Some of us hardly knew how to hoe, but now we consider ourselves experts. Then we cultivated onions. Of course we cut quite a few off, but we have learned much and would not do such a thing any more.

THE HOUSE AS WE FOUND IT

THE BARN AS WE FOUND IT

We all remember the time when we fertilized the tomatoes.

One of our most constant occupations was picking peas, of which there was a large patch.

Then came market days, when we took our produce to market. The first time the buggy was driven to market, it contained the general manager and the treasurer. These two officers went in their wide-brimmed rustic straw hats, upon which was showered a great deal of ridicule. Their first experience at marketing was not very pleasant. We all had a good laugh at their expense afterward. After that we took turns going to market, always taking care that we did not have our straw hats on. We hired a stand at the market, and there we could be found, selling our peas, beans, carrots, cabbages, beets, and other vegetables.

We carried our dinners, which we ate in the tent. Our suppers were cooked by Mrs. Honkomp, the lady of the place. We either ate them in the tent or in the shade outside. It is needless to say that we enjoyed the supper in the open, free air. We always slept well and feel that our condition has been physically benefited.

We did not work every day, sometimes three times a week, and sometimes only twice. During the hottest part of some days we played in the shade or rehearsed our band composed of such tin instruments as we could gather together. We had many lively debates, disputes, and discussions concerning our work, novels we had read, or topics concerning the welfare of the country; so you can see that we learned a great deal in discussing various things while we were working or taking a rest in the tent.

The most disagreeable part of the whole thing was the walk home. We did not fancy this journey, especially after the day's work.

There were many other boys that wanted to join, but we felt that there were no accommodations for so many, and that it would be too hard on Mrs. Honkomp to cook for them all.

We feel that to have a great many boys to take part it would be best to start early in spring with hotbeds and to have boys by fours to take plats of ground and start out in a scientific manner.

In the spring we will start early with hotbeds and incubators. We will work after school and Saturdays. We will engage in the raising of chickens, having, of course, a competent man to attend them in our absence. We will have a large number of new recruits, who, of course, will have their experience next summer, while we, the officers of the "Farm," and those who have had their experience last summer, will work in a more general way this summer teaching the new boys the things with which they are not familiar. There will also be a large number of boys who will join us, once the other boys inform them of their first taste of farm life.

We have suggested to Professor Horchem, and he has agreed to do all he can toward making arrangements by which we could have an orchard,

PREPARING FOR THE TENT

CIVIC IMPROVEMENTS

so that we could trim, prune, bud, and spray the trees. We would thereby get practice in taking care of fruit trees, and perhaps be able to make a little to help pay our expenses.

We are going to make an appeal to Professor Horchem to be permitted to edit a small journal, to which the boys and officers will contribute. It will be published monthly. It will inform the boys of all the markets, besides giving them helpful literature on farming.

We worked two or three days a week—that is, part of the time, for we were not without recreation. There was the cool, shady grove nearby, where we could play games, and the tent, where we could talk over the events of the day, and debate various questions, as stated above.

During the next summer, we will take short trips, such as the La Motte one, to various points of interest around here on the way to and fro noticing the methods of the most successful farmers and other things concerning our work.

And then, if we raise enough, which will not be improbable, we will go by wagon to the wilds of Wisconsin, the Dells of the Wisconsin River, for instance, for a week or two's camping.

Next summer a new barn will be erected in place of the old one seen in the cut. This will be quite an improvement on the old one.

Each boy will have so much ground to cultivate. He will be allowed to grow on it whatever he likes. At times all the boys will set to beautifying the whole place. They will have a taste of all kinds of work. If the roadway needs fixing, the boys will do it. A gate might be mended, or a fence repaired. The tents will have to be put up, the canvas mended. A small park should be laid out around the tents. The flowers would need care.

The cities and towns produce ten no-accounts and criminals where the country produces one or two, and this seems to be almost entirely due to the fact that on the farm the boy has something to do and does not spend his time loafing on the streets. It is a matter of common observation as well as of statistics that the bums and criminals with which the country is cursed come almost entirely from boys and girls who do not go to school or have no regular and definite work during the formative years, from nine to eighteen.

The life of the student is dissociated from the life of his home and his neighbors. He is taken away from and unfitted for the duties of his home and community. The school helps to make him feel strange in his own home and neighborhood instead

Fixing the Roadway

Going to Work

of helping him the better to understand and more thoroughly to enter into life about him.

There is no more edifying, dignified, and profitable occupation than that of agriculture, which is conducted in an intelligent, scientific, and painstaking manner. Through a "beautiful and bountiful garden" or a small farm, the working-classes can be shown how to shun the evils which arise from unsanitary and insufficient housing conditions, and how to secure after working hours and at their leisure some advantages of outdoor garden life, with opportunities for natural and beautiful occupation. By cultivating the soil, enough vegetables can be raised in a small garden, and enough eggs and meats can be secured from the poultry to pay more than half the grocery bill. Such gardens should lead many to see the advantages of land and cause many of them to leave the dark, dusty, and unhealthy city for fresh air and profitable undertaking. It is equally true that the children of the wealthy dwellers in hotels or apartment houses are in need of the freedom, the habit of work, and the interests that are developed by this outdoor life of productive activity.

Beside creating a love for the beautiful in nature, a love for a garden will in turn cause a love for a home and the desire to keep it up and improve it, and indirectly create a sentiment for larger public improvements, such as parks. We must begin with children, if we desire to continue and develop our civic pride.

The school ought to be a great beehive, buzzing with industry. We must find ways of letting the child live a more natural life, consisting of work and play, in both of which he will have more and more chance for initiative in proportion as he develops power of self-control and of controlling others.

By the time a boy has finished his eighth school year he should know whether he wants to be a carpenter, a farmer, or a professional man. He should therefore be placed in environments that permit observation of varied occupations. He should not only see the growing of fruits, vegetables, and grains for pleasure, but for profit, and he should be brought into contact with many industries, that he may have some intelligent basis for choice of the one he has the interest and capacity to follow. This experience should enable him to take more intelligent direction of his own course and thus save valuable time and costly experience.

Our present system of education is a terrible mistake. It is a mistake from every point of view. It is a mistake in so far as the mere acquirement of knowledge is concerned. The mind cannot assimilate beyond a certain rate. If forced with facts faster than it can master them, they will soon be rejected again. They will not be permanently built into the intellectual fiber, but fall out of recollection after the examination for which they were gathered. It is a mistake because it makes study distasteful. It is a mistake to weaken and to destroy energy without which a trained intellect is useless. Success could not compensate for ill-health, which would make failure doubly bitter. Herbert Spencer gave these facts over a half-century ago.

In our present system of study the children are not the determining factors in planning the course of study. The course of study is the main consideration. In every school teachers are specializing more and more from year to year. The curriculum is specialized, but not upon any rational grouping of children, or the innate power or ability of the children.

Someone must break away from tradition. The public schools cannot do it. If it has to come through the normal school the process is too slow. It must be started by those who have taught in the country schools, graded schools, and high schools, and who have made a study of the "doctrine of interest." Who can say what would be the power for good in the establishment of a farm school, by one who knows what he wants, what men and women he wants; one who prepares his pupils through them in such a way that each pupil will feel that he has a part to play in life, and that he should know his part and play it well, instead of preparing for a special mark from grade to grade, from grades to high school, and from high school to the colleges and the universities?

We cannot make artists out of pupils by placing them in an art gallery. They must understand the sentiments and conception of the artist before they can really understand the picture. So it is with work; so it is with play; so it is with study; so it is with nature. The boy does not appreciate the work of the soil, heat, and moisture until he gets in contact with work in the garden, or on the farm. He can be made to understand how an apparently worthless piece of ground can be made into one of the most attractive, pleasing, and profitable places in the community.

While the boy studies the growth of things, he also studies physics, chemistry, and botany. When he studies birds, trees, and animals, his love and desire for the beautiful is developed. When he builds his fences and pigeonhouses, and helps to make sidewalks, he secures a technical training which will involve mathematics. He will learn all about board-measure and the composition of concrete. He will look at plans and specifications and obtain the best authorities by consulting the best local architects and contractors, and read books and magazines on the subjects in which he is most interested. It will cause him to write to men of affairs, which will put him in business relations with the wider world. Natural conditions will be established, and each pupil will play his part, the part he can play best in life.

The kitten uses its paws and so learns how to handle them when compelled to. So the boys in this business course are coming into closer touch with real business, which now is growing up with the school and the world outside of it. The boys are not supposed to work all the time.

During twenty-five years of experience as a high-school teacher, county superintendent, and principal of a ward school, the writer has observed that not 65 per cent. of the boys finish the eighth grade. They are usually boys that wish to do things. They don't care about our superlatively correct language. They not only want to know things but have the habit of doing things. They don't want our present dose of education. All our pleading and forcing cannot retain them, even the best of them. Our methods are too bookish. If any change is made, it must be made by someone who has had the experience in grade work and who has been accustomed to consider the gradual development of the child through the grades, one who is not dominated by college entrance examinations, one who will do away with much drill, too much cram, and too narrow a range of subjects, but will always consider the development of the child. The man who makes a success of the new school must have the qualifications of a president of a university. According to Dr. Jordan's view

it will be the duty of such a man to create a peculiar school-atmosphere. He must set the pace, must frame its ideals, choose the men in whom those ideals can be realized. It is through the men he chooses that the new school will become a living thing. This man must co-operate with his helpers. His noblest work is that of maker of leaders. It is not what he himself can do, that first concerns the school. His personal powers, skill, or versatilities are of little moment. It will be what he can discern and divine in others that will gauge his success. It will be his instinct to know what the best work of others may be, and how he can use it in the fabric he is building. Long head and long patience he must needs have, for he will often wait years for men to grow to what he expects of them, and others to whom he can look for the right kind of growth. He must have the instinct to judge men, and to estimate what men say of men. He must be keen to recognize in others qualities of worth, which he himself may not possess. He must have the wisdom to foster individual freedom and the firmness to check that freedom that spends itself in futile, erratic, and sentimental effort.

GENERAL PLAN FOR PRACTICAL EDUCATION

1. Schools to be in the suburbs of our cities.

2. Schools to be in session the entire year, but only half the time to be spent indoors. Schoolroom work to be done chiefly in the winter and in bad weather.

3. Less deskwork. More laboratory, shop, and garden work. The active aspect of education now seen chiefly in the kindergarten to be maintained throughout the grades.

4. Initiative to be taken by children. All the leading trades, occupations, and professions to be carried on and opportunities to be open for the study of the same under trained workers. When at work under this direction, in field or shop, the need of further theoretic study or knowledge is found by the pupil and he will go to the schoolroom to get the needed work.

5. No written examinations. The test of ability will be found in the work done. If work is well done, examination is unneces-

sary; if poorly done, there is evident need for further study and effort. There should be no more need of formal examination here than in the business world.

Education is life—not preparation for life.

Interest is wanting to know what to do next.

Wisdom consists in knowing what to do next.

Virtue is the doing.

Civilization has not advanced by *words,* but by *acts* and *deeds.*

To plan *action* is the duty of the school.

EDITORIAL NOTES

History in the elementary school presents a problem and an opportunity. The problem has been ably discussed by Professor Henry Johnson of the Teachers College. He has criticized the imaginative history which looks for its construction largely to the child and insists that real history from the hands and heads of competent historians is a pabulum that if properly presented is quite digestible for children in the elementary school, and he has presented illustrations in his study on "History in the Elementary School." It is not too much to say that the material which Professor Johnson suggests can be unhesitatingly recognized as proper for the school and its pupils. The question is rather whether the material is adequate to the task which history has to meet in the elementary school.

The Problem of History in the Elementary School

History is the philosophy of the child and of many who are no longer children. It is history which must interpret the curriculum if it is to be interpreted to the elementary-school pupil. It is history which must connect the conceptions of the child with the institutions and life of the community about him. Consider for example how essential history is to such an admirable textbook in civics as that written by Professor Dunn, *The Community and the Citizen,* with its outline of the beginnings of the community, its site, what the people are seeking in the community, the family, and the services rendered to the community by the family, the making of Americans, etc. The great difficulty is that our histories are as yet histories only of politics. It is only a few of the industries, such as that of cotton on account of its vivid political interest, that are given their real value in the making as life of the community.

The Teaching of History as an Opportunity

The nub of the problem is found in the relation of this material to the child's intelligence. It is true that such material as that which Professor Johnson presents, can be made intelligible to the child. The question is whether this is the material which the child needs. And the answer to this question can only be given when we know what the child needs to have explained to him. In this sense it is important that the child should be almost as active in the direction of his historical study as is the graduate student who is at work on some historical problem that has become his own. For this function of history there is no study that should be so flexible and so pervasive in the whole curriculum, none in which the child's easy passage from imaginative processes to those of observation and reasoning should be more evident. History in the elementary school should be what was called "music" in the Greek child's education, the meaning of the life and the institutions about him, stated in social terms.

Social Situations the Terms in which Children think

The most important phase of history as the groundwork of the child's instruction is its concrete social character. We are just beginning to appreciate to what an extent children do and must do their thinking in social forms. If a child undertakes to define an object or a situation his irresistible tendency is to describe it as part of the activity of some person—e. g., a crime is "when a cop arrests you." It is through social situations that children carry out their generalizations and draw their conclusions, and it is the province of the school to make a continuous intellectual discipline out of this native capacity of children, through the historical treatment of as many subjects in the curriculum as possible. As the method of children's thinking history is not only the philosophy but the logic of the elementary-school curriculum.

NOTES AND NEWS

Reports from London give some interesting details of some experiments, which could be duplicated, partially, at least, in many schools, showing the conditions under which children can do their best work. A schoolroom was fitted with apparatus by which the temperature could be regulated and kept at any point between fifty and eighty degrees. Other apparatus was used to increase the humidity, and to secure movement and change of air, whenever desired.

The results of the experiments given briefly are as follows: When the atmospheric conditions are favorable, mental alertness, and accuracy are improved by two or three hours of work. Temperatures in excess of sixty-five degrees indicate hurtful conditions, giving rise to symptoms of inattention, slackness, and headaches. But if the air is kept constantly moving temperatures in excess of sixty-five will not prove harmful; and even at higher temperatures movement and change of air ameliorate the harmful conditions somewhat. But at seventy and above marked symptoms of deterioration in alertness and accuracy are very evident, whatever the atmospheric conditions.

Commissioner Draper has recently supplemented his late report on Industrial Education with an address on "Agricultural Education in the Public School System;" he sums up the conclusions as regards the work of the rural elementary school as follows, which he calls "suggestions concerning the educational basis of agricultural interests":

There should be a complete and interrelated system of schools, elementary, secondary, and higher, open to all, and essentially under the control of the people of the state.

The elementary school should be within reach of every farmer's home. So long as the school is adequately sustained and competently taught, the location may be left to the people of the district. It is more a question of expediency than of educational principle, and there is no balance of advantages in school-concentration to justify forcefully overthrowing an established order.

The elementary schools are to teach the elements of an all-around English education. They cannot specialize much and they are not to be in any sense exclusive. They are to aim at fitting children for the choice of any vocation they may prefer and for beginning the preparation therefor. They are always to preach the gospel of work, and to use books and objects and methods to stimulate quite as much interest—in the country, perhaps, more interest—in agriculture as in any other industry. This should be guarded in making the elementary syllabus. The work of the elementary schools in the country as in the city should not dawdle and waste time through the multiplicity of books and the idle exploitation of pedagogical theories and methods. It should be definite quantitatively as well as efficient qualitatively. The attendance laws should be enforced in the country as in the city, even though the extent of child labor on the farm and the distance from the school make neglect of the law very frequent and the difficulties of enforcement very great. The course should be simplified and shortened and the child brought to the end of it, with the assurance that he has some definite knowledge and measure of efficiency by the time he is fourteen years old. Better professional supervision should establish some satisfactory basis of graduation from the country elementary school, and graduation should qualify the pupil for admission to the high school, or a district agricultural school.

Massachusetts has a playgrounds act which should prove suggestive to other states. Every city or town in the state which has a population of 10,000 or more, and which shall vote to accept the provision of the act, shall be privileged, after July 1, 1910, to provide and maintain one public playground, conveniently located and of suitable size and equipment, for the recreation and physical education of the minors of the community; and at least one additional other playground for every additional 20,000 of population. The communities may appoint their own qualified supervisors and determine their compensation. Land may be secured for these purposes by public condemnation, as for other public purposes, and the community is empowered to raise the money therefor by taxation; and the community may, in order to meet the situation, incur indebtedness beyond the limit of municipal indebtedness to an amount not to exceed ½ of 1 per cent. of the assessed valuation. It will not be necessary to establish a sinking fund for the payment of this increased indebtedness, unless the community so desires. A majority of the voters in any city or town can make the act effective. Twenty-three communities have already voted to take advantage of the provisions of the act.

Advance sheets of the *Report of the Commissioner of Education* give some very interesting data as to educational progress during 1908. The schools of the country enrolled, last year, about nineteen millions of pupils of all grades and classes. That is to say, about 20 per cent. of the total population of the country attended the common schools for a longer or shorter period. The total expenditure by the public schools for the year was about three hundred and thirty millions of dollars.

A remarkable feature of the past year is found in the public interest in education as shown in the great number of educational commissions which have been and are at work investigating various phases of the educational situation. Ten states appointed such commissions. The work which they have undertaken is too varied to be specified in detail here but it is a subject well worth attention on the part of those interested in our larger public pedagogy. Technical and vocational education is one of the more prominent factors to be investigated. Massachusetts, Maryland, and

New Jersey each appointed a commission to provide better plans for this work.

A most encouraging phase of the work of the year is seen in the large number of voluntary educational organizations that have been established. These are both local and national in extent and import. This method of bringing issues to the larger social consciousness is being used more and more. It used to be thought that there must be something wrong with the interest that had to rely upon voluntary support in a country where the people rule, and where they ought to be able to get everything they want. But it is seen, now, that this is the best way of determining what it is the people actually do want.

But educational forces and issues are taking on an international aspect, also. During 1908 at least nine great international congresses, devoted to the problems of public and social education, were held. Congresses on the welfare of the child, on industrial education, moral education, household economy, popular education, etc., were very prominent. It is becoming more and more apparent that the problem of education is a world-wide problem, and not a merely local issue.

Recent numbers of the *Psychological Clinic* have contained considerable material of service to teachers. In the January number Dr. Roland P. Falkner, ex-commissioner of education for Porto Rico, presents "Some Uses of Statistics in the Supervision of Schools." He is chiefly interested in the economic results that follow from the proper employment of statistical data by the superintendent. He shows that in 1904–5 Porto Rico had fewer schools than in the previous year, but over 3,000 more children were in these schools. This result was obtained by the efforts of the district superintendents, spurred on by the admonitions and the reports of the commissioner's department. As another illustration Dr. Falkner finds in a school-report for an American city that the average registration per teacher was 42.08, the average roll per teacher 32.01, and the average attendance 30.3. These figures show that the school-system is not utilizing these teachers to the full extent, and yet a considerable number of children were in half-day sessions.

Whether half-day sessions are a detriment to the progress of the pupils or not, requires statistical examination. In three rooms in Camden, N. J., half-day pupils in 1905–6 made better percentage of promotions than the all-day pupils of the preceding year under the same teachers. In one case a contrary result was observed. Under these circumstances—and these are the only records of the kind available—Dr. Falkner contends that we cannot be sure that half-day classes for beginners in the first grade are a positive evil.

Another article takes up the question of "Elimination of Pupils from School," classifying some of the cities of the United States according to the percentages of loss throughout the grades. The city of Worcester, Mass., is in the class which loses less than 40 per cent. before the eighth grade. New York, Chicago, and Minneapolis lose between 65 and 70 per cent.; Cincinnati and St. Louis lose between 75 and 80 per cent.; whereas Philadelphia and Baltimore lose over 80 per cent.

The conclusions of the White House Conference on Children should be of interest to every teacher. Professor Henderson said once: "There is only one thing nobler than being a school-teacher, and that is to be a teacher." Interest in such work as that done by President Roosevelt's White House Conference indicates the teacher as distinct from the mere school-teacher. The full report of the conference appears in a current number of *Charities and The Commons* as "A Programme of Child-Caring Work." It should be in the hands of every teacher, and every school-teacher, too. This report deals with home care, preventive work, home-finding, state inspection of child-saving agencies, physical care of children, undesirable legislation, and the formation of a federal children's bureau. A thoroughgoing programme is outlined. When summarized it amounts to this: "The particular conditions and needs of each destitute child should be carefully studied and he should receive that care which his individual needs require, and which should be as nearly as possible like the life of the other children of the community." Has the teacher any responsibility in connection with this programme?

School Hygiene, the journal of the American School Hygiene Association, has been presenting some most valuable materials on the subject which it represents. But the journal has reached the point where it must have increased support if it is to continue its work. Its aim is "to secure improved school conditions for children, to awaken public interest in their welfare so that needed improvements can be obtained, and to report progress in this movement." The movement is worthy of more liberal support.

The editor of the *Psychological Clinic* has been attempting to criticize the so-called "Emanuel Movement" out of existence. He contends that "Dr. Worcester and his collaborators have reported no results as yet which establish satisfactory proofs of the efficiency of their methods." But his criticisms of what he calls the "Yellow Psychology" of Professor Münsterberg and the revived "occultism" of Professors James and Royce, are especially interesting. He contends that Professor James has been, throughout his course, "distinguished by an unscientific attitude, and that he has produced no results which have had any effect upon the development of modern psychology." All of which, of course, reads like the questions which Rip Van Winkle asked after his twenty years of sleep.

BOOK REVIEWS

Systematic Study in the Elementary Schools. By LIDA BELLE EARHART, PH.D. New York: Teachers College, Columbia University, 1908. Pp. 90+9 Tables.

The century-old emphasis upon psychology as the guide in education is destined to yield sooner or later to some direction inherent in the current revival and reconstruction of logic. This study is a pioneer in its special field of analysis of teaching practice. It presents a more or less psychological account of the conditions and the emergence of logical dependence among pupils in the elementary school. At the same time it shows one source of the pedagogical waste of time and effort, and becomes a criticism of the logical aspects of textbooks in the hands of pupils. The first two chapters sketch inductive and deductive procedure; the next two present the textbook and the schoolroom processes of study; while the last two (with the nine tables), which are the most interesting part of the work, state the results obtained by several methods of observation as to what continues to be the typical school practice and what is possible with children from the fourth to the seventh grades. The experiment of training some of the pupils tested in systematic study in order to show its possibility in general stands in need of greater control before it can be expected to yield results that would be either more uniform or accepted as conclusive. The author happily recognizes the limitations in this study. But it is important to be shown anew the regrettable situation that teaching too frequently leaves pupils helpless, and to have the theory of study illuminated by facts more or less negative. The early doom of "soft pedagogy" is not heralded by the discovery that "teachers lack a clear conception of what proper study is" (p. 66). Reading this monograph should be helpful to every teacher; but the reader will find difficulty in following the text and the tables which are not most conveniently arranged for ease of reference.

EDWARD FRANKLIN BUCHNER

JOHNS HOPKINS UNIVERSITY

An Algebra for Secondary Schools. By E. R. HEDRICK, Professor of Mathematics in the University of Missouri. New York: American Book Co., 1908. Pp. x+421. $1.00.

The number of good scholars turning their hand to the preparation of secondary texts in mathematics is rapidly increasing. Something more than a dozen secondary texts in algebra and geometry have appeared from the press during the summer and autumn just passed, all of which purport to be recognizing the spirit of the new movements for the improvement of the teaching of mathematics in high schools and academies. The volume before us makes the common claim. The author alleges that while "it meets the entrance requirements of American colleges and universities generally, this book is written essentially for those for whom the high-school course is to be the last." A point of not a little importance has been gained of late years in inducing men who prepare textbooks to take the point of view that the thing needed for high schools must be determined mainly by the requirements of students who are not going to colleges.

The distinctive features of this book are the metrical introductions to algebraic number; the early and extended use of graphs of numerous types; the care with which concepts are placed back of the operations applied to signed number; the condensation of certain topics, such as parentheses, into a much smaller compass than is usual; the great care given to work in the translation of English into algebra and algebra into English; the wide use of geometrical pictures to illuminate the algebra; the use of graphs in the teaching of simultaneous linear equations and quadratic equations rather than an appended chapter after the teaching service has been entirely performed, as is usually done by more timid teachers than Mr. Hedrick, and a rather full summary of the substance of the chapters. It should be mentioned that graphs are made to do valuable service in the presentation of logarithms. In the writer's opinion it is difficult to justify the treatment of logarithms as the last chapter of any school year. To make the subject of logarithms of value to a learner it is quite important that the development of the subject be followed up at once, by considerable application to calculations which impress the advantage gained by the use of logarithms.

There is also an appendix treating of detached coefficients, the remainder theorem as used in factoring, the factor theorem, choice and chance, permutations and combinations, factorials, Euclidean methods of H. C. F. and L. C. M., cube root and higher roots, limits, infinite series, imaginary and complex numbers, simultaneous quadratics graphically exhibited, and a summary of this rather heavy appendix. A valuable feature of the book is the tables of common weights and measures, including metric units with their English equivalents, also tables of geometrical mensuration formulas that come after the appendix, and then follows an index of a little over four pages.

As an example of the care with which the author presents some matters which are really difficult for the student but which the teacher usually passes over with no attention whatever, the following will serve: "A tin box is to be made from a square piece of tin by cutting out square corners and then folding up the flaps. Find the size of the piece of tin that must be used to make a box four inches high that must contain one hundred cubic inches volume. Let us first become familiar with the problem by trying several numbers. Suppose the original plate were eighteen inches square in the figure AB=BC=18 in., and we cut out the shaded corners each four inches square, etc."

After figuring the volume of the box from this trial it is found that it contains 400 cubic inches instead of 100 cubic inches, as required. Then the author suggests that it is easier to try the problem by calling the length of the required piece l and seeking to find l than to continue by this cut-and-try plan until the answer is happened upon. He then carefully carries through the solution of the problem on the unknown length l, getting the solution much after the customary fashion. Then he argues that the student must at the close of the solution "see which, if any, of the several possible answers are correct ones and if there may be answers that cannot possibly mean anything, as seen above." In the reviewer's opinion, this is a skilful way of impressing the learner with the importance of the algebraic plan of introducing an unknown number to facilitate problem-solution. There are many good pedagogic things of the type just alluded to.

A general criticism against the book is that it is very highly condensed, the statements in many cases being very succinct, making the book pretty hard reading for the students of the first and second years of high-school work. There are some instances of too great punctiliousness for formal correctness of logic, and evidences of a little too much nervousness lest some college critics may not find the book sufficiently high toned mathematically. This, however, is a weakness that "leans to virtue's side." Perhaps President Hall would find this book less open to the objection of being padded with explanations to make the way plain for the easy-going student than are most textbooks used in the public schools today. It can hardly be said that Mr. Hedrick has shown in this excellent little book a desire to "whip two ounces of soap into two hogsheads of lather."

The publishers have done their part of the book well. Much good would come from replacing books of the prevailing type by such a book as Mr. Hedrick's. Every secondary teacher of algebra should study this book.

G. W. M.

The Eleanor Smith Music Course. By ELEANOR SMITH, Head of the Department of Music, School of Education, The University of Chicago. New York: American Book Co., 1908. Book I, pp. 112, $0.25; Book II, pp. 145, $0.30; Book III, pp. 192, $0.40; Book IV, pp. 255, $0.50.

It is with a sense of elation that one opens a book bearing the name of this author. Miss Smith has won for herself a place among those interested in the musical education of children which guarantees the value of what she offers. The material contained in this series is strikingly attractive both as to music and texts. Especially happy is its adaptation to the needs of our cosmopolitan schools through folk-songs of many lands, the texts of these being translations from the original. It is interesting to note that although carefully graded, the illustrative songs never depart from the high standard of excellence, even the exercises introducing and elaborating technical points having rich musical content. The first sixty-nine pages of Book I are devoted to short melodies for reading and writing, while rote-songs selected from German, French, Norwegian, Bohemian, Danish, as well as American sources complete a charming volume. Book II continues this sight-reading material and rote-songs while technical problems are introduced in well-arranged sequence. A preparation for two-part singing appears in the form of rounds and canons. In Book III, two-part songs are introduced. Studies by Taubert, Reinecke, and other well-known composers promise aesthetic pleasure while new problems are being solved. In Book IV an unusual group of songs for bass voices, by breezy texts and stirring melody, will satisfy the exacting taste of the larger boys. Taken together, the series is an important contribution to educative musical literature for children.

M. R. KERN

BOOKS RECEIVED

AMERICAN BOOK CO., NEW YORK

Nature Study by Grades. Teachers' Book for Primary Grades. By HORACE W. CUMMINGS. Cloth. Illustrated. Pp. 180. $1.00.

Essentials in Civil Government. A Textbook for Use in Schools. By S. E. FORMAN. Cloth. Illustrated. Pp. 224. $0.60.

Aiken's Music Course. In One Book. By WALTER H. AIKEN. Cloth. Pp. 208. $0.50.

Schiller's Jungfrau von Orleans. Edited, with Notes and Introduction, by WARREN W. FLORER. Cloth. Pp. 375. $0.70.

C. W. BARDEEN, SYRACUSE, N. Y.

Report on the Teaching of English in the United States. By M. ATKINSON WILLIAMS. Cloth. Pp. 88.

John Brody's Astral Body, and Other Stories About Schools. By C. W. BARDEEN. Cloth. Pp. 195.

HOUGHTON, MIFFLIN & CO., BOSTON

The Life of Abraham Lincoln, for Boys and Girls. By CHARLES W MOORES. Cloth. Illustrated. Pp. 132. $0.25.

THE MACMILLAN COMPANY, NEW YORK

The Rhetoric of Oratory. By EDWIN DUBOIS SHURTER. Cloth. Pp. 309. $1.10.

A History of Education Before the Middle Ages. By FRANK PIERREPONT GRAVES. Cloth. Pp. 304. $1.10.

Kidnapped. "Macmillan's Pocket Classics." By ROBERT LOUIS STEVENSON. Edited, with Introduction and Notes, by JOHN THOMPSON BROWN. Cloth. Pp. 271. $0.25.

The Spy. "Macmillan's Pocket Classics." By J. FENIMORE COOPER. Edited, with Introduction and Notes, by SAMUEL THURBER, JR. Cloth. Pp. 424. $0.25.

CURRENT EDUCATIONAL LITERATURE IN THE PERIODICALS[1]

IRENE WARREN
Librarian, School of Education, The University of Chicago

ABBOTT, ALLEN. High-school dramatics. School R. 17:119–25. (F. '09.)

BARTO, D. O. Problems in secondary-school agriculture. Sch. Sci. and Math. 9:226–34. (Mar. '09.)

BIRGE, EDWARD A. A change of educational emphasis. Atlan. 103:189–200. (F. '09.)

CALDWELL, OTIS W., GALLOWAY, T. W., AND NORRIS, N. W. A consideration of the principle that should determine the courses in biology in the secondary schools. Sch. Sci. and Math. 9:244–8. (Mar. '09.)

(The) California textbook plan. Jour. of Educa. Bost. 69:173–4. (18 F. '09.)

CARLETON, E. F. Public-school libraries of Oregon. Sch. and Home Educa. 28:207–9. (F. '09.)

CHANDLER, ELMA. Elementary science in the high school. School R. 17:89–96. (F. '09.)

CLAPP, HENRY LINCOLN. Self-government in public schools. Educa. 29: 335–44. (F. '09.)

CLUTE, WILLARD N. Making botany attractive. School R. 17:97–8. (F. '09.)

COULTER, JOHN M. What the university expects of the secondary school. School R. 17:73–84. (F. '09.)

CROWE, JOHN M., BROADUS, E. K., AND HOSIC, JAMES F. Report of conference committee on high-school English. School R. 17:85–8. (F. '09.)

DE GARMO, CHARLES. Relation of industrial to general education. School R. 17:145–53. (Mar. '09.)

FAGAN, JAMES O. The industrial dilemma. The railroads and education. Atlan. 103:326–35. (Mar. '09.)

FALKNER, ROLAND P. Elimination of pupils from school. Psycholog. Clinic. 2:255–9. (15 F. '09.)

GILES, F. M. The teaching of agriculture in the high school. School R. 17:154 65. (Mar. '09.)

[1] *Abbreviations:* Amer. Educa., American Education; Atlan., Atlantic Monthly; Educa., Education; El. Sch. T., Elementary School Teacher; Journ. of Educa. Bost., Journal of Education, Boston; Journ. of Geog., Journal of Geography; Out., Outlook; Pop. Sci. Mo., Popular Science Monthly; Psychlog. Clinic, Psychological Clinic; Sch. and Home Educa., School and Home Education; School R., School Review; Sch. Sci. and Math., School Science and Mathematics; Teach. Col. Rec., Teachers College Record.

Glover, Katherine. Working for an education in a southern school. Craftsman. 15:707–17. (Mar. '09.)

Gummere, Francis B. A day with Professor Child. Atlan. 103:421–7. (Mar. '09.)

Hale, Edward Everett. Harvard. Out. 91:453–61. (Mar. '09.)

Hobbs, William H. New laboratory methods for instruction in geography. Journ. of Geog. 7:97–104. (Ja. '09.)

Hutchins, Jr., E. B. How may instruction in elementary chemistry be made more efficient? Sch. Sci. and Math. 9:252–61. (Mar. '09.)

Lodge, Gonzalez. Vocabulary of high-school Latin. School R. 17:128. (F. '09.).

Maddocks, Mildred. Schools of home economics. Good Housekeeping. 58:278–84. (Mar. '09.)

Manny, Frank A. American schools as seen by a Belgian educator. El. Sch. T. 9:322–7. (F. '09.)

Manny, Frank A. A study in adult education. School R. 17:174–7. (Mar. '09.)

Mead, George H. Industrial education, the working-man, and the school. El. Sch. T. 9:369–84. (Mar. '09.)

Mental healing and the Emmanuel movement. Psycholog. Clinic. 2:212–24. (15 D. '08.)

Munroe, James P. The American public school. Pop. Sci. Mo. 74:300–7. (Mar. '09.)

Myers, G. W. The year's progress in mathematics in the university high school. School R. 17:99–119. (F. '09.)

Nelson, J. C. Discussion: testing high-school pupils' knowledge of the Bible. School R. 17:126–8. (F. '09.)

Page, Mary Boomer. The present point of view of the plays and games of the kindergarten. El. Sch. T. 9:341–58. (Mar. '09.)

Payne, Bertha. The kindergarten programme. II. El. Sch. T. 9:309–22. (F. '09.)

Remsen, Ira. The problems of science teaching. Sch. Sci. and Math. 9:281–4. (Mar. '09.)

Smith, David Eugene. The teaching of mathematics in the secondary schools of the United States. Sch. Sci. and Math. 9:203–19. (Mar. '09.)

Stowe, A. Monroe. The school club: its relation to several educational ideals. El. Sch. T. 9:364–8. (Mar. '09.)

(The) teaching of arithmetic. Teach. Col. Rec. 10:1–100. (Ja. '09.)

Travis, S. S. High-school fraternities. Amer. Educa. 11:301–5. (Mar. '09.)

Whitaker, Nellie Comins. The physical needs of the grammar-school girl. El. Sch. T. 9:287–92. (F. '09.)

Woodhull, John F. How the public will solve our problems of science teaching. Sch. Sci. and Math. 9:267–84. (Mar. '09.)

VOLUME IX NUMBER 9

THE ELEMENTARY SCHOOL TEACHER

MAY, 1909

GETTING OUR BEARINGS ON INDUSTRIAL EDUCATION

JESSE D. BURKS, PH.D.
Principal Teachers Training School, Albany, N. Y.

The industrial-education craft has steered a devious course during her eventful voyage. Twenty-five years ago she was flying the flag of manual training at her main mast. Against headwinds—through heavy seas—sometimes apparently with faulty chart and compass, her pilots have brought her through—somewhat battered and scarred but still seaworthy. She has lately been dry-docked, scraped, and painted; equipped with twin propellers; provided with a new figure-head; renamed; compass adjusted; and now flies the pennant of industrial education.

That she is the same old craft will be evident, however, to anyone who will read the specifications of the old vessel and compare them with those of the repaired and re-christened ship that has so recently and so gallantly put out to sea. To one accustomed to the uncertainties of tacking against headwinds in a sailing vessel, and of drifting idly on a calm sea, waiting for favoring breezes, there seems to be magic in the resistless headway that our ship is making under the driving force of her engines. If only her course be true and her charts trustworthy, there can be little doubt that the newly launched craft will bring us surely and speedily toward our home port. The perils of the sea are numerous, however, and not always to be anticipated. Like the watchful mariner, we should seize every opportunity for determining our exact position by getting our bearings on a light, a point of land, a barren rock, a fixed star, or the sun itself.

Without pursuing further this fanciful figure, let us examine directly some of the bearings of the present national agitation for industrial education. It would certainly be hazardous to make any single statement designed to give the present attitude of the country at large toward industrial education and manual training. It is possible, nevertheless, for us to find some fairly definite indications of a few tendencies and to examine very briefly the significance of these tendencies in the general educational movement of today.

The past few years have seen the organization of divisions of industrial education within state education departments; the establishment of independent commissions on industrial education, of national and state associations for the promotion of industrial education, and of a national commission on country life. The need of industrial education has been emphasized again and again by the United States Commissioner of Education, by many leading state and city superintendents of schools, by the governors of numerous states, and by the President of the United States in at least two of his messages. It has been vigorously urged by manufacturers' associations, labor organizations, associations for civic betterment, charity organizations, and political parties. State legislatures have passed favorable laws and periodical publications have given to the industrial education propaganda a degree of publicity and support that they have rarely accorded any similar public movement. Teachers' associations have given increasingly large attention to the question. The manual training department of the National Education Association has given over its programmes almost wholly to its consideration and a new department of technical education has been organized. The general programmes of the Association and of its department of superintendence have given much time to the subject and many speakers of high ability have discussed its social, economic, and educational bearing. In short, we have had almost all of the possible accompaniments of a system of industrial education except industrial schools; and doubtless we shall have a plentiful supply of these in the very near future.

There are, in the United States, about one hundred and fifty schools of secondary grade which may properly be designated manual-training or industrial-training schools. Of this number, thirty are public high schools and are known variously as manual-training high schools, technical high schools, and mechanic-arts high schools. Most of them give from five to nine hours a week to manual, technical, and industrial instruction. Some give as little as four hours, and a few as much as twelve hours a week to such instruction. Six of the thirty schools report that they give all of their time to technical, industrial, and trade instruction; which indicates that these schools may be dealing in a serious way with genuine vocational problems and may be called industrial schools in the sense attached to that term in current discussion. In general, however, it may be said that high schools of the manual-training type are dominated by the same purpose that controls ordinary high schools and that this purpose is distinctly not vocational, unless we include attendance upon college among the vocations. It may confidently be asserted, furthermore, that with the exception of the new Cleveland high school and possibly one other, there does not exist today in the United States a public secondary school that with strict accuracy should be termed a technical high school.

Of the thirteen hundred city-school systems in the United States, almost exactly one-half have introduced, somewhere in their curricula, various forms of constructive activity known as handwork or manual training. In about one hundred and fifty of these cases handwork extends through all of the grades of the elementary school, and in about one hundred cases it is given in the high schools. In some cases handwork is given in the kindergarten only; and between this extreme and the other extreme of manual training in every grade, there are all possible differences in practice.

While on the whole, the manual-training movement has had a salutary effect in directing attention to the right relation between theory and practice in education, it is nevertheless true that handwork in the schools is still mainly abstract, isolated, impractical, and unsocial in character. It is very largely lacking in rational content and therefore in educational worth. As "busy work" and relaxation, it no doubt performs a function of some value. The very name "manual training," however, is suggestive of a discredited psychology. With a few gratifying exceptions, handwork is a fungus growth on an otherwise ill-proportioned and misshapen curriculum that needs not so much to be pruned and trained as to be uprooted and replaced by a more vigorous and more productive plant.

To put the matter positively, the great educational need at this point is for us to recognize in our practice what many of us profess to accept in theory: that constructive handwork is an indispensable means of developing intelligent ideas, sympathetic appreciation, and executive efficiency in relation to the industrial side of human society. "Manual training," in other words, should be replaced by intelligent study of the constructive, industrial factors of social progress.

It should be noted that the kind of study here proposed might as properly be termed "industrial education," as the training for skill in industrial vocations that is everywhere now being so vigorously demanded. It may indeed be doubted whether without a basis such as that suggested, industrial education can be saved from the isolation, the unsocial, and even anti-social tendencies with which the present curricula have been charged.

A few weeks ago, I was inspecting one of the largest manufacturing establishments in New York state, which had recently organized a school for apprentices; provided it with a thoroughly modern equipment; and placed in charge a well-educated man of high ideals and practical ability. Here, I thought, I had found an enterprise that might have something to teach the schools concerning their effort to meet concrete social needs. The master-mechanic to whose initiative this school was due told me, however, that he had serious doubt as to the practical value of his apprentice school. He thought he would direct the teacher to use the machines for demonstration purposes only, as the boys spent too much time "figuring out how to get a piece of work set up and how to get the thing done." "These boys," he said, "will work all their lives for our company and we want them to do things our way. We don't want the boys to draw; we want them to read drawings. We don't want them to figure; we want them to read figures. We don't want them to boss; we want them to be bossed." And he might have added, we don't want them to think but to become automatic machines.

The objection of this master-mechanic was to any system of training that develops initiative and independence. While his view is certainly not that of the most far-sighted manufacturers who are joining in the cry for industrial education, his attitude does represent a somewhat common tendency to regard industrial efficiency as the sole standard by which to measure the value of industrial education. There is need for a resolute stand against every attempt to exploit the efficiency of the rank and file in the interest of private greed. Education must never lend itself to any movement that ignores the fundamental truth that to make a life is of greater consequence than to make a living. By every proper means, education must seek to rectify the standards of industry itself and to promote a genuinely social consciousness among our people.

The ideals of industrial, as of all other forms of education, can be stated then only in terms of social intelligence, social appreciation, and social service. Any attempt to isolate completely the problems of industrial education must accordingly fail; for society is essentially organic and every truly social problem is shot through with a thousand threads of social complexity. In all of its essential qualities therefore, industrial education, in common with education of every other type, must conform to the great underlying needs of men and women composing a human society.

To say that industrial education introduces no fundamentally new principles, and that every important principle applicable to industrial education applies also to education in all of its aspects, is not however to overlook the necessity of working out in detail the application of such principles to the peculiar requirements of those boys and girls who are looking toward industrial vocations. A few general ideas will here be suggested which should help us to keep our bearings in making this application.

First, it is important that we make a clear distinction between elementary and secondary education. Neither in our thought nor in our practice have we thus far drawn this distinction with sufficient clearness, but have merely assumed that during the period of early adolescence the minds of boys and girls are sufficiently "mature" to warrant them in entering upon the study of Latin, algebra, geometry, and the various other subjects prescribed for admission to American colleges. From this point of view, elementary education is that uniform régime imposed upon all boys and girls who have not yet entered upon a college-preparatory course. I am sometimes disposed to think that if we had the courage to face the truth we should be compelled to admit that the present function of the elementary school is to eliminate 65 per cent. of its pupils so that the secondary schools shall not be overcrowded; and that the function of the latter, including the manual-training high schools, is to eliminate all of the residue who do not readily run into the mold handed out by the colleges.

I would propose the following as a rational as opposed to a purely formal distinction between elementary and secondary education. In the early stages of mental and social development, the similarities of children, for educational purposes, are more significant than their dissimilarities. This is the period of elementary education, when children may properly participate in a relatively uniform régime. When differences in taste, capacities, and ambitions become more significant for education than likenesses, whatever may be the arbitrary and external organization of education, the secondary stage in the development of boys and girls has *de facto* begun. Obviously this period begins at a much earlier point than is recognized in our present educational practice. The difference between elementary and secondary development is thus primarily a matter of mental and moral variation; not a mere matter of convenient arrangement. Differences in abilities and in interests will always demand corresponding variations in form of activity. If we persist in our inexcusable failure to provide such variations during the last years of our so-called elementary course, when individual differences appear with unmistakable and increasing force, we may expect boys and girls to continue as they now do to seek in the more tolerable occupations of street, factory, shop, office, and mercantile house, the kind of interests for which they feel an instinctive though vaguely defined need.

It should be clear, then, that industrial education is properly but one constituent of an organic *system* of secondary education. Like the various other members of such a system, industrial schools should be designed to meet the specific needs of a well-defined group of children who, by reason of common interests, common capacities, and common opportunities, are looking toward a common vocation.

In the current discussion of industrial education, it is surprising that no more strenuous protest has been made against the early specialization that is clearly involved in the proposed programme. At the risk of seeming to set up a man of straw, we shall notice very briefly some important considerations in this connection.

The arguments against "early specialization" were first brought forward with great vehemence in the discussion of the "elective system" in colleges that loomed up so large on the educational horizon a generation ago. They next appeared in the debate concerning the introduction of elective courses into our high schools. While the ultimate outcome of this later contest is no longer doubtful, the voice of protest has not yet been altogether quieted. The old familiar arguments are still urged against wider opportunity and greater freedom for pupils in high schools. We may expect these same arguments to be directed in turn against every effort to extend the elective system backward to the logical beginning of the secondary stage of education.

The outcome of the struggle between rigid prescription and free election must eventually be the same in all three of these fields; for the conflict is really one and not three. The question is whether human beings who differ widely in native gifts and acquired tendencies shall be forced to pursue a single conventional course of training, or have the privilege of choosing a course that will equip them not only for the worthy use of their leisure but for the intelligent pursuit of their vocations. Life itself is from the beginning an elective process—each individual selecting from the complex whole of experience those elements that accord with his native and acquired interests, and rejecting those elements that serve no useful purpose in his life.

In a very real sense then, it is a condition and not a theory that confronts us; for an elective system is already firmly established even in our elementary education. One of the alternatives open to a pupil is to continue in the single course offered by the schools; the other is to withdraw from school and, without adequate preparation, to enter at once upon some low-grade vocational pursuit that offers little educational advantage and a meager wage. The question is not, therefore, whether we shall extend the privilege of election to pupils now in the elementary schools; but whether, by introducing courses for industrial and domestic training within the school, we shall widen the field within which election may be made.

A rational system of secondary education, furthermore, must provide not only for the training of special capacities but for making children conscious of their individual abilities. One of the most serious weaknesses of the present organization of education is that the range of experience provided for in the schools is so narrow that many of the latent powers of children are not stimulated to activity. In order that a child may be placed in position to make proper choice of a school course and ultimately of a vocation, it is often essential that means be taken to ascertain what are his native capacities upon which success in every undertaking must very largely depend. These capacities cannot always be determined with reference merely to the desires of parents and of pupils or to such general advice as teachers and principals of schools are commonly qualified to give. Teachers must be equipped to recognize, to search for, and to interpret the evidences of special aptitude. This will necessitate a fuller recognition than is now given to the influence of heredity upon mental and moral traits, and a more vital and practical view of genetic psychology than is yet widely prevalent.

To summarize briefly, then, we have evidences of a widespread and almost unprecedented demand for industrial education; and this demand is but one aspect of the educational unrest that is now so widely felt. While manual training has done much to vitalize the educational thought of the country, it is still largely isolated and unsocial in practice and should be replaced by a more intelligent study of the industrial element in social life. There is a noticeable tendency to set up industrial efficiency as the final standard and to look upon industrial education as a means of exploiting this efficiency in the interest of the private gain of employers of labor. Such tendencies must be steadily resisted by leaders in education.

Industrial education properly constitutes an organic part of a rational system of secondary education which should meet the specific needs of various groups of children who, on account of differing tastes and capacities, must look toward widely different vocations. Such a system will make it necessary for children, with the guidance of parents and teachers, to make choice of a career at a much earlier age than is now regarded by many as prudent. Even under existing conditions, however, children are obliged to choose between continuing in the uniform course provided by the elementary school, and entering upon vocational pursuits without adequate preparation. One of the main functions of secondary education should be to make children aware of their special aptitudes and thus to make it possible for them to choose wisely the vocations for which by nature they are best adapted.

The whole argument for vocational training is of course open to the familiar charge that it is basely utilitarian. As to the charge that it is utilitarian, why should not the answer be what the common law terms "confession and avoidance"? Such training *is* utilitarian; but why *basely* so? Most men devote more than half of their waking hours to their vocations. Are their lives necessarily on that account basely utilitarian? Our war for independence had its origin in a question of taxation.

Was it for that reason a basely utilitarian struggle for selfish ends? Almost every great national policy involves some matter of industry or commerce. Is our national life therefore unworthy of our loyal affection? The intellectual and moral progress of the race has always been in large measure dependent upon material and commercial prosperity. Are the achievements of the human spirit on that account insignificant or base? As a people we profess a belief in the dignity of work. Shall we hesitate to exemplify our belief by making it possible for every man to find his work and in his work to find a worthy means of enlarging and completing his life?

MEDICAL INSPECTION IN ENGLISH PRIMARY SCHOOLS

HERBERT LEATHER
Manchester, England

Portents are not lacking which augur a complete revolution of the system which governs the primary schools of England.

When the industrial revolution of the eighteenth century hurled down the ancient supremacy of the manual crafts, reducing the sturdy workers of England to dependence upon the whirling machinery of the factory or workshop their position was analogous to that of a man who enters life with capital intact. The markets of the world were open to their products; the physical capacity of the workers to produce was boundless; work was plentiful. Yeoman farmers, no longer able to coax subsistence from the soil, sold their holdings and rushed to the centers of industry; the fishermen of Cornwall and Devon with their families flocked to the towns of Lancashire and Yorkshire where work at fabulous wages could be secured in abundance. Even the children could earn, untrammeled by inconvenient restrictions; and the nation spent recklessly of its inherited physical capital.

Then followed that period of commercial expansion the like of which has only been equaled in the development of the New World. The desolate wastes of the North became busy hives of industry; first the factory, then the houses, then the towns.

Coal fields, iron foundries, ship-building yards sprang up as though by magic; canals, new roads, and railways quickly connected the various centers, so that whole districts became in effect large towns. Fortunes were made freely, and if lives were lost among the busy wheels of industrial strife, if the young and helpless went down, if the workers began to age prematurely and to become marked with the deep-scored lines which stamp an impress upon the third and fourth generations, what mattered it so long as fresh supplies of bone and muscle rushed eagerly in from the country?

When improved methods of work were required there sprang up a demand for education which resulted in the passage of the act of 1870. That the perspective of its framers was limited almost solely to the training of the mind, ignoring the problem of physical development, was unfortunate; that the stage of mental development should be assessed and paid for, after the manner of the buyer in a great cotton or woolen concern, was a calamity the consequences of which are yet being bitterly felt.

Despite high rates of wages and the wider knowledge of healthy conditions of living which prevail today as compared with those of yesterday nearly all the great centers of population are faced with the presence of large numbers of unemployable men. While the workhouses are full, 5 per cent. of the present population being paupers, lunacy is increasing at an appalling rate. The terrible effects of town life are illustrated by the significant fact that the percentage of pauperism in London exceeds seven; and that such things should be in face of the enormous number of charitable organizations which are actively at work indicates the gravity of the problem which confronts the English nation.

Of the various social questions having for their object the elimination of physical deterioration the educationist is naturally chiefly interested in those which concern the welfare of the child.

Since the abolition of the system of payment by results, increasing attention has been paid by the Board of Education to the policy of improving the physical development of school children, especially in recent years. Provision must now be made in all school time-tables for a recreation interval during morning and afternoon sessions; in infant schools this interval may be prolonged, and lessons in all departments must be so arranged as to avoid any risk of undue fatigue in the pupils.

For very many years an elaborate system of military drill was encouraged in the schools, and this has recently been elaborated into a scheme more consonant with modern ideas of physical development. Every primary-school pupil is now taught to breathe correctly, and, if the existing scheme be persisted in, there should in time be a considerable diminution in the number of mouth-breathing children.

The inspectors of the Board have effected vast changes in the structural arrangements of schools by means of recommendations to managers in their annual reports; many schools which are condemned today would have been regarded as thoroughly satisfactory only a few years ago.

The splendid work of the inspectors in this department has been so gradually wrought that it is frequently overlooked altogether by prominent educationists. Not only is the practical hygiene of the school strictly supervised, but courses of well-graded instruction in personal hygiene are organized for the benefit of the pupils in attendance. There is, too, the provision in the Primary-School Code which sanctions gardening as an ordinary subject of the curriculum, and one which is being widely taken up in suburban and rural schools. Outdoor teaching is also sanctioned when suitable schemes are submitted by teachers, in all schools. The Board's encouragement of outdoor teaching has recently been extended by the inclusion of organized games in the general curriculum. The teaching of special subjects, as manual work for boys, and cookery and laundry work for girls, is also recognized by the Board by the payment of special grants.

It would appear therefore that the policy of the Board of Education, as distinct from that of the general government, is strongly in favor of securing sound physical development among the children in so far as this may be secured without interfering with the purely educational work of the schools—*vide Suggestions to Educationists:* "The duty of safeguarding the health of children of school age is only in a limited degree a duty of the school."

Had the present policy of the Board been inaugurated with the introduction of the industrial revolution it is possible that the problem of physical degeneracy would not have arisen in its present urgent form. The terrible tales told by the recruiting returns of disease and low vitality, in conjunction with a steady and alarming decrease in the national birth rate, have caused serious disquiet among all active workers on public administrative bodies. Earnest educationists have brought forward the whole question as it concerns the rising generation. "Begin with the child," they argue; "once given a fair start he will attain sound physical development and perform his share in the world's work."

In the last annual report of the London Education Committee it was pointed out that a process of selection had been introduced by the establishment of special schools for defective children. The process was carried out under the supervision of skilled medical advice and for the first time there was systematic medical inspection of a section of primary-school children. In order adequately to assess the value of the special work of schools, a medical specialist was appointed by the Board of Education. It was soon ascertained that children classed as defective were of many types; there were those so closely related to idiocy that while they could derive no benefit from the ordinary curriculum of special schools they greatly impeded the progress of those who could. For such cases the policy of permanent segregation under healthy conditions is being actively advocated. Other defectives were discovered to be of the epileptic class, and for these also separate schools are advised. Mental defect was often found to be the result of parental neglect or ignorance, and after simple surgical treatment was administered the defect gradually disappeared.

When medical officers were more generally appointed by the progressive educational areas for the purpose of inspecting cases for special schools it was discovered that the physical condition of school children throughout the country was marked in many respects by grave weakness; and in order that all the children under their control might be subjected to medical examination, additional doctors were appointed. As a result it became a statutory obligation on education committees to provide medical inspection for *all* children, on and after January 1, 1908. Many education committees as yet have not decided to take up the question thoroughly on grounds of expense, although children who suffer from grave defects of sight and hearing, if neglected, usually develop into the unemployable men and women whose ultimate destination is the poorhouse; so that the cost of initial neglect falls very heavily upon the general community.

It may prove interesting to record the experience of some of the pioneer education authorities in the field of medical inspection of school children.

One of the most comprehensive schemes is that drawn up by the committee of the Govan School Board. Ten medical officers are employed and the average number of children under the charge of each is about 3,000. The duties of officers are to advise the Board as to the ventilation, heating, lighting, and cleanliness of the schools; to inspect periodically all school lavatories and sanitary arrangements and to report to the headmaster any defects discovered; on receiving notice of an outbreak of infectious disease among the pupils attending any school the officers are to inquire and take such action as may be necessary to prevent infection, for which purpose they must co-operate with the Medical Officer of Health for the district; special schools and classes are to be reported on twice a year and the officers are to give the necessary certificates of admission to defective children seeking entry to such schools. They are to examine all scholars on admission and twice thereafter during their school life, and for the purpose of these examinations the schools are to be visited as often as may be necessary, but at least once a fortnight; they are to make reports on children submitted for examination by headmasters and to give such directions as may be required; they are to supervise such systematic measurements of heights and weights as the Board shall approve, inspect the physical exercises given in the schools, and medically examine candidates appointed to positions under the Board; finally they are by lecture, demonstration, or otherwise to instruct teachers in the methods of recognizing the common ailments and defects of school children, in the practice of first aid for school accidents, in the general hygiene of the school, and in the physiological principles that underlie physical training.

The teachers render assistance to the medical officers in filling up those parts of the Health Schedule, one of which is filled up for each child examined, relating to height, weight, chest measurement, etc. When a child is found to be suffering from any disease or defect, the medical officer informs the parent of the nature of the malady and urges upon him the necessity of placing the child under the care of a doctor. Medical or surgical treatment is no part of the medical officer's duty.

Although the School Board of Glasgow has not yet made arrangements for the medical inspection of all the children attending its schools the services of four special doctors have been employed for (1) testing the eyesight of the children, (2) examining scholars for admission to special schools, (3) examining the blind and the deaf mutes, (4) examining scholars for admission to physically defective classes, and for visiting and reporting on children who are absent from school on account of illness.

Under the supervision of Dr. Wright Thomson the eyesight of 52,493 children was recently tested, of whom 18,565 or 35 per cent. were found to be below the normal standard, and 11,209 or 21 per cent. had ocular defects. The proportion of these cases was highest in the poor and closely built districts and in old schools, and was lowest in the better-class schools and in those near the city outskirts. Dr. Thomson points out that defective vision, apart from ocular defect, seems to be due to want of training of the eyes for distant objects and partly to exhaustion of the eyes induced by working in a bad light. He strongly advises teachers to train the eyes of children for long vision by the introduction of competitive games involving the recognition of small objects at a distance of 20 feet or more.

The Manchester Education Committee has for many years taken an active interest in the treatment of backward and defective children. In addition to several special schools staffed by teachers possessing the highest educational qualifications, a residential school for cripples has been established in a spacious mansion surrounded by wide stretches of well-wooded country at Swinton. Here the children are nursed back to health, and during the process they receive instruction under ideal conditions.

On suitable days the pupils are taught on the lawn or in the shady spots which abound.

Mention must also be made of the summer school worked by the same authority. This institution is situated at Mobberley in the open country; and during the spring, summer, and autumn months, boys and girls from Manchester schools visit the country for a fortnight in charge of their teacher. Instruction of a suitable nature is given and there are long walks into the surrounding country. The parents of the visiting scholars contribute toward the expense of the visit and the success of the experiment has been so pronounced that the country school is now regarded as a permanent educational asset.

Quite recently several additional medical officers have been appointed to Manchester schools and the work of medical inspection is about to be organized upon a thoroughly comprehensive plan. Many of the more serious cases of mental defect and epilepsy in Manchester are transferred to the permanent home for the feeble-minded at Warford Hall, and the David Lewis Colony for Epileptics.

In Liverpool where the work of medical inspection is in the experimental stage there are three doctors for 133,000 children at the present time, but only children recently admitted, those about to leave school, and special cases are medically examined.

The Birmingham authorities have appointed three doctors with nurses to assist in the weighing, measuring, etc., of the children. There is a thorough medical examination with a high standard, equal to that adopted by the best insurance companies. A file index of all cases requiring supervision is kept for reference.

The splendid work done by Dr. James Kerr and his colleagues in the London County Council schools is only slightly indicated in the last report[1] which is worthy of deep study from every educationist. In clear statistical form, the various ills from which school children suffer are set forth. For example it was discovered that only 20 of 700 infants examined had sound teeth;

[1] *London County Council, Minutes of Proceedings* (No. 33), December, 1908. London: P. S. King & Son, Gt. Smith St., Westminster, S. W. $0.06.

in two secondary schools 62 per cent. of the pupils had two or more defective teeth, and in the training colleges 43 per cent. were returned as having dental defects. The urgency of prompt remedial treatment is illustrated by the statement that if the dental cases alone were taken in hand all the hospitals in London could not provide for one-tenth of the afflicted children, and a similar lack of accommodation is shown for the treatment of eye and ear defects. For absence from school attendance through ringworm alone, £5,650 is lost annually in grants.

The whole report was submitted to a special subcommittee for further consideration with the result that the London County Council Education Committee has now recommended the establishment of school clinics where common diseases of the eye, ear, teeth, and skin may receive immediate medical treatment; and convenient centers are about to be erected.

In this respect London has given a notable lead to the rest of the country, for the introduction of school clinics can scarcely fail to mark an epoch in educational progress. For in England, after generations of aimless wandering in the wilderness of social and industrial conflict, it would appear at last to be clearly established that all national progress and educational vitality are dependent upon the physical fitness of the nation's children.

A LANGUAGE-EXERCISE IN DRAMATIZATION

EMMA SIEBEL

No material presented for a language-exercise and no form of language-work has awakened in the children a more intense interest or provoked them to greater effort than have the stories of the gods and the Trojan war, and especially the writing of the play which follows.

The exercise is classwork, and all the children are represented, some contributing more than others; all, however, working with earnestness and each doing his part.

There was quite a heated discussion as to the subject to be chosen—some favoring the "Wedding Feast," others contending that that would be too simple, that it would only necessitate allowing the characters to say "in their own words" what the story had told them. They wished to "make up" their play, and the suggestion that we write on "Laomedon's Broken Promises," that being a story from which "a good lesson could be learned," carried the day. I had some misgivings as to the outcome, but would not discourage their enthusiastic effort.

The story of Cinderella, so familiar to all, was acted out to give them the "play-idea" and to familiarize them with the terms "exit," "enter," "act," "scene," "speech," "action," etc. We then spent one lesson "practicing," as they said, "the language of the gods," and another in changing sentences, "to make them sound more poetical."

The suggestion to substitute "Persons of the Play" for "Cast of Characters" came from a little girl who thought that "we are only children, and we want it to be all our own." They then selected the characters needed, deciding that we could easily add others should we have need of them.

They wished to know why Neptune and Apollo had been banished to earth, and when the stories had been told them, they unanimously decided that Mt. Olympus with its "golden palaces," and Jupiter in the act of banishing the offending gods would be a beautiful and effective scene with which to open the play. In this scene there was quite a difference of opinion as to Apollo's entering with "bowed head," some insisting that he would feel that his offense against Jupiter was justified. It was finally decided, however, to let him enter in this way, as, being sc beautiful, it would "make every one feel sorry for him." "He should go out," said one, "playing the lyre, as he is the god of music." "Oh, no," said another, "do you think he would feel like playing?" "Then," suggested a third, "let us say, 'softly playing the lyre,' as soft, sad music would express his grief for his son and sadness because he had to leave Olympus."

The second scene, they decided, must be the meeting of Neptune and Laomedon, as the audience must hear Laomedon make the promise which he afterward breaks.

The mountain-side with Neptune at work was the best suggestion offered for scene iii, and it immediately found favor. They were quick to see that it would offer an opportunity to show in Neptune's first speech that he was sorry for what he had done, and that "we must always pay in some way when we are not satisfied with what we have." This scene afforded them great pleasure, and they made special effort to have the language "poetical" as there were "no mortals, only gods speaking."

There was no difference of opinion as to scene iv; all agreed that it must represent the completed walls and the Scaean Gate. "That," thought one of the boys, "will be a beautiful scene, and a good place for Laomedon and the gods to meet, when they ask for their reward." Some thought that Laomedon might really have felt that Neptune did not deserve the reward as he had been helped by Apollo, but the great majority scornfully rejected this, insisting that "when anyone has made a promise, it must be kept, there must be no excuses." All thought, however, that Laomedon must have feared to refuse the god outright, and that "people of that kind always do try to make excuses."

Act II, scene i, was the most difficult part of the work. The first part of it was developed in this way:

"What shall be our next scene?"

"It should show the sea-shore, a crowd of people and Laomedon's daughter ready for the sacrifice."

"Why should this be represented?"

"It will be a beautiful scene." "I think it will show the Trojans how Laomedon is to be punished." "It will be the best place to let Laomedon make his promise to Hercules."

"Would what happens in this scene follow shortly after what happened in the last?"

"No, this would be years after."

"How do you know this?"

"The story tells us that the monster devoured one maiden a year, and that at last the lot fell on Hesione, Laomedon's beautiful daughter."

"How will the audience know this, since they do not know the story?"

"We will say at the beginning of the scene, 'Some years after' (later)."

"What division can we make here, then, in the play?"

"This can be the beginning of the second act."

"Who will be the persons in this scene?"

"Laomedon, because he will want to be near his daughter to save her if he can." "Hesione must be there." "There must be many people, because all the Trojans know of it." "The dragon must be there, too."

"Why will you have the dragon?"

"He must come up from the sea to devour the maiden."

"Would you like to see this?"

"Oh, no!"

"Would the audience enjoy it?"

"I think not, but how would they know about the dragon if they do not see him?"

"Who can tell us what to do?"

"We can have him behind the curtain, or only pretend to have him, and some one can tell the audience."

"Will the player tell it to the audience?"

"No, people on the stage only talk to one another."

"To whom can the story be told—to one of the Trojans?"

"No, they all know of it." "It must be told to a stranger."

"Will it be a stranger from one of the places near Troy?"

"No, he should come from a far-away country."

"Who, then, must be added to this scene and to the 'Persons of the Play?'"

"We must take away the dragon and put in the stranger."

"Will merely the word 'stranger' do?"

"I think it would sound well to say, 'A stranger from a foreign shore.'"

"The stranger" was accordingly added, and the "dragon" regretfully dropped. Having overcome this difficulty, the "Trojan's" story was easily composed, and the climax of the scene, "Honor to great Hercules," etc., gave great satisfaction.

In Act II, scene ii, the sympathy of some went out to Laomedon. They thought he would really have cause to fear Jupiter's anger were he to give up the steeds, and suggested that Hesione's hand might be offered to Hercules as a fitting reward.

Act II, scene iii, again presented the problem of telling the audience of a harrowing scene which could not be presented. They had learned to solve the problem, however, and the suggestion was soon offered to let servants running from the palace call to passing Trojans, who, of course, would not know what events were taking place in the castle.

The concluding lines of this scene were their supreme effort; they were determined that the last lines should be "poetry," and many and varied were the suggestions and criticisms made before this last difficulty was overcome.

The completed task was a source of great pride to the class, *all* feeling that they had worked faithfully and well. The fact that it had served to bring out the powers of the less able pupils was evidenced when one, whose work had always been below the average and whose interest, during one of the lessons, seemed centered in something upon his desk, brought up, when reprimanded for inattention, the lines:

> And I, the god of the silver bow,
> Will help thee, if thou so dost wish—

adding that he "might have gotten the other two lines," had he been left undisturbed.

LAOMEDON'S BROKEN PROMISES, OR THE REVENGE OF THE GODS

A PLAY IN TWO ACTS

Written by the pupils of the Fifth Grade (Room 1), Twenty-Seventh District School, Cincinnati, Ohio

PERSONS OF THE PLAY

Laomedon, ... King of Troy
Neptune, ... God of the Sea
Podarces, ... Son of Laomedon
Hesione, ... Daughter of Laomedon
Jupiter, ... Father of Gods
Apollo, ... God of Music, Sun, and Poetry
Hercules, ... A Hero
A Trojan.
A Stranger.
Followers of Hercules, Servants, Trojans.

ACT I—Scene 1

Mt. Olympus—Palace of Jupiter (Jupiter seated on his throne), Neptune.

Jupiter: Thou hast tried to dethrone me, exalt thyself, and rob me of my throne and power.

Neptune: Nay, not so, great Jupiter.

Jupiter: How darest thou dispute what I and all the gods well know! Thou shalt now pay the penalty for this offense by serving a mortal, King of Troy, for one long year. (*Rises.*) Go, now, and do my bidding and come not again into my presence until thy task is completed or I will deprive thee of thy power. (*Exit Neptune, enter Apollo, with bowed head.*)

Jupiter: Knowest thou, Apollo, why I have brought thee here?

Apollo: Aye, great Jupiter, I know that I have displeased and angered thee, but grief for my beloved son has almost maddened me.

Jupiter: Thy sorrow gave thee no right to injure another. For this deed I now banish thee from Mt. Olympus and the presence of the gods to serve for a time a mortal, King Admetus. (*Exit Apollo, softly playing his lyre.*)

Apollo: Farewell to Mt. Olympus and its palaces of gold,
My chariot and its fiery steeds I now no more behold,
I see no more Aurora, fair goddess of the morn.
Once happy as the other gods, but now I am forlorn.

(*Curtain.*)

Scene 2

The beautiful city of Troy. (Laomedon driving slowly along in his chariot. Enter Neptune, who steps up to the chariot.)

Laomedon: Who art thou, who darest to step so boldly up to my chariot?

Neptune: Thou knowest me not, oh, King; I am Neptune, great god of the sea. I have displeased Jupiter, our great father, and he, as punishment, has banished me from Mt. Olympus to serve thee for a year. What task shall I perform for thee?

Laomedon: Oh, great Neptune, I have long wished for walls to surround and protect my beautiful city. For mortals this would be a task of many years; but if thou wilt fulfil my desire I promise thee rich rewards.

Neptune: Be it so, Laomedon, thy wish shall be granted; soon strong walls will protect thy city. (*Curtain.*)

Scene 3

A mountain-side. City of Troy in the distance. (Neptune at the task of tearing a heavy stone from the mountain-side—sighing as he works.)

Neptune: This task seems endless! Oh, were it but completed! Had I been satisfied with the power given me and not displeased great Jupiter

I might even now be in the banquet halls of the gods, feasting on ambrosia and nectar. (*Stops suddenly, listening intently.*) What heavenly sounds do I hear? The strains seem to herald the approach of Apollo. They seem to soothe my weary spirit. (*Looks eagerly in the direction from which the sounds come. Enter Apollo, playing his lyre. He slowly approaches.*)

Apollo: Greetings to thee, Neptune. Why do I see thee at this heavy task?

Neptune: I return thy greetings, fair Apollo. Thy beautiful melody comforts and cheers me. Thou knowest well that I was banished from Olympus to serve for a year the mortal, King Laomedon. To build walls around his city is the task he has set for me. It is an endless one, but rich rewards await me when it is completed.

Apollo: Knowest thou that I, too, was banished from Olympus and sent to serve Admetus, King of Thessaly? My task is finished and gladly will I help thee at thy heavy labor.

And I, the god of the silver bow,
Will help thee if thou so desire,
I can so charm the stones, in row,
They will dance to the strains of my lyre.

Neptune: Oh, Apollo, to show my gratitude to thee, thou shalt receive a portion of the rich rewards that await me, for,

I cannot enough my gratitude show,
Beautiful god of the silver bow. (*Curtain.*)

Scene 4

Walls of Troy, showing the Scaean Gate. (*Laomedon and his attendants driving out of the Scaean Gate, admiring the walls.*)

Laomedon: What a grand structure! Such beautiful walls no mortal could have built. I now defy my strongest and fiercest enemy. My greatest foes must yield to me. (*Enter Neptune and Apollo.*) Lo! here come Neptune and Apollo. (*Salutes the gods.*) Greetings to ye, fair and noble gods. Your work has been well done and ye shall be my honored and welcome guests until the wrath of Jupiter is appeased.

Neptune: For thy offered hospitality we thank thee, but if thou wilt grant us the promised reward we will gladly depart.

Laomedon: When I made my promise to thee it was to be a reward for heavy labor. Thy work has been lightened by Apollo. Ye gods have all that can be desired; what can you want from a mortal? Beside, were ye not sent by Jupiter to serve me? Would not his wrath fall upon me were I to reward thee for a task done at his bidding?

Neptune: King of Troy, I see that thy word is not sacred to thee. As a god I will not dispute with thee, but thou shalt feel my wrath and power. (*Curtain.*)

ACT II—Scene 1

Some years later. Sea-shore. Laomedon's daughter ready to be sacrificed. Laomedon, soldiers, and people of Troy. Stranger from a foreign shore.

Stranger (to one of the Trojans): What mean this great gathering of sorrowing people and this beautiful maiden ready for the sacrifice?

Trojan: Knowest thou not of the dreadful sacrifice we must make every year?

Stranger: Is it a sacrifice demanded by the gods?

Trojan: Aye, stranger, and one that each year brings a great burden of sorrow to some one. Laomedon, our king, once broke a promise to the gods. For this Neptune sent up from the sea a great monster who devoured many of our people. In great fear and distress we fled to the temple, where the oracle announced that the monster would be satisfied to devour one maiden each year. To this we agreed. Each year one of our beautiful maidens has been delivered to this dreadful sea-serpent, and now the lot has fallen on beautiful Hesione, daughter of Laomedon. The king, in great sorrow, has sent out heralds to proclaim to the people that a great reward awaits the one who will slay the monster and save Hesione. (*Confusion among the people.*) But see! It is too late! Even now they are chaining Hesione to the rock and none has come to her rescue. But, lo! who comes here in such haste? Let us press forward and see. (*Enter Hercules, breathing hard. Steps up to Laomedon.*)

Hercules: Laomedon, great King of Troy, I have heard through thy heralds of thy daughter's great peril. Grant me the four immortal steeds received from King Tros and the monster shall be slain and thy daughter saved.

Laomedon: The steeds shall be yours! Save my daughter! (*Breathless silence for a few moments. Then a great cheer arises from the throng.*)

People: Honor to great Hercules! Hesione is saved! The monster is slain! (*Curtain.*)

Scene 2

Court of Laomedon's castle. Laomedon and attendants. Hercules.

Laomedon: Thou hast the monster braved,
And my daughter, Hesione, thou hast saved.
Thou art great, a hero grand,
Would I could give thee Hesione's hand.

Hercules: For the great honor thou art willing to bestow upon me I thank thee, but the immortal steeds thou didst promise me will be a rich enough reward.

Laomedon: My anxiety for my beloved daughter was so great that it made me give a hasty promise. The horses were a gift from great Jupiter to my grandfather Tros, and I would have cause to fear the wrath of the Father of Gods were I to part with them.

Podarces: Oh, my father, if thou didst make this promise thou shouldst fulfil it.

Laomedon: No son of mine need give me advice.

Hercules: Thou hast broken thy word to me.
As to Neptune, great god of the sea,
And if the wrath of Jupiter thou dost fear,
Thy broken promise to me shall cost thee dear.

(*Curtain.*)

Scene 3

Courtyard of Laomedon's castle. (Hercules and his followers entering the castle.) Podarces, Hesione, several servants. (Cries of distress coming from the castle. Servants fleeing from the castle.)

First Servant: Our king, Laomedon, is dead!

Second Servant: Where shall we flee for safety! Hercules in his anger has slain our noble king and all the royal family.

Trojans: To the rescue! Our king and the princes are being cruelly slain! (*Trojans press into the courtyard. Hercules appears at the castle gate with Podarces and Hesione.*) Back, Trojans! It is the great hero, Hercules.

Hercules: Trojans, ye have heard what has happened. So must all pay the penalty who break a promise to the gods. Podarces I have saved as he appealed to Laomedon to keep faith with me.

Podarces: Oh, great Hercules, what shall be our fate?

Hercules: Hesione shall remain, but thou Podarces, must leave with me. (*Hesione weeps, and kneels at Hercules' feet.*)

Hesione: Oh, Hercules, wouldst thou but hearken to my prayer to take me and leave my brother, Podarces, to rule over our beloved city of Troy.

Hercules: Thy prayer would e'en please the gods above,
As "Priam" bought back by a sister's love;
Thy brother, Podarces, here shall remain
And over the home of his fathers shall reign.

(*Curtain.*)

THE SEVENTH TO TENTH GRADES A UNIT IN MATHEMATICS

R. L. SHORT
Technical High School, Cleveland, Ohio

Since this paper is intended for educators interested in public-school work, it may be proper first to define the topic. This may be done best by giving an explanation of present conditions in our elementary and secondary courses.

The present course is: 7th and 8th grades, 1 unit; 9th grade, 1 unit; 10th grade, 1 unit. The paper is written to call attention to the defects of the course as now given and to raise the question: How may these defects be remedied?

For the past five years mathematics associations have taken up the cry for better mathematics teaching. A Professor Perry of England offered the first remedy by suggesting the teaching of physics and chemistry in algebra and the use of many measurements and experiments in the mathematics class. As a result, the disciples of this movement went up and down the land demanding correlation. But where are those disciples? You can't find them now. There was a fundamental error in the scheme. The material given the pupil to *use* in mathematics was beyond him, often beyond his comprehension. The result was, the student was so confused by the mass of new facts and new surroundings that he got no science and no mathematics.

We all teach some physics notions—it's the fashion—and a little such is well. But the teacher who tries to lead his pupil to discover and develop physics laws which cost the life-endeavor of some of the greatest intellects this world has known and to discover the equations governing those laws, certainly harms the pupil, the subject, and the cause of education.

There is a relation, a simple one, one that is easily within the grasp of every pupil, that has been entirely overlooked. With Professor Perry, I firmly believe that mathematics should not be set off in compartments. However, I am of the opinion that the articulation must be made with *known subjects* rather than with *unknown subjects*.

In the grammar school we teach arithmetic—just arithmetic—such as has been taught in grades IV and V. So far as my observation goes there is little or no thought-work done, no development of principles, no application made. In the ninth grade we teach algebra—just algebra. No application is made; the arithmetic does not help the algebra nor does the algebra help the arithmetic; geometry is not anticipated. In grade X we teach geometry. Little or no use of algebra is made, the equation is neglected, and pure reason introduced. Arithmetic is too far in the past to get even a hearing.

Such teaching during these four years is, to my mind, sheer waste of time. A few illustrations may strengthen the assertion. Your seventh-grade pupil, eighth-grade pupil, ninth-grade pupil, tenth-grade pupil knows nothing of the constitution of number, of the relation of numbers, of the use of number. He knows a few combinations of numbers. He knows a few rules and no *reasons why*. He may know $6 \cdot 8$ but when asked for $6 \cdot 18$ he frantically grasps a pencil or crayon. He may know the square of 32 but $16 \cdot 64$ is impossible without pencil and paper. He knows that $a^2 \cdot a^3 = a^5$ but he cannot tell you what power of 3 is $9 \cdot 27$. He will tell you that the square on the hypothenuse equals the sum of the squares on the two legs of the triangle but he cannot tell you whether the diagonal of a square whose side is 8 is 14, 15, or 16, even though he may possibly know that diagonal to be $8\sqrt{2}$. To multiply a fraction he is not quite sure whether to multiply the numerator or the denominator of the fraction by an integer, so to make certain that he does all that he should do he multiplies both. He knows the square of $a+b$ but he cannot tell you the square of $30\frac{1}{4}$. None of these defects is the fault of the child. They are chargeable directly to the teacher and to the courses offered.

Now for the remedy. A closer knitting together of arithmetic, algebra, and geometry, an articulation, if you please, of these subjects, and an understanding of principles rather than of rules will settle these troubles. For example, when your grammar-school pupil knows that $c(a+b)=ac+bc$, he should also know that $6 \cdot 18=6(10+8)$ and that $16 \cdot 17$ is also the product of a binomial and a monomial, namely $16(10+7)$. Mental arithmetic, rapid and accurate, is then possible. When your pupil knows how to write the product of $16 \cdot 17$, $(3x-17)(5x+16)$ needs no pencil and paper. You teach $32 \cdot 32=1024$, but do you teach $2^5=32$, $2^4=16$, $2^6=64$? You teach $(a^5)^2=a^{10}$, also $a^4 \cdot a^6=a^{10}$. Do you teach $(2^5)^2=2^{10}=(32)^2$ and $2^4 \cdot 2^6=2^{10}=(32)^2=1024$?

$a^2 \cdot a^3=a^5$. Does that mean to your pupil $3^2 \cdot 3^3=3^5$? That is, is $9 \cdot 27=3^5$?

$(a^2)^3=a^6$ and $\sqrt{a^6}=a^3$. Does 9^3 mean 3^6, and does $\sqrt{9^3}=\sqrt{3^6}=3^3=27$?

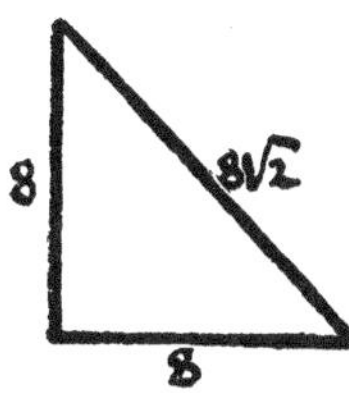

The side of a square is 8. The diagonal is $8\sqrt{2}$. Does your pupil have *any* idea of how long a line $8\sqrt{2}$ is? Does he know $8 \cdot 14$? Does he know that $8\sqrt{2}=8(1.4+)$?

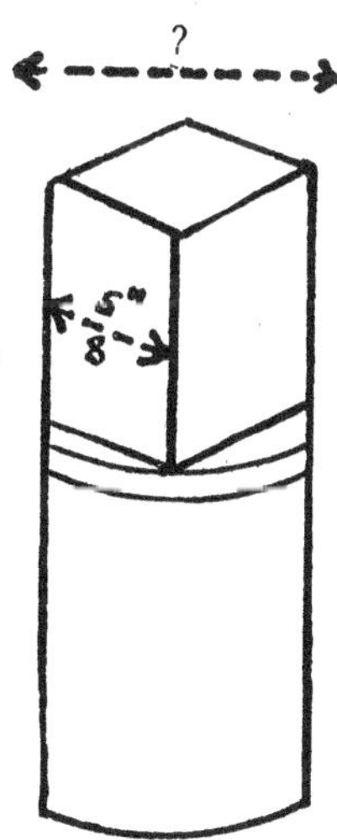

The stock for milling machine purposes is usually cylindrical. Try your pupil on this one: A piece of iron is to be milled so that one end is a square $\frac{5}{8}''$ on a side. What size stock must be selected? (See diagram.)

The problem is simply the application of the relation between the diagonal of a square and its side.

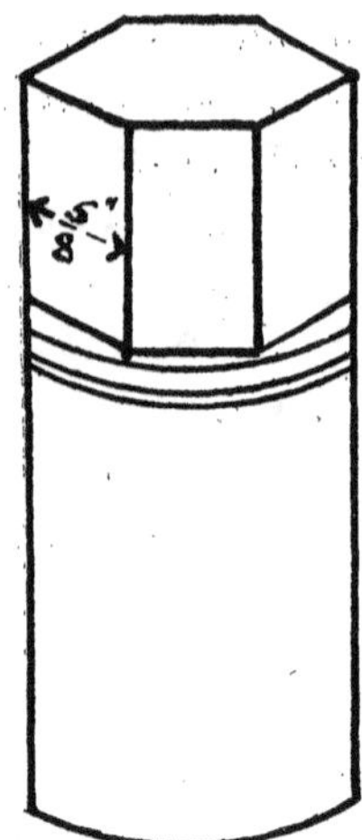

Now put the same question to the pupil making the end hexagonal, $\frac{5}{8}''$ on one side. Have you taught him why multiplying the numerator of a fraction multiplies the fraction or did he just learn the rule? Does he know that a mixed number is a binomial and that there are two kinds—the $a+b$ and the $a-b$—or does he square $30\frac{1}{4}$ by reducing to $\frac{121}{4}$ and squaring both numerator and denominator? I would suggest that the square of a mixed number be obtained mentally by means of, say,

$$(30\tfrac{1}{4})^2 = (30+\tfrac{1}{4})^2 = (900+15+\tfrac{1}{16}).$$

In reducing fractions to the lowest common multiple do you permit your pupils to follow this process:

$$\frac{5}{48}+\frac{11}{36}+\frac{8}{45}+\frac{7}{54}=\frac{\qquad\qquad}{2160}?$$

$$\begin{array}{r|rrrr}
2 & 48 & 36 & 45 & 54 \\ \hline
2 & 24 & 18 & 45 & 27 \\ \hline
3 & 12 & 9 & 45 & 27 \\ \hline
3 & 4 & 3 & 15 & 9 \\ \hline
 & 4 & 1 & 5 & 3
\end{array}$$

Or would you combine algebra and arithmetic in this manner?

$48 = 2^4 \cdot 3$
$36 = 3^2 \cdot 2^2$
$45 = 3^2 \cdot 5$
$54 = 3^3 \cdot 2$

Select for your L. C. M. each factor which appears, giving to each the highest exponent appearing in any number concerned, i. e., $2^4 \cdot 3^3 \cdot 5$.

$2^4 \cdot 3^3 \cdot 5 \div 48$ is $2^4 \cdot 3^3 \cdot 5 \div 2^4 \cdot 3 = 3^2 \cdot 5$. The first numerator is then $3^2 \cdot 5^2$. Similarly the second numerator is $2^2 \cdot 3 \cdot 5 \cdot 11$. The third numerator, $2^4 \cdot 3 \cdot 8$ or $2^7 \cdot 3$. The fourth numerator, $2^3 \cdot 5 \cdot 7$.

Then $\frac{5}{48}+\frac{11}{36}+\frac{8}{45}+\frac{7}{54} = \frac{3^2 \cdot 5^2 + 2^2 \cdot 5 \cdot 11 \cdot 3 + 2^7 \cdot 3 + 2^3 \cdot 5 \cdot 7}{2^4 \cdot 3^3 \cdot 5}$

$$= \frac{225+660+384+280}{2160}$$

$$= \frac{200+600+300+200+20+60+80+80+5+4}{2160},$$

all of which may be performed mentally.

Such a course will not only help the arithmetic but will be of infinite service in the manipulation of algebraic fractions and in the reduction of surd polynomials: e. g.,

$$\sqrt{(a^2-a-12)(a^2+2a-3)(a^2-5a+4)}.$$

A similar articulation and application of subjects should extend through algebra and geometry. It may necessitate some rearrangement of courses in both grammar school and high school. But is it not worth while? Will it not teach the pupil to think? Will it not give him some opportunity to estimate his answer and to know within some limit at least how nearly right he is? Will such articulation not bridge over the chasm between grammar school and high school and save some of that wholesale slaughter that now occurs in the freshman year?

It is my opinion that such course can be carefully and successfully worked out. The mathematics for college, for business, for scientific lines will then be built on the foundation laid in the third to sixth grades, will be one continuous course, the various phases of secondary mathematics being brought in naturally and as rapidly as the pupil can assimilate the material. Usable mathematics can be taught and that is the only kind of mathematics that belongs to the pupil.

EDITORIAL NOTES

We regret to state that the article in the Series upon Kindergartens, by Mrs. Alice H. Putnam on "Moral Controls in the Nursery and the Kindergarten," which should have appeared in this number, was delayed in the mail for so long a period that its appearance has been necessarily postponed until the next number.

G. H. M.

The Subn rmal and Defective Child in School

No educational movement is more deserving of vigorous support than that which is now gaining headway in the effort to care properly for the subnormal and defective child. It ought to call forth the most generous financial backing and it certainly requires the very best of scientific experts for its successful prosecution. One of the most effective means for expediting such pioneer work—and pioneer work it is in most of our communities—is the intelligent demand for it by the teachers in our great school systems. Every teacher may well feel under obligation to learn something of the facts with which we are confronted and the methods thus far proposed for dealing with the situation.

A few comments on certain obvious features of the case are distinctly in place at this time.

The Presence of These Children a Seri us Injury to the School

It should be clearly recognized that the obligation which we are under to give the subnormal child special care rests quite as much upon our duty to the normal child as to the defective one. To put subnormal or defective children into the classes with normal children is often a great wrong to both. The normal child is retarded in his progress by the class necessity of keeping step and going forward abreast, while the defective child is under a strain to which he ought not to be submitted. The writer has repeatedly been in classes where it was perfectly clear that the whole tone of the grade had been sapped and debilitated by the presence of a few very backward children to whom for various reasons the teachers felt obliged to give special attention. Children with serious nervous disorders ought never to be admitted to the regular classes. The nervous effect of such contact on highly organized but perfectly normal children is often cruelly disastrous.

A sharp distinction should also be drawn between the mentally retarded and backward child on the one hand and the truant or morally defective child on the other. The moral delinquency often springs from mental defect, but the retarded child is by no means necessarily a moral delinquent and to group the backward children with the chronic "bad boys" in joint classes, as has occasionally been done, is most immoral and unjust. The retarded child is very likely to be imitative in high degree and to respond eagerly to forceful leadership. Such leadership the confirmed truant is more than willing to furnish.

The Retarded Child and the Morally Defective Should Be Separated

We must expect to pay at a higher rate for the teaching of subnormal children than for that of normals, because they require more individual attention and this means more teachers per group. But as a people we are not wont to hesitate long on the score of cost, once we have convinced ourselves that a measure is socially essential.

Teaching of Subnormals Expensive

Whether the training of our subnormals can best be done in separate schools or in special rooms connected with each large school is a problem depending on many circumstances which vary from locality to locality. Such questions, of which there are many, are after all of small consequence compared with the securing of an adequate number of specially trained and thoroughly devoted teachers, who will save to the community the great wastage in human happiness and human efficiency which society is now permitting through the neglect of these retarded children.

Wastage Involved in Neglect of These Children

J. R. A.

NOTES AND NEWS

The first work of the Leipzig Institute for Experimental Pedagogy and Psychology is a translation of Kirkpatricks' *Fundamentals of Child-Study* under the title of *Grundlagen der Kinderforschung.* (Leipzig: A. Hahn. M. 3.50.)

Full reports of the recent meetings of the Depar ment of Superintendence of the N. E. A., and societies affiliated or connected with it, have already appeared, but it may be advantageous to emphasize here the work which is being done by the National Society of College Teachers of Education, and the National Society for the Scientific Study of Education. The former considered the problems of "Observation and Practice Teaching in College and University Departments of Education;" and while nothing startlingly new was said, yet the fact that the leaders in education from all parts of the country are pressing hard upon the practical aspects of preparation for education is, in itself, significant, and almost new. The movement to make preparation for teaching mean actual familiarity with the teaching situation, by means of observation of the best models, by practice under the criticism of the best teachers, and by theoretical consideration of the problems which arise in the student's own experience through this actual contact with real situations, is likely to grow until it completely occupies the field of the training of elementary teachers.

The second of the above-mentioned societies is continuing its work of calling attention to the moral elements involved in the school as it relates to the complete life-situation. The subject of education with relation to sex problems is becoming more insistent. It is easy enough to say that the child must be made to know; but How? and When? and What? Many periodicals are taking up this problem, more or less wisely. The work of this society ought to be in the possession of every teacher. Dr. C. R. Henderson, of the University of Chicago, long noted for his work in connection with civic morality, is the editor of the present yearbook.

Renewed attention is called to the work which a public library is able to do as an educational means in the recently published report of the New York Public Library for the year 1908. As related to the public schools, and to all schools, the work of this library is notable. It has a department devoted to work with schools, under the supervision of a competent man. In this department are a total of 411 branches which are regularly visited.

Bulletin boards have been erected in the schools of the Children's Aid Society, in parochial schools, in the Hebrew Technical Institute for Girls, in some corporate schools, and in recently completed public elementary and high schools, to the total number of 254 in schools, colleges, and universities. On these over 7,000 library notices have been posted. To those too far from any branch for regular visits notices are sent by mail, consisting of lists of new books of interest to teachers and the announcements of various library privileges for teachers and pupils.

Special effort has been made to equip the branches with books that would be useful in connection with the reference work of the elementary and high schools. In addition to the usual works of reference, dictionaries, encyclopaedias, almanacs, atlases, and so on, a list of books has been compiled that includes all of the required reading of these schools, with books related to the courses of the various grades and departments, including almost every subject in which the average boy or girl may be interested. . . . . When these collections are complete a teacher may send any pupil to the nearest branch with the assurance that the desired book will be immediately at hand, and the boys and girls will acquire the habit of a very free use of the library. . . . . Four new children's libraries have been opened and there are now forty such libraries. The circulation of books from children's libraries in 1908 was 2,175,347. In 1907 it was 1,871,800. The increase in volume of circulation is marked by far more gratifying increase in the quality of the books circulated and the amount of actual reading reported by the children on returning their books, or at the story hours.

The *Playground* in its current number contains the following:

The Third Annual Playground Congress will be held in Pittsburgh, Pa., on May 11 to 14. Already the Local Committee on Arrangements, the Programme Committee, and the committees on special subjects are busy at work preparing an unusually strong programme and an extensive series of novel exhibits and festivals for Congress week. Carnegie Music Hall, one of the most beautiful and convenient places for gatherings in the United States, has been secured for the use of the Congress. The Exhibition features will be particularly emphasized. Winter work and activities will be shown as of interest in the present movement for the all-year work of playgrounds. Another exhibition will deal with dramatics, folk dancing, and games, while the value of music in playground work will be developed at a musical feature in which playground children will sing Italian, Russian, German, Irish, and Negro folksongs. Folk dancing also will be a special feature of the festival work. The Pittsburgh Congress, moreover, will offer an excellent opportunity to study at first hand the way in which a municipality and a private organization can co-operate successfully, for the city of Pittsburgh has placed the management of its playgrounds in the hands of the Playground Association.

The general meetings will be held in the evening. The present plan is to have fewer addresses and to place greater emphasis on exhibition features. The speakers will be men and women recognized nationally as having an important message to offer on the play question and significant data to contribute to the working-out of the great educational, physiological, and civic problems, the solution of which is believed to lie in the field of properly conducted playgrounds. The topics at the general meetings will be limited to fields which have a truly national application. Each address will deal authoritatively with some phase of the question which has a national bearing and which is significant to all classes of playground advocates. The detailed discussion of questions applicable to limited fields will be held in connection with the special conferences and committee sessions. The reports of the special committees and the conference discussions will be each in its own field comprehensive. These committees for months past have been thoroughly canvassing their fields for all information. Each report will be a complete résumé of playground progress and discovery in all parts of the country. The chairmen of these committees report that all of their members are actively considering the problems. In addition, each committee has had the benefit of the suggestions in the field made by the entire membership of the Playground Association of America. The several committees and the chairmen who will present reports at the Congress are: Athletics for Boys, Dr. A. K. Aldinger; Equipment, E. B. De Groot; Festivals, Lillian D. Wald; Folk Dancing, Elizabeth Burchenal; Normal Courses in Play, Professor Clark W. Hetherington; Play in Institutions, Dr. Hastings Hart; Playgrounds as Social Centers, Mrs. Vladimir Simkhovitch; State Laws, Joseph Lee; Playground Statistics, Leonard P. Ayres; Storytelling in the Playground, Maud Summers.

The estimates of appropriations for the United States Bureau of Education for the fiscal year ending June 30, 1910, as transmitted to Congress, included under the general head of salaries estimates for additional employees as follows: Expert in higher education, $4,000; expert in industrial education, $3,000; expert in the welfare of children, $3,000; editor, $2,000, additional clerks, $12,100. Of the new employees requested, Congress made provision for an editor at $2,000; one clerk at $1,200; and one clerk at $1,000. The salary of the Commissioner of Education was increased from $4,500 to $5,000, making a total increase in the appropriations for the general work of the Bureau of $4,700 over the appropriations for the current fiscal year. The requests for a lump-sum appropriation of $40,000 for educational investigations; for an increase of $1,500 in the appropriation for the library; for an increase of $8,000 in the fund for collecting statistics; and of an appropriation of $39,000 for rent, metal shelving, additional furniture, and removal of the Bureau to new quarters, did not receive the favorable consideration of Congress.

The appropriation for the education of the natives of Alaska remains the same as for the present year, $200,000. The appropriation for reindeer in Alaska was reduced, on the recommendation of the Commissioner of Education, from $15,000 to $12,000. Provision was made by Congress for the designation of employees of the Alaska school service as special peace officers to assist in the enforcement of law in Alaska. It is expected that this legislation will be of great value in promoting the general welfare of the Alaskan natives.

The schoolhouse in Birr, beside which Pestalozzi lies buried, and on whose north wall hangs his memorial (1846), has been raised one story. To prevent the wall over the memorial from appearing too bare, the addition has been decorated with a fresco-painting in three parts, whose execution was undertaken by a young painter from the Aargau. The memorial has thereby lost repose to a certain extent but the impression of the whole surface is not as confusing as was feared.

In the spring of 1908 the French count, Béon, who owned "Neuhof," the home of Pestalozzi, died. In November Dr. Glaser-Lohner, an enthusiastic admirer of Pestalozzi (his father was a pupil at Hofuyl), purchased the whole area. Not speculation but reverence induced him to buy "Neuhof." The condition of affairs at "Neuhof" in the last year was a desecration of the home of the Pestalozzi charity school. Several years ago the directors of the Swedish Teachers' Association considered the matter of buying the "Neuhof," but the price, which was set at 165,000 francs, was judged by all to be too high. A training school in the spirit of Pestalozzianism, conducted on the principles of the Landerziehungsheim, would be an ideal use for the "Neuhof;" not an extensive institution, nor a money-making establishment, but a model school in the spirit of Pestalozzianism would be worthy of the place. Would it be impossible to secure the means for this purpose and to assure such a school at "Neuhof"?—*Die Deutsche Schule.*

Principal Robert L. Cooley, Sixteenth District School, No. 1, Milwaukee, has declared war on disease germs in schoolrooms in the following direct fashion:

We are all familiar with the necessity for protecting our water-supply from contamination. We gladly bear our portion of the enormous expense entailed in bringing pure water, in abundance, to our door.

We are acquainted with the necessity for pure-food legislation, and offer no objection, upon the ground of convenience, or expense, to any real safeguard to the public food-supply.

Public-school authorities have long been concerned with the problems of ventilation which deal with the forms of air-contamination involving its gaseous constituents. At great expense city schools have been equipped with large fans, operated by engines, or motors, for the positive delivery into the classroom, each minute, of a predetermined number of cubic feet of outdoor air per pupil.

Air, water, and food are further protected from contamination by carefully installed plumbing.

Have all of the necessities of public-school sanitation been met? Do we get clean air?

Dust is the great vehicle for the distribution of many pathogenic germs. The dust-evil is the greatest problem of sanitation remaining for public-school authorities to solve.

Without great care the schoolhouses become the disease-clearing-houses of the community.

Teachers and school-boards have come to regard the presence of dust in the schoolroom as a normal condition. It has seemed a hopeless thing to contend against. They are like the father who came to school to remonstrate with the principal who had sent his little girl home because of vermin in her hair.

"Everybody has them," he replied, as he insisted upon her being left undisturbed in her uncleanly condition.

Why this serene disregard of an undoubtedly grave condition?

Fire has never claimed a victim in the public schools of this city, and yet fire-escapes, at great expense, are being placed, as they should be, upon every school-building.

There is not a physician of repute, with a knowledge of conditions, who would dare to assert that deaths and serious illness have not been directly traceable to the dust in our schoolhouses.

Smallpox will throw a community into a panic. It is spectacular in its attack and effects. Cause and effect lie close together and the relation is recognized.

Tuberculosis is insidious and stealthy. The relation between cause and effect is difficult to make people understand and appreciate. Even when understood it seems to be but an intellectual appreciation, without any body of feeling back of it to give force to the conviction, and cause precautions to be taken at the expense of mere convenience.

It is so with the danger from germ-bearing dust. It performs its evil mission so stealthily and insidiously that the cause is looked for elsewhere. There is a tremendous inertia, an inherited lack of fear of this form of infection to be overcome, and a consequent disregard of proper methods of dealing with the problem.

What can teachers do? What are their responsibilities?

Let us consider some of the elements of this phase of the problem.

In any class of forty or more pupils, there are always some for whom today is the time of low resistive vitality. Not only is attendance at school compelled by law, but pale-faced, nervous, and anaemic children are daily drawn into attendance by over-stimulated pride and interest in their work. The very virtue of efficient teaching is the magnet that lures them into the schoolroom, when, for their own health, they would better be elsewhere.

Don't make a fetich of attendance.

Punctuality and regularity in attendance have been elevated among the cardinal virtues.

Concern yourself with the whole welfare of the pupil.

Establish no rewards that are absolutely cut off by a brief absence.

Acquaint yourselves with the valuable literature published by the state tuberculosis commission and assist in its understanding and distribution.

Constitute yourselves an extension of the state tuberculosis commission.

Agitate for "clean air" in the schoolroom.

Compulsory attendance at school carries with it an obligation, upon the part of the community, to maintain consistently wholesome conditions in our school-buildings. The resistive vitality of the pupil may vary from day to day, but the wholesome condition of the schoolroom must be maintained a constant factor.

Until recently no means of ridding a building of dust and dirt was known, except that of sweeping up and carrying out. By that crude method the fine, impalpable, but most dangerous, germ-infected dust was left behind to be beaten into suspension by improper methods of dusting and the tramp of many feet.

The writer of this paper, having had charge of a city school for a number of years, and having been a member of the Society for the Prevention of Tuberculosis, has been forcibly impressed with this neglected phase of schoolroom sanitation. As a result he has had installed in his building of fourteen rooms, a vacuum air-cleaning plant.

The work of this plant has been so effective, the conquest of the dust-problem has been so complete, that description of what it accomplishes will be of interest to all readers of this paper.

It sweeps the schoolhouse more rapidly than can be done with brushes.

It sweeps cleaner than can be done with brush or broom.

It does away with any dusting necessitated by sweeping.

It raises no dust in the process of sweeping and dusting.

It sucks the dirt and fine dust of the schoolroom through hose and pipes into a closed receptacle in the basement where it is destroyed by fire.

It sucks dust and dirt from places inaccessible to brush or broom.

It enables the janitor to sweep at any hour of the day, when corridors or certain rooms are not in use.

It is the ideal method for cleaning a school-building after the dismissal of the pupils.

It is now mechanically perfected and is a blessing to the community.

It costs considerable money.

How much is it worth?

Government has long fought tuberculosis in cows, trichinosis in pigs, foot-rot in cattle. We are quick to avail ourselves of the teachings of science when it will increase dividends, and attention to these matters has been found to pay.

The government is likewise committed to the policy of educating our children.

If it pays for the government to educate the child, it is certainly worth its while to protect his health which alone can make that education useful later on.

Any really important problem of public sanitation will not have its solution long delayed on the grounds of expense.

We have thousands in money for defense from preventable disease, but not one life of the most humble within our city, for tribute to it.

Enlighten the public and money will flow like water.

BOOK REVIEWS

A History of Education before the Middle Ages. By FRANK PIERREPONT GRAVES, PH.D. New York: Macmillan, 1909. Pp. 304. $1.10.

This book is not of the skimmed-milk, peptonized type of elementary history of education nor does it present an abstract history of philosophy for beginning students as does Davidson's otherwise admirable work. It is also free from the petty criticisms of great educational systems and the ideas of great thinkers that are so disgusting in some histories of education.

The chief topics to be considered, according to the author, are aim, content, method, and organization of education in each nation and period considered. This plan is followed throughout but a large proportion of the space is in every case given to historical facts showing the origin of educational ideals and aims. As in all other histories of education many of the facts given, although of significance to general history, have no direct bearing upon the problem of education.

This book, like nearly all others, does not in the opinion of the present writer give sufficient prominence to the more or less unconscious and unintentional education that is given the members of each new generation through their contact with the occupations, institutions, and traditions of their people. For similar reasons the intentional teaching of the young by directing their activity in accordance with the national needs, customs, and ideals does not seem to be appreciated at its full value. It is perhaps only natural that we who have always associated education with book learning cannot fully appreciate the most valuable features of such education as that carried on by the Greeks.

The matter is well arranged in topics and the facts are presented with clearness and accuracy. Part 1 treats of non-progressive education and Part 2 of the beginnings of individualism in education. After considering education among savages and peoples of primitive civilization the author treats of education in the historical nations of Egypt, Babylonia, Assyria, Phoenicia, China, Persia, Israel, Sparta, Athens, and Rome. The last chapter treats of early Christian education.

A writer of a history of education, like the good biographer, should be primarily appreciative and only secondarily critical. This Dr. Graves is to a greater extent than many other writers, yet the good points of the systems considered might have been brought out with greater clearness. The criticism of the education of any nation should not be based on present ideals and practices as is usually the case with most writers. The true basis of criticism is the correspondence or lack of correspondence between the aims of an educational system and the means used for attaining those ends. Only when one realizes that the ideal of the people of China was not like our own, one of progress, but of preserving everything as it had been, can he appreciate how admirably suited was the old Chinese system of education for the attainment of the desired end. One of the results of the study of the history of education should be to see more clearly the aims of modern education and judge more accurately how well our studies and methods are suited to the attaining of those ends.

Since to present clearly the historical facts that reveal education as a phase of the history of civilization is utterly impossible in a brief work designed for beginning students, it is the opinion of the present writer that the author of an introductory history of education is justified in overemphasizing the peculiarities of the ideals and practices of each nation in order to make the pictures more distinct. Dr. Graves is more careful than most such writers as to his historical facts but he fails as a literary artist in making the characteristics of each educational system stand out with sufficient distinctness to strongly impress elementary students. Considered in all respects, however, the book will rank high among histories of education.

E. A. KIRKPATRICK

FITCHBURG NORMAL SCHOOL, MASS.

The "Appleton" Arithmetics. Primary book. By J. W. A. YOUNG AND LAMBERT L. JACKSON. New York: D. Appleton & Co., 1909. Pp. 264.

"To teach arithmetic from the standpoint of the child," is the purpose this book sets itself. A broad purpose; indeed, is it very well possible in our days to *teach* anything from any standpoint, but that of the ones to be *taught?* The purpose is so broad, however, that further specification is necessary for a thorough understanding of the aim. What is the "standpoint of the child," with respect to arithmetic? Has it been clearly understood? What is there in the child's experience, that seems to call for arithmetic? In how far, or in what ways can arithmetic contribute to the unfolding and testing of the child's powers? Does it not seem necessary to answer these and many other related questions, in a somewhat definite fashion, before it can become clear, what we mean when we speak about the "standpoint of the child" with respect to arithmetic?

Perhaps the raising of these questions sends us out into terra incognita; at any rate, they open a broad field for scientific activity: to devise methods of investigation by means of which they may be adequately answered, to carry on such investigations in the classroom, and to put together manuals to be given to the children whose adaptability for arithmetic teaching we are trying to learn.

The *Appleton Arithmetics* are not intended for such purposes, however; they take for granted that the child's standpoint with respect to arithmetic is what it has generally been taken to be—eagerness to learn the fundamental processes on whole numbers and simple fractions, and their applications. They are "conservative, but not reactive. They represent what is sane in quality and safe in quantity for everyday classroom use under average conditions." They rather make fruitful use of the experience of the last ten years, then consciously try to gather new experience. They will contribute in a large fashion to bring into general application some of the things which have thus far been used by the people of advanced thought in education.

Every process, every idea is introduced by some "preparatory work," concrete in nature and intended to lead to an abstraction. Then follow, in many instances, oral exercises, mostly abstract, and after those come written exercises in which the abstract work is dissolved in applications. Such an arrangement surely ought to work well. Only, I would like to see about five times as many exercises in the preparatory work before any abstract notion is introduced. Can we reasonably expect children in the second year to attach any meaning to an addition table such as is found on p. 5, after nine concrete exercises, all with one set of objects? Why not present at least four or five *different* concrete situations before making attempt at an abstraction? The purpose of this book is finally to enable the child to use the fundamental processes of arithmetic in *concrete* situations. Is it altogether certain, that this cannot be reached in any other way except through an ill-digested abstraction? Can such an abstraction be expected to be a good tool for the applications?

The first chapter containing subject-matter for the first two years deals with numbers through twenty; chaps. ii and iii, designed for the third year, work with numbers through one hundred and one thousand respectively; chaps. iv and v, giving the work for the fourth year, lead the child through one million and give an introduction to the operations with common and decimal fractions. The reviews are frequent and thorough. The applications to practical problems are numerous and interesting, sometimes artificial. Multiplication by any number is immediately followed by division by the same number. Could not a similar interweaving have been carried out with the other topics?

The book is clearly printed and looks very attractive. I do not know whether the illustrations are always adapted to a child's understanding.

ARNOLD DRESDEN

SCHOOL OF EDUCATION

First Course in Biology. Part I, Plant Biology; Part II, Animal; Part III, Human. By L. H. BAILEY AND W. M. COLEMAN. New York: Macmillan, 1908. Pp. 204; 224; 164. Illustrated. $1.25.

Books in so-called general biology have been added to by Professors Bailey and Coleman. This book is made up of three parts, Plant Biology, Animal Biology, and Human Biology. It is really three small courses, one on botany, one on zoölogy, and one on human physiology bound within the same covers, separately paged, the whole constituting further evidence that the term "biology" means very different things to different people. An attempt is not made to study a biological topic by use of illustrative materials from both plants and animals, including men, but rather to study characteristics of the three divisions entirely separately. Furthermore, as evidence that the authors do not conceive of the task that they have assumed as one in which biological problems are to be found primarily in a study of living plants and animals we may cite their chapter of preliminary experiments upon compounds, oxygen, and air, study of acid and alkaline substances, test for starch, for nitrogenous substances, and for fats and oils, making and liberating oxygen, etc. It would seem that these experiments in a general biological course should arise in connection with real problems associated with plants and animals.

In the first part of the book, which is given to plants without any study as to what a plant is and what it must do in order to live, the student is soon plunged into "plant societies." Throughout this part detailed leaf, stem, and flower terminology finds abundant presentation, while the real work—the excuse for existence of these things—is less prominent than is desirable.

The discussion of the principles of biology, meaning of the term, and source of energy, appears, at the beginning of the second section, no explanation being offered as to why, if this is desirable at all, it was not presented before beginning the study of plants. Following this the groups of animals are considered in the order of increasing complexity.

The section on human physiology apparently is intended to mention practically all the topics one would find in any large work upon this topic, plus the discussion of alcohol and narcotics usually found in books designed to meet the trade. From the point of view of one interested in education it would seem there is no good basis to justify so inchoate a mass of material as found in this last part of the book.

In subject-matter the book contains many things with which specialists would find fault but these will not now be recounted.

O. W. C.

Public-School Relationships. By JOHN SOGARD; with an Introduction by HOMER SEERLEY. New York: Hinds, Noble & Eldredge, 1909. Pp. xxiv+197.

Public-School Relationships is a recent book that attempts briefly to discuss from a teacher's point of view "The Community and the School Officers," "The School Authorities and the Teacher," "The Teacher and the Pupil," and "The Employment of Teachers." The school officers, who "represent either the intelligence or the indifference of the community," are, in a sense, the exponents of the opportunity that the school may possess of becoming an organic factor in the life of the community. The school-board is entitled to the respect of the community, the author claims, since directly or indirectly the community makes the school-board. In a very true sense the *personnel* and ideals of the school-board are true representatives of the ideals of the community. When most of the people of a community thoughtfully accuse a board of ignorance, negligence, or corruption, the temporarily unrepresentative board will soon be exchanged for a representative one, while commendation by a majority means in a broad way that the board already stands for the community's educational thought. The wide differences that prevail relative to the functions of the school-board are presented by the author by means of replies to a *questionnaire* upon the duties of school-boards. The replies represent the entire range from a totally inactive and innocuous board, depending entirely upon superintendent and teacher, through a condition represented by a board that regards its functions as ending with attention to the material side of the schools, to one which looks upon the superintendent and teacher as hirelings to do the bidding of an over-functioning board.

In "The Teacher and the Pupil" some excellent educational philosophy is presented of which a single illustration may here be given. Mr. Sogard has investigated the question of amount of attention and time that shall be given to the "slow" pupils and here presents results of his inquiry. Although some teachers continue to believe that "while there is life there is hope" and consequently that they should seek the lost one even if the ninety and nine may meanwhile stray considerably, fortunately many teachers are discovering that it is quite as important to urge to his limit the exceptionally strong pupil, as to consume an undue proportion of time in trying to pull up a backward pupil until he reaches a respectable average.

The section on "Employment of Teachers" contains much valuable suggestion for superintendents, school-boards, and communities. O. W. C.

BOOKS RECEIVED

AMERICAN BOOK CO., NEW YORK

Standard Songs and Choruses for High Schools. By M. F. MacConnell. Cloth. Pp. 256. $0.75.

Nineteenth-Century English Prose. By Thomas H. Dickinson and Frederick W. Roe. Cloth. Pp. 495. $1.00.

D. APPLETON & CO., NEW YORK

The "Appleton" Arithmetics: Grammar-School Book. By J. W. A. Young and L. L. Jackson. Cloth. Pp. 450.

HOUGHTON, MIFFLIN & CO., BOSTON

A Primer of Nursery Rhymes. By Leota Swem and Rowena Sherwood. Cloth. Illustrated. Pp. 124. $0.30.

THE MACMILLAN COMPANY, NEW YORK

Beginners' Botany. By L. H. Bailey. Cloth. Illustrated. Pp. 208. $0.60.

Two Years Before the Mast (Pocket Series). By Richard Henry Dana. Edited by Homer Eaton Keyes. Cloth. Pp. 412. $0.25.

PRIVATELY PUBLISHED

Freehand Perspective and Sketching. Principles and Methods of Expression in the Pictorial Representation of Common Objects, Interiors, Buildings, and Landscapes. By Dora Miriam Norton. Illustrated. Pp. 172. Published by the author, Pratt Institute, Brooklyn, N. Y.

CURRENT EDUCATIONAL LITERATURE IN THE PERIODICALS[1]

IRENE WARREN
Librarian, School of Education, The University of Chicago

ADDAMS, JANE. The reaction of modern life upon religious development. Relig. Educa. 4:23–30. (Ap. '09.)

AYRES, LEONARD P. Irregular attendance a cause of retardation. Psycholog. Clinic. 3:1–9. (15 Mr. '09.)

BAGLEY, WILLIAM C. The pedagogy of morality and religion as related to the periods of development. Relig. Educa. 4:91–107. (Ap. '09.)

BAWDEN, WILLIAM T. Outline of a one-year course in mechanical drawing for high schools. Man. Train. Mag. 10:334–37. (Ap. '09.)

BENSON, ARTHUR CHRISTOPHER. The personality of the teacher. Educa. R. 37:217–31. (Mr. '09.)

BREED, MARY BIDWELL. The private boarding house. Relig. Educa. 4:60–65. (Ap. '09.)

BRISTOL, GEORGE P. Foreign languages in the high school. Educa. R. 37: 243–52. (Mr. '09.)

BRYCE, JAMES. Religion and public education. Relig. Educa. 4:30–34. (Ap. '09.)

BURKS, JESSE D. Need for a comprehensive restatement of educational theory. School R. 17:244–55. (Ap. '09.)

CAMPBELL, W. H. The value of industrial training in the elementary schools. Educa. Bi-mo. 3:285–98. (Ap. '09.)

CANFIELD, JAMES H. The library's part in education. Pub. Lib. 14:120. (Ap. '09.)

CARY, C. P. Proposed changes in the accrediting of high schools. School R. 17:223–30. (Ap. '09.)

CLARK, F. H. The influence of the report of the committee of seven on history work in the high schools. Educa. R. 37:331–42. (Ap. '09.)

[1] Abbreviations: Amer. Educa., American Education; Amer. Phys. Educa. R., American Physical Education Review; Atlan., Atlantic Monthly; Atlan. Educa. Journ., Atlantic Educational Journal; Educa., Education; Educa. Bi-mo., Educational Bi-monthly; Educa. R., Educational Review; El. Sch. T., Elementary School Teacher; Journ. of Geog., Journal of Geography; Liv. Age, Living Age; Man. Train. Mag., Manual Training Magazine; Prog. Journ. of Educa., Progressive Journal of Education; Psycholog. Clinic, Psychological Clinic; Pub. Lib., Public Libraries; Relig. Educa., Religious Education; School R., School Review; South. Educa. R., Southern Educational Review.

CLARK, LOTTA A. A good way to teach history. School R. 17:255-67. (Ap. '09.)

COE, GEORGE ALBERT. Annual survey of progress. Relig. Educa. 4:7-23. (Ap. '09.)

COLLINS, JOSEPH V. Religious education and the Sunday school. Educa. R. 37:271-84. (Mr. '09.)

COVERT, PAUL W. A college credit course in machine shop. Man. Train. Mag. 10:289-99. (Ap. '09.)

DEWEY, JOHN. History for the educator. Prog. Journ. of Educa. 1:1-5. (Mr. '09.)

"DOMINIE." A problem for boys' boarding schools. Educa. 29:453-60. (Mr. '09.)

ELIOT, CHARLES W. Educational reform and the social order. School R. 17:217-23. (Ap. '09.)

EMERSON, HENRY P. The English elementary school system. Amer. Educa. 12:358-62. (Ap. '09.)

FENNEMAN, N. M. Problems in the teaching of physical geography in secondary schools. Man. Train. Mag. 10:145-58. (Ap. '09.)

GILLETTE, JOHN M. Preparation of the college student for social service. Relig. Educa. 4:74-83. (Ap. '09.)

GREENE, FRANCES NIMMO. State support for library extension. South. Educa. R. 5:219-28. (D.-Ja. '08-'09.)

GREENWOOD, James M. Retardation of pupils in their studies and how to minimize it. Educa. R. 37:342-49. (Ap. '09.)

HADLEY, ARTHUR T. The library in the university. Pub. Lib. 14:115-17. (Ap. '09.)

HORN, P. W. City schools under the commission form of city government. Educa. R. 37:362-75. (Ap. '09.)

HOUSE, R. T. A neglected phase of practical education. Educa. 29:447-50. (Mr. '09.)

HUGHES, RICHARD CECIL. Factors in the dormitory problem. Relig. Educa. 4:47-51. (Ap. '09.)

JEWELL, AGNES. The public library and the school problem. Pub. Lib. 14:117-19. (Ap. '09.)

JOHNSON, GEORGE E. The playground as a factor in school hygiene. Psycholog. Clinic. 3:14-21. (15 Mr. '09.)

JOHNSTON, CHAS. Tutoring law-makers. Harp. W. 53:15. (27 Mr. '09.)

KARPINSKI, LOUIS C. Reform in the teaching of mathematics. School R. 17:267-72. (Ap. '09.)

KEOGH, ANDREW. The training of college students in bibliography. Pub. Lib. 14:124. (Ap. '09.)

KING, CHARLES A. The public school and industrial education. Educa. 29: 407-19. (Mr. '09.)

KINNE, HELEN. Some phases of household arts in the secondary schools, Man. Train. Mag. 10:307-13. (Ap. '09.)

MCANDREW, WILLIAM. The schoolman's dismissal. Educa. R. 37:252-71. (Mr. '09.)

MCCURDY, PERSIS HARLOW. The history of physical training at Mount Holyoke college. Amer. Phys. Educa. R. 14:138-51. (Mr. '09.)

MACDOWELL, THEODORE L. An outline of a plan for utilizing the salary schedule as a means for improving the efficiency of teachers in the elementary schools. Educa. R. 37:349-59. (Ap. '09.)

MANNY, FRANK A. Notes on English education. Atlan. Educa. Journ. 4:15-16. (Mr. '09.)

MARTIN, GEORGE H. A lesson from medical inspection of schools. Psycholog. Clinic. 3:9-14. (15 Mr. '09.)

MERIAM, J. L. Fundamentals in the elementary school curriculum. Educa. R. 37:390-99. (Ap. '09.)

PEABODY, FRANCIS GREENWOOD. The social conscience and the religious life. Relig. Educa. 4:1-7. (Ap. '09.)

PINE, JOHN. The origin of the University of the State of New York. Educa. R. 37:284-92. (Mr. '09.)

PRICE, HELEN U. Possibilities for work with children in smaller libraries. Pub. Lib. 14:121-23. (Ap. '09.)

REINSCH, PAUL S. The new education in China. Atlan. 103:515-23. (Ap. '09.)

ROSS, E. ATHELSTAN. The influence of the teacher on the child's interests. Man. Train. Mag. 10:313-17. (Ap. '09.)

RUEDIGER, WILLIAM C. Teaching pupils to study. Educa. 29:437-47. (Mr. '09.)

ST. JOHN, G. B. Rating of constructive work. Man. Train. Mag. 10:331-34. (Ap. '09.)

SANFORD, E. M. The origin, function and direction of play. Amer. Educa. 12:345-52. (Ap. '09.)

SCHNEIDER, OTTO C. The hand as a factor in education. Educa. Bi-mo. 3:278-85. (Ap. '09.)

SCHROEDER, H. H. The religious element in the public schools. Educa. R. 37:375-90. (Ap. '09.)

SCOTT, FRED NEWTON. A brief catechism on textbooks in English. Educa. R. 37:359-62. (Ap. '09.)

SMALL, WILLARD S. High-school secret societies and the psychology of adolescence. Atlan. Educa. Journ. 4:5-6. (Mr. '09.)

SMITH, CHARLES F. Industrial training in the grade workshop. Man. Train. Mag. 10:326-31. (Ap. '09.)

SMITH, FRANK WEBSTER. The normal school ideal. Educa. 29:432-36. (Mr. '09.)

SNEDDEN, DAVID. The combination of liberal and vocational education. Educa. R. 37:231-43. (Mr. '09.)

STARBUCK, EDWIN D. Agencies for deepening the spiritual life of the college. Relig. Educa. 4:83-90. (Ap. '09.)

STECHER, WILLIAM A. Play and playgrounds: The playgrounds under the Philadelphia board of public education. A paper read at the playground congress, municipal section, New York. Mind and Body. 16:61-64. (Ap. '09.)

STEINER, B. C. The library as an agency in religious education. Relig. Educa. 4:107-12. (Ap. '09.)

STOREY, THOMAS A. The organization of the department of physical instruction in the College of the City of New York. Amer. Phys. Educa. R. 14:132-38. (Mr. '09.)

STOWE, A. MONROE. The school club: the school garden, and the correlated school activities. El. Sch. T. 9:416-21. (Ap. '09.)

STRAYER, GEORGE D. Teaching children to study. Atlan. Educa. Journ. 4:5-7. (Ap. '09.)

TALBOT, MARION. Dormitory life for college women. Relig. Educa. 4:41-47. (Ap. '09.)

TEMPLE, ALICE. The occupations of the kindergarten. El. Sch. T. 9:397-410. (Ap. '09.)

THWING, CHARLES F. Dormitory life for college men. Relig. Educa. 4:34-41. (Ap. '09.)

TYLER, JOHN M. The place of physical training in the public schools. Educa. Bi-mo. 3:271-78. (Ap. 09.)

WEEGE, C. F. An appeal for sound educational physical training. Mind and Body. 16:41-45. (Ap. '09.)

WEEKS, ARLAND D. The two aims of high schools. Educa. 29:420-22. (Mr. '09.)

WHITTEN, W. W. Recent developments in school ventilation. Mind and Body. 16:45-49. (Ap. '09.)

WILBUR, THERESA M. The Young Woman's Christian Association and the problem of religious influence in colleges. Relig. Educa. 490-91. (Ap. '09.)

WINSTED, HULDAH. School excursions as a means of teaching patriotism in our public schools. Journ. of Geog. 7:131-34. (F. '09.)

WOODWARD, CORA STRANAHAN. The college sorority as a substitute for the woman's dormitory. Relig. Educa. 4:65-74. (Ap. '09.)

WORST, EDWARD F. Industrial arts in the primary schools of Germany. Educa. Bi-mo. 3:298-304. (Ap. '09.)

YUST, W. F. Library extension in the South. South. Educa. R. 5:211-19. (D.-Ja. '08-'09.)

VOLUME IX NUMBER 10

THE ELEMENTARY SCHOOL TEACHER

JUNE, 1909

MORAL "CONTROLS" IN THE NURSERY AND THE KINDERGARTEN

ALICE H. PUTNAM
Kindergarten College, Chicago

I have borrowed the word "controls" from Dr. W. C. Bagley's paper on "Controls of Conduct in the Schoolroom," published in the *Elementary School Teacher,* March, 1908. I like the word, because it implies many opportunities for learning wisdom both in the training of ourselves, and of our children. A consideration of the necessary elements of time, of circumstance, and of repetition, in a little child's ever-growing adjustments of himself to the requirements of nature and of society will make us grateful for Richter's suggestion: "You need not give any *edicta perpetua,* but your law-giving power can each day issue new decretals, and new pastoral letters."[1]

Because the nursery is the baby's first home, playground, school, social center, church, and sometimes the battle-ground where important questions are settled for better, for worse, we find there the experiences which are the raw material out of which his ideals of conduct will be woven. Slowly, very slowly, are the threads singled out of his small daily behaviors; yet, seen or unseen, the work is being done, and the child is himself the chief workman.

Our first and best aid can be given by a careful and frequent taking-account-of-stock of our children's physical ma-

[1] Jean Paul Richter, *Levana,* chap. vi.

chinery; for that, we are to hold ourselves largely responsible. If there is neglect, waste, or friction here, there will be explosions more or less serious all along the line. Fortunately, science comes to our aid here, and our personally conducted efforts, while somewhat experimental, generally are reasonably successful with normally born children. Henry Ward Beecher is reported to have said that if he "could be born well the first time, he would willingly take his chances of a second birth." But just as the body must be nourished, so must the inner nature of the child have its sustenance. Moral health and goodness do not come, nor will they stay of their own momentum. Only through the right and the constant use of the means of growth will there be an increase of power. The nutrition, air, exercise, rest, etc., which the body needs, all have their moral analogues. The nursery needs its moral and ethical "airs" temperatures; its pabulum of happy play, song and story, its laws of constraint as well as its laws of freedom. And even then, with the right knowledge, the right desire, there is the everlasting problem of its right application to each child in the home and school; for after all, the "meaning of life is in the individual."

The wisdom of the twentieth century shows us no better place to begin this sort of training than did Plato, when he said: "The best way to train the young, is to train yourself at the same time; not to admonish them, but to be always carrying out your principles in your own practice."[2] There can be no shilly-shallying here, without the loss of an enormous amount of "perfectly good" energy on the part of parents, teachers, and children. The child is a "behaving organism," which absorbs its stimuli far more from the lives of the people about him, than from their words. The child who sees father and mother living out true ideals of justice, temperance, industry, and religion (I mean by the latter the soul's relationship to God and man) will not lack for inspiration. "Inspiration" says Emerson, "is like yeast. 'Tis no matter in which of half a dozen ways you procure the infection, you can apply one or the other equally well to your purpose. And every earnest workman, of whatever sort, knows

[2] Jowett, *Plato's Laws,* Book V.

some favorable conditions for his task." Should the question be asked, "How can I attain this power?" the answer might be that given by the southern revivalist, who, when asked by some woman how she could "get religion," replied, "Act like you had it!"

Having gotten oneself somewhat in hand (we need not wait to be perfect), one naturally asks when and where and how the more definite work with the children should begin. Shall we find that moral growth has its nascent periods, as do instincts and impulses, muscles and cells? Are there some virtues which are more needed in childhood than at any other time, and which, because of the general plasticity of mind and spirit, can be better fostered at this time? Dr. Adler takes up these and similar problems, and his answers are definite and rational. He feels, as do most sane people, that the cradle is the place to begin; that regularity in the child's life, while not in itself morality, is conducive to moral development, because it sets a check on mere impulse, which like all good things is capable of abuse. He feels that a child of eighteen months can be taught obedience to its parents, and that this is necessary, for without the knowledge that there is a higher will than his own, no one can ever become a truly moral person.[3]

Froebel takes as his starting-point, the development in the child of what (for want of a better name) I like to call passive *courage*. It is really the beginning of lessons in endurance or fortitude, but these words appear a bit formal and rather severe when applied to a baby. He states the idea somewhat in this way. In the child's very first crying there is no self-will; it is an expression of unrest. The wilful and obstinate element comes into it, when the attendant is negligent or indolent in regard to a child's real discomfort. This may be fanciful, it may be real. Therefore the mother or attendant must be able to discriminate. Finding that all has been done that can be done, she may leave the little one to "find himself;" for if the persistent crying has brought attention and sympathy when not needed, the child soon learns to use his energy to govern those about him, rather than

[3] See Felix Adler, *Moral Instruction of Infancy,* chap v.

to use it to control himself.[4] A long experience with children in the nursery and out of it convinces me that the child who has learned something of this element of submission, who can in some degree take things as they are, who early learns to take his place as a member of the family rather than the part of a young monopolist, has made no small headway in his moral controls. But our rational and effectual requirements should be steady and inexorable. Here again Froebel points out a course so simple and so effective, so truly in harmony with that side of child nature which, instead of being hostile to law, shows that he has, at least, an innate respect for custom, (and is not this one of the child's early spellings of "morals" and "ethics?"):

> All true education [says Froebel] should at every moment be simultaneously double-sided; giving and taking, prescriptive and following, active and passive. . . . . Between education and pupil, between request and obedience, there should rule an invisible third something, to which educator and pupil are equally subject. This third something is the right, the best, necessarily conditioned and expressed without arbitrariness in the circumstances.[5]

Many a heartache comes to many parents because they have not been able to call forth habits of response, trust, and confidence from their children. Honest self-examination would show that the parents do not deserve it; they have not earned it, because of their thoughtless, inconsistent, and ignorant methods of procedure. To illustrate this, let me give an incident used by the author of *Parents and Pedagogues:*

> "Roger, come right back here this minute! Snake down there!" called out a young mother, neighbor of mine, yesterday. I naturally looked to see what danger my little friend Roger was getting into. The two-year-old adventurer was hesitating before his mother called him; but at this lie I was revengefully glad to see him start forward with neck outstretched, "Snake! snake! want see snake!" "If I have to come down there, I shall whip you," came from the mother. But the child continued peering round after the snake, and the mother came down. She snatched him up in her arms and kissed him rapturously. "Why don't you come when mamma calls, you darling little idiot?" Two lies in one lesson for this child's first course in mendacity![6]

[4] See Froebel (Hailman's trans.) *Education of Man*, pp. 22, 23.

[5] *Ibid.*, p. 14.

[6] Wilson, *Pedagogues and Parents*, p. 273, H. Holt & Co.

We need make no comment, except this: How often we have seen like inconsistencies and weaknesses!

Referring again to the question of nascent periods of child-like virtues, one can hardly fail to notice a child's natural attitude of respect for things that are true and good and lovely. Is this not the heart of reverence? Will life be worth very much to anyone without this spirit? Is it a noticeable trait in the child of today? Lecky says in his *History of European Morals:* "Of all the forms of moral goodness, a reverential spirit is that to which the epithet 'beautiful,' must be most emphatically applied. Yet the habits of advancing civilization are, if I mistake not, inimical to it." Because some good men and women have come to feel that the idea of it is so wound about with outward forms and conventionalities, rather than the living pulsating one, which would keep us in the state of humility in which alone we may acquire knowledge and wisdom, they seem to think it has no place in the education of our children any longer. I believe that this, like other virtues, can only be taught children in the concrete, and as it is too fine a thing for a child to miss, he should be much in the presence of people whom he cannot fail to love and respect, and his work, too, should be with objects which have for him a content that he can value and respect.

But, however good may be the habits which the child has acquired more or less unconsciously, something more is needed. The time comes when these habits must be made his own, through choice, as well as through use. His own personal feeling for the right must influence the habitual action.

Now comes the time when what we might call the vicarious element in the mother's teaching begins to fade into the background. Little by little she takes her hand from the helm, and lets baby use his own little steering oar. He bumps into rocks of various kinds—capsizes, perhaps, but the mother knows just how deep the water is, and that the child is not beyond his depth. "Look ahead," says Froebel's "Falling, falling" play. "Use your eyes and hands carefully and skilfully." "You can do it." "Try again!" And what courage it gives to be allowed to try again, and to feel that someone has faith in you in spite of your blunders! We sometimes behave as if we expected a child to acquire his little "controls" immediately, rather than mediately. Someone (?) has said that Nature is a thorough believer in the installment plan in relation to the individual; that it would be an injustice to the poor and weak were she to require cash payments in full for anything!

As the child grows toward adolescence, he may begin to exercise himself in moral gymnastics, somewhat as Mr. James has suggested in his chapter on "Habit," but this can hardly be expected during the years we are considering. The daily "stents" in cleanliness, order, obedience, the performance of little duties, etc., have to be set by parent and teacher, who stand to the child as embodiments of public opinion. Yet the growth and development of the child's selfhood should not lessen the mother's continued training of herself. His self-centeredness, his irregularly bold self-assertiveness, need to be balanced. This is generally done more effectively in the society of other children than in the family group alone, especially if the children are in the care of someone who has a true perspective of child-life. Haweis says: "there is one thing more important than knowing self, it is governing self; one thing more important than using impulse, it is governing impulse;" but this cannot be done until self is known, and in this process of becoming acquainted with self, both child and adult have many surprises. Dr. Bagley's paper, to which I have already referred, comes to our aid again, just here, in its plea for something more to live by than habit alone:

> Impulse and emotion [he says] are so closely related as genetically to be indistinguishable; and unless one can oppose an impulse with an idea just as powerfully colored with emotion, the impulse is bound to conquer. . . . . It is the *emotionalized idea*, the *ideal,* which will hold the reins of conduct when instinct is battling for control.[7]

Elsewhere in the same article he uses the term "emotionalized prejudice" to express the same thought. I think his argument holds as well for the nursery and kindergarten as for the school.

> There must be developed a prejudice highly colored with positive emotional force toward truth . . . . impersonal observation, dispassionate

[7] *Elementary School Teacher,* March, 1908.

judgment, *an emotional attitude against emotion, a prejudice against prejudice*. . . . . The early discipline of the family life is the great breeding-ground of these prejudices, because of the positive, profound, emotional factors that operate. (I mean by positive factors, those that operate in favor of the virtues in question.)

Who that has studied Froebel can fail to see this idea running through all of his writings—especially in the *Mother Play Book?* Miss Poulssen once said that this book might be called the "Book of the Evolution of Virtues." And mightn't we also call it "A Book of Ways and Means to Call Forth a Child's Prejudices in Favor of Clear Thinking, Right Feeling, and Noble Doing?"[8]

But just how does Froebel set about this? First, by the mother's use of the child's instinctive movements and sense activities, interpreting them not only in the language of the child's world, but in that of the larger one in which he is already involved, and from which he must evolve—the world of nature, of society, and again into that which is within him, the Kingdom of Heaven.

Much is said now-a-days about leaving the children in freedom to work out their own ideas in gift, occupation, and game, and undoubtedly they should have time for experimentation. But there are certainly ideas *not* yet their own, to which they also have a right because of the pleasure and skill which will come through them. I think that there can be a very definite relation in the very definitely dictated work of the kindergarten materials, and a child's moral controls. If through such work children reach ends which are thoroughly satisfactory; ends which have lasting value not only while they are in kindergarten but long after; if these ends are such as they would not be likely to "evolve from the depths of their own consciousness," such a method will not interfere with any self-activity and meantime a great deal has been gained. First, we have strengthened the child's

[8] Just here I am interrupted by an anxious psychological-pedagogical parent, who asks: "Have you any right to exercise this sort of hypnotic influence on your child? *Dare* you undertake to 'emotionalize' his prejudices?" Yes, my friend, I dare, because I believe that this is one thing parents are here for, and that this is one reason why a child has so long a period of immaturity. A child like an adult needs the sympathetic, wise guidance of those who have learned larger lessons than he himself has learned.

faith in our understanding of his tastes, as well as his belief that we know how to guide him to a new realization of ways and means to ultimate his desires. The child, it is true, may not feel what is often called the logical method of the plan, but he enjoys the facts, the little surprises; he uses his attention and skill in a new way; he becomes interested in details for which there is now a specific need; and that is worth while.

Secondly, through the close union of hearing and doing, habits of attention are set up, and through the co-ordinations of brain and hand, results are reached which again react on the intention, and he really enjoys doing, for the time being, the things *he is told to do;* and that is worth while.

Thirdly, the constant repetitions of language which call into consciousness definite ideas of form, size, number, position, and other elementary attributes which are common to all objects—attributes for which he has an immediate use, make for an understanding of them which he can carry into all his constructive and aesthetic work—and that is worth while.

Fourthly, to the foreign-born child this practical use of language, the *active* use of it, the very definiteness and constant repetition, counts for a very great opportunity, which means much, especially to those who must leave school early.

This special plan or method of work is no experiment; it is as old as the kindergarten itself; and I know it is good and true for, as Mr. Dooley says, "it wurruks," and I believe that a neglect of it is exactly as bad as too much of it!

All of the exercises of the kindergarten have definite possibilities as well as limitations, and it is in the meeting of just such extremes that the child finds a certain stimulus to his own activity, and in the exercise of it under right conditions he acquires certain controls; he learns to act as of himself. With the development of his individual will there comes the growth of his social will, and a child soon realizes that this is quite as important a factor in his well-being, as that which concerns himself alone.

Hidden away in all of this training, there is something which it is the end of education to develop; and to reach this end, there must be positive experiences of law and order, as well as experiences of freedom. These, if selected on the basis of a true understanding of child nature—not only on a knowledge of his natural instinctive loves, but with a realization of his possibilities—will be neither foreign nor irksome to him.

The child lives every day in the domain of morals and ethics, though he is unconscious of the fact. He must make good his claim to a "God-heredity" as he does that of his human relationships, through the exercise of that law of which he is at one and the same time the subject and the agent, viz., the law of service, as opposed to the law of self. Froebel understood very well that the child could not reach this ideal without at first running what Mr. Barnes calls "the tentacles of his selfhood," deeply into all that concerns him. In song and story, work and play, he must be given time to establish his own personal "inner connection" with his environment. The whole world appears at first to exist for him alone, and he so uses it. But as he comes in contact with other young persons of his own age who are like-minded, the conflict begins, which, if wisely directed, is to free him from the dominion of so unsatisfactory a master as self alone.

This is the end which Froebel has in view: an organized plan, which with the co-operation of the child will bring him into an ever-growing conscious relation to a larger life of nature, of man, and to a loving and living realization of that Image in which man is created. It is not a difficult thing to develop a feeling of respect for those who stand to the child as the interpreters of this larger outlook, provided they stand sympathetically, rationally, and consistently for it. For a homely example of this: a child will have much less to contend with if a command is given him in a positive yet gentle tone, than in the form of a weak invitation to do the thing which he knows perfectly well ought to be done; especially if it comes bearing the subtle suggestion that mother or teacher have little faith that the idea will be carried out. To illustrate definitely: "Now John, darling, mother has waited for you a long time, won't you *please* [rising inflection] put on your shoes?" (ditto). Compared with the father's strong, fearless—"John, stop fooling and put on your shoes at once!" The latter is far more effective, for it carries with it an assurance of faith that the order will be executed.

Another important thing for parent and pedagogue to bear in mind is the tendency of the child to hold to the thing he is doing. This has much to do with his response or his indifference to the request or command. A great deal has been wisely said in regard to the evil of breaking into a child's activities when they are under full headway, and switching his interest to other tracks. If the work has been wisely planned—if too much time hasn't been wasted on non-essentials, the probability is that when the time for a change of play or work has come for the majority of the children, the individual child who has a timely warning given can easily adjust himself to it in a perfectly psychological fashion. Here as elsewhere the adult example is stronger than words. The father who lingers to finish the newspaper column, or the mother who stops to cut out the second sleeve of Mary's dress, after the luncheon bell has rung, not only preaches an effective sermon against the law and habit of punctuality to the children, but also to the cook and other members of the household.

The good of the social whole must act as a check at times in individual interests. And we come back again and again to the fundamental law—not of the "greatest good to the greatest number" but to that larger thing, the "greatest good of the whole," and that again leads to the daily practice of the law of use, which means the greatest thing on earth put into living concrete forms. This idea is essentially as simple as it is true and strong.

> This law of use [says a recent writer,] is essentially different from the theory which declares the end of life and man's existence to be the glory of God, in the sense of a selfish delight of an arbitrary and powerful Being in experiencing the abject subjection and servitude of inferior creatures. God's glory has no higher or nobler manifestation than in the uses of the universe—in the mutual service of creature to creature. It is in the interchange of human uses that man finds at once the most intense and the highest happiness.[8]

[9] Rev. Frank Sewall, *The New Ethics*, G. P. Putnam's Sons.

"Billions of years," may alter our ideas of Christ, but they cannot alter the fact that now, to us, and to our children, the story of his life of service to all with whom he came in contact will endure, provided we practice it; for "there is no lost good." It is to this end that we would develop "moral controls" in our children's daily lives, first through the external vicarious control, till in due time the child shall "be predisposed to the higher direct obedience to law itself, of which obedience to the mother is the first stage."[10]

[10] Emilie Poulssen, *Love and Law in Child Training,* p. 147.

FIELD NOTES IN READING

I. A METHOD WITH WORDS

MARY E. LAING
Boston, Mass.

The primary teacher initiates the language habit in the two-fold aspect of reading and written expression. In the primary school, both these functions, so vital for intelligence, receive that fundamental bent which we call "attitude toward."

The teacher who stands at the entrance of this new life with books needs to have a simple vigorous hold on language; a sincere feeling toward it; an intelligent insight into its significance for the child.

From both the psychological laboratory and the writings of Helen Keller we have received some interesting facts that should enlighten us in our method with words.

Helen Keller, as only a blind-deaf-mute could do perhaps, gives us a valuable answer as to the meaning of the word for the mind.[1] This is illustrated in the story of her first word. When Miss Sullivan, her teacher from the Perkins Institute for the Blind, came to Helen, she found a nervous, passionate child, living in a dark and silent world into which only "wordless sensations" of touch, taste, and smell could enter.

The attempt to teach her the alphabet for the blind was at first fruitless, so difficult was it to bring to her shut-in mind the idea of the relation between the word and the thing it symbolized. One day after a "tussle" in trying to make the child see the relation between the word "doll" and the object, Helen seized her new doll and dashed it on the floor. She had not loved the doll and was keenly delighted when she felt the fragments at her feet. "In the still, dark world in which I lived," she says, "there was

[1] See Helen Keller, *The Story of My Life*, Doubleday, Page & Co., and *The World I Live In*, The Century Co.

no strong sentiment or tenderness." Her teacher brought Helen her hat and they walked down the path to the well-house.

> Someone was drawing water [writes Miss Keller] and my teacher placed my hand under the spout. As the cool stream gushed over my hand she spelled into the other the word "water," first slowly, then rapidly. I stood still, my whole attention fixed upon the motion of her fingers. Suddenly I felt a misty consciousness as of something forgotten—a thrill of returning thought; and somehow the mystery of language was revealed to me. I knew then that water meant the wonderful cool something that was flowing over my hand. That living word awakened my soul, gave it light, hope, joy; set it free! There were barriers still, it is true, but barriers that could in time be swept away.
>
> I left the well-house eager to learn. Everything had a name, and each name gave birth to a new thought. As we returned to the house every object that I touched seemed to quiver with life. That was because I saw everything with the strange, new sight that had come to me. On entering the door I remembered the doll I had broken. I felt my way to the hearth and picked up the pieces. I tried vainly to put them together. Then my eyes filled with tears: for I realized what I had done, and for the first time I felt repentance and sorrow.

The gift of language gave back to Helen Keller her own rightful worlds, intellectual, social, and ethical, from which she had been an outcast. As she says in *The World I Live In,* "with the dropping of a little word from another hand into mine, a slight flutter of the fingers, began the intelligence, the joy, the fulness of my life."

This wonder of language comes to the child so early and so innately that it is lost in forgetfulness. The nearest approach to it comes when he is initiated into a written or printed language that opens to him the world of books.

When we say that a word is a symbol we have said very much indeed. Helen Keller found it fairly entertaining play when Miss Sullivan began to talk into her hand. Nevertheless she tired of it. Babies in much the same way amuse themselves with vocal and speech play, but they could never learn a language as long as it was play and nothing more, since without meaning words cannot make interesting play. A symbol is something that in itself alone is utterly devoid of significance.

But when Helen Keller felt the meaning of the word, the

case was changed; at a flash, the symbol as the bearer of an idea came. In that discovery lay all the difference of being in possession of mind or being dispossessed of mind. For the mind seizes innately on this word-symbol as something which belongs essentially to itself. Well might it say, "Now I can think!" "Now I can grasp the world!" "Now my feelings become coherent, my voice is shaped, I can know and be known!"

The word is a bearer of an idea: it stands for something besides itself. The point of conquest in Helen Keller's case lay in relating the symbol to the thing for which it stood. *The word can be known in and through the idea and in no other way.* When Helen learned that that particular flutter of the fingers meant "water," it became a word to her: until then it was just "finger play."

The case is exactly paralleled when one helps a child in the first primary class to bring meaning to a strange word; meaning robs the shape of its strangeness and the unintelligible form becomes intelligible. We call that flashing instant when meaning and word come together, "recognition." Word-recognition is joining the word-form to the idea for which it stands. If we do it for the first time and do it well, we rightly call it learning the word: if we have power to do it automatically as a part of a thinking-expressing process we have mastered the word.

The way in which the word is originally apprehended determines the character of the subsequent recall. Miss Sullivan exhibited the wise-foolishness of motherhood when she put one of Helen's hands under the flowing water while she spelled the word into the other. In the schools where reading is being most thoughtfully studied the early words are motor. But the important point is that the child is encouraged to make them motor. The vivid imaging of the printed word is made a matter of first importance. But the interest which will give the word significance must come from the content side. Thus from the first there is an effort to make written language the bearer of imagery, a means for dramatization, and it is associated always with a vivid, virile meaning. The "moment" of getting the new word is made living, intent, where awareness of the word in and through the idea fills the mind.

The mind has little use for the word in isolation. On the form side there is no reason why we should not be as interested in isolated as in related words. But there again the symbol shows its impotency apart from use or function. The word represents the idea and the idea never remains isolated. Ideas are related to form thoughts. The mind thinks, and ideas when they assume a vital, virile form always do it as a part of a thinking process. So words must get them to the work of helping forward the mind's own activities. However a word may be introduced, it is never mastered except as it is used in connection with other words.

In this respect the work of the psychological laboratory has corroborated with singular clearness the observations of thoughtful educators and both are in substantial agreement with. Miss Keller's report.

Professor Cattell found that on an average—

> Consciousness can at one time grasp four numbers, three to four letters, two words, or a sentence composed of four words. The letters are slightly more difficult to grasp than the numbers, every combination of numbers making a number that "gives sense." Not as many words as letters can be grasped at one time, but three times as many letters when they make words as when they have no connection. Twice as many words can be grasped when they make a sentence as when they have no connection. *The sentence is taken up as a whole; if it is grasped, the words appear very distinct;* this is also the case when the observer constructs an imaginary sentence from the traces he has taken up.[2]

Dr. Zeitler,[3] after careful experiment, reached the conclusion that the definite fixing of the letters in the word is secured only through a knowledge of its meaning. The mind sees in the word the form that the meaning calls for. If the word is not known, the "letters fall into confusion." The word-form remains uncertain until the meaning is grasped. Therefore the "letter complex" *is seized on by the eye but established by the sense.*

This agrees with the experiments of Dr. Pillsbury[4] who found

[2] *Brain,* Vol. VIII. The italics are not in the original.

[3] Wundt's *Philosophische Studien.*

[4] *American Journal of Psychology,* Vol. VIII.

that there was a definite "moment" between the presentation of the word to the eye and its recognition, which came "in a flash." The visual image of the word is not clearly perceived, i. e., understood until its meaning is grasped. "Until meaning is associated with it, the word looks strange."

We read from the inside, outward: the inside indicating the meaning. The idea gives the word meaning and *in giving it meaning it makes it a living symbol.* Rapid recognition of words takes place only in sentences. This suggests that the smallest unit in the reading process is the sentence. We *recognize* isolated words: we *read* sentences. This puts the "alphabet method" out of count and also robs the "word method" of authority. We recognize written and printed words through their content. This power of recognition works most rapidly and normally when words are in such relation as to give them significance for the reader. *The sentence is the reading unit.*

Reading is a process of relating, thinking, imaging—getting meaning. Words in organic relation make this process possible. The work done in the psychological laboratory confirms what has been called the "thought method" or method of concentration in reading. It is safe to say that in our most enlightened schools this is the method employed. The child begins with a sentence or with the word having a sentence value: this always signifies a "story" to him. He reads for thought and his interest in content is made the dynamic of reading.

No experimental tests so far discredit the work of training children to power in getting word-forms. Word training is an important adjunct to the reading process. Such training falls under three important devices: phonic analysis without the use of diacritical marks: an acquaintance with word families that give power of quickly analyzing the word: training in getting new words through the context.

These devices give the child readiness in making out new words for himself. With this training the best schools recognize the need of inducing from the beginning a habit of self-help. *The teacher never tells the child a word that he can find out for himself.* If he has had the word before, he is encouraged to look it up. If the context does not help and he can get the word by phonic analysis or by seeing in it a familiar phonogram, he is encouraged to do that. *The habit of self-help is recognized as essential to word-mastery.* The best schools today have not a word-method so much as a method with words and this method is a method of word-mastery into which the child is trained.

By far the most important feature of this method with words should be the training of the child into the habit of getting new words through the context. This is the method that every good mind uses. We do not often come on printed words that are not already in our oral vocabulary. What we need when we are reading is a suggestion that will call the word to consciousness through its meaning, and the context will do that better than any other means whatever. The work of Cattell and Zeitler points to word perception through context as the right habitual impulse to establish in getting at the new printed word, simply because it is in harmony with the mental process in reading. Training in both phonics and phonograms carries with it the tendency to secure recognition through form alone; it should be supplemented always by a training which makes meaning enlighten form.

During the reading activity the value of any method with words must be determined by its power of becoming tributary to that particular thinking process that is reading. If the word can be recognized without analysis by means of context it should always be done.

After the work is well begun consciousness of the word does not normally enter into the reading process. The perception of the word is purely automatic. This reflex power is the surest sign of word-mastery. Every teacher of primary reading recognizes its apearance, by the way the child directs his attention. When the attention tends to center on content, word-recognition is getting into the fringe of consciousness where it belongs. A method with words should lead to: (1) reflex power over the word; (2) a self-trustful attitude toward words; (3) the power of making words alive with thought and imagery.

The good master likes the young apprentice to take up his

new tools with fearless hands. To want to use the tool, to believe he can use the tool, and above all to desire to do something through it—that is the attitude that makes for growing skill; and words are tools.

Giving the child a method with words saves him from the most serious "arrest" of the reading class, viz., the danger of becoming a reader of words. He must grasp ideas, get images, read "stories," and he must from the beginning be *expected to do this*. Two things have helped to produce that monstrosity of the schoolroom—the word-pronouncer; the first is the lack of mastery of the word so that the child is forced to read spelling-wise. The second, and by far the more dangerous, is the over-emphasis of oral reading.

The test of reading work should be made through the power of the individual to grasp thought accurately and with a good degree of rapidity. He only has mastered the word who makes the word a means of mastering the idea.

CHILD-LABOR LEGISLATION

SOPHONISBA P. BRECKINRIDGE
The University of Chicago

In 1802 the first child-labor act was placed upon the statute books of England; in 1909 a leading actress and intelligent woman can seriously argue that a statute prohibiting the employment of children under the age of sixteen in theaters is not only futile but opposed to the artistic and dramatic interests of the community, and can openly admit that the success of her engagement in one of the great cities of America is dependent upon her successful evasion of the laws of the state.[1] In 1879 Illinois succeeded in prohibiting the employment of children under fourteen in underground mining operation,[2] but at the present time the distribution of the morning papers in Chicago is accomplished through the utilization of twelve-year-old boys from two until seven o'clock, and the sight of boys and girls between the ages of ten and sixteen on the streets of the city until midnight is familiar to all members of the community. In 1843 Mrs. Browning was moved by a parliamentary report upon the condition of the child workers in English mines to write "The Cry of the Children." In 1908 Harriet Monroe was similarly moved by the condition of the child workers in American cotton mills to voice their helplessness and their fatigue in "The Shadow-Child." [3]

[1] See letter from Mrs. Minnie Maddern Fiske to *Chicago Evening Post,* March 6, 1909.

[2] Illinois Revised Statutes, 1903, chap. 93, § 22.

[3] *The Century,* December, 1908:

THE SHADOW-CHILD

BY HARRIET MONROE

Why do the wheels go whirring round,
Mother, mother?
O mother, are they giants bound,
And will they growl forever?
Yes, fiery giants underground,
Daughter, little daughter,
Forever turn the wheels around,
And rumble, grumble ever.

Why do I pick the threads all day,
Mother, mother,
While sunshine children are at play?
And must I work forever?
Yes, shadow-child; the live-long day,
Daughter, little daughter,
Your hands must pick the threads away,
And feel the sunshine never.

A National Child-Labor Committee is therefore clearly at the present time not a superfluous agency in working out the purposes of the nation to conserve its resources not only of mines and forests but of child life, for the sake of the coming generation.[4] Such a committee has been organized for five years, and the proceedings of the fifth conference are now in the hands of the public.[5]

The discussions at such a conference would naturally take a wide range. Since for the present, at any rate, the protection of the children is at the mercy of the legislatures of the various states, the most interesting portion of the conference would be the reports of the progress in the different sections of the country

Why do the birds sing in the sun,
Mother, mother,
If all day long I run and run—
Run with the wheels forever?
The birds may sing till day is done,
Daughter, little daughter,
But with the wheels your feet must run—
Run with the wheels forever.

Why do I feel so tired each night,
Mother, mother?
The wheels are always buzzing bright!
Do they grow sleepy never?
O baby thing, so soft and white,
Daughter, little daughter,
The big wheels grind us in their might,
And they will grind forever.

And is the white thread never spun,
Mother, mother?
And is the white cloth never done—
For you and me done never?
Oh, yes, our thread will all be spun,
Daughter, little daughter,
When we lie down out in the sun
And work no more forever.

And when will come that happy day,
Mother, mother?
Oh, shall we laugh and sing and play
Out in the sun forever?
Nay, shadow-child, we'll rest all day,
Daughter, little daughter,
Where green grass grows and roses gay,
There in the sun forever.

[4] The objects of the committee are stated as follows: To promote the welfare of society, with respect to the employment of children in gainful occupations; to investigate and report the facts concerning child labor; to raise the standard of public opinion and parental responsibility with respect to the employment of children; to assist in protecting children by suitable legislation against premature or otherwise injurious employment, and thus to aid in securing for them an opportunity for elementary education and physical development sufficient for the demands of citizenship and the requirements of industrial efficiency; to aid in promoting the enforcement of laws relating to child labor; to co-ordinate, unify, and supplement the work of state or local child-labor committees, and encourage the formation of such committees where they do not exist.

[5] *National Child-Labor Committee: Child Workers of the Nation.* Proceedings of Fifth Annual Conference on Child Labor, Chicago, Ill., January 21–23, 1909 (New York, 1909; 105 E. Twenty-second Street, New York City). (Supplement to the *Annals of the American Academy of Political and Social Science,* March, 1909.)

toward an adequate safeguarding of its child life against economic exploitation. The reports are on the whole fairly encouraging. The Illinois law, in spite of its failure to prohibit the employment of children in the street trades, appears with certain exceptions to be a fair model toward which other states are more or less rapidly approaching. That law is summarized by the factory inspector of Illinois in the following brief statement (p. 153):

It (1) prohibits the employment of minors under the age of 14; (2) abolishes night work for all minors under the age of sixteen; (3) limits the employment of children to eight hours a day; (4) requires an educational test, consisting of an ability to read and write legibly simple sentences (these need not be in the English language), and provides that in the absence of such ability the child must go to night school if he wishes to be employed; (5) prohibits the employment of minors under the age of sixteen in any occupation which may be considered hazardous or dangerous to the child or which may injury its health or morals, and specifically prescribes what are considered hazardous and dangerous employments; (6) makes it unlawful for an employer to employ children under sixteen in any place of amusement where intoxicating liquors are sold; (7) prohibits the employment of children under the age of sixteen on the theatrical stage after 7 o'clock at night; (8) provides that a fine of from $5 to $25 be imposed upon any parent who permits a child to be employed contrary to the provisions of the law, and a fine of from $5 to $100 be imposed upon any employer violating the law.

It should be said that the exemption of the children who are engaged in the street trades is due not so much to a defect in the law as formulated by the legislature as to the interpretation of that law by the courts, which have held that the child who sells newspapers, though selling them on a commission, is not an employee of the person from whom he has secured the papers, but is himself an independent trader, free to conduct his mercantile operations at any hour of the day or night. That the street trades are not regulated by an enactment similar to the child-labor law is perhaps due to the fact that any agitation in behalf of such protective measures must depend for its success on publicity given by the newspapers, and that it has been impossible up to the present time to secure the co-operation of the newspapers in any attempt to exclude these youthful merchants from this form of dealing.[6]

The children of New York receive a more complete protection in that, before they are allowed to go to work, they must have fulfilled the requirements of the fifth grade of the public schools. The laws of Ohio require that they shall have a fairly adequate equipment in the use of the English language. Progress slow, but more or less assuring, is reported from the southern states, which have been subjected to peculiar temptations because of the necessity under which they have felt themselves of attracting capital from the North and West, by which they have been seduced into unrighteous pledges which could be fulfilled only at the cost of the weaker members of their working groups. Kentucky, Alabama, Georgia, and Louisiana all report the enrolment of child-labor laws upon their statute books. The western states, too, have been realizing the fact that they are not free from the dangers confronting the eastern and southern communities. Oregon, for example, which has "tried to believe that it has no child labor, has realized that the employment of children in candy, cracker, tin can, rope, wire, broom, bag, bolt, box, chair, gum, glass, fruit canning, and cigar factories, stores of every description, messenger service, office service, hotels and boarding-houses"[7] was evidence of the need of regulation, and has prohibited the employment of children under fourteen in all factories. The citizens of the District of Columbia have succeeded in obtaining from Congress a child-labor law. And while everywhere, as in the state of Illinois, there remain problems of child conservation to be attacked, it is evident that the realization of the need is now country-wide. It is however likewise evident from the presentation of these reports and from the general discussion of the problem that the nation is confronted with a danger which cannot successfully be resisted by the legislatures of the various states acting independently. The theatrical child sent out from New York to play perhaps in cities of every state in the Union is evidence enough that the problem is an interstate problem which can finally be solved successfully only by a resort to congressional legislation. Under our present

[6] See pp. 238, 239.

[7] P. 193.

notions of the constitutional limitations resting upon Congress, it will for a considerable time be impossible to secure a federal child-labor law. In the meantime it is proposed to make use of the federal power to give information, and intelligent co-operation among states can be greatly fostered by the establishment of a children's bureau, in the Department of the Interior, which shall have for its function the investigation of all subjects affecting the health, the efficiency, the character, the happiness, and the training of children, together with legislation undertaking to regulate these matters in the various states.[8]

No discussion of the employment of children would be complete without a reference to those other forms of legislation which have been found necessary in order to supplement the child-labor laws. There is therefore a paper upon "Child Labor and the Juvenile Court," [9] an institution providing for the care of dependent, neglected,[10] and delinquent[11] children. There is

[8] P. 23. [9] P. 111.

[10] ". . . . any male child who while under the age of seventeen years or any female child who while under the age of eighteen years, for any reason, is destitute, homeless, or abandoned; or dependent upon the public for support; or has not proper parental care or guardianship; or habitually begs or receives alms; or is found living in any house of ill-fame or with any vicious or disreputable person; or has a home which by reason of neglect, cruelty, or depravity, on the part of its parents, guardian, or any other person in whose care it may be, is an unfit place for such a child; and any child who while under the age of ten (10) years is found begging, peddling, or selling any article, or singing or playing any musical instrument for gain upon the street, or giving any public entertainments, or accompanies or is used in aid of any person so doing."

[11] " . . . . any male child who while under the age of seventeen years or any female child who while under the age of eighteen years violates any law of this state; or is incorrigible, or knowingly associates with thieves, vicious, or immoral persons; or without just cause and without that (the) consent of its parents, guardian, or custodian absents itself from its home or place of abode, or is growing up in idleness or crime; or knowingly frequents a house of ill-repute; or knowingly frequents any policy-shop or place where any gaming device is operated; or frequents any saloon or dramshop where intoxicating liquors are sold; or patronizes or visits any public poolroom or bucket-shop; or wanders about the streets in the night time without being on any lawful business or lawful occupation; or habitually wanders about any railroad yards or tracks or jumps or attempts to jump on to (any) moving train; or enters any car or engine without lawful authority; or uses vile, obscene, vulgar, profane, or indecent language in (any) public place or about any schoolhouse; or is guilty of indecent or lascivious conduct."

perhaps no better illustration of the haphazard way in which the community has for the last one hundred and twenty-five years attempted to answer questions of such social importance as the employment of children and of women, the care of the poorer members of society, the protection of the wage-earning group, than the way in which it has failed to take advantage of the school system which lay ready to its hand, to meet all the demands in behalf of the child, until the evils of child labor and of dependency and delinquency had become acute. Had the principle of the compulsory-education law, which is now looked upon largely as the handmaid to the child-labor and the juvenile-court laws, been applied, had the community seen to it that its children were in school as a political party sees to it that its voters are at the polls, the crimes of child labor and of child delinquency could never have been laid at its door.

THE OPEN SCHOOLHOUSE: ITS PART IN THE VACATION OF THE STAY-AT-HOME

FLORENCE K. GRISWOLD
Teachers College, Columbia University, New York City, N. Y.

Each year the Board of Education of New York City strives to make the school an actual part of the life, not only of the children but of their parents. The buildings are open for lectures for people of all ages on all subjects. Boys and girls now have their clubs in the same rooms in which they learned the three R's. All these things go on in the winter, but in the summer, during the long vacation, when the schoolhouse used to rest, the blinds are no longer down, but every day may be seen the same children of the winter, thronging to school because they want to go—for summer school is not compulsory.

These schools are real homes to both children and parents of the congested districts. Their first great purpose is to keep the children off the streets by furnishing them with pleasant and practical employment. But their work is of a more far-reaching character than to teach actual trades. They aim to bring about a better understanding of what the good things in life are, and to help the children onward. In the summer school the discipline is very light, hence the teacher comes into closer contact with her little charges than in regular school. She knows more of their actual lives, of their thoughts and feelings, thus she has greater possibilities and can really be of more assistance in bringing about a better condition.

The open schoolhouse in the summer is divided into three different departments. There is first the summer school from nine to twelve in the morning in which the children are taught the manual arts principally. This is for children of all ages. In the afternoon from one until five o'clock, there is the playground. Here games are played, there is no work—"just fun." The gymnasium is open for the larger boys. While both of these are good and enjoyed by the children, it is the evening that both parent and child alike look forward to. At seven-thirty the vari-colored electric bulbs on the roof of the schoolhouse begin to light and shed a soft radiance far out like that of a lighthouse; only its mission is different, for it bids the people to come, not to keep off. The tired people of the neighborhood watch for it; it means to them the school roof-garden is open. Soon the band begins to play and the people go trooping up for a waltz or a quiet chat with the neighbors. Until ten o'clock, an orderly throng come and go, waltz and promenade, talk and laugh. Then the school-building becomes quiet again, darkness reigns, but the rest is of short duration, for at eight o'clock in the morning the baths are open; the child not only may go to school in summer, but he may go clean, a luxury that is not always appreciated by the East-sider, although the baths have a large patronage.

In the morning the classes are given over to the practical needs of life, to which, in winter, lack of time prevents giving more than an hour or two a week. There are classes in elementary and advanced sewing, knitting, cooking, dressmaking, embroidery, millinery, and nursing for the girls; while the boys are taught carpentry, chair-caning, weaving, basketry, and bookbinding. The leather-tooling classes are generally very large; poor parents are practical, particularly the Jewish and Italian, who readily see what is good and free, and will help them "on" in life.

Boston was the first city to grasp the idea of keeping the schools open in summer. New York soon followed, and has so perfected the idea, that educators from other cities are now studying her schools as models. The latter city, after a severe financial struggle, has been able to keep open over thirty schoolhouses. These are in the congested districts all over Greater New York and are well equipped for teaching industrial subjects.

To illustrate what the open schoolhouse means to a certain class of children, the following story was told by one of the teachers: When twelve o'clock came, the hour for dismissal, one tiny child did not rise from her seat, but sat still looking disconsolately around. When the teacher asked her why she did not go home, she looked at her and answered with a plaintive voice, "I ain't got no place to go; my mamma, she went out early this morning and locked up the room. Please teacher, can I stay here, the boys beat me on the street, and my mamma will not be home for a long time, not until dark." Only the teacher and the settlement worker know how many children are locked out from morning until night sometimes by worthless mothers, who go their own way, and leave the children to the mercy of anyone who will give them a few pennies, or a place of refuge from the cruelty of the children of the street, but mostly by parents who must leave their homes in order to provide bread to fill the always-hungry mouths.

EDITORIAL NOTES

The *Elementary School Teacher* has always maintained a close relation with the Elementary School of the School of Education in the University of Chicago. It is the purpose of this school to deal with those problems in elementary education whose solution are of importance not only to the theory of elementary education but may be of practical value to elementary schools throughout the country. It will therefore be of interest to readers of this journal to note certain important changes which will be made in this school at the beginning of the coming year.

The Elementary School in the School of Education of the University of Chicago

The school will be divided into three general sections, the first consisting of the first three grades, the second of the fourth and fifth grades and the third of the three highest grades in the school. Three supervising teachers will be added to the present staff of the school to take charge of these sections. It will be the duty of each of these general teachers to supervise closely the work of the grades in his or her section. In addition it will be the function of this general teacher to give individual attention to any pupil who is either behind his class or in advance of the regular work of the grade. It is hoped that this element of individual attention may reinforce very largely the efficiency of the grade work. It will render possible individual promotions in the middle of the year in the case of children who are in advance of their class sufficiently to go into the class above, and it will make it possible for children who have difficulty with a single subject to keep up with the class through special instruction in this difficult subject.

Supervising Teachers and Their Functions

In the second place a closer organization is to be established between the elementary school and the college and graduate departments of education. Professor Sargent, for example, will be a member of the graduate department of education and will at the same time organize the work in art and manual training throughout the elementary grades. Associate Professor Parker, who has been appointed to a position in the graduate

Relation of the Departments of the University and the School

department of education, will have full charge of the practice teaching. These examples of relation between the college and university department and the elementary school will serve to make clear the general policy whereby the various university and college departments will be brought into the most intimate relation with the elementary school curriculum. In the past the departments of history, geography, nature study and mathematics have exercised some influence in the organization of the elementary school course, but this relation will be made more intimate and effective and the course of study of the elementary school will, during the coming year, be thoroughly organized under the general supervision of all the officers of the School of Education.

Reduction of Numbers and School Period

Third, some reduction will be made in the number of students in the elementary school. The school has in the past experienced a large demand for the duplication of the upper grades. This involved the admission of pupils who have never had the advantage of the training given in the lower grades and is evidently disadvantageous from that point of view. Next year there will be only one sixth grade instead of two, as in the past, and in general it will be the policy of the school not to duplicate the upper grades. Further than this, it is expected that within a very limited period of time the whole course of the elementary training will be reduced to seven years.

C. H. J.

NOTES AND NEWS

No more important problem, or series of problems, is before the general social conscience today than that which deals with the elements and conditions of public health. As this problem affects the school, attention has been called to it frequently in these notes. The demand grows for the application of a greater amount of intelligence to the school situation in order to secure greater immunity from those forms of unhealthfulness which are the sure results of ignorance and unsanitary conditions. It is reported that Des Moines has banished the general towel from the washrooms of the schools, and insists that he who will not bring his own individual towel, or use the individual towel provided for him by the school, shall not use the washrooms. But the general drinking-cup is still found in most schools, though we have been warned for years as to the dangers which lurk in the cup that is passed from mouth to mouth. Such conditions as these are so easily remedied as to make toleration of them almost criminal.

The institution of positive agencies for the control of undesirable conditions in the schools goes on rapidly. The Cambridge (Eng.) Education Committee has founded a free dental clinic for the use of the primary-school children attending its schools. In Boston, says an article in the *Survey*, 82,255 children were examined by the school medical inspection, in 1908. The results of this inspection may be seen by a few comparisons. In 1907, 32 per cent. of the pupils were found to be suffering from defective eyesight. In 1908 this percentage had sunk to 23. The percentage of those defective in hearing had sunk from 8.1 per cent. to 7.6 per cent. in the same period. Of course, this improvement may not all be owing to the medical inspection, but at least these figures suggest that this system must be given a complete trial. "Communities are beginning to see the matter in a new light. They are asking themselves not whether they can afford to take steps to safeguard in the schools the welfare of their children, but rather whether they can afford not to take such steps."

But not only as a matter of health and physical welfare does this problem present its importance; the whole problem of mental efficiency and moral control is closely related to it. Dr. George H. Martin, secretary of the State Board of Education for Massachusetts, says, in a recent number of the *Psychological Clinic*,

> The lesson which I have learned is that in addition to all the other forces making for a better understanding of health conditions, it is the imperative duty of the schools of all grades to broaden and make more vital their teaching of physiology and hygiene. . . . . We hear about "essentials" in school educa-

tion. A sound body kept sound by right living is the essential which underlies and conditions all the rest.

Mr. George E. Johnson, superintendent of the Playground Association of Pittsburg, says, in the same journal, that 70 per cent. of all school children suffer some physical handicap. The schools betray the children in their ignorance and innocence to the deadly foes, disease and disability. To combat these enemies of childhood the community must expend more thought. Sunshine, air, and play must be provided for.

The Wisconsin State Horticultural Society has made the following announcement relative to the work of beautifying of rural school grounds:

> The great need of systematized effort which would lead to the general improvement of the grounds of the rural schools of this state has long been evident to the officers of the State Horticultural Society, but as with many other similar departments no funds have been available for the work. In 1907, however, the legislature very graciously increased the annual appropriation to this society so that we find it possible to undertake in a systematic manner this work which we have long had in view. The following is a brief outline of the plan recently adopted by the executive committee of the society:
>
> A committee of three, consisting of the president and secretary of the State Horticultural Society and one other person appointed by the president, will this year select six schools and for these landscape plans will be prepared, and in co-operation with the school boards trees and shrubs will be planted under the direction of an expert. In brief the society aims to establish this work on a basis similar to the trial and model orchard work of the society which has now grown to cover the entire state and become a most useful factor in the development of the fruit industry of Wisconsin.

In the city of Milwaukee a work is being quietly carried on by some philanthropic spirits which contributes much to the effectiveness of the school work and to the comfort and happiness of many school children. A committee of three ladies found upon investigation that there were many children whose mothers and fathers were both away at work during the day with no one at home to prepare food for the little ones. In many cases the doors were locked and the children not allowed to enter the houses. Public school kitchens were opened. Tickets are issued to the principals. If the child has a penny, he gives it to the matron with his ticket; if he has no penny he still receives the ticket, which has been marked by the principal, to the matron—thus no child knows whether his neighbor does or does not pay the penny. Soup and hot rolls are served every school day, excepting Friday, when rice and milk, with cocoa, are served. Ten kitchens have been kept open the past season, all but one in public school buildings. During the month of January last seven thousand lunches were served. The children are asked for the penny so that they may not think it possible to get food for nothing. The average of those who do not bring pennies is about 10 per cent. of those served. As a consequence of the penny lunches, the principals and teachers report better work and better attendance, two vital factors in the efficiency of public schools.

BOOK REVIEWS

The Administration of Public Education in the United States. By SAMUEL T. DUTTON AND DAVID SNEDDEN. New York: Macmillan, 1908. Pp. 601. $1.75.

To every director of public educational work, as well as to every American citizen, who has come to regard education as a great social and political activity of a democratic people, the recent volume by Professors Dutton and Snedden, of the Teachers College of Columbia University, will make a direct appeal. In spite of its evident deficiencies, it makes accessible for the first time a connected account of the machinery of public education, together with some interpretation of the forces operating this machinery. While one may reserve objections to the statement that "school administration is not merely a description of machinery, it is primarily a study of human evolution and the progress of communities toward a more highly civilized life" (p. 10), it may fairly be said that the authors have succeeded in accomplishing an acceptable and useful piece of work for American education.

The opening chapters, dealing with the national, state, and local organization, administration, and finance of public education present in a concise way the more prominent features of the American educational system. The manner of organizing and presenting the mass of necessarily difficult detail is clumsy and confusing and has resulted in a number of instances in merely a jumble of disconnected statements, from which it is difficult to disentangle any broad general principles of American educational administration.

The chapters on the construction and the adaptation of the schoolhouse, textbooks and supplies, the superintendent of city schools, the teaching staff, supervision, the course of study, and the grading and promotion of pupils present in brief space much valuable material which cannot but be immediately serviceable to students and school officers.

Special chapters are devoted to the administration of high schools, of normal schools, of vocational education, of correctional education, of the educa tion for defective and subnormal children, and of evening and continuation schools. In view of the general comprehensiveness of the treatment attempted, one regrets to note the absence of any discussion of the organization of higher education, of its relationship to the lower schools, or of its rapidly expanding educative influence now so well exemplified in the great majority of state universities.

The large contemporary importance of the relationship of high schools to higher educational institutions renders very noticeable the absence of any discussion of the standardization and inspection of our state secondary-school systems.

The bibliographies appended to each chapter are presented in such a way as to be almost useless. The titles are merely thrown together without any reference to importance or value.

The difficult style of the book as well as the peculiar mode of treatment will limit its ready use as a textbook in college and university classes. This fact is mentioned because today there is large need for an effective textbook for students who are preparing for participation in the directive activities of public education.

At a number of points the work is marred by errors, typographical and otherwise, destructive of both accuracy and clearness. More careful proof-reading would have obviated many of these errors.

President Butler, of Columbia University, has written a brief and characteristic introduction. While the *Administration of Public Education in the United States* has its defects and limitations, these are, in the majority of cases, of the sort necessarily imposed upon a bit of pioneer work treating of such a rapidly changing field of human action. EDWARD C. ELLIOTT

UNIVERSITY OF WISCONSIN

Arithmetical Abilities and Some Factors Determining Them. By CLIFF WINFIELD STONE, PH.D. Published by Teachers College, Columbia University, New York City. Pp. 101. $1.00.

This book is a practical research thesis. It represents the modern tendency toward scientific study of educational problems. It develops a scientific method by which the efficiency of the arithmetic teaching in any school system may be accurately determined. Every school superintendent or supervisor of arithmetic teaching should have a copy of this book, and it may be read with profit by teachers of arithmetic everywhere.

It is a study of the relation between distinctive educational procedures and the resulting products. It investigates the nature of the product of the first six years of arithmetic work, and the relation between distinctive procedures in arithmetic work and the resulting abilities.

Tests were given in twenty-six representative school systems, geographically distributed over a large area of the country. These tests measured the abilities of sixth-grade children in arithmetical processes and in problem-analysis. The results of the tests are tabulated and studied to determine their bearings upon the following topics: (*a*) variability in the products of the different school systems; (*b*) variability of abilities among children as to the amount accomplished and as to accuracy; (*c*) relationship of abilities among systems and among individual pupils; (*d*) what we should mean when we speak of the product of arithmetic teaching; (*e*) practical suggestions for grading and for grouping. The study shows that the net result of the arithmetic work is several products, rather than a product. Arithmetic is largely a training of special abilities. The lack of uniformity among systems is great, and the variability among individuals within a given system is even greater than among systems. The variability among boys does not differ appreciably from that among girls. "Ability in any fundamental except addition implies nearly the same ability in other fundamentals in both systems and individuals; but ability in any fundamental implies ability in reasoning in individuals to a less degree than ability in such a subject as English implies ability in such a subject as geography."

Part of the study is devoted to the relation between time-expenditure and abilities. There is little relation between the two. The use of time for the enrichment of the content of arithmetic work is not necessarily detrimental to the mastery of the essentials. The book considers also the relation between arithmetical abilities and the excellence of the course of study in arithmetic. While the excellence of the course of study doubtless is a factor in producing abilities, "systems vary so widely in the uses they are making of courses of study that the chances are about even that if one were to choose a system of schools with a good standing in abilities, that system would rank among the poorer systems as to course of study."

The tests used in the study are given in the book. The method of the study is given fully in Part I, and there should be no difficulty in adapting it in any school system. This scientific study provides the educational world with a means of beginning to standardize its products.

J. F. M.

BOOKS RECEIVED

AMERICAN BOOK COMPANY, NEW YORK

Coe's School Readers. By FANNY E. COE. Cloth. Illustrated. Third Grade Reader, pp. 284, $0.40; Fourth Grade Reader, pp. 360, $0.50.

Harvey's Practical Arithmetics. By L. D. HARVEY. Cloth. Book I, pp. 300, $0.35; Book II, pp. 400, $0.50.

Famous Men of Modern Times. By JOHN H. HAAREN AND A. B. POLAND. Cloth. Illustrated. Pp. 352. $0.50.

A. S. BARNES & CO., NEW YORK

Plays and Games for Indoors and Out. Rhythmic Activities Correlated with the Studies of the School Programme. By BELLE RAGNAR PARSONS. Cloth. Illustrated. Pp. 215. $1.50.

The Folk Dance Book. For Elementary Schools, Classroom, Playground, and Gymnasium. Compiled by C. WARD CRAMPTON. Cloth. Pp. 81. $1.50.

GINN & CO., BOSTON

The Body at Work. Book IV, "The Gulick Hygiene Series." By FRANCES GULICK JEWETT. Cloth. Illustrated. Pp. 247. $0.50.

HINDS, NOBLE & ELDREDGE, NEW YORK

Famous Poems Explained. Helps to Reading with the Understanding. By WAITMAN BARBE; with an Introduction by RICHARD G. BOONE. Cloth. Pp. 237. $1.00.

Writing the Short-Story. A Practical Handbook on the Rise, Structure, Writing, and Sale of the Modern Short-Story. By J. BERG ESENWEIN. Cloth. Pp. 441. $1.25.

THE MACMILLAN COMPANY, NEW YORK

The Psychology of Thinking. By IRVING ELGAR MILLER. Cloth. Pp. 303. $1.25.

WORLD BOOK CO., YONKERS-ON-HUDSON, NEW YORK

Human Physiology. An Elementary Textbook, of Anatomy, Physiology, and Hygiene. ("New-World Science Series.") By JOHN W. RITCHIE. Cloth. Illustrated. Pp. 362. $0.80.

New-World Speller. By JULIA HELEN WOHLFARTH AND LILLIAN EMILY ROGERS. Cloth. Illustrated. Pp. 160.

CURRENT EDUCATIONAL LITERATURE IN THE PERIODICALS [1]

IRENE WARREN
Librarian, School of Education, The University of Chicago

Actual co-operation between libraries and schools. Pub. Lib. 14:142–46. (Ap. '09.)

AYRES, LEONARD P. The money cost of the repeater. Psycholog. Clinic. 3:49–58. (15 Ap. '09.)

——Physical defects and school progress. Amer. Phys. Educa. R. 14:197–207. (Ap. '09.)

BARNES, EARL. Child-study in relation to elementary art education. Kind. Mag. 21:261–67. (My. '09.)

BINGHAM, MRS. KATE STEVENS. The playgrounds of greater Boston. New Eng. Mag. 39:185–93. (Ap. '09.)

BISHOP, AVARD LONGLEY. Geography in the universities abroad. Educa. R. 37:477–82. (My. '09.)

BOSTWICK, ARTHUR E., MAXWELL, WILLIAM H., AND BUTLER, NICHOLAS MURRAY. James Hulme Canfield. Lib. Journ. 34:143–45. (Ap. '09.)

BURKS, JESSE D. Getting our bearings on industrial education. El. Sch. T. 9:445–55. (My. '09.)

BUTLIN, IVA M. Honor system in college libraries. Pub. Lib. 34:162–64. (Ap. '09.)

CANFIELD, JAMES H. The library's part in education. Pub. Lib. 14:120. (Ap. '09.)

CHAMBERLAIN, ALEXANDER F., AND CHAMBERLAIN, ISABEL C. Studies of a child. IV. "Meanings" and "definitions" in the forty-seventh and forty-eighth months. Pedagog. Sem. 16:64–104. (Mr. '09.)

CLARK, ALICE WEMOTT. The story hour. Pub. Lib. 34:164–65. (Ap. '09.)

[1] Abbreviations: Amer. Phys. Educa. R., American Physical Educational Review; Educa., Education; Educa. News, Educational News; Educa. R., Educational Review; El. Sch. T., Elementary School Teacher; Good Housekeep., Good Housekeeping; Harp. W., Harper's Weekly; Indian Educa., Indian Education; Journ. of Educa., Journal of Education; Kind. Mag., Kindergarten Magazine; Kind. R., Kindergarten Review; Lib. Journ., Library Journal; Liv. Age, Living Age; New Eng. Mag., New England Magazine; Out., Outlook; Pedagog. Sem., Pedagogical Seminary; Psycholog. Clinic, Psychological Clinic; Pub. Lib., Public Libraries; Teach. Coll. Rec., Teachers College Record; Tech. World Mag., Technical World Magazine; Utah Educa. R., Utah Educational Review.

DEVEREUX, HELENA T. Report of a year's work on defectives in a public school. Psycholog. Clinic. 3:45–49. (15 Ap. '09.)

DICKINSON, ASA DON. The encouragement of literature in libraries. Pub. Lib. 34:166–67. (Ap. '09.)

DOLL, LOISE M. A Cincinnati special class. Psycholog. Clinic. 3:34–45. (15 Ap. '09.)

DOWNEN, JOHN M. The Renaissance of the three R's. Educa. R. 37:449–56. (My. '09.)

DRIGGS, H. R. What the eighth Utah legislature accomplished for education. Utah Educa. R. 2:7–11. (Ap. '09.)

EARLE, E. LYELL. A problem of the kindergarten today. Kind. Mag. 21:247–49. (My. '09.)

EGGLESTON, PERCY COE. Yale and her president. 1775–95. New Eng. Mag. 39:137–48. (Ap. '09.)

ELLISON, LOUISE. The acquisition of technical skill. Pedagog. Sem. 16:49–64. (Mr. '09.)

FORDYCE, CHARLES. College ethics. Educa. R. 37:492–501. (My. '09.)

FOSTER, WILLIAM TRUFANT. The American college on trial. School R. 17:330–44. (My. '09.)

GULICK, LUTHER H. Constructive medicine. How it has grappled with a single problem in school hygiene. Amer. Phys. Educa. R. 14:261–71. (My. '09.)

GULICK, LUTHER HALSEY. Why have playgrounds? Good Housekeep. 48:567–70. (My. '09.)

HADLEY, ARTHUR T. The library in the university. Pub. Lib. 14:115–17. (Ap. '09.)

HALL, G. STANLEY. What college for my daughter? Good Housekeep. 48:549–52. (My. '09.)

HOFFMAN, U. J. What the library means to the school. Harp. W. 53:24, 25. (24 Ap. '09.)

HOLMES, HENRY W. Educational progress in 1908. School R. 17:289–330. (My. '09.)

JASTRO, JOSEPH. Psychology and psychotherapy. Dial. 46:292–95. (1 My. '09.)

JEWELL, AGNES. The public library and the school problem. Pub. Lib. 14:117–19. (Ap. '09.)

KEOGH, ANDREW. The training of college students in bibilography. Pub. Lib. 14:124. (Ap. '09.)

KIP, KATHRYN ROMER. Is the kindergarten injurious? Kind. Mag. 21:249–53. (My. '09.)

LARUE, DANIEL WOLFORD. The church and the public school. Educa. R. 37:468–77. (My. '09.)

LEAHY, E. M. Some educational aims in a school for girls. Journ. of Educa. 40:285–89. (1 Ap. '09.)

LEATHER, HERBERT. Medical inspection in English primary schools. El. Sch. T. 9:455–63. (My. '09.)

LEE, JOSEPH. Growth through achievement. School R. 17:353–63. (My. '09.)

Library instruction in normal schools. Pub. Lib. 14:147. (Ap. '09.)

LIVERIGHT, ADA F. How may the use of books and library catalogues be made a subject of study in normal schools? Pub. Lib. 34:160–62. (Ap. '09.)

Public libraries and libraries in schools; contributed from various libraries. Lib. Journ. 34:145–53. (Ap. '09.)

M., A. C. Cleveland public library's children's work. Pub. Lib. 34:165, 166. (Ap. '09.)

MCKENSIE, R. TAIT. The regulation of physical instruction in schools and colleges from the standpoint of hygiene. Amer. Phys. Educa. R. 14:224–28. (Ap. '09.)

MACVAY, ANNA PEARL. Report of a classical teacher's visit to Great Britain and Ireland. Educa. R. 37:501–16. (My. '09.)

MAXWELL, WILLIAM H. The necessity for departments of hygiene within boards of education. Amer. Phys. Educa. R. 14:301–8. (My. '09.)

MEYLAN, GEORGE L. The contribution of physical education to national health and education. Amer. Phys. Educa. R. 14:191–97. (Ap. '09.)

MISAWA, TADASU. A few statistical facts from Japan. Pedagog. Sem. 16:104–13. (Mr. '09.)

OPPENHEIMER, CARROL P. The relation of the kindergarten to the home. Kind. Mag. 21:253–55. (My. '09.)

Orthogenics in the public schools. Psycholog. Clinic. 3:29–34. (15 Ap. '09.)

O'SHEA, M. V. Sympathy *vs.* sentiment in the kindergarten. Kind. R. 19:515–18. (My. '09.)

PERRIN, MARSHALL LIVINGSTON. The institutional school. School R. 17:344–53. (My. '09.)

PRICE, HELEN U. Possibilities for work with children in small libraries. Pub. Lib. 14:121–23. (Ap. '09.)

Qualifications and training of modern language teachers. Journ. of Educa. 40:247–48. (1 Ap. '09.)

Recent movements in the teaching corps of German universities. Educa. R. 37:482–92. (My. '09.)

RICE, RAYMOND F. New link between industry and education. Tech. World Mag. 11:227–35. (My. '09.)

ROOD, HENRY EDWARD. The newer education. Harp. W. 53:16–18. (17 Ap. '09.)

SELLERS, EDITH. A high school of Danish peasants. Liv. Age. 43:149–56. (17 Ap. '09.)

SHORT, R. L. The seventh to tenth grades a unit in mathematics. El. Sch. T. 9:471–76. (My. '09.)

SIEBEL, EMMA. A language-exercise in dramatization. El. Sch. T. 9:463-71. (My. '09.)

SMALL, WALTER H. An educational brief. Journ. of Educa. 69:427-29. (22 Ap. '09.)

STECHER, WM. A. Determining principles which should decide the content of the public-school curriculum in physical education. Mind and Body. 16:101-4. (My. '09.)

STOWE, LYMAN BEECHER. The government as a teacher. Out. 91:870-77. (17 Ap. '09.)

SIRUTHERS, J. Medical inspection. Educa. News. 3:357, 358. (9 Ap. '09.)

Studies in secondary education. Teach. Coll. Rec. 10:1-78.

SACHS, JULIUS. Introductory note. Pp. 1, 2.

STEVENS, ROMIET. Primitive history. Pp. 3-15.

MILLIS, JAMES F. Real problems in geometry. Pp. 16-45.

BROOKMAN. First-year high-school mathematics. Pp. 46-63.

INGLIS, ALEXANDER J. Co-operation and correlation in language teaching in the high school. Pp. 64-78.

THOMAS, ISAAC. The waste of life in college. Educa. 29:503-7. (Ap. '09.)

TILDSLEY, JOHN L. School reports as they are: a rejoinder. Educa. R. 37:433-49. (My. '09.)

TOMLINSON, EVERETT T. The great public schools of England. Scrib. 45:515-50. (My. '09.)

TRAVIS, SEWARD S. High-school fraternities. Educa. 29:517-27. (Ap. '09.)

TYLER, JOHN M. Physical training for girls of high-school age. Amer. Phys. Educa. R. 14:271-77. (My. '09.)

VARNEY, JOSHUA D. The basis of ethics. Pedagog. Sem. 16:113-19. (Mr. '09.)

WARDEN OF WADHAM COLLEGE. The Oxford undergraduate, past and present. Liv. Age. 43:267-74. (1 My. '09.)

WHIPPLE, MR. AND MRS. GUY MONTROSE. The vocabulary of a three-year-old boy with some interpretative comments. Pedagog. Sem. 16:1-23. (Mr. '09.)

WIMMS, J. H. The teaching of psychology to students in training. Journ. of Educa. 40:253-56. (1 Ap. '09.)

WITMAR, LIGHTNER. Are we educating the rising generation? Educa. R. 37:456-68. (My. '09.)

Work with schools. Pub. Lib. 14:141, 142. (Ap. '09.)

The Elementary School Teacher

June, 1909

Vol. IX, No. 10

THE UNIVERSITY OF CHICAGO PRESS
CHICAGO AND NEW YORK
OTTO HARRASSOWITZ, LEIPZIG

Beauty

Doctors regard beauty from the point of view of health, and tell you that a good natural complexion and a fair, soft skin are necessary essentials of beauty. They never disagree about that, nor do they disagree about the merits of

Pears' Soap

which is the most perfect beautifying agent known, being pure in every particle and possessing those special and unique qualities which render the skin pure, clear and of exquisite softness. The beauties of six generations have acknowledged PEARS' to be

The Best Aid to Beauty

From the Doctor's Point of View

PEARS

OF ALL SCENTED SOAPS PEARS' OTTO OF ROSE IS THE BEST.

"All rights secured."

The Elementary School Teacher

PUBLISHED MONTHLY EXCEPT IN JULY AND AUGUST

EDITORIAL BOARD

JAMES H. TUFTS

GEORGE H. MEAD, *Secretary* OTIS W. CALDWELL
EMILY J. RICE JOHN M. CROWE
LILLIAN S. CUSHMAN BERTHA PAYNE

WITH THE CO-OPERATION OF

THE FACULTY OF THE UNIVERSITY OF CHICAGO SCHOOL OF EDUCATION

AND

THE FACULTY OF THE FRANCIS W. PARKER SCHOOL

Vol. IX CONTENTS FOR JUNE, 1909 No. 10

The Elementary School Teacher is published monthly from September to June. ¶The subscription price is $1.50 per year; the price of single copies is 20 cents. ¶Postage is prepaid by the publishers on all orders from the United States, Mexico, Cuba, Porto Rico, Panama Canal Zone, Republic of Panama, Hawaiian Islands, Philippine Islands, Guam, Tutuila (Samoa), Shanghai. ¶Postage is charged extra as follows: For Canada, 30 cents on annual subscriptions (total $1.80), on single copies, 3 cents (total 23 cents); for all other countries in the Postal Union, 46 cents on annual subscriptions (total $1.96), on single copies, 6 cents (total 26 cents). ¶Remittances should be made payable to The University of Chicago Press, and should be in Chicago or New York exchange, postal or express money order. If local check is used, 10 cents must be added for collection.

Otto Harassowitz, Querstrasse 14, Leipzig, Germany, has been appointed agent for the European continent and is authorized to quote the following prices: Yearly subscriptions, including postage, M.8.25 each; single copies, including postage, M.1.10 each.

Claims for missing numbers should be made within the month following the regular month of publication. The publishers expect to supply missing numbers free only when they have been lost in transit.

Business correspondence should be addressed to The University of Chicago Press, Chicago, Ill.

Communications for the editors should be addressed to them at The University of Chicago, Chicago, Ill.

Entered October 12, 1903, at the Post-Office at Chicago, Ill., as second-class matter, under Act of Congress March 3, 1879.

Copyright, 1909, The University of Chicago

PROFESSOR IRVING KING'S

The Psychology of Child Development

In use at

Vassar College
University of Wisconsin
Milwaukee Normal
Columbia University
Pratt Institute
Georgia State Normal
Humboldt College
Iowa College
Franklin & Marshall College
Washington State Normal School
Cornell College

and many other institutions

THIS book is a study in the psychology of the growing mind designed to meet the needs of those educators and students who do not believe that a study of adult psychology is sufficient preparation for the teacher. Its point of view is that mental growth is a phase of children's activities, and hence that it must be studied in connection with them. The question of the beginning of consciousness is treated, and the development of grasping is traced as a typical activity involving growth in mental function. From the same point of view are discussed the emotional life of the child, his moral ideas, etc. One of the most notable chapters is that on imitation and its place in mental growth. The treatment of the subject is entirely new, and the interests of the school years are treated at length. The author here attempts to organize and present in a readable form the scattered material of child-study. The book closes with a valuable chapter on Adolescence and an extremely suggestive chapter on the educational implications of this activity-view of mental development.

12MO 288 PAGES $1.00 NET, POSTPAID $1.11

"I regard King's *Psychology of Child Development* as presenting child psychology from one point of view more effectively than any book that has yet appeared. And this point of view is one which every student of mental development ought to get. I am confident that the book warrants your making it known to all students of childhood. I think, too, that the better class of teachers found in teachers' reading circles would be able to appreciate much of the book at any rate."—M. V. O'SHEA, Madison, Wis.

"It is without question the best general view of the mental development of childhood that has yet been published."—W. G. CHAMBERS, State Normal School, Moorhead, Minn.

"It is a book sound in theory, full of suggestion, and valuable alike to the practical teacher and the educationalist."—*Educational News.*

"It will be of great value to normal schools as well as to the teachers in elementary and secondary schools."—*Journal of Pedagogy.*

Published by

The University of Chicago Press

Chicago, and 156 Fifth Avenue, New York

Plan Your Summer Trip *NOW* to

Colorado

the greatest Summer resort state in the Union and which offers the greatest variety of outdoor sports. Ideal place for camping out at small expense. The **Burlington Route** is the shortest line and with its three splendid daily trains offers the best service thereto. $30.00 round trip daily all summer.

Yellowstone Park

the national playground, containing nature's greatest wonders and where large game animals are constantly seen, in their native wild state. $46.50 round trip to Mammoth Hot Springs. $50.00 more including staging and hotels for 5½ days—or to the

Alaska-Yukon-Pacific Exposition

the most interesting exposition ever held—where meet the Occident and Orient, the South Seas and Alaska, and where the marvelous development of the great Northwest may be partly realized. $62 round trip on any of the electric lighted limited trains of the **Burlington Route, the only line running through trains from Chicago to Seattle.**

Send for handsome illustrated folders free, specifying the one or ones wanted.

Burlington Route

P. S. EUSTIS, Passenger Traffic Manager
C., B. & Q. R. R.
209 Adams Street, Chicago.

5417 6

BOOKS BY JOHN DEWEY

Studies in Logical Theory (*edited*)
xiv+388 pp., 8vo, cloth, net, $2.50; postpaid, **$2.67**

The School and Society (*fourth edition*)
130 pp., 12mo, cloth, postpaid . . . **1.00**

The Educational Situation (*second edition*)
104 pp., 12mo, cloth, net, 75 cents; postpaid **.80**

The Logical Conditions of a Scientific Treatment of Morality
27 pp., 4to, paper, net, 50 cents; postpaid . **.54**

Significance of the Problem of Knowledge
00 pp., royal 8vo, paper, net, 35 cents; postpaid **$0.37**

Psychology and Social Practice
42 pp., 12mo, paper, net, 25 cents; postpaid **.27**

The Child and the Curriculum
40 pp., 12mo, paper, net, 25 cents; postpaid **.27**

Interest as Related to Will
40 pp., 8vo, paper, net, 25 cents; postpaid . **.27**

At all booksellers or direct from

The University of Chicago Press

CHICAGO and 156 Fifth Avenue NEW YORK

SUMMER SCHOOL

UNIVERSITY OF PENNSYLVANIA

TERM: JULY 6TH TO AUGUST 17TH

Special Courses for Elementary School Teachers, High School Teachers, Supervisors and Principals, Instructors in Commercial High Schools, Social Workers, and Teachers in charge of School Playgrounds and Gardens.

School of Observation, with eight grades and an ungraded room, in charge of experts representing a variety of Training Schools and City Systems. Seminar for the discussion of work observed. Lectures by Noted School Men.

Psychological Clinics, Botanical Gardens, Chemical, Physical and Biological Laboratories.

Both Undergraduate and Graduate Courses in the usual subjects leading to the degrees of A.B., B.S., M.A., and Ph.D. including Music, Economics, and Commercial Geography.

For circular and information address A. DUNCAN YOCUM, Director of the Summer School, Box 12, College Hall, University of Pennsylvania, Philadelphia. Pa. 5

THE PERRY PICTURES

ONE CENT EACH

for 25 or more. Size 5½x8

(6 to 8 times size of this picture)

Send 25 cts. for 25 art subjects, or 25 Madonnas.

Catalogue of 1,000 miniature illustrations, two pictures and a Colored Bird picture for 3 two-cent stamps.

THE PERRY PICTURES CO., Box 501 Malden, Mass.

Normal College of the North American Gymnastic Union

415-419 East Michigan St., Indianapolis, Ind.

Two-year and four-year courses, leading to academic title and degree, open to high school graduates.

Competent teachers of physical training recommended by **Physical Training Teachers' Bureau of the N. A. G. U.**, 415-419 E. Michigan St., Indianapolis, Ind. Registration restricted to graduates of Normal College (1868-1909). 4

University of Illinois

The State University

Summer Session

June 21 to August 20, 1909

Large Faculty. Better facilities than ever before. Courses in all departments of science and arts. Tuition for the session $12.00. A free scholarship is offered to every high school teacher in Illinois, or to any other teacher in the state who can matriculate in the University. Circular and full information on application to

THOMAS ARKLE CLARK, DIRECTOR

URBANA, ILLINOIS 3

VALPARAISO UNIVERSITY

VALPARAISO, INDIANA

SUMMER SCHOOL WILL OPEN MAY 18; MID-SUMMER SESSION WILL OPEN JUNE 15

Catalog mailed free. Address, H. B. BROWN, President, or O. P. KINSEY, Vice-President 5

LITERATURE IN THE COMMON SCHOOLS

By Prof. John H. Cox. A book for teachers, with a model course of study. Cloth, 90 cents.

LITTLE, BROWN & Co. BOSTON.

University Summer School

Minneapolis, Minn. June 21 to July 31,'09

Elementary teachers' courses in all common school subjects. College courses in history, mathematics, languages, literature and science for high school teachers. Special courses in domestic art and science, manual training, music, drawing, and physical culture. For Bulletin, address

The Registrar, University of Minnesota

Minneapolis, Minn. 3

THE SCHOOL REVIEW

Edited by the Department of Philosophy and Education of the University of Chicago. Published monthly, except in July and August. Subscription price, $1.50 a year; single copies, 20 cents; foreign postage, 52 cents

The University of Chicago Press

CHICAGO NEW YORK

In Press

Little Stories About Little Animals for Little Children

BY SUSAN HOLTON

Illustrated in color by Katharine Maynadier Browne

Ten delightful little tales of the "domestic jungle" by a professional teller of stories to children.

The purity of Miss Holton's diction makes this book an excellent supplementary reader for children from five to eight.

Binding: Boards. 24mo. 75 cents net, postage extra.

If possible order through your local bookseller.

The Children's Publishing Company

Cincinnati 5

The Place of Industries in Elementary Education

By KATHARINE ELIZABETH DOPP

". . . We can only wish that this book may have the wide-reaching influence that it deserves.— *The Nation.*

270 pp., illustrated, net, $1.00; postpaid, $1.11

Address Dept. P

The University of Chicago Press

Chicago and New York

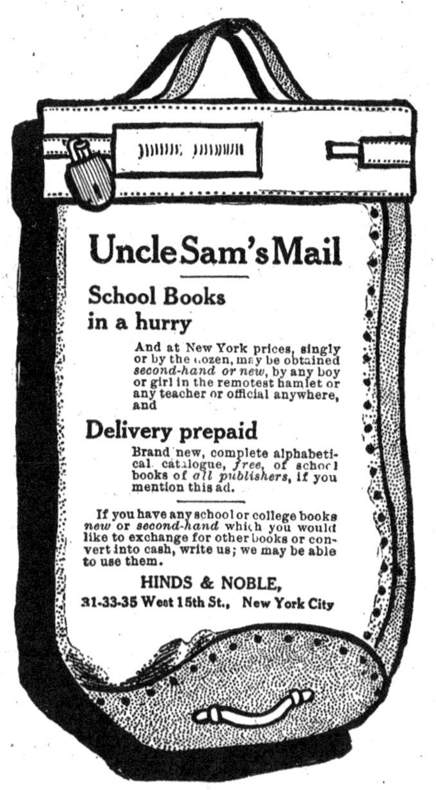

Magic Lanterns
with the
Alco-Radiant Light
for use where
Electricity Cannot be Had

The Alco-Radiant is the only practical, brilliant light for lantern use where electricity is not available. It burns alcohol, costs little to use and but a trifle to buy; weighs 3 lbs.; adaptable to any lantern. We also make

Electric and Calcium Lanterns,
Projecting Microscopes,
Projecting Spectroscopes,
Projecting Polariscopes
and Reflectoscopes

for showing Post Cards, Engravings and Cuts. We also carry **40,000** Lantern Slides for sale or rent. Send for lists stating your requirements.

WILLIAMS, BROWN & EARLE,
Dept. 22 918 Chestnut St., Philadelphia, Pa.

SOCIAL DUTIES FROM THE CHRISTIAN POINT OF VIEW

BY CHARLES RICHMOND HENDERSON

DESIGNED for use as a textbook in Bible classes and similar organizations. It introduces the reader to the following fields of thought and effort: (1) social aims; (2) the family; (3) material conditions of domestic life; (4) neglected children; (5) the working men; (6) rural communities; (7) the public health of cities; (8) urban economic interests; (9) urban education; (10) churches and religion in cities; (11) municipal government; (12) charities and correction; (13) great corporations; (14) the business class, the leisure class, and socialists; (15) national and state government and taxation; (16) international studies. In connection with each topic references are given for further reading; directions are offered for personal observation of local problems; many points are suggested for independent investigation and discussion by members of the class.

The author has sought to present the material in language free from technicalities, clearly and compactly. The problems are those which all young men and women at the threshold of actual responsibility are called upon to face.

330 pages, 12 mo, cloth. Postpaid, $1.25

Address Dept. P **The University of Chicago Press** Chicago New York

GLOBE TEACHERS' AGENCY

RECOMMENDS GOOD TEACHERS

Registration Free **Box 926** **ST. LOUIS, MO.**

6

THE CLARK TEACHERS' AGENCY

B. F. Clark Chicago, Steinway Hall Spokane, Wash., 225 Peyton Block **21st Year**

James F. McCullough Teachers' Agency

RAILWAY EXCHANGE BUILDING, CHICAGO

A Successful School and College Bureau

NOW is the time to **Register.** Good teachers wanted in all departments. **No Registration** fee to pay until position is secured. We make direct recommendation of our candidates. **Write us today.**

The Western Educational Agency wants **Specialists** in Drawing, Music, Manual Training, Domestic Science, Athletics, Physical Training, and Commercial Branches for **California Schools.** During the first week in May we had twenty calls for SPECIAL TEACHERS. Register Now. References: Stanford, or University of California. Address, WILLIAM HENRY HENSEY, B.A., B.S., Los Angeles, Cal.

CHILDREN PAY MORE ATTENTION

TO LESSONS ILLUSTRATED than to mental pictures from oral lessons

Our Catalogue of School Lanterns and Slides will suggest ideas to you.

It is FREE for the asking.

This Special School Lantern $45.00

McINTOSH STEREOPTICON COMPANY

421-22 ATLAS BLOCK CHICAGO, ILLINOIS

1

JERUSALEM IN BIBLE TIMES

BY LEWIS BAYLES PATON

An Archaeological Handbook for Travelers and Students

Fully illustrated, 150 pages, 12mo; flexible covers. Net, $1.00 Postpaid, $1.09

The University of Chicago Press
Chicago and New York

Preserve Your Magazines

Have them bound in Cloth or Leather. It will improve the appearance of your Library at a small expenditure. The University of Chicago Press has a well-equipped job bindery and will be pleased to quote prices + + + + + +

The University of Chicago Press

Mfg. Dept. Bindery Chicago

TEXT-BOOKS

Which You Will Wish to Consider When Making Changes

BEGINNERS' READING BOOKS

A Primer. *30 cents net, postpaid.*

A First Reader. *30 cents net, postpaid.*

These two books constitute a most satisfactory introductory course in reading. Difficulties in learing to read have been minimized by carefully graded exercises containing as reading material selections from the classic literature of children, which because of its inherent charm has been read for generations.

CHILDREN'S CLASSICS IN DRAMATIC FORM

By Augusta Stevenson

The author of this reader for the fourth grade is an experienced teacher who has received careful training in the playwright's art. She has prepared these dramatized versions of favorite tales from Anderson, Grimm, Æsop, and other sources for the pursose of arousing greater interest in oral reading and developing an expressive voice. *Illustrated by E. Boyd Smith.*

40 cents net, postpaid.

A PRIMER OF NURSERY RHYMES

By Leota Swem *Kindergarten Director* **and Rowena Sherwood** *Primary Teacher at Cedar Rapids, Iowa*

This is an original and delightful reading book for the first year of school. It is composed entirely of classic selections from the jingles which should form a part of the heritage of every child. Fully illustrated by reproductions from paintings of child life. *30 cents net, postpaid.*

WEBSTER-COOLEY LANGUAGE SERIES

By Alice Woodworth Cooley and W. F. Webster

(1) It is the only Series which provides a sufficient amount of language material.
(2) It is the only Series which makes a real, vitalizing use of literature.
(3) It is the only Series which emphasizes oral drill exercises (to teach correct habits of expression) throughout the entire grade course.
(4) It is the only Series whose parts are bound in a sufficient number of combinations to meet the special needs of every system of schools.
(5) It is the only Series which provides for a systematic course in English from the Fourth Grade through the High School.

A circular affording full and detailed information will be mailed upon request.

BAILEY-MANLY SPELLING BOOK

Price, Complete Edition, 25 cents

Part One, Grades 2-4, 16 Cents **Part Two, Grades 5-8, 20 cents**

This book represents a plan for the teaching of spelling which has been in successful use for several years. Its main features were determined ten years ago in the basis of long experience in teaching, and the details have been subjected to the test of actual use ever since. The success of the plan in the school in which it was first tried and in which the details were worked out, lead to its use in manuscript form in other schools.

The following points are of special interest:—

(1) Method of selecting the vocabulary. (2) Economy in teaching new words. (3) High literary quality of selections. (4) Review Words grouped as "Ear Words," "Ear and Eye Words," and "Eye Words."

HOUGHTON MIFFLIN COMPANY

BOSTON NEW YORK CHICAGO

The Hartford Fire Insurance Company
and
The National Association of Credit Men

The National Association of Credit Men, representing the leading mercantile houses of the United States, in addressing merchants throughout the country on the need of adequate and responsible fire insurance protection says:

> **"Through the guarantee which it has given you an insurance company may suddenly become your debtor. Might it not be well to know ahead of time what kind of debtor is it likely to be?"**

The points which the Credit Men say ought to be considered in a fire insurance company are given below. See how well they describe the Hartford.

What Credit Men Ask	What The Hartford Is
1. "What is the net surplus above capital and all liabilities?"	1. The Hartford's surplus January 1st, 1909, above capital and all liabilities—$5,061,592.
2. "Has it (the insurance company) a record of paying its debts (losses) promptly and without unjust deductions?"	2. After San Francisco, in putting the Hartford on its **Roll of Honor**, this same National Association of Credit Men said, "Considering that its gross loss was the immense sum of $10,275,000, the company is worthy of the highest commendation.
3. "Are the men who manage its affairs men of character and high standing in the community, upholding the principles of business which assure a long and honorable existence?"	3. The Hartford's reputation for commercial honor is its most cherished asset, and its continued observance of good faith with its policy-holders is attested by its popularity and success. It is 99 years old and does the largest fire insurance business in the United States.

The service which the Hartford affords the public continues throughout the year and is not limited to payment of losses. It has published a book, "Fire Prevention and Fire Insurance," with separate chapters for Householders, Merchants and Manufacturers, showing each how danger of fire may be reduced in his particular property. The book also gives valuable advice concerning insurance and may save you thousands of dollars no matter in what company you are insured. It is free. Send for it.

The Hartford Fire Insurance Company
Hartford, Conn.

Headache

The use of **Horsford's Acid Phosphate** is especially recommended in the relief of Nervousness and Headache caused by impaired digestion, prolonged wakefulness or overwork. It acts as a general tonic and vitalizer, promoting digestion and restoring the nervous system to healthful vigor.

Horsford's Acid Phosphate is agreeable to the taste and is the same phosphate that occurs in wheat and other cereals.

HORSFORD'S
Acid Phosphate
(Non-Alcoholic.)

SPENCERIAN STEEL PENS

ARE THE BEST

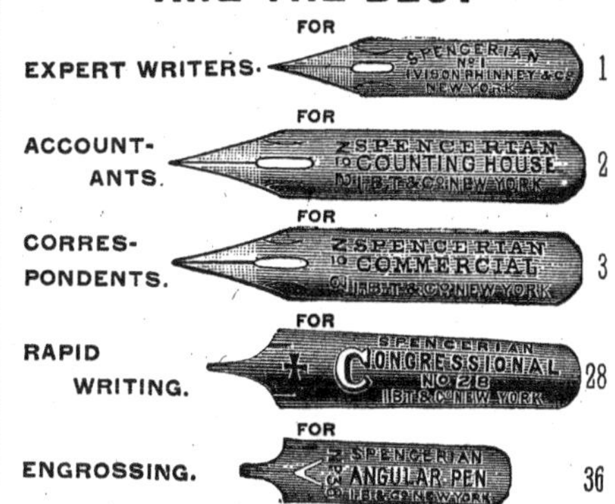

Select a Pen to Suit Your Handwriting

from a sample card of 12 pens sent on receipt of 6 cents in postage

SPENCERIAN PEN CO.
349 Broadway NEW YORK

MENNEN'S
BORATED TALCUM TOILET POWDER

"Baby's Best Friend"

and Mamma's greatest comfort. **Mennen's** relieves and prevents **Prickly Heat, Chafing and Sunburn.**

For your protection the **genuine** is put up in **non-refillable** boxes—the **"Box that Lox,"** with **Mennen's** face on top. Sold everywhere or by mail 25 cents—*Sample free.*

Guaranteed by the Gerhard Mennen's Chemical Co., under the Food and Drugs Act, June 30, 1906. Serial No. 1542.

Try Mennen's Violet (Borated) Talcum Toilet Powder—It has the scent of Fresh-cut Parma Violets. *Sample free.*

GERHARD MENNEN CO., Newark, N. J.

Mennen's Borated Skin Soap (blue wrapper) Specially prepared for the nursery } *No Samples*
Mennen's Sen Yang Toilet Powder, Oriental Odor
SOLD ONLY AT STORES

Intending purchasers of a *strictly first-class* Piano should not fail to examine the merits of

THE WORLD RENOWNED
SOHMER

It is the special favorite of the refined and cultured musical public on account of its unsurpassed tone-quality, unequaled durability, elegance of design and finish. Catalogue mailed on application.

THE SOHMER-CECILIAN INSIDE PLAYER SURPASSES ALL OTHERS
Favorable Terms to Responsible Parties
SOHMER & COMPANY
Warerooms Cor. 5th Ave., 22d St. NEW YORK

Ter-Centenary Celebration---Discovery of Lake Champlain---July 4, to 10, 1909

Ideal Summer Resorts

Vermont's Green Hills with its numerous Lakes and Streams and beautiful Lake Champlain have a thousand or more charming spots. *Village and Farm Homes, Summer Camps, First-class Hotels.* Excellent opportunity for real rest and recreation. Picturesque villages which offer rest to the seekers desiring a change from the city environment

Delightful diversity of mountain scenery is a constant source of enjoyment.

Excellent facilities afforded for entertaining guests at Vermont summer resorts.

Mountain Climbing, Fine Boating, Fishing and Hunting.

LOW RATE EXCURSIONS TO ALL POINTS OF INTEREST

Send 6c in stamps for 150 page booklet with 150 camera pictures, containing full information. Ter-Centenary Celebration Discovery of Lake Champlain, by Samuel de Champlain, published by the CENTRAL VERMONT RAILWAY, to SUMMER HOMES No. 14, at St. Albans, Vt.; or 360 Washington St., Boston, Mass.; or 385 Broadway, New York City. 6

FOR SUMMER HOME VACATION OUTING

LONG ISLAND, N.Y.

Long Island embraces all the conditions conducive to Health, Recreation, and Pleasure: BOATING, SURF AND STILL WATER BATHING, FRESH AND SALT WATER FISHING, GOLFING AND TENNIS; with unexcelled roads for AUTOMOBILING AND DRIVING.

Over 400 Miles of Shore Line on Ocean, Sound, and Bays

The hilly, tree-clad North Shore, bordering on Long Island Sound and indented with small bays, ideal for boating.

The South Shore, with its perfect beaches on the Ocean, and Great South Bay, affording the fullest opportunity for aquatic sports.

The Central Section, with its running streams and charming little lakes.

"Long Island Resorts," for 1909, brimful of helpful information about the resorts on the island, with list of hotels and boarding cottages, mailed on receipt of 6 cents by addressing the General Passenger Agent, "Department U."

LONG ISLAND RAILROAD
263 FIFTH AVENUE, NEW YORK 6

Scripture and Song in Worship

A SERVICE BOOK FOR THE SUNDAY SCHOOL

Arranged by
FRANCIS W. SHEPARDSON
and
LESTER BARTLETT JONES

A series of services, each based on a central idea and comprising responsive readings and songs. The hymns and music represent the very best in existence, and the selection is the result of long experience. There are special services for Christmas, Easter, etc.

152 pages, 12mo, cloth; net 50 cents, postpaid 59 cents

Address Dept. P

The University of Chicago Press
Chicago New York

The University of Chicago Press

THE books and periodicals published by the University of Chicago Press appeal particularly to purchasers of books other than fiction; and every dealer should familiarize himself with our list, so that he may present appropriate books to interested customers. Our publications are also especially desirable for libraries who aim to supply their patrons with the more solid current books and magazines. Consult our catalogues for particulars, or write to either our eastern or home office

CHICAGO and 156 Fifth Avenue NEW YORK

CLEANLINESS OF OPERATION

is one of the strong features that has helped to earn the present world-wide reputation and endorsement of the

DAUS IMPROVED TIP TOP DUPLICATOR

No printer's ink used, thus avoiding soiled hands and clothing. No expensive supplies. Always ready for use.

100 Copies from Penwritten and 50 Copies from Typewritten Original

SENT ON TEN DAYS' TRIAL Without deposit

Complete Duplicator, cap size (prints 8¾x13 in.), contains 16 feet of rolled printing surface (which can be used over and over again), 2 bottles of ink, Rubber and Powder. Price $7.50 less special discount of 33⅓% net............................ **$5.00**

Circular of larger sizes upon request. Take advantage of our Trial Offer

FELIX E. DAUS DUPLICATOR CO., DAUS BUILDING, 111 JOHN STREET, NEW YORK 6

The Wars of Religion in France—1559-76

THE HUGUENOTS, CATHERINE DE MEDICI, AND PHILIP THE SECOND

By JAMES WESTFALL THOMPSON

THE volume, representing nearly seven years of study, including two prolonged visits to France, is based upon a careful examination of original sources, and contains a valuable appendix of hitherto unpublished documents from the archives of Paris and London. It treats of the epoch of the Reformation, but does not attempt to deal with the religious conflict except in so far as it influenced the political, diplomatic, and economic activities of the period. Our whole interpretation of the sixteenth century, of course, has been profoundly changed by the recent progress in economics; and in the matter of industrial history and of the retroactive effect of wretched existing conditions, as also in the development of the Holy League of France out of certain political and social forces, the book makes decidedly new and valuable contributions. 618 pages, 8vo, cloth; illustrated; net $4.50, postpaid $4.84.

Address Dept. P

The University of Chicago Press
Chicago New York

LEISURE • CULTURE • ECONOMY

University Travel

Tours to Europe, under the guidance of scholars who make interpretation, not information, their chief aim. Systematic lectures by specialists in Art, History, Archaeology, Economics, are a part of our plan. These in no wise interfere with, but enhance the pleasure of, a general tour.

SEND FOR OUR ANNOUNCEMENT

University Prints

For the Student of Art. 2,000 separate reproductions of the masterpieces in Greek, Italian, Dutch, and Flemish Art at one cent each; 80 cents per hundred. Also Handbooks for the Student. Send two cents for complete catalogue and sample prints.

Bureau of University Travel

65 Trinity Place, BOSTON, MASS.

The Biblical World

ERNEST D. BURTON, Editor-in-Chief. Published monthly, with illustrations. Subscription price, $2.00 a year, single copies, 25 cents; foreign postage, 68 cents

The University of Chicago Press
Chicago and New York

JUDSON FREIGHT FORWARDING CO. Reduced rates on household goods to all Western points. 443 Marquette Bldg., Chicago; 1501 Wright Bldg., St. Louis; 736 Old South Bldg., Boston; 206 Pacific Bldg., San Francisco; 200 Central Bldg., Los Angeles. 2

Get "Improved," no tacks required

Wood Rollers
Tin Rollers

HARTSHORN SHADE ROLLERS

Bear the script name of Stewart Hartshorn on label for your protection.

Modern Constitutions

A collection of the fundamental laws of twenty-two of the most important countries of the world, with historical introductions, notes, and bibliographies.

By WALTER FAIRLEIGH DODD, PH.D.

2 vols. 750 pages. 8vo, cloth. Net, $5.00; postpaid, $5.42

THIS volume contains the texts, in English translation where English is not the original language, of the constitutions or fundamental laws of the Argentine nation, Australia, Austria-Hungary, Belgium, Brazil, Canada, Chile, Denmark, France, Germany, Italy, Japan, Mexico, Netherlands, Norway, Portugal, Russia, Spain, Sweden, Switzerland, and the United States. These constitutions have not heretofore been available in any one English collection, and a number of them have not before appeared in English translation.

Each translation has been carefully made, and the constitutional texts are given as now in force. Notes to the constitutions have been given sparingly, and have been confined almost entirely to information regarding constitutional amendments, election laws, and other matters absolutely necessary for the understanding of the texts. Each constitution is preceded by a brief historical introduction, and is followed by a select list of the most important books dealing with the government of the country under consideration.

ADDRESS DEPT. P

THE UNIVERSITY OF CHICAGO PRESS

CHICAGO AND NEW YORK

EDUCATION WITH REFERENCE TO SEX

EIGHTH YEARBOOK OF THE NATIONAL SOCIETY FOR THE SCIENTIFIC STUDY OF EDUCATION
By CHARLES RICHMOND HENDERSON

THIS study, which was made at the request of the Executive Committee of the Society, and published after their critical examination, and upon the approval of three medical advisers who have read it, is divided into two parts. The first part is chiefly medical and economic, and seeks to prove the necessity for social control of some kind.

This argument demonstrates the necessity for education with reference to sex—the theme of the second part of the work. In this part is found a careful discussion of educational aims, the scope of educational activities, the co-operating agencies in education, the care of infancy, personal hygiene and training, the influence of ideal interests, the principles of formal instruction in relation to sex—its necessity, difficulties and methods.

Part I, 75 pages, 8vo, paper; net 75c, postpaid 78c
Part II, 100 pages; net 75c, postpaid 80c : : :

Address Dept. P.

The University of Chicago Press

CHICAGO NEW YORK

Industrial Insurance in the United States

THIS book, revised and enlarged for the English-speaking public, has already been published in a German series. The introduction contains a summary of the European laws on workingmen's insurance against accident, sickness, invalidism, and old age, with statistics to 1908. The text describes the various forms of social insurance known in the United States and Canada; local clubs and associations, fraternal societies, trade union benefit funds, schemes of large firms, corporations, and railways. One chapter is directed to labor legislation and another to employer's liability laws. Illustrations of the movement are given in chapters on municipal pension plans for policemen, firemen, and teachers; also the military pensions of the federal government and southern states. The appendix supplies bibliography, forms used by firms and corporations, text of bills, and laws on the subject.

448 pages. 8vo cloth. Price, $2.00 net; postpaid, $2.19

Published by

The University of Chicago Press

CHICAGO NEW YORK

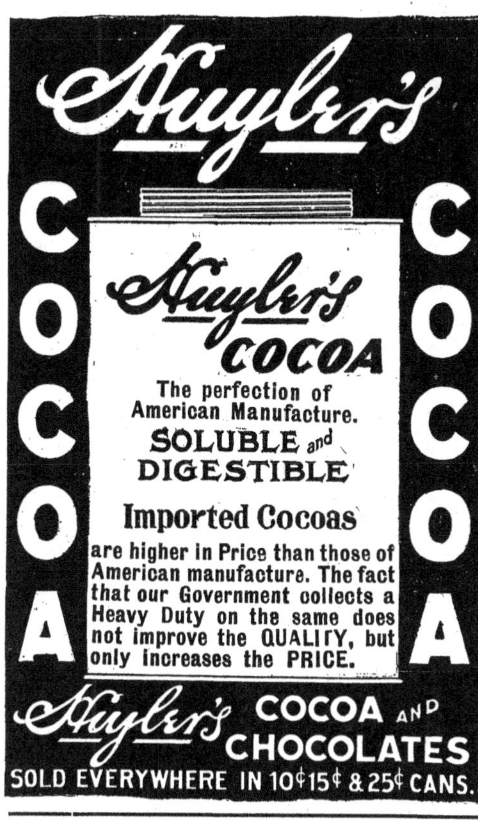

The Function of Religion in Man's Struggle for Existence

By GEORGE BURMAN FOSTER

A POPULAR embodiment of reconstructive religious thought. The book traces the evolution of religion from its past physical and intellectual interpretations to the voluntary and intuitive concepts of modern psychology. It is designed especially for young men and women to whom knowledge of science and of the higher criticism has made a new philosophy essential. The author lays stress upon the enduring quality of religion. He writes in a style of peculiar power and expresses so well the trend of present-day religious thought that his work will appeal to students of philosophy everywhere.

306 pages 16mo, cloth net $1.00 $1.10 postpaid

ADDRESS DEPT. P

The University of Chicago Press

CHICAGO NEW YORK

BAUSCH & LOMB
NEW OPAQUE PROJECTOR

HAS been made in response to the demand for a reliable instrument for the projection of opaque objects. It is not a toy, but a scientific apparatus projecting with brilliancy and even illumination and sharp definition pictures 4 x 4½" to distances up to 75 feet, dependent upon the lens.

¶ Projection by direct or reflected light at will. Price of apparatus complete, with lens of ten inch equivalent focus, $70.

¶ We have also a new combined opaque and lantern slide projector in which the change from one form of projection to the other can be easily and instantaneously made.

¶ Descriptive circular on request.

¶ PRISM is our little lens expositor. Send for Copy D, free on request.

Our Name on a Photographic Lens, Microscope, Field Glass, Laboratory Apparatus, Engineering or any other Scientific Instrument is our Guarantee.

Bausch & Lomb Optical Co.

NEW YORK WASHINGTON CHICAGO SAN FRANCISCO
LONDON ROCHESTER, N.Y. FRANKFORT

DENTACURA

Tooth Paste

Cleanses the teeth, hardens the gums, and perfumes the breath. It differs from the ordinary dentifrice by destroying the harmful bacteria in the mouth, thus minimizing the causes of decay. Endorsed by thousands of dentists. In tubes, deliciously flavored and a delightful adjunct to the dental toilet. Sample and literature free.

Dentacura Tooth Powder

is now offered to those who prefer a dentifrice in form of powder. For sale at best stores everywhere or direct.

Price 25 cents for either

Dentacura Company, 265 Alling St., Newark, N. J.

Grit

is an excellent thing to have, but it is terribly out of place in a **Lead Pencil.** An unevenly graded pencil is an abomination and should not be tolerated for a moment. You may use any pencil you like, but is it not better to like the pencil you use?

On receipt of 16c in stamps samples will be sent you of the best pencils that are made in this or any other country.

Joseph Dixon Crucible Co.
Jersey City, N. J.

12

"HUMBUG MEMORY SCHOOLS EXPOSED"
AND ADDRESS ON DEVELOPMENT OF THE

MEMORY

To introduce a series of valuable educational works, the above will be sent to all applicants **FREE**

MEMORY LIBRARY
Room 810 14 Park Place, New York

THE ELEMENTARY SCHOOL TEACHER

Edited by the Faculty of the Elementary School of the University of Chicago. Published monthly, except in July and August, with illustrations. Subscription price, $1.50 a year; single copies, 20 cents; foreign postage, 46 cents

CHICAGO THE UNIVERSITY OF CHICAGO PRESS NEW YORK

S. D. Childs & Co.

200 Clark Street, Chicago

COPPER-PLATE ENGRAVERS AND PRINTERS

Wedding Invitations, Announcements
Fine Correspondence Stationery
Crests, Monograms, Address Dies
Stamping and Illuminating

CORRESPONDENCE SOLICITED

Genuine Mennen's Borated Talcum Toilet Powder

Mennen's Borated Talcum Powder lays claim to being the most perfect powder on the market both in materials and method of manufacture. It is the oldest of Talcum Powders put up for general use, and has established itself on its merits in every quarter of the civilized world.

The woman who buys Mennen's for toilet use or any other purpose may rest assured that she is getting the purest and most perfect powder that chemical knowledge can originate or skill manufacture.

There is a *difference* in Mennen's and those who have once used it are quick to appreciate that this difference is a difference of superiority which is easily perceived in comparison with any other powder.

Some people may say: The same ingredients are open to everybody, why can't others get the same results and produce a perfect powder?

Ask the woman who is famous for her cake why Mrs. Brown working with the same recipe can't produce the same article. She has the same ingredients, the same directions for making and yet she can't make good cake. It is this knack, this touch of skill and genius which makes the difference between all original productions and imitations. It is this same genius which makes Mennen's original Talcum Powder superior to every other. 6

The most popular pens are

ESTERBROOK'S

MADE IN 150 STYLES

Fine Points, A1, 128, 333
Business, 048, 14, 130
Broad Points, 312, 313, 314
Turned-up Points, 477
531, 1876

Esterbrook Steel Pen Mfg. Co.

Works: Camden, N. J. 26 John St., N. Y.

10

Remington

THE name which distinguishes the BEST Typewriter—the name which *means* Typewriter.

The name which stands for the latest and greatest development in writing machines.

See the new models 10 and 11

Remington Typewriter Company
(Incorporated)
New York and Everywhere

The American Sociological Society

PAPERS AND PROCEEDINGS OF THE THIRD ANNUAL MEETING

Dec. 28–30, 1908

General Topic: The Family

CONTRIBUTORS

William G. Sumner, Charlotte Perkins Gilman, Charles Zueblin, Prince A. Morrow, R. C. Chapin, Margaret F. Byington, Edward T. Devine, Charles Richmond Henderson, Kenyon L. Butterfield, D. Collin Wells, U. G. Weatherly, George Elliot Howard, James E. Hagerty, George K. Holmes. Many other noted people took part in the discussions, which are all reported.

226 pages, 8vo, paper; net $1.50, postpaid $1.60

Address Department P

The University of Chicago Press

Chicago New York

FINE INKS AND ADHESIVES
For those who KNOW

Higgins'
- Drawing Inks
- Eternal Writing Ink
- Engrossing Ink
- Taurine Mucilage
- Photo Mounter Paste
- Drawing Board Paste
- Liquid Paste
- Office Paste
- Vegetable Glue, Etc.

Are the Finest and Best Inks and Adhesives

Emancipate yourself from the use of corrosive and ill-smelling inks and adhesives and adopt the **Higgins Inks and Adhesives.** They will be a revelation to you, they are so sweet, clean, well put up, and withal so efficient.

At Dealers Generally.

CHAS. M. HIGGINS & CO., Mfrs.

Branches: Chicago, London

271 Ninth Street. Brooklyn, N. Y.

8

PIKE'S PEAK
Cool in July
Up in the Sky
Santa Fe
Where the N. E. A. meets this summer.
Go to Denver—attend the meeting of the N. E. A.—and spend the ensuing vacation weeks among the cool Colorado Rockies and beyond.
Climb mountains, fish, hunt, golf, motor, ride, tramp, explore strange places, live in the open, absorb the sunshine.
All this and more can be done, and at very small expense. The Santa Fe has arranged low fare excursions costing only **$30** from Chicago, **$25** from St. Louis, **$17.50** from Missouri River. On these tickets you have until October 31 for final return.
By traveling via the Santa Fe you pass along the old Santa Fe Trail, so rich in border history. Also, you pass in review the Front Range of the Rockies, the most magnificent panorama of mountain scenery on the continent.
While in the West, see it all. See the numerous mountain resorts, see the gorges, canyons, parks; but above all see the **Grand Canyon of Arizona,** it's the greatest, most wonderful of all.
Let me assist in planning your tour by mailing the Santa Fe '09 Summer books:
"A Colorado Summer," "Yosemite,"
"California Summer Outings," "Titan of Chasms" (Grand Canyon)
Also, special convention folders for N. E. A. at Denver.
G. T. Gunnip, Gen. Agt.,
A. T. & S. F. Ry.,
105 Adams St., Chicago.
H. Newman

BUFFALO LITHIA SPRINGS WATER

Is a natural spring water bottled at the springs only. It has been before the public for thirty-seven years and is offered upon its record of results accomplished. In *Bright's Disease, Albuminuria, Inflammation of the Bladder, Gout, Rheumatism*, and all diseases dependent upon a Uric Acid Diathesis, it has been tested by leading physicians at home and abroad. The testimony of these physicians and their patients—based on actual clinical test and not on theory—tells our story. Are they not competent witnesses?

DR. ALFRED A. LOOMIS, *Professor of Pathology and Practical Medicine in the Medical Department of the University of New York*, wrote: "For the past four years I have used **BUFFALO LITHIA WATER** in the treatment of **Chronic Bright's Disease of the Kidneys,** occuring in **Gouty and Rheumatic subjects, with marked benefit."**

DR. G. A. FOOTE, *Warrenton, N. C., Ex-President State Medical Society, formerly Member of the State Board of Medical Examiners, and also of the State Board of Health:* "In **Bright's Disease of the Kidneys** I have in many cases noted the disappearance of **Albumin and Casts** under the action of **BUFFALO LITHIA WATER, which I regard as the most efficacious of known remidies** in this distressing malady."

DR. JOS. HOLT, *of New Orleans, Ex-President of the State Board of Health of Louisiana*, says: "I have prescribed **BUFFALO LITHIA WATER** in affections of the **Kidneys and Urinary Passages,** particularly in **Gouty** subjects in **Albuminuria,** and in irritable condition of **Bladder** and **Urethra** in females. The results satisfy me of its **extraordinary value in a large class of cases** usually most difficult to treat."

GRAEME M. HAMMOND, M.D., *Professor of Diseases of the Mind and Nervous System in the New York Post-Graduate Medical School and Hospital:* "In all cases of **Bright's Disease** I have found **BUFFALO LITHIA WATER** of the **greatest service in increasing the quantity of Urine and in eliminating the Albumen."**

MEDICAL TESTIMONY ON REQUEST

FOR SALE BY THE GENERAL DRUG AND MINERAL WATER TRADE

Buffalo Lithia Springs Water Co.

BUFFALO LITHIA SPRINGS, VIRGINIA.

HIGHEST IN HONORS

BAKER'S COCOA

Registered, U. S. Pat. Off.

50 HIGHEST AWARDS IN EUROPE AND AMERICA

A perfect food, preserves health, prolongs life

WALTER BAKER & CO., Ltd.

Established 1780 DORCHESTER, MASS.

Purify your Refrigerator!

Foods absorb foul odors. Prevent this and sickness by Keeping in your refrigerator a sponge sprinkled occasionally with Platts Chlorides. Wash the sponge twice a week!

Platt's Chlorides

The Odorless Disinfectant.

Sold by Druggists Everywhere

Write to the manufacturer, Henry B. Platt, 42 Cliff Street, New York, for free book.

SAPOLIO

THE FOUNDATION OF GOOD HOUSEKEEPING IS IN THE CONSTANT USE OF SAPOLIO

CLEANS

VOSE PIANOS have been established over 55 YEARS. By o[ur] system of payments every family in moderate ci[r]cumstances can own a VOSE piano. We take o[ld] instruments in exchange and deliver the new pia[no] in your home free of expense. Write for Catalogue D and explanations.

VOSE & SONS PIANO CO., Boston, Mass.

www.ingramcontent.com/pod-product-compliance
Lightning Source LLC
LaVergne TN
LVHW010522100826
845148LV00001B/67

* 9 7 8 1 4 2 5 5 7 3 7 8 2 *